MOTIVATION AND ACHIEVEMENT

BY JOHN W. ATKINSON
THE UNIVERSITY OF MICHIGAN

and

JOEL O. RAYNOR
STATE UNIVERSITY OF NEW YORK AT BUFFALO

In collaboration with:

David Birch

Marvin Brown
Elliot E. Entin
Sheila C. Feld
Gerald Gurin
Matina Souretis Horner
Stuart A. Karabenick
Robert W. Moulton
Ira S. Rubin
James R. Sawusch
Robert A. Seltzer
Richard M. Sorrentino
Joseph Veroff
Bernard Weiner
Zakour I. Youssef

V. H. WINSTON & SONS
1974 Washington, D.C.

A HALSTED PRESS BOOK

JOHN WILEY & SONS
New York Toronto London Sydney

V. H. Winston & Sons, Inc., Publishers
1511 K St. N.W., Washington, D.C. 20005

Distributed solely by Halsted Press Division, John Wiley & Sons, Inc., New York.

Library of Congress Cataloging in Publication Data:

Atkinson, John William, 1923–
Motivation and achievement.

Includes bibliographical references.
1. Achievement motivation. I. Raynor, Joel O. II. Title.
BF683.A85 152.5 73-21754
ISBN 0-470-03626-5

Printed in the United States of America

CONTENTS

PREFACE

This book is the culmination of a 25-year program of research on the effects of individual differences in achievement motivation on behavior. It should be of significant interest to a wide audience of students, and particularly to practitioners in education and management for whom it includes the most up-to-date identification and theoretical analysis of the various components of achievement-related motivation.

In addition to the hope of success, the fear of failure, and the difficulty of a task as it affects an individual's subjective probability of success–all identified as determinants of achievement-related tendencies in *A Theory of Achievement Motivation* (Atkinson & Feather, 1966),–we now also examine the impact of fear of success (particularly among women), the way in which confidence (and hence subjective probability of success) is influenced by individual differences in ability, the way in which recent experiences of success or failure produce either gratification and relief or persisting unsatisfied tendencies to achieve or persisting resistance that is carried over into present activities; and perhaps of special importance because it is teachable, the way an individual's conception of some immediate task as a step in a longer path to future goals and threatening consequences can profoundly affect the intensity of whatever is most characteristic of an individual's achievement-related motivation–positive interest or anxiety about failure.

This book does more. It also puts all of the previous and familiar work on achievement motivation into the new and more general conception of motivation offered in *The Dynamics of Action* (Atkinson & Birch, 1970). This reconstruction of the theory of motivation breaks with the stimulus-bound tradition of psychological theories to yield a conception of an active rather than a merely reactive individual. It offers a coherent theoretical explanation of emitted, or operant behaviors (i.e., *actions*) in addition to accounting for behavior that is more obviously a reaction to some immediate change in the immediate stimulus situation. The new theoretical framework, which emphasizes more the molar stream of an individual's behavior than the short goal-directed incidents of our traditional conceptions, identifies the time spent in various activities, the relative frequency of various activities, and, of course, the rate (operant level) of particular activities, *all in a constant environment*, as a whole new set of behavioral problems to be studied as expressions of individual differences in personality.

Of particular interest are the kinds of problems dealt with in the concluding part of the book–motivation and career striving, and the relationship between *intellective performance* in the short run (an intelligence test) and *cumulative achievement* or level of accomplishment in the long run. These problems of motivation require a theory that can address itself to much longer temporal intervals than in the past. The typical modest correlation (.30 to .50) between ability test scores and criteria such as college grades is deduced from the theory of motivation developed in the book and a conception of how *ability* and *motivation* interact to account for achievement.

Another highlight of the book is the inclusion in the Appendix of programs for computer simulation of motivational problems. Some of these, such as the different kind of relationship to be expected between motivation and level of performance (because efficiency of performance is the matter of central importance) and between motivation and cumulative achievement (because persistence or sheer amount of time spent is equally or even more important a factor) are dealt with in the text.

Like the earlier books reporting progress in this program of work at the University of Michigan, *Motives in Fantasy, Action, and Society* (Atkinson, 1958*a*) and *A Theory of Achievement Motivation* (Atkinson & Feather, 1966), following the pioneer work by McClelland, Atkinson, Clark, and Lowell (1953) in *The Achievement Motive,* the present volume is a report of a sustained collaborative effort by members of a research seminar, the core of it accomplished from 1962 to the present. We hope, as always, that organizing these individual contributions into five sections or parts, each with an introductory statement by the editors, helps one to see the vital role of each contribution to the cumulative achievement.

The pattern of cooperative research was set and described by David C. McClelland in the preface of *The Achievement Motive* (1953). The value of programmatic research at the frontier was well understood and encouraged by Donald G. Marquis (1948). The need for a conception of personality in contact with a theory of action, so that an individual would be described in terms of potentialities for action for which there are known principles, was sharply defined by Robert R. Sears (1951). And we have always been keenly aware that the choice of concept and the development of methods for treating the effect of the situation on the individual can enhance or hinder the possibility of integrating the conceptions of personaltiy and of social structure in concrete research (Atkinson, 1958*b*, p. 616). These have always been the central themes of our work on this problem at Michigan.

Once again, the book is built on the solid foundation of six doctoral dissertations (Weiner, 1963; Brown, 1967; Entin, 1968; Horner, 1968; Raynor, 1968*a*; Sorrentino, 1971), the latter with Raynor at the State University of New York, Buffalo.

We are particularly grateful to Joseph Veroff, Sheila Feld, and Gerald Gurin for their willingness to have their independent work at the Survey Research Center included here to represent forcefully the methodological concern that has consistently characterized this work. Their use of the same tool in a nationwide survey study that is typically employed in experimental research conveys the conviction we share, that the use of the same methods in both experimental and field research, rather than ad hoc devices, is the only realistic way of overcoming the all-too-common specious review and attempted integration of literature in terms of words commonly used to describe findings rather than in terms of truly commensurable factual evidence.

The reader already familiar with the earlier works on achievement motivation may find it useful to scan the table of contents and introductions to the several parts of the book before turning to Chapters 6, 7, 11, 15, 17, 19, and 20 for the new theoretical developments and their implications. Then he may wish to move immediately to computer simulation using the programs in the Appendix.

Much of the work from 1963 to the present has been supported by project grants from the National Science Foundation (GS-9 from 1962 to 1965, GS-1399 from 1966 to 1969, and GS-2863 from 1970 to 1972), a U.S. Public Health Service Special Research Fellowship to John W. Atkinson (1969–70), predoctoral fellowships to Marvin Brown, Matina Souretis Horner, and Joel O. Raynor, and a grant-in-aid of our research from the American College Testing Research Institute (during 1971–73), for which we are all indeed very grateful.

We want to acknowledge with thanks the guidance and criticism provided by colleagues who were members of one or more of the six doctoral dissertation committees: David Birch, W. Robert Dixon (Chairman for Entin), Loren S. Barritt, Donald R. Brown, Dorwin Cartwright, Elizabeth Douvan, Edwin Engel, Robert L. Isaacson, Melvin Manis, James N. Morgan, Robert W. Moulton, J. E. Keith Smith, Joseph Veroff, and David R. Beach, Edwin P. Hollander, James W. Julian, and E. Neil Murray at Buffalo.

For help in the clerical and secretarial tasks associated with preparation of the manuscript, we thank Betty DeKarske, Jill Coppock, Mary Ellen Friedman, Lee A. Gordon, Linda Herith, and Susan John.

We thank David John Atkinson for contributing his photograph of *The Fountain* by Vigeland in Froggener Park, Oslo, Norway, and Lise Vislie in Oslo, and Tone Wikborg of the Vigeland Museum.

Permission to reprint selections from books or journals was kindly granted by the following publishers: American Psychological Association, Duke University Press, Rand McNally, John Wiley & Sons, and Praeger Publishers.

John W. Atkinson
Joel O. Raynor

Ann Arbor and Buffalo
February, 1974

Dave Atkinson

Achievement is a we thing, not a me thing, always the product of many heads and hands no matter how it may appear to one involved in the effort and enjoyment of it or to a casual observer. This is the truth of Vigeland's great work, *The Fountain*, in Oslo.

What emotions will some day temper the experience of pride in personal accomplishment? What feelings will accompany the achievement when the enlightenment of mature behavioral science has superseded myth and all of us comprehend the truth of *The Fountain*, that people are interdependent in becoming what they become and in doing what they do? And that other unavoidable truth, that luck plays a vital role in the full account of any individual's actions?

The emotions should be gratitude and thankfulness and a richer sense of vicarious pride in the cumulative human achievement.

J. W. A.

PART I
THE GUIDING THEORY AND METHODOLOGICAL CONCERN

1
INTRODUCTION AND OVERVIEW

> *A law is expressed in an equation which relates certain variables. Individual differences have to be conceived of as various specific values which these variables have in a particular case. In other words, general laws and individual differences are merely two aspects of one problem; they are mutually dependent on each other and the study of the one cannot proceed without the study of the other* [Lewin, 1946, p. 794].

This book is the product of 25 years of integrated study, at the University of Michigan, of the functional significance of individual differences in achievement motivation. It presents the coherent account we have long been seeking of how personality interacts with the motivational impact of the immediate environment to determine the motivational state of an individual—*his inclinations;* the various ways in which these inclinations, or tendencies, are expressed in activity; and how, together with individual differences in ability, individual differences in motivation are responsible for the great differences in the cumulative achievement of individuals.

Guided by *A Theory of Achievement Motivation* (Atkinson & Feather, 1966), we have, in the years since, continued to address ourselves to the two fundamental questions that any theory of motivation must answer coherently: (*a*) What are the various components or determinants of the strength of an inclination or tendency to engage in a particular activity? (*b*) How is conflict among mutually incompatible inclinations, or tendencies, resolved and expressed in the various measurable aspects of an individual's activity?

Our most complete and coherent answers to these questions, presented here, represent our specification of what is implied by the programmatic equation left to us as a legacy and guide by Kurt Lewin, viz., $B = f(P,E)$. The book as a whole constitutes, we think, an intimation of what psychology is to become when the two sets of half-truths of the traditionally isolated disciplines of scientific psychology to which Cronbach (1957) eloquently called attention (viz., correlational psychology and experimental psychology)[1] are superseded by a psychology that does not systematically eschew more than half of its subject matter but rather focuses on the joint influence or interaction between personality variables and situational variables.

We have begun to achieve "the shape of a united discipline" to which Cronbach referred. "It is not enough," he said, "for each discipline to borrow from the other. Correlational psychology studies only variance among organisms; experimental psychology only variance among treatments. A united discipline will study both of these, but it will also be concerned with the otherwise neglected interactions between organismic and treatment variables [see Shen, (1942)]."Our job," he added, "is to invent constructs and to form a network of laws which permit prediction. From observations we must infer a psychological description of the situation and of the present state of the organism. Our laws should permit us to predict, from this description, the behavior of organism-in-situation [Cronbach, 1957, pp. 681-682]."

THE DYNAMICS OF ACTION AND OPERANT CONDITIONING

We have referred to the important question concerning the various components or determinants of an inclination or tendency to engage in a particular activity. We use the term *inclination* deliberately, for we find it so frequently in the writings of B. F. Skinner, e.g., in *Beyond Freedom and Dignity* (1971). It is vitally important and certainly accurate to say that these inclinations are the product of the schedules of rewarding and punishing consequences of activities in the life history of an individual. But that is not a complete psychology. What an individual brings with him through the doorway into each new life situation, when the lawful antecedents have faded into history, is his personality. This personality is the product of the life history or, more accurately, of the interaction of an individual's heredity and formative environment, to which the term refers [i.e., $P = f(H, E_f)$]. In an effort to emancipate us from the traditional myth of "autonomous man", Skinner is wittingly or unwittingly contributing again to a confusion of the hard-won distinction between the problems of learning and performance or, more generally, of *development* and *motivation* within a scientific psychology (see Atkinson, 1964, Ch. 5-6).

[1] One involves the study of individual differences using the product-moment correlation, guided by the truncated notion that $B = f(P)$. The other involves the experimental and conceptual analysis of behavioral processes and scrutiny of how random samples of people react to some manipulated variation in the immediate environment, guided by the truncated notion that $B = f(E)$.

A unified psychology needs conceptions of individual differences in personality and adequate diagnostic tests, just as physics needed the concept of mass and a scale yielding the lawful measures called weight. This does not deny that the various properties of the subject of interest, a person for psychology as distinct from a physical object, all have an origin and a lawful natural history. But we must recall that Copernicus and Galileo turned their attention to the orderliness of the observable solar system and of the motions of physical objects, and Newton made some theoretical sense of both, without a complete and coherent account of the genesis and developmental history of the differences in the masses of various objects which, in the case of solar bodies, is now known to have taken millenniums of time.

We use the Skinnerian term *inclination* as a synonym for our own technical term *tendency* and give it emphasis in this introduction because we think that our conception of *The Dynamics of Action* (Atkinson & Birch, 1970 and Chapter 15) presents a plausible theory of operant (or voluntary) behavior. The convergence of behavioral *technology* and behavioral *science* is near at hand.

THE CONTENT OF THE BOOK

We report and elaborate the several important steps taken since the work on theory of achievement motivation summarized in 1966 and reviewed in Chapter 2. We now recognize that fear of success, particularly in women (Matina Souretis Horner, Chapter 6) must be added to hope of success and fear of failure, previously considered the only factors inherent whenever performance is undertaken with an expectation of evaluation in relation to some standard of excellence. We have begun to appreciate more fully the motivational implications (mediated by effects on subjective probability of success) of individual differences in ability or competence (Robert Moulton, Chapter 4). Both of these contributions extended the basic theory as it focused upon the psychological present, the motivational effects of the immediate expected consequences of skillful and effortful performance.

To this earlier formulation, restricted as it was to *the psychological present,* must now be added a major elaboration of the theory of achievement motivation in terms which embrace *the psychological future,* the impact on motivation for some present activity of perceiving its instrumental relationship, as a step in a longer path, to more distant future goals and threatening consequences (by Joel Raynor, and co-workers, Chapters 7-10).

And to complete the picture, we have also embraced the motivational impact of *the psychological past* with a new emphasis on the immediate and differential persisting motivational consequences of success and failure as distinct from their effects on cognitive learning. This problem was first studied by Bernard Weiner (Chapters 17-18).

All of these developments have to do with the first basic question concerning the components or determinants of the strength of an inclination, or tendency, to engage in some achievement-oriented activity.

Our answer to the second question, the one which has to do with the gap between inclinations (motivation) and actions, is entirely new. In *The Dynamics of Action,* Atkinson and Birch (1970) have reconstructed the general theory of motivation, parting company with the stimulus-bound traditions of both S-R behavior theory and the cognitive (Expectancy X Value) theory developed in the work of Tolman and Lewin, and formulated as modern decision theory (e.g., Edwards, 1954). In Chapter 15 of this book, all the previous work on achievement-oriented activity is recovered within this new and more general theoretical framework. It emphasizes the molar stream of activity that characterizes the behavioral life of an individual rather than the short episodic view that has been fostered on psychology by its historical foundation in the concept of reflex. The theoretical conception of the dynamics of action presents as coherent an account of *actions* (i.e., emitted, or operant, behaviors) and changes from one activity to another *in a constant environment,* as it does of behavior that is obviously a *reaction* to some change in the immediate stimulus situation. This conception of the dynamics of action has to do with which of several particular activities will be initiated by an individual (choice), when it will happen (latency), and for how long the activity will continue (persistence). In reference to longer temporal intervals of observation that are characterized by many changes of activity, it accounts for the distribution of time among various activities, their relative frequency of occurrence, and the operant level or rate of particular activities.

To complete our answer to the second big question concerning the gap between strength of inclination, or tendency, and overt behavior, we also finally come to share the view of others (see Yerkes & Dodson, 1908; Broadhurst, 1959; Eysenck, 1966a), on the basis of rather consistent empirical evidence, including the doctoral research of Elliot Entin (Chapter 12), Matina Souretis Horner (Chapter 13), and Richard Sorrentino (Chapter 14), that the relationship between strength of motivation and efficiency in the execution of an activity (e.g., solving arithmetic problems) is nonmonotonic and most adequately described by an inverted U-function (Chapter 11).

The book is organized to bring the reader, in a series of steps, from the theory of achievement motivation and evidence as summarized by Atkinson and Feather (1966) to our present, more comprehensive and coherent conceptual analysis of motivation and achievement and to its important practical implications for motivational problems in personal career planning, in education, and in industry.

The concluding part, which shares the title of the book, does what we have never been able to do before within the theory of achievement motivation. It explores the longer temporal units—motivation and career striving (Joel Raynor, Chapter 19), and the distinction between achievement in the short run, *intellective performance* (e.g., an ability test), and achievement in the long run, *cumulative achievement* (e.g., academic performance in a year of college, the level of educational attainment, social mobility, productivity in a career). It presents a systematic statement of how ability and motivation interact to influence both *the level of intellective performance* on a test and *cumulative achievement* so as to produce the modest correlations of .30 to .50 that are conventionally reported between the two (John Atkinson, Chapter 20).

A final highlight of the book is the Appendix. It contains computer programs written by Robert Seltzer and James Sawusch to allow computer simulation of motivational problems guided by the principles advanced concerning the dynamics of achievement-oriented activity (John Atkinson and David Birch, Chapter 15) and the effect of motivation on efficiency of performance (John Atkinson, Chapter 11), results from some of which are reported within the book.

HISTORICAL BACKGROUND

Readers who approach this work for the first time may be helped by a guide to the mainstream of it. Many questions which may seem to be arising for the first time have arisen before and have been dealt with before, perhaps as long as 20 years ago. We are particularly concerned that the firm methodological foundation of the work be appreciated by the student who is unaware of its history, and that the interested reader know where to look to become sufficiently informed about it, so as to be capable of evaluating for himself some of the superficial reviews of work on achievement motivation that have appeared in the recent literature.

The work began in the winter of 1947 when David C. McClelland and John W. Atkinson began to study the effects of hunger, and then of experimentally induced motivation to achieve (when joined by Russell Clark and later by Thornton Roby) on the content of thematic apperception, i.e., imaginative behavior (see McClelland & Atkinson, 1948; Atkinson & McClelland, 1948; McClelland, Clark, Roby, & Atkinson, 1949). They were concerned with whether or not, and if so, how, experimentally induced differences in strength of different kinds of motivation were expressed in thematic apperception (imaginative activity). Could the content analysis be done independently by different judges with a very high degree of objectivity (i.e., coding reliability)? If so, could the scores (frequency counts of a particular kind of motivational imagery in stories written by different people under standard conditions) be related to the behavior of these same people in meaningful ways?

The answers to all of these questions concerning validity and objectivity of the method were clearly affirmative. In *The Achievement Motive* by McClelland, Atkinson, Clark, and Lowell (1953), the first 5 years of work mainly on the development of a reliable measuring instrument, evaluation of its potentialities and limitations, and its use in explorations of the origins and behavioral consequences of n Achievement (the need for achievement) is reviewed.

By 1958 the effect of motivation on thematic apperception had been extended to studies of needs for affiliation, power, fear, sex, and aggression, in addition to hunger and achievement motivation. In *Motives in Fantasy, Action, and Society* (Atkinson, 1958a), the second 5 years of work, including studies by a variety of participants in the research, is reviewed. By this time the different questions that have engaged the primary interest of various investigators begin to be apparent. McClelland and co-workers at Wesleyan and later at Harvard had begun to concentrate on the social origins and consequences of achievement motivation (see McClelland, 1961, *The Achieving Society*), as did other social psychologists (e.g., Douvan, 1958) and sociologists (see Rosen, 1956, 1959; Rosen & D'Andrade, 1959; Crockett, 1962). This interest in the relationship of achievement motivation, as inferred from the literature of a society (e.g., deCharms & Moeller, 1962) and in other ingenious ways (e.g., Aronson, 1958), to the entrepreneurial activity and economic development of a society, is followed by McClelland and Winter's interest in the effects on entrepreneurial activity of attempts to change achievement motivation in *Motivating Economic Achievement* (1969) and the related work of Litwin and Stringer, *Motivation and Organizational Climate* (1968).

The 1958 book, *Motives in Fantasy, Action, and Society,* reflects a very strong methodological interest at Michigan, including manuals for content analysis to yield measures of three important social motives–n Achievement, n Affiliation, and n Power.[2] Pretested practice materials prepared by Charles P. Smith and Sheila Feld that were included in 200 pages of Appendix enable anyone with sufficient interest to practice on his own and achieve a high degree of coding validity, i.e., a correlation of near .90 with scores already obtained from the same imaginative stories by a consensus of already expert coders. This methodological concern emphasized the fact, obvious by then, that various direct or self-descriptive tests gratuitously called measures of n Achievement and the experimentally validated projective or indirect test of n Achievement yielded uncorrelated results (McClelland, 1958a). The literature had already begun to be clogged with the confusing results produced with various ad hoc and unvalidated "tests" of n Achievement (see, particularly, Atkinson, 1960, on this point). We had found that the traditionally defined equivalent-form and test-retest reliability of TAT n Achievement was modest but certainly adequate for productive research *when used appropriately* (Haber & Alpert, 1958), but that the predictive validity of a thematic apperceptive test was apparently limited to roughly 20 minutes of testing, i.e., to about four or five stories (Reitman & Atkinson, 1958), a fact at variance with clinical practice.

Perhaps the most important thing learned by those centrally engaged in the task of moving ahead to develop a coherent conception of the effects on behavior of individual differences in n Achievement, and at a very early date (see McClelland et al., 1953, Ch. 7, "The Measuring Instrument," particularly pp. 191-192), was that *the conventional premises of psychometrics needed to be seriously questioned*

[2] See recent revisions and extensions of research on n Power by Joseph and Joanne B. Veroff (1972) and David G. Winter and co-workers (*The Power Motive,* in preparation).

when employed in reference to the stream of spontaneously emitted (operant) imaginative behavior. The rule of thumb adopted by several generations of apprentice co-workers at Michigan, based on the earliest split-half and test-retest reliabilities, is that *when everything is done correctly* (including coding validity of .90 or better), the classification of subjects as relatively High or Low in n Achievement in terms of a median split of the distribution of scores will be correct about 75% of the time. (In simple terms, this means that for a two-level measure of the strength of motive, we fall halfway between total ignorance and total knowledge.)

This early-learned and published lesson is based on the fact that when two equivalent forms were administered on one occasion (in a latin square design to separate effects of pictures and serial location) and the product-moment correlation between the two three-story forms was a respectable .64 ($N = 32$), the High-Low agreement was 78.1% (Atkinson, 1950). When these same two forms were administered one week apart by Lowell (reported in McClelland et al., 1953, Ch. 7) and the product-moment correlation dropped dramatically to .22 ($N = 40$), apparently implying little or no stability in n Achievement over a period of a week, the extent of the High-Low agreement between forms was still 72.5%. Both of the cruder and less presumptuous tests of reliability and stability yielded the same inference concerning the measured group difference in motivation and at the same level of confidence ($p < .01$). A little simple arithmetic told us that 5.6% of 40 subjects (i.e., 2.24 persons) had changed their position with respect to the median of the distribution to bring about such a calamitous change in the product-moment correlation (and in the belief system among some for whom the premises underlying traditional practice in the mental test movement have the status, apparently, of religious convictions). Among the more pragmatic agnostics (regarding tests of individual differences in personality), it took only a little imagination to suspect that a few very highly motivated and/or intelligent college students might seek information in the interim between administrations about the rather unique test of imagination they had experienced. Instead of returning on the second occasion like the constant and unchanged block of metal presumed by traditional test theory borrowed from physics, they might be substantially spoiled for a retest. It seemed eminently clear and intelligible then, and it still does today, that validity (under optimal conditions) might outrun "reliability" as traditionally viewed (McClelland, 1958a). Twenty-five years of productive work with an admittedly crude tool attests the validity of that early insight. The use of a projective measure of n Achievement or any other social motive should, it is advised, be restricted to those who have a sensible appreciation of both its limitations and its potentialities, and a sufficient scientific interest to develop the technical competence that can begin to be evaluated by the coding reliability achieved and reported in the methods section of a scientific publication. Chapter 3, by Joseph Veroff et al., returns to this basic methodological theme in the context of a classic study of American national character, using the crude but valid tool to measure social motives in a nationwide survey research project.

In 1963, Heinz Heckhausen began to summarize the program of work on hope of success and fear of failure in Germany in *Hoffnung und Furcht in der Leistungsmotivation.* Then later, in *The Anatomy of Achievement Motivation* (1967), we have his more recent and scholarly treatment of a growing international literature. To this must be added the work at the Institute for Educational Research at the University of Oslo (Rand, 1963, 1965; Gjesme, 1971; Vislie, 1972) and of Hayashi and Habu (1962) in Japan.

The Michigan program on achievement motivation is put into a broader historical and theoretical perspective in *An Introduction to Motivation* (Atkinson, 1964). Another progress report emphasizing the evolving theory and coverage of relevant experimental work on risk preference, level of aspiration, and persistence is presented in *A Theory of Achievement Motivation,* edited by Atkinson and Feather (1966).

One of the theoretical issues that began to take shape is the comparison of the explanation of effects of individual differences in motivation on level of performance of competitional and non-competitional tasks within S-R behavior theory (see Spence & Spence, 1966) and one offered within the theory of achievement motivation concerning performance on "easy" and "more difficult" tasks (see Atkinson, 1960, pp. 263-271). It was studied experimentally first by Bernard Weiner (1966a, and Chapter 18) and then by Karabenick and Youssef (1968, and Chapter 5).

The growing interest in developmental problems and studies of children evident in the writings of Joseph Veroff (1965) is brought together by Charles P. Smith (1969) in *Achievement-related Motives in Children.* The further analysis of the nationwide survey study reported by Veroff, et al. in Chapter 3 has been extended by Veroff and Sheila Feld (1970) in *Marriage and Work in America: A Study of Motives and Roles.* Another independent, but related, line of work appears in *Fear of Failure,* by Birney, Burdick, and Teevan (1969).

The immediate precursor of the present volume is *The Dynamics of Action* by Atkinson and Birch (1970). This work represents a very fundamental change of focus for the study of motivation, one that was initially suggested in Norman T. Feather's (1960) doctoral research on achievement motivation and persistence (see Feather, 1961; Atkinson & Cartwright, 1964; Atkinson & Feather, 1966). In the present volume, the reconception of the problems of achievement-oriented action within the framework of the dynamics of action, which was interspersed throughout the 1970 volume, is finally elaborated in Chapter 15 with David Birch, though it had already been represented in the innovative doctoral research of Bernard Weiner (reported here in Chapter 17) and of Marvin Brown (Chapter 16).

PLAN OF THE BOOK

Part I presents the basic theory of achievement motivation, the paramount interest in methodological issues that has always characterized this work, and advances within the framework of the theoretical perspective of the early and middle 1960s. Part II contains Raynor's elaboration of this theory of achievement motivation so that it includes, explicitly, *future orientation,* and presents evidence that solidly supports his thesis. Part III, still within the framework of the cognitive theory of achievement motivation as elaborated in Part II, focuses on the long-unresolved problem of how strength of motivation influences efficiency of performance and, therefore, the level of performance, i.e., productivity in a given task. Part IV recovers all of the earlier work in the new and broader theoretical framework provided by *The Dynamics of Action* (Atkinson & Birch, 1970). And Part V, the final section of this book, attests the heuristic value of the theoretical advance we believe we have achieved. Here we deal explicitly with the problems of career striving, and the kind of discrepancy between intellective performance on a test of ability, and cumulative achievement that the mental testers refer to as the problems of overachievement and underachievement. This is our first explicit attempt at theoretical integration of ability and motivation as the joint determinants of achievement and is particularly timely, we believe, in light of societal interest and the oversimplifications in contemporary discussions of the real meaning of ability and intelligence test scores.

Finally, in the Appendix, we continue to express and update our concern with methodological innovations by including the programs developed by Robert Seltzer and James Sawusch for computer simulation of motivational problems based entirely and explicitly on the theoretical principles of motivation presented in this book. It gives a picture of a new direction of work in progress today.

We end, we think, foreshadowing psychology tomorrow, and particularly with the new guide that the mental test movement has long been seeking from a psychology of motivation.

2
THE MAINSPRINGS OF ACHIEVEMENT-ORIENTED ACTIVITY[1]

John W. Atkinson

A THEORY OF ACHIEVEMENT MOTIVATION

The contemporary guide for research on achievement motivation (as of 1965) bears a striking resemblance to the resultant valence theory of level of aspiration advanced about 20 years ago in the writings of Lewin, Escalona, and Festinger (see summary article by Lewin et al., 1944). It extends, elaborates, and refines their earlier ideas and, at the same time, brings into the discussion systematically the basic concept of psychogenic need or motive advanced in the writings of Murray (1938) and McClelland (1951) as a useful one for description of how individuals differ in disposition to strive for certain general goals. The ideas of the theory are based primarily on the results of experiments in which individuals are classified as relatively High and Low in need for achievement (n Achievement) in terms of the frequency of imaginative responses suggesting their concern over performing well in relation to some standard of excellence. These responses appear in stories they have told or written in response to pictures or verbal cues in a standard thematic apperceptive test situation. The scheme represents a specification of the nature of the interaction between personality and environmental determinants of behavior which Lewin proposed in the programmatic equation, $B = f(P, E)$.

The Tendency to Achieve Success

First, it is assumed that the strength of the tendency to achieve success (T_s), which is expressed in the interest and performance[2] of an individual in some

[1] Reprinted with minor abridgement, by permission of the author and publisher, from J. D. Krumboltz (Ed.), *Learning and the educational process.* Chicago: Rand McNally, 1965.

[2] This assumes that the relationship between strength of T_s and performance is best represented as a positive monotonic function. However, see Part III for arguments and evidence suggesting that this relationship depends upon the nature of the task and therefore is more complicated than originally thought.—Editors.

task, is a multiplicative function of three variables: motive to achieve success (M_S), conceived as a relatively general and relatively stable disposition of personality; and two other variables which represent the effect of the immediate environment—the strength of expectancy (or subjective probability) that performance of a task will be followed by success (P_s), and the relative attractiveness of success at that particular activity, which we call the incentive value of success (I_s). In other words, $T_s = M_S \times P_s \times I_s$.

The concept of motive here represents individual differences in liking for success in general. The concept of expectancy, which refers to degree of belief that some act will be followed by some consequence, and the concept of incentive value of the expected consequence or goal, are the basic building blocks in the kind of theory advanced earlier by Tolman (1955) and Lewin (1938) and by contemporary workers like Rotter (1954) and others in the field of decision making (see Edwards, 1954).

According to this kind of Expectancy X Value Theory, one can influence motivation by manipulating cues which define an individual's expectations concerning the consequences of his actions and/or the incentive value of the consequences (or goals) produced by action. Following the early proposal of Lewin et al. (1944), it is assumed that the incentive value or attractiveness of success is greater the more difficult the task. This idea is now stated as a relationship between the incentive value of success (I_s) and the strength of expectancy or subjective probability of success (P_s): viz., $I_s = 1 - P_s$. In light of evidence obtained by Litwin (1958) when the reported probability of success at a task is related to some independent estimate of the incentive value of success, it would appear that the notion $I_s = 1 - P_s$ has more the status of a general description of conditions which exist, for whatever reason, in the domain of achievement-oriented activity than the status of a theoretical assumption. Consider, for example, what happens in a ring-toss game when each subject in one group is asked to stand at various distances from the peg and indicate how many times out of ten he thinks he can hit the target from that distance and each subject of another group is asked to recommend a monetary prize for hitting the target from various distances. Figure 1 shows that the average estimate of P_s decreases with distance, and the average monetary prize proposed, which we assume to be symbolic of an individual's estimate of his reaction to success at that distance, increases with distance. The result is similar when immediately after success at tasks which differ in difficulty, subjects are asked to rate the degree of their pleasure in success (Brown, 1963).

The major theoretical implications of these two assertions, $T_s = M_S \times P_s \times I_s$ and $I_s = 1 - P_s$, are shown in Figure 2. Curves representing the strength of the tendency to achieve success (T_s), as a function of expectancy of success (P_s), are shown for two hypothetical individuals who differ in strength of achievement motive (M_S). The tendency to achieve is more strongly aroused by tasks having intermediate probability of success than either very easy or very difficult tasks. When difficulty is held constant for a group of individuals, tendency to achieve

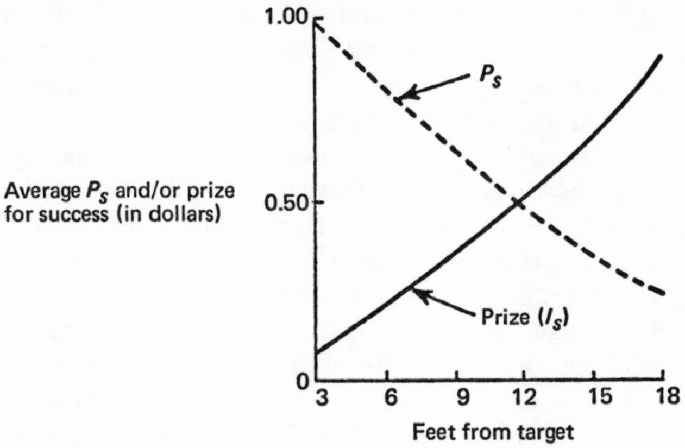

FIG. 1. Estimated probability of success (P_s) and prize recommended for success (I_s) by 20 college students in ring-toss game. (*After Litwin, 1958, with the permission of the author.*)

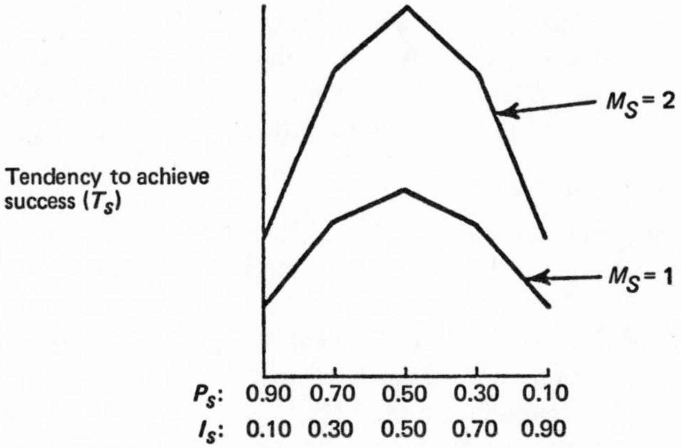

FIG. 2. Theoretical implications of assuming that $T_s = M_S \times P_s \times I_s$ and that $I_s = 1 - P_s$.

will be more strongly aroused when the motive is strong than when it is weak. And, finally, the differences in behavior due to differences in strength of tendency to achieve in individuals who differ in strength of achievement motive are most pronounced when the task is one of intermediate difficulty. The differences in strength of the tendency to achieve success at very easy and very difficult tasks as a function of strength of motive are not, as you can see in Figure 2, very substantial.[3]

[3] However, see Chapters 6 and 7 for discussions concerning the conditions under which this bell-shaped relationship between T_S and P_S may not hold.–Editors.

Figure 2 serves to summarize the results of a number of studies which show stronger preference for intermediate risk or moderate difficulty among persons scoring high in n Achievement and generally high level of performance of these persons in achievement-oriented situations. Since many of the experiments undertaken before we arrived at this theoretical scheme did not specify the degree of difficulty of the task, it is little wonder that they do not always show large differences between the performance levels of high and low n Achievement groups. We should expect little correlation between the n Achievement scores of individuals and their performance level when the task is easy or very difficult, given our present only moderately reliable tool for assessment of the personality variable.[4]

It is my belief that the current theory of achievement motivation is better than the method of assessment and that the time is ripe for a renewed attack on the problem of developing better techniques for assessing differences in strength of achievement motive. The pendulum swings in scientific work. The thematic apperceptive method led us to this conceptual scheme and still is the most useful and valid technique for assessment of differences in achievement motive and other social motives. But now, with some theory to guide our effort, we can turn again to the problem of developing more reliable diagnostic tools, hopeful of better results than those of earlier trial-and-check efforts to do the same thing (see McClelland, 1958a). The virtue of a theory is that it specifies what particular behavioral indicators we might use, and under what conditions, to assess relatively stable differences in the theoretical term M_S.

The Tendency to Avoid Failure

For some years, our studies focused only on the behavioral consequences of differences in achievement motive until the unsolved problems and accumulated evidence in them, as well as in the independent programs of work employing the Manifest Anxiety Scale and the Test Anxiety Questionnaire, made it patently clear to us that whenever performance is evaluated in relation to some standard of excellence, what constitutes the challenge to achieve for one individual poses the threat of failure for another. The tendency to avoid failure associated with anxiety is as fundamentally important a factor in achievement-oriented action as the tendency to achieve success. We treat this tendency, which is conceived as an inhibitory tendency that functions to oppose and dampen the tendency to undertake achievement-oriented activities, as the source of the conscious experience of anxiety. The tendency to avoid failure is also considered a multiplicative function of a motive, an expectancy, and an incentive. We speak of the motive to avoid failure (M_{AF}) and refer to a disposition which is separate and distinct from the achievement motive. It might be thought of as a capacity for reacting with humiliation and shame when one fails. This is considered the

[4] See Part III for treatment of another possible reason for the now-you-see-it-now-you-don't nature of the relationship between n Achievement and level of performance.—Editors.

source of individual differences in the anticipatory emotional reaction called anxiety or fear of failure. The tendency to avoid failure (T_{-f}) is aroused and expressed when there is an expectancy that some act will lead to failure (P_f), and it is also influenced by the incentive value of failure at that particular activity (I_f). That is, $T_{-f} = M_{AF} \times P_f \times I_f$. The incentive value of failure is negative, signifying that it functions like shock for a rat. It is a noxious event to be avoided. It is assumed that the negative incentive value of failure, i.e., the repulsiveness of failure, is greater the easier the task. No one feels very bad when he fails at a very difficult task, but to fail when a task appears easy is a source of great embarrassment. This idea is summarized in the assertion, $I_f = -P_s$. The previously unpublished evidence we have obtained by asking subjects to estimate expectancy of success and to recommend a suitable monetary penalty for failure at tasks which differ in difficulty (Figure 3) suggests that here again we are dealing with a description of the conditions that exist in achievement-oriented activities and not a theoretical assumption.

It should be apparent that the implications of these two assertions about the tendency to avoid failure, $T_{-f} = M_{AF} \times P_f \times I_f$ and $I_f = -P_s$, are described in curves looking very much like those already presented in Figure 2 except that the behavioral implications are just the opposite. That is, if you will look again at Figure 2 but imagine that the two curves are labeled "tendency to avoid failure when M_{AF} equals 1 and 2," we can say the following things. The tendency to avoid failure, which produces inhibition and decrement in performance,[5] is most strongly aroused when the probability of success (and so, therefore, also of failure) is intermediate. (We assume that the sum of the

[5] However, See Part III, Chapter 11, and Part IV, Chapter 15, for arguments suggesting that under certain conditions there are "paradoxical" effects of inhibition on both level of (immediate) performance and performance over time.–Editors.

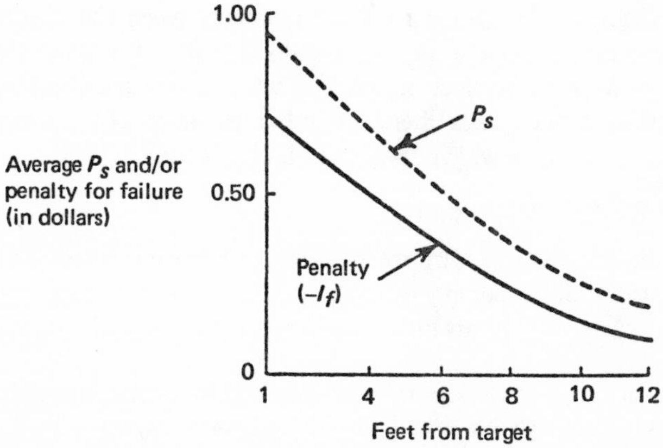

FIG. 3. Estimated probability of success (P_s) and penalty recommended for failure ($-I_f$) by 37 college students in a target practice game.

subjective probabilities of success and failure is approximately equal to one, and use the assumption that $P_s + P_f = 1.00$ for computational purposes in deriving the implications of the theory). The tendency to avoid failure is generally stronger the stronger the motive to avoid failure, which in our experiments is assessed by means of the Mandler-Sarason (1952) Test Anxiety Questionnaire. And finally, as with the achievement motive, we expect the effect of differences in disposition to anxiety to be more apparent in tasks of intermediate difficulty than in very easy or very difficult tasks.[6] This follows from the assumption of a multiplicative interaction between the personality disposition and the situational determinants.

The Resultant Achievement-Oriented Tendency

We study achievement-oriented behavior today assuming that all individuals have acquired a motive to achieve (M_S) and a motive to avoid failure (M_{AF}). That is to say, all persons have some capacity for interest in achievement and some capacity for anxiety about failure. Both are expressed in any situation when it is apparent to the individual that his performance will be evaluated in reference to some standard. One of these motives produces a tendency to undertake the activity; the other produces a tendency not to undertake the activity. There is what we traditionally call an approach-avoidance conflict. It is suggested by the conceptual scheme that we might better begin to think of this as a conflict between an *excitatory* tendency and an *inhibitory* tendency. It is assumed that the two opposed tendencies combine additively and yield a resultant achievement-oriented tendency which is either approach (excitatory) or avoidant (inhibitory) in character and of a certain strength depending upon the relative strength of motive to achieve success and motive to avoid failure in the individual. That is, the resultant tendency equals $T_s - T_{-f}$. Figure 4 shows the resultant tendency when the achievement motive is dominant within the individual. Figure 5 shows the resultant tendency when the motive to avoid failure is dominant. Such a person should inhibit all achievement-oriented activity. Given a choice between alternatives which differ in difficulty, he should choose none of them unless there are other extrinsic positive incentives to undertake these activities which overcome his resistance.[7]

The Role of Extrinsic Motivation

If, for example, there is intrinsic interest or curiosity in a task, or a tendency to seek approval or to comply with an authority–all arbitrarily described as sources of "extrinsic" motivation when we have focused attention on the

[6] However, in Chapter 7 it is argued that under certain conditions involving pursuit of long-term future goals, this bell-shaped relationship between T_{-f} and level of performance does not hold.–Editors.

[7] However, see Chapter 15 for a discussion of circumstances where extrinsic motivation may not be needed for the individual dominated by the motive to avoid failure to engage in achievement-oriented activity.–Editors.

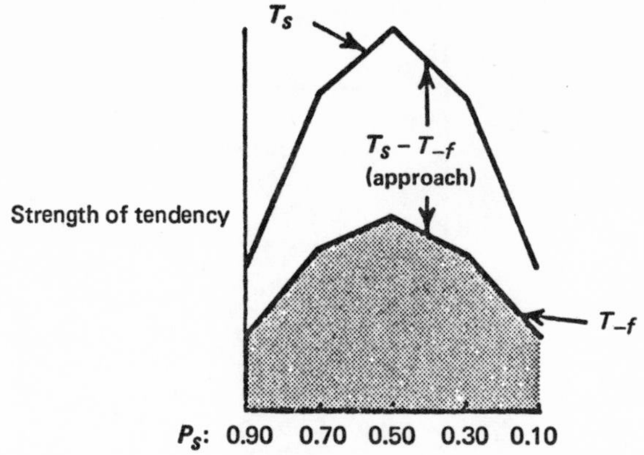

FIG. 4. Resultant achievement-oriented tendency ($T_s - T_{-f}$) when the motive to achieve is dominant in the individual, i.e., $M_S > M_{AF}$.

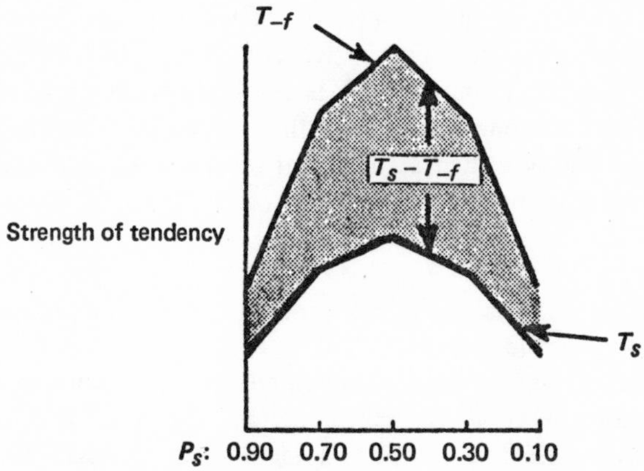

FIG. 5. Resultant achievement-oriented tendency ($T_s - T_{-f}$) when the motive to avoid failure is dominant in the individual, i.e., $M_{AF} > M_S$.

achievement-oriented process–then the tendency to avoid failure which would otherwise inhibit performance completely may be overcome by a stronger approach (excitatory) tendency. Except in very rare cases, there are always a number of different "extrinsic" components in the positive tendency to undertake activities that are viewed, by an observer, as achievement-oriented activities. In Figure 6 we see the effect of a constant amount of "extrinsic" excitatory tendency added to the resultant achievement-oriented tendency when the latter is negative, i.e., avoidant in character. The *difference* between the curves represents the *final strength of tendency* to undertake activities which

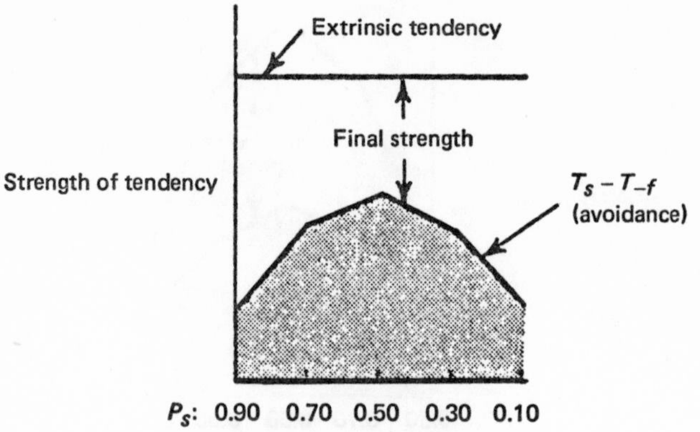

FIG. 6. Effect of constant extrinsic tendency to undertake an activity when the motive to avoid failure is dominant in the individual, i.e, $M_{AF} > M_S$.

differ in probability of success. You will note that the final strength of tendency is *weakest* in the intermediate range of difficulty. Thus the anxiety-prone person, when given a choice among activities which differ in difficulty, should prefer to avoid all of them, but should, if constrained, undertake either an easy task or a very difficult one because the final strength of his multidetermined tendency is then stronger than at the point of maximum challenge and threat where the subjective probability of success is near .50.

Implications Concerning Anxiety

A basic idea in this analysis is that a person who is dominated by a strong inhibitory tendency, the tendency that is expressed in anxiety when he is constrained to undertake achievement-oriented activities, may sometimes have a very high level of aspiration. He may undertake a very difficult task. But we conceive this as a defensive reaction, a mere going through the motions of achievement activities. He does it at all only because of other non-achievement-related sources of motivation. He is engaging in a compromise between the tendency to avoid failure and the sum total of his extrinsic motivation. If not constrained by extrinsic incentives, he would not undertake any activity when his performance might be evaluated. His tendency to avoid failure, by itself, does not tell us what he *will do* but what he *will not do.* His anxiety does not instigate avoidance behavior. His avoidant activity would take the form of complete inhibition of achievement-oriented activity were there not other sources of positive motivation which overcome his inhibition. The price this fellow pays for achievement-oriented action is the experience of anxiety, which I assume to be directly proportionate to the strength of the resistance, the inhibitory tendency, that is overcome.

These are some implications of the scheme concerning anxiety and avoidance. They represent a departure from the widely accepted view that anxiety is a source of excitation of responses and anxiety-reduction constitutes reinforcement. An Expectancy X Value formulation of the determinants of action suggests that "anxiety" is the consequence of inhibition that has been overcome, a symptom that a negative outcome is expected for the action being performed. When the individual performs an act with no anticipation of a negative consequence, there should be no anxiety. Thus we have a rationale for using a self-report test concerning anxiety in achievement situations to assess the strength of the motive to avoid failure. We assume that the amount of anxiety experienced by a person in a competitive situation is proportionate to the strength of his tendency to avoid failure. This inhibitory tendency must have been overcome by stronger positive tendencies, including the tendency to achieve, or else the individual would never have been present in the kind of achievement test situation about which he is later questioned on the Test Anxiety Questionnaire. When he reports how much anxiety he has experienced in test situations, he is telling us about the strength of his resistance to achievement-oriented action. From this we infer the strength of his motive to avoid failure. We cannot assess this motive very well through content analysis of the emitted behaviors which constitute a TAT story for the very reason that on a so-called projective device the subject is not constrained to undertake those preferably avoided activities in thought or to report them verbally. Perhaps if we explicitly instructed subjects always to tell achievement-related stories we could produce imaginative content *in all subjects* expressing the strength of the motive to avoid failure.

EVIDENCE CONCERNING ASPIRATION AND PERFORMANCE

Before discussing the theory in reference to changes in motivation produced by success and failure, let us consider some evidence that concretizes the static predictions of the theory.

n Achievement and Persistence

Table 1 shows results presented by French and Thomas (1958) relating the level of performance and persistence at a fairly difficult problem-solving task to strength of n Achievement in Air Force personnel. A number of studies have shown that n Achievement and Test Anxiety are uncorrelated in young college men when both tests are administered under neutral conditions. This means that the average strength of motive to avoid failure can probably be assumed equal in the high and low n Achievement groups of this experiment. Given the measured difference in strength of n Achievement, the resultant achievement-oriented tendency should be stronger in the high n Achievement group.

TABLE 1

Number of *S*s Strong (*N* = 47) and Weak (*N* = 45) in Achievement Motive Who Solved Complex Problem and Who Persisted at Task Until Time Limit (34 Minutes) Whether or Not They Had Solved It

Achievement motive	Performance level		Persistence	
	Solvers	Nonsolvers	Worked to limit	Stopped before limit
Strong	25	22	22	25
Weak	14	31	1	44

Note.–After French & Thomas, 1958, with permission of the authors and publisher, American Psychological Association.

n Achievement, Text Anxiety, and Performance

Results of a more recent study employing a measure both of n Achievement and of Test Anxiety are shown in Table 2. The main point of this study was to show the influence of achievement-related motives on all three of the traditional dependent performance variables in one study: direction of behavior (in the measure of level of aspiration or risk preference), performance level (the score obtained on the final exam in a college course), and persistence (time spent working on the final exam of a course before turning it in). The measure of aspiration or risk preference was obtained on an earlier occasion in a simple ring-toss game like the classic experiment of Hoppe (1930) with children and a more recent one by McClelland (1958b) which showed that even 5-year-olds who are high in n Achievement prefer to shoot from an intermediate distance. The same result appears in this study with college men and using other tasks (see Atkinson & Feather, 1966). This study (data shown in Table 2), also provides a very clear demonstration that Test Anxiety and n Achievement have diametrically opposite effects on achievement-oriented behavior. Each of the dependent variables is positively related to n Achievement and negatively related to Test Anxiety, and the correlation between the two motives in the study is insignificant. The study also included the measure called n Achievement on the Edwards Personal Preference Scale. Unfortunately, there was no evidence to attest the construct validity of this objective test. Thus it cannot be recommended as an economical substitute for the thematic apperceptive measure. In fact, those who scored high on the PPS variable called n Achievement, which would appear to have face validity given the conventional wisdom about motivation, behaved more like those the theory describes as motivated to avoid failure. The challenging task of developing a valid objective test of n Achievement still lies ahead. I can think of no reason why renewed effort should not be successful now that we have some theory to guide the construction of items and the logic of what is paired with what in a preference test. Some initial steps have been taken by Patricia O'Connor and me to develop an achievement risk preference scale by sampling real-life instances of achievement-oriented activity (e.g., if you were a relief pitcher would you prefer to come into the game when the score is tied or when you team is behind 5 to 2?). Preliminary results (Atkinson & O'Connor, 1966) show predicted correlations with TAT n Achievement and Test Anxiety scores, but this new test still lacks the predictive validity of the two other measures combined. We hope others trained in psychometrics will now be encouraged to undertake the task of developing *theoretically sound* objective tests of motivational dispositions. This will require greater interest in the conceptual and experimental analysis of the process of motivation than test makers have exhibited in the past.[8]

n Achievement, Social Class, and Grades

Table 3 shows results obtained by Rosen (1956) in a study of scholastic performance of high-school boys differing in n Achievement and coming from different social class backgrounds. Other studies of n Achievement and grades with ability controlled have produced similar positive results (Lesser et al., 1963; Morgan, 1952; Ricciuti & Sadacca, 1955). Several, however, have produced little or no evidence of a positive relationship (Krumboltz, 1957). Whether the negative results are to be attributed to some deficiency in methodology in administration or scoring of the TAT, to the overdetermined character of motivation for academic performance which masks or washes out differential effects of n Achievement (see Atkinson, 1958b), or to some other factor is unknown.[9] My hunch is that the quality of motivation in different classrooms and schools differs greatly depending upon the social organization of the school and instructional methods employed and that the relationship

[8] See Chapter 11, Footnote 3, for a further comment concerning the development of an objective (valid) measure of the achievement motive.–Editors.

[9] See Part II for the effects of future orientation on academic performance.–Editors.

TABLE 2

Three Measures of Achievement-Oriented Activity Obtained on the Same Group of Male College Students

n Achievement	Test Anxiety	*N*	Prefer intermediate risk	High persistence on exam	High performance on exam
High	Low	13	77%	73%	67%
High	High	10	40	40	60
Low	Low	9	44	43	43
Low	High	13	31	25	25

Note.–After Atkinson & Litwin, 1960, with permission of authors and publisher American Psychological Association. *Ss* classified in terms of median score on each variable.

TABLE 3

Scholastic Achievement of High-School Boys in Relation to Strength of Achievement Motive and Social Class Background

	Middle class[a]		Working class[b]	
Achievement motive	High	Low	High	Low
Average grades:	($N = 38$)	($N = 22$)	($N = 16$)	($N = 44$)
"B" or above	66%	32%	75%	36%
"C" or below	34	68	25	64

Note.–After Rosen, 1956, with permission of the author and of the publisher, the American Sociological Association.

[a]Hollingshead: Index I-II-III.

[b]IV-V.

between strength of any particular motive and level of achievement will vary markedly accordingly. We too often forget Lewin's guiding hypothesis, $B = f(P, E)$, which emphasizes interaction.

Rosen's results are particularly interesting in that they show that achievement motive is generally stronger in middle-class students, a finding replicated by a number of others, but that working-class boys who are strongly motivated to achieve do as well academically as their counterparts in the middle class. This fact fits well with Crockett's results concerning n Achievement and social mobility of men having working-class background to be considered later.

Educational and Vocational Choice

Of considerable interest for education is a study by Isaacson (1964) which shows that strength of n Achievement relative to Test Anxiety is related to choice of major field by college students, as shown in Figure 7. From college records showing the grades given students of known scholastic aptitude in the various departments of natural science, the humanities, social science, etc., and from estimates by students which confirmed his inferences, Isaacson ordered different fields of study in terms of difficulty, i.e., perceived probability of success. He ordered students in terms of a combination of normalized n Achievement score minus normalized Test Anxiety score ($M_S - M_{AF}$). His results show the extent to which the choice of major field is analogous to the choice of a task which represents a certain level of difficulty in a typical experiment on risk taking or aspiration. Men highly motivated to achieve relative to their anxiety about failure decide to major in fields which are perceived as intermediate in difficulty. Their more anxiety-prone peers more frequently select the easy or very difficult fields as defined by local scuttlebutt and grading practices.[10]

[10]However, see Chapter 7, particularly the discussion of results obtained by Wish and

(Continued)

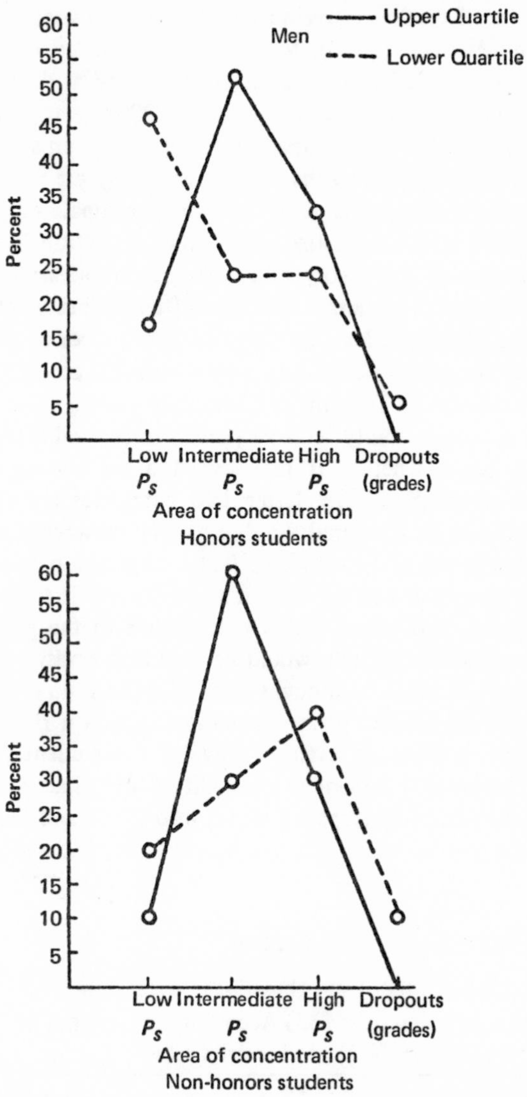

FIG. 7. Percentage of male Michigan students high and low in resultant achievement motivation who chose to concentrate in areas considered low, intermediate, and high in P_s. *(After Isaacson, 1964, with permission of the author and of the publisher, American Psychological Association.)*

Hazashi, which suggests that the results obtained in these studies depend upon whether or not the academic major is seen as importantly related to the achievement of future goals.—Editors.

The same pattern of results occurs in an earlier study of vocational aspiration of college men by Mahone (1960). Mahone's data showed that occupations which are normally accorded high prestige are perceived as difficult to attain. When college men were asked "How many out of 100 students have the general ability needed to succeed in this occupation?" and were given a randomized list of occupations whose positions on the prestige hierarchy are well known from national survey data, it was found that the average estimate of probability of success correlated—.85 with the prestige rank of the occupation. This means that the critical assumption of the theory of achievement motivation, $I_s = 1 - P_s$, applies to the occupational hierarchy which so often defines what is meant by success in life by sociologists. Mahone obtained two indices of preference for intermediate risk in vocational aspiration for men classified according to strength of n Achievement relative to Test Anxiety. He asked three clinical psychologists to consider each student's ability, college performance, and stated vocational aspiration and to judge whether it represented a realistic aspiration, over-aspiration, or underaspiration. The latter two categories are referred to as unrealistic. In addition, he measured the discrepancy between a student's own estimate of how many out of 100 students had enough ability to succeed at his chosen vocational aspiration and the student's own percentile rank on a measure of scholastic aptitude. This index, which corresponds to the goal discrepancy score of level of aspiration research, would be very high positive if the student aspired to an occupation which he thought demanded much more ability than he had, like shooting from 15 feet away from the target in a ring-toss game. It would be very low positive or even negative if the student aspired to an occupation which he thought demanded less ability than he had. Mahone divided the distribution of obtained discrepancy scores into thirds and found, as shown in Table 4, that the men in whom n Achievement is dominant more frequently

TABLE 4

Realistic (Intermediate) and Unrealistic Vocational Aspiration in College Men ($N = 135$) According to Strength of Achievement Motive (M_S) and Motive to Avoid Failure (M_{AF})

n Achievement	Test Anxiety score	N	Clinical judgments		Goal discrepancy	
			Realistic	Unrealistic	Intermediate third	Extreme thirds
High	Low	36	75%	25%	50%	50%
High	High	31	48	52	30	70
Low	Low	40	68	32	38	62
Low	High	28	39	61	18	82

Note.–After Mahone, 1960, with permission of the author and publisher, American Psychological Association.

have the realistic, moderately high aspirations; the men dominated by anxiety more frequently are unrealistic. They either set their vocational aspiration very low, or, what appears much more frequently, they appear to set their aspiration much too high for their ability.[11] We have replicated these results of Mahone's in a group of high-school seniors who were above the median in intelligence and part of an accelerated program which emphasized achievement-orientation in about the same way it is emphasized in college (Atkinson & O'Connor, 1963) but not in less intelligent high-school students.[12]

A national survey study (see Veroff et al., 1960 and Chapter 3) employed a thematic apperceptive measure of n Achievement and other social motives. The major importance of this study was its analysis of the method itself when given a severe test in a nationwide survey study. Veroff found, for example, that it is inadequate for the least verbal 17% of the population and that for the remainder of this very heterogeneous sample, the scores obtained from thematic apperceptive stories have to be adjusted to remove the effect of wide variations in length of protocol which correlated .20 with all motive scores obtained from the records. But we learned how to accomplish these adjustments and are satisfied with the general applicability and utility of the measuring instrument with a very heterogeneous population. Among the substantive results of interest is one showing that n Achievement is stronger among more highly educated groups (see Chapter 3, Table 3). I think this means, in part at least, that those who are most highly motivated to achieve are more persistent in the achievement-oriented activity we call getting an education. They are, in other words, less frequently to be found among the dropouts.

Crockett's (1962) analysis of social mobility in the same national survey data showed that men who are highly motivated to achieve more frequently have attained occupations higher in the status hierarchy than those of their father. Closer analysis locates the relationship between n Achievement and upward occupational mobility in men of working-class background, as show in Table 5. Why should this be? Crockett showed, in further analysis, that when the occupational status of the father is upper-middle or high, about 50% of the men have had some college education, and there is no relationship between getting a college education and n Achievement because, he argued, there are so many other sources of inducement for persons of middle-class background to go on to college. It is the expected thing to do, and the financial means are generally available. (Crockett's data show, in fact, that n Affiliation, or perhaps what might more appropriately be called the need for social approval, is a more significant factor in upward social mobility in this upper-middle segment of the

[11] Further analysis of Mahone's results in light of the proposed effects of future orientation on aspiration (see Chapter 7) indicates that the Low-High group predominately *overaspired.*–Editors.

[12] See Chapters 4 and 7 for a discussion of results reported by Shrable and Moulton (1968) in which predictions were supported for high-school students above their group median in intelligence but not for those below.–Editors.

TABLE 5

Strength of Achievement Motive and Occupational Mobility

Occupational prestige category of father	Strength of n Achievement	N	Occupational prestige category of respondent in relation to father: Below	Same	Above
High	High	20	55%	45%	0%
	Low	11	55	45	0
Upper-middle	High	50	42	32	26
	Low	43	42	35	23
Lower-middle	High	67	16	41	43
	Low	52	28	47	25
Low	High	60	0	33	67
	Low	65	0	54	46

Note.–After Crockett, 1962, with permission of the authors and publisher, American Sociological Association.

society.) Among men of working-class background, only about half as many manage to get some college education. And it is in this group, whose social values do not emphasize the central importance of education, and in which the financial means is so often lacking, that strength of need for achievement makes a difference in determining who gets a higher education. Crockett found that 27% of men from lower-middle and low status backgrounds who are high in n Achievement get some college education. Only 17% of the men in these social groups who are low in n Achievement had attended college. There is residual evidence of upward social mobility attributable to differences in strength of achievement motive among those who do not go on to college, particularly among lower status groups where one can move up in the occupational hierarchy without a college education, but it is quite clear that getting a college education, whatever the source of motivation for it, is almost always associated with upward movement for someone who has relatively low status background to begin with (see Crockett, 1964).

Crockett's results, then, show that strength of need for achievement is a factor in that form of persistence we call getting an education when there are not a lot of other inducements to do so and when the financial means are not easily available and that need for achievement is, in addition, a factor in upward mobility among those who do not get a college education.

These various studies of academic performance, choice of major field, vocational aspiration, and occupational mobility have produced results that are analogous to those obtained in studies of aspiration, performance, and persistence in controlled experiments. The same basic concepts–motive to achieve, motive to avoid failure, and expectancy of success–are useful in analysis of both sets of problems. A recent book by David McClelland, *The Achieving Society* (1961), surveys other social studies of the kind I have touched upon and extends their logic to the analysis of motivational problems of whole societies, e.g., the problems of economic development and the rise and fall of whole civilizations.

EXPECTANCY OF SUCCESS AS A MOTIVATIONAL VARIABLE

Let us turn now to the dynamics of achievement-oriented tendencies, the changes that are brought about by success and failure. It is assumed that when an individual undertakes an activity and succeeds, the expectancy of success at that task and similar tasks is increased; that when he fails, the expectancy of success at that task and similar tasks is decreased. Since the incentive value of success is inversely related to expectancy of success, the cognitive change produced by success and failure also produces a change in the incentive values of future success and failure. There is, subsequent to success and failure, a change in the strength of the tendency to engage in the same and similar activities, a motivational change.[13]

Effect of Success and Failure

Figure 8 shows the nature of this change, using a ring-toss game as our reference experiment, for an individual in whom the achievement motive is

[13] See Part IV for discussions of another effect of success and failure, namely, on the amount of achievement-related motivation that may carry over to influence motivation for some subsequent achievement-oriented activity.–Editors.

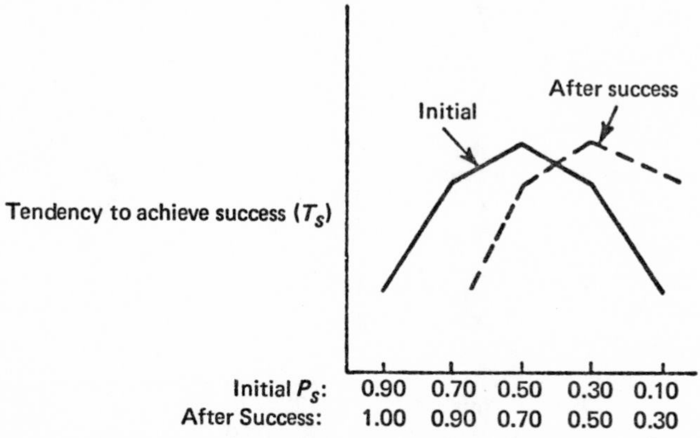

FIG. 8. Change in level of aspiration following success when motive to achieve is dominant, i.e., $M_S > M_{AF}$. Success produces an increase in P_s at the same and similar tasks. Since $I_s = 1 - P_s$, the change in motivation following success favors a change in activity, viz., raising the level of aspiration.

dominant. One of the curves shows the initial strength of the tendency to achieve at each of several tasks, as the subject approaches the task with only his past experience in similar situations influencing the strength of his expectancy of success at each level of difficulty. According to the theory, this individual will choose to undertake the task where P_s is .50. If he should do that and succeed, the change in expectancy of success and related change in the incentive value of success should produce the change in motivation shown in the curve labeled "after success."

Figure 9 shows the change in motivation predicted when the same individual fails in the curve labeled "after failure." His expectancy of success at the initially chosen task falls, this change generalizes to other similar activities, and so an initially easier task now appears the task of intermediate difficulty. You can see from the two figures how the theory of achievement motivation generates the hypothesis that among persons in whom the achievement motive dominates, the level of aspiration will generally tend to be raised after success and lowered after failure. Notice that the theory does *not* say that success will lead to a strengthening of the tendency to repeat the same action, which is what the empirical Law of Effect asserts.

Typical and Atypical Changes in Expectancy

The results of all the earlier work on level of aspiration which did not include assessments of individual differences in personality (see Lewin et al., 1944) clearly show that the changes described here are the "typical," i.e., most frequent, results of success and failure on level of aspiration. We explain these "typical" results of earlier studies by referring to what is known from contemporary surveys about the strength of achievement motive in college-

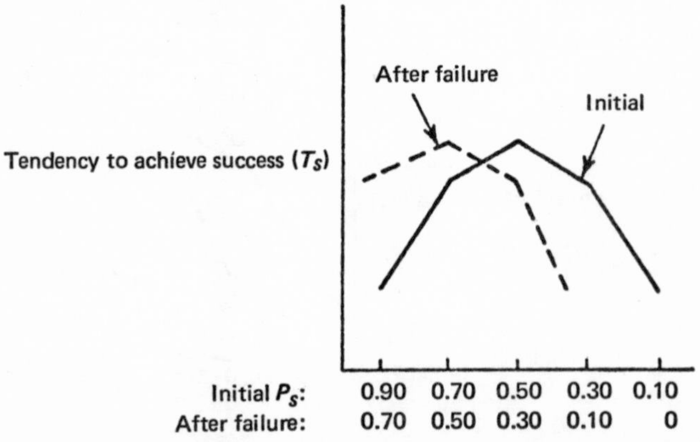

FIG. 9. Change in level of aspiration following failure when motive to achieve is dominant, i.e., $M_S > M_{AF}$. Failure produces a decrease in P_s at the same and similar tasks. Since $I_s = 1 - P_s$, the change in motivation following failure favors lowering the level of aspiration.

educated groups which have provided the subjects for the majority of studies of aspiration. The achievement motive is likely to be dominant in most persons who attend college.

The "atypical," i.e., less frequent, changes in level of aspiration–viz., lowering after success and raising after failure–are also explained by the current theory. Let us consider the individual who is dominated by the motive to avoid failure and refer back to Figures 5 and 6 for this discussion. His initial aspiration should be either a very easy task where failure is a rare event or a very difficult task where success is a rare event. If the most probable outcome occurs, success at the easy task and failure at the difficult task, there is no spur to change the level of aspiration. Success at an easy task raises the expectancy of success and reduces even more the tendency to avoid the task. Failure at the most difficult task lowers the probability of success and produces a similar motivational effect, a reduction in the strength of the tendency to avoid the task.

But note what should happen if the *improbable* outcome occurs. Suppose the anxiety-prone individual fails at the easy task. Then the probability of success is reduced from near certainty to some intermediate value closer to .50. As a result, the tendency to avoid failure at that task is greater on a subsequent trial. A few such failures and the task turns into the intermediate risk which this individual most wants to avoid. He should then do what might appear very irrational to the observer–shift from a very low to a very high level of aspiration. He should, in other words, choose the task for which the tendency to avoid failure is very weak. This happens to be the one where the P_s is very small at the other end of the continuum of difficulty.

What happens if this "anxious" individual has initially chosen a very difficult task and the unlikely thing happens, he succeeds? This atypical result should produce a very atypical change in his aspiration. Because he has succeeded at the task having a low P_s, the P_s is increased towards .50, and consequently the tendency to avoid this task is increased. He might be expected to shift his level of aspiration to a very easy task following success at a very difficult task.

These atypical changes in aspiration were present but infrequent in early studies of aspiration. Recently, Moulton (1965) has shown, as reported in Table 6, that they occur among persons who score high in Test Anxiety and low in n Achievement as the theory predicts. Moulton first ascertained each subject's initial preference among three tasks described to him as very easy, intermediate in difficulty, and very difficult, but without letting the subject perform the task he had chosen. Then, no matter which task was initially preferred, each subject performed the task of intermediate difficulty. Success and failure at this task were experimentally controlled. Following the experience of success or failure at the task of intermediate difficulty, the subject was then given the choice of working at either of the two remaining tasks–the easy one or the very difficult one. Moulton found that subjects in whom n Achievement was dominant, who normally preferred the task of intermediate difficulty, chose the very difficult task after success and the easy one after failure at that moderately difficult task.

TABLE 6

Number of Subjects Making Typical and Atypical Shifts in Level of Aspiration in Relation to n Achievement and Test Anxiety

n Achievement	Test Anxiety	Typical shift	Atypical shift
High	Low	30	1
Low	High	20	11

Note.–After Moulton, 1965, with permission of the author. "Typical" means raising following success and lowering following failure. "Atypical" means the opposite.

These are the typical changes in aspiration. But among the anxious subjects, those scoring low in n Achievement and high in Test Anxiety, he found the atypical shifts expected by the theory as shown in Table 6. The design was so arranged that half of the anxious subjects who had initially preferred the easy task as the one they wanted to perform were told they failed at the task of intermediate difficulty, and half of the anxious subjects who had initially preferred the very difficult task were told they had succeeded when they performed the task of intermediate difficulty. (A similar design was applied to the nonanxious subjects.) This meant that the P_s would be reduced for all tasks for the person who initially had chosen what appeared to be the easy task, and the P_s would be higher for all tasks for the person who had initially preferred the task that appeared very difficult. These anxious subjects, in other words, were faced with the problem of choosing between a task that would now appear more like a .50 risk (the one they had initially chosen) or another task, one of very high P_s for some of them, one of very low P_s for others. Table 6 shows that the subjects in whom motive to avoid failure was dominant did react defensively with the atypical shift in aspiration about one-third of the time and significantly more often than their more positively motivated peers.

Persistence after Continual Failure

The related problem of persistence following continual failure has been studied by Feather (1961, 1962). According to the theory, a person in whom n Achievement is dominant should be much more persistent following failure at a task which he believes initially to be easy than one he believes initially to be very difficult. Consider again Figure 4 to follow the argument. If the subject in whom n Achievement is dominant undertakes to solve a problem with P_s of .70 and repeatedly fails in successive trials, the P_s should at first drop toward .50–producing a heightening of interest–and then drop toward zero, causing a gradual decrease in the tendency to achieve at the task until finally the tendency to do something else will be stronger and the subject will quit. If this same person began the task thinking the P_s was only .05, a very difficult task, it should take only a few failures to reduce the tendency sufficiently so that he would prefer to do something else.

We should predict something very different for a subject in whom motive to avoid failure is dominant. Consider again Figure 6 to follow the argument for him. If he perceives the task as relatively easy to begin with, having a P_s of .70, and then begins to fail in successive trials, the immediate result should be an increase in the tendency to avoid failure as the P_s drops towards .50. Consequently, there is a reduction in the total strength of the tendency to perform the task. He should quit the task very soon after his initial failures if it seemed easy to begin with. On the other hand, if he began the task thinking it was very difficult, let us say with P_s of .05, and then fails, the effect of failure is, paradoxically, to reduce the strength of his tendency to avoid failure. The final strength of the tendency to undertake the task becomes stronger and stronger as the inhibition is reduced. The subject in whom the motive to avoid failure is dominant should, in other words, be very persistent in the face of failure at what initially appears to be a very difficult task. Feather's results, confirming these hypotheses, are shown in Table 7.

IMPLICATIONS

The Problem of Inadequate Motivation

These studies of change in aspiration and persistence following success and failure draw attention to the expectancy or subjective probability of success as a potent and manipulable motivational variable. When we consider the question of what is responsible for the inadequate motivation of particular individuals, we find that there are two possible answers. First, the deficiency in motivation may be the result of a deficiency in personality. The motive to avoid failure may be too strong and the motive to achieve too weak. This can produce a general resistance to achievement-oriented activity that must be overcome by other extrinsic sources of motivation if there is to be any spur to achievement-oriented

TABLE 7

Persistence Among College Men ($N = 35$) in the Face of Continued Failure as a Function of Personality and Initial Difficulty of Task

n Achievement	Test Anxiety	Percent above median in persistence	
		Task seen initially as easy ($P_s = .70$)	Task seen initially as difficult ($P_s = .05$)
High	Low	75	22
Low	High	33	75

Note.–After Feather, 1961, with permission of the author and of the publisher, American Psychological Association.

activity at all. Second, even when the personality is adequate, i.e., the achievement motive is relatively strong, there may be inadequate challenge. The task the individual faces may be too easy or too difficult *for him.*

Hopefully, we shall soon learn more than we now know about the antecedents of the personality dispositions called "motive to achieve" and "motive to avoid failure" so that practical steps can be taken to encourage change in basic personality structure. But until we know more than we now know it would appear that manipulation of the strength of expectancy of success is the most feasible means of bringing about changes in achievement-oriented motivation.[14]

Individual Differences in Expectancy of Success

Once the theoretical importance of expectancy of success is appreciated, we begin to be concerned about a new set of questions for research. For example, is the expectancy of success (P_s) the same for all individuals in a classroom as they face a particular task, or do they differ in P_s because of their past experiences with similar material as much or more than they may differ in the strength of the two achievement-related motives? We gain some insight concerning this kind of question from some results reported by Spielberger (1962) shown in Figure 10. These results, viewed through the spectacles of the present theory, suggest that a measure of an individual's scholastic aptitude or intelligence may also be taken as an index of his subjective probability of success in academic work.

Spielberger used the Manifest Anxiety Scale to assess the influence of anxiety on the academic performance of college freshmen. He determined the average grade point average of students who scored high and low in anxiety at five different levels of ability as measured by a scholastic aptitude test. We can assume that the average strength of n Achievement, not measured in this experiment, is equal in the two anxiety groups. Thus the low anxiety group is the one in which the resultant tendency to achieve is strongest. Compare the results obtained by Spielberger with what is expected according to the theory of achievement motivation if it is assumed that those who score very low in aptitude are persons who approach their college work with a very low expectancy of success and those who score high in aptitude are those who approach college work with a very high probability of success. The results fit the hypothesis that individual difference in disposition to anxiety will have very little effect on performance when the task is perceived as either very easy or very difficult but will have an effect when the task is one of intermediate difficulty, as it presumably is for those in the middle range on sholastic aptitude.[15]

[14] See Part II for how individual differences in the perceived importance or instrumentality of success or failure in a task for the achievement of distant future goals may affect motivation and hence level of performance.–Editors.

[15] See Chapter 5 for results when subjective probability of success was manipulated.–Editors.

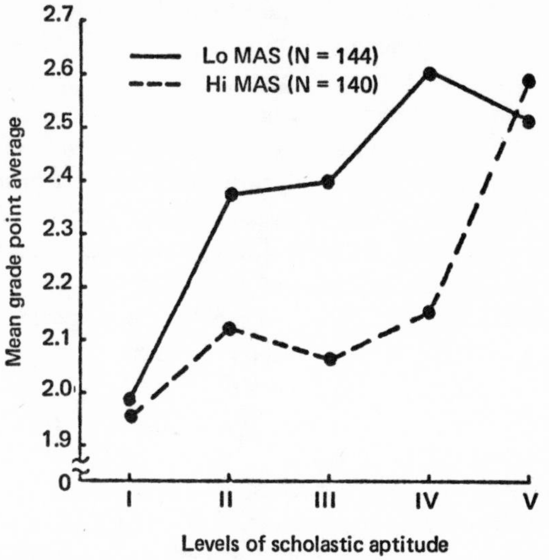

FIG. 10. Mean grade point average of college students at five levels of scholastic aptitude according to their manifest anxiety score (MAS). (*After Spielberger, 1962, with permission of the author and of the publisher, National Association of Mental Health, Inc.*)

Motivational Effects of Ability Grouping

The same basic idea provided the theoretical foundation for a study by Patricia O'Connor and me on the motivational effects of ability grouping. Our theoretical argument was quite simple. In the traditional heterogeneous class, where all levels of ability are represented, the chance of being a standout performer relative to peers must seem almost impossible for the student of low ability and is virtually assured for the student of very high ability. According to theory, when P_s is either very low or very high neither interest in achievement nor anxiety about failure will be aroused. Hence only the students of average ability are likely to be very motivated to achieve or anxious in the traditional heterogeneous class.

What happens when students of comparable ability are brought together in the same class? According to theory, the student of high ability now faces a more competitive situation. His P_s should drop from near certainty towards .50, an intermediate risk. Just the opposite should happen for the student of very low ability. Now, for the first time he is surrounded by peers of equal ability and so he has the opportunity for success relative to the others. His P_s is increased towards .50. In other words, homogenization in terms of ability should make the learning situation one of intermediate achievement risk for more students than the traditional heterogeneous class. Is this good? The theory asserts that ability grouping should enhance interest and performance when the achievement motive is strong and the motive to avoid failure is weak. But it should heighten the tendency to avoid failure when that motive is dominant in the person. The same treatment should, in other words, have *diametrically opposite motivational effects* depending upon the personality of the students.

Our study was conducted in sixth-grade classes of a midwestern city. The experimental classes were ability grouped for the first time in sixth grade. The control classes continued to be heterogeneous in ability in sixth grade. We measured amount of growth between fifth and sixth grade on achievement tests of reading and arithmetic. We measured amount of growth relative to average amount of growth among students comparable in intelligence. In addition, we assessed degree of interest and satisfaction in sixth-grade work as compared with fifth-grade work in one of our experimental schools by means of rating scales of various classroom activities. The results are shown in Tables 8 and 9. We expected and found that both boys and girls who were strong in n Achievement relative to Test Anxiety show evidence of greater learning and stronger interest in ability grouped classes than in control classes irrespective of the level of intelligence. We expected to find evidence of a decrement of interest and performance among the students who scored low in n Achievement relative to Test Anxiety when placed in ability grouped classes. Our results show the predicted decrement in reported interest and satisfaction but no significant change in scholastic performance when the anxiety-prone subjects in the experimental and control classes are compared. Ability grouping did not weaken the performance of these students, though they may have maintained the same level of performance as comparable students in the control classes at a greater personal cost if we take the ratings of interest and satisfaction seriously. It would be nice to know, but we do not, if they spent longer hours at homework.

TABLE 8

Students Showing Above-Median Growth for Their Level of Intelligence in Reading and Arithmetic on California Achievement Test

	n Achievement	Ability groups		Control classes	
	– Test Anxiety	*N*	%	*N*	%
(IQ 125+)	High	24[a]	71	37	46
	Low	10	50	27	37
(IQ 113-124)	High	11[b]	90	17	41
	Low	17	65	19	58
(IQ 112–)	High	8[b]	88	8	38
	Low	23	52	14	36

Note.–After Atkinson & O'Connor, 1963, with permission of the authors.
[a]Above median in both areas.
[b]Above median in one or both areas.

TABLE 9

Effect of Ability Grouping on Reported Interest in Schoolwork in Sixth as Compared with Fifth Grade

	Students above median			
n Achievement	Ability groups		Control classes	
- Test Anxiety	*N*	%	*N*	%
High	18	78	78	56
Moderate	22	41	82	43
Low	22	36	73	52

Note.–After Atkinson & O'Connor, 1963, with permission of the authors.

The results certainly suggest that ability grouping has important motivational implications and that what is so generally true of environmental manipulations in the domain of achievement-oriented activity is also true here: the same treatment may have diametrically opposite effects on different individuals. This, I believe, is one of the most important implications of contemporary research on human motivation–the challenge it poses for those who think there may be some *single* method of instruction or treatment which will produce optimal motivation for learning in all students irrespective of personality.

The Law of Effect–A Misleading Guide

Equally important is another general implication of the conceptual scheme which deserves some explicit comment. It is the argument that the Law of Effect is fundamentally inadequate as a guide to understanding in the domain of achievement-oriented activity. Success does not invariably produce a strengthening of the tendency to undertake the same activity on another occasion. Sometimes success weakens the subsequent tendency to engage in the same activity. The individual strongly motivated to achieve normally raises his level of aspiration following success: his behavior changes.

Gordon Allport (1943) noted this inadequacy of the Law of Effect more than 20 years ago, and now, at last, we have a reasonably clear explanation of why the traditional generalization does not hold. The law does not hold because in the domain of achievement-oriented activity an increase in the expectancy of success, which is the effect on the person of success, produces a change in the incentive value of success. Sometimes the effect of this change is an increase in the strength of the tendency to undertake the same activity. Sometimes it is just the reverse. It depends upon the personality of the subject–whether the motive to achieve or the motive to avoid failure is dominant in him–and it depends upon the initial strength of the expectancy of success at the task. The matter is complicated, certainly more complicated than the Law of Effect would ever lead us to imagine.

From the viewpoint of an Expectancy X Value theory of motivation, one which asserts that the tendency to undertake an activity is determined by the strength of the expectancy that the activity will produce certain consequences and the value of those consequences, the Law of Effect summarizes what is observed when there is no relationship between the value of the consequence of an action and the expectancy of attaining it. This is shown schematically in Figure 11. Holding the strength of motive and the incentive value of the consequence constant, we see that the strength of tendency to undertake an activity should increase as the strength of expectancy of attaining that consequence increases. This is what happens in a series of "reinforced" trials.

The Law of Effect should also provide an adequate summary of what happens when the value of the consequence of an action increases as the expectancy of attaining it increases. But the Law of Effect simply does not hold under the conditions of achievement-oriented activity when the incentive value of the consequence of activity (success) is inversely related to the strength of expectancy of producing it.[16]

How good is the evidence that the incentive value of success is inversely related to the expectancy of success: $I_s = 1 - P_s$? There are three sources of evidence. First, reported expectancies of success are found to be inversely related to estimates of the prize that ought to be awarded for success at a task (see Figure 1) and to reports of degree of satisfaction immediately after success at a task. Second, there are the

[16] However, see Chapter 7 for a discussion of complications to this relatively simple implication of an inverse relationship between P_s and I_s when future orientation is taken into account.–Editors.

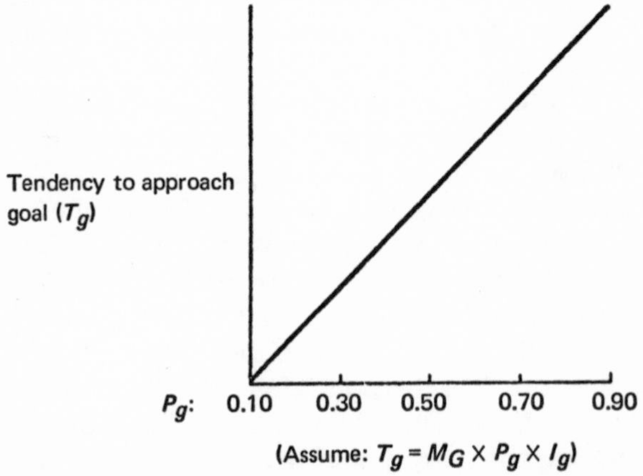

FIG. 11. Theoretical effect of increasing the strength of expectancy of attaining a goal (P_g) when the incentive value of the goal (I_g) is constant and not affected by a change in P_g (derivation of the Law of Effect).

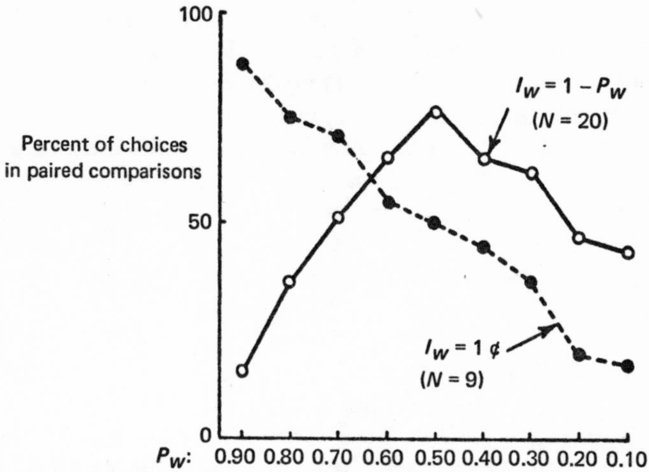

FIG. 12. Preference for various probabilities of winning (P_W) in a choice between lotteries when the monetary incentive was constant (I_W = 1¢) and when the monetary incentive (1¢ to 9¢ was inversely related to probability of winning ($I_W = 1 - P_W$).

results of all the studies of aspiration, change in aspiration, and persistence as a function of initial level of difficulty that are predicted and integrated when it is assumed that $I_s = 1 - P_s$. Finally, there is one more bit of indirect evidence which is previously unpublished. We have attempted to construct a simple money model of achievement-oriented activity. The subject is confronted with a set of containers each holding 100 beads. In each container there are a certain number of distinctively colored "lucky" beads. The subject cannot see the beads, but he can see a sign on top of each container which tells him how many lucky beads–10, 20, 30, 40, 50, 60, 70, 80, or 90–are in the container and how much money he will be given if he should pick a lucky bead from the container. Thus, for example, the subject must decide whether to put his hand into a container having a sign which says "10 lucky beads–lucky bead worth 9¢" or another container having a sign which says, "50 lucky beads–lucky bead worth 5¢." The value of the monetary incentive was arranged to fit the rule $I_w = 1 - P_w$. Thus the subject could win 9¢ if he picked a lucky bead when the probability was .10; 5¢ when the probability was .50; 1¢ when the probability was .90; etc. It was obvious to all the subjects that no skill or competence was involved in the task, yet, as the bell-shaped curve in Figure 12 shows, there was a very strong preference for intermediate risk in this lottery–comparable to the often observed preference for intermediate risk in achievement activity where the rule $I_s = 1 - P_s$ is assumed to hold. Every probability was paired with every other for each subject. The curve represents the percentage of times a given alternative was chosen in preference to all others.

The other curve in Figure 12, that relatively straight line having its peak where the probability of winning a lucky bead is .90, shows the results obtained *when the incentive value of the lucky bead was held constant at 1¢ no matter what the probability of winning.* When this condition exists in a state of nature—that is, when the incentive value of the consequence of an activity is constant—the effect of repeated reward should be a strengthening of expectancy of reward, and the Law of Effect is then a useful summary of what is likely to happen.

CONCLUDING COMMENT

If this essay had been prepared 10 years ago, I am sure the title would have been "The *mainspring* of achievement-oriented activity." It would have been concerned only with the achievement motive. You can look at a book published in 1953 under that title, *The Achievement Motive* (McClelland et al.), to see what would have been included.

Today's version, marking some progress in a decade of work, is called the *mainsprings* because our research has finally caught up with the relatedness of "anxiety" and need for achievement as determinants of activities when performance is evaluated. The present conceptual scheme gives equal emphasis to each of these motives and to the expectancy of success as the manipulable determinant of achievement-oriented motivation. You will find the beginnings of discussion along this line in *Motives in Fantasy, Action, and Society* (Atkinson, 1958a) and *The Achieving Society* (McClelland, 1961), and more thorough treatment in more recent publications, *An Introduction to Motivation* (Atkinson, 1964) and *A Theory of Achievement Motivation* (Atkinson & Feather, 1966).

Ten years from now, when we have sharpened and extended our conceptual analysis to embrace those other motivational factors that now are merely lumped in the category "extrinsic motivation," particularly the tendency to gain social approval in achievement activities which has already gained the special status of most neglected variable in research on achievement-oriented activity, a similar essay may have to be titled *the springs* of achievement-oriented activity.[17] Some may feel that would have been a more appropriate title and topic even for the present effort. I do not believe the current state of empirical knowledge supports that view. But if the reader feels that some extra justification is needed for the title and the special emphasis of tendency to achieve success and tendency to avoid failure as

[17]Editors' comment: Initially we planned to use this phrase as the title of the present volume. However, the complexities of the motivational determinants of achievement, which were unanticipated even just the short time ago when this paper was written (1965), compel a more sophisticated view of the relationship between the various sources of motivation for achievement and how they determine behavior (see Chapters 6, 7, 11, 15, 17, 19, and 20 for the new theoretical developments and their implications).

mainsprings of achievement-oriented activity, let the justification lie in the fact that they are wound up differently from the others, in a way that we would never have discovered if we had let our thought be constrained by that traditional notion, the Law of Effect, which has so long–too long–dominated thought about matters of learning and motivation in education.

3

THE USE OF THEMATIC APPERCEPTION TO ASSESS MOTIVATION IN A NATIONWIDE INTERVIEW STUDY[1]

Joseph Veroff, John W. Atkinson, Sheila C. Feld, and Gerald Gurin

In recent years, a number of important explorations of the use of projective measures in the survey interview setting (Campbell, 1950; Douvan & Walker, 1956; Lansing & Heyns, 1959; Maccoby & Maccoby, 1954; Sanford, 1950; Sanford & Rosenstock, 1952; Scott, 1956; Tompkins & Miner, 1958) have foreshadowed an inevitable direction of future research in social psychology: the common use in survey studies of assessment techniques developed in experimental and clinical studies of personality dynamics. This trend can be expected to promote a more meaningful integration than now exists of the societal data continually amassed in surveys of broad populations and the research findings accumulated in the clinics and laboratories of personality research. How quickly this integration will come about will depend in large measure upon the conscientiousness with which certain serious methodological problems are faced by the investigator who leaps from the laboratory or clinic to the doorstep of a startled housewife, interviewed because she happened to be selected by the magic of probability sampling. Conceptual integration of facts from field study, clinic, and experiment will be hastened if the personality assessment devices selected from the laboratory have already been investigated with some thoroughness.

[1] Reprinted and abridged by permission of the authors and the American Psychological Association from *Psychological Monographs,* 1960, 74 (Whole No. 499).

The investigations reported in this paper are based on data obtained within a national sample survey supported by the Joint Commission on Mental Illness and Health (Gurin, Project Director). Analysis of these data was supported by two grants from the National Institute of Mental Health, United States Public Health Service, Projects M2181 (Veroff, Principal Investigator) and M2280 (Gurin, Principal Investigator).

The present investigation is an attempt to foster such an integration. We present here an examination of the methodological problems faced in the first attempt to introduce thematic apperceptive measures of three motives (n Achievement, n Affiliation, and n Power) into a nationwide sample survey. Considerable research has been conducted to develop these measures in the experimental setting (Atkinson, 1958a; McClelland, Atkinson, Clark, & Lowell, 1953).[2] Consequently, in adapting these measures to the survey setting, we are in a position to be guided by a fund of research findings which define their validity and highlight the methodological issues to be given serious consideration.

A decade of experimental work has shown that experimentally induced motivational states influence the content of imaginative thought in ways that can be reliably coded to yield measures of important social motives–n Achievement, n Affiliation, and n Power. While results on hand attest to the validity of the approach (see Atkinson, 1958a) considerable further experimental refinement of the present measures is, without question, required. Nevertheless, several explorations using these measures in different cultural settings, i.e., in situations outside of the college laboratory (Child, Storm, & Veroff, 1958; Douvan, 1958; McClelland & Friedman, 1952; Rosen, 1956), have already suggested their promise for field research, particularly for survey studies. We realize, however, that a number of weighty methodological barriers stand in the way of using thematic apperceptive measures of motivation in a national survey, and that these barriers will only be overcome through direct study in field research.

The questions of immediate interest in this paper, therefore, have to do with methodological problems in using the thematic apperceptive method–known to require a modicum of verbal ability and known to be sensitive to the situational differences at the time of administration and known to require skill in content analysis–under the conditions of national survey interviewing.

METHODOLOGICAL PROBLEMS

Selection of Pictures

The particular pictures used to assess motivation by thematic apperception have important effects on the motivational content of stories (Birney, 1958; Haber & Alpert, 1958; Jacobs, 1958). Pictures will differ, depending on their content, in the average amount of motivational imagery they elicit from any group of subjects (*S*s). The amount of motive-related imagery that a picture elicits from a person is influenced both by the strength of his motive and by his past experiences in settings like the one portrayed in the picture.[3] Variability in

[2] See also Atkinson and Feather (1966) and Chapter 2.–Editors.

[3] Atkinson (1958b) has presented a theoretical scheme showing how cognitive expectations based on past experience in situations like the one portrayed in a particular picture together with the motives of the individual jointly determine the motivational content of an imaginative story.

over-all motivation scores which can be attributed to peculiar characteristics of the pictures used rather than to the strength of motive within the *S*s is a source of error we seek to avoid.

The population in the survey study to be reported in this paper is a sample of 1,619 adults (21 or over), a cross-section of Americans living in private households, selected by means of probability sampling (Kish, 1953). To construct a battery of pictures that will have similar significance for all social groups represented in this sample was the major problem of picture selection that we faced. Indeed, the sex difference is so important a factor (Angelina, 1955; Davenport, 1953; Field, 1951; Morrison, 1954; Veroff, Wilcox, & Atkinson, 1953; Vogel, 1954) that it was necessary from the very beginning to plan a different set of pictures for men and women.[4]

How then did we go about selecting pictures from the original list (see Atkinson, 1958a, Appendix III) available to us? We rejected pictures that were clearly oriented to the college setting (e.g., classroom scenes). We also rejected pictures suggesting themes that contained only one particular kind of motivational content. Then, based on a pretest (using college students) of the "cue" value of 40 pictures (see Birney, 1958; Haber & Alpert, 1958; Jacobs, 1958), we tried to select pictures in which one kind of motivation was rather strongly suggested but at least one or the other kinds of motivation was weakly suggested. We also wanted to select pictures portraying separately for men and women a *variety* of life situations with which, in one way or another, most people in this country have had some direct contact, viz., different types of work situations and interpersonal situations. Sampling from this variety of what appeared to us to be fairly universally relevant situations should minimize the bias in the measuring instrument.

Combining the ratings given by the students and our a priori conception of diverse situations for sampling pictures, we selected a large group of pictures for pretest in a Detroit residence survey. The stories told to these pictures were then scored for n Achievement, n Affiliation, and n Power. The pictures selected from this group for the final test forms, one for the men and one for the women, were those producing an adequate balance of scores for the three motives. The pictures finally decided upon are listed in order of presentation (numbers in parentheses refer to the list in Appendix III, Atkinson, 1958a):

Male Form:

1. Two men (inventors) in a shop working at a machine. (2)
2. Four men seated at a table with coffee cups. One man is writing on a sheaf of papers. (101)
3. Man (father) and children seated at breakfast table. (102)
4. Man seated at drafting board. (28)
5. Conference group. Seven men variously grouped around a conference table. (83)

[4] See also Horner's discussion of this issue in Chapter 6.–Editors.

6. Woman in foreground with man standing behind and to the left. (103)

Female Form:

1. Two women standing by a table and one woman is working with test tubes.
2. Woman (mother) seated by girl reclining in chair.
3. Group of four women. One standing, the others seated facing each other.
4. Woman kneeling and applying a cover to a chair.
5. Two women preparing food in the kitchen.
6. Same as item 6 above.

A striking feature of these pictures is that they all provide only moderate structure to the situation portrayed.

These two forms were administered to a group of 98 college students at the University of Michigan. The measures were administered in a latin square design controlling the order of presentation of pictures. Unlike the survey interview setting, the administration called for written stories according to procedures outlined elsewhere (Atkinson, 1958a, Appendix III). This study showed that order of presentation of pictures did not have any systematic effect on total motive scores and that the frequencies with which achievement, affiliation, and power imagery appeared in response to each form were approximately equal in the college group. The results of these several pretests seemed to justify going ahead with the proposed set of pictures in an initial study of a national sample.

We realize, however, that the pictures finally selected undoubtedly still have differential cue values for some respondents. Negroes, for example, have to respond to situations depicting white people. Very old and very young people have to make up stories about figures that are obviously not so old nor so young as they are. The work scenes do not include farming, surgery, ditch digging, sales, and countless other occupations, although both blue-collar and white-collar work situations are included. Despite these differences, our working assumptions are that the situations portrayed in the pictures finally selected are not altogether foreign to most of the people with whom we are dealing, and that, by and large, the pictures will be as suggestive of the three motivational content areas to a person of one social stratum as to a person in another. We had finally to recognize that only through intensive study of the motivational cue value of these pictures for different social groups would we sharpen our insight and discover criteria that might enable us to construct a better set and to evaluate the over-all merits of the present set of pictures.

In the second section of this monograph we present motive scores for various subgroups in the national sample. Differences we may find in the scores of various subgroups can be attributed to biased selection of pictures. Whether these differences in fact reflect something more than biases in picture selection is a problem we consider in that section.

The procedures followed in administration of the pictures and in the analysis for motivational content will be described subsequently. Table 1 presents some results from the national survey that are pertinent to an evaluation of the selection of pictures. It shows the frequency of imaginative stories told in response to each picture which contained each kind of motivational content.

Both male and female forms appear more strongly cued for affiliative imagery than for achievement or power imagery. To conclude, however, that the greater affiliative response is indicative of some trend in national character would require the gratuitous assumption that each set of six pictures represents equally the populations of life situations in which n Achievement, n Affiliation, and n Power are normally expressed. The differences among average scores can more

TABLE 1

Percentage of Stories Coded for Achievement, Affiliation, and Power Imagery (by Picture and Sex)

Sex	Picture	Affiliation imagery	Achievement imagery	Power imagery
Men ($N = 597$)				
	1	3%	32%	11%
	2	16	23	14
	3	17	2	38
	4	53	13	1
	5	33	13	30
	6	33	3	22
Average raw score[a]		4.85	2.90[b]	2.84
Standard deviation		3.65	3.29	2.73
Women ($N = 774$)				
	1	2%	45%	10%
	2	56	3	26
	3	44	10	6
	4	6	36	1
	5	40	30	6
	6	35	1	25
Average raw score[a]		5.31	3.97[b]	1.84
Standard deviation		3.54	3.30	2.19

[a]Scores based on manuals and procedures in Atkinson (1958a, Chs. 12, 13, 14).

[b]The category, "Unrelated Imagery," was scored 0 instead of −1. Scores obtained using 0 and −1 correlate .96.

appropriately be used as an index of the relative sensitivity of the present pictures to each of the motives and as a guide for improving the selection of pictures in subsequent studies.

In light of Haber and Alpert's (1958) definition of a strongly cued picture as one which elicits a particular kind of motivational imagery from 75% or more of the *S*s in a sample and a weakly cued picture as one which elicits imagery from between 25% and 50% of *S*s, we must conclude that the two six-picture forms employed in the present study are weakly cued for each of the three motives. None of the pictures can be considered strongly cued for any motive; and no more than four pictures in the set fall in the range Haber and Alpert designate as weakly cued for a given motive. Consequently, in the present study there should be fewer "false positives" which often occur when strongly cued pictures are used. On the other hand, the relatively low frequency of response has two important negative implications. First, scores from weakly cued pictures are necessarily less variable and therefore by themselves have less potential for generating strong relationships with other variables. Secondly, low average frequency of response to pictures is one of several considerations[5] that preclude the possibility of a meaningful split-half analysis of the reliability of the motive scores in this study. A split-half estimate of the reliability of the present measures is considered inappropriate because the average frequency of response is so low that even moderately motivated *S*s often respond to only one or two pictures of the set.

[5] Earlier systematic split-half and test-retest estimates have yielded coefficients as high as .78 (McClelland et al., 1953) and .74 when all the pictures were strongly cued for n Achievement and .53 (Haber & Alpert, 1958, p. 661) when all the pictures fell in the 25 to 50% (weakly cued) range for n Achievement. In these systematic studies of reliability, care was taken to construct subsets of pictures having qualitatively as well as quantitatively similar cues. In the present study the six pictures were not deliberately selected with an eye to having two equivalent subsets of three pictures with similar content for each motive. Rather, the choice of pictures was guided by just the opposite orientation of (*a*) presenting a variety of nonoverlapping life situations in which (*b*) three different motives might be expressed. For a fuller discussion of reliability of motivation scores, as distinct from reliability of coding which is taken up at length in a subsequent section, see Atkinson (1958a), Haber and Alpert (1958), McClelland (1958a), Reitman and Atkinson (1958), and Atkinson (1960).

(Since the basic method has not changed in any essential way in 20 years, those who approach this work for the first time should study the original and most intensive analysis of the question of the reliability of the TAT n Achievement score in McClelland et al., 1953, pp. 187-194. It was learned at this early date that the strong assumptions of traditional psychometrics can be misleading and counterproductive. We discovered that the product-moment correlation between scores from equivalent forms and in test-retest might vary from a respectable .65 to a dubious .22 when classification of persons as High (above median) and Low (below median) was remarkably stable, 78% and 73%, respectively, when coding reliability was excellent ($r = .90$). Those experienced in the use of the method find the tool productive in research assuming a High-Low classification is correct about 75% of the time, where 50% represents chance expectation.–Editors.)

Control of the Interview Setting for the Projective Measures of Motivation

In experimental studies using projective measures of strength of motivation, the experimenter controls the amount of time the *S* spends telling a story. When written forms of the test are employed, each *S* is given a booklet containing a sheet of paper for each story. On each page are four sets of questions, adapted from Murray (1953), which help to remind *S* to cover all elements of a plot (see Atkinson, 1958a, p. 857):

What is happening? Who are the persons?
What had led up to this situation? That is, what has happened in the past?
What is being thought? What is wanted? By whom?
What will happen? What will be done?

Recognizing that we could not ask a great many of the potential respondents in a national survey to write out the story, we were confronted with the task of fitting a procedure that was as similar as possible to the one above into the *interview* setting. We had to face the fact that we would be dealing with respondents who differed greatly in verbal fluency, with an individual administration rather than the usual group administration,[6] and with interviewers having different tendencies for probing. How could we command control over these differences to provide measures of motivation that would be comparable to those obtained in well-controlled experimental settings?

In the pretest already described, we explored different wordings of the usual leading questions and changed them slightly to elicit the most adequate imaginative protocols. The final wording of the questions for each picture and story was:

Who are these people? (Who is this person?) What are they (is he/she) doing?
What has led up to this—what went on before?
What do they (does he/she) want—how do they (does he/she) feel?
What will happen? How will it end?

The interviewers were instructed to write in verbatim transcript the story told to each picture as responses to each of the questions. The series of questions for each story appeared on one page with a space after each for the answers given. Each interviewer had a set of 4" × 6" pictures which he was to show to the *S*. Detailed instructions given to the interviewers reflected our decisions (*a*) not to make this a completely spontaneous story-telling situation but to have the interviewer ask the plot-guiding questions, and (*b*) not to allow the interviewers to engage in the spontaneous probing they usually engage in with open-ended questions but rather to be very specific about the conditions under which

[6] Lindzey and Heinemann (1955) have concluded from research studies of individual- and group-administered TATs that they are reasonably equivalent. (See also Walker and Atkinson, 1958, for an earlier field study using this method.—Editors.)

probing was permissible and what these probes should be (see Veroff et al., 1960, for excerpts from the specific instructions).

To approximate a "neutral" test condition,[7] the projective measure appeared at the beginning of the interview. [See Gurin, Veroff, and Feld, 1960, for the larger context of this study.] It was preceded only by a few questions about leisure-time activities, used to establish rapport and to avoid what might otherwise be too abrupt a beginning if the imaginative test was given first. Another survey study (Morgan, Snider, & Sobel, 1958) which included exactly the same measure of motivation but at the end of the interview (because of special rapport problems in that interview situation) found that the stories were considerably influenced by the specific nature of the material discussed in the questionnaire before the thematic apperceptive procedure was introduced.

The rationale given to respondents for introducing the novel storytelling procedure in a survey about "modern living" was:

> Another thing we want to find out is what people think of situations that may come up in life. I'm going to show you some pictures of these situations and ask you to think of stories to go with them. The situations won't be clearly one thing or another—so feel free to think of any story you want to.
>
> For example, here is the first picture. I'd like you to spend a few moments thinking of a story to go with it. To get at the story you're thinking of I'll ask you questions like: Who are these people? What do they want? and so on. Just answer with anything that comes to mind. There are no right or wrong answers.

The interviewers reported that no major difficulty arose with this testing procedure. However, the major question we must ask about the effectiveness of the procedure is whether enough standardization of interviewing was established to rule out possible interviewer effects on the measures of motivation obtained from the stories. Would different interviewers testing the same population elicit stories that were similar in motivational content?[8] This problem is treated in a later section.

Coding the Stories

Training the coders. One of the most important methodological contributions of previous work on these projective measures of motivation has been the continued concern of research workers with attaining high coding reliability. Feld and Smith (1958) have evaluated the training procedures used to teach novices the methods of content analysis for the three motives and report that conscientious use of the training materials they describe enables coders to score stories for n Achievement, n Affiliation, and n Power with reliabilities acceptable for research purposes. They review interjudge reliabilities reported in 14 published studies using the method of content analysis to be employed in this

[7] A "neutral" test condition is one in which the experimenter makes no deliberate attempt to arouse or relax a particular kind of motivation before administration of the test.

[8] Birney (1956) has reported evidence of an "*experimenter effect*" on the level of achievement-related content in stories written by college students.

analysis and find scoring reliabilities ranging from .66 to .96 with a median of .89. They also report interjudge reliabilities ranging from .73 to .92 with a median of .87 for 12 novice coders who had just finished learning how to score a set of familiar pictures using their training procedures (i.e., after about 12 hours of independent practice). This survey of the degree of objectivity in coding obtained in small-scale experimental studies provides a standard against which to evaluate the coding reliabilities attained in this first attempt with a national sample.[9]

A team of nine coders (three for each motive) with little or no previous contact with this kind of research was trained by the method prescribed by Feld and Smith. In addition to this training procedure, scoring seminars were held, mainly to establish consensus about scoring stories derived from pictures never before used in any study. Often the stories elicited from a new picture demand specific scoring conventions not treated in scoring manuals. Feld and Smith (1958) report that coders show a small but nevertheless statistically significant decrease in reliability when coding novel material. Novel types of imagery were thoroughly discussed in the light of previous practice and the coders annotated their scoring manuals accordingly.

To insure good coding reliabilities even further, each coder was trained as an "expert" on two pictures from the male form and two from the female form, and subsequently coded only those pictures. In this way the scoring of each individual coder contributed to potentially one-third of a particular motive score for each *S*. As a result, we ruled out bias of total scores attributable to the scoring idiosyncrasies of a particular coder. Further experience was given each coder on pictures for which he was finally responsible in the course of scoring 400 protocols gathered in another study at the Survey Research Center (Morgan et al., 1958). Check-coding was done on a sample of 240 stories from 40 *S*s by two other coders[10] who had previously been checked out as "expert" in motive scoring.

Scoring reliabilities from this "warm up" check-coding, and for others reported in this paper, were computed in two ways. First, we estimated the degree of agreement in noting the presence of any achievement, affiliation, or power imagery in the story—the single most important scoring decision for the coder. This agreement is expressed as a percentage (twice the number of agreements on the presence of motivational imagery divided by the sum of the total number of times motivational imagery was coded by the two coders). The

[9] A more recent count of coding reliability in the studies reported in Atkinson and Feather (1966), in this volume, and among several graduate classes in social motivation at Michigan, where 12 to 20 hours is spent learning the technique, shows the median for n Achievement still to be .89 and the lowest quartile at .85. We call this to the attention of researchers, e.g., Weinstein (1969), who reports completely negative results but fails to note that his coding reliability of .77 is the lowest in the literature since the .66 reported in 1952 before the scoring manual had been written.—Editors.

[10] Two of the authors—Sheila Feld and Joseph Veroff.

second estimate of the coding reliability was the rank-order correlation between motivation scores based on all six stories coded first by the three coders and then by the check-coding experts. Although the individual percentages of agreement on "imagery" (ranging from 50% to 90%) were not consistently as high as the customary agreements found in experimental research, we felt that the total score reliabilities (.74, .76, .87) showed that these coders had attained a degree of proficiency which, augmented by further clarification of scoring problems, was sufficient to begin systematic scoring of the stories in the national sample.

Assessing coding reliability of motivation scoring in the national survey sample. The nine coders, each a specialist on four pictures (two from the male form and two from the female form) for one of the three motives, coded two stories from each of the 1,619 respondent's protocols (or 3,238 stories). The criteria for scoring or not scoring a particular response are those specified in the available manuals for n Achievement, n Affiliation, and n Power (McClelland et al., 1953, 1958; Heyns, Veroff, & Atkinson, 1958; Veroff, 1958) plus specific conventions adopted for novel pictures.

Each coder's total scoring task was divided into three nearly equal sections (about 1,080 stories to be scored within each section). Furthermore, each coder scored the protocols in a different order, never scoring two stories from the same *S* in sequence.[11] These three sections each represents a coding period for which check-coding procedures were done. Within each third of the coding, a set of protocols were designated as reliability checks. The particular stories that were to be coded by the "expert coder" were unknown to the coders. From these protocols we estimated the reliabilities, again both as percentage of agreement in the coding of the presence of motivational imagery in the stories, and as rank-order correlations of total scores obtained from six stories. After each check-coding, differences between coder and "expert" were discussed. The three reliability checks provided an opportunity to follow the progress of coding reliability over the period of several months which it took each student coder, working part-time on an hourly basis, to complete approximately 100 hours of coding. The resulting percentages of agreement and total score reliabilities in the three different periods of coding are presented in Table 2.

The reliabilities of the coders were remarkably consistent over the three sections of coding. There are occasional shifts upward and downward, but there are no consistent trends indicating any drastic effects of coding over a prolonged period. It is our opinion that the downward trends in reliability often seemed to reflect the "expert" coder's lack of adaptation to these particular pictures.

[11] For a given motive each *S's* stories were scored in such a way that two were scored by one coder during the first third of coding, two in the next third by the next coder, and two in the last by the third coder. In this way any systematic bias of coding attributable to time of coding would be randomized over the *S*s. The exception to this procedure is the set of stories in the reliability checks. All of the stories of these *S*s were coded during the same period of coding.

TABLE 2

Scoring Reliabilities for the Nine Coders and the Three Motivation Scores in the National Sample Survey

Motive and coders	Pictures	Percentage of imagery agreement (60 Stories)			Total score reliabilities (30 *S*s)		
		Check 1	Check 2	Check 3	Check 1	Check 2	Check 3
n Achievement					.89[b]	.77	.81
Coder 1	1, 6[a]	80	82	90			
Coder 2	3, 4	71	75	63			
Coder 3	2, 5	87	55	82			
n Affiliation					.91	.76	.76
Coder 1	4, 5	80	80	89			
Coder 2	2, 6	83	89	78			
Coder 3	1, 3	80	73	80			
n Power					[c]	.72	.73
Coder 1	1, 5	[c]	75	67			
Coder 2	3, 6	[c]	73	77			
Coder 3	2, 4	[c]	77	84			

[a]To be read, Picture 1 and Picture 6 on male form and on female form.

[b]Spearman rank-order correlations.

[c]These figures were similar to those attained in the second and third reliability checks for n Power coding. Exact figures are unavailable because the check coding sheets were misplaced and cannot be reestimated since the coders changed their original codings in the direction of the consensus after discussion.

The extent to which this is true can be evaluated in light of a second set of reliability coefficients that were computed *after* the coder and the expert check-coder had discussed every instance of disagreement and had come to a consensus of opinion about final coding. Correlations between the coders' original scorings and this consensus of opinion[12] were uniformly higher indicating that at times it was agreed the "expert" had been in error. The postdiscussion score reliabilities for first, second, and third checks were: n Achievement–.91, .94, .88; n Affiliation–.94, .84, .81; and n Power[13]–.77, .77.

Consequently, we view the reliability coefficients reported in Table 2 as conservative estimates of the objectivity of the method of analysis employed. The median percentage agreement in coding motivation imagery is 80%, about 10% less than usually attained in small-scale studies with familiar materials. All of the total score reliabilities (median = .77) fall within the range found in published experimental studies, but only two of the eight are above the median of coding reliabilities reported in smaller-scale studies (viz., .89). Considering the anticipated loss in coding reliability attributable to the use of several new pictures here for the first time, we were encouraged by these results. Nevertheless we anticipate some loss in sensitivity of the measuring instruments due to some coding unreliability.

Correcting Motivation Scores for Variations in Length of Protocol

The correlation between motivation scores and length of protocol has been found negligible in studies with college students when 4 minutes are allowed for writing stories (Atkinson, 1950, p. 27). At least four studies, however, have shown significant relationships, requiring some sort of correction when somewhat different test conditions are employed. Ricciuti (1954) and Ricciuti and Sadacca (1955) found correlations ranging from .48 to .59 between n Achievement scores and number of words in the brief protocols of high school students when no structuring questions were asked and when only 2.5 minutes were allowed for writing stories. Walker and Atkinson (1958) found (and corrected for) a correlation of .41 between length of protocol and fear-related motivation scores in a very heterogeneous sample of soldiers when there was less than adequate control over the actual time spent writing stories. Child, Storm, and Veroff (1958) also found it necessary to correct achievement scores obtained from folk tales to remove the difference attributable to length of story. We had reason to anticipate that in this heterogeneous sample there would be gross differences in the length and adequacy of protocols that might be attributed to gross differences in verbal ability of *S*s and/or to uncontrolled differences in the behavior of interviewers. Two separate problems were anticipated: (*a*) how

[12]These "new" conventions have been integrated into scoring manuals for this set of pictures, which are available on request from Survey Research Center (Attention: Dr. Veroff), University of Michigan, Ann Arbor, Michigan.

[13]First reliability estimate on n Power coding unavailable (see Footnote c, Table 2).

to eliminate protocols because of inadequate responses, and (*b*) how to correct for anticipated correlations between motivation scores and length of stories in protocols otherwise judged to be adequate for further analysis.

Elimination of protocols. At the outset of scoring the protocols it was clear that some *S*s gave responses which had to be considered inadequate for arriving at valid motivation scores. What does an inadequate response mean for assessment of motivation? It means that the person gave no imaginative content that could possibly be scored for motivational content. The person, for whatever reason, has prevented the measuring instrument from being applied. If a person rejects the whole task (24 inadequate responses—four leads in six stories), his protocols are obviously not suitable for scoring. Even if the person rejects the task for only one picture (i.e., four inadequate responses in only one story), his protocols should not be considered, for he has not taken the complete test. Had he responded to that particular picture, his story might have been saturated with a particular kind of motivational imagery. But what of the other possibilities?

A judgment of the seriousness of omission was made on the basis of the extent to which each kind of omission might *potentially* affect the total motivation score. In light of our experience with practices informally employed in experimental studies, an *S*'s protocols were judged to be adequate when at least half the stories were complete and no more than one question was omitted from any or all of the remaining stories.

This criterion led to the elimination of 17% of the men and 14% of the women. Two things should be kept in mind in appraising the significance of this number of rejected protocols. First, we deliberately adopted a fairly stringent criterion for elimination. Secondly, these *S*s were eliminated not on the basis of just one set of responses to one picture, but on the basis of inadequacy of response *on any one of six pictures.* Consequently, we judge that the frequency of inadequate protocols is not out of line with the frequency of inadequate responses that would be obtained from any complex open-ended questionnaire in a nationwide survey setting if we were to eliminate *S*s giving an inadequate response on any *one* of a set of six complex open-ended questions.

The loss of data is most severe in the least educated groups (see Table 3). Of those who have little or no schooling, nearly one-third of the sample of men and women are rejected from further analysis. What these data suggest, therefore, is that the measuring device as here employed in a survey setting is less appropriate for certain segments of the population—particularly among the least educated groups. This is hardly a startling result. Practically any verbal measure runs into the same difficulty. Inadequate responses to open-ended attitude questions tend to stem largely from uneducated groups; inadequate answers (response sets) on certain forced choice questionnaires also are most apparent in uneducated groups (Christie, 1958).

We suspect that a failure to produce a meaningful protocol may also reflect deficiencies in the kinds of social motivation that are being assessed in this study—particularly achievement motivation. Hence, we may be overestimating

TABLE 3

The Relationship of Education to Percentage Loss of Subjects Due to Inadequate Protocols

Educational level	Men		Women	
	N in sample[a]	Percentage loss	*N* in sample[a]	Percentage loss
No schooling; grade school (1-6 years)	107	32	125	28
Grade school (7-8 years)	138	25	160	18
High school (9-11 years)	139	12	209	16
Completed high school	169	12	266	7
Attended college	157	7	136	7

[a]Does not include *S*s whose educational level was not ascertained.

the average level of motivation in any group from which a great many *S*s are removed because of their inadequate protocols. This additional possibility argues against using subsequent data from this analysis to estimate *absolute* norms in specific groups, but it does not vitiate the possibility of comparing social groups on average motivation scores, once we recognize that we may have biased estimates in certain groups.

Correction for correlation between length of stories in adequate protocols and motivation scores. The number of words in protocols accepted for 597 men and 774 women ranged from 80 to 823 as shown in Table 4. The median number of words was 291 for men and 279 for women, or about 46 to 48 words per story. This is exactly the same length obtained by Ricciuti and Sadacca (1955) from 2.5-minute stories written by high school students, but is approximately half the length usually obtained in studies with college students when 4 minutes are allotted for writing each story. Although there is no way to compare directly the time needed to write and to tell stories, one may note that the approximate time allotted for each story in the instructions given interviewers (3 to 3.5 minutes) is less than the 4 minutes normally allotted in studies of college students.

The raw n Achievement, n Affiliation, and n Power scores[14] obtained from the content analysis were correlated with length of protocol separately for men and women. The results show the anticipated significant relationships between length of protocol and raw motive scores, product-moment correlations ranging

[14]A total score is obtained by summing the frequencies of particular kinds of motivational content appearing in each of the six stories (see Atkinson, 1958a, Part II).

TABLE 4

Example of Correction Applied to Uncorrected n Achievement T Scores to Remove the Correlation between These Scores and Length of Protocol (Males Only)

Number of words in protocol	Female[c] ($N = 597$)	Male ($N = 774$)	Mean uncorrected n Achievement score[a]	Correction[b]	Mean corrected n Achievement score
80–169	(40)	32	45.75	3	48.75
170–229	(101)	117	47.95	2	49.95
230–289	(215)	147	50.04	1	51.04
290–349	(157)	127	49.96	0	49.96
350–409	(101)	77	52.90	-1	51.90
410–469	(49)	45	53.58	-2	51.58
470–529	(21)	23	52.96	-4	48.96
530–589	(10)	11	50.09	-5	45.09
590–649	(7)	11	55.82	-6	49.82
650 and above	(3)	7	56.43	-7	49.43
Median	291	279			

[a]Scores represent normal deviate equivalents using the T score conversion of percentile ranks, the mean is 50 and standard deviation is 10.

[b]Correction factor obtained from the regression line based on the average of correlations between n Achievement, n Affiliation, and n Power scores and length of protocol. (Correction factor equals mean n Achievement score of the whole sample minus mean "expected" n Achievement score for protocols of particular length.)

[c]Female distribution is included here for purposes of comparison with that for the males. However, the uncorrected and corrected scores in this table are for males only.

between .21 and .28. Clearly some correction of the raw scores is necessary to eliminate the obvious fact that a person who tells longer stories stands a greater chance of obtaining a high score based on a frequency count of particular kinds of motivational content in what he has said.

Before applying correction procedures, we simplified our considerations of the motivation scores by putting the n Achievement, n Affiliation, and n Power scores on the same scale within each sex by assigning percentile ranks to each motivation score (for men and women separately). When a number of persons had the same score, the median percentile rank of the interval covered was assigned to all tied scores. Each distribution of percentile ranks was normalized. Percentile ranks were converted to normal deviate scores based on a mean of 50 and a standard deviation of 10 (*T* scores). As before, each sex was considered separately.

These *T* score conversions of percentile ranks effectively remove the differences between average motivation scores for both men and women,[15] but they do not correct for the influence of length of protocol. The correlations between length of protocol and *T* scores are all within ± .01 of the original correlations between raw scores and length of protocol.

The question as to how to remove the effect of length of protocol was resolved in light of the following argument. The need for some kind of correction is obvious. A person's chance of getting a higher score on any motive is greater the longer the story he tells; the greater the amount of imagery he produces in an imaginative story, the greater the chance of it being coded as evidence of some motive. Theoretically, the best possible correction would be one based on the average of correlations between scores for many kinds of motives and the length of protocol. This average correlation would indicate the systematic relationship between length of protocol and score on any motive.

In this study, the stories have thus far been coded for only three motives. Hence the average of the three correlations provides the nearest estimate that can be made of the extent to which length of story influences opportunity to get a high score. The average of the three correlations is .22 for men and .24 for women. In each case, this average correlation was used to determine a regression line of motivation scores on length of protocol.[16] The average "expected"

[15]There were significant differences among the raw n Achievement, n Affiliation, and n Power scores both within and between sexes. These are readily explained in terms of the slight differences in degree to which the sets of pictures "suggested" each of the three motivational concerns. It seemed desirable to convert these scores immediately to the same scale, i.e., percentile rank, to avoid possible misinterpretation of the meaning of different average raw scores.

[16]We suspect that these three motives—n Achievement, n Affiliation, n Power—all might be expected to be more highly related to length of protocol given the interpersonal nature of the interview, than some other kinds of motivation (e.g., hunger). Hence we are well aware of the possibility that the correction employed may "over-correct" the scores. This seemed the lesser of two evils given the compelling a priori case that a longer protocol should increase the chance of getting a high score on any type of motivational content.

motivation score was determined for each length-of-protocol interval. The average expected score at each interval was then subtracted from the obtained average score for the whole sample on each motive separately. This difference score (obtained for each motive separately) was then used as a constant correction for all individual scores within particular intervals of length. Thus, a correction factor was added to scores that were too low because protocols were short, and a correction factor was subtracted from scores that were too high because of very lengthy protocols.

The effect of this correction was to remove the systematic expected difference in motivation scores as a function of the length of protocol. In Table 4 are presented the average *T* scores for n Achievement in men as a function of length of protocol before and after the correction described above was accomplished. Similar effects are obtained with women on achievement motivation and with both men and women on the other motives. The final corrected scores, no longer biased by length of protocol, will henceforth be referred to as the n Achievement, n Affiliation, and n Power scores in all further analyses. The correlation of these scores with length of protocol did not exceed ± .05 (n.s.). They are presented in Table 5 for males and Table 6 for females

TABLE 5

Mean n Achievement, n Affiliation, and n Power *T* Scores of Males before and after Correction for Verbal Fluency

Motive and education	Mean score[a]	
	Before correction	After correction
n Achievement		
Grade school	48.76	49.90
High school	49.49	50.23
College	51.95[b]	51.92[c]
n Affiliation		
Grade school	49.21	49.88
High school	49.97	50.22
College	51.27	51.27
n Power		
Grade school	50.97	51.38
High school	49.58	49.94
College	50.23	50.09

[a]Does not include *S*s whose educational level was not ascertained. Grade school $N = 176$, high school $N = 271$, college $N = 146$.

[b]College mean score significantly higher than high school and grade school means ($p < .05$).

[c]College mean score significantly higher than grade school mean score ($p < .05$).

TABLE 6

Mean n Achievement, n Affiliation, and n Power *T* Scores of Females before and after Correction for Verbal Fluency

Motive and education	Mean score[a]	
	Before correction	After correction
n Achievement		
Grade school	48.50[b]	49.46[b]
High school	50.41	51.18
College	51.49	51.67
n Affiliation		
Grade school	47.82[b]	47.86[b]
High school	50.82	50.33
College	51.57	50.43
n Power		
Grade school	48.77[b]	49.89
High school	50.50	51.09
College	51.56	51.47

[a]Does not include *S*s whose educational level was not ascertained. Grade school $N = 226$, high school $N = 428$, college $N = 127$.

[b]Grade school mean score significantly lower than both high school and college mean score ($p < .05$).

along with the uncorrected scores for each motive as a function of level of education.

What effect will this correction of motivation scores for length of protocol have on subsequent analyses? The relationship of motivation scores to any variable which is in turn highly related to verbal fluency, should now be uncontaminated by the factor of verbal fluency. Where previously there might have been an artifactual relationship between a given variable and motivation score (because both variables were related to verbal fluency), there should no longer be any relationship. Where a relationship between motivation score and a variable might previously have been obscured artifactually, there might now appear a significant relationship.

The Effect of Interviewers on Motivation Scores

Although we made a serious effort to standardize the interviewing procedure, we realize that having a group of 159 different interviewers (27 men and 132 women) collecting the protocols must necessarily introduce some variability into the measures that has hitherto been minimal when all protocols are collected at one time in a group administration. An estimate of the extent of this interviewer variability will help us to gain some perspective concerning how far the national survey interview departs from standardized administration procedures.

To establish such an estimate in survey data is a difficult problem. A valid test of the effect of different interviewers requires random assignment from the population of respondents to the interviewers. This is decidedly not the case with the Survey Research Center's field operation. While the selection of respondents is completely determined at the central office of the Survey Research Center by probability sampling techniques, these respondents are not assigned to interviewers at random. To the degree that the assignment is not random, there may be systematic differences in responses obtained by various interviewers that stem from differences in the composition of the samples interviewed, and not from differences attributable to the interviewers themselves. In spite of this danger of finding effects that are really attributable to respondents, we wanted to arrive at some estimate of interviewer effect. We therefore designed an analysis of "possible" interviewer effects which would be least subject to criticism that we had grossly confounded interviewers and characteristics of respondents. Our analysis undoubtedly still can be criticized on this score. But in any case, a violation of the assumption that the respondents of each interviewer represent a random sample of the population should in most cases contribute to an overestimation of interviewer effects. As a result the estimates to be described can probably be viewed as *maximal* estimates of interviewer differences.

We examined possible interviewer effects in a limited sample of the total population of interviewers (see Veroff et al., 1960, for the specific criteria that determined this sample). Given our limitations, we were able to find 8 pairs of interviewers for male *S*s and 15 pairs of interviewers for female subjects. (Each pair represents a different primary sampling unit or PSU.) We designed an analysis of variance[17] of motivation scores broken down to estimate the significance of the variance assignable to interviewer effects, and in addition, we segregate the component variance for interviewers and examine the extent of its effect on score variability.

These analyses showed that a "possible" interviewer effect on motivation scores is statistically significant in three instances: n Achievement scores for women, and n Power scores for both men and women. Furthermore, when component variance for interviewers is specifically segregated, its effect on score variability is estimated as an intraclass correlation from which we can derive the proportion of variance in motivation scores possibly contributed by interviewer differences (Snedecor, 1946, p. 243). These were negligible for men except for n Power where the percentage increase in variance was .29. Among women, the percentage increase was negligible for n Affiliation but .18 for n Achievement and n Power. Considering these estimates as maximal estimates, we feel safe in

[17]We are indebted to Leslie Kish for his suggestions with procedure.

concluding that we have achieved a fair degree of standardization in interviewing techniques for these measures of motivation.

One reason these maximal estimates of interviewer effects on motivation scores are low is that the motivation scores have been corrected for length of protocol. Similar analyses of variance were run using number of words in the protocol as the dependent variable. These show that for both men and women respondents there is a substantial interviewer effect on length of protocol. The effect is especially strong among male *S*s. The correction of motivation scores to eliminate the effect of differences in length of protocol has removed most of the possible interviewer effect on these scores.

Overall Evaluation of Methodological Problems Encountered

These, then, are the methodological problems encountered in the survey setting and our evaluations of the extent to which they remain as problems or as sources of error in subsequent uses of the thematic apperceptive measures of motivation. One problem was solved–the bias of motivation scores attributable to verbal fluency. One problem appears very difficult to solve–the inadequate protocols produced by uneducated persons. A third problem should be resolved by further empirical analysis–possible bias in the selection of pictures. The two remaining problems–lower coding reliability than in experimental studies and possible bias in motivation scores attributable to interviewers–are ones that lower the reliability of measurement in subsequent analyses using the motivation scores. But both of these sources of error appear to be ones that certainly can be greatly reduced in subsequent studies. Experimental investigations can be conducted to clarify the difficult scoring questions that arise with new pictures, as with those employed here for the first time, and to reduce the error in coding that is a normal consequence of trying to fit general scoring criteria to imagery produced by novel stimuli. Similarly, the influence of interviewers, particularly on length of protocols, should be greatly reduced by even more thorough briefing of interviewers. We can be guided by the results of this study concerning the conditions of administration, and, specifically, the desired length of stories.

INTERPRETATION OF MOTIVATION SCORES

If methodological problems of the sort we have discussed in the previous section are seriously considered, the use of thematic apperceptive measures of motivation, and other sensitive techniques of personality assessment, can be expected to begin to contribute to the study of important substantive problems in survey research. Yet even after methodological precautions are taken, there remains an important question: What conceptual meaning do we attribute to the motivation scores? This is the issue now to be considered.

The problem of interpretation of motivation scores obtained from thematic apperception is not a new one (Atkinson, 1958a; McClelland et al., 1953); but the broader setting of a national survey study exaggerates the difficulties that are normally encountered even in fairly well-controlled experimental studies.

Three factors are thought to influence the frequency of motivational imagery produced in stories elicited by pictures (taken as the measure of the strength of a particular kind of motivation): (*a*) individual differences in strength of motive, a relatively general and enduring disposition within the person to strive for certain kinds of goal satisfaction, affect motivational imagery; (*b*) cues in the pictures that are used to elicit imaginative thought may also heighten or dampen motivation for particular goals to the extent that the situation portrayed is relevant to the life experience of the respondent; and (*c*) the immediate life situation of the person may arouse or dampen motivation for particular goals. The latter influence may be some factor in the immediate test situation of the respondent, or some more general but transient influence on his life situation, or some more general and longer lasting influence on his life situation (e.g., constant achievement pressure of the job) at the time the measure is administered. Both pictures and a person's life situation provide cues that define expectations concerning what kinds of goals are relevant and reachable, and how attractive it would be to reach the goals.

While we attempted to remove biasing effects of pictures, we have no independent evidence that we have in fact removed all possible bias. For instance, can we assume that the pictures employed, which portray relatively young men and women in common life situations, will have the same meaning for young, middle-aged, and aged respondents? Furthermore, the standardization of the interview situation might control the immediate situational influences at the time the test was administered but obviously could have no effect on life conditions affecting the person at the time the survey was conducted. Can we assume, in advance, that the active young businessman is being tested under situational circumstances that are comparable to those of an older man enjoying retirement from business and the stress of day-to-day activities? Or must we conceive of the possibility that these gross differences in the total life situation in which the administration of our test of motivation is embedded will produce effects comparable to those produced by experimental manipulation of situational influences in studies of motivation in college students?

Therefore when our results show that a particular kind of motivation is stronger in one social group than another, our task is not finished; rather, the difficult task of interpretation is now thrust upon us. The inference that the result means the two groups differ in strength of a general and enduring disposition of personality requires the assumption, and supportive argument, that the effects of picture cues may be considered equivalent in the two groups and that the situational pressures for expression of the motive, whether transient or relatively enduring, are also equivalent.

It can be argued that certain life situations can have lasting effects on a person's disposition so that "situational" differences become "personality" differences. Little is known concerning how permanent are the effects of certain life experiences, particularly ones that occur later in life. The assumption of the primacy of early experiences in the generation of personality dispositions has been widely accepted. Facing frankly the paucity of evidence concerning dispositional versus situational factors in motivation, and their interactions, we can see that any one of the following arguments might be pursued in the interpretation of obtained differences between certain social groups.

1. The obtained difference is attributable to differences in enduring personality dispositions acquired early in life.
2. The obtained difference is the consequence of a change in personality disposition induced by important situational factors later in life.
3. The obtained difference is a consequence of exposure to differential temporary situational pressures affecting the level of aroused motivation regardless of equivalence in underlying personality disposition.

Thus two problems remain that must be faced in confronting the substantive results obtained with the thematic apperception instrument: assessments of the bias of picture cues and the influence of the *general* life situation on the motivation scores. These problems will be illustrated in the discussion of substantive results that follow.

In Tables 7 to 12 are presented some of the obtained differences in n Achievement, n Affiliation, and n Power scores when certain social groups in American society are compared. These tables are presented in the present context for two reasons: first, to illustrate concretely the issues which arise when we are finally confronted with the task of arriving at a valid interpretation of the motivation scores; and secondly, to provide researchers who are interested in particular social groups some descriptive information concerning potential differences in motivation among these groups. Under no circumstances should these data be considered unequivocal norms about strength of motives in particular social groups until the issue of the extent to which obtained differences are situational, dispositional, or artifactual is settled. Furthermore, under no circumstances should all of the differences presented in these tables be considered reliably different from one another. For readers who would like some bearings on the approximate differences in percentages required for a statistically significant comparison between two independent groups, we have included in the Appendix a table of differences required for significance (.05 level) with different sample sizes (*N*s). This Appendix table is presented merely to provide approximate estimates of the statistical significance of obtained differences.

In all of the tables, *S*s have been classified as "High" or "Low" in motivation score by dividing the distribution of corrected *T* scores as near to the median of the distribution for the whole sample as was possible. The tables indicate what percentage of particular subgroups are high (above the median) in the national sample. Direct cross comparisons between men and women are not justified since different test forms were employed for the two sexes and the distributions of scores for men and women were considered separately in designating high and low scores.

Education

Table 7 presents the percentage of scores in each of three educational levels that are above the median for the whole sample for each motive. The percentage of college-educated *S*s, whether men or women, with high n Achievement scores is substantially higher than the percentage of *S*s who have had only a grade school education. Among women, the same result appears in connection with affiliation scores and power scores.

Now how would one interpret these differences? Are the picture cues biased in favor of the college population? Has the life experience of a college education

TABLE 7

Educational Level Related to n Achievement, n Affiliation, and n Power

Motive[a] and education	Percentage[b] of high scores[c]	
	Men	Women
n Achievement		
Grade school	48	44
High school	49	49
College	62	52
n Affiliation		
Grade school	47	43
High school	47	53
College	51	52
n Power		
Grade school	55	42
High school	47	51
College	49	54

[a]Here and in all subsequent tables, the motive measures used are the *T* scores corrected for verbal fluency.

[b]Does not include *S*s whose educational level was not ascertained. Grade school *N*s, Men = 176, Women = 222; high school *N*s, Men = 271, Women = 422; college *N*s, Men = 146, Women = 127.

[c]Here and in all subsequent tables, high scores refer to the scores on each motive measure that are above the median for the total sample of men or women.

affected the achievement motive of college women? Or were college women high in achievement motivation from an early age, and thereby managed to get to college? We cannot resolve these different views. Later evidence, however, may bear on which interpretation is more appropriate.

Occupation

In Table 8 are presented the percentage of men presently employed on a full-time basis in various occupations who obtained high scores for each of the three motives. Achievement motivation scores are much more frequently high among persons in higher status occupations than among men in lower status occupations.

No systematic relationship between n Affiliation or n Power scores and occupational *status* is clearly apparent, though certain possibly meaningful differences in the different occupations may be discerned. Whereas 51% of managers and proprietors score high in power motivation, only 43% of professionals and 40% of clerical workers, the remainder of the white-collar occupation category, score high in power motivation. Should the difference here be considered a manifestation of differences in basic personality disposition which has led one group of men to positions of supervision and another not, or should the difference in motivation scores be considered a reflection of the difference in motivational influences contained in the day-to-day life situation of managers, as a group, versus those classified as professionals? Or, could the result conceivably be attributed to some biasing in the content of the picture cues favoring one group and not another with respect to the suggestion of

TABLE 8

Occupational Level Related to n Achievement, n Affiliation, and n Power (Men Employed Full-Time Only)

Occupation of respondents	*N*[a]	Percentage of high scores		
		n Ach	n Aff	n Pow
Professionals	67	60	54	43
Managers and proprietors	70	59	56	51
Clerical workers	30	57	47	40
Sales workers	34	59	47	47
Skilled workers	120	50	55	50
Semiskilled workers	88	52	41	53
Unskilled workers	38	45	37	50
Farmers	39	44	31	51

[a]Does not include *S*s whose occupational level was not ascertained or *S*s whose occupations were not codable into these categories.

TABLE 9

Age Related to n Achievement, n Affiliation, and n Power

Motive and age	N[a]	Percentage of high scores		N[a]
		Men	Women	
n Achievement				
21-24	32	66	47	53
25-34	165	50	50	205
35-44	119	57	50	184
45-54	123	54	45	152
55-64	82	42	52	98
65 plus	76	47	35	77
n Affiliation				
21-24		47	53	
25-34		48	53	
35-44		44	55	
45-54		49	53	
55-64		53	36	
65 plus		49	38	
n Power				
21-24		44	55	
25-34		45	52	
35-44		52	47	
45-54		51	49	
55-64		49	45	
65 plus		54	47	

[a]Does not include *S*s whose age was not ascertained.

power-related imagery? [See also Crockett, 1962, 1964; Rosen, Crockett, & Nunn, 1969.–Editors.]

Age

Perhaps the clearest illustration of the problem of interpretation of scores as effects of personality disposition versus situation effects is apparent in consideration of age trends, particularly in the achievement motivation scores of men (Table 9).

There are some notable differences between the age groups in achievement motivation (for both men and women). For example, the highest achievement motivation is found among the youngest men, and the next highest among a middle-aged group, (35–44 years), while the lowest achievement motivation scores appear in the older groups. A number of alternative interpretations of these differences can be offered. On the one hand, these differences may reflect some important generational differences in the strength of achievement motive dispositions. On the other hand, the stage of a man's life cycle may have a great deal to do with his current aroused achievement motivation, the eagerness of youth starting out in a career and the middle aged pressure to "achieve or else" may both lead to heightened achievement motivation in contrast to the pressures of old age that may detract from achievement arousal. From other results we have obtained thus far, relating achievement motivation to other variables (controlling for age), we do find that the age groups vary considerably in what achievement motivation signifies. One can at the present only speculate about a life cycle or a generation difference influencing these results, and perhaps both sets of factors are crucial.

The age differences obtained may reflect picture biases as well; the possibility of systematic age differences in the connotation of the pictures cannot be excluded. Very old people, for example, might have special difficulty in generalizing from the pictures presented to their own life situations since the figures in the pictures are not clearly old in appearance.

As a result of these obtained age differences in motivation scores and our speculations about their meaning, we have considered age as a critical variable for investigations of other substantive relationships to be reported in future papers. [See Veroff, 1961; Veroff, Feld, & Crockett, 1966; Veroff, Feld, & Gurin, 1962; Veroff & Feld, 1970.–Editors.]

Place of Residence

In Table 10 we present the distributions of motivation scores according to the place of residence–whether in a metropolitan area or their suburbs, a small city, a small town, or a rural area. These findings present some differences in scores that are not completely independent of status considerations noted in other comparisons–income, occupation, or education differences. Nevertheless there are noteworthy results: For both men and women there is greater concentration of high achievement motivation scores in small towns and rural areas than in larger communities. High affiliation motivation seems to be more prevalent among men from smaller communities, but highest in women living in metropolitan areas. Power motivation seems to be relatively high in metropolitan areas.

These differences may have important implications for the thesis that the type of community one lives in can determine the development of certain motivational interests. For example, one might want to say that a *consequence* of living in smaller communities is the development of a heightened interest in affiliation and yet there remains one possibility that such an interpretation is in error. Motivation can play a large role in *determining* the kind of community people live in, whether they are willing to remain in a city or in a rural area,

TABLE 10

Current Place of Residence Related to n Achievement, n Affiliation, and n Power

Motive and place of residence[a]	N	Percentage of high scores		N
		Men	Women	
n Achievement				
Metropolitan areas	86	48	45	104
Suburbs	87	52	42	97
Small cities	92	51	43	118
Small towns	180	56	49	152
Rural areas	225	53	49	230
n Affiliation				
Metropolitan areas		42	58	
Suburbs		44	49	
Small cities		48	49	
Small towns		48	54	
Rural areas		51	46	
n Power				
Metropolitan areas		55	57	
Suburbs		56	45	
Small cities		46	46	
Small towns		44	51	
Rural areas		50	48	

[a]Metropolitan areas and their suburbs are defined by the United States Census Bureau Classification: small cities have populations of over 50,000, small towns populations of under 50,000, and rural areas are open farm country not located in a standard metropolitan area.

whether they migrate to suburban areas, and the like. For example, men with high affiliation motivation may prefer small towns where intimacy is easier.

Broken Home Background and Death of a Spouse

We have already suggested that many of the differences in motivation scores obtained can be as plausibly interpreted as situational differences as they can as personality differences. The "correctness" of either interpretation, or the relative importance of each interpretation should be resolved in further study. There is evidence that the resolution of this problem will not be a general one; one or the other interpretation will not be uniformly appropriate, but both will be involved. This evidence comes from examining two other special groupings–broken home background, and death of a spouse.

All respondents were asked whether or not they had lived with both of their parents before the age of 16. Through further probing we were able to group respondents into three categories:

1. Coming from intact homes.
2. One or both parents died before the respondent was 16.
3. Parents were divorced or separated before respondent was 16.

These experiences in early childhood are likely to be profound catalysts for inducing basic personality patterns. We feel that differences found in adults with these three kinds of early backgrounds might reflect early personality integration of motivation. In these comparisons (Table 11), parental divorce seems to have had effect on achievement motivation–lowering it for males and raising it for females. Death in the family lowers affiliation motivation in males, but not in females, and either death or divorce raises power motivation in males and lowers it in females. We have found a sizable relationship between the age of the

TABLE 11

Broken Home Background Related to n Achievement, n Affiliation, and n Power

Motive and home background	Percentage of high scores[a]	
	Men	Women
n Achievement		
Intact home	54	48
Parent(s) died	45	42
Parents divorced or separated	38	60
n Affiliation		
Intact home	49	49
Parent(s) died	39	52
Parents divorced or separated	46	51
n Power		
Intact home	47	51
Parent(s) died	61	45
Parents divorced or separated	62	44

[a]Does not include *S*s whose home background was not ascertained or *S*s whose home background was not codable into these categories. Intact home *N*s, Men = 471, Women = 585; Parent(s) died *N*s, Men = 80, Women = 125; Parents divorced *N*s, Men = 24, Women = 45.

TABLE 12

Marital Status Related to n Achievement, n Affiliation, and n Power (Age 50 and Above Only)

Motive	Percentage of high scores			
	Men		Women	
	Married ($N = 169$)	Widowed ($N = 27$)	Married ($N = 122$)	Widowed ($N = 93$)
n Achievement	47	37	47	43
n Affiliation	50	41	43	39
n Power	48	63	47	43

respondents and experiences of family disruption by divorce. Proportionally more younger than older respondents make up the group from divorce backgrounds. Even with age controlled, however, most of the differences apparent in Table 11 remain; for the most part, the differences cited occur at each age group considered.

Explanations of these differences would rest, we argue, on considering what implications these early life experiences have on motive development. Having obtained differences in motivation scores for these groups, we could plausibly proceed with an interpretation of differences by assuming that the differences reflect enduring *personality* changes brought on by family disruptions in early childhood. What is perhaps most important is that these potential differences in motivation are attributable to dispositional differences. Therefore, the motivation score *can* reflect personality differences.

The last table we are going to consider is one which compares two groups of men and women–those presently married and those whose spouses have died (Table 12). We present this table only for older (50 and above) men and women because the number of widows and widowers under 50 is relatively low. Differences without this age control might be attributable to age rather than the loss of a spouse. There are interesting differences in the table. For all motives, except power motivation in men, the loss of a spouse yields a decrease in score which is primarily a situational change. The general conclusion might be that losing one's wife or husband in later life for most people has the effect of decreasing their motivational concerns–a conclusion not at all out of line with current thinking about problems in old age. At any rate we have evidence that a life situational factor in later life can have a strong effect on motivation scores.[18]

SUMMARY AND CONCLUSIONS

We have reviewed some of the methodological and interpretive problems attending the use of thematic apperceptive measures of motivation in a

[18] See Veroff et al., 1960, for data concerning income and race.–Editors.

nationwide interview study. In light of this exploration, it is possible to offer both evaluations of the difficulties encountered and a prognosis concerning these measures in substantive research within the survey setting.

Selection of Pictures

The selection of separate sets of six pictures for men and for women was guided by previous research concerning the effect of picture cues on thematic apperception. The percentage of stories elicited by these pictures which contained imagery related to achievement, affiliation, and power was lower than anticipated from pretests but sufficient, we believe, to allow for valid assessment of individual and group differences in the strength of the three motives.

We have no independent basis for evaluating the extent to which the objective was attained of providing a fair opportunity for persons in all strata of American society to express their motives. Only intensive analysis of the responses to particular pictures by particular segments of the population (reserved for a later paper) will provide the kind of evidence needed for further evaluation of the adequacy of the pictures that were employed and clarification of the issues to be faced in subsequent attempts of this sort.

Interviewer Effects

In light of the known sensitivity of thematic apperception to conditions of administration, we anticipated and found that despite our efforts to standardize the interviewing procedure, the interviewers did (apparently) contribute significantly to the variance of some (but not all) of the motivation scores. However, we were gratified to find that our estimates of interviewer effect—maximal estimates as a consequence of possible confounding of interviewer and respondent effects in survey data—were no higher than in fact they were. That interviewer effects on motivation scores were less than anticipated can be attributed to the correction employed to remove the relationship between raw motivation scores and length of protocol. Interviewers differed considerably in the average length of the imaginative protocols they obtained. Correction of motivation scores for this factor effectively eliminated much of an otherwise substantial interviewer effect.

As a consequence of bias attributable to interviewers still remaining in some of the motivation scores, we anticipate some loss in the sensitivity of the measures (i.e., an increase in error variance) in later analyses of substantive relationships, e.g., relationships of motivation to demographic variables.

Reliability of Coding

The reliability of coding attained by a team of nine relatively novice student coders, while less than that normally attained with this method of content analysis in small-scale experimental studies of college students, was nevertheless encouragingly high. The range of coding reliability coefficients for the motivation scores assigned to individuals was .72 to .91 with a median of .77. All of these estimates of coding reliability are within the range of reliabilities reported in earlier published studies. However, in comparison with the median standard of .89 attained in experimental studies, in this study with new pictures and other novel problems there is a loss in reliability of coding and hence some increase in the error of measurement. We expect, therefore, an additional loss in the sensitivity of the measures in later analyses of substantive relationships.

Inadequate Protocols

A substantial number of individuals produced protocols that were judged inadequate for further analysis. The overall loss of data amounted to 17% among men and 14% among women. In both sexes, the loss was heavy and serious, as might have been anticipated, only among the least educated groups. Hence, the average motivation scores of some subgroups in the population, specifically those in which level of education is very low, must be considered biased estimates–derived only from the most verbal members of those groups.

Verbal Fluency

One problem of considerable importance, the relationship between motivation scores and length of imaginative protocol, which is described by correlations of .20 to .28 in this national sample, seems to have been quite adequately overcome. The correction devised reduces these correlations to the range from −.04 to .05 and effectively removes the possibility that substantive relationships, like the significant positive relationship between n Achievement and education of respondent, can be considered spurious because of a dependency of motivation scores on verbal fluency. As mentioned earlier, this correction also produced a very substantial reduction in the extent of variability of motivation scores attributable to interviewer differences.

Interpretation of Motivation Scores

Differences in motivation scores in various subgroups of the population can be variously interpreted as reflecting differences in: personality, life situation, and the significance of the pictures for various groups. The relative importance of each of these interpretations may be evaluated only by further inquiry into the kinds of variables related to these scores within different subgroups. A particular network of interrelationships may be suggestive of which of these views may be supported. It might very well be that the interpretation of the scores will vary depending on which social group is being investigated. Or, one conclusion that seems likely is that for each social group the motivation score can be partially interpreted as personality assessment and partially as an assessment of reactions to ongoing life situations. There is evidence in the survey data that each of these interpretations may be operating in the scores. Motivation scores reflect differences both in early life experiences (broken home background) and later life experiences (death of a spouse).

These alternative considerations of the conceptual meaning of the motivation scores precludes the consideration of their relationships with demographic variables as unequivocal norms describing subgroup differences in personality. The results have been presented here with the hope that they can serve as background for exploring the significance of motivation differences in society.

If methodological precautions like those outlined here are seriously considered, the use of thematic apperceptive measures of motivation (and other sensitive techniques of personality assessment) can be expected to make marked contributions in the study of important substantive problems in survey research. Careful inquiries into the relationship of these measures to other psychological variables and to demographic indices in this survey, and in subsequent national studies, should greatly enhance our understanding of the social origins and consequences of motivation. At the same time, survey studies will provide insights that are needed to refine the thematic apperceptive method itself. The use of thematic apperception to assess motivation in survey studies of national character will mean that factual evidence concerning personality configurations within American society can be integrated with the fund of factual evidence concerning the dynamics of motivation already derived from experimental and clinical use of these same measures.

We are pleased to present you with

A REVIEW COPY OF

by

price

publication date

MOTIVATION AND ACHIEVEMENT

J.W. Atkinson & J.O. Raynor
(Editors)
$19.95
4/10/74

Two clippings of your reviews will be appreciated

HALSTED PRESS
A Division of JOHN WILEY & SONS, Inc.
605 Third Avenue, New York, N.Y. 10016

APPENDIX

Approximate Sampling Error Differences for Percentages from 35% to 65%

N	700	500	300	200	100	75	50	25
700	5.4–7.6	5.9–8.3	6.9–9.7	8.0–11.2	10.7–14.4	12.1–15.9	14.6–18.9	20.3–25.8
500		6.3–8.8	7.2–10.1	8.4–11.8	11.0–14.8	12.3–16.2	14.8–19.2	20.5–26.1
300			8.2–11.5	9.1–12.7	11.5–15.6	12.9–17.0	15.4–19.7	20.8–26.5
200				10.0–14.0	12.2–16.7	13.4–17.9	15.8–20.7	21.2–27.2
100					14.1–19.0	15.2–20.1	17.3–22.4	22.4–28.6
75						16.2–21.2	18.2–23.5	23.1–29.4
50							20.0–25.7	24.5–31.1
25								28.3–35.8

Note.–The values shown are the differences required for significance (two standard errors) in comparisons of percentages derived from two different subgroups of the current survey. Two values–low and high–are given for each cell. The lower estimates are based on simple random samples. The higher values are based on the computation of individual sampling errors carried out on the current study data, and allow for the departure from simple random sampling in the survey design such as stratification and clustering. The sampling error does not measure the total error involved in specific survey estimates since it does not include non-response and reporting errors.

4

MOTIVATIONAL IMPLICATIONS OF INDIVIDUAL DIFFERENCES IN COMPETENCE[1]

Robert W. Moulton

People differ widely in terms of the degree to which they believe themselves to possess various abilities. That is, we consider ourselves to be relatively well equipped to deal with some kinds of skilled tasks, and less well equipped to deal with others. I refer to these *beliefs* as competence judgments. They should be correlated with but not identical to actual abilities as measured. I will talk about some of the effects of these differences in self-ratings on attempts to test the theory of achievement motivation as it is currently stated (see Chapter 2).

Any meaningful application of the theory of achievement motivation depends on an accurate control or assessment of subjective probability of success, and techniques for meeting this requirement have been numerous and varied. An understanding of the problems involved in these techniques and of other points I would like to make depends on a distinction between two kinds of level of difficulty. First is the individual's subjective judgment as to the likelihood that he can succeed on a given achievement task. This is the subjective probability of success, or P_s, variable in the current theory. Judgments can also be made about the difficulty level of tasks in more general terms, e.g., how difficult the task is for the average man or what proportion of a given population can succeed. Thus, for example, the farther away subjects stand from a target in a dart-throwing experiment, the smaller the proportion of a given population that can succeed. Similarly, occupations can be ranked with a high degree of interjudge reliability with respect to the proportion of the population that has

[1] This paper was presented at the meetings of the American Psychological Association, Washington, D.C., September 1967, as part of a symposium entitled: "A Theory of Achievement Motivation: Problems and New Developments."

the requisite ability. I call these generalized judgments about difficulty level *consensual difficulty*. Typically, given a set of achievement tasks, subjective probability ranks will fall in at least roughly the same order as obtains for the consensual difficulty dimension. However, and this is a basic point in my argument, though the ordering may be the same, the locations of the range of values of subjective probability can fall at quite different points along the dimension of consensual difficulty, *depending upon competence,* i.e., the degree to which the individual believes he possesses the skills necessary for successful performance on the tasks of the type involved. For example, if one believes himself to be very good at a particular kind of task, he may have a high P_s on tasks for which only a small proportion of the population can be expected to succeed.

These differences in competence can and have created difficulties in applications of the theory of achievement motivation. If we present subjects with tasks which vary in consensual difficulty, we have no way of being sure as to what values of P_s are generated. Obviously, results can be distorted seriously by this factor. Adding to the importance of these considerations is the fact that competence judgments and achievement-related motives may be interrelated.

Several studies by Feather (1965, 1966), a study by Brody (1963), and data recently gathered by Shrable and myself (Shrable & Moulton, 1968) offer evidence showing that achievement-related motives are related to subjective probability of success. That is, given most kinds of information about level of difficulty, such as distance from the target in a dart-throwing experiment, or the proportion of the population that can succeed, etc., P_s tends to be positively correlated with measures of the motive to approach success (M_S) and to be negatively correlated with measures of the motive to avoid failure (M_{AF}). Thus when criterion differences between motive groups are examined, differences obtained may reflect differences in P_s rather than being an expression of the motive differences presumably under investigation. Precisely this set of events has been postulated to account for some anomalous results in previous research. Smith (1964) showed, for example, that predictions from the theory about degree of persistence on a final exam were supported only when differences in intelligence (used as a measure of relative competence) were taken into account.

There are various techniques for eliminating or controlling problems created by individual differences in competence. Actual frequency of success or failure can be controlled or assessed in an experimental situation, and subsequent strength of tendencies can be examined. Potential problems with this technique are suggested by recent work of Feather (1966), who has shown that when these sequences of success and failure are in marked contrast to initial expectancies, performance level is affected in ways which may obscure a test of the current theory. Weiner's (1965a, and Chapter 17) work also would suggest that effects of success and failure on the amount of persisting motivation or inertial tendency (see Part IV for theory and research concerning inertial motivation) would complicate the use of this technique. Another possible technique is simply to ask *S*s to state their own probability of success with respect to tasks. We have some evidence for the usefulness of this approach (see Shrable & Moulton, 1968), though other research suggests that introspection about the values of P_s of tasks creates special circumstances which we do not as yet understand (see Litwin, 1958).

In another attack on this problem, I devised an experimental situation in which the effects of motive-related differences in competence were apparently reduced to a minimum. I attempted to convince *S*s that an accurate assessment of their competence with respect to tasks used had been made, and that data shown to them concerning task difficulty represented an accurate statement of their own P_s for the tasks. On two occasions using this technique, the prediction that *S*s for whom M_S exceeds M_{AF} would show a relatively greater preference for tasks of intermediate difficulty than would *S*s of the opposite motive pattern was clearly confirmed (Moulton, 1965, 1967a). In another experimental condition similar to the first, except that information about level of difficulty did not preclude the influence of competence differences, the pattern of results could not be dealt with by theory unless the influence of differences in competence was assumed.

Another approach is to attempt to assess interindividual and intraindividual differences in competence with respect to the general class of achievement tasks in question. Morris (1966) used this approach in a study of the rated attractiveness of occupations. He developed a reliable measure of relative competence within various occupational clusters which hang together because they presumably require the same general class of abilities, e.g., mechanical, musical, scientific, etc. Within each of the clusters he selected jobs at roughly equivalent points along the dimension of consensual difficulty. He assumed that in areas of high competence the jobs with moderate P_s would have high consensual difficulty, while in areas of low competence, jobs with moderate P_s would fall at the easy end of the consensual difficulty scale. *S*s for whom $M_S > M_{AF}$ were expected to prefer jobs of high consensual difficulty in high-competence areas and of low consensual difficulty in low-competence areas. The opposite pattern was expected of *S*s for whom $M_{AF} > M_S$. Both sets of predictions were confirmed. Without a consideration of competence differences, relationships between achievement-related motive patterns and level of occupational aspiration were minimal, a finding which paralleled my experimental study of difficulty preference where such controls were not applied (Moulton, 1965, 1967a).

In further work with the competence variable, Shrable and I (see Shrable & Moulton, 1968) have been able to show that it has relevance even for the measurement of the achievement motive. We currently assume that the writing of fantasy stories from which the strength of motive is inferred is subject to the same rules as any achievement-related behavior. Thus the latent motive, in combination with subjective expectancies aroused by picture cues, produces achievement-related tendencies (see Atkinson, 1958b), the strength of which determines the likelihood of appearance of scorable achievement imagery (to obtain the n Achievement score) in the fantasies. The absence of achievement fantasy can thus reflect the absence of appropriate expectancies as well as the absence of the motive. Shrable and I selected pictures which were clear with respect to the type of abilities required for good performance on the activities portrayed. Using Morris' (1966) measure of competence, we examined differences in amount and type of achievement imagery associated with pictures portraying activities differing in the extent to which the individual felt he possessed the requisite competence. We reasoned that very high competence with respect to activities represented in a picture might be associated with fantasies of unique accomplishments at very high levels of consensual difficulty, such as inventions or discoveries, or alternatively with fantasies of future, high-level career activities. It should be these kinds of activities for which achievement-related tendencies would be maximal in high-competence areas because the moderate risk is represented by these activities when the individual is high in competence. These types of fantasies are a part of the established n Achievement scoring system (see McClelland et al., 1958). For pictures of low-competence activities we expected that the immediate and routine demands for simple good performance would approach the moderately difficult range, and that we would find themes presently scored for n Achievement simply because they meet the criterion of evidence of concern over competition with standards of excellence. Both expectations were confirmed. Additionally, we tentatively anticipated that low-competence pictures might show less total scorable n Achievement because there might be no activity, no matter how easy, for which the individual might have a P_s appreciably above zero. This expectation was clearly confirmed for *S*s (high-school-aged students) above the median on intelligence. They wrote more n Achievement fantasies in response to high- as contrasted to low-competence pictures. For low IQ *S*s the results were just as clear but reversed. We do not have any ready explanation for this reversal, but we feel it may represent a clue as to the circumstances under which achievement fantasies may represent substitutive or compensatory fantasy and when they may represent an indication of a persistent latent tendency to actively seek certain classes of incentives. In any event, this piece of work suggests that control of the competence variable in measurement of the motive demands further investigation; it may be an important source of error in the present procedure.

I should point out that the modifications of the theory to be put forward by Raynor (1967; see also Chapter 7) can deal quite elegantly with most of the results I have just reported, as well as some of the others I will describe.

Another important point on the effects of competence: According to the theory as presently stated (Chapter 2), the strength of the achievement-related tendencies aroused by tasks of the same P_s should be equal. The fact that they were drawn from areas differing in competence would therefore be irrelevant with respect to the strength of these particular tendencies. However, people have other reasons to succeed, of course, and it is recognized that the total strength of tendency to perform a task requiring skill includes tendencies associated with other incentives contingent upon successful performance. An important fact about many of these "extrinsic" incentives such as social approval, prestige, money, etc., is that the more difficult the task is perceived to be by others, the greater the magnitude and/or quality of these incentives received as a result of success. In high-competence areas the individual has a relatively high subjective probability of success on tasks of high consensual difficulty (tasks which others see as very difficult)–which consequently offer high incentive values for these other inducements to action. Generally speaking, then, "extrinsic" tendencies should be considerably stronger in these areas, because, though tasks of equal P_s may arouse equal achievement-related tendencies, the total tendency should be greater for the task from an area of high competence rather than low. Morris (1966) found in the previously cited study that almost all of his high-school-aged students stated a vocational choice which fell in an area of high competence. Subjects for whom $M_S > M_{AF}$ chose from among the jobs of very high consensual difficulty within areas of high competence. This was predictable from the assumption that these are the jobs most closely approaching the point where $P_s = .50$ for high-competence areas. My argument is that the strong "extrinsic" tendencies aroused by these particular jobs caused them to be preferred to other moderately difficult jobs in areas of low or moderate competence. *S*s for whom $M_{AF} > M_S$ also chose in areas of high competence, but they avoided the top-level jobs which we assume have a P_s approaching .50. By selecting jobs of moderate consensual difficulty in high-competence areas, they were in fact choosing jobs of relatively high subjective probability of success. Thus they were avoiding the moderately difficult level of occupational aspiration, as expected from the theory, while selecting jobs with relatively high extrinsic payoffs for which their probability of attainment was high.[2]

The manner in which the effects of success and failure may be mediated by the competence variable must also be considered. Note that success and failure not only change P_s for tasks at hand, but they also change competence; that is, they cause the 0.00 to 1.00 range of subjective probability to shift up or down on the scale of consensual difficulty. Thus success or failure not only can have an effect on the strength of achievement-related tendencies to perform any act of a given level of consensual difficulty, but also they affect the strength of total tendency to perform acts which fall in particular areas of competence through changes in the strength of extrinsic tendencies. Success or failure at some tasks may in fact have tremendous self-diagnostic implications. The information tells the individual the extent to which he can realistically aspire to attain the highly valued incentives which success at high levels of consensual difficulty affords.

[2] See Chapter 7 for a discussion of how competence, future orientation, and achievement-related motives are expected to influence risk taking (as in occupational choice), and recent data bearing on this issue.–Editors.

Much of what I have been saying depends on the assumption that there are relatively universally perceived, cohesive clusters of abilities and that people do recognize various tasks as falling within such clusters. To the extent that this is not true, an assessment of competence within an area is useless. However, the reasoning I have presented would assert that the assumption is subject to test. Success or failure on a task of a particular level of consensual difficulty would affect the subjective probability of other tasks to the extent to which the second task was seen as requiring the same abilities. Thus the strength of tendencies to perform the second task would be affected in predictable ways if it is the case that the two tasks do indeed fall in the same area of competence. Actually, one can reverse the logic and begin to learn about the degree to which tasks are perceived as requiring the same abilities by examining the degree to which success or failure on a given task affects the strength of tendencies aroused by tasks which presumably fall in the same area of competence.

In summary then, competence is an important and measurable mediator of the relationship between the external cues defining level of difficulty and the values of subjective probability that result. Consequently, it is an important determinant of variations in strength of achievement-related tendencies aroused by any objectively describable external situation. We have seen a number of possible ways in which the influence of the variable can be eliminated or assessed, including its operation in the measurement of the achievement motive itself. A number of studies clearly indicate that effective tests of the theory of achievement motivation are dependent on such steps. Finally, I have suggested that insofar as the total strength of the tendency to perform an achievement-related act is composed of tendencies aimed at incentives extrinsic to achievement, competence will have crucial effects on the strength of the total tendency to perform the act to the extent that these extrinsic incentives increase as a function of the level of consensual difficulty.

5

PERFORMANCE AS A FUNCTION OF ACHIEVEMENT MOTIVE LEVEL AND PERCEIVED DIFFICULTY[1]

Stuart A. Karabenick and Zakour I. Youssef

The present study was designed to test implications of Expectancy X Value Theory of achievement motivation (see Chapter 2) using a performance task that permitted the systematic variation of levels of subjective probability of success (P_s). This was done using a modified paired-associate (PA) learning task. By color-coding the word pairs, three groups of items known to be of equal difficulty were identified to subjects as being either very easy (E), very difficult (D), or of intermediate difficulty (ID).

Theory of achievement motivation leads to the predictions that (*a*) persons in whom the motive to achieve success is relatively stronger than the motive to avoid failure ($M_S > M_{AF}$) should select and perform better at ID tasks than at E or D tasks, and (*b*) persons with the opposite motive pattern ($M_{AF} > M_S$) should, if constrained, select and perform maximally at either E or D tasks, avoiding and performing more poorly at ID tasks ($P_s = .50$) (see Chapter 2). The theory has received support in studies of risk taking (Atkinson & Litwin, 1960; McClelland, 1958b; Moulton, 1965; Raynor & Smith, 1966; see also Chapter 2) and of persistence (Feather, 1961; see also Chapter 2). In studies of achievement motivation and performance, support for the theory has been obtained where P_s was deliberately manipulated (Atkinson, 1958c; Atkinson & O'Connor, 1963) and where assumptions can be made about P_s in cases where it has not been a variable (e.g., Atkinson & Litwin, 1960; Spielberger, 1962; see also Chapter 2).

According to the theory and in view of the empirical support it has received, it was predicted that persons for whom $M_S > M_{AF}$ would perform better on

[1] Reprinted and abridged by permission of the authors and the American Psychological Association from the *Journal of Personality and Social Psychology*, 1968, 10, 414–419.

word pairs designated as being of ID than on either E or D pairs (an inverted U-shaped function). Persons for whom $M_{AF} > M_S$ were predicted to perform better on either E or D pairs than at ID pairs (a U-shaped function). In other words, the model predicts a quadratic interaction between perceived difficulty level, or probability of success, and individual differences in achievement motive disposition.

METHOD

Pretest

Fifteen word pairs were used that were highly frequent nouns in the Thorndike-Lorge Count (1944). On the basis of previous studies[2] the pairs were placed into three groups so as to equate the mean and variance of the difficulty levels across groups as closely as possible. The groups were color-coded using red, yellow, and green transparent tapes.

A test for matching was conducted in which 12 *S*s learned the lists using standard PA instruction. This list of 15 pairs was presented to *S*s on a Lafayette memory drum with 2-second intratrial and 4-second intertrial intervals. Learning and test trials were alternated, and pairs were presented in three random orders to minimize serial position effects. An analysis of variance using total correct responses over the first 10 trials revealed no significant differences between the groups of word pairs ($F = 1.28, df = 2/22$).

Main Experiment

Subjects. Seventy-six male introductory psychology students at Eastern Michigan University served as *S*s in the main experiment. No pretest *S* participated in the main experiment.

Assessment of M_S and M_{AF}. Assessment of individual differences took place in a 1-hour session in a large auditorium. The session was conducted under "neutral" conditions (McClelland, Atkinson, Clark, & Lowell, 1953). Individual differences in the strength of M_S were obtained using the measure of thematic apperception (TAT) developed by McClelland et al. (1953) and scored according to the manual for n Achievement (McClelland et al., 1958). A four-picture set was used; each picture was projected on a screen for 20 seconds after which *S*s were given 4 minutes to write their story. Protocols were scored by one of the authors (S.K.) who had previously obtained a high scoring reliability with the n Achievement scoring manual. Individual differences in the strength of M_{AF} were measured by the Test Anxiety Questionnaire (TAQ–Mandler & Sarason, 1952). This is a self-report measure of anxiety aroused in a testing situation. The TAQ was presented immediately after the TAT.

[2] Z. I. Youssef. Transfer from serial to paired-associate learning. Unpublished study, 1967.

Persons were placed in four motive groups on the basis of their scores on both the TAT and the TAQ. According to the rationale presented by Atkinson and Litwin (1960), persons above the median on the TAT and below the median on the TAQ (High-Low) were classified as having $M_S > M_{AF}$. Those below the median on the TAT and above the median on the TAQ (Low-High) were classified as having $M_{AF} > M_S$. Persons high or low on both measures (High-High or Low-Low) were assumed to fall between the extreme motive groups, that is $M_S \approx M_{AF}$.

PA test procedure. The PA task was administered individually at least 2 weeks subsequent to the assessment session. The *E* in this part of the study was unknown to the *S*s, not having been involved in conducting the assessment session.[3] The *E* began the session with the following set of achievement-oriented instructions:

> The experiment that you are about to participate in consists of learning a series of word-pairs. This task is not unlike other tasks that you may have encountered requiring reasoning, the ability to think and act quickly and efficiently. This task has been given to other students at this and other universities and it will be possible to compare your score with the scores made by these other students. For this reason you should perform to the best of your ability so that your performance can be taken as an accurate measure of your ability.

*S*s were then given the same standard set of PA instructions that were used in the pretest except that they were now told that the colors served as an indicator of the difficulty level of each word-pair, namely: easy, intermediate, and difficult. The following instructions were used:

> The words in this experiment are covered with different colors. The colors are to indicate to you the different levels of difficulty of the words with which they correspond. The difficulty of these words has been determined by analysis of data acquired through previous experiments using people of similar background, interests, and scholastic standing as yourself. The easy words were all learned readily by all persons; the difficult words were learned by only a few people; and as may be expected, the intermediate words were learned well by about half of the people. On the chart before you are the colors you will find in the list, and indicated is the difficulty level with which each color corresponds. You may wish to refer to this chart from time to time.

Six different color-difficulty-level combinations were used. The particular combination for a given *S* was chosen at random and was displayed on a chart placed in front of him. This procedure was used to remove any systematic bias due to differences in difficulty between the word groups not removed by the matching procedure. *S*s learned the list to a criterion of three successive perfect repetitions with the restriction that at least 10 but no more than 30 trials were allowed.

[3]The authors wish to express their appreciation to Ralph Kirk and Steve Bedwell for their assistance during the assessment session and to John Nilan for conducting the individual PA testing sessions.

RESULTS

Figure 1 presents the mean number of correct responses made by High-Low and Low-High motive groups on E, ID, and D word pairs over Trials 1-10. It can be seen that performance differences between these two groups exist only on ID items, and, in addition, the High-Low group is shown to perform better than Group Low-High on all 10 trials on these items. The index used for analysis was the total number of correct responses over the first 10 trials. This measure was chosen since all *S*s received at least 10 trials and because it was judged as a more stable measure than those based on fewer trials.[4] The means over Trials 1-10 are presented in Table 1 for all motive groups. Inspection indicates that the performance trends of the four motive groups are in the directions predicted by the Atkinson model. The means indicate an inverted U-shaped function for the High-Low group and a U-shaped function for the Low-High group. In addition, Groups High-High and Low-Low fall in between the two extreme groups, and their performance is approximately the same over all levels of difficulty.

Table 2 presents an analysis of variance for Groups High-Low and Low-High. As predicted by the model, the Motive Groups X Difficulty interaction is significant ($F = 3.59$, $df = 2/52$, $p < .05$). Another analysis of variance, presented in Table 3, using all four motive groups, was conducted to determine

[4] All analyses were conducted with Trials as a third dimension. Total 10 trial score was considered sufficient to present since none of the interactions involving Trials were significant.

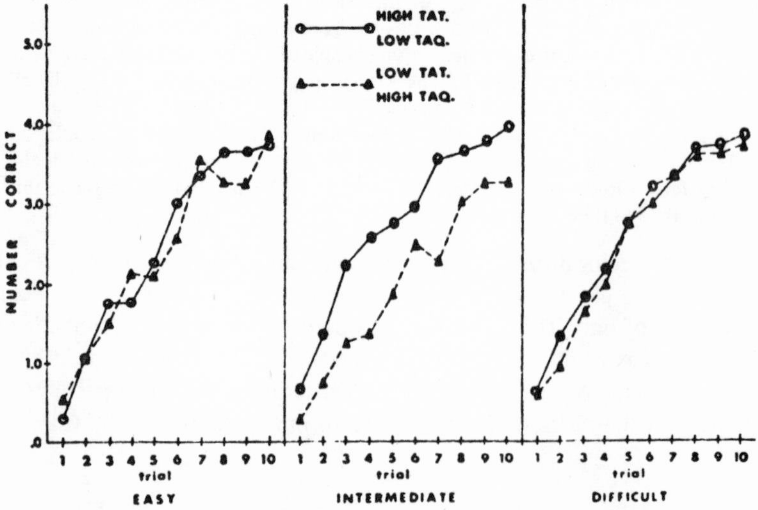

FIG. 1. Mean number of easy, intermediate difficulty, and difficult word pairs correctly recalled by extreme motive groups on Trials 1-10.

TABLE 1

Means for all Groups on Total Number Correct of 10 PA Trials

TAT-TAQ	Supposed difficulty level of word pairs		
	Easy	Intermediate	Difficult
High-Low	24.71	27.71	26.50
High-High	22.71	22.84	22.79
Low-Low	24.09	23.92	24.04
Low-High	23.21	20.00	25.43

TABLE 2

Analysis of Variance for the "Extreme" Motivational Groups X Perceived Level of Difficulty on the Total Number Correct of 10 PA Trials

Source	*SS*	*df*	*MS*	*F*
Between *S*s	7,108.24	27	263.27	
Motive groups (M)	246.86	1	246.86	.998
Error (between)	6,861.38	26	263.90	.94
Within *S*s	1,672.00	56	29.86	
Difficulty (D)	78.88	2	39.44	1.47
M X D	193.50	2	96.75	3.59*
Error (within)	1,399.62	52	26.92	
Total	8,780.24	83		

*$p < .05$.

whether Groups High-High and Low-Low would contribute to the interaction. When these groups are included, the Motive Groups X Difficulty interaction fails to reach significance. Furthermore, the difference between the two interaction sum of squares in Tables 2 and 3 is sufficiently small to preclude any significant interaction, however partitioned, other than that using only the High-Low and Low-High motive groups. This is consistent with the model that predicts that performance will be equal across difficulty levels for persons for whom it can be assumed that $M_S \approx M_{AF}$ as is the case for Groups High-High and Low-Low.

Subsequent trend tests were conducted to determine the relative contribution of linear and quadratic components of the interaction involving High-Low and Low-High motive groups. As shown in Table 4, the interaction was a function of the differing quadratic trends of the High-Low and Low-High groups ($F = 7.16$, $df = 1/52$, $p < .01$), the linear component accounting for a negligible portion of the variance ($F = .024$, $df = 1/52$). In addition to finding that the quadratic

TABLE 3

Analysis of Variance for all the Motivational Groups X Perceived Level of Difficulty on the Total Number Correct of 10 PA Trials

Source	*SS*	*df*	*MS*	*F*
Between *S*s	20,021.67	75	266.96	
Motive groups (M)	378.18	3	126.06	.46
Error (between)	19,643.49	72	272.83	
Within *S*s	4,027.33	152	26.49	
Difficulty (D)	30.64	2	15.32	.59
M X D	242.28	6	40.38	1.59
Error (within)	3,754.41	144	26.07	
Total	24,049.00	227		

TABLE 4

Orthogonal Polynomial Comparisons for the Two "Extreme" Motivational Groups X Perceived Level of Difficulty on the Total Number Correct of 10 PA Trials

Source	*SS*	*df*	*MS*	*F*
High-Low linear	22.32	1	22.32	.83
High-Low quadratic	41.44	1	41.44	1.54
Low-High linear	34.32	1	34.32	1.27
Low-High quadratic	174.30	1	174.30	6.47*
Motive Groups X Difficulty (linear)	.64	1	.64	.02
Motive Groups X Difficulty (quadratic)	129.86	1	129.86	7.16**
Error	1,399.62	52	26.92	

*$p < .05$.
**$p < .01$.

trends between High-Low and Low-High groups differed, tests on each group show that the U-shaped trend for the Low-High group was significant ($F = 6.42$, $df = 1/52$, $p < .05$). Thus, as predicted by the model, the Low-High group performed less well on ID than on E or D items. However, although the High-Low group performed slightly better on ID than on E or D items, the quadratic trend was not statistically significant ($F = 1.52$, $df = 1/52$).

DISCUSSION

The data present clear evidence for the interaction between resultant achievement motive strength and subjective probability of success in determining performance. Specifically, persons for whom $M_S > M_{AF}$ (the High-Low group) performed better than those for whom $M_{AF} > M_S$ (the Low-High group) at tasks designated as being of intermediate difficulty, but the performance of these groups did not differ when the tasks were either easy or difficult. In addition, whereas persons for whom $M_S > M_{AF}$ tended to perform better at intermediate difficulty tasks than at easy or difficult tasks, persons for whom $M_{AF} > M_S$ performed better on easy or difficult tasks than at those designated as being of intermediate difficulty. These trends are precisely as predicted by the theory of achievement motivation (Chapter 2) and thus provide direct evidence to support its validity to a degree not found in previous studies.

An important finding in this study is that the performance of persons classified as having $M_{AF} > M_S$ (the Low-High group) showed a relative aversion for intermediate difficulty items. In previous studies (e.g., Atkinson, 1958c; Atkinson & Litwin, 1960), persons classified as having $M_{AF} > M_S$ have shown lower motivation levels than persons classified as having $M_{AF} > M_S$ at intermediate difficulty tasks, but motivation for *both* of these groups have been highest at intermediate difficulty levels, failing to demonstrate the predicted avoidance pattern for persons with $M_{AF} > M_S$. Atkinson and Litwin (1960) proposed that this trend was due to the absence of persons for whom M_{AF} is truly greater than M_S in college populations from which, they reasoned, most of the highly anxious persons had been selected out. Due to broad admission standards, it is less likely that highly anxious persons were so eliminated from the population sampled in the present study. The presence of a greater number of "truly" anxious persons could account for the emergence of the avoidance patterns for persons in Group Low-High.

One factor that may have influenced the results was the positive correlation between TAT and TAQ scores, an uncommon finding since most correlations between these measures have been zero-order and typically negative (see Atkinson & Feather, 1966). A Pearson r of .04 between the two measures was not significant ($p > .10$), but an examination of the TAT and TAQ distribution showed them to be skewed and in opposite directions, indicating a non-parametric statistic. A Spearman rho of .19 was significant (one-tailed $p < .05$).

An examination of the mean TAT and TAQ scores of the four motive groups indicated that the correlation had no effect on the characteristics of the motive groups since it was found that the mean TAT scores of Groups High-Low and High-High did not differ significantly; the same was true for Groups Low-High and Low-Low. Neither did the TAQ scores differ significantly between Groups High-High and Low-High or between Groups High-Low and Low-Low. Therefore, it may be concluded that there is no reason to suspect that the small positive correlation produced an unusual set of initial conditions to qualify the results. The only manifestation of the correlation was the smaller number of *S*s in Groups Low-High and High-Low as compared to Groups High-High and Low-Low.

A second factor to consider is the assumption of equal spacing of perceived difficulty levels necessary for the orthogonal polynomial comparisons to be appropriate. The assumption would appear tenable, but even if it were not, since the interaction between motive levels and success expectation was obtained without resorting to orthogonal comparisons, the results support the hypothesis regardless of the validity of equal spacing assumptions. It is also of note that significance was obtained with small sample sizes ($n = 14$ for Groups High-Low and Low-High). To obtain statistically significant results with such sample sizes (the *SDs* are about 40% of their respective means on PA performance) attests to the powerful interaction effects of motive disposition and perceived difficulty on performance.

As for the theoretical implications, these data are not readily explained by S-R formulations relating anxiety level and performance (e.g., Brown, 1966; Farber & Spence, 1953; Montague, 1953; Taylor & Spence, 1952). Since the task used in this study can be considered a relatively complex one, the Taylor-Spence theory would predict that persons high in anxiety would not perform as well as those low in anxiety. Thus, subjects in Group High-Low and Low-Low (relatively low in anxiety) would be predicted to perform better than *S*s in Groups Low-High and High-High (relatively high in anxiety). The evidence does not support this prediction since the main effect for motive groups was not significant.

In addition, the Taylor-Spence theory would have predicted no differential performance on items differing in subjective difficulty. Again, the evidence is contrary to this prediction given the significant interaction between motive (anxiety) levels for Groups High-Low and Low-High and perceived difficulty. The results suggest further studies where task complexity and subjective difficulty levels are varied simultaneously so that both the Taylor-Spence and Atkinson predictions could be directly compared. The present design could be used for such a test.[5]

[5] See Chapter 18 for another test between the two theoretical positions.—Editors.

6

THE MEASUREMENT AND BEHAVIORAL IMPLICATIONS OF FEAR OF SUCCESS IN WOMEN[1]

Matina Souretis Horner

This study is an attempt to extend current theory of achievement motivation (Chapter 2) so as to embrace and comprehend some sex differences that have been previously observed. The concept of motive to avoid success is introduced as an additional, relevant variable to be considered in reference to the behavior of women in competitive achievement situations. It is one more step in the direction of identifying the various motives and incentives inherent in achievement-related activities of contemporary life.

The effects on performance of two different kinds of achievement situations are explored for both sexes: (*a*) noncompetitive achievement-oriented situations, viz., those which involve competition against a standard only, and (*b*) interpersonal competitive achievement-oriented situations which involve competition against others.

Since the publication of *The Achievement Motive* (McClelland et al., 1953), there has been extensive research to understand the contemporaneous determinants of achievement-oriented behavior (see Chapter 2). But relatively little progress has been made to resolve the sex differences that were identified almost at the outset of the research (Veroff, Wilcox, & Atkinson, 1953). Data related to achievement motivation in women have been very scarce, as evidenced by the fact that female achievement motivation occupies less than a page, in fact only a footnote, in Atkinson's (1958a) *Motives in Fantasy, Action, and Society,* a more

[1] This chapter is based on a portion of an unpublished doctoral dissertation (Horner, 1968) at the University of Michigan. The major part of this work was carried out while the author held a USPHS Pre-Doctoral Fellowship. Another part of the doctoral research is presented in Chapter 13.

than 800-page compilation of available theory, data, and method concerning achievement motivation. In that footnote, sex differences is referred to "as perhaps the most persistent unresolved problem in research on n Achievement." In *The Achieving Society* (1961), McClelland makes no mention of achievement motivation in women, though dealing with every other possible source of evidence for the motive, e.g., Indians, Quakers, Ancient Greeks, vases, flags, doodles, children's books, etc. The few comparable studies of achievement motivation in females that have been conducted are neither consistent with the theory, with the findings for males, nor even internally consistent with each other.

This chapter will focus upon implications of my study for this long unresolved problem. In a later chapter (Chapter 13), its contributions within the context of the fund of evidence regarding achievement motivation and performance among male subjects will be given separate treatment. Some of the procedures, common to the two chapters, are described in greater detail in Chapter 13.

In this study we posit a tendency to avoid success among females in competitive achievement-oriented situations, particularly those involving competition against males. The tendency is considered a potent motivational determinant of achievement-related activities for women, but not for men, in contemporary American society. Perhaps it is the factor primarily responsible for the major unresolved sex differences observed in previous research on achievement motivation.

The original problem involving sex differences in studies of achievement motivation (Veroff, Wilcox, & Atkinson, 1953) was the fact that women did not show an increase in thematic apperceptive n Achievement imagery as did men (McClelland et al., 1949) when exposed to experimental induction of achievement motivation stressing "intelligence and leadership" ability. This is shown in Tables 1 and 2. Under neutral conditions, however, the scores of the high-school-aged girls and college women were as high as and sometimes higher than those of young men under arousal conditions. This failure of females to show the expected increase under arousal was summarized by McClelland et al. (1953):

> Women do not show an increase in n Achievement scores as a result of achievement-involving instructions. . . . Why then don't women's scores increase under experimental arousal? This is the puzzler. Two possible explanations—invalidity of the scoring for women, [and] scores too high to go higher—have been eliminated. Apparently the usual arousal instructions simply do not increase achievement striving in women. . . [p. 178].

Today, almost 15 years later, the problem is still not completely resolved, although several attempts have been made to clarify it. Angelina (1955, cited in Atkinson, 1958a, p. 77) did find an increase in the n Achievement score of female Brazilian college students under achievement arousal conditions stressing intelligence and leadership ability. The results were explained by the fact that

TABLE 1

Mean n Achievement Scores of High-School Boys and Girls Obtained from Stories Written in Response to Pictures of Male and Female Characters Under Relaxed and Achievement Orientation Conditions

Subjects	N	Relaxed orientation				N	Achievement orientation			
		3 male pictures		3 female pictures			3 male pictures		3 female pictures	
		M	*SD*	*M*	*SD*		*M*	*SD*	*M*	*SD*
Boys	18	1.94	3.32	1.72	3.40	28	4.93	3.75	1.57	2.66
Girls	22	5.72	4.02	1.77	2.90	24	5.21	2.64	1.92	3.30

Note.–From Veroff et al., 1953, with permission of the authors and of the publisher, American Psychological Association.

TABLE 2

Mean n Achievement Scores of College Women Obtained from Stories Written in Response to Pictures of Male and Female Characters Under Relaxed and Achievement Orientation Conditions

	Relaxed orientation ($N = 27$)		Achievement orientation ($N = 26$)	
	M	*SD*	*M*	*SD*
Male pictures	5.70	3.93	5.77	4.20
Female pictures	.26	2.59	.38	3.12

Note.–From Veroff et al., 1953, with permission of the authors and of the publisher, American Psychological Association.

opportunities for higher education are very limited in Brazil and, therefore, only highly competitive girls who place great emphasis on intellectual accomplishment will succeed in enrolling in a university.

From this, Lesser, Krawitz, and Packard (1963) suggested that the American female subjects previously studied may not have been as concerned with standards of excellence as with achieving in the sense of "social acceptability," an idea previously suggested by Field (1951). So they undertook a study of achievement motivation at Hunter High School for girls in New York City. This is an institution which places great emphasis on the intellectual accomplishments of women and provides intense scholastic stimulation, including the pursuit of college training. Admission is very competitive. Only 150 of 4,000 highly selected candidates are admitted. More than 99% of their graduates proceed to college; a large percentage of these attain recognition and go on to pursue professional careers. It therefore seemed reasonable to assume that these subjects would show concern for competitive standards of excellence and achievement like that of the Brazilian college women and would show an increase in n Achievement scores under arousal conditions stressing intelligence and leadership ability.

Lesser et al. (1963) compared a group of girls who were meeting the academic demands of the school (i.e., the achievers) with a group, matched with the former on IQ, who were not (i.e., the underachievers). All *S*s were exposed to a set of thematic apperceptive pictures of males and females under both neutral and achievement-oriented conditions. The overall effect of the experimental induction of motivation on n Achievement score was nonsignificant. However, as shown in Table 3, the n Achievement scores of the achievers did increase significantly in response to the achievement-oriented conditions when they produced stories to pictures of females, but not to pictures of males. The opposite was true for the underachievers. The authors concluded that the achieving girls do perceive intellectual goals as a relevant part of their own female role, but that underachieving girls perceive intellectual achievement goals as more relevant to the male role than to their own female role (Lesser et al., 1963, p. 63).

This attempt to resolve the complexities of the problem of n Achievement in women in terms of differential perception of what kind of behavior is appropriate to their social role is a meaningful one, but not complete. For instance, in view of the nature of the school, it seems reasonable to assume that *all* the students at Hunter, achievers and underachievers alike, should see intellectual attainment as a relevant aspect of the female role. Yet the results of

TABLE 3

Mean n Achievement Scores of Achieving and Underachieving Girls Under Neutral and Achievement-Oriented Experimental Conditions to Pictures Containing Female and Male Characters

		Experimental conditions								Total for all experimental conditions and pictures	
		Neutral				Achievement oriented					
Group	*N*	3 female pictures		3 male pictures		3 female pictures		3 male pictures			
		M	*SD*	*M*	*SD*	*M*	*SD*	*M*	*SD*	*M*	*SD*
Achievers	40	4.80	2.39	5.43	2.61	6.03	2.82	4.78	2.17	5.26	2.56
Underachievers	40	2.93	2.40	4.18	2.82	2.25	2.22	6.20	2.47	3.89	2.91
Total for all subjects	80	3.86	2.58	4.80	2.56	4.14	2.91	5.49	2.44		

Note.–From Lesser et al., 1963, with permission of the authors and of the publisher, American Psychological Association.

the Hunter study showed that under intellectual achievement arousal "the scores of the achieving girls increased markedly for the female pictures and decreased for the male. The scores of the underachieving girls increased markedly for male pictures and decreased for females [French & Lesser, 1964, p. 127]." The explanation offered implies that the underachievers do not see achievement as relevant to the female role and therefore showed a decrease in scores to female pictures under arousal. When, however, the differential content of the cues with male and female figures is taken into account, the result raises more questions. Why should the underachievers show a decrease in score under arousal to female pictures primarily concerned with homemaking activity? Why do achieving girls increase their scores under intellectual arousal to female pictures depicting homemaking activities and decrease them to male pictures having more achievement-relevant content? Just because they see achievement as relevant to the female role is certainly no reason that they should fail to see it as also relevant to the male role.

It is useful to consider a number of other studies bearing on the question of differential responses of college women to male and female TAT n Achievement pictures and their relationship to performance. Veroff et al. (1953) found that more achievement imagery was projected to male as compared to female TAT pictures by students of both sexes enrolled at an urban Eastern high school and by women at a large coed Midwestern university. The result was interpreted as reflecting sex role differences in American culture where achievement and success are a definite part of the traditional male role but not of the traditional female role (Mead, 1949). Alper (1957) and Morrison (1954) found that the sex of the principal TAT figure affected the n Achievement scores of college women, but that under arousal conditions the increase in score was not always to the male pictures. Morrison (1954) showed that female pictures with high-achievement cues (e.g., female career pictures) did elicit as much achievement imagery as did similar pictures of males. Alper's work was carried out at a New England women's college–an all-female school at which academic achievement for females is highly valued. For these girls, n Achievement imagery was expressed in response to female cues only when achievement arousal was kept low and social acceptability was not at stake. French and Lesser (1964) found that regardless of value orientation (intellectual versus woman's role), women got higher n Achievement scores under intellectual arousal when male figures were used in pictures. Under traditional woman's role arousal, the scores were higher when female figures were used. Lipinski (1965) attempted to show that college females with various manifest and latent sex role orientations would respond differentially in amount of achievement motivation elicited under various achievement-arousal conditions. The university women in her study were given the TAT n Achievement measure in a classroom setting with both males and females present, under neutral and achievement-oriented conditions, 1 week apart. Six stories under neutral conditions and six under aroused conditions were obtained from each of the subjects. Three of the cues were male and three were female in each condition. As a group, the women showed an increase in scores from the neutral to the achievement-oriented condition, with male pictures eliciting a greater increment than the female pictures.

A further analysis in which individual differences in sex role orientation were taken into account is particularly important. Guided by previous data for males, Lipinski quite reasonably hypothesized that the more "masculinely-oriented" groups of women would, like the men do, show a greater increase in n Achievement scores than would the other sex role groups under the achievement-oriented condition. Despite the fact, however, that these subjects scored highest in n Achievement in the neutral conditions, they showed a decrement in the aroused condition. The female-oriented groups, on the other hand, showed an increment in the aroused condition. This study again raises questions about the adequacy of trying to explain female data on achievement motivation simply in terms of differential perception of social role. Why, for instance, should the male-oriented women in this study, who particularly value achievement in competitive intellectual endeavors, show a decrement in TAT n Achievement score under arousal?

Another area of divergence between male and female data has been with regard to the achievement motivation-performance relationship. Data available show that achievement motivation predicts several types of performance for males but lacks consistent predictive power for females, for whom the data are confusing (see Horner, 1968).[2]

From results presented above and elsewhere, it seems clear that to explain female responses on the TAT n Achievement measure or to account for the lack of a consistent motivation-performance relationship in female data in terms of differential perception of their social role among the subjects is at best premature. This is especially true in the absence of evidence with regard to how differential perception of social role in individuals functions psychologically to become reflected in behavior, whether that behavior be imaginative response to projective cues or performance on some other competitive achievement task. (See Chapter 19 for further discussion of this point.)

A number of the problems noted can be resolved if we do not restrict our attention to the achievement motive alone, but rather extend our analysis to include achievement-related anxieties and defenses associated with them in achievement-oriented situations. It has been argued that achievement-oriented situations simultaneously offer a chance of success and a threat of failure, thus engaging both the motive to achieve and the motive to avoid failure (the expectancies that good performance will create a feeling of pride and poor performance a feeling of shame). Using measures of both types of motivation together, rather than either by itself, has greatly enhanced the efficiency of

[2] Veroff et al. (1953) and O'Connor, Atkinson, and Horner (1966) did find that neutral n Achievement scores have the same behavioral implications for college-age females as males and for sixth grade children of both sexes. (See also Chapter 9.–Editors).

predicting behavior from the theory of achievement motivation in studies of men (Atkinson & Feather, 1966; Chapter 2).

One consistent finding for females has been that they get higher scores on measures of anxiety than do males. The explanations typically offered for this sex difference have been that women tend to react more emotionally. They tend to have stronger anxiety responses than men in situations where the negative consequences are similar. Men tend to defend against the admission of anxiety because it reflects adversely on their masculinity (Sarason et al., 1960). In a study restricted to test anxiety, Sarason (1959) found no real sex differences in the social desirability of the items on the Test Anxiety Questionnaire. It seems from this that admitting anxiety in test situations may not be as threatening to men as admitting anxiety in other, more general, types of situations.

A MOTIVE TO AVOID SUCCESS

Thus far, a test on achievement-related anxiety has been viewed mainly as a measure of motivation to avoid failure aroused by the expectancy that performing a task may lead to negative consequences, i.e., feelings of shame because of failure. It may be that females are in fact more anxious than males in testing or achievement-oriented situations because, for them, there are negative consequences associated not only with failure, but also with success and the implications of success in competitive achievement situations. This latter type of anxiety is here referred to as motive to avoid success (M_{AS}). If women are threatened by success as well as by failure in competitive achievement situations, it would not be surprising that their test anxiety scores are higher than those of men. This is especially likely on measures like the Mandler-Sarason (1952) Test Anxiety Questionnaire, which do not specify *what* one is anxious about, but simply that the person is anxious in a particular type of situation. The suggested presence of a motive to avoid success is based on the premise that, among women, an expectancy is aroused in competitive achievement situations that success will lead to negative consequences. It is therefore important to indicate just what these negative consequences of success might be for women.

Mead (1949) suggested the basis of the problem with her idea that intense intellectual striving can be viewed as "competitively aggressive behavior." The aggressive overtones of competition and success are evident in the vocabulary used to describe such situations and by the fact that (very often) each time one succeeds, someone else fails or is beaten. Freud (1933) pointed out that the whole essence of femininity lies in repressing aggressiveness. As a result, a woman is threatened by success because unusual excellence in academic intellectual areas is unconsciously equated with loss of femininity, the consequence of which may be social rejection. In other words, there are two potential sources for the negative consequences of success, i.e., *loss of one's sense of femininity and self-esteem* regardless of whether anyone finds out about the success or not and/or *social rejection* because of the success. The latter would also mitigate against the fulfillment of other needs. Kagan and Moss (1962) pointed out that the typical female has greater anxiety over aggressive and competitive behavior than the male and that she therefore experiences greater conflict over intellectual competition, which in turn leads to inhibition of intense strivings for academic excellence. It is suggested here that being successful in such competitive activities is the major source of threat or fear. Success in such situations implies that one has actively competed or been aggressive. Without the success, simple involvement in achievement activity does not carry the implication of intense striving or aggressive, unfeminine behavior.

It is therefore proposed that under achievement-oriented conditions which stress intellectual and leadership ability, the expression of achievement motivation aroused in women may become inhibited by the concurrent arousal of fear of success and fear of failure or, whenever possible (as in the Lesser et al. study), defensively projected into less conflictful situations such as (*a*) women engaged in homemaking types of activities or (*b*) men engaged in more intellectual and achievement types of pursuits. It is clearly evident in psychoanalytic literature that anxiety, and defensive reactions against that anxiety, should be considered together.

Distinction Between Competitive and Noncompetitive Achievement Situations

If anxiety about competitiveness and its aggressive overtones underlies the major differences detected in research on achievement-related motivation in women, then women should behave quite differently in competitive and noncompetitive achievement situations.

In the present study, the possibility that the achievement situation involves two distinct types of competitive aspects will be considered. The first aspect is competition against a standard of excellence inherent in a task, and the second is competition against another person or other people as well. The aggressive overtones of competition should be substantially stronger in the second case.

The typical achievement situations with which we are familiar such as schools, colleges, business, politics, etc., as well as most experimental situations, involve both aspects, either explicitly or implicitly. In order to succeed or to do well in school, one must perform well on the tests and also in relation to the others in the class. As a result, any evidence that the two aspects have a differential impact on behavior is hidden, and the results are confounded.

In this study the two aspects are experimentally separated. There is a noncompetitive achievement-oriented situation in which subjects compete only against a standard of excellence; and, there are two competitive conditions in which they also compete against another person.

In the noncompetitive achievement-oriented condition, the experimenter tries to convince the subject that his/her behavior will in no way be compared with or judged against that of anyone else.

In the competitive conditions, the subject is in direct competition with someone else. The competitive, aggressive aspects of achievement are thus stressed, thereby maximally arousing fear of success if the hypothesis is correct.

It will be particularly interesting to note the extent to which behavior of the subjects varies in achievement situations when they are competing against another person and when they are competing only against a standard defined by the task and their own internal standards of excellence.

The theory of achievement motivation as presently formulated cannot readily make differential predictions between the conditions nor between the sexes. As noted in Chapter 2, the theory considers conflict between the tendency to achieve success (T_s) and the tendency to avoid failure (T_{-f}) inherent in any instance of achievement-oriented behavior, but does not embrace the concept of a tendency to avoid success (T_{-s}).

Before considering the functional significance of the tendency to avoid success, we must clarify just what assumptions are to be made about the motive to avoid success and how it is to be incorporated into the existing theory. Among the critical assumptions needed prior to deriving the specific hypotheses for the present study were those concerned with the conceptual analysis of motive to avoid success (M_{AS}), with the factors determining arousal and strength of the tendency to avoid success (T_{-s}), and with the relationship between the proposed negative incentive value of success (I_{as}) and subjective probability of success (P_s) (task difficulty) in any situation.

Assumptions Regarding M_{AS} and T_{-s}

The addition of T_{-s} to the theory and the hypotheses for the study will be guided by the following assumptions about motive to avoid success (M_{AS}) and about tendency to avoid success (T_{-s}):

1. Motive to avoid success is a stable characteristic of the personality acquired early in life in conjunction with sex role standards. It can be conceived as a disposition (*a*) to feel uncomfortable when successful in competitive (aggressive) achievement situations because such behavior is inconsistent with one's femininity, an internal standard, and (*b*) to expect or become concerned about negative consequences such as social rejection following success in such situations.

2. Motive to avoid success is much more common in women than in men. This assumes that being successful in competitive achievement situations has generally been consistent with masculine identity and other male goals and not antagonistic to them, as may be the case with women.

3. Motive to avoid success is probably not equally important for all women. Fear of success should be more strongly aroused in women who are highly motivated to achieve and/or highly able (e.g., who aspire to and/or are readily capable of achieving success). For women with less achievement motivation or ability (e.g., those for whom success is neither a major goal nor one readily

within their reach), there is no reason to feel anxious about succeeding. In approach-avoidance gradient terms, the former women are typically much closer to the threatening goal than are the latter.

4. Motive to avoid success is more strongly aroused in competitive achievement situations where performance reflecting "intellectual and leadership" ability is to be evaluated against some standard of excellence *and* against someone else's performance than in noncompetitive situations where competition is directed only against an impersonal standard.

5. Once aroused, the tendency to avoid success (T_{-s}) either (*a*) will function as a negative inhibitory tendency acting against the expression of the positive tendency to achieve success which is also aroused in achievement-oriented situations, or (*b*) may lead to the expression of defensive responses which serve to relieve the anxiety aroused when for extrinsic reasons the T_s must be expressed. That is, $T_A = (T_s - T_{-f}) - T_{-s} + T_{ext}$.

6. The best assumption we can make at the present time about the strength of the tendency to avoid success is to follow the principle used for T_s and T_{-f}, i.e., that the strength of the tendency is a multiplicative function of motive strength, incentive value, and probability of success:

$$T_{-s} = M_{AS} \times P_s \times I_{as}$$

It is further assumed that *the strength of the negative incentive value of success* ($-I_{as}$) *will be greater for women in competitive than in noncompetitive achievement situations, when their competitors are males rather than females,* especially if they are "important" males, and when the tasks involved are generally considered masculine, such as tasks of mathematical, logical, spatial, etc., ability.

7. One of the major problems in making specific predictions about behavior in terms of the tendency to avoid success (T_{-s}) is what assumptions to make about how the negative incentive value of success (I_{as}) is related to difficulty of the task (P_s), if at all. Factors other than P_s which are assumed to influence the strength of I_{as} have already been discussed. There are several possibilities for the relationship between I_{as} and P_s, and these are discussed fully elsewhere (Horner, 1968).

METHOD

Subjects

The *S*s were 178 undergraduate students enrolled in nine introductory psychology sections at the University of Michigan during the winter of 1965. Their part in this experiment served to fulfill a course requirement for 3 hours of experimental participation. After an initial assessment period, 90 female and 88 male *S*s were randomly assigned to the three experimental conditions (see Chapter 13 for a report of results for the male *S*s). The *S*s were predominantly freshmen of whom about 40% of each sex were honors students.

Following the initial assessment period, a personal appointment for the rest of the experiment was arranged for each *S*. Over 90% of the *S*s kept their appointments.

Procedure: Initial Assessment Period

Two early evening sessions were scheduled 4 days apart. Each of these involved 100 *S*s with about an equal number of men and women present. Men were directed to one side of the room and women to the other. The seating instructions were given verbally and were also written on the board at the front of the room. The *E* for the two initial sessions was a male graduate student in psychology who has had considerable experience in the assessment of achievement-related motivation.[3]

Assessment of the achievement motive. Verbal leads rather than pictures were used to elicit imaginative stories for the measurement of the achievement motive. *This made it convenient to test males and females at the same time.* With verbal leads, the problem of finding pictures with similar cue value for males and females is to a large extent avoided. In this way the possible influence of such extraneous factors as the age, race, appearance, dress, etc., of the persons depicted on the kinds of stories elicited is also eliminated. We have already discussed some of the problems involved with the female pictures that generally have been used in previous research. Verbal leads have been used successfully in previous work by Winterbottom (1953), Lowell (1952), French (1955), and Atkinson and Litwin (1960).

The verbal leads selected for this study were the following:

1. David (Carol) is looking into his (her) microscope.
2. A young man (woman) is talking about something important with an older person.
3. At the end of the school day, Richard (Barbara) is going back to the chemistry lab.
4. John (Anne) is sitting in a chair with a smile on his (her) face.
5. Steven (Nancy) and the girl (boy) he (she) has been dating for over a year have both applied to the same highly selective university.
6. After first term finals John (Anne) finds himself (herself) at the top of his (her) med school class.

Only the name of the lead character(s) differed for the men and women.

In obtaining individual n Achievement scores, only the first four verbal leads were used. Previous work has shown that the first four of eight pictures provides the most valid measure of the achievement motive (Reitman & Atkinson, 1958).

The critical cues. The fifth and sixth verbal leads were explicitly included to explore differences between the sexes in response to cues about competitive achievement situations. The sixth verbal lead was intentionally cued to focus

[3] I wish to thank Joel Raynor for giving so generously of his time.

upon possible conflict involving a motive to avoid success. It was included for development of a method of content analysis that would hopefully assess individual differences in this motive.

The assessment of the achievement motive was carried out under standard neutral conditions as described by McClelland et al. (1953, p. 101) and Atkinson (1958a), except that verbal leads were substituted for pictures. The subjects were instructed to read printed instructions to themselves as the experimenter read them aloud. Each verbal lead was printed slightly above the middle of a single page in the booklet, and following each page with a verbal lead was one for writing the story to that particular cue identical to those used for picture cues (Atkinson, 1958a, p. 837).

The stories were coded for n Achievement according to the content analysis scoring system described in detail in McClelland et al. (1958). The interjudge scoring reliability of the author, who scored all protocols, with an independent expert scorer (PAO)[4] was a rank-order correlation of .91 for n Achievement scores assigned to 30 protocols and 89% agreement in scoring achievement imagery. The rescore reliability of the author for 30 other stories was .93. The range of n Achievement scores obtained from these verbal leads was from 0 to 25 with median score of 8.5 for men, and from 0 to 24 with median of 7.3 for the women.

These same stories were also scored for n Affiliation by an expert scorer (SK)[5] who had a rescore reliability of .92 for n Affiliation scores assigned to the protocols.

Assessment of test anxiety. Immediately following the thematic apperception measure of the achievement motive, *S*s took an Achievement Anxiety Test (AAT) (see Alpert & Haber, 1960). They read the standard instructions to themselves as *E* also read them aloud and then were given 15 minutes to complete the test.

Only the 10 items of the *Debilitating Anxiety Scale* were used to obtain a measure of the motive to avoid failure. The mean debilitating anxiety scores were 26.01 (SD = 5.7) for males and 26.6 (SD = 5.9) for females. These were quite comparable to earlier results obtained by Mahone (1958). The Debilitating Anxiety scores were uncorrelated with the n Achievement scores for men (r = .13, N = 88) and for women (r = −.07, N = 90). These results are consistent with the generally found independence of test anxiety assessed by the Mandler-Sarason Test Anxiety Questionnaire (1952) and n Achievement (see Atkinson & Feather, 1966, Ch. 20, p. 341).

Resultant achievement motivation. To provide a single indicator of the strength of the motive to achieve success (M_S) relative to the motive to avoid failure (M_{AF}), the standard score for Debilitating Anxiety was subtracted from the standard score for n Achievement. This combination of scores is logically

[4] I am very grateful to Patricia O'Connor. Her help throughout the study was invaluable.

[5] I wish to thank Stuart Karabenick for scoring the protocols for affiliative motivation.

consistent with the theory of achievement motivation and is referred to in the literature as a measure of *resultant achievement motivation.* The resultant score has been used successfully in a number of previous studies (see Atkinson & Feather, 1966).

Verbal performance. After the short break, the *S*s read instructions stating that they would be asked to perform a number of tasks designed to measure certain aspects of intellectual ability and that their performance on these tasks, together with other information available about their past performance, would be considered in the latter part of the research as a full and accurate measure of their abilities.

The first task was half of the Scrambled Words task designed by Lowell (1952), five pages with 24 words per page and a time allowance of 2 minutes per page indicated by *E*.

The second task, presented as a "general reasoning" test, involved four pages with six line puzzles per page, one or two of which were not solvable. Twelve minutes was allowed for this task.

The third task was a solvable mathematical puzzle, presented as a test of logical ability and mathematical aptitude. Eight minutes was allowed for this task.

Since the main purpose of these tasks was to give the *S*s reason to believe that the *E* did, in fact, have some first-hand information about their ability for use in the second part of the experiment, only the Scrambled Words Test, which has been used in previous research (Lowell, 1952) was even considered as a measure of performance level.

Second Test Period

For this part of the experiment, *S*s were randomly assigned to one of three conditions. Randomization was carried out within sex groups using a table of random numbers. The conditions were: the Noncompetitive achievement-orientation (NC); the Mixed Sex Competitive (MF and FM); and the Same Sex Competitive (MM and FF). In each condition, during the second testing session, a Level of Aspiration or Risk Preference task, three performance measures, and a personal questionnaire were administered.

Risk preference. In the noncompetitive condition, the *S*'s task was to choose one of seven tasks on which he or she would most like to work for the rest of the experiment. In the two interpersonal competitive conditions, *S*s were to indicate which one of seven possible competitors they would most like to compete against for the rest of the experiment. Each of the possible choices was placed along a scale of difficulty. The *S*s were led to believe that the exact level of difficulty of each choice was defined individually for each of them on the basis of their previous performance in the first session and from information available in their academic records.

In reality, the choices were distributed along the scale identically for all *S*s in all conditions as shown below:

(1)	(2)	(3)	(4)	(5)	(6)	(7)
			50-50			

Very easy FOR YOU	Moderately difficult FOR YOU	Very difficult FOR YOU

As is clearly shown, only the 50-50 point of moderate difficulty is numerically specified. Numbers representing the P_s of the other choice points were not included.

The *S*s were also asked to indicate on the same form which task or against which competitor they would *least* like to work.

Furthermore, to check on the possibility of biasing of P_s, the *S*s were also asked to indicate what they felt their chances were (out of 100) of doing well on the task or against the competitor they had selected.

Following Moulton (1965), every effort was made to convince each *S* that the choice points in fact reflected his own probability of success as accurately as possible. This was done to minimize the subjective biasing of probabilities.

The Noncompetitive Achievement-oriented condition (NC). Each *S* in the noncompetitive condition was run individually in a small experimental room under achievement-oriented instructions. This condition is similar to that used by Atkinson and Reitman (1956). The *S*s were given the booklet with their name on it and asked to read the instructions for the Level of Aspiration task to themselves. They were told that after they had worked on the task that they had selected, they would be told how well they had done.

The female *E* was in the room only long enough to be sure that the *S* understood the instructions and to emphasize the underlined portions, e.g., that the difficulty of each task on the scale was subjectively defined for *that* particular *S*. The *S* was then left alone to make his choices. Following this, the *E* explained:

> For the rest of tonight's session you will be asked to perform a number of tasks which, on the basis of your past performance, the experimenters feel are of *intermediate difficulty for you.* The tasks are in this folder, and the instructions for them are on tape. Don't open the folder until you are instructed to do so.

Every effort was made to convince *S*s that the research was being carried out by an experimental team. The *S*s were told that it was the "rest of tonight's session" rather than the rest of the experiment so that they would not feel that their choice of task difficulty was irrelevant and would not be considered at all. (See Chapter 13 for a more detailed presentation of these procedures.)

Procedures for competitive conditions. The general sequence of instructions followed those for the noncompetitive condition, but now the *S* was led to believe that a competitor rather than a specific task offered a certain level of risk with regard to success. The Risk Preference task for the competitive conditions was given to the *S*s in small groups of either six or eight in which there were always at least two *S*s of the opposite sex present, sitting around a very large rectangular table. The female *E* waited for all *S*s to come and then gave each one the appropriate form with his or her name written on it and with the sex of his or her potential competitor clearly indicated in the designated spot. The *S*s were asked to read the instructions to themselves. *E* then stressed the fact that the *S*s' potential competitors, e.g., those represented on the scale, may or may not have been one of the other *S*s in the room at that time. (See Chapter 13 for a detailed presentation of the procedures and instructions for the competitive conditions.) Then *S*s made their choices, the forms were collected, and plans for the next part of the experiment were explained:

> For the rest of tonight's session you have been paired with someone of approximately the *same* ability for performing the tasks involved; in other words, you have a 50-50 chance of doing better than one another. You will compete directly against each other on these tasks, and at the end of the session you will know which of you did best. We will have to go down to another group of rooms now where you can meet your competitor and work on the tasks.

The *S*s were then led to experimental rooms and paired in accordance with the condition to which they had been previously randomly assigned. They were asked to sit at the desk on which was the folder with their name but not to open the folders until they were told to do so.

Performance on verbal and arithmetic tasks. For this part of the experiment the instructions for all *S*s in all conditions were given by a male voice on a tape recorder, and a female *E* was present in the room only long enough to start the recorder.

In the noncompetitive condition, the *S*'s name and the level of difficulty of the tasks were written by hand in the upper right-hand corner. For the competitive conditions, the name of the competitor was also written in.

A similar procedure was followed for the instructions on each of the three tests in the booklet, and timing within and between tests was done by the tape-recorded male voice.

Generation anagram. The first performance measure given was the *generation anagram* as previously used by Clark and McClelland (in McClelland et al., 1953, Ch. 8), Veroff et al. (1953), and Lipinski (1965). Ten minutes was allowed for the test. The task was to make as many words as possible using the letters of a master word generation.

Performance scores on this task reflect the total number of words correctly made in 10 minutes using the letters of the word generation.[6] The scores ranged

[6] It has been previously reported (Clark & McClelland, 1950; Veroff et al., 1953) that only in the third 2-minute interval are there substantial individual differences in number of anagrams completed by *S*s differing in resultant achievement motivation. But Veroff et al. (1953) and Lipinski (1965) have both used the total output score successfully with female college students. Rather than discard the *S*s who misused the checkmarks identifying the minutes throughout the task, it was decided to use total output score in this study, even though the third 2-minute period may have provided a more sensitive measure.

from 27 to 89 with a mean of 48.06 (σ = 12.07) for males, and from 23 to 77 with a mean of 50.68 (σ = 10.74) for females.

Immediately following the generation anagram task was an arithmetic problems task (Atkinson & Reitman, 1956; Reitman, 1957; Smith, 1961) for 5 minutes.

The number of arithmetic problems attempted ranged from 5 to 51 with a mean of 29.41 (σ = 9.9) for males, and from 9 to 40 with a mean of 25.86 (σ = 7.2) for females. The number of arithmetic problems correctly done ranged from 2 to 50 with a mean of 26.2 (σ = 10.1) for males, and from 8 to 39 with a mean of 22.6 (σ = 7.8) for females. Immediately following the arithmetic test, *S*s were directed to a Digit Symbol Substitution task, *but since it is likely that scores on this task would be influenced by feelings of success and failure on the just-previous arithmetic task on which the Ss had been asked to predict how well they would do prior to actual performance, the measure was not scored for purposes of this experiment.*

Questionnaire. A brief questionnaire on *S*'s personal background, educational and vocational goals, and reactions to the experiment was administered. Only two of the questions in the questionnaire were considered in this part of the study. The first was the one asking each *S* how well he or she knew the competitor. Only one *S* had seen his or her competitor before, and that one only in a classroom setting.

The second question with which we shall be concerned asked: "How important was it for you to do well on the tests in this part of the experiment?" The *S* replied by putting an *X* along a line running from "not at all" to "very important," with only the "moderately important" point specified. It was assumed that these self-descriptions might also reflect the strength of the tendency to perform the tasks in each of the conditions.

Development of a Measure for the Motive to Avoid Success

The sixth verbal lead had been included at the end of the standard TAT n Achievement protocol to explore sex differences in thematic apperceptive responses to a cue reflecting success in a field traditionally populated by men. The analysis of these responses serves as a first step toward obtaining a measure of individual differences in strength of motive to avoid success. For the 90 females in the study, the verbal lead employed was: *"After the first term finals Anne finds herself at the top of her medical school class."* For the 88 males in the sample, the lead was: *"After first term finals, John finds himself at the top of his medical school class."*

Scoring criteria. In developing the scoring criteria for fear of success imagery, I was guided by Scott's (1956) results. He showed what happens in a thematic apperception test when a person is confronted with a cue or situation that represents a very real threat rather than a goal, or simultaneously represents both a goal and a threat.

A very simple present-absent scoring system was adopted for fear of success imagery. The stories were scored for fear of success if there was negative imagery expressed which reflected concern about the success. For instance:

1. Negative consequences because of the success
2. Anticipation of negative consequences because of the success
3. Negative affect because of the success
4. Instrumental activity away from present or future success, including leaving the field for more traditional female work such as nursing, school teaching, or social work
5. Any direct expression of conflict about success

Also scored was evidence of:

6. Denial of the situation described by the cue
7. Bizarre, inappropriate, unrealistic, or nonadaptive responses to the situation described by the cue

The author had 96% rescore reliability on imagery for 40 protocols and 91% reliability with an independent scorer[7] for 90 protocols.

The *S*s' responses to the success cue can be generally classified into three main groups, i.e.:

1. The first and most frequently occurring category was one in which negative affect and consequences are rooted mainly in affiliative concerns such as fear of being socially rejected, fear of losing one's friendships, the loss of one's datable or marriageable quality, actual isolation or loneliness as a result of the success, and the desire to keep the success a secret and pretend that intelligence is not a part of her.

2. The second category is comprised of the stories in which negative affect and consequences are free of any affiliative concern and independent of whether anyone finds out about it or not, such as doubting one's femininity, feeling guilty or in despair about the success, and wondering about one's normality.

3. The third group of stories involved denial of various types, such as denying the reality or possibility of the cue, stating "it is impossible," and denying effort or responsibility for attaining success. This was the second largest category and a particularly interesting one.

Examples of stories involving denial include the following:

> Anne is a CODE name for a non-existent person created by a group of med students. They take turns taking exams and writing papers for Anne . . . .

> Anne is really happy she's on top, though Tom is higher than she–though that's as it should be . . . . Anne doesn't mind Tom winning.

> Anne is talking to her counselor. Counselor says she will make a fine NURSE. She will continue her med school courses. She will study very hard and find she can and will become a good nurse.

[7] I wish to thank Sandra Tangri for scoring these stories and providing a reliability check.

> It was luck that Anne came out on top of her med class because she didn't want to go to med school anyway. [denial of effort]

An example from part of a bizarre story:

> She starts proclaiming her surprise and joy. Her fellow classmates are so disgusted with her behavior that they jump on her in a body and beat her. She is maimed for life.

The intensity, hostility, and symbolic quality of the language used by the *S*s in writing their stories is very clear. For example:

> Anne is an acne faced bookworm. She runs to the bulletin board and finds she's at the top. "As usual" she smarts off. A chorus of groans is the rest of the class's reply. Anne was always praised for her initiative and study habits–mainly because these were the only things one could praise her for. She studies 12 hours a day, and lives at home to save money. She rents her books. "Well it certainly paid off. All the Friday and Saturday nights with my books, who needs dates, fun–I'll be the best woman doctor alive." And yet, a twinge of sadness comes thru–she wonders what she really has. But, as is her habit, she promptly erases that thought, and goes off reciting aloud the 231 bones in her wrist.

(This story includes two very common themes: the physical unattractiveness of the student and her lonely "Friday and Saturday" nights.)

> Anne, the girl who swallowed the canary in her younger days, is pretty darn proud of herself. But everyone hates and envies her. People begin to connive so that she will fall down on her grades next semester. All the men she knows begin to put the pressure on in a very negative sort of way. She is continually having to justify her existence. Everyone, even girls and her own parents, say she is a grind. Anne thinks she knows how to comfort herself beautifully, but finds she doesn't when she's sticking out like a sore thumb. She finds that notoriety is not a graceful position. I don't know! Her problem is apparently insoluble, because she's really a good student. Will she humble herself? Wait and see.

RESULTS

Sex Differences in Fear of Success Imagery

The first striking characteristic of the results was the sheer magnitude of the differences between the male and female *S*s in the kind of responses made to the cues scored for fear of success. In accordance with the first hypothesis, the women showed significantly more evidence of fear of success imagery than did the men. Only 8 out of 88 or less than 10% of the men,[8] compared to 56 of the 90 or better than 62% of the women in the sample, expressed fear of success imagery ($\chi^2 = 52.26$, $df = 1$, $p < .0005$).

[8] Very literal use of the scoring criteria was made in getting a motive to avoid success score for the males. Without using the bizarre, inappropriate category or the cheating category as evidence of denial, only four men would have gotten a high motive to avoid success score.

Perhaps the best way to understand the sex differences found is by comparison of two of the typical male stories with two of the typical female stories.

Male stories:

John is a conscientious young man who worked hard. He is pleased with himself. John has always wanted to go into medicine and is very dedicated. His hard work has paid off. He is thinking that he must not let up now, but must work even harder than he did before. His good marks have encouraged him. (He may even consider going into research now.) While others with good first term marks sluff off, John continues working hard and eventually graduates at the top of his class. (Specializing in neurology.)

John is very pleased with himself and he realizes that all his efforts have been rewarded, he has finally made the top of his class. John has worked very hard, and his long hours of study have paid off. He spent hour after hour in preparation for finals. He is thinking about his girl Cheri whom he will marry at the end of med school. He realizes he can give her all the things she desires after he becomes established. He will go on in med school making good grades and be successful in the long-run.

Female stories:

Anne has a boyfriend Carl in the same class and they are quite serious. Anne met Carl at college and they started dating around their soph. years in undergraduate school. Anne is rather upset and so is Carl. She wants him to be higher scholastically than she is. Anne will deliberately lower her academic standing the next term, while she does all she subtly can to help Carl. His grades come up and Anne soon drops out of med-school. They marry and he goes on in school while she raises their family.

An example of a female story not scored for motive to avoid success:

Congrats to her! Anne is quite a lady–not only is she tops academically–but she is liked and admired by her fellow students. Quite a trick in a man-dominated field. She is brilliant–but she is also a lady. A lot of hard work. She is pleased–yet humble and her fellow students (with the exception of a couple of sour pusses) are equally pleased. That's the kind of girl she is–you are always pleased when she is–never envious. She will continue to be at or near the top. Will be as fine practicing her field as she is studying it. And–always a lady.

It was expected that Honors women, assuming this group has had a history of previous success in competitive achievement activity and perhaps also a higher level of ability, should have greater frequency of fear of success imagery than the non-Honors women. The data in Table 4 show the number of women classified according to Honors status who show evidence of fear of success imagery.

The trend of the data in Table 4 tends to support the hypothesis, though falling shy of the conventionally accepted level of significance. The trend suggests that fear of success imagery is more salient among women who are highly able, highly motivated to achieve, and competitively successful than for those less able, less motivated to achieve, and less successful (e.g., Honors versus non-Honors students).

It was also expected that women high in n Achievement would show evidence of stronger motive to avoid success than would women low in achievement

TABLE 4

Number of Women Classified According to Honors Status Who Show Evidence of Fear of Success Imagery

Fear of success imagery	Honors status*	
	Honors	Non-Honors
Low	10	24
High	26	30
Total	36	54

Note.–Observed frequencies were adjusted for expected frequencies of subjects high in M_{-S} and correction for continuity was made in getting χ^2.

*$\chi^2 = 2.57; p < .10$.

motivation because the former are the only ones aspiring to success. However, in the light of my hypothesis that motive to avoid success may influence thematic apperceptive performance, a meaningful direct test of this hypothesis is not really possible. A number of analyses were carried out from which no definitive conclusions could be drawn. No significant relationship exists between fear of success imagery and strength of achievement motivation as it is currently assessed. Females high in fear of success imagery may inhibit expression of achievement motivation on the TAT. This raises questions with regard to the predictive validity of the TAT n Achievement scores for women, at least as the measure is presently administered and scored.

Fear of Success Imagery and Performance of Women in Competitive and Noncompetitive Achievement Situations

The primary hypothesis states that motivation to avoid success will be more strongly aroused in competitive than in noncompetitive situations. If fear of success imagery is an index of the motive to avoid success, this measure should be related to performance as follows: females with a strong motive to avoid success perform at a higher level in the noncompetitive condition (when they are working alone against a standard) than in a competitive condition (when they are also competing against another person), especially if the competitor is a male.

In light of the hypothesized relationship between ability and motive to avoid success, it is particularly important to exercise control over initial ability differences. The best procedure would be to use each *S* as her own control; i.e., each *S* would perform in both a competitive and a noncompetitive condition. Unfortunately, the design of the experiment does not allow this comparison to be made for all *Ss*. Only the 30 *Ss* in the noncompetitive condition performed in both a competitive and noncompetitive setting.

The total female sample was used as a basis for determining standard scores for each of these 30 *Ss*[9] for their performance on the generation anagram and a scrambled words test. The latter test had been administered earlier in a large mixed sex competitive condition, and is considered most like the opposite sex competitive condition. The correlation between the scrambled words test and the generation anagram task is high and significant for both sexes (for females, $r = .58$). When organized according to the experimental conditions to which the *Ss* were later assigned, correlations correspond to a priori notions about the similarity of the conditions. In other words, the correlation is highest for the subjects in the mixed sex competitive condition ($r = .69$). This was also true of the male *Ss*.

Differences between standard scores on the two performance measures were obtained, and *Ss* were divided simply into those who did better working alone than in a competitive group ($N = 14$), and those for whom the opposite was true ($N = 16$). Table 5 shows that 77% of the female *Ss* high in fear of success imagery performed better in the noncompetitive condition, while 93% of those low in fear of success imagery performed better in the competitive condition ($\chi^2 = 11.37$, $p < .005$). Since two-thirds of the males performed at a higher level in the competitive than in the noncompetitive situation, the results for women low in fear of success resemble those for men while the results for women high in fear of success do not.

In order to determine whether individual differences in motive to avoid success were the ones primarily responsible for this result, it was decided to see how the other motive measures used in the study related to this same performance criterion. Table 6 summarizes these results. None of the other conventional motive measures was related to the performance criterion.

[9] The male distribution was used for assigning Z scores to the female *Ss* in order to avoid the problem that the results would be strongly influenced by one or two *Ss* in the sample.

TABLE 5

Relative Performance of Women in Competitive and Noncompetitive Situations as a Function of Individual Differences in Fear of Success Imagery

Fear of success imagery	Do better working alone	Do better working in competitive situations
High	13	4
Low	1	12

Note.—$\chi^2 = 11.37$; $p < .005$.

TABLE 6

Relative Performance of Women in Interpersonal Competitive and Noncompetitive Situations as a Function of Individual Differences on Various Diagnostic Tests

	Do better working alone	Do better working in competitive situation	χ^{2} [a]	p
n Achievement score				
High	5	9	.574	n.s.
Low	9	7		
Test Anxiety score				
High	8	6	.502	n.s.
Low	6	10		
Resultant Achievement Motivation				
High	4	9	1.338	n.s.
Low	10	7		
n Affiliation score				
High	7	8	.133	n.s.
Low	7	8		
Fear of success imagery				
High	13	4	11.374	$< .005$
Low	1	12		
Risk preference				
Intermediate	6	14	4.838	$< .05$
Extreme	8	2		
Honors	7	5	.452	n.s.
Non-Honors	7	11		

[a] Correction for continuity is included in the chi-square result.

However, female *S*s who performed at a higher level in the competitive than in the noncompetitive situation showed a significantly stronger preference when in the noncompetitive situation for tasks of intermediate difficulty than did those who performed at a higher level in the noncompetitive situation. The latter preferred the extremes, and when a midpoint break was used, they preferred easy rather than difficult tasks. (This may mean that the behavioral preference for risk, presumed to express the relative strength of M_S and M_{AF} in a person, may be a better way of getting at these motives in women, provided risk preference is measured under noncompetitive conditions, than via the combination of TAT n Achievement and Test Anxiety, both of which are confounded for women according to the present line of argument. This possibility certainly deserves further consideration in the future. The assumption here implied is that strength of achievement motivation as conventionally measured is validly represented by a higher level of performance in competitive than noncompetitive situations.)

The *S*s were further divided into three rather than two performance groups as follows:

1. Those who perform at a higher level in noncompetitive settings.
2. Those who perform at a higher level in competitive settings.
3. Those who perform at about the same level in both settings.

In groups 1 and 2, all standard score differences were greater than .6, and most were greater than 1.0. In the third group, no Z score difference was greater than .32.

In this refined analysis, all nine females who performed at a higher level in the noncompetitive condition had high fear of success imagery, and seven of the nine who did better in the competitive condition had low fear of success imagery. Six of the 12, or 50% of those who performed at about the same level in both conditions, scored high in fear of success imagery.

The overall pattern in this analysis is that the female *S*s who performed at a higher level in the noncompetitive than in the competitive situation (Group 1) wrote stories characterized by high fear of success imagery and low n Achievement imagery, and showed a preference for easy tasks in the noncompetitive condition. Those, on the other hand, who performed at a higher level in the competitive situation (Group 2) wrote stories characterized by low fear of success imagery, and showed a preference for intermediate tasks in the noncompetitive condition. Compared to the previous group where those with high fear of success imagery wrote low n Achievement stories, in this group those with high fear of success imagery wrote high n Achievement stories. The importance of these results lies in the consistent pattern of behavior emerging for female *S*s which can be related to differences in strength of motive to avoid success–including how they responded on a self-report questionnaire.

Subject's Self-Report on the "Importance" of Doing Well in Each Condition as a Function of the Motive to Avoid Success

Immediately following performance in each of the experimental conditions, *S*s were asked to indicate on a scale "How important was it for you to do well on the tests in this part of the experiment?" The mean level of "importance" reported by female *S*s classified according to experimental condition and fear of success imagery is shown in Table 7.

In both competitive conditions, the mean level of "importance" reported by *S*s with high fear of success imagery is significantly lower than that of *S*s with low fear of success imagery ($p < .05$). In the noncompetitive condition, the difference is in the same direction but falls short of the conventionally accepted level of significance ($p < .10$).

For *S*s with high fear of success imagery, differences in mean level of importance between the noncompetitive condition and each of the two competitive conditions are significant. (The *S*s in the noncompetitive condition

TABLE 7

Mean Level of "Importance" Reported by Women Classified According to Experimental Condition and Fear of Success Imagery in Response to the Question: "How important was it for you to do well on the tests in this part of the experiment?"

Fear of success imagery	Conditions								
	Noncompetitive (NC)			Competitive					
				Mixed Sex (FM)			Same Sex (FF)		
	N	*M*	σ	*N*	*M*	σ	*N*	*M*	σ
High	(17)	55.6	9.2	(19)	45.7	19.4	(20)	44.7	24.4
Low	(13)	66.5	24.0	(11)	61.1	27.1	(10)	56.5	12.3
	$t = 1.56$			$t = 1.66$			$t = 1.75$		
	$p < .10$			$p < .05$			$p < .05$		
Subjects with:									
High fear of success imagery	NC vs. FM			$t = 1.99$			$p < .05$		
	NC vs. FF			$t = 1.85$			$p < .05$		
							1 tail		
Low fear of success imagery				no significant differences					

report a significantly higher level of importance for doing well.) No significant differences are found between the conditions for *S*s with low fear of success imagery.

These results are consistent with the performance data in suggesting that women, especially those high in the motive to avoid success, will explore their intellectual potential to full measure only when they are in a noncompetitive setting and least of all when competing against men.

DISCUSSION

A scoring system was developed for the motive to avoid success from responses to the sixth verbal cue which had been included for exploratory purposes ("At the end of the first term final, John (Anne) finds himself (herself) at the top of his (her) medical school class"). A simple present-absent scoring system was adopted, and subjects were divided into two groups, those showing some evidence of having fear of success and those who gave no such indications.

With this admittedly simple scoring system the following results were obtained:

In accordance with the hypothesis, women showed significantly more evidence of fear of success imagery than did the men ($p < .0005$).

There was a trend for Honors women (e.g., those who are probably highly able and motivated to achieve and who have a previous history of success) to show more evidence of fear of success imagery than non-Honors women ($p < .10$).

With *S*s acting as their own ability control, those showing evidence of fear of success performed better when working in a noncompetitive setting for intrinsic reasons than when working in a mixed sex competitive setting against others ($p < .005$).

*S*s with high fear of success imagery reported on a questionnaire that it was significantly less important to do well in the competitive situations than in the noncompetitive situation ($p < .05$). No differences were found for *S*s low in fear of success imagery. Furthermore, those *S*s with high fear of success imagery reported a lower level of importance for doing well in each of the conditions than did those with low fear of success imagery. The differences between the two were significant only in the competitive conditions ($p < .05$), and in the noncompetitive condition ($p < .10$). Thus, there is consistency in the pattern of the *S*s' responses to the question of how important it is to do well and how they actually performed.

Other results for which there were trends in the data, i.e., for which the evidence is suggestive rather than conclusive, are briefly summarized here:

With ability controlled, female *S*s with low fear of success imagery (like the male subjects) performed at a higher level in competitive conditions in the presence of extrinsic factors than in noncompetitive situations. *S*s high in fear of success imagery may be inhibiting expression of achievement imagery on the

TAT n Achievement measure, making it difficult to identify those women truly high in achievement motivation. The possibility of using risk preference for this purpose was raised.

The results presented suggest that optimal performance for most women with high motive to avoid success can be obtained only if they work in achievement situations that are noncompetitive. In the absence of interpersonal competition and its aggressive overtones, the tendency to avoid success (T_{-s}) will be minimally aroused if at all. These women would, furthermore, be least likely to explore their intellectual potential when competing with men.

Previous Results in Light of Motive to Avoid Success

We have found that women show significantly more evidence of fear of success imagery than do men. Furthermore, the performance of women with high fear of success imagery is adversely affected in competitive achievement situations, whereas that of women with low fear of success imagery is not. So few men showed evidence of fear of success imagery ($N = 8$) that a meaningful test of its relationship to behavior in men could not be made. It is, therefore, not surprising that the results of women in the past have not been consistent with the results of men.

Nor is it surprising in light of the data relating motive to avoid success to initial ability and achievement motivation, and showing its effects on performance in different achievement-oriented conditions, that studies carried out on women at various schools under widely diverse achievement situations have not yielded a consistent pattern of information. The various schools differ not only in the level of ability and achievement motivation of their students, but also in terms of the presence or absence of male competitors, the size of the competitive groups, the subjective probability of success of the students, etc.[10] Thus, perhaps the effects of motive to avoid success on behavior should be seriously considered when attempting to understand and account for the behavior of women in achievement situations. In the past, the impact of a fear of success has been uncontrolled—and the results have been very difficult to interpret or understand.

The relationship between competitors in achievement situations. A variable of considerable importance not studied in the present work is the relationship between the competitors. Motivation to avoid success should be more strongly aroused, and therefore produce a greater decrement in performance if the relationship between the competitors is a close one so that social rejection (because of success) and its negative implications about one's femininity are significant threats. Of particular interest would be a comparison of the behavior of mixed sex competitive pairs who are seriously dating, engaged, or married, against that of those who neither know each other nor would particularly care

[10] Information on the various institutions at which data has been gathered came from A.W. Astin, *Who Goes Where to College?* (1965).

to. A comparison of the behavior of same sex competitive pairs who are close friends with pairs who don't know each other very well would provide a valuable control in such a study.

The impact of attendance at a coed or same sex school. On a broader and more general basis, a study of the influence of education at coed versus same sex institutions (with ability controlled) would also provide much useful information. I would be particularly interested in whether going to a same sex school, where there are no competitors of the opposite sex, reduces the impact of fear of success that is reflected in such things as choice of major and seriousness in pursuit of a career or higher education. Some control must, of course, be exerted with regard to initial choice between the two types of school.

If going to the same sex school is found to reduce the impact of motivation to avoid success on performance, then an important question remains as to whether this influence will continue once women leave the supportive environs of the school and enter a mixed sex competitive world; e.g., has this been only a moratorium on the arousal of fear of success, or has a change in "attitude or motivation" with long-term implications been effected?

PART II
FUTURE ORIENTATION: THE COGNITIVE ELABORATION OF THEORY OF ACHIEVEMENT MOTIVATION

The elaboration of the theory of achievement motivation to take into account explicitly the concept of *contingent future orientation*, as distinct from *expectancy*, began as an attempt to achieve more precision in defining the situational determinants of the values of success and failure to an individual. More generally, the aim was to define what is meant by "ego-involvement" or "importance" in achievement-oriented situations. The earliest studies conducted to validate the projective measure of the achievement motive (see McClelland et al., 1949) suggested that achievement imagery might profitably be defined in terms of long-term career striving. However, the theoretical implication of this finding was not appreciated for almost 20 years. During the intervening period, the empirical foundation for an Expectancy × Value theory of achievement motivation was provided (see Chapter 2). Then the initial statement of the theory, restricted as it was to the *immediate* consequences of an activity, was logically extended to take account of the effects of distant future goals on the motivation for *immediate* activity (Raynor, 1967, 1968a, 1969). The elaborated theory of achievement motivation now assumes that the strength of tendency, or inclination to act in a certain way, is a multiplicative function of the strength of expectancy that the act will result in a consequence, and the value of that consequence to the individual, *summed over all expected consequences of the act.* The circumstance under which this summation is expected to occur is also derived from this more general statement of an Expectancy × Value theory. It is now called a *contingent path*: when a series of steps are functionally related so that immediate success guarantees the opportunity to strive for future success(es) while immediate failure means loss of the opportunity to continue and therefore failure to achieve the future goal(s).

The initial paper in this section (Chapter 7) traces the development and gives the present status of theory and research on contingent future orientation. At issue is the earlier assumption that subjective probability of success in an immediate activity is the only determinant of the incentive values of success and failure. The more general statement of theory assumes, among other things, that the meaning (or value) of success and failure is also related to the long-term implications of immediate success and failure in the activity confronting an individual *when it is the immediate next step in a contingent path.* The arguments and evidence suggesting that future orientation and expectancy require distinct conceptual treatment, and research that has been guided by the elaborated theory, are presented. The theoretical analysis also recaptures and defines within the theory of achievement motivation such concepts as *psychological distance* and *instrumental value* of an activity, and it introduces a set of new distinctions between different kinds of future orientation (contingent, noncontingent, and one-step paths; open and closed, as well as increasing, decreasing, and constant probability contingent paths).

The second paper in this section (Chapter 8) presents one of the first studies to be explicitly guided by the general hypothesis that the characteristic effects of differences in achievement-related motives would be accentuated when an immediate activity (a final examination in a college course) was seen by the student as instrumentally related to achievement of his own future goals. It is unique in another respect: it asked students immediately prior to a final examination to describe, as accurately as they could, their own subjective motivational state at the time. This study was a direct outgrowth of research conducted by Isaacson and Raynor (1966), which was later replicated and extended (Chapter 9) to distinguish the effect of future orientation on performance in a specific college course and on overall academic performance for a semester.

Studies relating individual differences in achievement-related motives and academic performance point to the importance of research conducted in actual life situations for the development of ideas that can later be refined by experimental analysis in more controlled, laboratory situations. The last chapter in this section (Chapter 10) presents the first published study in which experimental induction of future orientation was carried out. It was based upon the initial (and unsuccessful) experimental work to validate the distinction between contingent and noncontingent future orientation presented among the studies in Raynor's (1968a) doctoral dissertation. The positive results obtained in this follow-up study helped to establish the experimental paradigm for a series of subsequent (and as yet unpublished) studies whose results are summarized in the first chapter of this section.

The concept of future orientation has provided an integrating link between the experimental analysis of achievement motivation in particular tasks and the more general societal implications of motivation for achievement (see Part V, Chapter 19). The experimental paradigm involving contingent future orientation has provided a means for arousal of substantially stronger achievement-related motivation in laboratory situations than previously. This leads on to the complication of specifying the nature of the relationship between strength of motivation and efficiency of performance that was uncovered in earlier research involving use of additional immediate extrinsic incentives to increase the arousal of motivation for a task. Sorrentino's (1971) doctoral dissertation, included with other studies of this problem in Part III, provides an important link between future orientation and the behavioral effects of overmotivation. His results suggest some caution in generalizing from findings reported in this section concerning the relationship between achievement-related motives and the level of performance. This critical problem, the relationship between strength of motivation and efficiency of performance in different kinds of tasks, is held for Part III.

7
FUTURE ORIENTATION IN THE STUDY OF ACHIEVEMENT MOTIVATION[1]

Joel O. Raynor

OVERVIEW

The basic idea that future orientation was separable from the concept of perceived task difficulty (i.e., subjective probability of success) and therefore represented a neglected variable in theory and research on achievement motivation (see Raynor, 1969) came initially from an analysis of previous research concerning the effects of different arousal conditions on both the content of imaginative stories (see McClelland et al., 1953) and the relationship between measures of achievement-related motives and behavior (see Atkinson & Reitman, 1956; Raynor & Smith, 1966). More direct evidence from two empirical investigations (Isaacson & Raynor, 1966; Raynor, Atkinson, & Brown, this volume, Chapter 8) bolstered the argument and suggested how individual differences in future orientation interact with individual differences in achievement-related motives to determine total strength of achievement motivation sustaining immediate activity. The principles of general expectancy-value theory (see Edwards, 1954) in conjunction with Lewin's (1938) analysis of behavior as a series of steps in a path to a goal were then used as the basis for an elaboration of initial expectancy-value theory of achievement motivation (see Atkinson, 1957; Atkinson & Feather, 1966; also Chapter 2). Algebraic statement of the basic assumptions of this elaboration of theory and their subsequent manipulation lead to predictions concerning risk taking, level of performance, and persistence in immediate activity of a contingent path—the basic situation in

[1] This paper was written while the author was supported by Grant GS-2863 from the National Science Foundation entitled "Effects of Distant Future Goals on Achievement Motivation."

which the theory applies, defined as a series of steps in which immediate success guarantees the opportunity to strive for future success(es) while immediate failure guarantees future failure through loss of the opportunity to continue along the path. Evidence reviewed here that is relevant to a test of some of these hypotheses (see Raynor, 1970, and Chapter 9; Raynor & Rubin, 1971, and Chapter 10; Sorrentino, 1971, and Chapter 14; Entin & Raynor, 1973; Raynor & Entin, 1972; Raynor & Sorrentino, 1972; Raynor, Entin, & Raynor, 1972; Raynor, 1972; Sorrentino & Raynor, 1972) suggests that the more general implications of the theory concerning enterpreneurial activity and career striving (see Chapter 19), as well as others discussed here, are worth taking seriously.

EFFECTS OF DIFFERENT AROUSAL CONDITIONS

There have been a number of studies in which manipulations of various kinds were first used to create different degrees of achievement orientation (i.e., ego involvement), to be followed by some response measure intended to reflect these differences. Two kinds of studies which employ this general procedure can be identified. The first kind was used to develop the n Achievement index of the achievement motive (see McClelland et al., 1953) while the second was used to validate it as a measure of individual differences in personality (see Atkinson, 1953).

Achievement Imagery

In the first kind of arousal study (e.g., McClelland et al., 1949), a battery of tasks was administered, followed by a story-writing task described as a "test of creative imagination." In the "ego-involved" (i.e., achievement-oriented) condition, the battery was described as a series of intelligence tests, while in the relaxed condition it was described as a series of tests in the developmental stage for which normative data were being collected. In the neutral condition the story-writing task was administered so as not to arouse or reduce motivation. Appropriate experimenter behaviors accompanied each set of instructions (see Klinger, 1967, for a further exploration of this point). Differences in the content of stories written under achievement-oriented, in comparison to neutral and relaxed, conditions were used to define the scoring categories of the n Achievement index. The scoring manuals for n Achievement can therefore be viewed as empirical summaries of the results of this kind of arousal study. The crucial scoring decision involves identifying "achievement imagery," first defined (in Scoring System A) as dealing with *some long-term problem of getting ahead at the ego ideal level* (*career, schooling, inventing something, etc.*) (McClelland et al., 1949), but later revised (in Scoring Systems B and C) to include explicit concern over competition with a standard of excellence and unique accomplishment as well as long-term involvement as the three expressions of achievement orientation (see Atkinson, 1950, and McClelland et al., 1953, respectively).

Note that future orientation, in the form of long-term striving to achieve a goal, has played a central role in the definition of achievement imagery. Examination of the original instructions used to create the condition of achievement orientation suggests why. The tests that preceeded story writing were described as though they were used as screening devices for the selection of Washington administrators and officer candidates during the Second World War. The implication to the *S* was probably that good performance on them would reflect future leadership potential. Thus, at the very least, both differences in future orientation and concern about doing well in the immediate activity contributed to the heightened state of motivational arousal and the subsequent effects on achievement imagery that were obtained.

Relationships Between Motives and Behavior

The second kind of arousal study was first used to help validate the n Achievement score as a measure of the achievement motive (see Atkinson, 1953; Atkinson & Raphelson, 1956; Atkinson & Reitman, 1956) and has since been used in a similar manner with n Achievement and Test Anxiety as a joint measure of the strength of resultant achievement-related motives (see Atkinson & Litwin, 1960; also Chapter 2). The motive measures are (usually) administered under neutral conditions. Response measures of various kinds (recall of interrupted tasks, risk preference, performance level, persistence, etc.) are then obtained under different arousal conditions. The relationship between motive measures (assumed to reflect relatively stable and enduring individual differences in personality when used in this manner) and behavior under these conditions has served as the basis for the evolution of theory of achievement motivation (Atkinson & Feather, 1966, Ch. 20; also Chapter 2). While the results of this second kind of arousal study have not been consistent, they show in general that the relationships between strength of resultant achievement motivation or each motive measure taken separately which can be derived from theory (*a*) are strongest under achievement-oriented conditions, (*b*) are stronger under achievement-oriented than relaxed conditions (however, see Smith, 1963), (*c*) are weaker, nonexistent, or reversed in relaxed conditions, and (*d*) are reduced or disappear when extrinsic incentives to perform (money, social approval) are offered, either by themselves or in conjunction with achievement-orienting instructions.

INITIAL THEORY OF ACHIEVEMENT MOTIVATION AS A LIMITED CONCEPTION

Atkinson (1964) has argued that "when there is no expectancy that performance will lead to pride of accomplishment, that is, when $P_s = 0$ because instructions or other cues rule out the possibility of expecting evaluation of performance and feelings of success as in "relaxed" conditions, there is, according to the theory, no incentive to achieve. Hence there is no basis for predicting that performance of persons scoring High and Low in n Achievement will differ under 'relaxed' conditions [p. 243]." However, it appears that a so-called "relaxed" condition fulfills the definition of achievement orientation provided by McClelland (1961)–a situation in which the individual feels responsible for the outcome of his activity, he anticipates unambiguous knowledge of results, and there is some degree of uncertainty or risk. Since the inherent properties of most skill tasks define a continuum of difficulty which is readily perceived, it seems that the mere presentation of such a task, as in a relaxed condition, should be sufficient to arouse an individual's achievement motivation. Furthermore, Smith (1963) and Raynor and Smith (1966) found the predicted relationship between achievement-related motives and risk preference (success-oriented individuals chose tasks of intermediate difficulty to a greater extent than failure-threatened individuals) in a relaxed condition.

It thus appeared that initial attempts to formulate expectancy-value theory of achievement motivation were unable to account for the results of both kinds of arousal studies. The problem arises from the fact that subjective probability of (immediate) success is the only situational determinant of resultant achievement motivation (see Edwards, 1962; Atkinson & Feather, 1966, Ch. 20; see also Chapter 2). Thus the theory could not account for differences in the degree of future orientation of achievement imagery in stories written under different arousal conditions, nor could it derive differences in strength of relationships between achievement-related motives and behavior obtained under different arousal conditions for a task that requires effort or skill–unless changes in subjective probability of success were systematically related to these different conditions such that P_s was always closer to an intermediate value (.5 on a scale from 0 to 1) under achievement-oriented arousal. While this explanation had not been ruled out, there was no evidence to support it, and it did not appear to be a fruitful way to account for the results described above.

Following the suggestion provided by the analysis of the effects of different arousal conditions on achievement imagery (specifically, the increase in long-term involvement under achievement orientation), the question was asked as to whether predicted relationships tended to be stronger in this condition because of the (important) future implications usually attributed by the experimenter to behavior when inducing the heightened state of achievement arousal. This called attention to the possible effects of the implications of immediate task performance for the achievement of future goals on the relationship between achievement-related motives and immediate behavior.

Empirical Evidence Concerning the Role of Future Orientation

Additional evidence bearing on the role of future orientation was provided by Isaacson and Raynor (1966). These investigators examined the effects on academic performance of achievement motivation and the perceived instrumentality of good grades (i.e., immediate success) for future career success. Male college students scoring in the lowest 15% of the obtained distribution of Debilitating Anxiety (DA) scores (Alpert & Haber, 1960) were assumed to be relatively stronger in the motive to achieve success than in the motive to avoid failure, while those in the highest 15% on DA were assumed to have the opposite motive pattern (see Atkinson, 1964, p. 250). Students were also divided into three groups based on their ratings of the perceived instrumentality ("helpfulness" and "importance") of grades to future career success (termed PI). The groups low in DA received significantly higher grades than the groups high in DA within the High ($p < .01$) and intermediate ($p < .05$) PI groups, but not within Low PI. In addition, students low in DA tended to receive higher grades, while students with high DA tended to receive lower grades as PI increased.

The results of the Isaacson and Raynor (1966) study led to the investigation of the subjective reactions of male college students when faced with a final course examination in introductory psychology as a joint function of achievement-related motives and the relationship between their examination performance and their own future goals (PI) (see Raynor, Atkinson, & Brown, this volume, Chapter 8). The dominant trend of the preliminary results was reported as follows: "Strength of motivation expressed in the self-descriptive ratings, whether approach or avoidant in action implications, is also a function of whether or not a subject views his performance on the examination as related to his own future goals. If he does not, then even though he is confronted by an obvious test on which his performance will be evaluated, he described himself as less concerned about his performance. The kind of differences expected among individuals who differ in achievement motivation . . . are greater among those who view the examination as related to future goals [Atkinson, 1966, p. 28]."

The two studies just cited suggested that the effects of an individual's characteristic achievement motivation, determined by the relative strengths of motive to achieve success and motive to avoid failure, are accentuated when immediate skill activity is perceived to be the immediate next step in a path to the achievement of distant future goals. In fact, this kind of result was anticipated in earlier work and arguments (see Lewin, 1938; Peak, 1955; Thomas & Zander, 1959; Vroom, 1964). While Expectancy × Value theory of achievement motivation (Chapter 2) did not specifically exclude possible effects of an individual's extent of future orientation on motivation of immediate activity, it appeared to lack the conceptual tools to deal with it. Still, the available data failed to rule out the possibility that differences in (immediate) subjective probability of success which were correlated with ratings of perceived instrumentality could not account for the apparent accentuation of motivation in the studies cited above, especially since they left open the possibility that experience in the immediate activity had influenced ratings of perceived instrumentality, which were obtained at the end rather than the beginning of the semester in both studies. In fact, subsequent research replicated the dominant pattern of interaction obtained in these early studies while obtaining ratings of PI at the beginning rather than at the end of the semester (see Raynor, 1970, and Chapter 9). Also, later experiments in which the same values of subjective probability of success were induced for immediate activity in contingent paths (the "high-importance" condition) as well as noncontingent paths (the "low-importance" condition) also yielded a pattern of interaction (e.g., see Raynor & Rubin, 1971, and Chapter 10) that makes it unlikely that this and/or the earlier research could be accounted for in terms of differences in perceived task difficulty (see also Entin & Raynor, 1973). Thus the decision to give explicit theoretical consideration to future orientation as separable from the concept of expectancy or subjective probability as a determinant of total motivation sustaining immediate activity appears to have been justified.

AN ELABORATION OF THEORY OF ACHIEVEMENT MOTIVATION

The logic of a *general* expectancy-value theory of motivation provided a way of overcoming the limited conception that strength of achievement motivation of individuals who are equivalent in strength of achievement-related motives depends entirely upon expectations of success and failure in the activity they are immediately faced with. In such a theory, the strength of tendency to act in a certain way depends upon the strength of expectancy that an activity will result in a consequence, and the value of that consequence to the individual, *summated over all expected consequences of the activity* (see Edwards, 1954, 1962; Vroom, 1964). Theory of achievement motivation had moved toward this more general conception when it noted that incentives for good performance (money, power, the approval of others, etc.) whose attainment was dependent upon immediate success aroused *extrinsic* tendencies to act which summate with the resultant tendency to achieve to determine total strength of tendency sustaining immediate activity (see Chapter 2). An elaboration of theory of achievement motivation referred to here (see Raynor, 1969) extended this analysis so that motivation aroused by anticipation of some number of *future* (achievement-related and extrinsic) as well as immediate consequences of activity could be specified in terms of Expectancy X Value theory.

This elaboration built upon the analysis provided by Lewin (1938), which conceived of behavior as a series of steps in a path to a goal. However, Lewin considered and rejected as implausible the possibility that more immediately expected outcomes in a path could be valued as "ends" in themselves rather than merely as "means" of getting on to the final goal in the path. In Lewin's scheme, the value of the "subgoals" is totally derived from their instrumental relationship to the final goal of the path. On the other hand, the analysis provided in the elaboration eliminated the qualitative distinction between subgoals and goals by use of an algebraic statement which, given certain assumptions (see below), specifies the relative values of each anticipated success and failure and derives the relative strengths of component tendencies aroused by each in a series of immediate and more distant, future (anticipated) outcomes of immediate activity. Thus the distinction between outcomes which serve as means to an end and those which serve as ends in themselves becomes a quantitative rather than a qualitative issue, depending upon their relative magnitudes and their anticipated order of occurrence. This point is discussed further in a subsequent section dealing with the distinctions between means-end striving and intrinsic versus instrumental motivation.

Algebraic Statement of the Elaboration

The basic assumptions of this elaboration (Raynor, 1969) can be summarized in following manner. A particular activity is considered the immediate next step in a path. A path consists of a series of steps. Each step represents an activity (task) and its expected outcome(s) or consequence(s). A step is achievement-related if skill activity can result in success or failure. Any achievement-related step may have as expected outcomes one or more extrinsic reward (positive incentives) or threat (negative incentives). A consequence is called a "goal" when it has positive incentive value. Steps in the path are identified by their anticipated order of occurrence and by the kind of consequence that is expected. The individual's knowledge of what activities will lead on to what outcomes within a class of incentives determines the length of path.

The tendency to achieve success in immediate activity (T_s) is determined by the summation of component tendencies to achieve (T_{sn}), each a multiplicative function of motive (M), subjective probability (P), and incentive value (I):

$$T_{sn} = M_S \times P_{1sn} \times I_{sn} \tag{1}$$

and

$$T_s = T_{s_1} + T_{s_2} + \ldots + T_{s_n} + \ldots + T_{s_N} \tag{2}$$

where the subscripts 1, 2, . . . n . . . N represent the anticipated order of steps (activities and outcomes) in a path, from the first (1) to the last (N), and n represents a general term for any particular position in this anticipated sequence. In a similar manner the tendency to avoid failure (i.e., not to engage in achievement-related activity) is assumed to be additively determined by component inhibitory tendencies:

$$T_{-fn} = M_{AF} \times P_{1fn} \times I_{fn} \tag{3}$$

and

$$T_{-f} = T_{-f_1} + T_{-f_2} + \ldots + T_{-fn} + \ldots + T_{-fN} \tag{4}$$

The resultant achievement-oriented tendency (also referred to as resultant achievement motivation) is obtained by the summation of the tendencies to achieve success and to avoid failure, and is written symbolically as $T_s + T_{-f}$. The most useful algebraic statement of the determinants of resultant achievement motivation is the following:

$$T_s + T_{-f} = (M_S - M_{AF}) \sum_{n=1}^{N} (P_{1sn} \times I_{sn}) \tag{5}$$

which indicates that it is determined by the resultant strength of an individual's characteristic achievement motivation (M_S - M_{AF}) and a summed situational component which, given certain assumptions relating subjective probabilities and incentive values of success and failure in a contingent path (see below), can be determined by knowledge of an individual's perception of the difficulty of each activity (step) in the path.

The Distinction Between Contingent and Noncontingent Paths

While the conditions under which future orientation should influence strength of resultant achievement motivation (namely, contingent paths, to be discussed below) have thus far been derived *from the logic of the theory,* as implied in the above set of equations, there may be other circumstances to which the theory applies that are not deducible in an equivalent fashion. The argument can be stated in words as follows. If an individual believes that immediate activity does not influence the opportunity to strive for some future success, strength of expectancy or associative link (see Atkinson, 1964, Ch. 10) between the immediate activity and the future consequence is zero (i.e., P_{1s_2} = 0, etc.). Also, if immediate failure is not related to future failure, then P_{1f_2} = 0, etc. In this instance, future orientation should not affect strength of motivation sustaining immediate activity, since the multiplicatively determined value of component tendencies will be zero. This situation is called a *noncontingent path,* defined as a series of steps in which prior success or failure has no bearing on the opportunity to engage in subsequent activity in that path—hence these have no influence on future success or failure, except insofar as immediate success or failure may alter the perceived difficulty of that subsequent activity.

On the other hand, if an individual believes that immediate success is necessary in order to guarantee the opportunity to strive for some number of future successes while immediate failure means future failure by guaranteeing loss of the opportunity to continue in that path, as in what is called a *contingent path,* the strength of expectancy or associative link between the immediate activity and the future success (i.e., P_{1s_2}, etc.) is represented by the product of the subjective probability of immediate success (P_{1s_1}) and the subjective probability of future success, given the opportunity to strive for it (P_{2s_2}). In other words, the combined difficulty of immediate success and future success, given the opportunity to strive for future success, determines the probability that immediate activity will lead on to future success. More generally, the strength of expectancy that immediate activity will result in some future success (P_{1sn}) is assumed a multiplicative function of the subjective probabilities of success in each step of the path:

$$P_{1sn} = P_{1s1} \times P_{2s2} \times P_{3s3} \times \ldots \times P_{nsn} \tag{6}$$

This can be written in shorthand in terms of sequential multiplication:

$$P_{1sn} = \prod_{n=1}^{N} (P_{nsn}) \tag{7}$$

Consequently, component tendencies to achieve success (and to avoid failure) will be aroused in a contingent path to influence strength of motivation sustaining immediate activity, their particular strength being determined by P_{1sn} and I_{sn} for each anticipated success (s_n) and failure (f_n), respectively. The special assumption relating P and I will be introduced and discussed shortly.

Expectancy and Psychological Distance

At this point it is worth noting that the (total) subjective probability that immediate activity in a contingent path will eventually result in some future success seems appropriately interpreted by use of the concept of *psychological distance,* a variable incorporated into earlier statements of expectancy-value theory within the Lewinian framework (see Frank, 1935; Lewin, 1938, 1943) but neglected in its later formulations (see Cartwright & Festinger, 1943; Festinger, 1942; Atkinson, 1957). The meaning of this equivalence is that when subjective probability of immediate activity leading to some future success is low, it can be said that the psychological distance between the individual who is faced with the immediate task and the anticipated future success is large. In other words, the degree of perceived difficulty and psychological distance are directly proportionate (or, subjective probability of success and psychological distance are inversely proportionate). This seems quite similar to Heckhausen's (1967) assumption that "psychic distance" is a determinant of what he terms the "expectation gradient."

Failure to recognize the equivalence of expectancy and psychological distance in previous statements of expectancy-value theory may have been due to an emphasis on experimental situations in which immediate activity has no long-term implications (i.e., meaning) to the subject. Studies of level of aspiration (see Lewin, Dembo, Festinger, & Sears, 1944) and decision making (see Cartwright & Festinger, 1943) which were conducted within this theoretical framework were restricted to concern over the immediately expected consequences of activity. Little regard was given to the potential implications to the *S* of success and failure in the experimental activity for the achievement of his own future goals, or even to the effect of success or failure on the opportunity to strive for subsequent goals in later phases of the experiment. In other words, the tasks that were used might be described by the *S*s as "trivial" *in terms of their life situation.* As already pointed out, focus on the future implications of immediate academic performance for the student's future career success (see

Isaacson & Raynor, 1966; Raynor, 1970, and Chapter 9) paved the way for dealing explicitly in the theory with "important" aspects of the immediate task situation in terms of a general expectancy-value framework.

Subjective Probability and Incentive Value

Consistent with earlier analyses (see Festinger, 1942; Atkinson, 1957; also Chapter 2), in this elaboration of theory it was assumed that the incentive value of some anticipated success (s_n) in a contingent path is an inverse linear function of the (total) subjective probability that immediate activity will (eventually) result in that success,

$$I_{sn} = 1 - P_{1sn} \tag{8}$$

and that the incentive value of some anticipated failure (f_n) is represented by the negative value of (total) subjective probability of success,

$$I_{fn} = -(P_{1sn}) \tag{9}$$

Subjective probabilities of success and failure are assumed to vary between 0 and 1 and summate to 1 for computational purposes to determine the implications of algebraic manipulation of the above equations (1 through 9).

The above set of assumptions is a direct extension of those made in initial theory of achievement motivation (Chapter 2). They may prove to be incorrect in their mathematical statement, and even in their general implications for behavior in immediate activity of a contingent path. However, they have the virtue of allowing for the derivation of component tendencies to achieve success and to avoid failure, given that the perceived task difficulty at each step in the path can be specified and that these probabilities combine multiplicatively to determine total difficulty, and they either (*a*) are directly subject to empirical test and/or (*b*) lead to hypotheses which can be tested experimentally (see below). Rather than wait for final empirical verification of the exact nature of the relationship between probabilities and incentives in a contingent path, the implications of the present set of assumptions have been derived and now serve as a guide to research. The self-corrective process of scientific inquiry will no doubt indicate the extent to which this has been a useful strategy. At this point there can be little doubt that these assumptions have served as a valuable impetus to begin the experimental analysis of the effects of differences in nature and extent of future orientation on motivation sustaining immediate activity.

COMPARISON OF CONTINGENT AND NONCONTINGENT FUTURE ORIENTATION

We now distinguish between contingent, noncontingent, and one-step path situations. These differ in the type and extent of an individual's cognitive stucture relating immediate activity to the opportunity for future striving and therefore to the possibility of future achievement. Contingent and noncontingent paths can involve the same degree or extent of future orientation (have the same length of path), but differ in the perceived relationship between immediate and subsequent activities and their outcomes (steps) along the path. A noncontingent path presents a series of anticipated activities, but the individual's skill or effort in the immediate activity is known not to influence the opportunity for subsequent striving along the path. In a contingent path, immediate success is believed to guarantee the opportunity to strive for future success(es), while immediate failure guarantees future failure through loss of the opportunity to continue.

While the present elaboration is a direct extension of previous theory to contingent path situations, and its implications for level of performance in a particular immediate activity differ only in degree with those of the initial theory, other behavioral implications increasingly differ as the length of contingent path increases so that, under certain circumstances, the two positions yield opposite predictions for behavior in contingent path situations. Before proceeding to a discussion of component tendencies and their calculation based on the particular set of assumptions stated thus far for contingent paths, it is worth viewing some general behavioral implications of the concept of length of contingent path, and contrasting these to the predicted effects in noncontingent paths of equivalent lengths. Anticipation of future success or failure should influence strength of motivation sustaining immediate activity in a contingent path, while it should not effect motivation in a noncontingent path.

It is important to remember that component tendencies aroused by some particular step in a contingent path do not determine behavior directly, but rather summate to yield a resultant achievement-oriented tendency sustaining immediate activity in the contingent (but not the noncontingent) path. Thus each anticipated success in a contingent path is assumed to arouse a component tendency to achieve, and these summate to determine the (total) tendency to achieve success in the immediate activity. Component tendencies aroused by the anticipation of each possible failure summate to yield the total (inhibitory) tendency not to engage in the immediate activity. Individuals in whom the motive to achieve success is stronger than the motive to avoid failure ($M_S > M_{AF}$), who are assumed to be primarily motivated to achieve, should become increasingly more motivated to do well as the length of a contingent path increases, while individuals who are assumed to be primarily motivated not to engage in immediate activity (i.e., are inhibited by the threat of failure) ($M_{AF} > M_S$) should become even more inhibited as the length of a contingent path increases. Thus an increase in length of a contingent path should increase an individual's characteristic achievement motivation and therefore increase the difference in motivation between success-oriented and failure-threatened individuals, although we shall see later that this accentuation should become progressively smaller with each further increase in length, for most contingent paths. If an increase in positive motivation increases performance efficiency, and an increase in negative motivation decreases performance efficiency (but see Part III), then individuals in whom $M_S > M_{AF}$ should do better, while individuals in whom $M_{AF} > M_S$ should do worse in immediate activity of (*a*) a contingent than a noncontingent path, and (*b*) the longer of two contingent paths. Hence the superiority in performance of the success-oriented over the failure-threatened individual should be greater in contingent than in noncontingent paths of equivalent length, and in the longer of two contingent paths.

Two kinds of studies have tested these hypotheses. The first has already been described in reference to the Isaacson and Raynor (1966) study, where the nature of the path faced by the individual was inferred from ratings of the importance of doing well in an immediate activity (an academic course) for the achievement of a student's own future goals. Several similar studies have since been conducted. *S*s high on rated importance (also termed perceived instrumentality or PI) are assumed to face a contingent path relating immediate activity to subsequent achievement, while those low on PI are assumed to face a noncontingent path. Studies by Raynor, Atkinson, and Brown (Chapter 8), and one of two reported by Raynor (1970, and Chapter 9), provide data consistent with predictions of an accentuation of characteristic achievement motivation within the presumed contingent path. College students classified high in n Achievement and low in Test Anxiety ($M_S > M_{AF}$) received higher grades in an introductory psychology course, and were relatively more concerned about doing well than anxious, when the grade was seen as highly related to future goals than when it was not.

Raynor, Cosentino, and Edwards recently obtained data (not as yet reported) from a survey of college students in which the same pattern of interactions just described was obtained, using students' standing on a two-item measure of test anxiety (low anxiety assumed to indicate $M_S > M_{AF}$, while high anxiety $M_{AF} > M_S$) and their rating of the *necessity* of getting good grades for their future plans to work (PI)—with the students' reports of their overall grade-point average in college as the dependent measure. Thus this study provides a direct link between those which used ratings of helpfulness and importance to assess PI and the variable of contingent future orientation, since the clearest way to assess this variable seems to ask about the *necessity* of doing well for later success. Note that an average of grades in this study yielded the pattern of interaction previously found only for a single grade. On the other hand, Raynor (1968b) reported that high-school students received higher grades regardless of motive status when their *overall* high-school grades were seen as important for their own future success than when they were not. Also, in the second study reported by Raynor (1970, and Chapter 9), the accentuation of expected results served to eliminate within the high rated importance group an apparent reversal for low importance of the expected superiority of the success-oriented over the failure-threatened group—when grades in introductory psychology were used as the measure of performance—while when the *overall* average for the semester was calculated, all subjects received high grades within high than within low rated importance.

The results for the failure-threatened group in the above studies have not been consistent, but they are of particular theoretical (as well as practical) importance, since evidence supporting a simultaneous increment for the success-oriented group and a decrement for the failure-threatened group provides a pattern of results which requires consideration of the interaction between individual differences in achievement-related motives and contingent future orientation rather than a more intuitive appeal to an overall "increase in arousal" when immediate performance is importantly (i.e., contingently) related to distant future achievement.

The second kind of study that has been conducted is designed to deal directly with the manipulation of different kinds of future orientation. Raynor and Rubin (1971, and Chapter 10) present the first published test using this procedure. They experimentally induced contingent and noncontingent paths, each having four steps. As predicted, success-oriented individuals performed significantly better while failure-threatened individuals performed significantly worse in a complex (three-step) arithmetic task when it was the first step in the contingent path than when it was the first step in the noncontingent path. The success-oriented group performed substantially better than the failure-threatened group, as expected, within the contingent condition, but this difference was negligible within the noncontingent condition. In addition, within the contingent condition, the performance of groups for whom it was assumed that the two motives are of equal strength fell intermediate between that of the two extreme motive groups, which is the expected ordering if the motives to achieve and to avoid failure yield a resultant motive strength of zero when they are equal.

In another experimental study, Entin and Raynor (1973) investigated whether the shortest possible contingent path (of only two steps) would produce the predicted pattern of interaction in comparison to a noncontingent path of the same length. They also made several changes in procedure which tend to rule out alternative explanations of the results reported by Raynor and Rubin (1971, and Chapter 10). Their results replicated the earlier findings. These two experimental studies taken together suggest that a path of two steps is sufficient to produce effects of contingent future orientation, and that these become even stronger as the length of path is increased from two to four steps. A study by Raynor, Entin, and Raynor (1972) tested this hypothesis directly by inducing contingent paths of two and four steps using a sample of sixth and eighth grade boys and girls from an inner city school who were mostly black and Spanish-speaking Americans. The results showed the predicted pattern of interaction when groups extremely low and high on the Test Anxiety Scale for Children (Sarason et al., 1960) were used to infer success-oriented and failure-threatened groups, respectively, even when performance scores on a simple arithmetic task were corrected to reduce to zero the correlation between performance and standing on a measure of verbal "ability" (see Chapter 20 for a discussion of a motivational interpretation of performance in such so-called "ability" tests). However, the difference within the shorter path was not significant when the correction for "ability" was used.

Sorrentino (1971, and Chapter 14) has continued the experimental investigation of future orientation by viewing, among other things, individual performance in a group task presented as a contingent or a noncontingent path. He extended the analysis to consideration of individual differences in n Affiliation as well as achievement-related motives (as inferred from n Achievement and Test Anxiety scores). His findings replicate the general pattern of interaction found by Raynor and Rubin (1971, and Chapter 10), *but only for subjects low in n Affiliation. Results for Ss high in n Affiliation showed a significant reversal of the predicted pattern of interaction.* While this reversal is interpretable in terms of performance decrement due to too much positive motivation for success-oriented individuals also high in n Affiliation, and a performance increment due to the dampening effect of inhibition for the failure-threatened individuals high in n Affiliation (see Sorrentino, Chapter 14; see also Chapter 11 for a general discussion of these points), his results caution against the continued use of a simple linear assumption to relate positive motivation and performance efficiency that has thus far been employed in discussions of the behavioral implications of future orientation. On the other hand, a pre-performance measure of anticipated interest in the task that was obtained by Sorrentino showed the predicted increase with the addition of both n Affiliation and contingent future orientation to the success-oriented individuals. Thus the experimental evidence presented thus far suggests that while contingent future orientation accentuates characteristic differences in aroused achievement motivation, use of performance efficiency to infer differences in motivation requires further systematic study to specify the conditions under which such a relationship can be expected to be linear. Other evidence to be described in later sections of this paper (dealing with predictions derived from more specific assumptions of the theoretical elaboration presented here) use measures of persistence and risk preference, which presumably are not subject to the complications of overmotivation suggested by Sorrentino's important research.

COMPONENT TENDENCIES AND TOTAL MOTIVATION TO ACHIEVE IN CONTINGENT PATHS

Use of Equations 1 to 9 (above) permits the derivation of the magnitudes of component (intrinsic and instrumental) tendencies aroused in a contingent path. While not so restricted by theory, for the present illustrations it has been assumed that the perceived task difficulty at each step in a particular contingent path is the same. Substitution of numbers that range from 0 to 1 for values of subjective probabilities and incentive values yields a family of curves depicted schematically in Figure 1 for individuals with $M_S - M_{AF} = +1$ (considered to be "success-oriented") and in Figure 2 for individuals with $M_S - M_{AF} = -1$ (considered to be "failure-threatened"). These curves show the relative magnitudes of component resultant tendencies to achieve that are aroused by each anticipated step in a contingent path, for constant probability paths in which each task is perceived to be either very easy ($P_{nsn} = .9$), moderately difficult

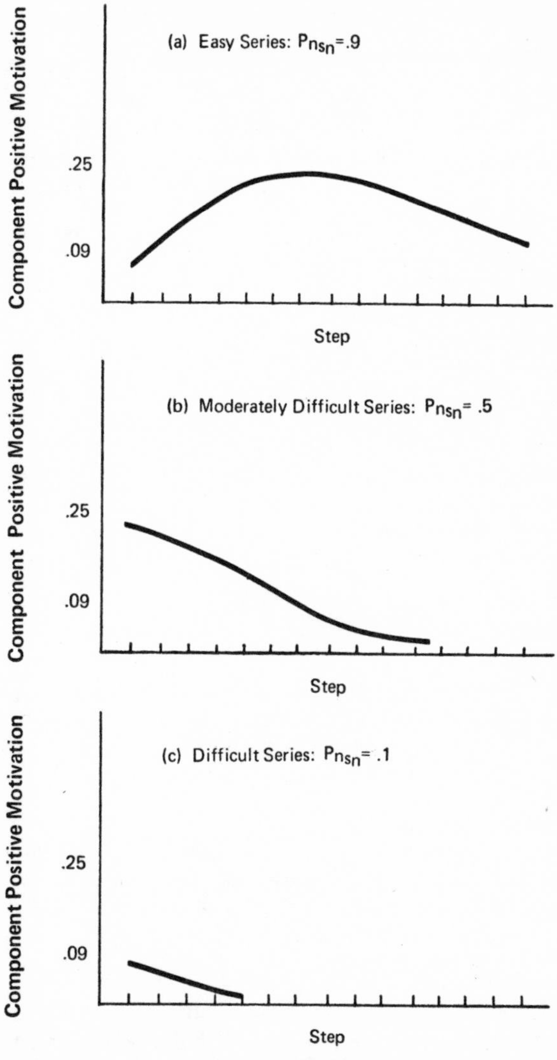

FIG. 1. Components of *positive* motivation (resultant tendency to achieve) aroused by each task of a series of easy, moderately difficult, and difficult tasks in a contingent path. $M_S - M_{AF} = +1$ in this example.

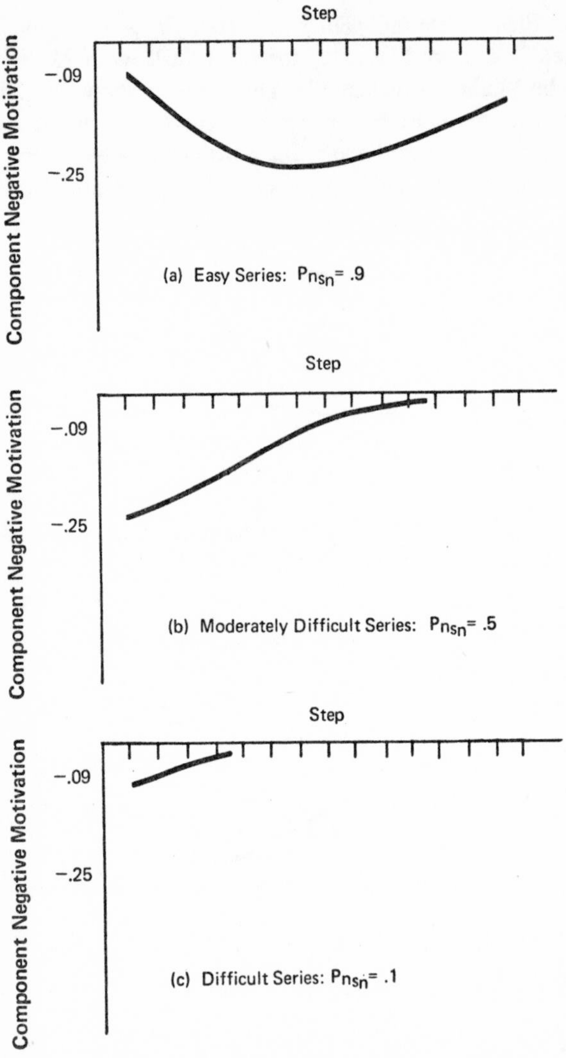

FIG. 2. Components of *negative* motivation (resultant tendency to achieve) aroused by each task of a series of easy, moderately difficult, and difficult tasks in a contingent path. $M_S - M_{AF} = -1$ in this example.

(P_{nsn} = .5), or very difficult (P_{nsn} = .1) that are relatively short (e.g., $N = 2$), of moderate length (e.g., $N = 5$, 7, or 9) and very long (e.g., $N = 15$).

Figures 1 and 2 show that for constant-probability paths consisting of a series of *easy tasks* (P_{nsn} = .9), both positive and negative achievement motivation aroused *by the task itself* that is confronting the individual (Step 1 taken alone) is relatively small in comparison to the strengths of component motivation aroused for that task by the subsequent tasks perceived to be part of the contingent path. We see that components of motivation increase as the length of the contingent path increases, up to step 7, where they reach their respective positive and negative maximum values. These then decrease more slowly as the length of path continues to increase up to 15 steps. On the other hand, for constant-probability paths consisting of a series of difficult tasks (P_{nsn} = .1), not only are components of positive and negative motivation aroused by Step 1 relatively weak, but they drop off rapidly to even smaller values as the length of path increases.

While Figures 1 and 2 do not relate directly to behavior, if we assume that the largest component of positive tendency that is aroused in a contingent path defines the content of the "phenomenal goal" (i.e., the goal consciously attended to) of immediate activity of the path, we can then make predictions concerning the extent of future orientation that an individual should be consciously aware of when faced with immediate activity of a contingent path. If we further assume that the constant value of task difficulty along a contingent path can be taken to indicate the degree of confidence which an individual has with regard to success in that path (i.e., rated competence; see Moulton, Chapter 4), we can then describe the individual who is both motivated to achieve and highly confident of success as primarily motivated to achieve *future* rather than *immediate* success–in Figure 1a, the largest component tendency is aroused by Step 7 rather than Step 1. He should engage in immediate activity not because it offers any great challenge in itself (the intrinsic component tendency aroused by Step 1 is relatively small), but because immediate success is necessary in order to strive for his primary goal, seen to be success in the future. Note also that the component tendency aroused by Step 15 is also smaller than that aroused by Step 7, so that we may describe the phenomenal goal as being in the "realistic" or "moderate" future, rather than in the far-distant future. In contrast, the individual who is primarily inhibited by the threat of failure and who (perhaps because of his high ability) happens to be highly confident of success at each step, should lack a phenomenal goal entirely, insofar as it concerns anticipated success qua success. If constrained to view the future steps of a contingent path by anticipation of a (constant) extrinsic reward at each step in the path, we then expect that the phenomenal goal of immediate activity should be focused on attainment of extrinsic rewards in the immediate present *or* in the distant future. Both would then yield a sum of extrinsic and negative achievement motivation which is more positive than that for the realistic future. If, more probably, extrinsic motivation is stronger for the later than the earlier steps (see Chapter 19), he should be concerned about attainment of extrinsic rewards in the distant future, avoiding concern about the realistic future, which might be said to arouse greatest "phenomenal threat" as a consequence of anticipation of engaging in immediate activity in a contingent path.

Now consider the individual primarily motivated to achieve who, because he is only moderately confident of success, believes himself faced with a contingent path consisting of moderately difficult tasks (P_{nsn} = .5). His phenomenal goal should be to succeed in the immediate present, since the first step of the path arouses the largest component tendency to achieve (see Figure 1*b*). For the success-oriented individual who lacks confidence completely and therefore sees the contingent path as consisting of a series of difficult tasks (P_{nsn} = .1), we expect an absence of future orientation. Component tendencies are small even for anticipated success in the immediate present or close future (see Figure 1*c*). Conversely, the failure-threatened individual who lacks confidence should, given constraints toward viewing the future due to extrinsic motivation, be concerned about future extrinsic rewards, yet lack a clear-cut phenomenal threat.

If we assume that the phenomenal goal of immediate activity is revealed by the future orientation of an imaginative story, and that the strength of resultant achievement motivation sustaining immediate activity is revealed by the total amount of achievement imagery included in an imaginative story, results reported by Shrable and Moulton (1968) are relevant to an evaluation of the hypotheses just derived for those individuals primarily motivated to achieve. These investigators measured the perceived competence of high-school students for different vocational areas using an instrument developed by Morris (1966). Each *S* estimated his chances of success in each of four areas of achievement skill. We can assume that the higher this value of total perceived difficulty in an area, the higher the value of constant subjective probability of success for a contingent path in that area. Extensive pretesting had identified a picture stimulus seen as depicting one of these areas by at least 80% of the respondents. Imaginative stories were obtained using these pictures, following the usual procedures developed in research on achievement motivation (see Atkinson, 1958a, Appendix III). Stories were then coded using the three primary scoring categories of the n Achievement scoring manual C (see McClelland, Atkinson, Clark, & Lowell, 1958). The total n Achievement score for each picture was also obtained. *S*s who wrote at least one story containing achievement imagery were assumed to be primarily motivated to achieve. Only those students who rated one picture area high and one low in subjective probability of success for that skill were included in the data analysis. The results indicated that for those students above their group median on intelligence, there was significantly more achievement imagery indicating concern over achieving distant future goals (scored "long-term involvement" and "unique accomplishment")[2] and more overall achievement imagery (a higher n Achievement score), in stories written to pictures portraying areas of *high* rated subjective probability of success. However, results were reversed for those below the group median on intelligence. It is not clear at present what implications this reversal has for the conceptual analysis of future orientation. It may be that the present elaboration of theory

[2] Data for these two categories were considered together by Shrable and Moulton and were not available for separate analysis. However, unique accomplishment would usually occur only after more limited mastery in earlier steps of a contingent path, so that both kinds of imagery should reflect future orientation.

applies only when an individual has sufficient ability to have acquired well-articulated cognitive expectations concerning the long-term implications of immediate activities (see also Chapter 19). Without this capacity, the imaginative story may represent substitutive or compensatory fantasy (see Moulton, 1967b, and Chapter 4).

A more general implication of the above analysis is that, insofar as there is a positive correlation between measures of achievement-related motives and the rated confidence of individuals faced with skill activity (see Atkinson & Feather, 1966, Ch. 20), we expect to find a positive correlation between extent of (achievement-related) future orientation and achievement motivation (see McClelland, 1961). However, this relationship is not due to the achievement motive per se (although present measurement confounds the motive and extent of future orientation, as already noted), but is mediated through differences in confidence to influence the phenomenal goal of immediate activity of perceived contingent paths (see also Chapter 4).

Joint Effects of Length of Path and Subjective Probability of Success

In order to move from the consideration of the phenomenal goal of immediate activity in a contingent path to total strength of achievement motivation sustaining immediate activity in the path, it is necessary to depict the summation of component tendencies which are shown in Figures 1 and 2 in terms of the joint influence of length of path and subjective probability of success, thus yielding total resultant achievement motivation sustaining immediate activity. When this is done algebraically, Figures 3 and 4 are obtained. They represent the areas under each of the respective curves in Figures 1 and 2. The implications of these values of positive and negative resultant achievement motivation are discussed in the sections which follow.

For any length of contingent path (two or more step paths), an individual's achievement motivation should become stronger with an increase in magnitude of constant subjective probability of success along the path in conjunction with an increase in the length of the path. Thus individual differences in achievement-related motives should affect immediate behavior to the greatest extent in *long* contingent paths which are perceived to be relatively *easy* (P_{nsn} = .9), to the least extent when each step is perceived to be relatively difficult (P_{nsn} = .1), and to an intermediate extent when each step is perceived to be of moderate difficulty (P_{nsn} = .5). As the length of contingent path *decreases*, the point at which the difference in resultant achievement motivation between success-oriented and failure-threatened individuals is greatest moves toward intermediate difficulty so that, when the length of path is 1, earlier predictions that the difference between these two motive groups should be maximal when P_s = .5, and minimal where P_s = .1 or .9 (see Atkinson, 1957; Atkinson & Feather, 1966, Ch. 20; see Chapter 2), are recaptured as the simplest case of the more general theory.

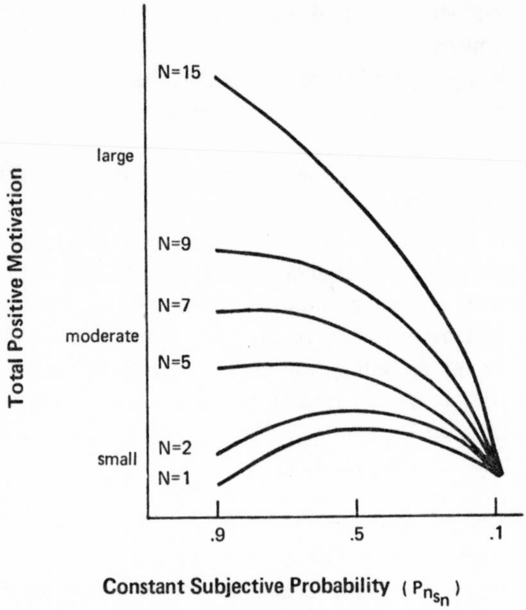

FIG. 3. Schematic representation of total *positive* motivation (resultant tendency to achieve) aroused in a contingent path as a function of the length of path (N) and constant level of perceived difficulty ($P_{n s_n}$) along the path. $M_S - M_{AF} = +1$ in this example.

Performance Level

It follows from the curves shown in Figures 3 and 4 that if individuals are constrained to perform in immediate activity of contingent paths and the length of path is made progressively shorter, the point at which the greatest difference between success-oriented and failure-threatened groups in level of performance should occur moves toward immediate activity of moderate difficulty (see Karabenick & Youssef, 1968, and Chapter 5)—if performance efficiency is a positive linear function of total positive motivation. On the other hand, for long contingent paths which differ in the constant value of perceived difficulty at each task, those in whom $M_S > M_{AF}$ should work harder and perform better (again, if positive motivation is directly related to performance efficiency) when each step is perceived to be *easy* than when each step is perceived to be difficult, with performance intermediate between these extremes when each task is perceived to be of moderate difficulty. These predictions are reversed for subjects in whom $M_{AF} > M_S$; that is, immediate performance should be highest for the difficult series, lowest for the easy series, and between these extremes for the moderately difficult series. Thus the greatest superiority of success-oriented over failure-threatened individuals should occur in immediate activity of the *easy* series rather than the moderate series as the previous theory implies, or in the difficult series as recent arguments by Heckhausen (1968) suggest.

Raynor and Sorrentino (1972) conducted two studies to test this hypothesized interaction between perceived difficulty at each step along a contingent path and individual differences in achievement-related motives. In the first study, male *S*s were recruited from two summer employment offices in London, Ontario (Canada). They ranged in age from 16 to 21 and were paid for their participation. After measures of n Achievement and Test Anxiety were obtained in group testing sessions, contingent paths of four steps each were induced according to the procedures used by Raynor and Rubin (1971, and Chapter 10). One group was presented a series of easy tasks (P_{ns_n} = .8), another a series of moderately difficult tasks (P_{ns_n} = .5), the other a series of difficult tasks (P_{ns_n} = .2). As predicted, the greatest superiority of the success-oriented (high in n Achievement–low in Test Anxiety) over the failure-threatened (low in n Achievement–high in Test Anxiety) group was found for the first task of the easy contingent series ($p < .05$), while this difference was negligible for the moderately difficult series (n.s.) and reversed for the difficult series. This yielded the predicted pattern of interaction as far as between motive-group differences in the easy versus the difficult series is concerned ($p < .10$). When the two motive measures were viewed separately, results for n Achievement (high versus

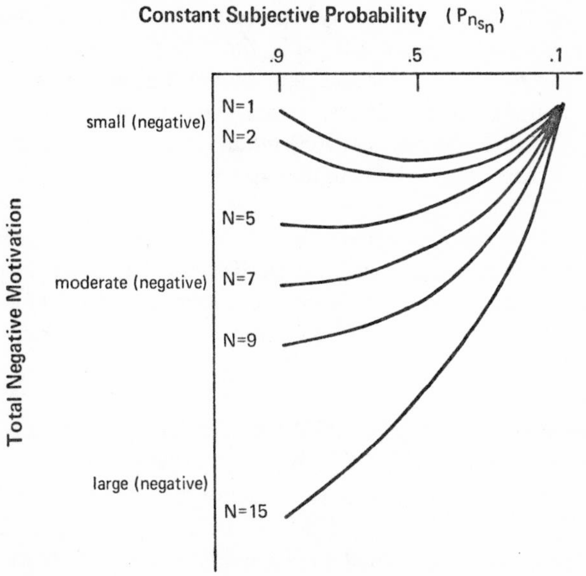

FIG. 4. Schematic representation of total *negative* motivation (resultant tendency to achieve) aroused in a contingent path as a function of the length of path (*N*) and constant level of perceived difficulty (P_{ns_n}) along the path. $M_S - M_{AF} = -1$ in this example.

low thirds) closely resembled those for the combined motive measure, while those for Test Anxiety showed no systematic effects of perceived difficulty along the path. In the second study, seven-step contingent paths were presented as very easy ($P_{n^s n} = .9$), moderately difficult ($P_{n^s n} = .5$), or very difficult ($P_{n^s n} = .1$) to three groups using instructions modified from those first used by Entin and Raynor (1973) to create contingent paths. *S*s were male college students drawn from an introductory psychology subject pool to fulfill a course requirement. Results were very similar to the positive findings of the first study for low and high groups on Test Anxiety (based on thirds), but showed no effects of perceived task difficulty when thirds on n Achievement were viewed.

While the inconsistencies for n Achievement and Test Anxiety taken alone in the data just presented and the modest levels of significance that were obtained when results were as expected suggest that more research is needed on this question, these studies by Raynor and Sorrentino are important because no statistically reliable evidence was found in support of the expected superiority in level of immediate performance of the $M_S > M_{AF}$ over the opposite motive group *except under experimental conditions where an attempt was made to induce high subjective probability of success* (i.e., *to create an easy task*) *at each step of a contingent path.* Thus the results did not conform to what would be expected if initial statements of theory of achievement motivation (Chapter 2) were extrapolated without modification to a contingent path situation, in which case it would be expected that the superiority in performance of the success-oriented over the failure-threatened individuals should be the same for both high and low values of subjective probability of success, and largest for moderate levels of task difficulty. In addition, the positive results are generally opposite to what would be expected based on Heckhausen's (1968) modification of theory of achievement motivation, since this position leads to the expectation that the greatest superiority in performance of success-oriented over failure-threatened individuals should occur for low rather than high values of subjective probability of success. In fact, in all but one comparison made in both studies, the difference in performance between success-oriented over failure-threatened groups was either smallest in the predicted direction, or in the opposite direction, for the difficult series.

Persistence

The implications of Figures 3 and 4 for persistence in the face of *failure* in immediate activity of a contingent path (prior to the point at which the failure means loss of the opportunity to continue) are in general similar to those derived from initial theory (see Feather, 1961, 1963; see also Chapter 2). However, persistence in the face of continued *success* in immediate activity of a contingent path (prior to the point at which the success means a guaranteed opportunity to move on to subsequent activity in the path) is viewed quite differently by initial theory and its present elaboration. For example, if immediate activity is initially perceived to be of moderate difficulty, the elaboration predicts that success-oriented individuals faced with a long contingent path should persist to a greater extent in the face of continued immediate success than failure-threatened individuals, whereas initial theory predicts just the opposite. This implication is seen by viewing (in Figures 3 and 4) the magnitude of resultant achievement motivation for the two groups as one moves from low to high subjective probability of success (i.e., difficult to easy along a task difficulty dimension). Both positive and negative achievement motivation *increase* in immediate activity, according to the elaborated theory, for long contingent paths, whereas both positive and negative achievement motivation *decrease* in immediate activity, according to the initial theory, for one-step paths.

Raynor and Entin (1972) tested these hypotheses by presenting a purported test of ability to subjects as either a three-step contingent or noncontingent path. Three booklets were constructed, the first with 35 pages, the second with 30 pages, and the third with 25 pages. Each page contained a number of complex (three-step) arithmetic problems previously used by Raynor and Rubin (1971, and Chapter 10) and by Entin and Raynor (1973), among others. Each booklet was called a test item, and each page was called a subset of that test item. *S*s were told that the experimenters were collecting final data for some similar kinds of items taken from a larger abilities test. These items were described as ordered from easiest to most difficult, but since they were taken from the last part of the test, "even the first kind of item you will work on is not easy. Our research has shown that it should be of moderate difficulty for a college group of this age and ability." *S*s were then told that the test was constructed like many other tests of ability so that failure, defined as doing below the established average for that particular subset and trial, marked one's level of ability. In the contingent condition, *S*s were told that they could have as many tries (do as many pages) on an item as they wanted, *as long as they were successful on each subset (page)*, while *S*s in the noncontingent condition were told that they could have as many tries as they wanted on a particular kind of item, *even if they happened to fail on a particular subset (page)*. *S*s were further told that when they felt they had mastered a kind of item, they could go on to the next more difficult item, but that they could not return to an easier item once they had moved on to a more difficult one—"so make sure you are good enough before you move on." *S*s were given feedback after each trial that insured that each subject succeeded on every page of the first booklet. After 35 trials the experiment(s) were ended. The number of pages attempted in the first booklet (item) was taken as the measure of persistence.

Two studies were conducted, one using male college students, the other female college students, as *S*s. Both studies yielded similar results. Based on the present elaboration of theory, it was predicted and found in both that *S*s classified high in n Achievement and low in Test Anxiety would (*a*) persist longer in the contingent than the noncontingent condition ($p < .05$ and $< .005$, respectively for the male and female samples) and (*b*) persist longer than the low-high group in the contingent condition ($p < .01$ and $< .05$, for males and females, respectively). These results are opposite to what would be expected based on the initial theory if it were extrapolated without modification to contingent path situations. However, the hypothesis for the noncontingent condition, namely that the low-high group would persist longer than the high-low group, was not supported. In the first study the trend was slightly in the opposite direction to that predicted, and in the second study there was a nonsignificant trend in the expected direction. Also, the prediction that the low-high group would persist longer in the noncontingent than in the contingent condition was not supported in either study; these subjects persisted about the same (moderate) extent regardless of condition in both studies.

Risk Preference

The implications of the curves shown in Figures 3 and 4 for risk preference are that in long contingent paths an individual in whom $M_S > M_{AF}$ should prefer immediate activity which is perceived to be relatively *easy*, while individuals in whom $M_{AF} > M_S$ should, if constrained to do so, prefer immediate activity that is perceived to be relatively *difficult*. This contrasts with the predictions of initial theory of achievement motivation (and those made by elaborated theory for one-step paths, to which the initial theory addresses itself), which suggest that success-oriented individuals should prefer (immediate) activity perceived to be of moderate difficulty, while failure-threatened individuals should, if constrained by extrinsic sources of motivation to remain in the situation, prefer (immediate) activity perceived to be either very easy or very difficult (see Chapter 2). The differences between the two sets of predictions can be understood in words as follows. Individuals in whom $M_S > M_{AF}$ should act to guarantee immediate success in a contingent path so as to insure the opportunity to strive for success in subsequent skill activities in the path, since the magnitude of positive instrumental tendencies aroused by the future steps, when combined, is far greater than the positive intrinsic tendency that is aroused by the immediate task (alone) of moderate difficulty. Individuals in whom $M_{AF} > M_S$ should act to guarantee immediate failure in a contingent path by choosing an immediate task of great difficulty so as to not be exposed to the possibility of further failures in the path, since the magnitude of negative instrumental tendencies aroused by the future steps, when combined, is far greater than the negative intrinsic tendency aroused by an immediate task perceived to be easy or difficult. Choice of an easy task means further exposure to later steps, since success in an easy task is assured, while preference for a difficult task will almost always lead to (*a*) the approval of others for undertaking a difficult endeavor but (*b*) loss of the opportunity for further exposure to achievement-related activity, which is less noxious than constrained skill performance.

Raynor (1972) has conducted a series of seven studies dealing with these risk-taking hypotheses, using at times either and/or both a game of chance and a game of skill and various lengths of contingent and noncontingent paths and single-activity control conditions. The results are fairly consistent in showing that the results expected for the success-oriented individual are found for all *S*s, regardless of motive group, with some weak suggestions of support for the predicted interaction between individual differences in achievement-related motives and kind and length of path.

On the other hand, a recent study by Wish and Hasazi (1972) provides striking confirmation of the predictions made by the elaboration of theory discussed here using the actual curricular choices of male college juniors enrolled in a school of management to infer immediate risk taking in a contingent path. Students were tested on the same day they were required to choose a major. Each student rated the chances out of 100 on an 11-point scale (in increments of 10) of students "much like themselves" or receiving their degrees in each of the six major areas offered by the school. Prior to that, measures of n Achievement and Debilitating Anxiety were administered in the usual manner. An independent behavior criterion was also obtained (an anagrams task–Horner, Chapter 13) which subsequently correlated +.43 ($p < .05$) with a measure of resultant achievement motivation (standard score on n Achievement minus standard scores on Debilitating Anxiety) to yield construct validation of the motive scores. The students' actual curricular choices made later that day were subsequently analyzed as a function of resultant achievement motivation (positive versus negative scores) and a categorization of curricular choices as easiest, moderately difficult, or most difficult. Specifically, each student's curricular choice was placed as either falling (on his own ratings of the six major areas) as closest to the difficult end of the scale (0 chances out of 100), closest to the middle (50 chances out of 100), closest to the easy end of the scale (100 chances out of 100), or not falling into one of these three (termed the "other" category). The data are shown in Table 1. The result is striking. Students with positive resultant achievement motivation (assumed here to mean they were success-oriented) are seen to have overwhelmingly preferred the easiest program

TABLE 1

Choices of Major Area Categorized into Three Levels of Perceived Difficulty Based on Each Student's Own Rating of the Chances of Receiving the Degree in That Area for "Students like Himself"

Resultant achievement motivation	Level of difficulty*			Other
	Most difficult (closest to 0.00)	Intermediate (closest to 0.50)	Easiest (closest to 1.00)	
Positive	1	12	55	23
Negative	28	8	1	14

Note.–Based on Wish and Hasazi (1972), who initially analyzed their data by comparing the Intermediate to the combined Most difficult and Easiest categories. This table is based on a personal communication, and is included here by permission of the authors.

*$\chi^2 = 75.41, df = 2, p < .001$.

of study, which has the greatest number of cases even when the "other" category is included, while those with negative resultant achievement motivation (assumed here to mean they were failure-threatened) chose the most difficult program of study, even when the "other" category is included. When the "other" category is disregarded, the opposite trends showing the preference of the success-oriented group for those majors seen as easiest and the failure-threatened group for those majors seen as most difficult are both apparent ($\chi^2 = 75.41, df = 2, p < .001$).

ACHIEVEMENT MOTIVATION, ENTREPRENEURIAL ACTIVITY, AND CAREER STRIVING

It is now possible to examine some more general implications of the hypotheses which have thus far been derived from the present elaboration of theory of achievement motivation. Consider an individual who is primarily motivated to achieve success ($M_S > M_{AF}$). While the elaborated theory recaptures the prediction that he should prefer moderate risks when immediate activity has no future implications (as in a one-step or noncontingent path), the analysis for contingent path situations suggests that he should become much less speculative (i.e., more conservative) in immediate risk taking involving achievement-related activity so as to guarantee the opportunity to strive for future success(es) in that path. This hypothesis has a direct bearing on the analysis of the relationship between achievement motivation and entrepreneurial activity (see McClelland, 1961). Businessmen who are success-oriented should be much less speculative in their every-day (i.e., immediate) decisions which involve risk than McClelland's analysis suggests, since such activity is here conceived to represent immediate activity in a long contingent path, where failure means loss of the opportunity to continue (i.e., bankruptcy). If the previous ideas were completely correct, it would seem that most success-oriented businessmen and other entrepreneurs would be "failures" in a relatively short period of time. While this may be the case, and can be tested empirically, the elaborated theory suggests that it is the *long-term* challenge of success (i.e., success as the phenomenal goal in the realistic future) which provides the attraction for these individuals to engage in immediate activity in situations (contingent paths) where immediate failure has such disastrous consequences.

More generally, the career decisions of success-oriented individuals should not, according to elaborated theory, consist of a series of immediate risks in which there is a 50-50 chance of failure, but rather should reflect a much lower degree of risk (i.e., preference for immediate activity in which the chances of success are relatively high) in activity of a contingent path leading on to the chosen career, since immediate failure has the consequence of failure to achieve the career goal through loss of the opportunity to continue its pursuit. Again, it is the future challenge which offers the moderate risk, given the necessity of guaranteeing "staying in the ballgame" long enough to achieve future career success.

This elaboration of theory suggests that any skill activity inherently offers a challenge (i.e., inevitably arouses some degree of intrinsic achievement motivation) whose action implications depend upon an individual's characteristic achievement motivation. But what should happen to an extremely success-oriented "novice" (newcomer) in an area of achievement skill who, because he is strongly motivated to do well, succeeds at his preferred moderate risk in a one-step situation? Soon he will no longer find much interest and challenge in immediate activity in this area, because all tasks will be perceived to be easy and will arouse minimal positive intrinsic achievement motivation. Should this individual now switch to another area of achievement skill, to begin again to develop his level of competence, as the initial theory of achievement motivation implies? Elaborated theory suggests not. Rather, he should move toward engaging in what will now begin to constitute the kind of contingent path commonly known as a career (see Chapter 19 for a more detailed discussion of contingent career paths). With continued success, his confidence should increase, and his phenomenal goal should become increasingly fixed on the realistic future rather than the immediate present. As he continues to succeed and becomes extremely confident of his increasing skills in this area, his phenomenal goal should be fixed at higher and higher levels of consensual difficulty (see Moulton, Chapter 4). That is, the goals this individual pursues will be perceived by others to be difficult ones. His immediate activity, which appears to him to offer little inherent challenge now that he has become an "expert" in this area, should be seen by others as being of great difficulty, requiring tremendous skill and offering great immediate risk, and his phenomenal goal will appear to others to be unattainable, a case of "overaspiration." Thus the subjective view of the individual and that offered by others should differ markedly. Persons at the forefront of their chosen professions, particularly those involving activities which allow the perception of an inherent continuum of task difficulty, should exhibit the developmental history just described.

In subsequent sections concerning open and closed contingent paths, we will view the dynamics of motivation of immediate activity as a function of continued success. However, at this juncture an additional observation is in order. We have already emphasized that in a relatively long contingent path of high constant subjective probability of success, the success-oriented individual should be relatively uninterested and lack a feeling of challenge for the immediate activity of this path taken by itself. His conscious phenomenal goal of immediate activity should be focused on success in the moderate future, for it is here that the individual perceives that attainment of success should provide greatest satisfaction and feelings of accomplishment. Hence we find the paradoxical situation of an individual choosing tasks that would ordinarily be boring and uninteresting, not as ends in themselves, but as means to the achievement of future success; *but pursuit of this future goal never provides that great satisfaction, because immediate achievement merely puts off the challenging future goal to an equally distant later goal in the path, since it leads to an increase in confidence and a shift in the phenomenal goal to a new, slightly more distant, anticipated achievement.*

The above description of the developmental dynamics of motivation in a career path, derived as it is from an interpretation of the meaning of the algebraic implications of elaborated theory, offers a systematically coherent, yet plausible, explanation of the motivational history of individuals who are perceived by others to be at the forefront of their chosen careers. It is important to remember that motivation aroused in the present for such an individual should be determined by perceived rather than consensual (view of others) difficulty, so that the apparent contradiction between others' view of the contingent path confronted by the person and his own view (which is used to predict his behavior) is not really a problem, given the theoretical vantage point taken here. This position consistently pursues the Lewinian analysis in terms of the life space of the subject, rather than how others view that life space. The latter view becomes important only insofar as it determines the magnitude of extrinsic rewards offered for, and hence what can be anticipated in attainment of, achievements of an extraordinary nature, the "unique accomplishment" included in the present coding of achievement imagery (see Chapter 4).

The above analysis therefore suggests why achievement imagery reflecting *both* long-term striving and unique accomplishment were found to increase in attempts to create heightened states of achievement-orientation and makes more understandable the treatment of both as expressions of subjective probability of success in an area of achievement skill, as reported by Shrable and Moulton (1968) and discussed earlier in this chapter.

PSYCHOLOGICAL DISTANCE AND PERCEIVED INCENTIVE VALUE OF SUCCESS

With regard to the direct implications of an inverse relationship between incentive value of success and (total) subjective probability of success in a contingent path, it follows from the assumptions stated thus far that the value of an anticipated success is determined by its anticipated order of occurrence and by the particular values of subjective probability of success in the steps which intervene between the individual and the particular activity which can result in that future success. When the strength of achievement-related motives and the magnitudes of subjective probability of success are held constant, the incentive values of some anticipated future success should vary in direct proportion to the number of steps which intervene between the individual and that success. As the "psychological distance" between the individual and the success increases, so should the incentive value of that success, and vice versa. For example, if an individual were to succeed at the immediate activity in a contingent path, and the subjective probabilities of success in subsequent steps were not to change from what they were prior to that success, then the incentive value of the last anticipated success (or any other future anticipated success) should decrease. This apparent contradiction of a goal-gradient hypothesis (see Hull, 1932) should occur for the incentive value of success qua success in a contingent path, but not for the incentive value of an outcome which is determined by extrinsic concerns, such as anticipated money, power, or the approval of others, unless the anticipated size of these rewards is also inversely related to the total subjective probability of success in a contingent path. In addition, when achievement-related motives and the number of steps in a path are held constant, the greater the perceived difficulty of steps along the path which intervene between the individual and the particular anticipated success in question, the greater should be the perceived incentive value of that success. Both of these implications of the presumed inverse relationship between incentive value of success and (total) subjective probability of success should be subject to experimental tests, preferably in situations where the effects of extrinsic rewards are minimized so as to reduce their predicted shifts (which are generally opposite to those specified for achievement-related outcomes).

OPEN AND CLOSED CONTINGENT PATHS

In the present elaboration of theory, the degree or extent of an individual's future orientation is represented by the length of a path. This variable has been emphasized by Lewin (1951), Heckhausen (1967), and Nuttin (1964; see also Nuttin & Greenwald, 1968) among others, as an important determinant of human motivation. In particular, Nuttin (1964) has distinguished between two kinds of task: "Some tasks are accomplished by giving only one response to a situation or stimulus, while other(s) . . . remain unaccomplished after this first response because they have a further goal: something remains to be done: the response is only the first step [p. 73]." The former task is termed "closed," the latter "opened." The distinction between opened and closed tasks made by Nuttin corresponds to immediate activity of a one-step, as compared to a many-step, path in the present elaboration of theory. However, it fails to make the crucial distinction between contingent and noncontingent paths, which has already been shown to be important in the experimental analysis of achievement-oriented behavior.

There is another distinction that is appropriately dealt with by the use of open and closed path situations, that is, whether or not there is the possibility for new (not previously considered) striving in a contingent path as a consequence of an immediate success. Thus, an open contingent path is defined here as a series of steps in which the occurrence of each immediate success leads to the anticipation of one or more additional consequences of (new) immediate activity in the path which become apparent and add on to the end of the previously conceived path. Therefore the length of the path does not decrease when an individual achieves immediate success, but remains fixed or even increases in length as new possibilities for future achievement become apparent after an immediate success. A closed contingent path is defined here as a series of steps in which there is a clearly-defined final, or ultimate, goal (see Thomas & Zander, 1959) whose achievement is expected to signal the end of activity in that particular contingent path.

At this point it is necessary to again emphasize that when we refer to a contingent path with some values of subjective probability of success at each step in the path, we mean those values which are anticipated to exist in the future, as seen by the individual who is faced with immediate activity in the path. In following the dynamics of motivation as a function of continued immediate success in a contingent path, it is necessary to make assumptions concerning how these anticipated future levels of difficulty are affected by continued immediate success. These may be assumed to remain constant in order to simplify the calculation of total motivation sustaining (new) immediate activity as the individual moves successfully through the path (the issue is irrelevant in the face of immediate failure since subsequent striving in that path is ruled out). However, this is not a plausible assumption, since success will most likely increase the perceived chances of future success along the path. But since the theory is concerned only with the life space of the individual when confronted with the immediate next step in the path, these changes do not create any conceptual problems. They merely make it necessary to reapply the theory for each (new) activity that is confronted by the individual, taking into account those perceived levels of difficulty at each of the remaining steps in the path. The simplifying assumption of no change in subjective probability along the path as a function of continued success can be handled experimentally by appropriate instructions (see Raynor & Rubin, 1971, and Chapter 10), and therefore will be made here to keep the already complicated analysis at a manageable level. The reader can, however, anticipate that tests of the theory which do not insure a constant rather than changing cognitive structure with regard to perceived difficulty will have to take account of these changes in making predictions (see Raynor & Entin, 1972).

When other determinants of motivation are held constant, the initial strength of resultant achievement motivation for immediate activity in open and closed contingent paths will be equal when their lengths are equal. But after an initial success, the strength of motivation for (new) immediate activity will be greater in an open than in a closed contingent path, since the length of the closed path will have decreased while the length of the open path will have remained the same or even increased. This difference in relative strengths of motivation should be even greater after a second success, etc., because the length of the closed path will have further decreased, but not that of the open path. Thus after a series of immediate successes we should expect that differences in positive and negative achievement motivation of success-oriented and failure-threatened individuals will be much smaller for immediate activity in the closed path than for immediate activity in the open path.

After each success in the open path, the *success-oriented individual* should face the same or a greater number of possible future successes which provide continued interest and arouse additional components of positive achievement motivation, which compensate for the loss of motivation due to the achievement of immediate success. However, after each success in a closed path, he would face a decreasing number of potential opportunities to strive for success, resulting in an eventual loss of interest in immediate activity in the closed path as a function of continued success along the path. He might never reach the final goal (unless constrained to pursue it due to large extrinsic rewards contingent upon final goal attainment) because he might be motivated to select and initiate immediate activity in a different path which offers greater potential pride of accomplishment. An open path provides such an alternative. It also insures that continued shifting to seek out achievement-related activity that provides sufficient positive motivation can be eliminated. Therefore we expect that, other things equal, individuals primarily motivated to achieve success will learn to prefer and eventually will end up engaging in immediate activity in open (career) paths.

On the other hand, while the *failure-threatened individual* should initially be equally resistant to engaging in immediate achievement-oriented activity in open and closed contingent paths, he should encounter less resistance (i.e., experience less aroused inhibition and hence anxiety, since the former is assumed to produce the latter–see Atkinson, 1964, Ch. 10; see also Chapter 2) after an initial (unlikely) success in a closed than an open path. Other things equal, the failure-threatened individual should learn and come to prefer, when constrained to engage in achievement-oriented (career) activity, immediate behavior in closed contingent paths. He could then strive for those extrinsic rewards which are contingent upon (career) goal attainment, with minimal inhibition aroused by the inevitable tests of ability which contingent paths require at each step in order to continue.

INCREASING AND DECREASING PROBABILITY PATHS

Treatment of contingent paths thus far has assumed, for purposes of easier derivation of hypotheses using the algebraic statements of elaborated theory, that perceived difficulty is constant along a particular path. This need not be so, but the increased complexity resulting from consideration of all possible combinations of subjective probabilities of success along the path can be reduced if we consider two special cases. In one, perceived difficulty in the first step is low (i.e., subjective probability of success is high) but increases in regular fashion for each anticipated step, as seen by the individual when faced with the first step. In the other, perceived difficulty in the first step is high, but decreases in regular fashion for each anticipated step, as seen when faced with the first step.

These are termed, respectively, decreasing and increasing probability paths. By applying the equations of elaborated theory (which were used earlier to deal with constant probability paths, each having a different value of subjective probability of success), we find that the difference in positive and negative motivation sustaining immediate activity in long *decreasing* probability contingent paths is far greater than in long *increasing* probability paths. This leads to the prediction that success-oriented individuals should prefer and perform better in immediate activity in decreasing probability paths than increasing probability paths, whereas failure-threatened individuals, if constrained to do so, should prefer and perform better in those with increasing rather than decreasing probabilities.

INTRINSIC AND INSTRUMENTAL MOTIVATION

While the distinction between means and ends in this elaboration of theory is a quantitative matter, it is still useful to distinguish between *intrinsic* tendencies aroused by anticipation of immediate success and failure in skill activity, and *instrumental* tendencies aroused either by anticipation of future successes or failures, or by anticipation of future extrinsic outcomes. Referring back to the earlier discussion of means and ends, it can be said that immediate activity in a contingent path serves the individual both as a "means" with "instrumental value," in that immediate success is necessary in order to guarantee the opportunity to strive for future successes, and as an "end in itself" with "intrinsic value," in that immediate success is a desired possible consequence (see Thomas & Zander, 1959). The terms "intrinsic and instrumental tendencies" are used to refer to the components of motivation (i.e., component tendencies) aroused by anticipation of immediate and future consequences, respectively, with the exception that the term "immediate tendency" rather than "intrinsic tendency" is used when referring to motivation aroused by anticipation of an immediate extrinsic reward whose occurrence is dependent upon immediate success. The notion of an "intrinsic" (achievement-related) tendency is meant to convey the belief that the mere presentation of a skill task in which there is the possibility of success or failure in relation to some standard of excellence should arouse a component of resultant achievement motivation. However, the relative magnitude of this tendency is often small compared to the total of component instrumental tendencies presumed to be aroused in long contingent paths. The fact that many "life" contingent paths offer substantial extrinsic rewards should also be kept in mind (see Chapter 19), since predictions derived from this theory may be altered substantially by the concurrent arousal of extrinsic (immediate and instrumental) tendencies. It will be understood that all predictions concerning (total) resultant achievement motivation sustaining immediate activity in a contingent path presume a minimum of extrinsic motivation, unless otherwise specified.

Given the above interpretation of means-ends striving in conjunction with the concepts of intrinsic-instrumental motivation, it is worth noting here that prior to its elaboration, expectancy-value theory of achievement motivation had no concepts having the functional significance of "means" activity having instrumental "value." Thus the limitation of previous theory can now be viewed in a more general way. The behavior of a subject in a laboratory situation is not often related to the achievement of future success or failure, with "future" referring either to subsequent outcomes in that situation or in later "life" situations, thereby leading to the conclusion that its determinants, and behavior in general, might be adequately conceptualized merely in terms of tendencies aroused by the inherent properties of a task and the immediate rewards expected for participation in the experiment (see Chapter 2). However, many life situations require consideration of both intrinsic and instrumental (both achievement-related and extrinsic) tendencies because present performance is conceived by the individual as but a step in a (contingent) path to some future goal. Thus, for example, the college freshman who wants to become a psychologist and enrolls in an introductory psychology course might believe himself faced with the first step in a hierarchy of prerequisite courses which, if all goes well, will lead on to his chosen career (see Chapters 8 and 9). Previous theoretical accounts of the determinants of this immediate behavior were forced to deal with the total situation faced by the student as a one-step path, thus neglecting the role of instrumental motivation in determining immediate behavior, or, at the other extreme, considering immediate behavior as nothing but instrumental to the attainment of the future goal. While these points are made explicitly within the context of expectancy-value theory of motivated behavior–from the earlier Lewinian analysis to the initial theory of achievement motivation–the general criticism applies to most of motivational theory, with the exception of a few earlier positions already cited. Thus the theoretical analyses of Tolman (1932) and Hull (1932, 1935, 1937) are in fact applicable only to one-step situations, and then only if it is assumed that the value of a goal and its anticipated difficulty of attainment are either positively related or independent. The elaboration provided here, in its general form, can apply to any incentive system, which is of particular relevance for the field of social psychology, where immediate behavior that is studied is often related to important future goals of the individual.

CONCLUDING REMARKS

The present paper has traced the development and given some of the major implications of an elaboration of theory of achievement motivation (Raynor, 1968a, 1969) designed to overcome an important deficiency of previous statements of theory (Atkinson & Feather, 1966, Ch. 20; see also Chapter 2) which failed to distinguish between future and more immediately expected consequences of immediate activity. The concepts of contingent future orientation, instrumental value, and psychological distance, among others, have been identified within this elaboration. Implications and current evidence concerning immediate risk preference, performance level, and persistence have been discussed, as well as the effects of continued success on motivation along a path.

Murray and Kluckholm (1953) have suggested that one of the general functions of personality is "to form serial programs for the attainment of distant future goals [p. 39]." A serial program refers to the arrangements of subgoals which stretch into the future and which, if all goes well, will eventually lead to some desired end state (Hall & Lindzey, 1957, Ch. 5). The concept of serial program can readily be identified with the conception of a series of anticipated steps in a path leading on to some distant future goal that has been emphasized here in the definitions of noncontingent and contingent future orientation. The importance of *contingent* paths in the analysis of life striving is therefore seen as relating both to the functions of the individual to plan his immediate and long-term activity, and to those of society in general, which, after all, sets up those particular alternative contingent paths to the achievement of success in a culture, and provides the accepted standards of good performance and the "gatekeepers" to see that these standards are met in the pursuit of achievement goals (see Chapter 19 on motivation and career striving, where these points are further elaborated).

The study of future orientation in the context of theory and research on achievement motivation suggests the general point that attempts to create "ego-involvement" of subjects in laboratory experiments are successful to the extent to which they involve use of the subject's life goals, or those aspects of motivation related to them. Put another way, we must recognize the limitations of a laboratory psychology of motivation in simulating the conditions under which motivation of an individual is expressed in his life behavior. This is *not* to say that we should give up the control of artificially created situations to instead investigate the whole of an individual's life experiences "in the raw." Rather it suggests that we be modest in terms of the inferences that can be drawn from such experiments for when the individual is engaged in behavior as an interrelated series over time which is importantly related to attainment of goals that he has committed himself to pursue, for whatever reason (see Chapters 19 and 20). It further implies that we will never achieve a full understanding of human motivation if we are tied completely to the laboratory experiment. We must engage in conceptual analysis and perform experiments concerning motivation in life over a long period of time, taking advantage of the fact that such life situations often arouse the motivational constructs we seek to investigate. While the laboratory situation is "real," and would be ideal if we could reinstitute life goals and commitment to their pursuit under such circumstances without the subject being aware of taking part in an experiment, both ethical and practical considerations often make this impossible.

8

SUBJECTIVE ASPECTS OF ACHIEVEMENT MOTIVATION IMMEDIATELY BEFORE AN EXAMINATION[1]

Joel O. Raynor, John W. Atkinson, and Marvin Brown

The study of achievement motivation provides a promising opportunity for theoretical integration of traditionally disparate interests among psychologists. Some investigators are primarily concerned with the content and cognitive structure of an individual's goals and beliefs, what he has to say about himself, his objectives in life, or his conceptions of the causes of his own actions (e.g., Heckhausen, 1963; Nuttin, 1964; Weiner et al., 1971; Nisbett & Valins, 1971; Heckhausen & Weiner, 1972). Others, particularly those of us involved in this sustained program of research on the functional significance of individual differences in achievement-related dispositions of personality, have always been much more explicitly concerned with an individual's actions, *what he does when he knows that his performance will be evaluated.* Quite some time ago, McClelland (1955) argued for the development of a new psychology of mental content, one that would employ categories of analysis that have some systematic theoretical significance. We are encouraged to think that now is the time for serious efforts to bridge the conceptual gap between research concerned with the subjective aspects and the overt-behavioral aspects of achievement motivation.

In a sense, a first step toward such an integration was taken with the development of the projective measure of n Achievement (McClelland et al., 1953). Subsequent research using both this and the self-descriptive Test Anxiety Questionnaire (Mandler & Sarason, 1952) has been focused on developing theory

[1] This study was supported by grants from the National Science Foundation (GS-1399 to J.W.A. and GS-2863 to J.O.R.). A preliminary discussion of the results and their implications was presented at the 18th International Congress of Psychology in Moscow (Atkinson, 1966).

to explain how differences in personality inferred from these "subjective" measures and manipulable influences in the immediate environment *jointly* influence behavioral phenomena such as level of performance, risk preference, and persistence (see Chapter 2; Atkinson, 1964, Ch. 9; Atkinson & Feather, 1966). The present study is much more explicitly concerned with introspective reports of college students. They were asked to describe their own thoughts and feelings immediately before a final examination in a college course, the kind of achievement-oriented situation in which actions have been systematically studied. Candor was assured by a foolproof method of guaranteeing anonymity.

The present study was undertaken as those of us working out of the same ongoing research seminar began to see how an individual's perception of the relation of his immediate task to his own future goals might influence motivation for that activity (Raynor, 1967, 1969). Thus, it was possible to turn to an integration of the study of the process of motivation (already thought to be influenced by certain cognitive factors) to an explicit analysis of the content of the conscious experience of motivation using the systematic theory that had been worked out in studies of action as our guide.

The early theory of achievement motivation (Chapter 2), which had restricted attention to the immediate expected consequences of an activity, had already been challenged by the results of an unpublished study done by Isaacson and Raynor (1966) when the present study was being conceived. They had found that the differences in academic performance expected by the early theory of achievement motivation for persons who differed in strength of achievement-related motives tended to be accentuated when students conceived their present activity as also instrumental to the achievement of more distant future goals. The results of the study now to be described presented a similar challenge when the descriptive reports of the thoughts and feelings of students facing a final examination were related to both the conventional measures of achievement-related motives and to a measure of their perception of the relationship of the examination they were about to take to their own future goals. The result obtained is explicitly implied by the elaboration of the theory of achievement motivation (Chapter 7): whatever are found to be subjective correlates of an individual's characteristic achievement motivation should be intensified and individual differences should be accentuated when the task has important implications for the achievement of the individual's future goals.

Whether these subjective reactions would be expressions of the positive (M_S) and inhibitory (M_{AF}) motives taken separately or of their resultant strength ($M_S - M_{AF}$), as is overt action, was less clear. If the quality of subjective reactions obtained by introspective report is determined by each motive separately, those which might characterize an individual who is strongly motivated to achieve, such as concern about doing well, eagerness, and enthusiasm when faced with a test of ability, should be more clearly evident within such students who also perceive the exam as related to their future goals than among those who do not. And particular subjective reactions which might characterize an individual who is strongly inhibited by the threat of failure, such as anxiety, worry, and dread when faced with a test of ability, should be more clearly evident in such students who also perceive the exam as related to their own future goals than among those who do not.

On the other hand, if subjective reactions are expressions of resultant motivation, only those students who are primarily motivated to achieve ($M_S > M_{AF}$) should be relatively more concerned about doing well than anxious, more eager than worried, more enthusiastic than full of dread, and even more so when the exam is related to their future goals. For example, reports of concern about doing well in relation to reports of anxiety should be much greater for this group when the exam is viewed as important for future success than when it is not. Conversely, only students primarily inhibited by the threat of failure ($M_{AF} > M_S$) should be relatively more anxious than concerned about doing well, more worried than eager, more full of dread than enthusiastic, if subjective reaction is an expression of resultant motivation. They should become even more negatively concerned when the exam is related to their future goals. Thus, for example, the amount of anxiety reported in relation to concern about doing well should be much greater when the exam is important for future success than when it is not. Finally, students who are relatively indifferent to the alternative achievement-related outcomes ($M_S \approx M_{AF}$) should be about as concerned about doing well as they are anxious, as eager as worried, and they should not differ in these reactions whether the exam is related to their future goals or not.

Whether subjective reactions are related to the two achievement-related motives (M_S and M_{AF}) separately or jointly, we expect the differences in subjective reactions which characterize groups of students who differ in the two motives to be greater among those who perceive an examination as related to their own future goals than among those who do not.

METHOD

Assessment of Motives

A projective measure of n Achievement (McClelland et al., 1953) followed by the Test Anxiety Questionnaire (Mandler & Sarason, 1952) was administered in large testing sessions during the first part of the Fall semester (1965) to about 350 male college students enrolled in introductory psychology at the University of Michigan (see also Brown, Chapter 16, who used the same parent population). Pictures were presented in the following order to elicit stories: 2, 48, 1, 7, 100, 24 (see Atkinson, 1958a, Appendix III). Stories were scored for n Achievement in the usual manner (McClelland et al., 1953; Atkinson, 1958a, Ch. 12) by one of the authors (J.O.R.) who had already established his expertise by correlating above .90 with (*a*) the n Achievement practice materials (Smith & Feld, 1958) and (*b*) another expert scorer (see Raynor & Smith, 1966). Total scores on Test

Anxiety were obtained by summing scores for the individual items. The distributions of n Achievement and Test Anxiety scores were each broken at their median to obtain groups high and low on each measure. Students were also classified simultaneously high and low on both measures, creating four subgroups: those high on both measures (High-High), low on both (Low-Low), high on n Achievement and low on Test Anxiety (High-Low), and low on n Achievement and high on Test Anxiety (Low-High), as in earlier work (Chapter 2). The correlation between n Achievement and Test Anxiety in this sample was -.02 ($N = 324$).

Assessment of Subjective Reactions

As students who had been previously invited to come early appeared to take their final examination in introductory psychology, they were handed a questionnaire with the following set of general instructions:

> *Please take about 10 minutes to complete this questionnaire anonymously before beginning to work on your examination, if you are willing,* or sometime within the first half-hour of the exam, if you are unwilling to do it before beginning the exam. Your instructor has agreed to allow you extra time to complete your exam should it be necessary, so you will not be under unusual time pressure. May I remind you that this is a voluntary task and not a requirement of the course. I sincerely hope you are willing to do that and, particularly, before beginning the exam, for it is our judgment that introspections at that time would provide the most useful information. Wait until things settle down so that you are not distracted, or begin immediately if you are early. At the end of the period, deposit your unsigned questionnaire in the large envelope addressed to me on the desk up front. Then address the brown envelope to yourself and leave it, separately, among the other envelopes on the desk. I will send you a descriptive report in several months.
>
> Thank you.
>
> [Signed]
> John W. Atkinson
> Professor of Psychology

Three kinds of items were devised to assess students' subjective reactions. The first part of the questionnaire adapted a technique used by Nuttin (1964) to obtain introspective reports. It presented a series of incomplete sentences:

Right now, I . . .
I feel . . .
I hope . . .
I expect . . .
In a couple of hours . . .
This final exam . . .

Below each was a space of about an inch for students to complete the sentences, which were introduced by these written instructions:

> Use common everyday language. Use the words and phrases that best describe your thoughts and feelings to *complete* the following sentences:

The next part of the inquiry consisted of a series of more structured, self-descriptive items. Below each appeared a graphic rating scale subdivided into six equal parts. Students were instructed:

> For the following questions, put an X on that point on the line which best indicates the strength of your feeling right now. Put the mark anyplace along the line.

The word "Midpoint" appeared below in the middle of the line, and appropriate statements anchored the ends of each rating scale. The items relevant to the present paper and the anchoring statements were as follows: To what extent do you feel enthusiastic about the exam? (Feel very enthusiastic, Do not feel at all enthusiastic); To what extent are you worried? (Not at all, A lot); To what extent are your feelings related to how others will react to your exam grade? (Not at all related to how others will react, Very much related to how others will react); To what extent is the exam important for your own self-evaluation? (Not at all important for self-evaluation, Very important for self-evaluation).

The last item in the questionnaire read as follows:

> The way I feel about the exam, compared to how I generally feel is (check one):
>
> ____less involved and less interested than usual.
> ____more feeling of dread and apprehension than usual.
> ____more feeling of eagerness and enthusiasm than usual.

At the bottom of the questionnaire was a place to mark whether the introspective questionnaire was completed before the exam or, if not, how many minutes after the exam started.

Anonymity

Each student had been handed a questionnaire with a code number which identified his appropriate motive classification but which otherwise guaranteed his anonymity. The *E*s were unaware of the motivation classification during their content analysis of results. Of the 191 students who were invited to participate, 152 (80%) returned completed questionnaires: 82% of the High-Low group, 85% of the High-High group, 73% of the Low-Low group, and 78% of the Low-High group.

Content Analysis of Introspective Reports

Each student's completions of all open-ended sentences were scored for the presence of two kinds of content: statements indicating (A) concern over doing well and/or getting a good grade; (B) descriptions of states of anxiety that were either unqualified or elaborated in intensity. For each subject a score of 1 was given for the presence of a category, while a score of 0 was given for its absence. Responses to the sentence "In a couple of hours . . . " were scored 1 for the presence of statements indicating achievement interest such as (C) "working again" or 0 for its absence, and 1 for an indication that the subject would (D) be "relieved, happy, or relaxed" or 0 for its absence.

Protocols were scored, one category at a time, by two independent judges (J.W.A. and K.B.W.)[2] with a 5-year interval between codings. The percentage agreements for the presence of statements in each category for the entire sample of completed questionnaires ($N = 152$) were as follows: (A) 89%, (B) 93%, (C) 87%, (D) 91%.

Assessment of Future Relatedness

The relatedness or *Perceived Instrumentality* (PI) of the exam to a student's future goals was inferred from his response to the question "To what extent does your exam performance relate to your own future goals?" Students were divided into three groups: scores of 1 and 2 were considered low, scores of 3 and 4 were considered intermediate, and scores of 5 and 6 were considered high.

Treatment of the Data

Several indices were developed from the questionnaire responses to reflect a student's subjective reactions. One kind simply consisted of the raw scores obtained from the content analysis of the sentence completions (scores A, B, C, and D above) and the scores obtained from the graphic rating scale items. A second kind consisted of composite scores reflecting the predominate reaction of an individual. This includes the scoring of responses to the final question concerning present feeling as compared to usual feeling.

The composite measure obtained from the sentence completions reflected a student's concern about doing well and/or getting a good grade (score A) relative to his report of unqualified or elaborated anxiety (score B): +1 was given for the presence of score A coupled with the absence of score B; −1 was given for the absence of score A coupled with the presence of score B; 0 was given for either the presence or absence of both scores A and B. Thus, a positive score reflects relatively more concern about doing well than anxiety, a negative score reflects greater anxious concern, and a 0 score reflects equivalence of the two reactions. The more positive a group mean, the greater is the concern about doing well relative to anxiety. The more negative a group mean, the greater is the anxiety relative to concern about doing well.

Another composite measure reflected a student's enthusiasm in relation to his worry, as indicated by the scale for the objective items. First, responses for enthusiasm were categorized so that scores of 1, 2, or 3 were considered to indicate high enthusiasm, and scores of 4, 5, and 6 were considered to indicate low enthusiasm. Responses to the item dealing with amount of worry were also categorized. Scores of 1, 2, and 3 were considered to indicate a high degree of worry, and scores of 4, 5, and 6 were considered to indicate a low degree of worry. Then a student was given a score of +1 if high in enthusiasm and low in worry, a score of −1 if low in enthusiasm and high in worry, and a score of 0 if

[2] The authors thank Kenneth B. Wegman for scoring the protocols to obtain the reliability checks.

either high or low on both enthusiasm and worry. Interpretation of these indices is analogous to that described earlier for the composite measures reflecting concern about doing well relative to reported anxiety.

For the last item, which focused upon present feelings compared to usual feelings, a score of +1 was given if the student checked the response "more feeling of eagerness and enthusiasm than usual," a score of 0 was given for checking "less involved and less interested than usual," and a score of −1 was given for checking "more feeling of dread and apprehension than usual."

In summary, each composite measure reflects a continuum of positive relative to negative resultant affective reaction to the examination. The more positive a mean for a group of students, the greater is the dominance of positive over negative subjective reactions. The more negative a mean for a group, the greater is the dominance of negative over positive subjective reactions.

RESULTS

Table 1 presents the percentage of students in each motive group that indicated concern about doing well and/or getting a good grade in their sentence completions. Both motives influenced the results. Students high in n Achievement, low in Test Anxiety, and particularly those classified simultaneously as high n Achievement-low Test Anxiety (the High-Low group) showed much greater concern about doing well when the exam was perceived as highly instrumental to future goals than when it was not. The significance of the predicted trends between those highest and lowest in PI were $p < .05$ for those high in n Achievement ($t = 1.93, df = 146$); $p < .005$ for those low in Test Anxiety ($t = 3.09$, $df = 146$); and $p < .01$ for those classified high n Achievement-low Test Anxiety ($t = 2.61, df = 140$).

Among those who viewed the exam as importantly related to their future goals (i.e., high PI) those high in n Achievement tended to express more concern about doing well and getting good grades than those low in n Achievement ($t = 1.29$, $df = 146$, $p < .10$ in this direction); those high in Test Anxiety tended to express this concern less frequently than those low in Test Anxiety ($t = 1.62$, $df = 146$, $p < .10$ in this direction); and for the extremes in resultant achievement motivation, High-Low versus Low-High, the expected difference was significant ($t = 1.82, df = 140, p < .05$).

The expected interaction involving strength of motives and the extreme groups on PI, though apparently quite substantial in each case, approached statistical significance ($p < .10$) only for the comparisons including the measure of Test Anxiety.

Table 2 shows that students high in Test Anxiety, low in n Achievement, and particularly those low in n Achievement and high in Test Anxiety (the Low-High group), increase in expression of felt anxiety as the exam is perceived more instrumental to future goals. In the latter case the expected trend is significant ($t = 2.26$, $df = 140, p < .025$). When PI is high, the expected difference between

TABLE 1

Effect of Individual Differences in n Achievement, Test Anxiety, and Perceived Instrumentality of a Final Exam to Future Goals on the Percentage of Subjects Indicating Subjective Concern about Doing Well and/or Getting a Good Grade (Score A) in Sentence Completions

	Perceived Instrumentality of exam						
	Low		Intermediate		High		Difference
	N	Mean	*N*	Mean	*N*	Mean	H–L
n Achievement							
High	24	54%	29	66%	31	83%	29%
Low	27	56	17	41	24	63	07
Difference H–L		-02		25		20	22
Test Anxiety							
High	20	60	28	57	34	65	05
Low	31	52	18	56	21	86	31
Difference H–L		12		01		-21	-26
n Achievement–Test Anxiety							
High-Low	15	47	9	56	16	94	47
High-High	9	67	20	70	15	67	00
Low-Low	16	56	9	56	5	60	04
Low-High	11	55	8	25	19	63	08
Difference (H-L)–(L-H)		-08		31		31	39

TABLE 2

Effect of Individual Differences in n Achievement, Test Anxiety, and Perceived Instrumentality of a Final Exam to Future Goals on the Percentage of Subjects Indicating Expression of Unqualified or Elaborated Anxiety (Score B) in Sentence Completions

	Perceived Instrumentality of exam						
	Low		Intermediate		High		Difference
	N	Mean	*N*	Mean	*N*	Mean	H–L
n Achievement							
High	24	33%	29	48%	31	52%	19%
Low	27	33	17	35	24	71	38
Difference H–L		00		13		-19	-19
Test Anxiety							
High	20	40	28	54	34	74	34
Low	31	40	18	28	21	38	-02
Difference H–L		00		26		36	36
n Achievement–Test Anxiety							
High-Low	15	27	9	22	16	38	11
High-High	9	44	20	60	15	67	23
Low-Low	16	31	9	33	5	40	11
Low-High	11	36	8	38	19	79	43
Difference (H-L)–(L-H)		-09		-16		-41	-32

TABLE 3

Mean Composite Scores (A and B) Indicating Concern about Doing Well and/or Getting a Good Grade (+) Relative to Unqualified or Elaborated Anxiety (−) in the Sentence Completions

	Perceived Instrumentality of exam						
	Low		Intermediate		High		Difference
	N	Mean	*N*	Mean	*N*	Mean	H−L
n Achievement							
High	24	.21	29	.17	31	.29	.08
Low	27	.22	17	.12	24	-.08	-.30
Difference H−L		-.01		.05		.37	.38
Test Anxiety							
High	20	.20	28	.04	34	-.09	-.29
Low	31	.23	18	.33	21	.48	.25
Difference H−L		-.03		-.37		-.57	-.54
n Achievement–Test Anxiety							
High-Low	15	.20	9	.33	16	.56	.36
High-High	9	.22	20	.10	15	.00	-.22
Low-Low	16	.25	9	.33	5	.21	-.04
Low-High	11	.18	8	-.13	19	-.16	-.34
Difference (H-L)−(L-H)		.02		.46		.72	.70

the extreme motivational groups (High-Low versus Low-High) is significant (t = 2.41, df = 140, $p < .005$).

The clearest picture of the interactive influence of the motives of an individual and his conception of the instrumentality of the immediate task to future goals is shown in Table 3. Here we make use of the composite measure indicating concern about doing well (+) relative to expression of anxiety (-). When *S*s are classified in terms of n Achievement by itself or Test Anxiety by itself, we see the by now familiar diametrically opposite trends as perceived instrumentality (PI) increases. It is most dramatically apparent when the most extreme groups are compared. Among *S*s classified High n Achievement-Low Test Anxiety, there is a regular increase in concern about doing well relative to anxiety from low to intermediate to high PI. The increase of .36 (comparing high versus low PI) approaches significance (t = 1.57, df = 140, $p < .10$ in this direction). For those classified Low n Achievement-High Test Anxiety, there is just as regular an increase in reported anxiety relative to concern about doing well from low to intermediate to high PI. The decrease of -.34 (comparing high versus low PI) is also fairly reliable (t = 1.36, df = 140, $p < .10$ in this direction). The difference between these diametrically opposite trends of the two extreme motive groups, +.36 versus -.34, is statistically significant (t = 2.06, df = 140, $p < .025$, one-tailed test).

Within the group of *S*s who view the exam as highly instrumental to future goals, those simultaneously high in n Achievement and low in Test Anxiety feel much more concerned about doing well than anxious (.56), while the feelings of those low in n Achievement and high in Test Anxiety lean the other way (-.16) (t = 3.27, df = 140, $p < .001$, in predicted direction). The other two groups, more equivalent in relative strength of the two opposing motives, fall between these significantly different extremes. On the other hand, among those for whom PI is low, the four motivational subgroups are not ordered as expected, and the differences among them are negligible. When PI is intermediate, the motive subgroups are ordered as when PI is high and the difference between the extreme groups H-L (.33) versus L-H (-.13) begins to appear (t = 1.48, df = 140, $p < .10$ in this direction).

Scores indicating mean enthusiasm and worry, and enthusiasm relative to worry, were analyzed as a function of motive groups and standing on PI. None of the overall analyses of variance revealed significant effects, and specific comparisons failed to reveal any differences in the predicted direction that approached significance. In short, there is no evidence that either motives or standing on PI influenced self-description of enthusiasm and worry taken alone or in terms of a composite measure reflecting resultant reaction. The same was true when n Achievement and Test Anxiety were employed separately for motive classification.

Table 4 presents mean composite scores derived from the last question which reflect relative eagerness and enthusiasm (+), involvement and interest (0), and dread and apprehension (-) felt about the exam in comparison to how the

TABLE 4

Mean of Measure Indicating More Eagerness and Enthusiasm (+1), Less Involved and Interested (0), or More Feeling of Dread and Apprehension (−1) than Usual When Asked for Comparison of Feeling before the Exam with Usual Feeling

	Perceived Instrumentality of exam						
	Low		Intermediate		High		Difference
	N	Mean	*N*	Mean	*N*	Mean	H−L
n Achievement							
High	23[a]	−.17	28[a]	−.43	30[a]	−.30	−.13
Low	26[a]	−.04	17	−.24	23[a]	−.35	−.31
Difference H−L		−.13		−.19		.05	.18
Test Anxiety							
High	20	.10	27[a]	−.37	33[a]	−.33	−.44
Low	29[b]	−.26	18	−.33	20[a]	−.35	−.09
Difference H−L		.36		−.04		.02	−.35
n Achievement–Test Anxiety							
High-Low	14[a]	−.21	9[a]	−.44	16	−.38	−.17
High-High	9	−.11	19	−.42	14[a]	−.22	−.11
Low-Low	15[a]	−.13	9	−.22	4[a]	−.25	−.12
Low-High	11	.27	8	−.25	19	−.37	−.64
Difference (H-L)−(L-H)		−.48		.19		.01	.47

[a]One subject in this group did not answer this question or checked more than one of the three possible responses.
[b]Two subjects had missing data in this group.

students usually feel. On the whole, it is apparent that students tend to feel more apprehension and dread immediately before a final examination than they usually do. All *S*s tended to feel more dread and apprehension when PI was high than low. This trend is most dramatic among those classified low n achievement-high Test Anxiety, for whom the difference was −.64 ($t = 1.69$, $df = 134$, $p < .05$ in this direction).

Two additional questions were included. One asked, "To what extent are your feelings related to how others will react to your exam grade?" (See Table 5.) The other asked, "To what extent is the exam important to you for your own self-evaluation?" (See Table 6.) Each involved self-rating on a six-point scale.

Most obvious and easily interpreted are results in Table 5 concerning the influence of both Test Anxiety and Perceived Instrumentality on how feelings are related to how others will react to the exam grade. Analysis of variance among all groups in Table 5 in the Test Anxiety comparison showed that both main effects, Test Anxiety ($F = 13.37$, $df = 1$ and 146, $p < .001$) and PI ($F = 7.13$, $df = 2$ and 146, $p < .01$) were significant.[3]

In Table 6, concerning importance of the exam for self-evaluation, the ratings are generally substantially higher than those concerning importance of the reaction of others, but only the main effect of PI is statistically significant ($F = 8.11$, $df = 2$ and 149, $p < .001$). As PI increases, so does the importance of the exam for self-evaluation.

In response to the incomplete sentence, "In a couple of hours . . . ," those high in n Achievement and the high n Achievement-low Test Anxiety subgroup indicated, within each level of PI, that they would be working again (Score C) to a greater extent than those low in n Achievement and low n Achievement-high Test Anxiety respectively ($F = 5.69$, $df = 1$ and 72, $p < .025$, and $F = 10.37$, $df = 1$ and 146, $p < .01$, respectively). None of the differences attributable to Test Anxiety, the PI of this particular exam, nor any of the interactions were significant. This would appear to indicate that quite independently of the present activity, those who are highly motivated to achieve normally anticipate spending more time than others in achievement-oriented activity (see Chapter 15). None of the comparisons indicating "relief, happiness, or relaxation" in response to this question (Score D) yielded significant differences.

DISCUSSION

The introspective reports obtained from the sentence completions immediately before a final examination in a college course suggest that the resultant strength of achievement-related motives ($M_S - M_{AF}$) and PI interact to influence both concern about doing well and the feeling of anxiety. This pattern

[3]The interactions involving motivation and PI were significant in the other two comparisons but are less easily interpreted.

TABLE 5

Mean Scores Concerning the Extent to Which Feelings Are Related to How Others Will React to the Exam Grade

	Perceived Instrumentality						
	Low		Intermediate		High		Difference
	N	Mean	*N*	Mean	*N*	Mean	H–L
n Achievement							
High	24	2.38	29	3.62	31	3.23	.85
Low	27	2.89	17	2.47	24	3.79	.90
Difference H–L		-.51		1.15		-.56	-.05
Test Anxiety							
High	20	2.55	28	3.57	34	4.12	1.57
Low	31	2.71	18	2.61	21	2.43	.28
Difference H–L		-.16		.96		1.69	1.29
n Achievement–Test Anxiety							
High-Low	15	2.20	9	2.89	16	2.38	.18
High-High	9	2.67	20	3.95	15	4.13	1.46
Low-Low	16	3.19	9	2.33	5	2.60	-.59
Low-High	11	2.45	8	2.25	19	4.11	1.66
Difference (H-L)–(L-H)		-.25		.64		-1.73	-1.48

TABLE 6

Mean Scores Concerning the Extent to Which the Exam Is Felt Important for Student's Own Self-Evaluation

	Perceived Instrumentality					
	Low		Intermediate		High	
	N	Mean	N	Mean	N	Mean
n Achievement						
High	24	3.75	29	4.38	31	4.48
Low	27	2.89	17	4.24	24	4.71
Test Anxiety						
High	20	3.40	28	4.36	34	4.74
Low	31	3.23	18	4.28	21	4.33
n Achievement-Test Anxiety						
High-Low	15	3.67	9	4.33	16	4.38
High-High	9	3.89	20	4.40	15	4.60
Low-Low	16	2.81	9	4.22	5	4.20
Low-High	11	3.00	8	4.25	19	4.84

of results is consistent with the expectation that an individual's characteristic achievement-related motivation will be accentuated when success in an immediate test is perceived as instrumental to achievement of future goals.

There is rarely, if ever, a significant difference in the subjective descriptions of the motivational state when PI is low or even moderate. This does not necessarily mean that there is no difference. One must be mindful of the crudity of the tools we use to diagnose motivational differences and the crudity of the introspective report as a measure of the subjective state. Given crude measuring instruments, only substantial differences in the strength of motivation are recorded as significant differences with a small sample of cases. And these substantial differences occur where they are expected to occur. As elaborated in Chapter 7, the theory of achievement motivation predicts accentuation of whatever are the typical differences among people in subjective aspects of motivation when the present activity is perceived as a step in a contingent path in which present success is believed necessary to continue the pursuit of more distant future goals.

There are no surprises in the descriptive characteristics of the subjective state of persons in whom $M_S > M_{AF}$ and $M_{AF} > M_S$. We get from these direct introspective reports essentially the same conception of the subjective state of motivation of the more positively motivated person that is suggested by the achievement-related concerns expressed as achievement imagery in imaginative stories. And the unqualified and elaborated reports of felt anxiety correspond closely to what the person who scores high in Test Anxiety says about himself retrospectively in taking that test. Here we have the inside view of the effect of future orientation on motivation to complement the overt-behavioral consequences that have been reported concerning academic performance (Isaacson & Raynor, 1966; Raynor, 1970, and Chapter 9) and level of performance on specific tasks (Raynor & Rubin, 1971, and Chapter 10; Entin & Raynor, 1973; Raynor & Sorrentino, 1972). Although the results of some studies do not fit the pattern (see Raynor, 1968b; also the second study reported in Raynor, 1970, and Chapter 9), and some details of others deviate from the expected pattern, the theoretical elaboration in Chapter 7 seems the most coherent explanation for the results of research thus far conducted.

It should be noted that in both the Isaacson and Raynor (1966) and the present study, the ratings of the relationship between immediate activity and future goals were obtained at the end of the semester rather than at the beginning. However, results reported by Raynor (1970) which replicate the interaction effects reported by Isaacson and Raynor (1966) suggest quite clearly that whether these ratings are obtained at the beginning or at the end of the semester does not influence their functional significance.

Results for the questions concerning "importance for self-evaluation" and "feelings dependent upon reactions of others to the exam," both of which showed an increase in mean score with an increase in PI, provide independent evidence that those who rate the exam as important for their own future goals (high PI) face a more "ego-involving" situation than those who rate the exam as unimportant for their own future goals. The "importance" of the exam for a person's evaluation of himself increases with an increase in the relatedness of the exam to future goals. For some individuals this implies greater concern about doing well and higher positive self-evaluation (those who are success-oriented). For others, who are threatened by failure, heightened concern about self-evaluation is associated with an increase in reported anxiety implying the greater weighting of negative feelings.

The results of the present research may have important implications for the assessment of individual differences in achievement-related personality dispositions. Typically, we have administered the TAT measure of n Achievement under *neutral* conditions, in which nothing is done either to arouse or to reduce achievement motivation. The present findings suggest that the situation which allows for the greatest discrimination between reactions of individuals who differ in strength of achievement-related motives involves an explicit relationship between immediate performance and *their own* future goals. A diagnostic test which maximally discriminates the resultant achievement motivation of individuals will obviously enhance the prediction of other behavioral differences which are directly proportionate to resultant achievement motivation. Other things held constant, both the reliability and validity of measures of individual differences in achievement-related dispositions should be increased if they are assessed in the context of behavior that is related to an individual's future goals. To do this in a group administration might require that there be some homogeneity in future goals.

Perhaps the Test Anxiety Questionnaire generally provides a more sensitive and reliable indicator of individual differences in motivation than TAT n Achievement because *S*s are specifically asked to report how they feel taking intelligence tests as well as examinations in courses. The set for retrospective description of one's own feelings may focus more sharply on episodes in which there typically is future orientation than the usual neutral classroom atmosphere in administration of the TAT to assess n Achievement.

Data for the two composite measures obtained from the structured items reveal a pattern of interaction between extreme motive groups and standing on PI which is generally similar to that obtained from the composite measure of the sentence completions, except that the former tend to reduce an apparent reversal of expected differences between motive groups within low PI rather than to accentuate the generally expected differences within high PI. The results for the structured items also fail to yield statistically reliable interaction effects. This may merely reflect the fact that the structured items came later in the questionnaire, and represent some kind of sequence effect, or it may indicate that the coding of emitted reactions provides a superior measure of the subjective motivational state of an individual. Since the questionnaire was designed with the specific purpose of getting at subjective reactions using the open-ended technique developed by Nuttin (1964), and the more structured items were included only as a secondary interest, their equivocal interpretation reflects our primary concern with the first rather than the second part of the data collected.

9

RELATIONSHIPS BETWEEN ACHIEVEMENT-RELATED MOTIVES, FUTURE ORIENTATION, AND ACADEMIC PERFORMANCE[1]

Joel O. Raynor[2]

Prior to a recent elaboration (Raynor, 1969; see also Chapter 7) the theory of achievement motivation (Atkinson & Feather, 1966, Ch. 20; see also Chapter 2) concerned only immediately expected success and failure as achievement-related consequences of an activity. This elaboration of theory, however, takes into account the important effects of expected future outcomes on the strength of motivation of the task or activity immediately confronting the individual. The present study concerns the prediction of current academic performance as a joint function of a student's achievement-related motives and his conception of a relationship between his grades and his own future career success. Hypotheses are derived from this elaboration of theory of achievement motivation (see Chapter 7).

A student in whom the motive to achieve success is stronger than the motive to avoid failure ($M_S > M_{AF}$) should be more motivated to achieve and hence should receive a higher course grade when the grade is related to his future career

[1] Reprinted and abridged by permission of the author and the American Psychological Association from the *Journal of Personality and Social Psychology,* 1970, **15**, 28–33.

[2] Data reported in this paper were included in an unpublished doctoral dissertation (Raynor, 1968a) carried out at the University of Michigan as part of a continuing program of research on achievement motivation supported by a grant (GS-1399) from the National Science Foundation to John W. Atkinson, chairman of the doctoral committee. The first was conducted with support from the United States Office of Education Research Contract SAE-8451 to W. J. McKeachie, J. E. Milholland, and R. L. Isaacson. The second was carried out while the author held a research fellowship from the National Institute of Mental Health, United States Public Health Service. Preliminary results of the first study were presented in an earlier, unpublished paper (Raynor, 1967). The author wishes to thank James W. Julian and Bernard Weiner for their helpful editorial comments on the manuscript.

success than when it is not. Anticipation of other future rewards (money, power, or the approval of others) as a result of future career success should further accentuate this predicted superiority. On the other hand, a student in whom the motive to avoid failure is stronger than the motive to achieve success ($M_{AF} > M_S$) should be more inhibited and hence receive a lower course grade when the grade is related to his future career success than when it is not. However, other incentives dependent upon future career success may arouse motivation which is sufficiently positive to overcome inhibition caused by the possibility of future career failure. In this instance the theory cannot make predictions unless the relative strengths of (inhibitory) achievement-related motivation and other (excitatory) motivation are known. Nevertheless, the increment in total positive tendency which is aroused by the perceived relation between good performance in the course and the achievement of future goals should be greater for students in whom $M_S > M_{AF}$ than for the opposite motivation group. It is therefore predicted that (*a*) students with $M_S > M_{AF}$ who conceive a course to be related to future career success should receive a higher grade than those who do not, and (*b*) this difference in grades should be greater for students with $M_S > M_{AF}$ than for those with $M_{AF} > M_S$.

Two studies are reported using an extension of the procedures described by Isaacson and Raynor (1966). Tests of n Achievement and test anxiety were used in both studies. Students classified simultaneously high in n Achievement and low in test anxiety (the High-Low group) were assumed to have $M_S > M_{AF}$. Given the student population from which subjects were drawn, the majority of those low in n Achievement and high in test anxiety (the Low-High group) were assumed to have equal strengths of the two motives; only a minority of this group should have $M_{AF} > M_S$ (see Atkinson & Feather, 1966, p. 342). Failure to obtain a substantial number of subjects with $M_{AF} > M_S$ in a particular sample would tend to attenuate the strength of relationships between the motive measures and academic performance predicted here.

STUDY I

Method

Subjects. Sixty-nine men and 52 women enrolled in an introductory psychology course (Psychology as a Social Science) at the University of Michigan participated in separate testing sessions during the first half of the semester as part of their course requirement.

Assessment of motives. The thematic apperceptive measure of n Achievement (McClelland, Atkinson, Clark, & Lowell, 1953) was administered first, following the standard procedures described by Atkinson (1958a, Appendix III). Six pictures were shown in the following order to elicit stories: 2, 48, 1, 7, 100, 24. Numbers are from Atkinson (1958a, Appendix III). n Achievement scores were obtained in the usual manner (see McClelland, Atkinson, Clark, & Lowell,

1958). The *r*s between scores of the author and the suggested practice materials (Atkinson, 1958a, Appendix I), and an expert scorer (see Raynor & Smith, 1966), have been established at above .90.

The Mandler-Sarason (1952) Test Anxiety Questionnaire (TAQ) was administered next. Below each item was a graphic rating scale subdivided into five equal parts. Items were scored so that a 5 indicated highest and a 1 indicated lowest amount of anxiety. A total Test Anxiety score was obtained by summing scores for the individual items.

The product-moment correlation between n Achievement and Test Anxiety scores was $-.05$ ($N = 67$) for males and .13 ($N = 52$) for females.

Assessment of perceived instrumentality of grades. A Student Plans Questionnaire was then administered. One question asked, "How important to you is getting a good grade in introductory psychology for having your career plans work out?" Five statements describing various degrees of importance were provided: very important, important, fairly important, not too important, and not at all important. These were scored so that 1 indicated highest and 5 indicated lowest rated importance. Another asked, "To what extent do you believe getting a good grade in the introductory psychology course will help you to do well in your chosen career?" Four statements describing various degrees of helpfulness were provided: A score of 1 was given "be a great help," 2 was given "be of some help," 3 was given "be of little help," and 4 was given "practically irrelevant." A total score was obtained by summing the scores from the two questions. The lower the score the greater the perceived instrumentality of a good grade in introductory psychology for future career success (PI-Psych). Those students below the median on PI-Psych were assumed to face a contingent path, while those students above were assumed to face a noncontingent path, relating the introductory psychology course to future career success.

Treatment of the data. Grades were obtained at the end of the semester. They were treated numerically so that the higher the letter grade, the higher the number: A = 4, B = 3, C = 2, D = 1, F = 0. Comparison of mean scores between men and women did not reveal significant differences in n Achievement, test anxiety, PI-Psych, or grades. Therefore, high and low groups were obtained by using the combined group median for each variable (except grades). Mean grades in introductory psychology were then analyzed for men and women separately. Analysis of variance indicated that sex was not significantly related to grades, either alone or in interaction with motives and/or PI. Inspection of the data indicated that the pattern of results for the two sexes was in general similar. Since male and female students did not differ significantly on any variables, their data were combined for all subsequent analyses. Hypotheses were evaluated by means of a priori comparisons using the within-cell error (weighted by the number of subjects in each comparison) and the degrees of freedom of the appropriate analysis of variance (see Winer, 1962, p. 244).

Results

Table 1 presents the mean grades in introductory psychology in terms of the combined motive classification and PI-Psych. Analysis of variance reveals a significant effect due to motives ($F = 5.56$, $df = 1/58$, $p < .05$). There is also a significant interaction between motives and PI-Psych ($F = 5.24$, $df = 1/58$, $p < .05$). The pattern of results in Table 1 indicates that the High-Low group received higher grades than the Low-High group, but only within high PI. PI-Psych by itself was not related to grades ($F < 1$, $df = 1/58$, *ns*). As predicted, within the High-Low group students high in PI-Psych received higher grades than students low in PI-Psych ($t = 1.76$, $df = 58$, $p < .05$).[3] Also as predicted, the difference in grades between high and low PI-Psych was larger in the positive direction (high-low) for the High-Low than for the Low-High group ($t = 2.29$, $df = 58$, $p < .025$).

STUDY II

Method

Subjects. Male college students from two introductory psychology courses at the University of Michigan were tested using procedures which were similar to those of Study I.

Assessment of motives. The thematic apperceptive measure of n Achievement was administered first, followed by the TAQ and the Student Plans Questionnaire. Pictures used to elicit TAT stories were the same as described in Study I, and were presented in the same order. The TAQ was administered and scored as before. The product-moment correlation between n Achievement and Test Anxiety scores was $-.007$ ($N = 199$).

Assessment of perceived instrumentality of grades. The Student Plans Questionnaire differed somewhat from that used in the first study. The critical question read, "... please list each of the courses that you are taking for credit

[3] *p* values of *t* tests are for one-tailed levels of significance.

TABLE 1

Study I:
Mean Grades in Introductory Psychology as a Function of Achievement-Related Motives and Perceived Instrumentality

n Achievement-test anxiety	Perceived instrumentality (PI-Psych)			
	N	Low	*N*	High
High-Low	15	2.93	19	3.37
Low-High	11	3.00	17	2.59

this semester in the left column below. Then indicate opposite each course how important to you is getting a good grade in that course for having your future career plans work out." Opposite each space appeared the five degrees of importance described previously. In this way a rating was obtained for each student of the importance of a good grade for future career success in each of the courses taken in the semester.

Treatment of the data. Several indexes of PI were obtained. Of the 168 subjects then enrolled in introductory psychology, 81 rated the course as either "very important" or "important" and were considered high in PI-Psych; the remainder were called low. Thus, as in Study I it was possible to evaluate the relationship between achievement-related motives and grades in this course with its rating of PI taken into account.

In addition, a PI score was calculated for each student's 3-or-more-credit courses. This index was taken to represent a rating of the PI of the grade-point average obtained in the semester for future career success (PI-GPA). It made possible a test of the relationship between achievement-related motives and the grade point average for the semester with ratings of PI-GPA taken into account.

Finally, students who rated at least one course as either "very important" or "important" (a high-PI course), and at least one course as "not too important" or "not at all important" (a low-PI course), were identified. Only 94 out of 189 subjects for whom complete data were available fulfilled this criterion. The grade-point averages for each subject's high- and low-PI courses were then calculated separately. This made it possible to evaluate the relationship between academic performance in high- and low-PI courses for different motive groups, using each subject as his own control.

Results

For grades in introductory psychology. The mean grades in introductory psychology are presented in Table 2. The analysis of variance reveals a significant effect due to PI-Psych ($F = 6.18$, $df = 1/77$, $p < .05$). Both motive groups received higher grades within high than within low PI-Psych. There is also an interaction between motives and PI-Psych ($F = 3.84$, $df = 1/77$, $p < .10$). Within

TABLE 2

Study II:
Mean Grades in Introductory Psychology as a Function of Achievement-Related Motives and Perceived Instrumentality

n Achievement-test anxiety	Perceived instrumentality (PI-Psych)			
	N	Low	*N*	High
High-Low	21	2.95	20	3.50
Low-High	16	3.38	24	3.42

the High-Low group, students high in PI-Psych received higher grades than students low in PI-Psych ($t = 3.06$, $df = 77$, $p < .005$), and the difference in grades between high and low PI-Psych is larger for this group than for the Low-High group ($t = 1.96$, $df = 77$, $p < .05$). However, motive classification by itself is not related to grades ($F = 1.29$, $df = 1/77$, *ns*). Inspection of Table 2 indicates that contrary to Study I, the High-Low group did not receive substantially higher grades than the Low-High group within high PI-Psych. As in the first study, within low PI-Psych the High-Low group received *lower* grades than the Low-High group.

For the grade point average: Between-subjects design. Analysis of variance reveals a main effect due to PI-GPA ($F = 2.95$, $df = 1/97$, $p < .10$), while the effect of motive classification and the interaction between motives and PI-PGA are both negligible (*F*s < 1). The High-Low group received higher overall grades for the semester when they were high (2.89) than when they were low (2.62) in PI-GPA ($t = 1.64$, $df = 97$, $p < .06$). However, the difference in grades between groups high and low in PI-GPA was not significantly greater for the High-Low group (.27) than for the Low-High group ($2.84 - 2.71 = .13$; $t = .61$, $df = 97$, *ns*).

For the grade point average: Within-subjects design. Subjects in both motive groups received higher grades in their high- than in their low-PI courses ($F = 4.72$, $df = 1/51$, $p < .05$). This difference was slightly larger for the High-Low group ($2.81 - 2.43 = .38$) than for the Low-High group ($2.91 - 2.67 = .24$), but the interaction between motives and PI does not approach significance ($F < 1$, *ns*). Motive classification by itself did not affect grades ($F < 1$). Thus for both the between- and within-subjects analyses of the joint effects of motives and PI-GPA on the grade point average, the predicted interaction effect was not found.

DISCUSSION

The following pattern of relationships was found in both studies: (*a*) Students of the High-Low groups received significantly higher grades in a college introductory psychology course when they rated the grade high in career importance (high PI-Psych) as compared to those who saw the grade as low in importance (low PI-Psych); (*b*) this difference was larger than for students of the Low-High groups. These results suggest that the predictive efficiency of achievement-related motive scores depends upon the moderator-variable effect of an individual's future career orientation. The first finding appears to indicate that individuals in whom $M_S > M_{AF}$ (the High-Low groups) are more motivated to do well when immediate activity may result in both immediate and future success than when it is expected to lead only to immediate success. The second finding suggests that individuals for whom M_S and M_{AF} are presumed to be of about equal strength (the Low-High groups) are less motivated to do well than those with $M_S > M_{AF}$ when both immediate and future success can result from immediate activity.

According to theory of achievement motivation, students of the High-Low groups should receive higher grades than students of the Low-High groups. In both studies (particularly Study II) future orientation tended to reduce an apparent reversal of the expected effect: the High-Low group received lower grades than the Low-High group within low PI-Psych, while the opposite was true within high PI-Psych. The pattern of results suggests that a student's characteristic achievement motivation for this particular course is revealed only when immediate performance is important for future career success.

Hypotheses were extended in Study II to take account of overall academic performance in a semester and a combined rating of PI. Both the between- and within-subjects analyses indicated a main effect of PI on average grades rather than the predicted interaction between motives and PI. Students of both motive groups tended to receive higher grades when they rated the grades as relatively important for future career success. A recent study (Raynor, 1968b) also reported a similar finding. Measures of n Achievement and test anxiety were included in a nationwide study of adolescent boys (see Bachman, Kahn, Mednick, Davidson, & Johnston, 1967). Verbal reports of the average grade received by each student in the previous year were obtained. In addition, the perceived instrumentality of grades for future success was measured by asking each student to rate the importance of his overall high school grades for making his future plans work out. The results indicate that although the High-Low group reported significantly higher grades when high than when low in PI, the Low-High group did also. Here again there was a failure to obtain the predicted interaction between motives and PI.[4]

There are several possible reasons for the failure to obtain an interaction between achievement-related motives and future orientation when an average of grades is used to measure academic performance. Hypotheses of the present paper were derived for the case where achievement-related rather than "extrinsic" motivation was assumed to be the primary determinant of academic performance in a particular course. If the reverse were true for one or more of the other courses used to obtain a measure of *overall* academic performance, anticipation of rewards (such as money) dependent upon future career success would lead to an overall increment in immediate performance and reduce rather than accentuate the characteristic effects of an individual's achievement-related

[4] P. M. O'Malley has made a preliminary report of the results of his secondary analysis of the level of educational achievement of adolescent boys whose motivational characteristics were measured by Bachman et al. (1967) when they were high school sophomores. Both the differences in the achievement-related motives and in the perceived instrumentality of education are positively and significantly related to the percentage of students in some form of post-high school education as of 1970. (Report of results directed to J. W. A., August 27, 1973, and included here with permission.) (See Chap. 20, this volume, for theory concerning cumulative educational attainment.)—Editors.

motives. This would eliminate the interaction between motives and future orientation and produce a main effect due to PI. All students would receive higher grades when primarily motivated to attain future extrinsic rewards than when not so motivated. This is the result obtained in the data reported here, using both the between- and within-subjects analyses. It was also found in the sample of adolescent boys referred to earlier.

It may also be that some courses are not easily relatable to a specific career. In addition, students may not be equally certain of their future career plans in different academic areas. In these instances the future implications of immediate performance would be less clear, perhaps arousing less concern about the possibility of future failure. This would reduce the inhibitory effect of future orientation on immediate performance and eliminate the interaction between achievement-related motives and PI.

10

EFFECTS OF ACHIEVEMENT MOTIVATION AND FUTURE ORIENTATION ON LEVEL OF PERFORMANCE[1]

Joel O. Raynor[2] and Ira S. Rubin

A recent elaboration of theory of achievement motivation (Raynor, 1969; see also Chapter 7) is concerned with the effects of future orientation on motivation of immediate activity in two kinds of situations. A person may believe that success in an immediate skill activity is necessary in order to guarantee the opportunity to strive for some number of future successes, while immediate failure guarantees future failure, or he may believe that immediate success or failure will not influence his opportunity for future achievement. This is the difference between a *contingent* and *noncontingent* path relating immediate success-failure and future success-failure. The person's conception that skill activity is the immediate next step in a contingent path should enhance the characteristic effects of his resultant achievement-related motives. Persons in whom the motive to achieve success is stronger than the motive to avoid failure ($M_S > M_{AF}$) should be more motivated to do well and therefore attain higher levels of performance in the immediate activity of a contingent than a noncontingent path. Conversely, persons in whom $M_{AF} > M_S$ should be more inhibited and hence attain lower levels of performance in the immediate activity of a contingent than a noncontingent path. Strength of achievement motivation of persons in whom $M_S \approx M_{AF}$ should not be affected by future orientation, so that their performance should not differ in different kinds of path.

[1] Reprinted and abridged by permission of the authors and the American Psychological Association from the *Journal of Personality and Social Psychology,* 1971, 17, 36–41.

[2] This study was supported in part by a grant (GS-2863) from the National Science Foundation to Joel O. Raynor, entitled "Effects of Distant Future Goals on Achievement Motivation."

Evidence concerning the effects of contingent future orientation on level of performance has thus far been indirect (see Chapters 8 and 9). In the present research future orientation was directly manipulated by experimental induction of different kinds of path. A contingent path was created by leading subjects to believe that success on a prior "test" in a series of four similar arithmetic "tests" was necessary in order to guarantee the opportunity to take the next tests, while failure on any test ruled out the possibility of taking additional tests. A noncontingent path was created by telling subjects that they would have the opportunity to take each of the four tests, regardless of their performance on any one of them. Each subject was led to believe that his chances of success were intermediate (about .5) for each of the four tests. Level of performance was measured on the first test in each experimental condition.

Previous arguments (see Atkinson, 1964, Ch. 9; Atkinson & Feather, 1966, Ch. 20) imply that those college students classified in the high n Achievement-low Test Anxiety (High-Low) group should have characteristic resultant motivation to *approach* success ($M_S > M_{AF}$), those classified in the low n Achievement-high Test Anxiety (Low-High) group *may* have characteristic achievement motivation that is negative in sign and *inhibitory* in action implications ($M_{AF} > M_S$), and those classified in the High-High and Low-Low groups have relatively *neutral* achievement motivation ($M_S \approx M_{AF}$). The recent results reported by Karabenick and Youssef (1968, and Chapter 5) are consistent with these assumptions, particularly that their Low-High group actually had $M_{AF} > M_S$.

It was expected that our results would replicate the previously described pattern of relationships predicted by theory of achievement motivation (Atkinson & Feather, 1966, Ch. 20): highest performance by the High-Low group, lowest performance by the Low-High group, and performance intermediate between these extremes by the High-High and Low-Low groups. In addition, specific hypotheses of the present study were that (*a*) the High-Low group would perform at a higher level in the contingent than in the noncontingent condition, (*b*) the Low-High group would perform at a lower level in the contingent than in the noncontingent condition, and (*c*) the High-High and Low-Low groups would perform at the same levels in the contingent and in the noncontingent conditions. Hypothesis *b* is based on the assumption that the majority of subjects classified Low-High have $M_{AF} > M_S$.

METHOD

Assessment of Motives

All students enrolled in introductory psychology courses at the State University of New York at Buffalo participated in large testing sessions at the beginning of the semester in which the projective measure of n Achievement (McClelland et al., 1953) was administered first, following standard procedures

(Atkinson, 1958a, Appendix III). In each session men sat toward the front and women toward the back of a large lecture hall. Descriptive sentences rather than pictures were used in the following order to elicit stories: (2) two men in a factory are working at a machine, (48) a man is working with a typewriter and books, (1) an older man is talking to a younger man, (7) a boy is standing: a vague operation scene is in the background. Numbers in parentheses identify corresponding pictures (Atkinson, 1958a, Appendix III). Protocols were scored for n Achievement in the usual manner (McClelland, Atkinson, Clark, & Lowell, 1958) by one of the authors (J.O.R.), who has been established as an expert scorer by correlating above .90 with (*a*) the n Achievement practice materials (Smith & Feld, 1958) and (*b*) another expert scorer (see Raynor & Smith, 1966). The use of sentences rather than pictures to obtain stories has previously been shown to yield an index of n Achievement which has construct validity (Horner, 1968, and Chapters 6 and 13; Raynor, 1968b).

The first third of the Mandler-Sarason (1952) Test Anxiety Questionnaire was also administered. A graphic rating scale appeared below each item and was scored so that 5 indicated the highest and 1 indicated the lowest amount of anxiety. A Test Anxiety score was obtained by summing scores for the individual items. Scores on the first third of this questionnaire have correlated between .84 and .90 with total scores (see Smith, 1964).

Students were classified simultaneously high and low on both motive measures, based on medians obtained from the distributions of male scores only. This procedure resulted in four motive groups: students high on both measures (the High-High group), low on both (the Low-Low group), high on n Achievement and low on Test Anxiety (the High-Low group), low on n Achievement and high on Test Anxiety (the Low-High group). The product-moment correlation between the two motive scores was .06 ($N = 588$).

Subjects and Experimental Conditions

Approximately equal numbers of male students from each combined motive classification were randomly selected to participate in this study[3] as part of their introductory psychology course requirement. All students from this preselected pool were contacted and agreed to participate. Sessions were conducted at least 1 month after motive scores were obtained according to the compatibility of subjects' and experimenter's (I.S.R.) free time. One subject from the High-Low group and 3 from the High-High group were not run because they could not be scheduled. Half of each motive group was to be run in each experimental condition. However, 2 more subjects of the Low-Low group than planned were inadvertently run in the noncontingent rather than the contingent condition. The motive groups of subjects were not known by the experimenter.

[3] Several other studies were also conducted using subjects drawn from this population (e.g., see Chapter 14). They will not be mentioned further here. Also, only students with regular or transfer status were included in the present study.

Subjective probability of success. In the present study each subject was led to believe that his chances of success were about .5 for each of the four tests. An ability group norm procedure (see Moulton, 1965; also Chapter 4) was used to induce this subjective probability of success. It involved making clear to the subject his chances of "success" (solving 20 out of 25 problems on each test) in relation to a group of peers of his own ability. Each subject was first placed in an ability group based on information he provided; his quantitative (mathematical) score on the College Board Examination and his cumulative grade point average. Subjects were then told the following:

> On the basis of extensive pretesting of a large number of students at this and other universities, five test booklets–one for each ability group–have been developed. Each booklet contains four tests: each test is composed of 25 separate problems. The items on each test have been preselected to give you a 50-50 chance of completing at least 20 of the 25 items in 2 1/2 minutes. The later tests have been adjusted for practice and learning effects to maintain this 50% level of difficulty on each of the four tests. This estimate of your chances of success is based on a computer analysis of the performance of a large sample of students. Later experimentation has confirmed the validity of the estimate: that is, within each ability group approximately 50% of the respondents were able to complete 20 out of 25 items on each test.

In fact, this information was entirely fictitious.

Experimental conditions. Subjects in the contingent condition were then told:

> You will have 2 1/2 minutes to work on each test. The opportunity to take the next test in the series depends on how well you do on the previous test. In other words, in order to take Test 2, you must complete 20 out of 25 items on Test 1 within 2 1/2 minutes. Similarly, in order to take Tests 3 and 4, you must complete 20 out of 25 items on the tests which came before them within each test's time limit. If you fail to complete 20 out of 25 items on any test, you cannot continue on to the next test. Instead, you will remain in your seat until the end of the test period.

Subjects in the noncontingent condition were told:

> You will have 2 1/2 minutes to work on each test. You will have an opportunity to take each of the four tests, regardless of your performance on any one of them.

Level of performance. Each subject then received the booklet appropriate for his ability group. All test booklets contained identical sets of problems. Each test in the booklet consisted of 25 three-step arithmetic problems (see Wendt, 1955) on a single page. Each problem consisted of two lines of three numbers. The numbers on each line were to be added and/or subtracted. To solve a problem the first line had to be solved first, the answer kept in mind, the second solved, and its answer kept in mind. If the answer to the first line was larger than the answer to the second, the second was to be subtracted from the first. If the answer to the second line was larger than the answer to the first, the two answers were to be added. A written set of test instructions accompanied each booklet. Just before starting the first test, subjects were given the following reminder:

The only thing that you are permitted to write down on the paper is the final answer. Do each problem in your mind and write down the answer. Remember, you will have 2 1/2 minutes to do as many problems as you can.

After the first test was completed, the experiment was ended and subjects were completely debriefed.

Treatment of the Data

Scores on the first test indicating the number of problems attempted and the number of problems correctly answered were obtained for each subject. The two measures correlated .93 (N = 58). Scores were first analyzed to determine whether reported ability influenced the results. The obtained distribution of ability groups was split at the median. Analysis of variance indicated that ability group was not significantly related to the dependent measures, either alone or in interaction with motives or conditions. Inspection of the data indicated that the pattern of results was similar for the two ability groups. Therefore their data were combined for all subsequent analyses.

Hypotheses were tested by means of a priori comparisons (t tests) using the within-cell error (weighted by the number of subjects in each comparison) and the degrees of freedom of the analysis of variance of all four motive groups (see Winer, 1962, p. 244). Since directional hypotheses were formulated for the High-Low and Low-High groups, they were evaluated using one-tailed tests of significance. On the other hand, two-tailed tests of significance were used for comparisons within the High-High and Low-Low groups, since no differences between experimental conditions were expected.

RESULTS

Table 1 shows the mean number of problems attempted and Table 2 the mean number of problems correctly answered for all motive groups in each experimental condition. Inspection indicates that the High-Low group attempted more problems and answered more correctly than the Low-High group, and the

TABLE 1

Mean Number of Problems Attempted as a Function of Motive Groups and Experimental Conditions

	Condition			
Motive group	Noncontingent		Contingent	
	N	*M*	*N*	*M*
High-Low	8	15.63	7	18.43
High-High	6	11.67	6	14.17
Low-Low	10	14.40	6	12.67
Low-High	7	14.14	8	8.38

TABLE 2

Mean Number of Problems Answered Correctly as a Function of Motive Groups and Experimental Conditions

Motive group	Noncontingent		Contingent	
	N	*M*	*N*	*M*
High-Low	8	13.00	7	17.43
High-High	6	8.83	6	12.00
Low-Low	10	12.70	6	11.33
Low-High	7	11.86	8	7.00

differences are greater in the contingent than in the noncontingent condition. Analysis of variance of the data for the extreme motive groups (High-Low and Low-High) reveals significant effects due to motives (F = 23.68 and 15.43, df = 1/26, $p < .001$) and significant interactions between motives and conditions (F = 13.09 and 9.95, df = 1/26, $p < .005$). Comparisons between the High-Low and Low-High groups within experimental conditions indicate highly significant differences in the contingent condition (t = 5.98 and 5.01, df = 26, $p < .001$ for both scores) and nonsignificant differences in the noncontingent condition ($ts < 1$).

The specific hypotheses of the present study concern trends within motive groups, which are, in general, as predicted. The High-Low group attempted more problems and answered more correctly in the contingent than in the noncontingent condition (t = 1.35 and 1.91, df = 50, $p < .10$ and .05, respectively). The Low-High group attempted fewer problems and answered fewer correctly in the contingent than in the noncontingent condition (t = 2.77 and 2.10, df = 50, $p < .005$ and .025). The Low-Low group attempted about the same number of problems and answered about the same number correctly in the two conditions ($ts < 1$). These findings are as predicted. However, the means for the High-High group were higher in the contingent than in the noncontingent condition, although the differences for both number of problems attempted and answered correctly were not statistically significant (t = 1.08 and 1.22, df = 50, *ns,* two-tailed tests). The fact that the expected ordering of motive groups was found within the contingent condition (both High-High and Low-Low intermediate between High-Low and Low-High) suggests that the means for the High-High group in the noncontingent condition were *lower* than expected, rather than that the means for the High-High group in the contingent condition were higher than expected. That is, the results for the High-High group do not suggest an increment in performance due to contingent future orientation.

DISCUSSION

The results provide direct confirmation of hypotheses derived from an elaboration of achievement motivation theory (Raynor, 1969, and Chapter 7) concerning the effects of contingent future orientation on level of performance, particularly as measured by the number of problems answered correctly in a three-step arithmetic task. As predicted, subjects for whom it was assumed $M_S > M_{AF}$ (the High-Low group) answered significantly more problems correctly in the contingent than in the noncontingent condition ($p < .05$), while subjects for whom it was assumed $M_{AF} > M_S$ (the Low-High group) answered significantly fewer problems in the contingent than in the noncontingent condition ($p < .025$). Also as predicted, contingent future orientation did not significantly affect the number of problems answered correctly by subjects for whom it was assumed $M_S \approx M_{AF}$ (the High-High and Low-Low groups), although this was more apparent for the Low-Low than for the High-High group. Results using the number of problems attempted in the task as the measure of performance followed the same pattern, but the significance tests do not confirm hypotheses in as clear-cut a manner.

Note that level of performance of the High-Low group was significantly higher than that of the Low-High group in the contingent condition ($p < .001$), *but not in the noncontingent condition,* despite an attempt to arouse maximum achievement motivation for the first test by setting subjective probability of success for each subject at .50. Many experimental studies which employ test-like ("achievement-oriented") instructions seem to imply to the subject some contingent relationship between immediate performance and future achievement (see Raynor, 1968a, and Chapter 7). Previous research on achievement motivation may have confounded sources of motivation which are aroused by the inherent properties of a skill task (intrinsic tendencies) and sources of motivation which are aroused by the contingent relationship of immediate task success to the attainment of future goals (instrumental tendencies). Raynor's (1969) elaboration of theory of achievement motivation assumes that these sources of motivation summate to determine the total strength of tendency sustaining immediate activity. It would then be expected that differences between High-Low and Low-High motive groups would vary from very small to substantial, depending upon the proportion of subjects who believed that their immediate behavior was instrumental to the achievement of their own future goals.

PART III
MOTIVATION AND THE LEVEL OF PERFORMANCE

One question that has been central in much of the research on achievement motivation during the past 25 years is a simple one: *What are the behavioral effects of relatively general and enduring differences between individuals in strength of motive to achieve*? The effects of this particular motive on both preference and persistence of behavior have been clarified in recent conceptual and experimental developments (covered in Chapters 2 and 7). Yet findings concerning the effects of individual differences in strength of motive to achieve on the effectiveness or level of performance in a given activity have been inconsistent and sometimes contradictory (Klinger, 1966). Our intention in Part III is to examine the nature of the relationship between strength of motivation and *efficiency* of performance and the implications for studies of individual differences in motivation.

The theoretical conception of achievement motivation which has guided research in recent years is obviously far more complicated than the simple hypotheses which spurred McClelland and coworkers in 1947 to undertake experiments that would establish the validity of thematic apperception as a method for assessment of individual differences in strength of motive to achieve (McClelland et al., 1949, 1953). The determinants of strength of the tendency to undertake a given activity with the intent of performing well, then viewed as a relatively simple function of the strength of an individual's need for achievement, is now known to be a complex function of a number of interrelated variables. In addition to the relatively general and stable personality disposition called motive to achieve in terms of which individuals differ, there are these other significant influences on the strength of tendency to achieve success: the individual's subjective probability of success in a given activity, which is influenced by both the objective difficulty of the task and his ability or competence in that kind of activity; the individual's conception of the relationship between the particular activity and his future goals; and, still to be introduced in Part IV, is the strength of his inertial tendency to achieve, i.e., the persistent unfulfilled wish to achieve carried over to the present from recent occasions in which achievement motivation has been aroused but inadequately gratified (Weiner, 1965a, and Chapter 17). All these now constitute the known determinants of the strength of the tendency to achieve success in a given activity. But the final strength of the tendency which motivates performance of a particular task includes even more than this as presently conceived. It involves a summation of a set of component motivational tendencies, depending upon the environmental conditions at the time of performance, including in addition to the tendency to achieve success, the tendency to avoid failure, and other *extrinsic* tendencies such as the tendency to gain social approval, or to earn money, and even a tendency to avoid success! And each of these other tendencies has a comparable set of determinants. It is a complicated yet probably still incomplete specification of the typical components of motivation for achievement-oriented action. Yet it is enough to have produced some sophistication concerning what order of magnitude one should *ever* expect between a single motivational variable (e.g., n Achievement) and any behavior. It has yielded a realistic tolerance (and respect) for correlations on the order of .30 to .40 that isn't shared by those who know less about motivation.

Looking back over the research on effects of individual differences in need to achieve on level of performance, which was spurred by Lowell's (1952) early finding that men who scored high on thematic apperceptive n Achievement apparently tried harder and thus performed at a higher level than others on verbal and arithmetic tasks, and early recognition of the interactive effects of personality and situation (Atkinson, 1950, 1953), one can see a rather fatal flaw. Despite the guiding suggestion of the old Yerkes-Dodson (1908) hypothesis that discriminative performance might suffer when motivation is too intense, and early suggestions that this might be more obvious in certain tasks than in others (e.g., McClelland, 1951, Ch. 13; Wendt, 1955), the step-by-step experimental work on need for achievement and performance level initially assumed a simple monotonic relationship between the final strength of tendency (motivation) and efficiency of performance—and this in the face of rather inconsistent and sometimes contradictory evidence. Why? Probably because it seemed to us unlikely that really very intense levels of motivation were ever being produced in the laboratory. Perhaps because in a survey of the historical evolution of thought about motivation (Atkinson, 1964), we did not then see the Yerkes-Dodson law as an important part of the mainstream, a deficiency correctly noted in Eysenck's (1966a) review. Whatever the reasons, we had not looked as hard at the question of *what is required to perform well* as we had at the question of *what are the several determinants of motivation to perform well.* Our behavioral criteria defining actual achievement have sometimes been specific tasks undertaken for a relatively short period of time in the laboratory, where the key issues are the actual speed and efficiency of performance. But sometimes lumped in the same discussion of achievement motivation and performance have been studies using school and college grades, which depend as much or more on persistence in study and care in preparation of outside work as on efficiency in test taking. Even more cumulative measures of achievement such as social mobility and success in life have sometimes crept into the discussion. Unfortunately, added to this confusion about motivational effects on performance is the continually repeated error of reviewers, who consider themselves impartial observers (e.g., the annual reviews of psychology; Klinger, 1966), to ignore the well-documented fact that various ad hoc tests arbitrarily called measures of n Achievement in the literature do not share the unique experimental validation of thematic apperception coded in a particular, well-defined way (McClelland et al., 1953, 1958) and that they typically yield indices that are uncorrelated with TAT n Achievement (see McClelland et al., 1953, p. 327; McClelland, 1958a, pp. 38–41; Atkinson, 1960, pp. 275–277; Atkinson & Litwin, 1966, pp. 77 and 88; Atkinson & Feather, 1966, pp. 348–351). Still another common failing in some reviews of work on behavioral effects of achievement motivation is to disregard the major upgrading of the scientific usefulness of a projective technique by insisting that coding reliabilities of .85 to .95, and nothing ever as low as the .77 reported in Weinstein's work (1969), are the minimum display of expertise in technique required for serious consideration of experimental results and arguments about motivation based on them.[1]

We shall put off consideration of long-term or cumulative accomplishment until the final section of the book. Our interest in this section is restricted to discussion of a rather general guiding hypothesis for study of the effects of intensity of motivation on efficiency of performance of a given task. We refer, specifically, to how well a person will perform in a given activity when some measure of work actually accomplished in a given period of time is taken as the index of level of efficiency of performance. The ideas hark back to the Yerkes-Dodson hypothesis and to more recent interest in an inverted U-shaped relationship between behavioral efficiency and level of arousal (Hebb, 1955; Broadhurst, 1959; Cofer & Appley, 1964; Eysenck, 1966b). Our main interest in the present context is some suggestive findings—none of them definitive by itself—in some of our most recent studies to the effect that persons who are strong in motive to achieve (n Achievement) and also strong in motive for approval (n Affiliation) show a decrement in performance when in a situation which offers as attainable incentives both success at the task (achievement) and immediate social approval from an observer or audience.

[1] The simple point is that when coding validity coefficient is .90, the n Achievement scores obtained by some investigator have 81% of variance in common with scores that would be obtained by other experts in the method. When the coding validity drops to .70, the common variance with experts is then only 49%. There has been a loss of 32% in common variance. That is roughly 40% less competence than what is required for productive experimental research. A simple check of all the work published in Atkinson and Feather (1966), and in this book, together with Feld and Smith's (1958) earlier survey of interjudge coding reliability in the published literature again defines the median at .89 and the upper edge of the lowest quartile at .85. Weinstein's .77, and his unique manner of computing it, is the worst since 1952, when one investigator had completed a study before the coding manual had even been written by McClelland et al.

Graduate students at Michigan learn to code n Achievement and n Affiliation as a normal part of their exposure to technique in courses on social motivation. With this degree of interest in learning the skill, their median coding validity (i.e., agreement with materials precoded by consensus of experts) after use of the published practice materials (see Smith & Feld, 1958) is also .89.

Perhaps journal editors are too easily intimidated by the accusation that negative results are not allowed to be published which often appears, or is suggested, in some reports that are obviously technically incompetent.

11
STRENGTH OF MOTIVATION AND EFFICIENCY OF PERFORMANCE[1]

John W. Atkinson

The question to which I direct attention is this: *What should be the relationship of individual differences in need for achievement, as presently measured, and performance level, as a function of the overall level of motivation to undertake a task in a given situation?* The conception of the final strength of tendency to engage in some activity as presented in Chapters 2 and 7 involves the algebraic summation of these and other components: tendency to achieve success, which is in part a function of individual differences in strength of motive to achieve; tendency to avoid failure which, because it is negative in sign, functions as resistance to achievement-oriented activity; and any extrinsic tendency to undertake an activity, which depends upon the presence in a given situation of the opportunity to gain social approval, a monetary reward, or some other extrinsic incentive for undertaking the activity in question ($T_A = T_s - T_{-f} + T_{ext}$).

The tendency to achieve success and the tendency to avoid failure are conceived as inherently related to the evaluation of performance. Hence they are invariably present whenever there is some standard of excellence against which the individual can measure his success or failure. The so-called extrinsic tendencies depend upon the presence in a given situation of, for example, an audience to provide social approval, or the offer of a monetary prize or income for work accomplished. Thus, the final strength of tendency to undertake an

[1] This is an elaboration of papers presented in a symposium on achievement motivation at the annual meeting of the American Psychological Association, and at the Ann Arbor meeting of the National Academy of Sciences in the fall of 1967.

activity *in a given situation* is likely to be greater when there are extrinsic incentives in addition to the challenge to achieve provided by the task itself.

Let us assume, to begin with, that the relationship between the final strength of tendency that is expressed in an activity and performance level is an increasing monotonic function as shown in Figure 1. This has been the implicit assumption in most previous research on achievement motivation. You note that we invariably expect a positive correlation between n Achievement score, the measure of motive, and performance level except when there is some obvious upper limit that cannot be exceeded for physical reasons. The graph shows the effects of individual differences in strength of motive to achieve in points labeled *a, b,* and *c,* corresponding to three individuals in three different conditions in which either the parameters of achievement motivation itself, or of extrinsic sources of motivation, account for (1) a weak, (2) a moderate, or (3) a very intense average level of motivation among the *S*s.

In Figure 1 it is assumed that the final strength of tendency to undertake the particular task (T_A) is overdetermined. That is, it is influenced by the tendency to achieve (T_s), the tendency to avoid failure (T_{-f}), and some source of extrinsic motivation (T_{ext}) such as the tendency to gain social approval in additive combination. Since failure is an aversive anticipated consequence of undertaking the activity, this tendency, as previously stated, functions as a source of resistance to achievement-oriented activity. It dampens enthusiasm. It subtracts

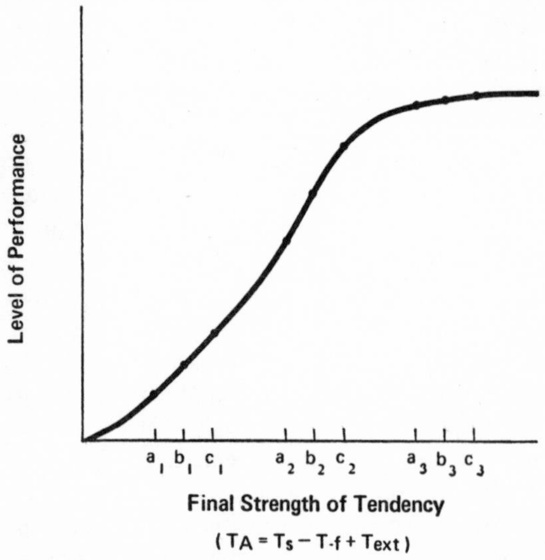

FIG. 1. The assumption that efficiency of performance (and therefore level of performance holding ability constant) increases monotonically as strength of motivation increases until some physical limit or ceiling is reached.

from the sum of the positive tendencies to undertake the activity ($T_s + T_{ext}$) and therefore always functions to diminish the final strength of the tendency to undertake the task. Given the premise of a monotonic relationship between final strength of tendency and performance level, we should always expect strength of motive to achieve to be positively related to performance, and individual differences in anxiety (taken as the measure of motive to avoid failure) always to be negatively related to performance level, except when an upper physical limit has been reached, in which case differences in neither motive will have any effect.

This was the general hypothesis when Atkinson and Reitman (1956) sought to demonstrate, and did, that the generally expected positive relationship between n Achievement and performance would occur if persons were given an achievement-oriented instruction and then left alone in a room to work at a task, but could be washed out completely by having them work in a coacting, competitive group situation under achievement orientation, but with two conspicuous proctors (an audience) and, additionally, a substantial monetary incentive. The number of three-step arithmetic problems attempted and solved correctly by college men who differed in n Achievement when working alone versus in the multi-incentive condition for 14 minutes is shown in Table 1. These writers suspected that there might have been an intensity-produced decrement among those high in n Achievement in the multi-incentive condition but had to discount the possibility because of a flaw in their procedure. To remind *S*s of their presence in that condition, they had asked them to make a check on their answer sheet (a pacing operation) at the end of each minute. This could have disrupted the performance of both groups.

To justify the assumption that the multi-incentive condition had introduced an incentive to gain social approval by working hard, it was shown that *S*s classified low in n Achievement but high in n Affiliation had shown a gain of 16.7 between conditions as compared to a loss of 5.8 for all other subjects combined ($p < .05$). They found, though they had not expected it, a nearly significant positive relationship ($p = .10$) between n Affiliation score and correct arithmetic performance in the multi-incentive condition concerning which they said: "The positive trend, while statistically very tenuous, suggests that the expectancy of pleasing the *E*s by working hard was most salient in the multi-incentive condition [Atkinson & Reitman, 1956, p. 365]."

Follow-up studies by Reitman (1957, 1960) and Smith (1961, 1966) showed replications in part, but introduced complications that may take on a new light as we continue our analysis.

Reitman (1957) was mainly concerned with an attempt to standardize (and thus to rigorize) the experimental induction of motivation by use of printed instructions alone, rather than relying on spoken ones and the kind of subtle role-playing by an investigator to create an effect which depends so much (for replication) on the personality and skill of an investigator. It was and still is a worthy objective. I have always felt that the form and tone of his published

TABLE 1

Arithmetic Performance (14 Minutes) as a Function of Achievement Motive and Experimental Condition

Achievement motive	Achievement-orientation (alone)				Multi-incentive (coacting group)			
	N		Attempted	Correct	N		Attempted	Correct
High	21	M	78.1	71.6	24	M	67.1	60.3
		σ	24.8	24.1		σ	19.6	19.3
Low	30	M	60.3	55.5	21	M	69.1	60.1
		σ	15.7	16.4		σ	22.3	23.0
Difference			17.8[a]	16.1			-2.0	.2
(H-L)			$p < .01$	.01			n.s.	n.s.

Note.–After Atkinson & Reitman, 1956, with permission of the authors and of the publisher, American Psychological Association.

[a] σ difference derived from estimate of within group variance, $df = 92$.

TABLE 2

Mean Correct Arithmetic Performance (9 Minutes) as a Function of Achievement Motive and Experimental Condition

Achievement motive	Achievement-orientation (alone)		Achievement-orientation (coacting group)	
	N		*N*	
High	14	49.50	10	44.70
Low	9	41.33	11	45.00
Difference		8.17		-.30
		$r = .37$*		$r = -.09$

Note.–After Reitman, 1957, Tables 7 and 14, with permission of the author.
*$p < .05$ in predicted direction.

report (Reitman, 1960) was more negative, and therefore misleading, than it should have been. In my own reanalysis of the study, restricted to that portion of the data which meets the investigator's own previously stated criteria for its inclusion in the analysis of effects of individual differences[2] and which deals with conditions that were explicitly intended to approximate those of Atkinson and Reitman (1956), the result is an encouragingly similar pattern as shown in Table 2.

My secondary analysis once again reveals that *S*s classified low n Achievement-high n Affiliation had shown a gain of 10.69 as compared to a loss of 5.20 for all other motivational subgroups combined between working alone and in the group setting with a pacing proctor. (The latter was intentionally made less obvious than in the earlier study but was, nevertheless, still present.) And in this case, the correlation between n Affiliation and arithmetic performance (an insignificant $r = -.22$, as before, in the alone condition) was a significant .53 ($p < .05$) in the "multi-incentive" condition. The magnitude of difference when *S*s worked alone corresponds very well to that in Table 1 when one notices that the work period was only about 64% as long as in the earlier study. (And once

[2] Reitman stated the requirement of homogeneity in average level of TAT n Achievement among several classes given a particular form of the test as a prerequisite to combining scores into a single distribution, and also evidence of a mean difference between the performance levels of different treatments to justify the presumption that instructions had produced the intended effect among subsets of his sample (e.g., members of a particular class). Unfortunately, several subsets of his sample did not meet one or the other of these sound criteria. That fact is not given enough emphasis in the published report, in my view, to help a relatively uninformed reader or reviewer of literature to understand why only half his results (those for one of two forms of the test he had included) are consistent with earlier work.

again, there is a hint of the possibility of performance decrement among those highly motivated to achieve in the "multi-incentive" condition.)

Consider now Figure 2, which is constructed on the premise that a task may be such that for some unspecified reason trying very hard to perform well may have a detrimental effect on the efficiency of performance. This might be the kind of task at which precipitate action may not pay off. What do we now expect concerning the relationship between an individual's n Achievement and performance? When the final strength of tendency to undertake the task is in the range of weak to moderate (1), as would probably be the case if a person were left alone in a room to work on a task without an audience (Atkinson & Reitman, 1956; Reitman, 1957), the relationship between n Achievement (a_1, b_1, c_1) and performance would be positive as so generally expected. But now suppose that other factors in the personality of the individual (e.g., other motives, competence, future orientation concerning the task, etc.) and in the situation he confronts (e.g., incentives) serve to heighten the final strength of tendency systematically so that it falls in the middle range (2) on our graph for all the *S*s (a_2, b_2, c_2) among whom we are making the comparison. We now would expect the correlation between strength of n Achievement and performance to be zero. And if the presence of still other aroused motives, for example, the need for social approval, or stronger incentives in the situation produced a very intense average level of final motivation for the task (3), we

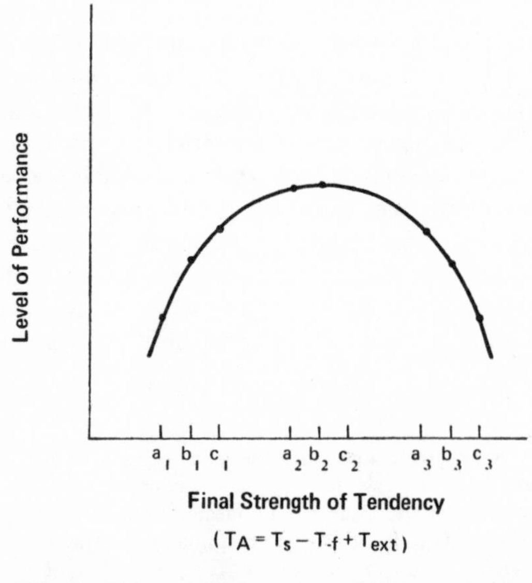

FIG. 2. The assumption that efficiency of performance (and therefore its level holding ability constant) increases up to some optimal level after which efficiency decreases as motivation increases still further.

would paradoxically expect that the person who scores highest in n Achievement (c_3) would perform least well. The relationship between strength of achievement motive (a_3, b_3, c_3) and performance would now be negative.

Paralleling these three hypotheses, but exactly opposite in direction, are the expectations we should have concerning the effects of individual differences in anxiety on performance if, as the theory of achievement motivation supposes, anxiety tests measure the strength of motive to avoid failure, and the tendency to avoid failure functions as resistance to achievement-oriented activity by diminishing the final strength of tendency to undertake the task. When the performance situation produces only weak to moderate final tendency to undertake the task, the relationship between anxiety and performance should be negative as so often is found. But given additional sources of motivation–some combination of other motives in the person and other attainable incentives in the situation–which bring the final strength of tendencies into the moderate range, we should expect no correlation between anxiety in the individual and the level of performance. And finally, when the final strength of positive motivation to undertake the task becomes very strong, we come to the *nonobvious* hypothesis that persons who are most anxious (a_3 in the set of a_3, b_3, c_3 of Figure 2) should perform best. The dampening effect of their inhibitory tendency should, under these special circumstances of excessive positive motivation for the task, prevent the occurrence of an otherwise expected performance decrement. This is to say, specifically, that if a certain task is sensitive to performance decrement when a person is "overmotivated", and the person in question is both highly motivated to achieve and highly motivated for social approval (as might be inferred from personality tests), and both of these incentives are immediately attainable in the situation, then he should perform better if he is also high in anxiety than if he is low in anxiety.

I would probably be much more cautious and qualified in offering this nonobvious hypothesis if we had not already seen some broader hints of the effect in the work by Smith (1961, 1966), and by Atkinson and O'Connor (1966), and in several other studies that were in progress when this paper was first being prepared–the work of Elliot Entin (Chapter 12) and Matina Souretis Horner (Chapter 13).

The more general guide provided by the old Yerkes-Dodson hypothesis is that the shape of the curve describing efficiency of performance in relation to strength of motivation will depend upon the nature of the task–e.g., what is required of the *S* (Figure 3). A simple, overlearned task that involves very little response competition may, perhaps, produce the monotonic increasing function we have traditionally assumed (e.g., Task A in Figure 3). A more complex activity in which discrimination among alternatives or deliberation plays a major role in effective performance may produce the kind of curvilinear relationship we have just been describing (Task B). Still other tasks, perhaps those which require a very cautious, deliberate, or relaxed approach, might produce a decreasing function for most of the range of motivation (Task C in Figure 3).

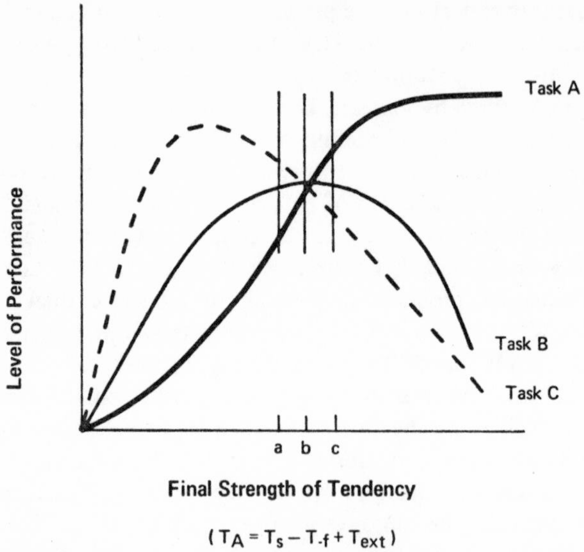

FIG. 3. The most general statement that can be made about the effect of strength of motivation on efficiency of performance: it depends on the nature and requirements of the task. Persons who are stronger in motivation (*a, b, c*) may perform better, worse, or the same as others on different kinds of tasks.

The important point is—*we must discover all this empirically since it is not already known.* And to do it, we must be able to define a number of points along a continuum of increasing motivation for performance of a task.

Here, I think, is where the conceptual development in study of achievement motivation can now provide a useful guide. It can identify the kind of people (in terms of their measured motives) and the kind of situation (in terms of incentives made available), and combinations of these with still other conditions (e.g., future orientation) which define an order of points along the continuum of intensity of motivation. We can thus begin systematic study of this old, unresolved problem with human *S*s (instead of being limited to data from shocked, starved, or half-drowned air-gasping animals—Birch, 1945; Broadhurst, 1959). Until now, we have not had enough in the way of useful theory or technique for study of human motivation even to consider a broad-scale attack on the problem.

To summarize: If the relationship between intensity of motivation and efficiency of performance is curvilinear, as so often supposed for particular kinds of task even though a specification concerning the kind of task is relatively vague, then the relationship of individual differences in n Achievement and Anxiety to performance can be positive, negative, or zero, depending upon the conditions and the requirements of the task (see Figure 3). This possibility now seems one of the most plausible explanations of the now-you-see-it-now-you-don't character of the relationship between n Achievement and level of performance in much of the earlier work in which the nature of the conditions and requirements of the task were relatively ignored, if not in the studies themselves, certainly in the nondiscriminating reviews of the literature.

The decrement in performance among persons highly motivated to achieve to which I have referred, if it exists, is produced by "overmotivation," by trying too hard, by caring too much about performing well. The decrement in performance that we have so frequently observed in relation to strong anxiety is different. According to the theory of achievement motivation, it is produced by "undermotivation" resulting from resistance, the inhibiting effect on performance of expecting to fail. The least obvious of the several hypotheses among those presented is that *the inhibitory effect of the tendency to avoid failure (or any other inhibitory tendency) should enhance performance when positive motivation would otherwise produce a greater than optimal level of intensity of motivation for the task.*

AN EMPIRICAL PARADIGM GROUNDED IN A THEORETICAL CONCEPTION OF MOTIVATION

Table 3 outlines a general plan for research concerning the effect of strength of motivation on efficiency of performance. It presumes that the final or total strength of motivation for performance of a task (T_A) is a summation of component motivational tendencies (e.g., $T_A = T_s - T_{-f} + T_{\text{app}}$) and that each component tendency depends upon interaction of characteristics of personality (viz., strength of motive) and the nature of the immediate environment (viz., expectation or not of attaining a relevant incentive) as specified in Chapters 2 and 7.

One of the earliest studies of n Affiliation established very clearly that college men who are highly motivated for affiliation (or social acceptance) are described as *approval seeking,* by persons who know them well, significantly more often than men who score low in n Affiliation (Atkinson, Heyns, & Veroff, 1954). National survey data (Veroff et al., 1960, and Chapter 3) has established that n Achievement and n Affiliation are uncorrelated in a representative sample of male adults. So the fourfold classification of personality, in terms of relative strength of resultant n Achievement (n Achievement–Test Anxiety) and n Affiliation (taken as a measure of need for social approval in this context) presupposes division of the distribution of scores obtained from subject samples at the median to identify those who are relatively strong (high) and weak (low) in the several motives.[3] This should yield approximately equal numbers of *S*s for each of the four rows in Table 3. The two columns represent two experimental

[3]The combination of TAT n Achievement and Test Anxiety is accomplished by converting raw scores to standard scores and subtracting the latter from the former (Atkinson & Feather, 1966).

TABLE 3

A Paradigm for Experimental Analysis of the Effects of Strength of Motivation (+ to ++++) on Efficiency of Performance

Personality (Motives)		Environment (Incentives)			
Resultant n Achievement (n Achievement–Test Anxiety)	n Affiliation	Achievement related only		Achievement-related and social approval	
High	High	(A)	++	(E)	++++
High	Low	(B)	++	(F)	+++
Low	High	(C)	+	(G)	+++
Low	Low	(D)	+	(H)	++

Note.–It is assumed that strength of motivation for the task, $T_A = (T_s - T_{-f}) + T_{app}$, and that motives (*P*) and incentives (*E*) combine multiplicatively in determination of component tendencies. For simplicity, High = 2 and Low = 1 in reference to strength of motives; and presence of a relevant incentive = 1 and its absence = 0. The number of +s indicates strength of T_A for each subgroup in the table.

treatments (or situations), one offering only the incentives to achieve success and to avoid failure that are inherent in any achievement-oriented task, the other offering an additional incentive to gain social approval by performing well.

It is assumed that putting *S*s alone in a room to work at a task following an achievement-orienting instruction meets the requirement of achievement-related incentives but not of social approval. In contrast, the same achievement orientation coupled with an audience (an immediate potential agent of social approval) would meet the requirement of the second treatment. The multi-incentive condition of the initial Atkinson-Reitman experiment (Table 1) included an attentive audience of two proctors, a competitive coacting group setting, and also a monetary incentive.

To simplify the motivational implications of this eight-celled table, I have arbitrarily assumed that High = 2 and Low = 1, concerning relative strength of motives, and that the presence of the relevant incentive is indicated by 1 and its absence by 0 in the treatment columns. The number of + signs in each of the eight cells represents the sum of the products of the interaction of personality (motive) and environment (incentive) that is normally assumed in the expression, $T_A = T_s - T_{-f} + T_{ext}$.

This combined use of diagnostic tests of strength of motives in an individual and experimental control of incentives in the work environment yields four distinguishable levels of intensity of motivation for performance of a task. Within the first treatment (e.g., working alone with achievement orientation), those *S*s classified L-H (i.e., low n Achievement-high n Affiliation) should not be any more strongly motivated than *S*s classified L-L (low in both motives) because there is no incentive to gain social approval in that setting. Within the second treatment (e.g., achievement orientation plus an incentive for social approval), the most highly motivated *S*s are those who are strong in both of the corresponding motives. There is no a priori basis for ordering the H-L and L-H groups relative to each other in this condition. But we can be assured that each of them should be more strongly motivated than the L-L group and less motivated than the H-H group in that setting. That is the general logic of the table.

If it were plausible to assume that groups of *S*s who differ in motives do not also differ systematically in average level of ability required to perform a task, one could combine various subgroups to form a four-point continuum of intensity of motivation for performance of a task. These combinations, in order of increasing strength of motivation, would be: (C,D), (A,B,H), (F,G), and (E). Entin (1968), whose work is reported more fully in the next chapter, did just that regarding performance on a rather simple and a more complex arithmetic task (from Atkinson & Reitman, 1956) for a sample of junior high school boys. Half received *private feedback.* They were told that their scores would be posted on the bulletin board next day by code number (analogous to working alone in a room). The other half received *public feedback.* They were told the scores would be posted by name (analogous to having an audience). His results are shown in

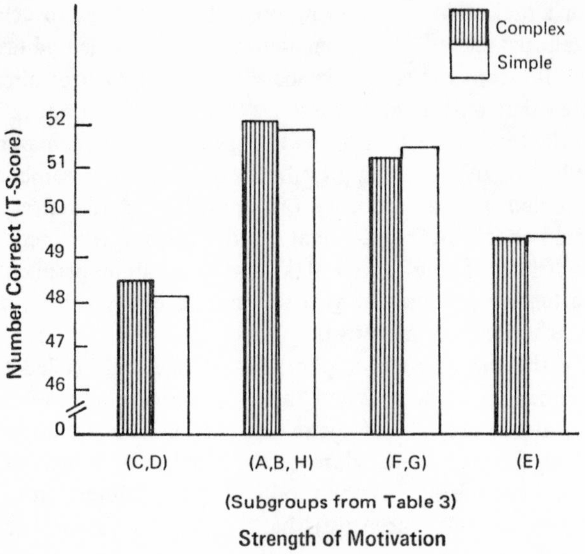

FIG. 4. Mean number correct arithmetic problems on a simple and more complex task by junior high school boys classified on resultant n Achievement and n Affiliation and performing with private versus public anticipated feedback. (*After Entin, 1968, with permission of the author.*)

Figure 4. The level of performance for both the relatively simple and the more complex task (which were interspersed during the work period) is related to strength of motivation in a way that is consistent with the hypothesis that overmotivation may produce a loss of efficiency.

Equally suggestive of the inverted U-shaped function relating efficiency of performance to strength of motivation are some results presented by Smith (1961, 1966). One aspect of his much broader study corresponded very closely in procedure and intention to the early Atkinson-Reitman experiment. I focus on that part of his study only. Both n Achievement and Test Anxiety were assessed under *neutral* conditions. Then performance on the same three-step arithmetic problem employed in both studies already cited, and for 14 minutes as in the Atkinson-Reitman study, was undertaken by different *S*s under these four conditions:

1. *Relaxed.* The *E* informally asked *S*s to bear with him as he sought to get some information on how long it would take to do some pretty simple and rather dull tasks. They were told that they wouldn't have to work them all, that he wanted only group scores, and that no one would receive an individual score. He then left the room, leaving the group of *S*s to work at the tasks.

2. *Extrinsic.* An effort was made to exclude explicit achievement incentives but to give the *S*s an extrinsic reason for working fast (see also French, 1955).

The group was scheduled very late in the afternoon so they would feel pressure to hurry to make the scheduled evening meal. An irrelevant task was introduced first to fill time and create additional time pressure. Then *E*, looking at his watch, mentioned there were several more tasks to work on, that they would take quite a while, but that *S*s could go as soon as they had finished. The tasks were described as simple, "once you get the hang of them," and *S*s were told no one would receive an individual score. They were simply urged to get on with it as quickly as possible so as to get on to still other tasks.

3. *Achievement.* The *S*s, in a group, were told they would be assigned to individual work rooms for the next test, which was described to them as similar to other ones developed to measure critical abilities, etc. Following this achievement orientation, *S*s were placed alone in rooms for 14 minutes of work replicating the Atkinson-Reitman alone condition very closely.

4. *Multi-incentive.* Again replicating the earlier experiment, *S*s in a group setting were given the same achievement orientation, the additional offer of a $5.00 prize for the highest score on the test, and were proctored by *E* as they worked in a coacting, competitive group atmosphere. The *E* paced around, stopwatch in hand, and tried to look concerned when any *S* slackened up.

Smith (1961, 1966) had a thorough postexperiment questionnaire in which he asked *S*s to indicate the various reasons they had worked, how hard they had tried, etc. He found that the incentive to achieve was significantly more salient in the latter two conditions than in the others, that money was an incentive where offered, and that finishing quickly to have time for other things distinguished his extrinsic condition. Following Smith (1961, p. 135), I have used the average rating of *S*s concerning how hard they felt they had worked on the arithmetic task, as a basis for ordering the conditions in Table 4 according to presumed average intensity of motivation. The results are plotted separately according to differences on neutral n Achievement score (Smith, 1966, p. 290), differences in Test Anxiety score (Smith, 1961, Table 22), and simultaneous classification of *S*s in terms of both measures. The results again suggest a decrement in performance among the particular subgroup of *S*s that would be likely to be the most highly motivated (assuming a comparable level of n Affiliation for each subgroup in Table 4).

Among *S*s scoring low (below median) in n Achievement there is an orderly increase in level of performance reaching its maximum in the Multi-incentive condition. Among those high in n Achievement, there is a comparable increase reaching a maximum in the achievement-oriented condition and then dropping substantially in the Multi-incentive condition. The pattern of results for the Achievement and Multi-incentive conditions corresponds to that of the earlier experiment (Table 1), except that now the statistically significant difference is the reversal ($p < .02$) in the Multi-incentive conditions. One need only assume that the high n Achievement group in Smith's *Achievement* condition is already beyond the optimal level of motivation (see Figure 2), where the comparable group in the earlier experiment (Table 1) was not, to explain both the

TABLE 4

Mean Correct Arithmetic Performance (14 Minutes) According to Strength of Achievement-Related Motives under Various Conditions

Mean Post-test rating by *S*s: how hard they had worked	Relaxed (3.41)	Extrinsic (3.97)	Achievement (4.00)	Multi-incentive (4.39)
n Achievement				
High[a]	52.07	56.47	70.69	58.39
Low	51.43	55.93	64.93	76.94
Difference	.63	.54	6.36	-18.55
Test Anxiety				
High[b]	48.33	56.00	58.92	70.31
Low	55.43	56.38	75.71	64.74
Difference	- 7.10	- .38	-16.79	5.57
n Achievement–Test Anxiety				
High-Low[c]	53.0	51.7	78.8	55.3
High-High	55.1	60.6	66.0	58.7
Low-Low	56.4	60.0	71.3	71.5
Low-High	34.8	49.8	55.8	85.3

Note.–After Smith, 1961, 1966, with permission of the author and of the publisher, John Wiley & Sons.

Differences attributable to n Achievement here are smaller than when one picture of questionable validity is eliminated from the set of six (Smith, 1961, Table 15). This picture is removed for the joint classification based on Smith, 1961, Table 58. Generally the differences are somewhat smaller but the pattern is unchanged with quantitative ability controlled statistically (Smith, 1961).

[a] N_s = 14 to 18 in each subgroup.
[b] N_s = 13 to 19 in each subgroup.
[c] N_s = 4 to 10 in each subgroup.

correspondence of the pattern in the two experiments and the fact that the relationship of n Achievement to performance is, in fact, significantly *negative* in Smith's Multi-incentive condition.

The pattern of results for differences in Test Anxiety is diametrically opposite as generally expected. When results are arranged for *S*s simultaneously classified on n Achievement and Test Anxiety (following Smith, 1961, Table 58), again there is a rather striking suggestion of the nonmonotonic hypotheses. The most extreme groups are outlined for easy reference. Furthermore, the hypothesis that strong anxiety, in dampening motivation, should function to enhance performance efficiency when an individual might otherwise be "overmotivated" is certainly supported by the trends of the differences between subgroups alike in n Achievement but different in anxiety in the Multi-incentive condition when compared with their counterparts in the achievement (alone) condition.

The main impetus for reanalysis of some of this earlier work on n Achievement and level of performance in terms of the assumption of an optimal level of motivation (Figure 2) comes from a study conducted by Atkinson and O'Connor (1966). They identified three different behavioral symptoms of differences in strength of resultant achievement motivation (performance level, preference for intermediate risk, and lack of persistence under certain conditions after Feather, 1962). All of these could be derived as legitimate behavioral indicators from the theory of achievement motivation (Chapter 2), and all had been studied in earlier work using TAT n Achievement and Test Anxiety measures. Their primary aim was to validate a newly constructed achievement risk preference scale, hopefully the long-sought, short, objective test that might replace the cumbersome combination of thematic apperception and test anxiety questionnaire for assessment of motivation. This primary aim of the study was not achieved. The new test simply did not work.[4] An intensive analysis of the results in terms of TAT n Achievement, Test Anxiety, and TAT n Affiliation did, however, yield the central theme of this paper. It was found, in brief, that resultant achievement motivation (n Achievement–Test Anxiety) was related as expected to each of the behavioral variables *but only among Ss who scored below the median in n Affiliation.* This would correspond to a comparison of groups H and F in Table 3, since each male *S* was tested individually but in the immediate presence of a female examiner. In retrospect, it seems obvious that the situation must have offered both incentives to achieve and for immediate social approval in the eyes of a subject.

In addition, it was found that TAT n Affiliation was also related in exactly the same way to each of these presumed behavioral symptoms of achievement motivation *among Ss for whom resultant achievement motivation was weak.* This would correspond to a comparison of groups H and G in Table 3. In both comparisons, the intensity of motivation is in the relatively low to moderate range.

Furthermore, the significant relationships between n Affiliation and two behavioral indicators (preference for moderate risk and lack of persistence), ones that normally require the assumption that $I_s = 1 - P_s$ in their theoretical derivation, forced us to consider seriously the possibility that "*the incentive value of any extrinsic reward that appears to S to be contingent upon the*

[4] Further failures, even to make productive use of the valid available tools, are reported in Weinstein (1969), or to make any substantial progress in developing better ones, in Atkinson (1969a). Some evidence of progress in this endeavor, though still much less than definitive evidence, appears in the work of Mehrabian (1968, 1969, 1970), Hermans (1969, 1970), Veroff, McClelland, and Marquis (1971), and Veroff, Hubbard, and Marquis (1971). Several reviews by McClelland (1958a, 1971), Atkinson (1960), and Atkinson and Feather (1966) elaborate the dimensions of this problem. See especially Atkinson and Litwin (1960) and Atkinson and O'Connor (1966).

adequacy of his performance when skill and effort is demanded may be proportionate to the apparent difficulty of the task. Specifically, this hypothesis means that a person who produces very little imagery having to do with excellence of performance in thematic apperceptive stories under neutral conditions might display all the behavioral symptoms of 'an entrepreneurial risk-taker' if some extrinsic reward like love or money, for which he does have a strong motive, were offered as a general inducement for performance [Atkinson & O'Connor, 1966, pp. 317-318]."

Analysis of those results, then explicitly guided by the assumption that *S*s highly motivated both to achieve and for social approval must have suffered a decrement in performance attributable to "overmotivation," yielded the hypothesis and suggestive supportive evidence (with a small number of cases) that among these very highly motivated *S*s, the additional presence of a strong tendency to avoid failure (i.e., High Anxiety), functioning to dampen motivation, would paradoxically enhance the efficiency of their performance. It is an important hypothesis in search of *definitive* evidence.

The most interesting application of the hypothesis of a nonmonotonic relationship between strength of motivation and efficiency of performance (Figure 2) coupled with the logic of the research design presented in Table 3, lies in careful consideration of some results obtained by Matina Souretis Horner (1968). Her procedures and analysis of results will be described in detail in Chapter 13. Briefly, the experiment, a part of a comparative study of men and women in various competitive conditions, considered the level of *verbal* performance of college men in three conditions: (*a*) working alone in a room following *achievement orientation* and against a standard which implied $P_s = .50$; (*b*) in direct *competition with a female student* presented as equivalent in ability; (*c*) in direct *competition with a male student* presented as equivalent in ability.

We may assume that the "alone with achievement orientation" condition is a refined replication of the similar treatment studied by Atkinson and Reitman (Table 1). But what about the two face-to-face competitive settings? Do they intensify achievement-related motivation? Do they introduce extrinsic incentives, e.g., to gain social approval? The *E* had informed the *S* in these competitive conditions, "'After you have worked on the tasks, you will be told which one of you did best and how much better' [Horner, 1968, p. 49]."

We have two justifiable bases for deciding whether or not an incentive for social approval is introduced in the competitive settings and, if so, in which of the two treatments it was more salient or stronger. First, you will recall that Atkinson and Reitman (1956) found the greatest gain between working alone and working in a proctored, coacting, competitive group setting was among those classified low n Achievement-High n Affiliation. Second, inspection of Table 3 tells us that if an incentive for approval *is* introduced, the change in level of performance by *S*s classified low in n Achievement-High in n Affiliation (subgroups C and G in Table 3) will be most diagnostic. Why? Because there is a large increase in strength of motivation (+) to (+++) but it occurs within the low to moderate range. Thus performance level should not yet be affected by an *over*motivation decrement. A comparison of subgroups A (++) and E (++++) would involve a comparable large increase in motivation, but we anticipate the possibility of a decrement in the performance of the most highly motivated *S*s, subgroup E. So comparison of performance levels of subgroups A and E might hide a real motivational difference.

With this argument as justification, the three treatments of the Horner experiment with male college subjects can be arranged in the order shown in Table 5. The measure reported in the table is response output on a 10-minute anagrams task for which raw scores were normalized to yield a distribution having a mean of 50 and standard deviation of 10. The distribution for resultant n Achievement (n Achievement-Test Anxiety) is divided at the median, as is the distribution of n Affiliation scores.

The results for the critical diagnostic groups (low resultant n Achievement-High n Affiliation) are enclosed by an outline for emphasis so that the increase from 41.8 to 53.6 to 56.1 is clearly apparent. This is the basis for ordering the treatments according to presumed average strength of motivation. Now the implications of the assumptions in Figure 2 and Table 3 are vulnerable to disproof.

Let us take the analysis in stages. First, consider the overall results when *S*s are classified only according to n Achievement-Test Anxiety at the bottom of Table 5. Compare these results with those in Tables 1, 2, and 4. They are essentially the same. A positive difference attributable to achievement motivation appears in all studies when *S*s are working alone and not when there are multi-incentives.

Next, consider the trend across treatments of *S*s classified low in both motives in comparison with that of *S*s who are low in resultant n Achievement but high in n Affiliation. There should, according to Table 3 (which implies a multiplicative combination of motive and incentive), be some improvement in the performance of the low resultant n Achievement-low n Affiliation groups but less improvement than when n Affiliation is high. There is the expected smaller gain of 6 or 7 compared to one of 12 or 14, twice as large.

Next, consider the results within the *achievement-orientation alone* condition. Note that the difference in n Affiliation makes no difference, nor should it, since there is no incentive for social approval in that condition.

Now let us examine the results for *S*s who are high in resultant achievement motivation. The difference in n Affiliation makes no difference (nor should it) in the alone condition. But as we move across to the first competitive condition, we expect the subgroup high in n Affiliation to show evidence of a greater increase *in motivation* than the subgroup low in n Affiliation. The former group goes from 46.5 to 53.9; the latter group from 48.4 to 53.4. There is no difference between the gains in performance. Is this the first sign of the inadequacy of our analysis? Not at all. The subgroup high in n Affiliation could

TABLE 5

Mean Anagrams Performance of Men Working Alone and in Competition According to Resultant Achievement Motivation and Affiliative Motivation

	Alone		Competition with female		Competition with male	
	N		N		N	
High Resultant n Achievement (n Achievement–Test Anxiety)						
High n Affiliation	(10)	46.5	(7)	53.9	(7)	48.4
Low n Affiliation	(8)	48.4	(6)	53.4	(5)	53.7
Low Resultant n Achievement (n Achievement–Test Anxiety)						
High n Affiliation	(6)	41.8	(7)	53.6	(6)	56.1
Low n Affiliation	(6)	40.8	(10)	47.7	(10)	46.7
Resultant n Achievement (n Achievement–Test Anxiety)						
High	(18)	47.4	(13)	53.7	(12)	50.3
Low	(12)	41.3	(17)	49.4	(16)	50.2
Difference		+ 6.1		+ 4.3		+ .1
		$p < .025$		n.s.		n.s.

Note.–After Horner, 1968, with permission of the author.
Raw scores on 10-minute anagrams task were normalized to yield a mean of 50 and an *S. D.* of 10.

have increased more in strength of motivation, but not in performance, if it had gone beyond the optimal level of motivation and is now beginning to manifest a performance decrement. We shall have to assume this: that in the *competition with females,* the 53.4 of the High resultant n Achievement-Low in n Affiliation subgroup is on the weak or left side of optimal motivation in Figure 2 (marked *a*) and the 53.9 of the High resultant n Achievement-High n Affiliation subgroup is on the strong or right side of optimal motivation in Figure 2 (marked *c*).

Now the final values in the table must come out a certain way, or the whole argument fails. The most highly motivated subgroup (High resultant n Achievement-High n Affiliation) *must* perform even less adequately in the *competition with a male,* for they are already presumed to be beyond the optimal level of motivation in *competition with a female.* And they do perform less adequately. The performance drops from 53.9 to 48.4. The final result, the level of 53.7 of *S*s high in resultant n Achievement but low in n Affiliation, is easily interpreted as the result of an increase in motivation from the weak or left side of optimal motivation in Figure 2 (see above) to the strong or right side of optimal motivation. All the pieces of the puzzle have fallen into place!

One can see the nonmonotonic relationship between strength of motivation and efficiency of performance in two places. First, look across the three conditions for those having strong motives for both achievement and social approval. The level of performance goes from a relatively high 46.5 to 53.9 (interpreted as already beyond optimal motivation) down to 48.4.

Now look within the treatment producing strong incentives both to achieve and for social approval. Those low in both motives perform at 46.7. Then each of the subgroups having one strong motive does better: 53.7 for the subgroup having high resultant n Achievement but low n Affiliation, 56.1 for the subgroup having high n Affiliation but low resultant n Achievement. You will recall that earlier we said that the 53.7 already represented some decrement in performance. The 56.1 is the highest level of performance in the table, implying that this particular subgroup, this combination of personality and situation, produced a level of motivation closest to the optimal level of motivation for the given task. Finally, consider the drop from around 54 to 56, when only one strong motive is involved, to 48.4 when both motives are strong in the situation producing both of the relevant incentives. The differences in performance attributable to motivation in this table are often equal to one or one and one-half times the standard deviation of the distribution of performance scores. *What if it had been an intelligence test* (see Chapter 20)?

The cumulative weight of the evidence from these six Michigan studies gives credence, I think, to my claim that *much of the now-you-see-it-now-you-don't character of earlier studies of n Achievement and performance is to be understood in terms of the implications of a nonmonotonic relationship between strength of motivation and efficiency of performance and one that may be very much influenced by the particular requirements of the task* (as suggested in Figure 3.)

Another more recent study by Sales (1970) is particularly relevant to the role played by requirements of the task. He showed a linear correlation of .33 ($p < .05$) between n Achievement and productivity by male college students in decoding anagrams for an hour when each, working alone under achievement orientation, was given a new set of seven to do every 5 minutes. This allowed on the average about 30% of the time to rest and wait. But other *S*s, also working alone, were *overloaded* by being presented with 12 anagrams each 5 minutes, approximately 35% more than could be accomplished in that time. The average productivity was increased by this overload, but the linear correlation between n Achievement and productivity dropped to zero as the relationship between the variables shown by Sales took the very form of a symmetrical inverted U as shown in Figure 2[5] (see also Poulton, 1971).

POSSIBLE CAUSES OF INEFFICIENCY IN THE EXECUTION OF AN ACTIVITY

Strictly speaking, a blow-by-blow account of what is involved in the efficient execution of an activity, i.e., the details of performance, is a problem that lies outside the psychology of motivation. It is quite generally assumed (e.g., Vroom, 1964, p. 203) that Performance = f (Ability X Motivation). We shall take a penetrating look at the implications of that programmatic proposition in our final chapter. Here, let us treat an individual's level of ability as equivalent to his level of performance when he is optimally motivated. That would be the best he is ever capable of doing at a particular task.

What ideas have been proposed that might help us to understand why a moderately strong inclination to undertake a particular task might yield the most efficient execution?

One hypothesis, offered by Easterbrook (1959) and frequently cited, has to do with the effect of utilization of available cues for performance and effective organization of the behavior that is required for performing a task well. The central idea is that as motivation increases, there is increased concentration, essentially a reduction in the range of cue utilization. The field of attention narrows. There is less utilization of more peripheral or incidental cues and more importance attached to the central ones. Accordingly, whether a course of action is facilitated or disrupted by increased motivation depends entirely on the complexity of the task, the number of cues that must be utilized simultaneously to achieve the behavior required by the task. Easterbrook's conception is that in any situation there are a range of task-relevant cues (represented here by the

[5] In the underload condition, *S*s were more often successful (having accomplished what was expected). In the overload condition, *S*s always failed. Systematic intensification of achievement motivation following failure, as discussed by Weiner (Chapter 17), seems a likely explanation of the source of the overmotivation decrement produced by the requirements of the task.

inner circle of Figure 5) and a number of task-irrelevant cues that reduce effectiveness of performance of the task to some extent (the shaded zone between the inner circle and outer rim of the larger circle which defines the totality of cues in Figure 5). One can imagine that when strength of motivation for the task is relatively weak, and the person is not much involved in it, his range of attention is rather broad so that it encompasses both task-irrelevant cues (the shaded portion) and task-relevant cues (the inner circle). As strength of motivation increases, the reduction in range of cue utilization reduces the proportion of irrelevant cues employed and so performance improves. This restriction of range continues as motivation and involvement in the task increase until the degree of concentration corresponds exactly to the requirements of the task. All the task-irrelevant cues that reduce effectiveness are outside the range of attention, and all the important task-relevant cues are within the range of attention. Any further reduction in the number of cues employed can only mean the loss of some relevant and important ones. If a further increase in motivation causes a further concentration of attention that has this effect, the organization of the required behavior will suffer and the efficiency of performance will diminish.

Another viable hypothesis comes straight out of the traditional Hullian presumption that a nonspecific drive has a multiplicative influence on all of the specific habits of responding that are elicited in a particular stimulus situation to produce excitatory tendencies for each of the various competing responses. When we consider the final strength of tendency to undertake a particular activity as conceived here (e.g., $T_A = T_s - T_{-f} + T_{ext}$), we are referring to the strength of motivation *to engage in a particular activity,* e.g., to solve arithmetic problems, to make a list of anagrams, etc., instead of doing something else, such as looking

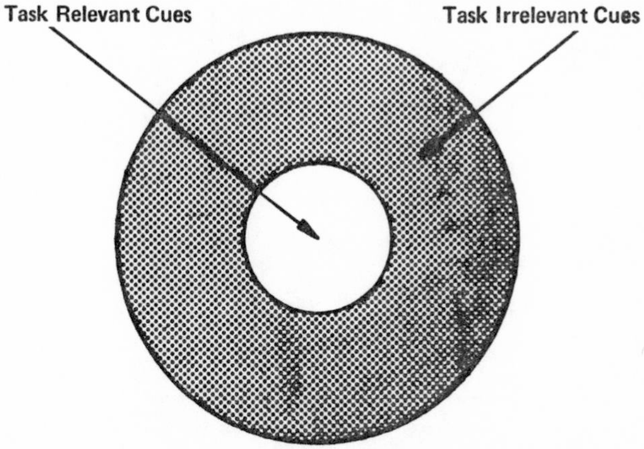

FIG. 5. Graphic presentation of task-relevant and task-irrelevant cues. Easterbrook (1959) proposes that cue utilization becomes more concentrated as intensity of motivation increases.

out the window at fluffy white clouds in the sky. *This T_A may be considered a nonspecific influence on any and all of the more molecular responses whose temporal order, organization, and occurrence constitutes the activity A in question.* In other words, the implications of Hullian theory concerning competition among task-relevant responses, or intratask response competition, may be employed, if they are useful, in analysis of the efficiency of performance of a task or in execution of the activity referred to by T_A.

Most frequently, the point is made in applications of the Hullian principle, ${}_SE_R = D \times {}_SH_R$, that the probability of occurrence of the dominant (or stronger) of two competing habits is enhanced by any increase in drive as shown in Figure 6. Employing this logic as a basis for interpreting much of the old literature in the field of social motivation (particularly the average effect on performance of an audience in samples not differentiated according to dimensions of personality), Zajonc (1965) concluded that an audience must increase the level of drive. He unraveled much evidence to support the notion that performance (of previously well-learned responses) was enhanced by an audience, but that learning (which requires the occurrence of responses for which habit strength is initially subordinate or weak) is impaired by an audience. His penetrating analysis has spurred a new interest in old matters of social motivation (audience, coaction, competition) among workers who think about motivation in traditional Hullian terms (see also Cottrell, 1968; Weiss & Miller, 1971). Much of the new work overlaps the domain of earlier work on achievement motivation and anxiety, but with greater attention to specific social influences and more refinement in experimental manipulations.

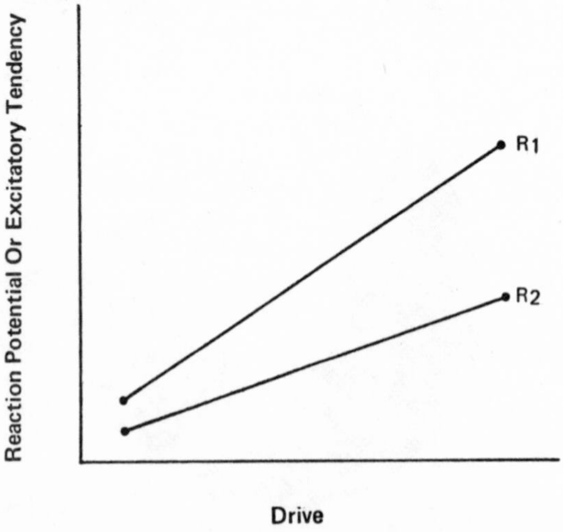

FIG. 6. Effect of increased drive on responses of different (R_1 and R_2) habit strength according to Hull and Spence [$E = f(D \times H)$].

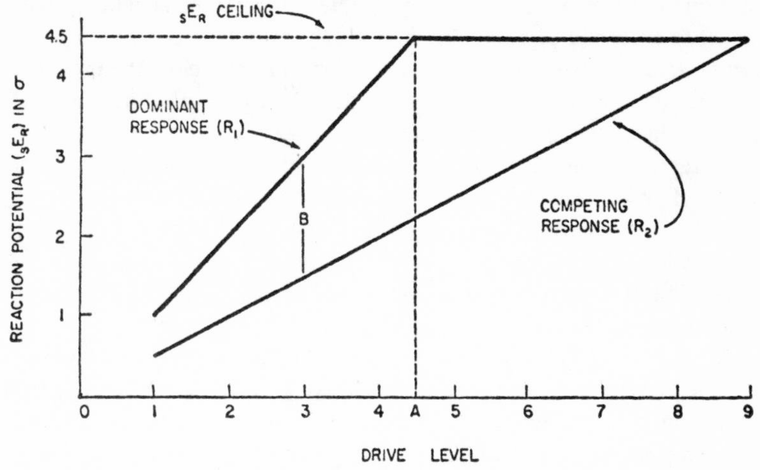

FIG. 7. Effect of increased drive level on reaction potentials of dominant and subordinate habit with hypothesized ceiling on $_SE_R$. *(After Broen & Storms, 1961, with permission of the authors and of the publisher, American Psychological Association.)*

This conventional application of the Hullian conception does not provide much help in understanding why performance of a well-learned task (like solving simple arithmetic problems) should be enhanced by increased motivation up to a certain point but then be impaired by still further increases in motivation. Typically, the research guided by this scheme has emphasized the single point that increased drive enhances the performance of relatively strong habits (simple noncompetitional tasks) and impairs the performance of relatively weak ones (complex competitional tasks) (see also Taylor, 1956; Spence, 1958; Spence & Spence, 1966).

A theoretical argument by Broen and Storms (1961) provides a more heuristic guide in the use of the Hullian scheme as a model of what might be happening to competition among task-relevant responses, the ones that must be performed correctly, quickly, and in a certain order, etc., to produce the molar outcome or effect we describe as doing the task well. Broen and Storms advanced *the hypothesis of a ceiling or upper limit on reaction potential or excitatory tendency* with the theoretical effects shown in Figure 7.

They follow the general logic of Hull (1943) and Spence (1956) concerning momentary fluctuations or oscillations in the strength of excitatory tendency (E) for any particular response, and the assumption that the probability of occurrence of a given response depends upon the magnitude of the (average) difference between E_1 and a competitor E_2 (as drawn in Figure 7). They point out that the probability of the dominant response (the one having greater habit strength) will increase as strength of motivation increases up to the point at which E_1 reaches the ceiling and cannot increase further. Thereafter, as motivation continues to increase, its probability of occurrence will decline as E_2 continues to grow and decreases the $E_1 - E_2$ difference.

Figure 8, also taken from Broen and Storms (1961), plots the probability of occurrence of the dominant and subordinate responses whose motivational viscissitudes have been described in Figure 7.

May I repeat that in my view the task of giving a blow-by-blow causal account of efficient execution of a molar activity lies outside the psychology of motivation. But some generalization is needed concerning how efficiency (defined as level of performance relative to level of ability) is related to strength of motivation in order to explain how achievement is influenced by motivation (Chapter 20).

If we think of the abscissa (or horizontal axis) in Figures 7 and 8 as referring to the final strength of tendency to undertake a task ($T_A = T_s - T_{-f} + T_{\text{ext}}$), remembering the interaction of personality dispositions and immediate situational influences that produce T_A, we have another possible explanation, in this application of a modified Hullian scheme, of why the relationship between level (or efficiency) of performance and strength of motivation for a given task may be nonmonotonic and normally take the form of an inverted U.

In reference to Figure 7, one need only imagine that the dominant habit (R_1) were even somewhat stronger to begin with to see that the point of optimal motivation would then be weaker than what is shown in the figure. In fact, one can be led to some other rather amazing and novel hypotheses. Suppose, for example, that good performance of some task requires the frequent occurrence of a relatively weak or subordinate response. Perhaps a task requiring creativity,

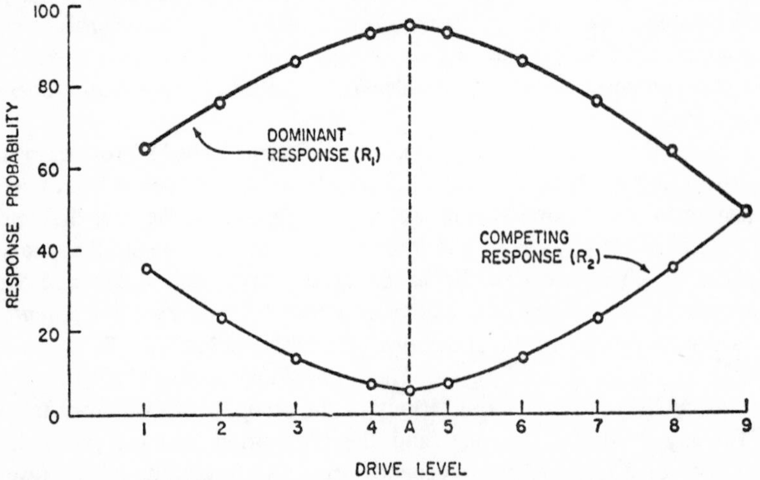

FIG. 8. Expected probabilities of a dominant response (R_1) and a competing response (R_2) as a function of magnitude of difference between ${}_SE_{R_1} - {}_SE_{R_2}$ in Figure 7. (*After Broen & Storms, 1961, with permission of the authors and of the publisher, American Psychological Association.*)

the occurrence of relatively bizarre or rare responses, is an interesting possibility to have in mind as an example. When, according to Figure 8, would this "creative" response be most likely to occur? Apparently, when T_A is either very weak (but then the person might be vulnerable to interruption by some stronger T_X to engage in some other kind of activity instead), or when T_A is exceedingly strong and the person is therefore totally involved in his work and (because T_A is so strong) he is not vulnerable to interruption by tendencies to undertake other kinds of activities instead.

In this strange case, we would have to plot a U-shaped curve to describe the relationship of strength of motivation to efficiency of performance. Perhaps that is why creativity has been such a hard nut for psychologists to crack!

FINAL COMMENT

By now one of my strongly held views has probably become apparent. I believe it is rather nonsensical routinely to run product-moment correlations (which tell us only the degree of *linear* relationship) between every possible measure of motivation and/or performance merely because our new genie, the computer, can perform the trick instantly (and with factor analysis as a dividend) even at the click of a college sophomore's fingers. Like atomic energy, the computer has power to greatly amplify the effects of human enlightenment or stupidity. In the war on ignorance in the behavioral sciences, let us try to bring some enlightenment to the great weapon. Creative thinking must occur before data is processed blindly, automatically. It should be anchored in the most discerning analysis we are capable of making of the descriptive details of experimental observations that contain the clues concerning motivation and behavior. As Freud once pointed out in an eloquent defense of the importance of small signs in the inferential work of a psychologist–the detective does not expect to find an autographed photograph of the murderer pinned to the shirt of his victim!

How does strength of motivation influence efficiency of performance? We now have the conceptual analysis of the problem, some adequate diagnostic tests of personality, and enough experimental know-how for a frontal attack on the questions that Yerkes and Dodson raised back in 1908. The solution will most probably involve a triple interaction involving the nature of the task, the motives of the individual, and the incentive character of the work situation. It promises to be a profitable program of empirical research and one of fundamental importance for education, vocational guidance, and the optimal use of human resources in personnel selection.

If the main implications of this analysis are correct, it means that no work situation is optimal for everyone, no type of personality is most productive in all situations, no single generalization about the effects of strength of motivation will apply to all tasks. It means, more specifically, that for every particular occupational role (if we take role to be a combination of task and work situation), there is a different kind of most productive personality. And for every personality, the anxiety-prone no less than the most positively motivated, there is a particular role which offers an opportunity for relatively greater productivity and relatively greater contribution than others as a solid foundation for the individual's self-esteem.

We know what it is we need to find out. How to proceed to find it out has finally come into focus. The task is technically feasible. The implications are important.[6]

[6]One should consult the review of animal literature of Broadhurst (1959) and contemporary work by Eysenck (1966b) and co-workers, which have the same general thrust as recommended here. I feel that our systematic program of work on achievement motivation has yielded a more coherent conceptual analysis of the determinants of strength of human motivation. Thus it offers a more promising general guide for operational definition of strength of motivation in future systematic experimental analysis of this problem.

12

EFFECTS OF ACHIEVEMENT-ORIENTED AND AFFILIATIVE MOTIVES ON PRIVATE AND PUBLIC PERFORMANCE[1]

Elliot E. Entin

Two hypotheses are proposed to relate the theory of achievement motivation (see Chapter 2) to performance: a "monotonic" hypothesis that predicts performance on an achievement-oriented task to be monotonically related to strength of tendency, and, in contrast, a "curvilinear" hypothesis that stipulates that the relationship between strength of tendency and performance is contingent upon the nature of the task, perhaps its complexity (Atkinson & O'Connor, 1966; Atkinson, 1967; see also Chapter 11).

Intuitively, it would seem that achievement motivation should be related to the vigor of performance or performance efficiency. During the formative years of the theory of achievement motivation (Atkinson, 1957, 1964, Ch. 9; Atkinson & Feather, 1966, Ch. 20), it was simply assumed that a positive monotonic relationship existed between strength of the achievement motive as measured by the n Achievement score and vigor of performance. Early studies by Lowell (1952), French (1955, 1958a), Wendt (1955), Atkinson (1953), and Atkinson and Raphelson (1956) bolstered support for that notion. However, it was also noted that "the results obtained in some of these experiments have not always been consistently replicated by other investigators... [Atkinson, 1964, p. 237]." An adequate explanation of why this is so is not yet available.

[1] This chapter is adapted from an unpublished doctoral dissertation (Entin, 1968) carried out at the University of Michigan. The research was partially supported by Grant GS-1399 from the National Science Foundation to John W. Atkinson. Study I was presented in a paper, "The Effect of Achievement-oriented Tendencies and Extrinsic Tendencies on Performance," published in the *Proceedings of the American Psychological Association*, 1971, and is included here by permission of the author and of the American Psychological Association.

Probably some of the difficulty lies in replicating the experimental conditions used or in the reliable assessment and/or coding of n Achievement. Atkinson (1964) and Atkinson and O'Connor (1966) have suggested yet another possibility, one concerning the role of extrinsic sources of motivation in determining the relationship between achievement-related motives and level of performance.

Atkinson and O'Connor (1966) addressed themselves to this possibility in discussing an unexpected performance decrement, apparently due to the arousal of an intense level of motivation. They suggested that an optimal level of motivation might exist for most efficient performance and that, once this level is exceeded, performance declines. This is similar to the curvilinear hypothesis discussed by Yerkes and Dodson (1908) in their classic study.

The impact of a curvilinear hypothesis would be to point out that the form of the function describing the relationship between final strength of tendency to act (T_A) and performance efficiency is in part dependent upon the nature of the task that the *S* is required to perform and in part dependent upon the intensity of T_A. A monotonically increasing function might be observed if the task were of the "simple," highly practiced variety that involved very little conflict among competing responses. However, a more "complex" task that required more careful discrimination among alternatives might produce some kind of curvilinear relationship. Here the optimal level of motivation for maximum performance efficiency falls at some intermediate level. Atkinson (1967, and Chapter 11) also notes that there may be tasks which require a very careful, cautious, deliberate approach on the part of the *S*. For most of the range of motivation this kind of task might produce a decreasing function.

The assumption that a curvilinear relationship exists between performance and strength of T_A is, at best, tentative. No clear evidence for such a relationship exists in research on achievement motivation. Nor is there an unambiguous demonstration that a significant decrement in performance occurs in a group very high in T_A in comparison to a group more moderate in strength of T_A. However, the possibility of a curvilinear relationship provides one of the more plausible explanations for the results obtained by Atkinson and Reitman (1956), Smith (1961), and Atkinson and O'Connor (1966) in their multi-incentive conditions.

The present research was designed to investigate the general hypothesis that the joint contribution of achievement-related motives and some other motive extrinsic to achievement such as the affiliative or approval motive may be too great for efficient performance, producing a performance decrement. Individuals were categorized high or low on resultant achievement motivation (standardized n Achievement score minus standardized Test Anxiety score) and high or low in n Affiliation (Heyns, Veroff, & Atkinson, 1958), and performed in either a private or public condition. Since both private and public conditions were achievement-oriented, the class of achievement-related incentives (success and failure) was assumed to have been aroused for all *S*s. Those assigned to the public condition were considered to perceive a large, unambiguous approval or affiliative incentive since these subjects were led to believe that their performance outcome would be known to peers, teaching personnel, and parents. The private condition attempted to reduce the affiliative or approval incentive and to minimize all possibilities of gaining it by guaranteeing to the *S* that his performance outcome would be strictly personal and available only to him.

A complete ordering of the eight groups that result from the combination of resultant achievement motivation (high or low), n Affiliation (high or low) and experimental condition (private or public) with respect to the strength of final positive tendency to act (T_A) is not possible. However, the assumption of additivity of tendencies (specifically, $T_A = (T_s - T_{-f}) + T_{\mathrm{app}}$) in conjunction with those above concerning the incentives aroused in the private and public conditions does yield a partial ordering of groups. The ordering was obtained by assigning a weight of 2 to a relatively strong (above the median) motive, a weight of 1 to a relatively weak (below the median) motive, a weight of 2 to the public condition, and a weight of 1 to the private condition. Combining resultant achievement-affiliative-condition combinations having the same total weights yields four composite groups:

I. Consisting of the group with *S*s high in resultant achievement motivation, high in n Affiliation, that performed in the public condition (High-High-Public). This group was assumed to be highest in T_A.

II. Composed of the following groups: *S*s high in resultant achievement motivation, high in n Affiliation, that performed in the private condition (the High-High-Private group); the High-Low-Public group, and the Low-High-Public group. This composite group was assumed to be the second highest in T_A.

III. Composed of the following groups: High-Low-Private, Low-High-Private, and Low-Low-Public. This composite group was assumed to be third highest (or next to lowest) in T_A.

IV. Composed of the Low-Low-Private group, assumed to be weakest in T_A.

The "monotonic" and "curvilinear" assumptions relating strength of T_A to performance can now be stated in terms of the ordering of the composite groups. If the relationship between T_A and performance is (positive) monotonic, then performance scores should be ordered as follows, from lowest to highest: composite groups IV, III, II, and I. However, if this relationship were curvilinear, and more specifically, in the general form of an inverted U-shaped curve (see Chapter 11), then composite groups IV and I would be expected to be lower than composite groups III and II, or, at least, that IV would be lower than III, and I would be lower than II. Finally, while not expected in the present study, if the relationship between T_A is such that any increase in T_A over its lowest value produces too much positive motivation for performance efficiency (see Chapter 11), then the ordering of composite groups would be, from lowest performance to highest: I, II, III, and IV.

Two studies were conducted. The first represented a preliminary investigation of the relationship between achievement-related motives and performance in both a private and a public condition using the n Affiliation measure of the approval motive to further differentiate *S*s into groups presumably high and low in their sensitivity to incentives offered by the public condition and therefore differing in the extent to which incentives in the public condition (but not the private) should influence strength of T_A. Study II represented a further refinement of the procedures developed in Study I for inducing the private and public experimental conditions. Also, in Study II *S*s worked on both a "simple" and a "complex" task, the rationale being that the complex task should be more susceptible to effects of too much positive motivation on level of performance and hence results for it should support the curvilinear hypothesis to a greater extent than results for the simple task, which were expected to support the monotonic hypothesis.

STUDY I

Method

Subjects and assessment of motives. One hundred and fifteen male high-school students were administered the projective measures of n Achievement and n Affiliation, and the Test Anxiety Scale for Children (TASC), under neutral conditions (see Atkinson, 1958a, Appendix III) and scored according to the pertinent literature concerning each (McClelland et al., 1958; Heyns et al., 1958; Sarason et al., 1960). The protocols were scored for n Achievement by the author, whose product-moment correlation with the training materials (see Feld & Smith, 1958) has been established at .90 and with another expert scorer at .89, and for n Affiliation by a trained expert scorer.[2] *S*s were assured that these measures would in no way affect their school grades, but rather that these questionnaires were a continuation of the personality inventories they had already taken for counseling purposes.

Scores from the above three instruments were transformed into T-Scores (standard scores with a mean of 50 and S.D. of 10). The T-Score distribution for n Affiliation was rank-ordered and split at the median to obtain high and low groups. A measure of resultant achievement motivation was obtained for each *S* by subtracting his T-Score on TASC from his T-Score on n Achievement. This distribution was also broken at the median to obtain high and low groups.

Each *S* in the sample had taken the Differential Aptitude Test (DAT) sometime during the school year as part of the school's testing program. Nonverbal scores on this standardized test were subsequently obtained. Since the

[2] The author wishes to thank Allison Arscott of the Institute for Social Research for scoring the protocols for n Affiliation. She is an established expert whose scoring correlates above .90 with the training materials and with another expert scorer.

DAT (as are all aptitude or intelligence tests) was administered under conditions perfectly replicating the description of an achievement-oriented task (see McClelland et al., 1949), scores on it were viewed as a dependent measure reflecting the effects of individual differences in achievement-related and affiliative motives, but free of the specific effects of the experimental manipulations of the present study.

Experimental conditions. A week later students who had participated in the earlier assessment were randomly divided into the public and private conditions, and administered a "timed arithmetic test" (see below). Verbal instructions pointed out that this was an important test of basic arithmetic ability, that it would affect students' placement in high-school classes, and therefore that they should try to do their best. Written instructions on page two of the arithmetic booklets reiterated the achievement-arousing instructions and provided the information inducing the experimental conditions. Those in the *public condition* read:

> Your grade on this test will be posted on the wall outside the room. A list including your full name, followed by your number and letter grade, will appear at 3:00 P.M. today. This is a test of your ability so try your best.

Those in the *private condition* read:

> Your grade on this test will be private and of the strictest confidence. After all the tests handed out are returned, the name sheets will be torn away and only the code number retained. Only you will know your results. At 3:00 P.M. today, a list including your private code number,[3] followed by your number and letter grade, will appear on the wall outside this room.

Performance task. The arithmetic task consisted of four different kinds of problems (addition, subtraction, multiplication, and division) constructed from a table of random numbers. Problems were arranged 36 to a page: 9 of each kind of problem, randomly ordered. There were five pages, for a total of 180 problems. Each problem, regardless of kind, consisted of six digits. The *S*s were allowed 3 minutes per page. It was explained verbally that *S*s would be asked to turn the page at the end of a certain time limit and that they should do so rapidly so as not to waste time. Total testing time was 15 minutes.

Treatment of the data. Scoring of a 30% subset of the arithmetic task indicated that the number of problems attempted and the number solved correctly were almost perfectly correlated ($r = .98$). It was arbitrarily decided to use the number of problems attempted as the measure of arithmetic performance. Both this distribution and that of the nonverbal DAT scores were transformed into T-Scores.

Results

Table 1 presents mean nonverbal DAT scores and mean arithmetic performance scores as a function of resultant achievement and affiliative motivation.

[3] In the private condition, a four-digit ID number was placed on the second instruction page.

TABLE 1

Study I: Nonverbal DAT Score and Number of Problems Attempted on the Arithmetic Task as a Function of Resultant Achievement Motivation and n Affiliation

Resultant achievement motivation	n Affiliation	*N*	Mean nonverbal DAT score	Mean number of problems attempted: arithmetic task
High	High	(20)	53.5	52.2
High	Low	(25)	54.2	54.2
Low	High	(24)	49.2	51.0
Low	Low	(27)	46.4	43.5

As predicted by theory of achievement motivation and found in previous research (see Atkinson & Litwin, 1960), *Ss* high in resultant achievement motivation had higher nonverbal DAT scores and attempted more arithmetic problems than *Ss* low in resultant motivation ($F = 17.22$ and 7.62, $df = 1/88$, $p < .001$ and $< .005$, respectively). Also, *Ss* high in n Affiliation had higher nonverbal DAT scores than those low ($F = 5.14$, $df = 1/88$, $p < .05$), but did not differ in performance on the arithmetic task.

Table 2 shows the mean arithmetic performance as a function of resultant achievement motivation and experimental conditions. The pattern of results appears similar to that obtained by Atkinson and Reitman (1956) and Smith (1961). In the private condition the group high on resultant achievement motivation performed significantly better than the low group ($F = 10.69$, $df = 1/92$, $p < .01$), while in the public condition there is little difference between these two groups ($F = 1.69$, $df = 1/92$, n.s.). Note that the difference in results between the two conditions is due entirely to the lower performance in the public than in the private condition of the group high in resultant achievement motivation ($F = 3.10$, $df = 1/92$, $p < .10$).

Table 3 shows arithmetic performance as a function of achievement-related and affiliative motivation as well as experimental conditions. Only for *Ss* low in resultant achievement motivation within the private condition was there any noticeable difference due to n Affiliation, but there is no statistically reliable evidence to suggest that n Affiliation functioned as a positive motive to influence arithmetic performance. Therefore the data were not analyzed further according to the composite groups described earlier since there was no basis to discriminate between groups high and low on n Affiliation.

TABLE 2

Study I: Mean Number of Problems Attempted by Groups High and Low on Resultant Achievement Motivation in the Public and Private Conditions

Resultant achievement motivation	Condition			
	Private		Public	
	N	Mean	*N*	Mean
High	(20)	56.7	(25)	51.6
Low	(27)	47.4	(24)	48.0
Difference (H–L)		9.3		3.6

TABLE 3

Study I: Number of Problems Attempted as a Function of Resultant Achievement Motivation, n Affiliation, and Experimental Condition

Resultant achievement motivation	Condition			
	Private		Public	
	Low n Affiliation	High n Affiliation	Low n Affiliation	High n Affiliation
High	(12) 56.8	(8) 56.5	(13) 51.8	(12) 51.4
Low	(14) 45.2	(13) 51.3	(13) 47.6	(11) 47.3

Note.–Numbers in parentheses represent *N*.

STUDY II

Method

Subjects and assessment of motives. The sample consisted of 169 male students, drawn from the seventh and eighth grades of a junior high school, who were present on both testing days. The assessment of motives took place 1 week before the administration of the performance tasks. The projective measure was administered first (using pictures 2, 7, 8, and 100; numbers are from Atkinson, 1958a, p. 834) according to the standard procedures (see Atkinson, 1958a, p. 836) and was subsequently coded for n Achievement and n Affiliation according to the appropriate scoring manuals.[4] The Test Anxiety Scale for Children was administered as in Study I. The correlations between the three motive measures were distributed about zero and were nonsignificant.

Experimental conditions. The *E* or one of his four male assistants[5] entered each of the seventh and eighth grade math classes held during the school day and administered the performance tasks under achievement-oriented conditions. *S*s were informed that the test was timed and that they should work as quickly and accurately as possible. An explanation and demonstration of the simple and complex arithmetic problems followed. Several example problems were worked by *S*s, and an example of each kind of problem was left on the blackboard. *E* next instructed *S*s to read a set of instructions to themselves, which created either the public or the private condition (determined by random distribution of the test booklets). *S*s in the *public* condition read the following:

> Your grade on this test will be posted outside this room. A list including your full name followed by your number score and its equivalent letter grade will appear tomorrow at this time. Your teacher and counselor will also receive copies of your results, so try to do your best so that they can be proud of you.

*S*s in the *private* condition instead read the following:

> Your score on this test will be private and of the strictest confidence. Neither your teacher, your counselor, nor any school official will learn your results. Only you will know your results. You will be able to learn your score tomorrow by picking up a sealed envelope bearing your private ID number on a table just inside this room.

Ten pages of the performance tasks followed. Two minutes were allowed for each page. A pretest had shown that it was virtually impossible to finish all of the problems on a page in this time. The total testing time was 20 minutes.

Performance tasks. The simple task consisted of the addition of a two-digit number to another two-digit number. The problems were constructed from a

[4] The author thanks Sharon Lucas and Allison Arscott for coding n Achievement and n Affiliation, respectively. Miss Lucas had previously been established as an expert scorer for n Achievement in the usual manner (see also Footnote 2).

[5] The author would like to thank Terry Davidson, Lloyd Johnson, Joel Raynor, and Jerry Syzmanski for their assistance.

table of random numbers and arranged 72 to a page. Five different pages were constructed and arranged in the test booklets in 10 different orders.

The Wendt (1955) three-step arithmetic task was used as the complex task of this study. It had previously been employed by Atkinson and Reitman (1956) and Smith (1961). Problems were arranged 24 to a page. Five different pages were constructed and presented in 10 different orders. The pages of simple and complex problems were alternated in all test booklets, with a complex page always coming first.

The simple and complex tasks used here are assumed to represent a gradient of complexity primarily determined by an increase in the number of steps necessary to arrive at the correct solution. However, the quality of steps involved in a solution was also assumed to be a factor. Complexity was assumed to increase if the quantity of steps increased or the quality of the steps called for represented a higher learning type (see Gagne, 1965). It was assumed that the complex task required quantitatively more steps and that it called for steps of a qualitatively higher learning type than the simple task.

Treatment of the data. The distributions of simple and complex problems solved correctly were each standardized by conversion to T-Scores to facilitate comparison of performance on the two tasks. Resultant achievement motivation was determined as described in Study I. Planned comparisons were used to test those hypotheses suggested by the original argument that performance on the simple task would be a positive monotonic function of strength of final tendency to act (T_A), while this relationship would be curvilinear for the complex task. These a priori tests were computed according to the procedure described by Winer (1962, p. 208) using the appropriate mean square error.

Results

Tables 4 and 5 show the mean number of problems solved correctly for both the simple and the complex tasks respectively, as a function of groups high and low on resultant achievement and affiliative motivation in the private and public conditions. Inspection of these data shows that the group assumed to be most positively motivated (the High-High-Public, where the first term represents resultant achievement motivation, and the second, n Affiliation) did not solve the greatest number of problems on either task. Comparison of this High-High-Public group with the equivalent group in the private condition (the High-High-Private group) reveals a marginally significant difference in favor of the latter for the complex task ($t = 1.32$, $df = 161$, $p < .10$, one-tailed test). An equivalent test for the simple task did not reach the accepted level of significance ($t < 1$, n.s.). Thus the results for the complex task offer *tenuous* support for the curvilinear hypothesis that predicts too intense levels of motivation might be counterproductive when compared to some group more moderate in total positive motivation. The results for the simple task contradict the initial expectation of a monotonic relationship between strength of motivation and level of performance for such a task. That is, the results for *both* tasks are consistent in offering no

TABLE 4

Study II: Mean Number of Problems Correct on the Simple Task as a Function of Resultant Achievement Motivation, n Affiliation, and Experimental Condition

Resultant achievement motivation	Condition			
	Private		Public	
	Low n Affiliation	High n Affiliation	Low n Affiliation	High n Affiliation
High	(19) 53.3	(23) 51.7	(19) 51.8	(18) 49.6
Low	(28) 46.9	(18) 50.2	(24) 50.5	(20) 51.4

Note.–Numbers in parentheses represent *N*.

TABLE 5

Study II: Mean Number of Problems Correct on the Complex Task as a Function of Resultant Achievement Motivation, n Affiliation, and Experimental Condition

Resultant achievement motivation	Condition			
	Private		Public	
	Low n Affiliation	High n Affiliation	Low n Affiliation	High n Affiliation
High	(19) 52.4	(23) 53.5	(19) 51.9	(18) 49.4
Low	(28) 46.4	(18) 51.4	(24) 49.6	(20) 50.3

Note.–Numbers in parentheses represent *N*.

support for the monotonic hypothesis. Furthermore, inspection of the data yields no basis to discriminate between the two arithmetic tasks. The pattern of results for each is what would be expected of a complex task.

If the assumption is correct that n Affiliation produced a positive tendency that by itself is monotonically related to performance on the tasks used in this study, then at least within *S*s low in resultant achievement motivation, those high in n Affiliation should perform better than those low. Furthermore, this difference should be greater in the public than in the private condition. For both tasks there is an overall tendency within the low resultant motivation group for those high to perform better than those low in n Affiliation (as in Study I). However, the differences in the private condition ($t = 1.14$, n.s., and $t = 1.67$, $df = 167$, $p < .10$, one-tailed test, for the "simple" and "complex" tasks, respectively) were *larger* rather than smaller than those within the public condition (ts < 1, n.s.). This suggests that n Affiliation was not a very salient incentive within the public condition, so that if we are to entertain the possibility that the decrement of the High-High-Public group was produced by too much positive motivation for optimal performance efficiency (the curvilinear hypothesis), then other positive extrinsic tendencies would appear to be responsible for the purported increase in positive motivation.

Since there is some statistical evidence for n Affiliation as a positive motive, the mean performance scores of the four composite motivation groups whose derivation was described earlier were calculated. The composite groups represent a partial ordering on strength of final tendency to act (T_A); Group IV is assumed lowest, while Group I is assumed highest on T_A. Their mean level of performance is shown in Table 6. Inspection suggests that the relationship between strength of T_A and performance was curvilinear rather than positive monotonic on both tasks. However, several analyses (e.g., Bartholomew, 1959a, 1959b, 1961; Gaito, 1965) to contrast the two hypotheses failed to yield clear-cut (statistically reliable) support for one over the other (see Entin, 1968, for a presentation and discussion of these tests).

The data were next collapsed across n Affiliation groups and reanalyzed as in Study I as a function of resultant achievement motivation and experimental

TABLE 6

Study II: Mean Number of Problems Correct in the Simple and Complex Tasks for Each of the Four Composite Motivation Groups

Composite group	N	Mean number of simple problems	Mean number of complex problems
I	(18)	49.56	49.44
II	(62)	51.65	51.98
III	(61)	52.25	51.00
IV	(28)	46.86	46.43

TABLE 7

Study II: Number of Problems Correct for the Simple and Complex Tasks as a Function of Resultant Achievement Motivation and Experimental Condition

Resultant achievement motivation	Simple task		Complex task	
	Condition			
	Private	Public	Private	Public
High	(42) 52.4	(37) 50.7	(42) 53.0	(37) 50.7
Low	(46) 48.2	(44) 50.9	(46) 48.4	(44) 49.9
Difference (H – L)	4.2	-0.2	4.6	0.8

Note.–Numbers in parentheses represent *N*.

conditions (see Table 7). Inspection indicates that the pattern of results was similar to that obtained in Study I: *S*s high in resultant motivation performed better than those low on both tasks in the private condition ($t = 1.48$ and 1.56, $df = 165$, $p < .10$, for the "simple" and "complex" tasks, respectively), while these differences were negligible within the public condition ($ts < 1$, n.s.).

It was noticed that within the eighth grade sample, *S*s high on resultant achievement motivation performed significantly better than those low ($t = 1.70$, $df = 84$, $p < .05$; $t = 2.20$, $df = 84$, $p < .02$), but this was not so for the seventh graders ($ts \leqslant 1.0$) nor for the sample as a whole. A stronger resultant achievement motivation would contribute to a stronger final motivation. Thus as an ancillary analysis the eighth grade *S*s were isolated and their results examined. In addition, a crude measure of performance efficiency was devised for this sample and analyzed along with the other dependent variables. Essentially the same analysis procedure was followed as that described for the whole sample. The new efficiency measure was the percentage of problems worked correctly, transformed to T-scores. The new means are presented in Tables 8 and 9.

The contrast that should best discriminate between the two hypotheses in question is a comparison between the group highest in final tendency and the next more moderately motivated group, in this case the high resultant achievement motivation, high affiliation private group. This contrast showed that a difference in favor of the moderately motivated group, approached significance for the "simple task" number correct ($t = 1.37$, $df = 84$, $p < .10$) and the "complex task" number correct ($t = 1.29$, $df = 84$, $p < .10$), and was highly significant for the "simple task" percentage correct ($t = 2.89$, $df = 84$, $p < .005$).

It was expected that among *S*s low on resultant achievement motivation, those high on affiliation should perform better than those low. Only the comparison for "simple task" percentage correct yielded conforming significant results ($t = 1.90$, $df = 84$, $p < .05$). All other comparisons, however, were in the

TABLE 8

Study II: Mean Number Correct and Mean Percentage Correct for Simple Task as a Function of Resultant Achievement Motivation, n Affiliation, and Experimental Condition for the Eighth Grade Sample

Resultant achievement motivation	Affiliation	Number correct				Percentage correct			
		Private		Public		Private		Public	
		N	Mean	*N*	Mean	*N*	Mean	*N*	Mean
High	High	(9)	55.7	(10)	49.9	(9)	58.9	(10)	47.2
High	Low	(11)	54.9	(11)	55.2	(11)	53.2	(11)	54.5
Low	High	(11)	50.9	(11)	50.4	(11)	52.2	(11)	51.8
Low	Low	(16)	49.4	(13)	49.8	(16)	44.5	(13)	49.8

TABLE 9

Study II: Mean Number Correct and Mean Percentage Correct for Complex Task as a Function of Resultant Achievement Motivation, n Affiliation and Experimental Condition for the Eighth Grade Sample

Resultant achievement motivation	Affiliation	Number correct				Percentage correct			
		Private		Public		Private		Public	
		N	Mean	*N*	Mean	*N*	Mean	*N*	Mean
High	High	(9)	55.3	(10)	49.9	(9)	52.8	(10)	52.8
High	Low	(11)	55.2	(11)	55.1	(11)	53.7	(11)	55.6
Low	High	(11)	51.3	(11)	49.3	(11)	52.4	(11)	50.0
Low	Low	(16)	48.4	(13)	48.8	(16)	48.8	(13)	48.2

expected direction. From arguments made above it was further expected that high n Affiliation *S*s who are low in resultant achievement motivation should perform best in the public condition. There is no support for this from the data.

In summary, results from the eighth grade sample present a bit stronger and more consistent picture that the group strongest in final motivation to perform suffered a decrement when compared to the performance of a more moderately motivated group. There is also some evidence that affiliation must have been a positive (but weak) source of motivation for subjects in this sample.

DISCUSSION

In reviewing the above results a consistent pattern emerges. The curvilinear assumption linking theory of achievement motivation to performance efficiency is only weakly supported, but far stronger is the implication that a simple positive monotonic relationship between strength of tendency (T_A) and level of performance is inadequate.

When individual differences in n Affiliation are discounted, the overall results of both studies replicate the general pattern reported by Atkinson and Reitman (1956; also described in Chapter 11) and Smith (1961; described in Chapter 11). That is, *S*s high on resultant achievement motivation performed better than *S*s low on this measure in a private (achievement-oriented) condition where the outcome of an *S*'s performance was to be known only to him; this difference was negligible in a public condition, where the outcome of performance was to be known to parents, teachers, and peers. In Study I the critical difference to note occurred for the group high on resultant achievement motivation, which performed lower in the public than in the private condition–thus showing the performance decrement. However, the performance of the group low on resultant achievement motivation was about the same in both conditions. In Study II the overall results for the "complex" task were similar to those obtained for the task in Study I. Overall results for the "simple" task depicted a similar but smaller performance decrement for the high resultant motivation group coupled with an increment of similar magnitude for the group low in resultant motivation from the private to the public condition. Thus the instructions used to induce these public conditions had the same general effect of reducing the expected positive relationship between resultant achievement motivation and level of performance–just as occurred in the multi-incentive conditions of the Atkinson and Reitman (1956) and Smith (1961) studies. If it is correct that the public condition introduced some positive incentive to act that was extrinsic to achievement-related concerns, then the apparent decrement of the groups high in resultant achievement motivation from the private to the public condition cannot be readily reconciled with the assumption of a (positive) monotonic relationship between strength of total positive motivation (T_A) and level of performance.

The results in Study II for the composite ordering of motivation groups suggest that the relationship between strength of T_A and performance may be curvilinear rather than monotonic for the two tasks. They also suggest that there is no justification for describing one task as more or less "complex" than the other. However, independent behavioral evidence fails to provide a solid confirmation of the functional significance of scores of n Affiliation as a positive source of motivation. While previous research suggests that this is the case (see Atkinson, Heyns, & Veroff, 1954; French, 1955, 1958b; Atkinson & Raphelson, 1956), and *S*s high in n Affiliation received higher scores on the nonverbal Differential Aptitude Test in Study I, the results of both studies failed to show the expected interaction within the group low on resultant achievement motivation. That is, those high in n Affiliation should outperform those low in n Affiliation to a greater extent in the public than in the private condition. Such evidence would appear necessary to substantiate the argument that too much *positive* motivation was aroused for the group high on both resultant achievement and affiliation motivation in the public condition to produce the performance decrement compared to the private condition. On the other hand, there is no evidence from the low resultant motivation groups to support arguments that a negative motive was aroused. Examination of the groups low on resultant motivation across experimental conditions shows their performance scores to be essentially the same. Thus we are left to speculate about the reason for the apparently lower performance of the groups high in resultant motivation in the public condition. Smith (1961) has suggested that the public instructions (i.e., multi-incentive) might introduce some negative incentive for those high but not for those low on resultant achievement motivation. However, such an assumption cannot be tested in the present studies. It would therefore appear that unequivocal demonstration that an intense level of positive motivation can be counterproductive awaits future research.

13
PERFORMANCE OF MEN IN NONCOMPETITIVE AND INTERPERSONAL COMPETITIVE ACHIEVEMENT-ORIENTED SITUATIONS[1]

Matina Souretis Horner

This study is concerned with the confounding influence of other motives and incentives on the relationship between achievement motivation and performance. The importance of situational factors in determining this relationship has already been stressed (see Atkinson & Reitman, 1956; Reitman, 1960; Smith, 1961; and Chapters 11 and 12). All these studies emphasize that only under conditions where extrinsic motivation has been minimized can we expect the relationship between achievement motivation and performance to be consistently positive.

Atkinson and Reitman (1956) suggest that the positive relationship between strength of achievement motivation and performance will exist only when subjects believe that their performance will lead to an achievement incentive, that it will not be found when other kinds of "extrinsic" incentives are also expected. They report that under multi-incentive conditions, when extrinsic factors such as affiliative and/or money motives were also thought to be aroused, the relationship between achievement motivation and performance was obscured. *S*s low in n Achievement and high in n Affiliation were found to profit most by the addition of extrinsic incentives. There is a suggestion that those high in both motives may have suffered a performance decrement due to the presence of a greater than optimal level of motivation. Trends in a study by Smith (1961) were very similar, but were originally interpreted differently by him. The

[1] This chapter is based on a portion of an unpublished doctoral dissertation (Horner, 1968) at the University of Michigan. The major part of this work was carried out while the author held a USPHS Pre-Doctoral Fellowship. Another part of the doctoral research is presented in Chapter 6.

confounding influence of extrinsic factors was further emphasized by Atkinson and O'Connor (1966), who considered the effects of n Affiliation in terms of social approval as an added incentive in the experimental situation when an observer is present. They reported an adverse effect on performance when high n Affiliation was coupled with high resultant achievement motivation. This again suggested the possibility of a performance decrement when motivation to perform well is too intense.

The design of the present study attempts to unravel further some of the complications noted in previous research of this kind. Specifically, the effects on the performance of men in two kinds of situations are studied: (*a*) a noncompetitive achievement-oriented situation involving competition against a standard only; and (*b*) an interpersonal competitive achievement-oriented situation involving competition against another person or persons. (Chapter 6 has reported some effects of these same situations on the behavior of women.)

Typical achievement situations in life (i.e., in schools, business, politics, etc.), as well as most experimental situations, either explicitly or implicitly involve both of these aspects of competition. For example, in order to succeed or to do well in school, one must usually perform well on tests in relation to some basic standard but also in relation to others in the class. If the two kinds of competition have different effects on behavior, they would be systematically confounded most of the time.

In the present study, these two aspects of competition are experimentally separated. In the noncompetitive achievement-oriented condition, *S*s compete only against a standard of excellence. The experimenter tries to convince each *S* that his behavior will in no way be compared with or judged against that of anyone else. It is assumed, therefore, that extrinsic motivation in this condition is negligible. In two interpersonal competitive achievement-oriented situations, *S*s must compete against another person, either a male or a female. Here the *S* is quite obviously in direct competition with someone else. Extrinsic motivation is thus assumed to be much greater in the interpersonal competitive than in the noncompetitive achievement-oriented condition.

The theory of achievement motivation (see Chapter 2) does not address itself explicitly to the distinction between different kinds of competition, nor does the scoring of thematic apperceptive stories for n Achievement (McClelland et al., 1953). It therefore does not explicitly make different predictions for noncompetitive and interpersonal competitive achievement-oriented situations. However, the assumptions just made concerning the strengths of extrinsic motivation aroused in the two situations, in conjunction with existing theory concerning achievement motivation, allow us to derive (for men) the following specific hypotheses: (*a*) the total strength of motivation to perform will be stronger and hence level of performance (*assuming a monotonic relationship*) will be higher in the interpersonal competitive than in the noncompetitive achievement-oriented condition; (*b*) regardless of competitive condition, *S*s high in resultant achievement motivation will perform at a higher level than those low in resultant achievement motivation, but this difference will be clearest in the noncompetitive achievement-oriented condition, where extrinsic motivation is at a minimum; (*c*) regardless of competitive condition, *S*s high in resultant achievement motivation will take moderate risks (select tasks of intermediate difficulty), while those low in resultant motivation will take extreme risks (select either very easy or very difficult tasks).

The above risk-taking hypothesis would not hold if the strength of the negative incentive value of failure in interpersonal competitive achievement-oriented conditions, especially when men compete against women, were more than a simple function of subjective probability of success due to an increase in the threat of failure in such conditions. In fact, it seems reasonable to assume that failure against a woman in a mixed-sex competitive achievement-oriented situation would tend to be more threatening to a man than failure when alone (noncompetitive) or (perhaps) even failure against another man. Perhaps an exponential relationship would be an appropriate model relating the negative incentive value of failure to subjective probability of success (see Horner, 1968, for a detailed treatment of this possibility). If this were the case, men should prefer competitors against whom it is believed there is a small chance to win.[2]

METHOD

General Procedure

*S*s were administered diagnostic tests for n Achievement and Debilitating Anxiety (Alpert & Haber, 1960) and several purported measures of their ability in large-group testing sessions conducted several weeks prior to an invitation to appear at a second session. On the latter occasion, each *S* was assigned to one of three achievement-oriented experimental conditions: noncompetitive (alone); interpersonal competition with a male; or interpersonal competition with a female. *S*s were then given a risk-preference task in which each was asked to select from among either tasks which differed, as described, in difficulty (in the noncompetitive condition), or from among competitors who differed, as described, in the chance or probability they offered the *S*s of being able to win against them in the interpersonal competitive conditions. The difficulty of the tasks as described to each *S* was purportedly based on his own ability scores (viz., those obtained in the prior group-testing session) and from his academic record. Three performance tasks (generation anagrams, complex arithmetic problems, and digit symbol substitutions) were then administered. This was followed by

[2] If extrinsic motivation (e.g., to gain social approval) entered into the choice among tasks that differ in difficulty, one might develop an argument that (*a*) the secondary gain of appearing to try difficult tasks would influence the choice, or that (*b*) the expectation of greater approval for success at a difficult task would accentuate preference for moderate risk even among those normally weak in resultant achievement motivation.–Editors.

questions concerning personal background and other questions pertaining to the experiment.

Subjects

The male *S*s were among 178 undergraduate students enrolled in nine introductory psychology sections at the University of Michigan during the winter of 1965. Their part in this experiment served to fulfill a course requirement for 3 hours of experimental participation. After an initial assessment period, 90 female and 88 male *S*s were randomly assigned to the three experimental conditions (see Chapter 6 for a separate report of results for the female *S*s). The *S*s were predominantly freshmen of whom about 40% of each sex were honors students.

Following the initial assessment period, a personal appointment for the rest of the experiment was arranged for each *S*. Over 90% of the *S*s kept their appointments.

Procedure: Initial Assessment Period

Two early evening sessions were scheduled four days apart. Each of these involved 100 *S*s, with about an equal number of men and women present. Men were directed to one side of the room and women to the other. The seating instructions were given verbally and were also written on the board at the front of the room. The *E* for the two initial sessions was a male graduate student in psychology who had had considerable experience in the assessment of achievement-related motivation.[3]

Assessment of the achievement motive. Verbal leads rather than pictures were used to elicit imaginative stories for the measurement of the achievement motive. The procedure and cues were fully described earlier in Chapter 6.

In obtaining individual n Achievement scores, only the first four of six verbal leads were used. The latter two were introduced to study fear of success as described in Chapter 6. The assessment of the achievement motive was carried out under standard neutral conditions as described by McClelland et al. (1953, p. 101) and Atkinson (1958a, pp. 606-661) except that verbal leads were substituted for pictures.

The stories were coded according to the content analysis scoring system described in detail in Atkinson (1958a, Ch. 12) and also in McClelland et al. (1953, Ch. 4). The interjudge scoring reliability of the author, who scored all protocols, with an independent expert scorer (P.A.O.)[4] was a rank-order correlation of .91 for n Achievement scores assigned to 30 protocols and 89% agreement in scoring achievement imagery. The rescore reliability of the author for 30 other stories was .93. The range of n Achievement scores for men was from 0 to 25 with median score of 8.5.

[3] I wish to thank Joel Raynor for giving so generously of his time.
[4] I am very grateful to Patricia O'Connor. Her help throughout the study was invaluable.

These same stories were also scored for n Affiliation by an expert scorer (S.K.)[5] who had a rescore reliability of .92 for n Affiliation scores assigned to the protocols.

Assessment of test anxiety. Immediately following the thematic apperception measure of the achievement motive, *S*s took an Achievement Anxiety Test (AAT) (see Alpert & Haber, 1960). They read the standard instructions to themselves as *E* also read them aloud and then were given 15 minutes to complete the test.

Only the 10 items of the *Debilitating Anxiety Scale* were used to obtain a measure of the motive to avoid failure. The mean Debilitating Anxiety scores were 26.01 ($SD = 5.7$) for the male *S*s. These were quite comparable to earlier results obtained by Mahone (1958, 1960). The Debilitating Anxiety scores were uncorrelated with the n Achievement scores for men ($r = .13$, $N = 88$). These results are consistent with the generally found independence of Test Anxiety assessed by the Mandler-Sarason Test Anxiety Questionnaire (1952) and n Achievement (see Atkinson & Feather, 1966, Ch. 20, p. 341).

Resultant Achievement Motivation

To provide a single indicator of the strength of the motive to achieve success (M_S) relative to the motive to avoid failure (M_{AF}), the standard score for Debilitating Anxiety was subtracted from the standard score for n Achievement. This combination of scores is logically consistent with the theory of achievement motivation and is referred to in the literature as a measure of *resultant achievement motivation.* The resultant score has been used successfully in a number of previous studies (see Atkinson & Feather, 1966).

Verbal Performance

After the short break, the *S*s read instructions stating that they would be asked to perform a number of tasks designed to measure certain aspects of intellectual ability and that performance on these tasks together with other information available about their past performance would be considered in the latter part of the research as a full and accurate measure of their abilities.

The first task was a 10-minute Scrambled Words task designed by Lowell (1952), five pages with 24 words per page and a time allowance of 2 minutes per page indicated by *E*.

The second task, presented as a "general reasoning" test, involved four pages with six line puzzles per page, one or two of which were not solvable. Twelve minutes was allowed for this task.

The third task was a solvable mathematical puzzle, presented as a test of logical ability and mathematical aptitude. Eight minutes was allowed for this task.

Since the main purpose of these tasks was to give the *S*s reason to believe that the investigator did, in fact, have some first-hand information about their ability

[5] I wish to thank Stuart Karabenick for scoring the protocols for affiliative motivation.

for use in the second part of the experiment, only the Scrambled Words Test, *which has been used in previous research* (Lowell, 1952) was even considered as a measure of performance level.

SECOND TEST PERIOD

For this part of the experiment, *S*s were randomly assigned to one of three conditions. Randomization was carried out within sex groups using a table of random numbers. The conditions were: the Noncompetitive achievement-orientation (NC); the Mixed Sex Competitive (MF and FM); and the Same Sex Competitive (MM and FF). In each condition, during the second testing session, a level of aspiration or risk-preference task, three performance measures, and a personal questionnaire were administered.

Risk Preference

In the noncompetitive condition, when working alone, the *S*'s task was to choose one of seven tasks on which he would most like to work for the rest of the experiment. In the two interpersonal competitive conditions, *S*s were to indicate which one of seven possible competitors they would most like to compete against for the rest of the experiment. Each of the possible choices was placed along a scale of difficulty. The *S*s were led to believe that the exact level of difficulty of each choice was defined individually for each of them on the basis of their previous performance in the first session and from information available in their academic records.

In reality, the choices were distributed along the scale identically for all *S*s in all conditions as shown below:

(1) (2) (3) (4) (5) (6) (7)

50-50

Very easy FOR YOU — Moderately difficult FOR YOU — Very difficult FOR YOU

As is clearly shown, only the 50-50 point of moderate difficulty is numerically specified. Numbers representing the P_s of the other choice points were not included.

The *S*s were also asked to indicate, on the same form, on which task or against which competitor they would *least* like to work.

Furthermore, to check on the possibility of biasing of P_s, the *S*s were also asked to indicate what they felt their chances were (out of 100) of doing well on the task or against the competitor they had selected.

Following Moulton (1965; see also Chapter 4), every effort was made to convince each *S* that the choice points, in fact, reflected his own probability of success as accurately as possible. This was done to minimize the subjective biasing of probabilities. The instructions for the task in each of the conditions indicate how this was done.

Noncompetitive (alone). Each *S* in the noncompetitive condition was run individually in a small experimental room under achievement-oriented instructions. This condition is similar to that used by Atkinson and Reitman (1956). The *S*s were given the booklet with their name on it and asked to read the instructions for the Level of Aspiration task to themselves. The instructions stated that *S* would have a *chance to choose on which of seven possible tasks he would most like to work during the last part of the experiment.* The tasks were described as similar to tests with which they were familiar, as frequently used to measure intellectual abilities and to predict future success in academic and vocational areas. *S*s were told that on the basis of the information available concerning their performance in school and performance on the tests given at the previous session their ability to perform each of the tasks involved had been accurately determined. With this information *each* of the tests had been placed on a scale from very easy "FOR YOU" to complete successfully to very difficult "FOR YOU" to complete successfully.

> By moderately difficult is meant that YOUR chances of doing the task successfully are about 50-50.
>
> By very easy is meant that YOUR chances of doing the task successfully are much greater than 50-50.
>
> By very difficult is meant that YOUR chances of doing the task successfully are much less than 50-50.

Finally, they were told that after they had worked on the task selected, they would be told how well they had done.

The female *E* was in the room only long enough to be sure that the *S* understood the instructions and to emphasize the underlined portions, e.g., that the difficulty of each task on the scale was subjectively defined for *that* particular subject. *The S was then left alone to make his choices.* Following this, the *E* explained:

> For the rest of tonight's session you will be asked to perform a number of tasks which, on the basis of your past performance, the experimenters feel are of *intermediate difficulty for you.* The tasks are in this folder and the instructions for them are on tape. Don't open the folder until you are instructed to do so.

Every effort was made to convince the *S*s that the research was being carried out by an experimental team. The *S*s were told that it was the "rest of tonight's session" rather than the rest of the experiment so that they would not feel that their choice of task difficulty was irrelevant and would not be considered at all.

Procedure for competitive conditions. The Risk Preference task for these conditions was given to the *S*s in small groups of either six or eight in which there were always at least two *S*s of the opposite sex present, sitting around a very large rectangular table.

The female *E* waited for all *S*s to come and then gave *each* one the appropriate form with his or her name written on it and with the sex of his or her potential competitor clearly indicated in the designated spot. They were asked to read the instructions on the top page to themselves and then, as in the NC condition, *E* emphasized the underlined portions of the instructions, stressed the fact that his or her potential competitors, e.g., those represented on the scale, may or may not have been one of the other *S*s in the room at that time. The instructions for the *S*s in the competitive conditions were as follows:

> Today you will have a *chance to choose against which of 7 possible persons you would most like to compete* on a number of tasks during the last part of the experiment. The tasks are similar to tests with which you are familiar, frequently used to measure intellectual abilities and to predict future success in academic and vocational areas. It is felt that predictions would be even more accurate if abilities were measured in direct competitive situations.
>
> On the basis of the information we have about each of you with regard to your previous performance in school and by your performance on the tests given at the previous session, YOUR ability and that of each of the possible competitors to perform the tasks involved has been accurately determined. With this information, each of the possible competitors has been placed on a scale from very easy FOR YOU to compete against successfully to very difficult FOR YOU to compete against successfully.
>
> By moderately difficult is meant that YOUR chances of successfully competing against him/her on the tasks involved are about 50-50.
>
> By very easy is meant that YOUR chances of successfully competing against him/her on the tasks involved are much greater than 50-50.
>
> By very difficult is meant that YOUR chances of successfully competing against him/her on the tasks involved are much less than 50-50.
>
> NOTE: You may not really want to compete against any of the persons, or on the other hand all of them may be appealing to you. In either case, make a special effort to decide on and select the ONE about which you feel *least* negative or the one that is most appealing to you.
>
> *After you have worked on the tasks, you will be told which one of you did best and how much better.*

The *S*s made their choices, the forms were collected, and plans for the next part of the experiment were explained:

> For the rest of tonight's session you have been paired with someone of approximately the *same* ability for performing the tasks involved; in other words you have a 50-50 chance of doing better than one another. *You will compete directly against each other on these tasks and at the end of the session you will know which of you did best.*[6] We will have to go down to another group of rooms now where you can meet your competitor and work on the tasks.

Again the *S*s were told that it was the "rest of tonight's session" rather than the rest of the experiment so that they would not feel the choices they had just made were completely irrelevant.

The *S*s were then led to experimental rooms and paired in accordance with the condition to which they had been previously randomly assigned. They were

[6] Italics added by editors.

asked to sit at a desk on which was the folder with their name but not to open the folders until they were told to do so.

Performance on Verbal and Arithmetic Tasks

For this, the critical part of the experiment, the instructions for all *S*s in all conditions were given by a male voice on a tape recorder, and a female *E* was present in the room only long enough to start the recorder.

In the noncompetitive condition, the *S*'s name and the level of difficulty of the tasks were written by hand in the upper right-hand corner. For the competitive conditions, the name of the competitor was also written in.

A similar procedure was followed for the instructions on each of the three tests in the booklet, and timing within and between tests was done by the tape-recorded male voice.

Generation Anagram

The first performance measure given was the *generation anagram* as previously used by Clark and McClelland (in McClelland et al., 1953, Ch. 8; Veroff et al., 1953; and Lipinski, 1965). Ten minutes was allowed for the test. The task was to make as many words as possible using the letters of a master word generation.

Performance scores on this task reflect the total number of words correctly made in 10 minutes using the letters of the word generation. The scores ranged from 27 to 89 with a mean of 48.06 ($\sigma = 12.07$) for the males.

Immediately following the generation anagram task was an arithmetic problems task (Atkinson & Reitman, 1956; Reitman, 1957; Smith, 1961) but for only 5 minutes.

The number of arithmetic problems attempted ranged from 5 to 51 with mean of 29.41 ($\sigma = 9.9$) for the males. The number of arithmetic problems correctly done ranged from 2 to 50 with mean of 26.2 ($\sigma = 10.1$) for males. Immediately following the arithmetic test, *S*s were directed to a Digit Symbol Substitution task, *but since it is likely that scores on this task would be influenced by feelings of success and failure on the just-previous arithmetic task on which the subjects had been asked to predict how well they would do prior to actual performance, the measure was not scored for purposes of this experiment.*

Questionnaire

A brief questionnaire on *S*s personal background, educational and vocational goals, and reactions to the experiment was administered. Only two of the questions in the questionnaire were considered in this part of the study. The first was the one asking each *S* how well he or she knew the competitor. The second question with which we shall be concerned asked: "How important was it for you to do well on the tests in this part of the experiment?" The *S* replied by putting an X along a line running from "not at all" to "very important," with only the "moderately important" point specified. It was assumed that these self-descriptions might also reflect the strength of the tendency to perform the tasks in each of the conditions.

RESULTS

Risk Taking

Table 1 shows the number of *S*s classified according to resultant achievement motivation and experimental condition who selected tasks or competitors of intermediate (points 3, 4, and 5) versus extreme (1, 2 or 6, 7) levels of difficulty. The main hypothesis that men with high resultant achievement motivation would more frequently prefer moderate risks than would those with low resultant motivation is not supported. There are no significant differences in risk

TABLE 1

Number of Male Subjects Classified According to Resultant Achievement Motivation and Experimental Condition Who Selected Tasks or Competitors of Intermediate versus Extreme Levels of Difficulty

Condition	*N*	Level of difficulty	
		Intermediate	Extreme
Noncompetitive (alone)	(30)	16	14
Resultant achievement motivation			
High	(18)	9	9
Low	(12)	7	5
Competition with female	(30)	17	13
Resultant achievement motivation			
High	(13)	7	6
Low	(17)	10	7
Competition with male	(28)	16	12
Resultant achievement motivation			
High	(12)	6	6
Low	(16)	10	6
All Men	(90)	49	39
Resultant achievement motivation			
High	(43)	22	21
Low	(45)	27	18

preference between the two motivation groups in any of the experimental conditions. Nor are there any significant differences between the conditions.

Table 2 shows the risk-taking results for Honors and non-Honors groups separately. Again, no significant differences were found between *S*s high and low in resultant achievement motivation among Honors or non-Honors *S*s.

One reason why the risk-taking hypothesis was not supported may be that the attempt to reduce differences in subjective probability of success that might be due to differences in ability was not effective (see Moulton, 1965, and also Chapter 4). If such differences existed, men in the Honors program should more frequently select difficult tasks and competitors than non-Honors students. They did ($\chi^2 = 15.02, p < .001$). Honors *S*s preferred the extreme to the intermediate risk option to a greater extent than did the non-Honors *S*s ($\chi^2 = 9.53, p < .005$). Furthermore, this difference was found only among those Honors *S*s who were high in resultant achievement motivation. Comparison of confidence levels that were obtained immediately after the *S* made his choice revealed that the Honors *S*s reported a higher expectation of doing well; the difference is significant for the most difficult alternative ($t = 3.01, df = 17, p < .005$) but is not for the next most difficult one ($t = 1.15, df = 16, p < .15$). While this effect is not consistent throughout all levels of difficulty, it suggests that Honors *S*s who selected what were described as difficult tasks may have actually chosen tasks that seemed close to intermediate difficulty. Since among the Honors *S*s only those high in resultant achievement motivation preferred the "difficult" alternatives, the Honors data may in fact support the initial expectation that this group would prefer those tasks which, for them, offered an intermediate risk.

Performance Level

Anagrams. The number of words correctly unscrambled by a sample of Honors ($N = 28$) and non-Honors ($N = 28$) *S*s matched for achievement motivation was used as a basis for assessing any initial differences in ability between Honors and non-Honors *S*s. This showed that the Honors group had a higher mean than the non-Honors group ($t = 1.76, df = 54, p < .05$). Therefore it was necessary to control for initial ability differences attributable to the disproportionate representation of Honors and non-Honors *S*s in the various experimental conditions. Raw scores on the number of correct generation anagrams problems were normalized for the Honors and non-Honors groups separately, based on the performance of the motivationally matched samples referred to above. This use of standard scores having a Mean of 50 and S.D. of 10 eliminates the mean difference between Honors and non-Honors *S*s attributable to difference in verbal ability among those who are comparably motivated. The mean number of anagrams completed is shown in Table 3 as a function of resultant achievement motivation (n Achievement-Anxiety), affiliative motivation, and experimental conditions. Analysis of variance reveals a significant effect due to experimental conditions ($F = 6.75, df = 2/76, p < .01$). Inspection of Table 3 indicates that, as predicted, *S*s constructed substantially

TABLE 2

Risk Preference of Male Subjects Classified According to Resultant Achievement Motivation and Honors Status under Different Experimental Conditions

Condition	Honors		Non-Honors	
	Intermediate	Extreme	Intermediate	Extreme
Noncompetitive (alone)	2	7	14	7
Resultant achievement motivation				
High	1	5	8	4
Low	1	2	6	3
Competition with female	3	8	14	5
Achievement motivation				
High	0	5	7	1
Low	3	3	7	4
Competition with male	8	9	8	3
Achievement motivation				
High	4	5	2	1
Low	4	4	6	2
All Men	13	24	36	15
Resultant achievement motivation				
High	5	15	17	6
Low	8	9	19	9

TABLE 3

Mean Number of Anagrams Constructed by Men in 10 Minutes as a Function of Resultant Achievement Motivation, Affiliative Motivation, and Experimental Condition

Motivation	Conditions					
	Noncompetitive (alone)		Competition: With female		Competition: With male	
	N	*M*	*N*	*M*	*N*	*M*
High affiliation						
High resultant achievement	(10)	46.5	(7)	53.9	(7)	48.4
Low resultant achievement	(6)	41.8	(7)	53.6	(6)	56.1
Low affiliation						
High resultant achievement	(8)	48.4	(6)	53.4	(5)	53.7
Low resultant achievement	(6)	40.8	(10)	47.7	(10)	46.7
Conditions	(30)	45.0	(30)	51.7	(28)	50.4

Affiliative motivation

Resultant achievement motivation	High		Low			
	N	*M*	*N*	*M*	*N*	*M*
High	(24)	49.2	(19)	51.4	(43)	50.2
Low	(19)	50.7	(26)	45.7	(45)	47.8
	(43)	50.1	(45)	48.1		

Note.–Results are given in standard scores derived from a motivationally matched sample of Honors and non-Honors subjects. Each distribution has mean of 50 and S.D. of 10.

more anagrams in both the competitive conditions than when working alone in the noncompetitive condition ($t = 3.20$, $df = 58$, $p < .005$ and $t = 2.56$, $df = 56$, $p < .01$, respectively). These findings are consistent with the hypothesis that the tendency to perform would be generally stronger, and hence level of performance higher, for male *S*s in interpersonal competitive than in noncompetitive conditions. However, an expectation that *S*s high in resultant achievement motivation would generally construct more anagrams than those low in resultant motivation is not supported ($F = 2.39$, $df = 1/76$, n.s.). Only when working alone in the noncompetitive condition is the predicted difference between these two groups apparent ($t = 2.05$, $df = 28$, $p < .025$). Thus the data is consistent with that reported in previous studies where the predicted relationship between achievement motivation and performance was obtained when *S*s were left alone in a room to work, but was not found under multi-incentive conditions (Atkinson & Reitman, 1956; Reitman, 1957; Smith, 1961).

In light of the evidence from previous studies (see Atkinson & Reitman, 1956; Atkinson & O'Connor, 1966) concerning the confounding influence of affiliative motivation on achievement-oriented performance, the data for performance level were viewed taking into account individual differences in n Affiliation (see Table 3). While no significant difference is found between *S*s high and low in n Affiliation *per se* ($F < 1$, n.s.), there is a significant interaction between resultant achievement motivation and n Affiliation ($F = 4.12$, $df = 1/76$, $p < .05$). Subjects high on only one type of motivation constructed more anagrams than those high on both types of motivation when conditions were combined. The performance of this most highly motivated group was superior only to that of *S*s low in both types of motivation.

Further inspection (Table 3) reveals that while the influence of affiliative motivation was negligible in the noncompetitive condition, in the interpersonal competitive conditions the predicted relationship between resultant achievement motivation and performance is found only among those *S*s low in n Affiliation. For *S*s high in affiliation under the interpersonal competitive conditions, there is a reversal of the expected ordering of motive groups such that *S*s low in resultant achievement motivation constructed significantly more anagrams than those high in resultant motivation ($t = 2.49$, $df = 11$, $p < .025$).

The apparent performance decrement for *S*s high in both resultant achievement and affiliation motivation, together with the apparent increment for *S*s high in affiliation but low in resultant motivation, has been detected in previous research (see Atkinson & Reitman, 1956; Reitman, 1957; Smith, 1961; Atkinson & O'Connor, 1966; see also Chapters 12 and 14).

Arithmetic problems. Arithmetic performance scores were transformed as described for the anagrams task. Since the number of problems attempted and the number correctly solved are highly correlated ($r = .94$, $N = 88$) and the two measures yield similar results, only the latter is presented (see Table 4). Inspection shows a similar pattern of results as found for the anagrams task. *S*s tended to perform higher in the interpersonal competitive conditions than in the noncompetitive condition, although the differences are not significant ($F = 1.24$, $df = 2/76$, n.s.). Performance was higher for the high than for the low group on resultant achievement motivation ($F = 2.85$, $df = 1/76$, $p < .10$), with the difference reaching statistical significance in the noncompetitive ($t = 1.90$, $df = 28$, $p < .05$) but not in either interpersonal competitive condition. Within the low group on n Affiliation, *S*s tended to perform higher if they were high than if they were low in resultant achievement motivation, while within high n Affiliation this difference was either negligible (competing against a female) or reversed (competing against another male).

TABLE 4

Mean Number of Correct Arithmetic Problems Completed by Men in 5 Minutes as a Function of Resultant Achievement Motivation, Affiliative Motivation, and Experimental Condition

Motivation	Conditions					
	Noncompetitive (alone)		Competition			
			With female		With male	
	N	*M*	*N*	*M*	*N*	*M*
High affiliation						
High resultant achievement	(10)	50.9	(7)	50.4	(7)	48.5
Low resultant achievement	(6)	39.6	(7)	48.5	(6)	53.4
Low affiliation						
High resultant achievement	(8)	49.5	(6)	53.4	(5)	56.1
Low resultant achievement	(6)	48.5	(10)	49.5	(10)	46.7
Conditions	(30)	47.8	(30)	50.3	(28)	50.2

Affiliative motivation

Resultant achievement motivation	High		Low			
	N	*M*	*N*	*M*	*N*	*M*
High	(24)	50.0	(19)	52.5	(43)	51.1
Low	(19)	47.2	(26)	48.2	(45)	47.8
	(43)	48.8	(45)	50.0		

Note.–The results are given in standard scores derived from a motivationally matched sample of Honors and non-Honors subjects. Each distribution has a mean of 50 and S.D. of 10.

DISCUSSION

In the present study *S*s chose and then performed either on tasks in which there was only competition with an inherent standard of good performance (noncompetitive achievement-oriented condition) or on tasks in which there was also competition against another person (interpersonal competitive achievement-oriented conditions)–either another man or a woman. The expected preference of *S*s high in resultant achievement motivation for alternatives of intermediate difficulty was not found. Honors *S*s were significantly more confident of success than non-Honors *S*s for the most difficult alternative despite procedures designed to eliminate such a difference in subjective probability of success. However, consideration of this difference still fails to clarify the risk-preference results for the non-Honors groups since the predicted relationship was not found among these *S*s even in the noncompetitive achievement-oriented condition, where the risk-taking hypothesis would be most likely to be supported.

The expected superiority in performance of *S*s high over those low in resultant achievement motivation was found only in the noncompetitive condition where extrinsic sources of motivation were deemphasized by having *S*s work on tasks in a room by themselves directed only by taped instructions, and among *S*s low in n Affiliation, who are presumed to have lower extrinsic motivation for the task than *S*s high in n Affiliation. The hypothesis of a positive relationship was not supported within the interpersonal competitive achievement-oriented conditions; the expected difference was not found in competition with a female and was reversed in competition with another male. In light of previous arguments concerning the effect of multiple incentives on performance (Atkinson & Reitman, 1956; Reitman, 1960; Atkinson & O'Connor, 1966; Smith, 1961; also Chapters 11, 12, 14), this apparent decrement in performance deserves very close attention.

The present results suggest that the addition of a competitor in an achievement-oriented situation can have either a positive or a negative effect on performance *depending upon individual differences in resultant achievement motivation.* In the interpersonal competitive conditions, especially against men, high affiliative motivation appears to enhance the performance of *S*s low in resultant achievement motivation but to produce a performance decrement among *S*s high in resultant motivation. It is therefore important to consider the functional significance of affiliative motivation in achievement-oriented situations involving interpersonal competition. *The critical issue appears to be whether achievement of success or doing well in such a situation is compatible with or antagonistic to fulfillment of affiliative concerns.*

The pattern of results in the present study is similar to that obtained by Atkinson and O'Connor (1966), where a female *E* was present during performance of male *S*s in an otherwise noncompetitive achievement-oriented situation. These investigators suggested that successful achievement for men in competition with standards of excellence is not only compatible with but also instrumental to attaining affiliative ends, i.e., immediate social approval from an audience. In terms of the present results, this argument suggests that *S*s high in affiliative motivation and low in resultant achievement motivation performed at a higher level in the interpersonal competitive conditions because here *immediate* social approval for achievement could be obtained from the competitor, while this was not so in the noncompetitive condition. If we accept the idea that doing well in competition against another person in achievement-oriented situations is instrumental to both achievement and affiliative ends, the major unresolved problem concerns why *S*s high in both achievement and affiliative motivation show a decrement rather than an increment in the interpersonal as compared to the noncompetitive achievement-oriented conditions.

One possible explanation for this decrement was suggested by Atkinson and O'Connor (1966), namely, that there may be an optimal level of motivation for a given level of task complexity (Yerkes & Dodson, 1908). The performance decrement is thus attributed to a greater than optimal intensity of motivation for the particular task. One of the implications of this position concerns the effect of inhibitory motivation as conceived within the theory of achievement motivation. Subjects with greater than optimal level of *positive* motivation who are also high in the motive to avoid failure should perform at a higher level than those who are low in the motive to avoid failure because the total *resultant* motivation for the former will be lower (due to increased inhibition) and hence closer to the optimal level (see Chapter 11). Atkinson and O'Connor (1966) found suggestive evidence supporting this possibility (see also Sorrentino, Chapter 14). Unfortunately the size of the present sample prevents a direct test of this hypothesis. However, this argument may explain why the decrement effect is larger in competition with another male than with a female. Failure against a woman should be more threatening to a man's conception of masculinity than failure against another man. The level of fear of failure may therefore be greater in the mixed-sex condition because of an additional source of inhibitory motivation that is aroused when the competitor is a female. If this were true, the total level of anxiety that is aroused in mixed-sex competition should be greater and the total tendency to perform lower–and perhaps closer to optimal.

The above explanation of the performance decrement of male *S*s high in both achievement and affiliative motivation assumes that success in competitive achievement situations is instrumental to an affiliative goal such as social approval. But does a man high in affiliative motivation really expect to gain the "friendship" or "social approval" of a peer whom he defeats or outperforms? Perhaps, if the peer is female. Perhaps not, if he is male. If we assume that doing well against a male competitor, especially in a face-to-face situation in which the results will be known, is not consistent with attaining affiliative goals, an alternative explanation for the performance decrement in the same-sex condition of *S*s high in both achievement and affiliative motivation is that these *S*s experienced a conflict of motives or simply were distracted while trying to succeed by their simultaneous attempts to affiliate with their competitor. There are a number of suggestive trends in the data which support this view. Immediately following performance, *S*s were asked to indicate, "How important was it for you to do well on the tests in this part of the experiment?" When competing with a male subject, *S*s high in both affiliative and resultant achievement motivation report a significantly lower level of "importance" than those low in affiliation but high in resultant motivation ($t = 2.57, p < .05$). This difference was not significant within either of the other two conditions. If responses to this "importance" question reflect strength of tendency to do well, then the overmotivation hypothesis suggests that *S*s high in both achievement and affiliative motivation in an interpersonal competitive condition should have indicated a higher rather than a lower level of "importance" than other *S*s. In other words, they should have indicated that they were trying harder than anyone else to do well, and the decrement could then be attributed to "too much effort." The assumption that importance ratings reflect tendency to do well is of course rather tenuous.[7]

Another source of suggestive (though weak) evidence worth noting in favor of the conflict hypothesis concerns the number of errors made on the arithmetic problems. Men competing with a woman, in which case achievement may be consistent with affiliative goals, made significantly fewer errors than in both the noncompetitive condition ($\chi^2 = 6.86, p < .005$), where affiliative motivation is presumably not aroused, and when competing with a man ($\chi^2 = 8.30, p < .005$), where achievement may be inconsistent with attaining affiliative goals. The only way to make this data consistent with the overmotivation hypothesis would be to argue that the inhibition was high when competing with a woman, thereby reducing the level of total motivation of *S*s high in both achievement and affiliative motivation so that it was closer to an optimal level of performance efficiency. However, such an argument might have difficulty explaining why *S*s low in both types of motivation made so few errors.

The evidence just presented is merely suggestive and neither conclusive nor adequate for deciding between the idea of a conflict-induced decrement or a decrement due to excessive positive motivation. Both "conflict" and "overmotivation" may adversely affect performance under different circumstances. Since both would produce performance decrements, it is necessary to learn more about the functional significance of affiliative motivation under various conditions before a choice between the two alternatives can be made. Whether success in interpersonal competition serves or is antagonistic to affiliation needs appears to be a critical unanswered question that requires further experimental attention (see also Sorrentino, Chapter 14).

[7] Attempts to explain the importance ratings in terms of an attempt to reduce cognitive dissonance (Festinger, 1957) through importance ratings after performance is known does not appear to work.

14

EXTENDING THEORY OF ACHIEVEMENT MOTIVATION TO THE STUDY OF GROUP PROCESSES[1]

Richard M. Sorrentino[2]

The major purpose of the study on which the present chapter is based (see Sorrentino, 1971, 1973) was to demonstrate that achievement-related motives determine leadership behavior in task-oriented group situations. However, this paper is devoted to some rather unexpected findings that emerged concerning the interaction between achievement-related motives, the affiliative motive, and contingent future orientation. As will be seen, while the study demonstrates that achievement-related motives can serve as the source of determinants of leadership, the results also parallel those which Atkinson and O'Connor (1966) described as an *overmotivation effect* concerning the relationship between total motivation to act and level of performance. Ironically, these authors set out to investigate a quite different hypothesis from the one eventually suggested by their data–exactly what happened in the research considered here. It would appear more than coincidence that this was the case (see also Horner, Chapter 13). We will first examine the rationale and hypotheses of the study and then discuss the unexpected findings.

[1]This chapter is based on a doctoral dissertation (Sorrentino, 1971) completed at the State University of New York at Buffalo. It was supported in part by Grant GS-2863 from the National Science Foundation to Joel O. Raynor entitled "Effects of Distant Future Goals on Achievement Motivation." Parts of the study were presented in collaboration with J.O.R. in an unpublished paper (Sorrentino & Raynor, 1971) at the meetings of the Eastern Psychological Association, April, 1971, and in Sorrentino (1973). This chapter was prepared especially for this volume while the author was supported by Canada Council Grant No. S72-0639.

[2]The author wishes to thank Joel Raynor for his help in this study.

The lack of a clear relationship between achievement motivation and leadership has long been an enigma to researchers. While it seems reasonable to many that persons high in achievement motivation should emerge as leaders, the relationship has never been demonstrated experimentally. However, many descriptive studies suggest that such a relationship exists. Gardner (1948) and the American Management Association (1948), for example, found that the projective measure of n Achievement correlated highly with successful business executives. Similar results were recently reported by Wainer and Rubin (1969). A sampling problem for researchers studying achievement motivation is that college students are typically high in the motive to achieve success (M_S) and low in the motive to avoid failure (M_{AF}) as compared to the rest of the population (Zander & Forward, 1968; Raynor, 1969; Atkinson & Feather, 1966). Further, the person high in M_S tends to be more active in college and community activities (DeCharms et al., 1955; Kaltenbach & McClelland, 1957) and comes from a family in which there has been stress on early self-reliance and mastery (Winterbottom, 1953).

While earlier investigation of the relationship between achievement motivation and leadership has been sparse, the importance of such investigation has been strongly emphasized. Bass (1960), for example, citing the field studies of Gardner (1948) and the American Management Association (1948), concludes:

> If placed in interaction with others, persons high in need for achievement will, we expect, be more likely to attempt to solve the group's problems apart from all other considerations motivating members to attempt leadership [p. 147].

Furthermore, Bass suggests that a person high in n Achievement may exhibit an interaction orientation at a social gathering and a task orientation in a work group.

A review of the literature led Beer, Buckhout, Horowitz, and Levy (1959) to judge the following three personal attributes as important properties of a leader:

1. Self-acceptance (self-confidence)
2. Need achievement
3. Interpersonal skills

It is of interest to note that Beer et al. (1959) consider interpersonal skills, in part, a natural outgrowth of self-confidence and need achievement. The authors write:

> In part, interpersonal skills represent the mechanics of leadership. To some extent, they are the tools whereby self-acceptance and need achievement come to function [p. 50].

In an effort to relate n Achievement and n Affiliation to leadership, Pepinsky, Hemphill, and Shevitz (1958) investigated the attempts to lead in a task-oriented situation of persons High-Low or Low-High on the two variables. A person's attempts to lead were either accepted or rejected by the other members of the group. While differences between the conditions of acceptance and rejection were obtained (more attempts to lead under acceptance than rejection), no differences between personality attributes were found. The failure to obtain differences may be attributed to one or more of the following considerations:

1. The measures of n Achievement and n Affiliation were not those recommended by Atkinson (1958a), and to this date no alternative measures have been found to correlate highly with the projective measure (Atkinson & O'Connor, 1966).

2. Some evidence (see Atkinson & O'Connor, 1966) suggests that under conditions of evaluation *S*s high in n Affiliation and *S*s high in n Achievement behave similarly.

3. By failure to control or vary fear of failure and subjective probability of success, less precision is obtained (see Atkinson & Feather, 1966).

However strongly suggested, research to date has not clearly defined the relationship between achievement motivation and leadership. The primary reason for failure to find such a relationship may be the lack of strong theoretical underpinnings. That is, previous investigators have viewed n Achievement merely as a personality characteristic of a leader without cognizance of those situational determinants which serve either to arouse or to diminish the resultant tendency to achieve (e.g., "Contingent" versus "Noncontingent" activities). Further, they have largely neglected other personality characteristics (e.g., n Affiliation) which may serve to enhance or diminish its effect. Previous research on leadership, therefore, has not employed a theory which clearly specifies the interaction between the achievement motive, other motives, and situational determinants (for elaborated discussion of this issue, see Hollander, 1961; Hollander & Julian, 1968, 1969).

Theory of achievement motivation (Atkinson, 1964; Atkinson & Feather, 1966) together with an elaborated theory of achievement motivation (Raynor, 1969) does specify such an interaction, but primarily for nongroup activity. That is, the theories do not deal extensively with group task-oriented behavior or the leadership process.[3] There is, however, a large body of evidence directly or indirectly linking theory of achievement motivation with several characteristics which are seen to be of considerable importance to the leadership process: level of performance, self-confidence, interest, and quantity and quality of verbal interaction.

Level of Performance (Competence)

According to theory of achievement motivation (Atkinson, 1964; Atkinson & Feather, 1966), persons in whom the motive to succeed is greater than the

[3] Zander (1970) and Zander and Forward (1968) have investigated some aspects of group behavior using the theory of achievement motivation. They have, however, been primarily concerned with the group, rather than with the individual in the group, as the unit of analysis.

motive toward failure ($M_S > M_{AF}$) should perform better in an achievement-oriented task than persons in whom $M_{AF} > M_S$. This prediction is supported by research reporting that *S*s in whom $M_S > M_{AF}$ perform better than those with $M_{AF} > M_S$ on course grades (Atkinson & Litwin, 1960; Isaacson & Raynor, 1966; Raynor, 1970, and Chapter 9), word-problem tests (Raynor, 1968a), learning nonsense syllables (Karabenick & Youssef, 1968), and arithmetic problems (Smith, 1966; Atkinson & Reitman, 1956; Raynor & Rubin, 1971, and Chapter 10).

That level of performance or competence is an important determinant of leadership is amply illustrated by Julian, Hollander, and Regula (1969), who state:

> A . . . major determinant of group support for the leader is the leader's ability to contribute to group goals. Other things equal, more competent leaders are found to be more strongly endorsed by the group [p. 43].

Support for this statement is readily available in the literature. Bass and White (1951) found a direct relationship between problem-solving ability, word fluency, and ratings on leadership abilities. Dubno (1965) reports that groups tend to be more satisfied when leaders are demonstrably competent in a central function and do most of the work associated with that function. Using five-man discussion groups, Marak (1964) found that the rewards associated with the leader's ability on a task lead to greater perceived as well as actual influence. In a factor analysis of many studies, Stogdill (1948) reports the following five personal factors to be associated with leadership: capacity, achievement, responsibility, participation, status. The first two factors as defined by Stogdill may be seen as a function of competence, i.e., capacity–soundness of judgment and thought, insight and originality; achievement–better students, ability to get things done.

Self-Confidence

A person with $M_S > M_{AF}$ who is confronted by an ambiguous achievement-oriented task should have more confidence of success than a person in whom $M_{AF} > M_S$. Atkinson & Feather (1966) write:

> When he ($M_S > M_{AF}$) approaches a task in which there is considerable ambiguity about the probability of success, he will be more confident than others. Why? This is probably because his realistic approach to challenges in the past, his enthusiasm and persistence have made him more successful than others. He extrapolates the higher "batting average" (i.e., more frequent success) to the new venture when little concrete information about his chances is available [p. 368].

This prediction is supported by Brody (1963), who found that when approaching a task in which the P_S is fairly ambiguous, *S*s in whom $M_S > M_{AF}$ will have higher confidence (their subjective P_S) than those with $M_{AF} > M_S$.

A large number of studies show the importance of self-confidence for leadership. Stogdill (1948) cites 11 experimental studies which report leaders as rating higher on self-confidence and self-esteem than their followers (see Zeleny, 1939). Similarly, in summarizing the small-groups literature, McGrath and Altman (1966) report that leaderless group-discussion performance was highly related to ratings on self-confidence.

Interest

In an achievement-oriented situation, a person in whom $M_S > M_{AF}$ should display greater interest in the situation than one with $M_{AF} > M_S$ (Atkinson & Feather, 1966). That is, interest in the situation is assumed to be directly proportionate to the resultant tendency to achieve. In extending this assumption to a group situation, it would seem that this relationship would hold for any achievement-oriented activity in which the group may be engaged. Hence, persons in whom the resultant tendency to achieve is positive would be expected to have a stronger desire for group success at an achievement-oriented activity than persons in whom the resultant tendency to achieve is negative. Partial support for this prediction is provided by Zander and Forward (1968), who found that in a group task *S*s in whom $M_S > M_{AF}$ developed a strong desire for group success whether in a central or a peripheral role, whereas those with $M_{AF} > M_S$ developed similar desires only when in the central role. This suggests that in a leaderless group situation, that is, where the leadership role is not yet clearly defined, persons in whom $M_S > M_{AF}$ will be more interested in the group activity than those with $M_{AF} > M_S$. Failure to find differences between the two motive groups in the central role may be due to arousal of extrinsic sources of motivation (e.g., n Affiliation) when in the leadership role.

In reviewing the literature on leadership, Hare (1962) reports that high interest in the group activity was frequently found to characterize leaders (see Cleveland & Fisher, 1957; Van Dusen, 1940). Julian and Hollander (1966) report that, aside from the significance of task competence, leaders described as "interested in group members" and "interested in group activity" were significantly endorsed by the group to continue as leader.

Quantity and Quality of Interaction

Theory of achievement motivation makes no predictions concerning quantity and quality of verbal interaction, since the theory is usually restricted to nongroup activity. In view of the evidence, however, it does seem possible to make fairly logical predictions concerning quantity and quality of verbal interaction. The theory predicts, for example, that persons in whom $M_S > M_{AF}$ have a positive resultant tendency to act in an achievement-oriented situation, while those with $M_{AF} > M_S$ have a tendency not to act or to inhibit performance. One would expect that in a group task this tendency would carry over to influence verbal interaction. It has been shown, for example, that *S*s in whom $M_S > M_{AF}$ produce a greater quantity of performance as well as quality than those with $M_{AF} > M_S$ (Lowell, 1952; Atkinson, Bastian, Earl, & Litwin, 1960; Atkinson & Reitman, 1956; Atkinson & Raphelson, 1956; Raynor &

Rubin, 1971). Furthermore, Zander and Forward (1968) have demonstrated that predictions from theory of achievement motivation do carry over into group tasks (i.e., desire for individual success to desire for group success). Hence, given the assumptions (*a*) that achievement motivation operates similarly in a group (taking into consideration additional sources of extrinsic motivation), (*b*) that quantity of performance and quality of performance are characteristics of resultant achievement motivation, and (*c*) that verbal interaction is one way the individual may achieve individual as well as group success, quantity and quality of (at least) task-relevant verbal interaction should be greater for persons in whom $M_S > M_{AF}$ than for their counterparts.

Quantity of verbal interaction is clearly seen to be one of the most important determinants of leadership. That is, the high participator is usually identified by the group as the leader (Norfleet, 1948; Bales, 1953; Bass, 1949; Borgatta & Bales, 1956; Kirsch, Lodahl, & Haire, 1959; Riecken, 1958).

The status of *quality* of participation as a determinant of leadership is not as clear. Although competence or level of performance is seen as an important determinant of leadership, Riecken (1958) and Regula and Julian (1967) report that when manipulating both quantity and quality of interaction, main effects were obtained for quantity but not for quality of interaction, nor were interaction effects obtained. That is, the high participator emerged as leader, regardless of his quality of participation.

While quantity of participation is seen as most important, quality of participation cannot be ruled out. The abundance of evidence reported (when quantity was not controlled) supporting the importance of perceived and actual competence suggests that the two elements of participation may be confounded. For example, Jones and Gerard (1967) point out that quantity of participation may serve merely in the role of a mediator for more important processes such as self-confidence and ability (and according to Bass, 1960, achievement motivation).

EXTENSION OF THEORY OF ACHIEVEMENT MOTIVATION

The literature gives strong support to the assumption that resultant achievement motivation may serve as the source of several determinants of leadership. However, in extending theory of achievement motivation to a group context, careful attention must be given to other possible sources of motivation implied by a group situation, and to the effect of various situational determinants on resultant achievement motivation. A review of past research (Sorrentino, 1971, Ch. 1) indicates that two such variables are n Affiliation and "Contingent versus Noncontingent" paths.

Affiliation

It is assumed that affiliative tendencies are most likely aroused in a group situation regardless of whether the situation is achievement-oriented or socio-emotionally oriented. For example, Forward (1967) reports that persons high in n Affiliation are more likely to endorse the group's standard than persons low in n Affiliation. Atkinson and O'Connor (1966) argued that in situations where social approval is an additional incentive, differences in strength of affiliative motivation could systematically influence achievement-related behavior (see also Chapters 11, 12, and 13). For example, a person high in n Affiliation might be motivated to perform well regardless of his achievement-related motives. Since social approval may be contingent upon good performance in a group situation, individual differences in n Affiliation were examined.

A situational variable of considerable importance both to theory and to the leadership process is that of contingent as compared to noncontingent future orientation (see Raynor, Chapter 7). Consideration of future orientation broadens the initial theory to include situations where distant future goals may influence a person's immediate behavior. Raynor's elaboration derives that differences in performance between success-oriented and failure-threatened individuals will be accentuated when attainment of one or more future goals is contingent upon success at more immediate activity, as opposed to a situation where attainment of future goals does not depend upon prior success or failure. Contingent path situations may also represent a closer approximation to "life" situations than many previous laboratory studies concerned with the leadership process. Hence behavior under contingent and noncontingent future orientation was also viewed.

Specific hypotheses of the study were as follows: (*a*) *S*s High-Low (on n Achievement–Test Anxiety) will receive higher scores than *S*s Low-High on all measures of achievement-related behavior, while the opposite will occur for task-irrelevant measures; these differences will be greater (*b*) in a contingent than in a noncontingent condition and (*c*) for *S*s also high as opposed to low in n Affiliation.

The Study

Sixty-four male undergraduate students from introductory psychology courses at the State University of New York at Buffalo were selected as *S*s for the experiment on the basis of their TAT scores of n Achievement and n Affiliation[4] and scores on the Test Anxiety Questionnaire. Each *S* was assigned to one of 16 four-member groups in which each member of the group differed from the other members in his combination of achievement-related motives (High n Achievement–Low Test Anxiety versus Low n Achievement–High Test Anxiety) and the affiliation motive (High versus Low n Affiliation). Eight of the groups were assigned to the Contingent condition (they were told that they *must* succeed at the first of three games in order to continue on to the next two), and

[4] Assessment of n Achievement and n Affiliation followed standard procedures (Atkinson, 1958a, Appendix III).

eight groups were assigned to the Noncontingent condition (they were told that they would play all three games regardless of success or failure at the first game).

The game was a matrix variety (adapted from Hollander, 1960) with plus or minus points in each intersection of a row and column. Each group had 15 trials to achieve success. The criterion for success was that the group must end up with at least 200 points by the end of the last trial. Each trial consisted of 1 minute for each member to think individually about the next choice and 3 minutes of group discussion in order to reach a group choice. Twenty dependent measures in all were obtained. On 10 of these measures, differences between High n Achievement-Low Test Anxiety and Low n Achievement–High Test Anxiety groups were directly predicted or inferred from theory of achievement motivation (e.g., quantity and quality of task-relevant verbal interaction). The other 10 were included to test the generality of predictions to other possible determinants of leadership ability (e.g., amount of influence, contributions towards the group goal).

Analysis of variance revealed significant effects on 18 of the 20 dependent measures (the exceptions were the second measure of self-ratings of interest and others' ratings of interest, both obtained after the experiment). On 12 of these, a significant three-factor interaction between achievement-related motives, standing on the affiliation motive, and experimental conditions was found: performance on practice trials, $F = 4.60$, $df = 1$ and 56, $p < .05$; quantity of task-relevant verbal interaction, $F = 4.82$, $df = 1$ and 14, $p < .05$; quality of verbal interaction, $F = 6.51$, $df = 1$ and 16, $p < .025$; self-ratings of competence, $F = 11.29$, $df = 1$ and 14, $p < .005$; others' ratings of competence, $F = 3.83$, $df = 1$ and 14, $p < .10$; self-ratings of contribution, $F = 3.43$, $df = 1$ and 14, $p < .10$; others' ratings of contribution, $F = 3.35$, $df = 1$ and 14, $p < .10$; self-ratings of task leadership ability, $F = 4.30$, $df = 1$ and 14, $p < .10$; others' ratings of task leadership ability, $F = 8.18$, $df = 1$ and 14, $p < .025$.

The dominant pattern of interaction between achievement-related motives, the affiliative motives, and conditions on most of the dependent measures is represented by performance on practice trials, as shown in Figure 1*a*. Scores from this measure were obtained prior to group interaction and may be considered here as baseline data. As may be seen in Figure 1*a*, for *S*s low in n Affiliation, the High-Low group performed better than the Low-High group in the contingent condition, while the opposite is found in the noncontingent condition. Note that the High-Low group performed at a higher level while the Low-High group performed at a lower level in the contingent than in the noncontingent condition.

For *S*s high in n Affiliation, the reverse pattern of interaction is found. The High-Low group performed at a *lower* level while the Low-High group performed at a *higher* level in the contingent than in the noncontingent condition.

Once group interaction began the pattern of results shown for the practice trial's data for the High-Low and the Low-High groups across the conditions X affiliation motive combinations generally remained the same on most measures.

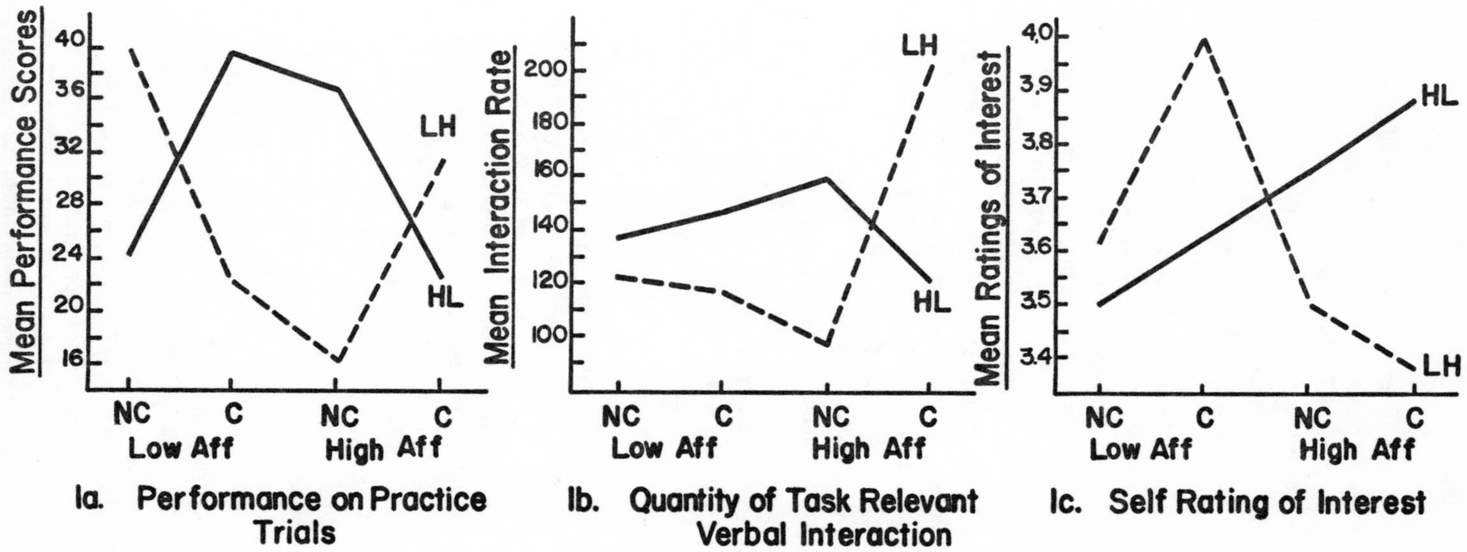

FIG. 1. Scores on three dependent measures for High n Achievement–Low Test Anxiety (HL) and Low n Achievement–High Test Anxiety (LH) subjects in the Noncontingent (NC) and Contingent (C) conditions who are also classified High and Low in n Affiliation (Aff).

The actual magnitude of difference between the High-Low group and the Low-High group, however, diminished for *S*s low in n Affiliation but was accentuated for *S*s high in n Affiliation. This difference between the practice trials data and the group interaction is most clearly seen in Figure 1*b*, where performance on practice trials is compared with quantity of task-relevant verbal interaction, the single best predictor of emergent leadership in previous research (see Regula & Julian, 1967).

One important exception to this pattern was for anticipated interest in the game, for which the analysis of variance showed a significant interaction between achievement-related motives and standing on the affiliative motive ($F = 4.67$, $df = 1/14$, $p < .05$). As can be seen in Figure 1*c*, for *S*s high in n Affiliation, the High-Low group had overall higher anticipated interest than the Low-High group, while for *S*s low in n Affiliation the reverse was true. Anticipated interest is the only task-relevant measure where the pattern of results within the *S*s high in n Affiliation is in the predicted direction: the High-Low group anticipated more interest and the Low-High group anticipated less. The other exception was for performance during the individual choice periods, for which a significant interaction was obtained between achievement-related motives and experimental conditions ($F = 14.24$, $df = 1$ and 14, $p < .005$). On this measure all *S*s performed at a higher level in the contingent than the noncontingent condition, except for the High-Low group high in n Affiliation, for which the reverse was true.

DISCUSSION

While the results of the Sorrentino (1971, 1973) study lend strong support to the general hypothesis that achievement-related motives are the source of determinants of emergent leadership, they lend only partial support to the specific hypotheses derived from initial and elaborated theory of achievement motivation. Significant difference between *S*s High-Low and Low-High (on n Achievement–Test Anxiety) were found, but were in the predicted direction in only two of the four possible combinations of standing on n Affiliation and experimental conditions. Also, while the predicted pattern of interaction between achievement-related motives and experimental conditions was obtained for *S*s low in n Affiliation, it was *reversed* for those high in n Affiliation.

Recent theoretical arguments and research findings suggest that the reversal of expectations that occurred in this research for *S*s high in n Affiliation when in a contingent condition may be attributed to the phenomenon termed "overmotivation" (see Atkinson & O'Connor, 1966; also Chapters 11, 12, and 13). For example, referring for the moment to the practice trials performance (see Figure 1*a*), the arousal of contingent future orientation in High-Low *S*s also low in n Affiliation produced a performance increment, as predicted, but produced a performance decrement for those High-Low *S*s with high n Affiliation. Thus the combination of both high affiliation and contingent future orientation may have led to too much positive motivation for optimal performance efficiency, producing a performance decrement. But the measures of anticipated interest in the task, which may reflect total positive motivation for it, showed a predictable stepwise increment in scores from lowest to highest positively motivated group within the High-Low *S*s. On the other hand, the arousal of contingent future orientation in Low-High *S*s also low in n Affiliation produced a performance decrement, as predicted (as measured by practice trials performance), but seemed to produce a performance increment for those Low-High *S*s with high n Affiliation. Here the inhibitory effects of contingent future orientation may have reduced the effects of too much positive motivation that would have otherwise been produced due to the arousal of strong affiliative motivation (as just described for the High-Low group also high in n Affiliation)–leading to a performance increment in comparison to the Low-High group also high in n Affiliation in the noncontingent condition. Again the measure of anticipated interest reflects the predicted direction of results for the high n Affiliation-Low-High groups, suggesting that positive motivation was lower within the contingent than the noncontingent condition among these *S*s. Thus, while the interest measure obtained prior to any performance orders seven of the eight experimental groups according to their predictable strength on total positive motivation (the exception is the Low-High group low in n Affiliation in the contingent condition), the data reflect the two possible effects of adding additional sources of motivation that were identified, but without reference to contingent future orientation, in Atkinson and O'Connor's (1966) research and in Atkinson's (1967, and Chapter 11) theoretical analysis. These performance effects were not predicted in the present research because it was not possible to determine a priori how much positive motivation would be "too much" for optimal performance efficiency on the particular task that was employed–a problem that still remains to be resolved (but see Atkinson, Chapter 11, for a suggested means of going about dealing with this very important issue).

One way in which the proposed effects of overmotivation may have operated in the present study is shown in Figure 2. Here the dominant pattern of interaction is schematically represented using the results of performance in the practice trials plotted on an inverted U-shaped curve. The horizontal axis represents increments in positive motivation, and the vertical axis represents mean performance scores for each of the eight experimental groups. The five points on the curve represent increment in units of positive motivation and fall approximately where the data for these groups would lie on an inverted U-shaped curve. In this explanation the affiliative tendency is assumed to be the strongest source of motivation aroused in an achievement-oriented group activity. The addition of high n Affiliation to any combination of achievement-related motives and experimental conditions increases positive motivation by 3 units. On the other hand, contingent future orientation is assumed to be less of a contributing factor, increasing resultant achievement motivation (positive or negative) by only 1 unit; for the High-Low group, the increase is positive,

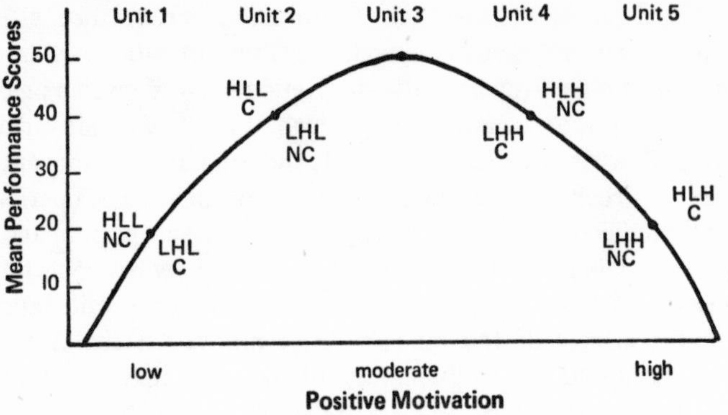

FIG. 2. Schematic representation of the dominant pattern of interaction using data from performance on the practice trials. Here it is assumed that n Affiliation was the major contributor of positive motivation to all groups (+3 to groups high in comparison to low in n Affiliation), while contingent future orientation changed the resultant tendency to achieve by only 1 unit (+1 added to the High-Low group and −1 to the Low-High group in the contingent in comparison to the noncontingent condition).

while it is negative for the Low-High group. As required by the data obtained in the practice trials for *S*s low in n Affiliation in the noncontingent condition, the Low-High group is assumed to have initially higher positive motivation than the High-Low group.

The above explanation is consistent with Raynor and Rubin's (1971, and Chapter 10) interpretation of the effects of contingent future orientation on motivation of immediate activity. According to this view, results for *S*s low in n Affiliation replicate the pattern of interaction predicted by Raynor's (1969; Chapter 7) assumptions, while results for *S*s high in n Affiliation represent an extension of the previous research to situations where too much positive motivation is aroused for the efficient performance of success-oriented individuals, while serving to increase performance efficiency of the otherwise inhibited failure-threatened individual also high in n Affiliation. The group situation where individuals interact in a face-to-face encounter is particularly likely to provide incentives for the satisfaction of affiliation motivation, especially when individual performance is known to contribute to the performance of the group as in the present task.

The explanation just proposed is consistent with the dominant pattern of interaction found in the present study, but cannot account for the pattern of results obtained for performance during the individual choice periods, specifically the substantial increase within *S*s low in n Affiliation of the Low-High group from the noncontingent to the contingent condition. Zander and Forward (1968) report a similar finding, that Low-High *S*s (on n Achievement–Test

Anxiety) actually increased their desire for group success when moving from a peripheral to a central position in the group. Since both studies were task-oriented, it would appear that either the tendency to avoid failure was not aroused or it was outweighed by other positive extrinsic tendencies. One similarity between the individual choice periods of the present study and the procedure used by Zander and Forward was that both allowed for a certain amount of anonymity in obtaining the particular measures being discussed. Under such conditions it is more likely that the tendency to avoid failure was not aroused because there was no perceived threat of failure, than that strong extrinsic motivation outweighed the inhibitory effect of anticipation of failure.

There is another possible explanation of the proposed effects of overmotivation to account for the dominant pattern of interaction (excluding data for the performance during individual choice periods). The addition of n Affiliation may have accentuated the characteristic differences in achievement-related motives while contingent future orientation served only as an additional source of positive motivation. Grosbeck (1958) noted that Low-High individuals (on n Achievement–Test Anxiety) also low in n Affiliation appeared extremely cautious in the presence of others. If n Affiliation served as a source of positive motivation, the Low-High group also high in n Affiliation should be less cautious rather than more so in comparison to the Low-High group also low in Affiliation. If a cautious stance with regard to tasks represents signs of inhibitory motivation producing lower performance, then we need only further assume that as in some previous studies (see Raynor, 1968b, 1970, and Chapter 9) the behavioral evidence suggests that contingent future orientation increases the performance of all *S*s, presumably because of the addition of sources of extrinsic rewards anticipated as contingent upon both immediate and future success. While the first explanation put forward is more consistent with existing theory and evidence, the alternative possibility could account for the dominant pattern of results and is perhaps worth further investigation.

As can be seen from the results of the present study, the issue of overmotivation is one in strong need of resolution, not only for its intrinsic value to the theory, but also in terms of extending the theory beyond the limits of traditional interests in individual performance in nongroup activity. Consider, for example, the consistency of results on theory-related and non-theory-related dependent measures in the present study. While this, as well as highly significant differences on most of these measures, leads to the conclusion that achievement-related motives can serve as the source of determinants of emergent leadership, *the issue of overmotivation is currently seen as a barrier to making precise predictions as to who will emerge as a leader in task-oriented group activity.* Resolution of this issue may lead to a fruitful extension of the theory of achievement motivation not only to the leadership area but also to other areas where additional situational and personality characteristics play a major role in determining behavior.

PART IV
A NEW THEORETICAL FRAMEWORK FOR THE STUDY OF ACHIEVEMENT MOTIVATION

In *The Dynamics of Action* (1970), David Birch and John Atkinson present a radical revision in definition of the problem of motivation and a reconstruction of the theory of motivation. Our aim in Part IV is to present this new conception, briefly and in outline, in order to achieve certain objectives. We want to show how various problems of achievement-oriented behavior are recovered within the new and more general framework, to give new interpretations of the meaning and functional significance of certain terms in the familiar theory of achievement motivation presented in Chapters 2 and 7 of this volume, and to lay the foundation for new directions in research on achievement-oriented activity.

A critical review of the inadequacies of traditional views of motivation, which provides both historical introduction and justification for this fresh view of the problem, is presented elsewhere (Atkinson, 1964, Ch. 10; Atkinson & Cartwright, 1964). Several preliminary statements of the new conception were prepared for special audiences (Birch & Veroff, 1966; Birch, 1968; Atkinson, 1969b; Atkinson & Birch, 1970). Chapter 15 by Atkinson and Birch will quote and paraphrase freely from these earlier essays and from their collaborative book, which is the definitive statement.

Most of us whose work in the continuing program of research on achievement motivation at Michigan is reported in the 1966 monograph (Atkinson & Feather, 1966) and in this volume had continued to conceive various studies within the familiar theory (i.e., Chapter 2) even as the new conceptual framework was being hammered into shape in seminars during the 1960s. But two doctoral dissertations specifically on achievement motivation, first by Bernard Weiner (1963) and then by Marvin Brown (1967), began to explore implications of the new conception even before a complete and systematic statement of it had been accomplished.[1] Chapter 15 presents a theoretical foundation for their work (presented in Chapters 16 and 17) and a useful introduction to it even though they did not have all of it explicitly in mind before their studies were conducted. In Chapter 18, Weiner

[1] See also the innovative work of Allison (1964), Birch (1966, 1968), Karabenick (1967), Valle (1967), Timberlake and Birch (1967), and Timberlake (1969) with animals and children.

extends his use of the new conception to a reinterpretation of the theoretical significance of effects of individual differences in anxiety in learning easy and complex tasks. He, like Karabenick and Youssef in a later study reported in Chapter 5, calls attention to the confrontation of S-R behavior theory (see Spence & Spence, 1966) and the theory of achievement motivation (see Atkinson, 1960, pp. 267–268) in the analysis of performance on tasks involving much (relatively difficult task) or little (relatively easy task) response competition.

15
THE DYNAMICS OF ACHIEVEMENT-ORIENTED ACTIVITY

John W. Atkinson and David Birch[1]

We begin with this premise: the behavioral life of an individual is a continual stream of thought and action, characterized by change from one activity to another, from birth until death. There are no behavioral vacuums except, of course, when an individual is literally unconscious for reasons of illness or accident and incapable of behaving at all. Otherwise, the individual is always doing something. *A simple change from one activity to another poses the fundamental problem for a psychology of motivation.* If we develop the conceptual tools needed to account for this simple fact, we shall be well on our way to explaining a series or sequence of changes from one activity to another even when the immediate environment of an individual, the stimulus situation, has remained constant for a substantial interval of time.

A CHANGE OF ACTIVITY

The conceptual analysis of a simple change from one activity to another recaptures all the traditional problems of motivation–initiation of an activity, persistence of an activity, vigor of an activity, and choice or preference among alternatives–but from a new and different theoretical perspective. All this became apparent to us after Feather's (1962) landmark study of persistence in achievement-oriented action. In using the familiar theory of achievement

[1]In this Chapter, we pull together the various discussions of achievement-related topics scattered throughout *The Dynamics of Action* (1970), quoting freely from our book and earlier presentations of the basic concepts, with permission of the authors and publisher, John Wiley & Sons.

motivation (Chapter 2), Feather was forced to the realization that one could not really derive a hypothesis about who would be more or less persistent when failing to solve a puzzle *without making an explicit reference to the strength of the individual's motivation to undertake some other alternative activity instead.*

Under natural conditions, whenever we begin to observe an individual, we note that he is already doing something. There is already an activity in progress. For example, a student is studying at his desk. Another student is immersed in a conversation with several friends in his room. We refer to this initial activity of a subject during an interval of observation as activity A. The fact that activity A is occurring, and not some other activity instead, implies either that this is the individual's only inclination to behave at the time or that the tendency to engage in this activity A (T_A) is stronger than any other competing tendency (T_B, T_C .... T_X). While the clock ticks, we continue to observe the individual. Some time later we note that activity A is no longer occurring. The student has ceased to study at his desk. The other one has terminated the conversation with friends. But when the initial activity A ceases, the individual does not stop behaving. We observe that some other activity, let us call it activity B, has been initiated to replace activity A. The one student who was studying is now going to join his friends in conversation. The other is returning to his desk to study.

The observed change of activity, from A to B, during an interval of observation (t), implies that there has been a change in the relative strength or dominance relations of the behavioral tendencies. The change is from $T_{A_I} > T_{B_I}$ to $T_{B_F} > T_{A_F}$, where I and F designate the initial and final strength of the tendencies in the interval of observation (t). The strength of one or both T_A and T_B must have changed during the interval of time such that the tendency that was weaker at the beginning has become the stronger one at the end of the interval (Figure 1).

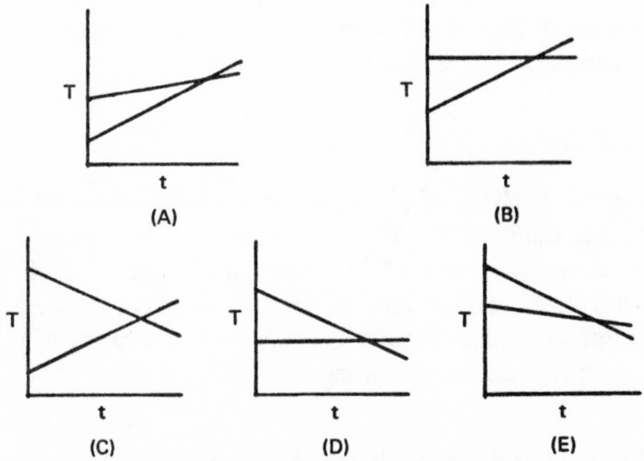

FIG. 1. Various ways in which a change in relative strength of T_A and T_B can come about during an interval of time (t).

It is the main business of a theory of motivation to explain how these changes in strength of tendencies come about to cause the change in activity exactly *when* it actually occurs. Common sense says the individual will change from one activity to another when he wants to do the one thing more than he wants to do the other. This explanation is a good beginning, but it ends where the need for scientific explanation begins. Unless we are to believe that tendencies can change in strength spontaneously, mysteriously, or on some kind of a random basis, we come to the problem with this conservative assumption: *tendencies do not change spontaneously.* Something must cause the change in the strength of a tendency. We expect to find that the cause is something that happens, a natural event, within the interval of observation preceding the observed change in activity.

We begin our analysis, then, conceiving an activity that is occurring as an expression of the behavioral tendency or inclination that is dominant at a particular time. We assume, as do the traditional theories of motivation, that the magnitude or intensity of an activity reflects the strength of the motivating tendency. And our initial conservative assumption, that no spontaneous change in the strength of a tendency can occur, may be rephrased in a way that acknowledges an indebtedness to Freud's notion that a wish persists until it is expressed: *A behavioral tendency, once aroused, will persist in its present state until acted upon by some psychological force that either increases or decreases its strength.*

What does happen during the interval in which a change of activity is observed? The individual is continuously exposed to his immediate environment, traditionally called a stimulus situation (S). And he is engaged in a particular activity, traditionally called a response (R).

Certain common changes of activity are well understood, and a pattern that fits ordinary intuition about them can be found somewhere in Figure 1. For example, the change from eating one's dinner to reading the newspaper fits the pattern of *C, D,* or *E* in Figure 1. All have in common a reduction in the strength of the tendency sustaining the initial activity of eating. And the change from reading the newspaper to answering the telephone fits the pattern of *A, B,* or *C* in Figure 1. All have in common an increase in the strength of the tendency for the newly initiated activity. In these and many other instances that come to mind, certain activities like eating obviously function to reduce the strength of a tendency, and certain stimuli, like the ringing of a telephone, obviously function to increase the strength of a tendency.

We suppose, more generally, that the *instigating force* (*F*), which increases the strength of a particular inclination to act, called an *action tendency* (*T*), is commonly attributable to exposure of the individual to some discriminable feature of the immediate environment, a stimulus. And we suppose that the *consummatory force* (*C*), which reduces the strength of a particular tendency, is attributable to the expression of that tendency in the activity itself. The change in the strength of a particular action tendency during an interval of observation should depend on the relative strengths of instigating force and consummatory force. That is,

$$\frac{T_F - T_I}{t} = F - C \tag{1}$$

It is clear that if $F > C$, there will be an increase in the strength of T. If $C > F$, there will be a decrease in the strength of T. If $C = F$, the strength of T will not change during an interval of time. It will become stable or remain constant.

But wait, one can think of other instances of a change in activity that do not seem to fit this simple picture of turning from some initial activity, either because the tendency which motivates it has been satisfied by some consummatory activity, or because some other inclination to act has been made stronger by the instigating force of an insistent call to action (a telephone ringing) or even a more subtle temptation, such as the sight of a familiar face in a crowd. Sometimes a change in activity, as intuitively understood, occurs for negative rather than positive reasons. The impact of some feature of the immediate environment is not so much instigation of activity as the opposite, suppression of an activity. For example, the ardor of a small boy to continue playing with his father's electric tools is dampened by the appearance of father, who has previously threatened punishment for this, and some other activity is initiated instead. And the appearance in the classroom of the teacher with a stack of final examinations in hand can—we have been supposing in recent years (Chapters 2 and 7)—increase the strength of a tendency *not* to undertake an activity that might eventuate in failure. We also recall, in this connection, how *S*s in whom $M_{AF} > M_S$ quickly moved away from failure at an easy puzzle to another in the Feather experiment, presumably because the tendency to avoid failure had become stronger as their initially high P_s dropped towards .50 following each successive failure (Feather, 1962).

The complete analysis of a change from one activity to another will involve not two but three motivational processes: *instigation of action, consummation in action,* and *resistance to action.* In the context of this book, the first two processes refer to the fate of the tendency to achieve success and other kinds of action tendencies (to gain approval, or some other extrinsic incentive) that spur action. The latter, *resistance,* refers to the dampening effect of the tendency to avoid failure or the tendency to avoid success (Chapter 6), or any other tendency that opposes an action tendency to reduce or weaken the strength of the *resultant* tendency ($\bar{T}$) for some activity. This much is acknowledged at the very outset, as well as that an activity is an expression of the *resultant* tendency when both instigation and resistance are taken into account. But let us postpone discussion of resistance in a change of activity until we have the dynamics of an action tendency clearly in mind and a good grasp of the principle which specifies *when* the change from one activity to another will occur. In this case, $\bar{T} = T$, since there is no resistance. We will bring resistance in later.

The Effect of Instigating Force on an Action Tendency

If the change in strength of an action tendency depends upon the relative strength of the instigating force (F) and consummatory force (C), as stated in Equation (1) above, the change in T_B, some subordinate tendency not then being expressed in behavior, will be an increase in strength whenever the individual is exposed to some instigating force for that activity since $C = 0$.

Figure 2 shows the effect of continuous and intermittent exposure to an instigating force for some particular activity. In each case the rate of increase in strength of the action tendency corresponds to the magnitude of the instigating force of the stimulus situation for that activity. This "arousability" of an action tendency depends upon the action implications of the stimulus situation for the individual as developed in his past experience in the same or similar situations (i.e., on learning). If he has learned, for example, that the consequence of some activity is success, there will be instigating force to engage in the activity and succeed. This will "arouse" and/or strengthen his tendency to engage in that activity.

An example of continuous exposure to an instigating force is the effect on the student, who is working at his desk, of the continuous low murmur of voices in friendly conversation somewhere nearby which call him to affiliative activity. An example of intermittent exposure to an instigating force is the periodic ringing of the telephone. This produces an increase in the strength of tendency to answer it, while it is ringing, which persists, while it is off, until the next ring produces a further strengthening, and so on.

The more spasmodic intermittent exposure to instigating forces of somewhat different magnitudes and durations during a longer time interval (also shown in Figure 2) produces an overall change in strength of T_B (i.e., $T_{B_F} - T_{B_I}$) that is equivalent to the change produced by supposing that the individual has been exposed to the *average instigating force* continuously throughout the whole time interval. This is shown graphically in Figure 2 by the dotted line superimposed

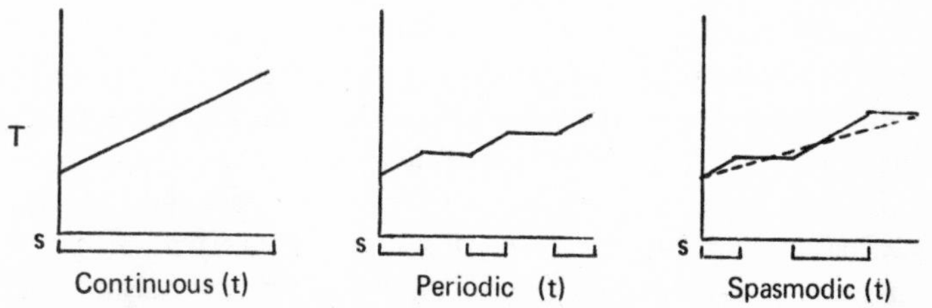

FIG. 2. The effect on strength of an action tendency of continuous, periodic, and spasmodic exposure to the instigating force of a stimulus when the tendency is not being expressed in activity. The overall effect of spasmodic exposure is equivalent to continuous exposure to the average instigating force.

on the irregular trend describing the actual effect on T of spasmodic exposure to F. Since an observer has no detailed knowledge of the actual path of growth of a tendency during an interval of observation, the assumption of continuous exposure to an average instigating force during an interval of observation is simple and useful.

When a tendency is not being expressed in activity and $C = 0$, the implication of Equation (1) above is that the final strength of an action tendency (T_F), at the end of some interval of time, will depend upon its initial strength (T_I), the magnitude of the (average) instigating force (F) of the immediate stimulus situation for that activity, and the duration of exposure to that instigating force (t). That is,

$$T_F = T_I + F \cdot t \tag{2}$$

Stimuli in the immediate environment need not be thought of as the only source of instigating forces to engage in different activities. Given a relatively rich immediate environment, an individual is exposed to instigating forces to engage in many different activities, certainly enough to produce a varied stream of behavior. But we suppose that instigation to action can arise more privately, as a consequence of an individual's covert activities and experience (Atkinson & Birch, 1970, pp. 333-337). For example, when one is remembering the warmth and joy of an activity together with friends, there is instigating force for affiliation. When one imagines, for whatever reason, a nice big piece of lemon meringue pie, there is instigating force to eat. When one is thinking of his chances of succeeding, there is instigating force to achieve, and so on. We focus on the instigating force of the immediate environment when our main interest is to understand why the same individual behaves differently in different situations and why different individuals behave differently in the same situation.

The Joint Effects of Instigating and Consummatory Force

Whenever an activity is initiated and in progress, the discriminable and manipulable features of the immediate environment with which the individual has commerce in doing whatever he is doing provide continual instigating force to sustain the activity. A person who is eating is in contact with food. A person at work has the work before him, etc. But in addition, we now assume that expression of a tendency in the activity serves to decrease the strength of that tendency. The consummatory force of some activities will be greater than others. Where the traditional view emphasizes the *qualitative* distinction between certain obviously consummatory activities (such as eating) and certain other activities that are preparatory or instrumental to it (such as walking to a restaurant and sitting down at a table), we view this difference as a *quantitative* one. The *consummatory value* (c) of an activity will depend upon the *kind* of activity, and this will influence the magnitude of consummatory force (C). But we assume, in addition, that the *intensity* of the activity will also influence the magnitude of the consummatory *force* of an activity. The intensity depends upon how strongly motivated the individual is, *how involved he is* in the activity. It corresponds to the strength of the tendency being expressed in the activity at the time. Thus, we propose

$$C = c \cdot T \tag{3}$$

An individual engaged in an activity is simultaneously exposed to forces that strengthen (F) and weaken (C) the tendency (T) motivating the activity. If $F > C$, then T increases, as in the case of T_A in graph A of Figure 1. If $C > F$, then T_A decreases, as in graphs C, D, and E of Figure 1. Eating salted peanuts, or any other good appetizer, is an example of $F > C$. Eating a thick chocolate cake, or equivalent dessert, is an example of $C > F$.

When $C = F$, then the strength of the action tendency will remain constant. We can be more specific about when this will occur. Since $C = c \cdot T$, C will equal F when $c \cdot T = F$. That will occur when $T = F/c$. This means that the strength of a tendency sustaining an activity will stabilize at a higher level when the instigating force is relatively strong compared to the consummatory value of the activity, for then the ratio of F/c will be high. If we suppose that normally the consummatory value (c) of so-called instrumental activities is much lower than of so-called goal activities, we might expect the typical trend in strength of action tendency during the phase of instrumental striving for some valent goal to correspond to the salted nut phenomenon, as illustrated by the lower curve in Figure 3. When the instrumental activity is initiated, $F > C$ so T will increase. But as T increases, so also does C, the consummatory force of the activity, because $C = c \cdot T$. As this continues to happen, the growth rate of T gradually diminishes, and finally T stabilizes when $C = F$.

If a particular activity were initiated when $C > F$, as might typically be the case for so-called goal or consummatory activities, both because the consummatory value of that kind of activity (c) is high and because T is strong, the

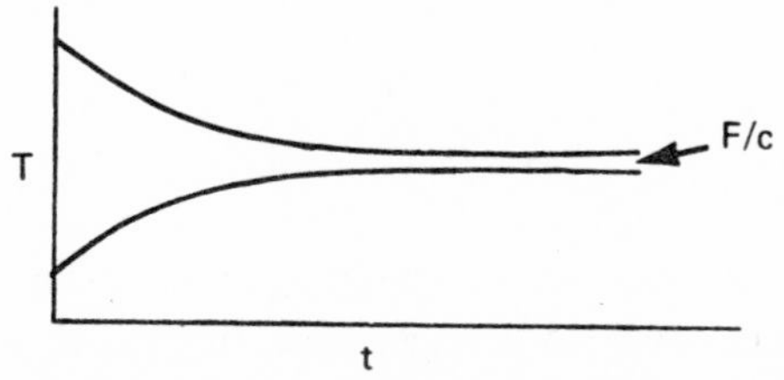

FIG. 3. The net effect on the strength of an action tendency when it is continuously instigated by a stimulus and continuously expressed in activity. The strength approaches a limit at which $F = C$ and therefore $T = F/c$.

strength of T will begin to decrease almost immediately. As its strength decreases, so also does C until finally $C = T$. In this case, the strength of T will again stabilize at a level corresponding to F/c, as shown in the upper curve of Figure 3. If the consummatory value (c) of an activity is very great, the F/c level will be substantially lower.

If these are the normal trends for the strength of a tendency that is being expressed in activity, then the shapes of the increasing and decreasing trends of T_A in Figure 1 should be redrawn (or imagined) to correspond to those in Figure 3.

The important implication of the idea that the strength of the tendency sustaining an activity will gradually become stable, if that activity continues, is that an interruption of activity and thus variability of behavior is guaranteed. Sooner or later, the strength of some other tendency that is instigated continuously or intermittently in that environment will catch up, become dominant, and cause a change of activity.

The Principle of Change of Activity

Let us return to the original problem: the change in relative strength or dominance relations of T_A and T_B that causes the change from activity A to activity B during the interval of observation (t). We can now derive a principle for this simple case.

At the beginning of the interval, when A is initially in progress, $T_{A_I} > T_{B_I}$. Some time later (t), activity A ceases and activity B is initiated, when $T_{B_F} > T_{A_F}$. This implies $T_{B_F} = T_{A_F}$ plus a very small and negligible quantity. We shall say, for simplicity, that the change occurs when $T_{B_F} = T_{A_F}$ (but not forget that very small extra quantity).

During the interval, when activity A is occurring but activity B is not, there is no consummatory force operating to reduce T_B. So the determinants of T_{B_F} are given by Equation (2) above as $T_{B_F} = T_{B_I} + F_B \cdot t$. When we substitute for T_{B_F} in the equation $T_{B_F} = T_{A_F}$, describing the state of the individual when the change in activity occurs, we have

$$T_{B_I} + F_B \cdot t = T_{A_F}$$

$$t = \frac{T_{A_F} - T_{B_I}}{F_B} \qquad (4)$$

This *principle of change of activity* identifies the several determinants of the time taken by an individual to change from the initial activity A to the subsequent activity B. It is apparent that the same reading of the clock provides a measure of the persistence of one activity (A) and the latency of the other activity (B). Two central problems in the psychology of motivation—persistence of an activity and initiation of an activity—are recovered as the two inseparable aspects of a single behavioral problem: a change of activity. Their interrelationship, lost in the traditional account of discrete goal-directed episodes each having a beginning in a state of motivation, a middle–the instrumental activity–and an end–either consummation or frustration–is now obvious when the focus of interest becomes the joint or juncture between successive activities in the stream of behavior.

Consider the earlier example of change in activity of a student from studying at his desk to going to join his friends in conversation. The principle states that persistence in the achievement-oriented activity of studying will be greater and/or the initiation of the affiliative activity less prompt when the tendency to continue studying (T_{A_F}) is very strong relative to the initial strength of the tendency to join his friends (T_{B_I}) and when the instigating force to join his friends (F_{B}) is also weak.

On the other hand, initiation of the affiliative activity will be most prompt (and persistence in studying minimal) when the initial strength of tendency to join his friends (T_{B_I}) is very strong in relation to the tendency to study (T_{A_F}), and when the instigating force to join his friends (F_{B}) is also very strong.

The dual role of the immediate stimulus situation is made apparent if we consider as fairly typical the case in which T_{A}, sustaining activity in progress, has become relatively stable at the level defined by $F_{\mathrm{A}}/c_{\mathrm{A}}$. Then, substituting for T_{A_F} in Equation (4) above, we get

$$t = \frac{F_{\mathrm{A}}/c_{\mathrm{A}} - T_{\mathrm{B}_I}}{F_{\mathrm{B}}} \tag{5}$$

In our illustration, F_{A} is produced by the desk, books, papers, and other items of work immediately before the student, c_{A} represents the consummatory value of the ongoing activity of studying, F_{B} is produced by the continual murmur of the conversation of friends in the hallway or room next door. And T_{B_I} represents the strength of a persisting or *inertial tendency* to join his friends that must be attributed to instigation that has occurred prior to the beginning of the interval of observation.

How, we may now ask, is this conception of the dynamics of action related to study of the effects of individual differences in the strength of motives to achieve, to affiliate, etc.? A motive (M_{G}) has been conceived as a variable that influences a whole family of functionally related activities. These are activities that are expected to lead to the same kind of goal. The strength of an individual's motive to achieve, we have been saying in the familiar theory (Chapters 2 and 7), functions to produce generally stronger or weaker tendencies to achieve than those of other people in a variety of different stimulus situations. We now can see that *the strength of an individual's motive to achieve must function as a determinant or component of a whole family of instigating forces to engage in activities that involve evaluation of one's performance in relation to standards of excellence.*

Looking at Equation (5) above, we can see that a strong motive sustaining an activity in progress (F_A) will, like the somewhat analogous concept of inertial mass in physics, tend to make it more difficult to induce the individual to move on to another activity. It will encourage persistence.

The same strong motive, but now considered a determinant of F_B when the individual is engaged in some other kind of activity, should promote greater willingness to initiate activity B promptly than would a weaker motive. In this position, the function of a motive is somewhat analogous to the gravitational mass of physics. Thus, other things equal, the person strong in achievement motive should be more willing than others to initiate achievement activities when engaged in or confronted with opportunities for other kinds of activity. And since the strength of tendency expressed in an ongoing activity will approach a higher level when F_A is strong, the person strong in motive to achieve should be more intensely involved (if not always more efficient–see Part III) and more persistent in his achievement activities.

The principle of change of activity thus becomes the integrative principle for studies of the behavioral effects of this kind of difference in personality. It provides *a theoretical foundation for expecting to find correlations among the many behavioral symptoms of differences in strength of achievement motive.* It implies more generally (as we shall see later in more detail) that personality, conceived in part as a hierarchy of relatively general motives, constitutes a specification of how an individual will distribute his time among different kinds of activities.

We have said all these things in reference to how strength of a motive should be conceived as a determinant or component of a family of instigating forces. Thus, a motive is an important influence on instigation of one *kind* of activity, or activities instrumental to one *kind* of goal. The very same points can be made in reference to the other variables we have identified in the familiar theory of achievement motivation (Chapter 2) and in Raynor's elaboration of it (Chapter 7). Some of these variables may refer to the whole family of activities to which the term motive refers. Others (e.g., competence in athletic versus intellectual activities) may refer to particular subsets of the family of instigating forces to which motive refers. Still others (e.g., future orientation concerning the field of psychology but not the field of economics) will refer more specifically to the instigating forces to undertake some intellectual activities but not others. And still others (e.g., the P_s at a given task) will refer very specifically to the strength of instigating force to achieve at a given task.

What this adds up to, in brief, is that *the familiar* (Chapter 2) *and elaborated theory of achievement motivation* (Chapter 7) *is now to be considered a theory about the determinants of instigating forces to achieve success* (F_S) *in various activities and not, as heretofore assumed, of the final strength of tendencies to achieve success in various activities in particular situations.* The familiar theory, in ignoring the systematic influence of inertial tendencies, i.e., the persistence into the present situation of tendencies previously aroused and strengthened, is as stimulus-bound as the more general cognitive theory (decision theory) on which it was based.

In a discussion of what is known about sexual behavior, Whalen (1966, p. 152) has distinguished the meaning of "sexual arousal" and "the momentary level of sexual excitation." "Sexual arousal" refers to "an individual's characteristic rate of approach to orgasm as a result of sexual stimulation." We make this very same distinction between the state or level of motivation (tendency) and the rate of change in its strength resulting from relevant stimulation (force). And we would tend to agree with Whalen's conclusion "that these two dimensions of sexuality comprise sexual motivation." These two dimensions, the rate of arousal or change in strength of a tendency (force) and its state, level, or strength at a particular time (tendency), comprise the essentials of any kind of motivation we may wish to analyze.

Displacement and Substitution

We have already introduced the concept of a family of functionally related activities to help establish contact with the familiar idea of relatively general and enduring motives to achieve, to affiliate, for power, to eat, etc., early in the discussion. Now let us arrive at the same concept another and less arbitrary way.

In Figure 1 there are three patterns of change in activity, those labeled *A*, *B*, and *C*, that have a common characteristic. Each involves an increase in the strength of T_B, the tendency motivating the second activity. Together these patterns show rather directly how the trend and strength of T_A affect persistence in activity A and/or the time to initiate activity B. One might imagine, looking at patterns A and C, that if T_A had already become stable at the higher or lower level before the interval of observation, the time taken for the change in activity would be the same as shown. Generally, T_A will be strong or rising when F_A is strong, and T_A will be weak or falling when F_A is weak.

The two other patterns of change in activity, patterns *D* and *E* in Figure 1, have something in common with pattern *C*, viz., a decreasing trend in T_A, the tendency sustaining the initial activity. Patterns *D* and *E* are particularly interesting. To fit pattern *D*, we must think of an example in which T_B had been aroused and strengthened by exposure to appropriate instigating forces before this interval of observation. But now, its persistence at a particular level (rather than some increase or decrease) implies that no feature of the immediate environment, no present stimulus, is influencing it. Nevertheless, at some point the inclination to undertake activity B, T_B, becomes dominant. This inclination must seem to the individual to arise spontaneously, for there is no immediately present stimulus to elicit it, to call it forth, or to strengthen it. Recall the illustration of the student who was initially having a conversation with his friends and then left them to study. We might assume that the affiliative activity had substantial consummatory value (c) to account for a decreasing T_A, and that the tendency to study, T_B, had previously been aroused by exposure to the books, desk, papers, etc., in his room before the conversation with friends began. At some point in the conversation, when the student has had enough talking with friends to last him for a while, *the inclination to study arises spontaneously from within.*

Here we see an important implication of assuming that something must cause a change in the strength of tendency, that it will otherwise (like a Freudian wish) persist at a given level. An individual can be motivated to act from within, without the immediate physical presence of any external goad, or stimulus, for that activity. The behavior is unambiguously *an action* and not *a reaction.* This justifies our claim of offering a theory of an active organism.

Since this kind of change can only occur when the strength of the tendency sustaining the activity in progress is diminishing, that is where we should look for our instances of it—after a period of obviously consummatory activity and when the immediate environment is relatively barren of features producing instigating forces for other activities. This illustrates how the strongest among previously aroused but unfulfilled wishes will have an important selective influence on what is done next in the stream of an individual's activity.

The last pattern of change, pattern *E* in Figure 1, would seem impossible given our discussion to this point, for the subordinate tendency T_B is becoming weaker even though activity B is not occurring. This could not happen unless certain tendencies, or the activities they motivate, were functionally related so that what happened to one directly might have a similar but indirect effect on another.

We know from common observation that this kind of thing does happen. The aroma of a charcoal steak, broiling over an open fire, increases not only the specific tendency to eat the steak but also tendencies to eat potato chips, pickles, and anything else that is soon made available. Direct instigation of one particular activity (e.g., to eat a steak) does have an indirect instigating effect on *some* other tendencies (e.g., to eat other foods, to go to the store to get some food, etc.) but not on *all* other tendencies (e.g., to study for an exam, to play the violin, etc.). And, similarly, the direct expression and consummation of one tendency in action (e.g., eating potatoes) does have an indirect consummatory effect on *some* other tendencies (e.g., to eat steak, to go to the store for some food) but, again, not on *all* other tendencies (e.g., to study for an exam, to play a violin, etc.).

In pattern *E* of Figure 1, we have a case in which activity A, in progress, is declining because $C_A > F_A$ and this is having an indirect *substitutive* effect on the strength of T_B. It, too, is declining but not as rapidly as T_A. Returning to our example of the student talking with some friends, this might be an illustration of what is happening to his inclination to talk to still some other one of his friends. He moves from his conversation with one set of friends to searching out a different one. Since both tendencies are declining, this pattern is likely to occur only when tendencies are relatively weak and, therefore, in situations that fail to instigate other attractive alternatives.

The indirect strengthening of the tendency for one activity that is attributable to the instigation of some other activity is called *displacement.*

The indirect weakening of the tendency for one activity that is attributable to the consummatory force of some other activity is called *substitution.* We refer to the capacity of one activity to reduce the tendency for another activity as its *substitute value* for the other.

The indirect instigation of an activity (displacement) will depend upon the magnitude of the direct instigating force for the activity to which an individual is exposed, and the degree of relationship between the two activities. We have supposed, in a more detailed and technical discussion of this (Atkinson & Birch, 1970, Ch. 2), that the closeness of the relationship between two activities can depend upon their association in the person's history, or their symbolic equivalence (both proposed by Freud), or their being two instances of essentially the same kind of consummatory activity (e.g., eating steak, eating pie, etc.), or their being alternative means to the same or similar ends or goal activities (e.g., to throw the ring from 5 feet to achieve, to throw the ring from 10 feet to achieve, to write an excellent exam to achieve, etc.).

The indirect reduction in the strength of tendency for one activity by actual occurrence of another, i.e., the degree of substitution, also depends on the magnitude of the force operating directly on the tendency for one and the degree of relationship between the two activities. Thus, for example, success in one activity may provide an indirect or *substitutive* effect, on the tendency to succeed in another activity. (See Atkinson & Birch, 1970, Ch. 2).

Thus broadened to include these more general and indirect effects of instigation of some specific activity and consummation in its occurrence, we systematically embrace the concept of *a family of functionally related tendencies* that will ordinarily tend to increase and decrease in strength together relative to other families of tendencies. The members of the same family will, in other words, tend to have a common fate.

In reference to families of tendencies, it often simplifies discussion and description of what is happening to use the family name, a class term such as tendency to eat, tendency to achieve, tendency to affiliate, etc., which embraces all the specific action tendencies that are affected by displacement and substitution, rather than trying to list exhaustively and in precise detail (which is probably impossible) what happens to the strength of each specific action tendency. This means that when we say the tendency to achieve is aroused by an intelligence test, we mean, specifically, that the effect of the direct instigation to achieve on the test spreads, i.e., is displaced, and thus indirectly influences the strength of a whole cluster or family of functionally related action tendencies.

The term motive to achieve is used in reference to the corresponding family of instigating forces. Individual differences in strength of motive to achieve are differences among individuals in the "arousability" of the tendency to achieve (i.e., the family of specific tendencies that have a common fate). Affiliation motive refers to individual differences in the "arousability" of a family of action tendencies that are economically described as tendency to affiliate, and so on.

The concepts of displacement and substitution take us from the specifics of particular life situations to description of the more general motivational implications for an individual. These concepts provide the theoretical foundation and justification for the use of more general class terms, such as motive to achieve, affiliative motive, power motive, etc., for economical description of how individuals differ in personality, that is, in their greater or lesser willingness to initiate and persist in different kinds of activity, etc.

Choice of Preference among Alternatives

We have made reference to the initiation of an activity, the intensity or vigor of an activity, and the persistence of an activity. To complete the coverage of traditional behavioral problems that have required a theory of motivation, let us turn to the more complicated problem of choice.

When the question is which of two (or more) alternatives will be chosen or preferred, the issue, as defined by this new conceptual scheme, is which of two (or more) competing tendencies will attain dominance first as shown in Figure 4. The study of preferential behavior is distinguished from the study of initiation and persistence in a particular activity in the eyes of the observer, not in the nature of the problem. In one case, the observer's bias is restricted to the initiation or cessation of some particular, critical activity. In the other case, he is prepared to notice and record which of two (or more) activities occurs, ignoring whatever else occurs in the individual's stream of activity.

The case of an individual engaged in some initial activity A and exposed to stimuli producing instigating force for incompatible activities X and Y is shown in graph A of Figure 4. In this case, alternative X occurs (is chosen) because the

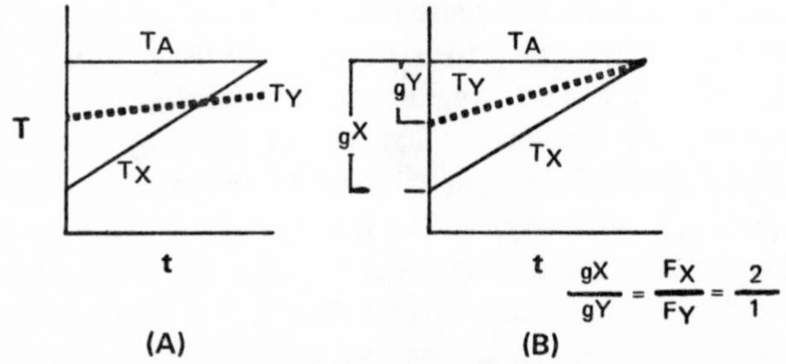

FIG. 4. *Choice.* Which of two competing tendencies attains dominance first? Preference follows the stronger force except when the ratio of the initial gaps (gX/gY) is greater than the ratio of the instigating forces (F_X/F_Y).

theoretical latency for activity X, given the conditions, is less than the theoretical latency for activity Y. (The theoretical latency is the time taken, *t*, to initiate an activity when there is no competing alternative.) In other words, activity X occurs because $t_X < t_Y$ where

$$t_X = \frac{T_{A_F} - T_{X_I}}{F_X} \quad \text{and} \quad t_Y = \frac{T_{A_F} - T_{Y_I}}{F_Y}$$

In graph A, the choice is for the activity instigated by the stronger force even though the initial strength of the two tendencies, prior to exposure to the stimuli for choice, favored preference for activity Y.

Will the activity motivated by the stronger instigating force always win out in competition? The answer to this question, derived from the principle of change of activity, is suggested in graph B of Figure 4. Here the condition depicted is the special case in which the theoretical latencies for the two activities are equal. That is,

$$t_X = t_Y$$

$$\frac{T_{A_F} - T_{X_I}}{F_X} = \frac{T_{A_F} - T_{Y_I}}{F_Y}$$

$$\frac{T_{A_F} - T_{X_I}}{T_{A_F} - T_{Y_I}} = \frac{F_X}{F_Y}$$

$$\frac{g_X}{g_Y} = \frac{F_X}{F_Y}$$

Both in Figure 4 and immediately above, we use the abbreviations gX and gY for $(T_{A_F} - T_{X_I})$ and $(T_{A_F} - T_{Y_I})$ in reference to the "initial gaps" for X and Y. The "initial gap" is the amount by which the strength of a tendency must increase in order to exceed T_A and be expressed in behavior.

In the special case shown in graph B of Figure 4, the ratio of the initial gaps (gX/gY) equals the ratio of the magnitudes of the respective instigating forces (F_X/F_Y). And in this particular case, activity X will again be chosen, because in the next instant T_X will increase more rapidly than T_Y and will become dominant. But one can now see that if T_{Y_I} were a little stronger, or T_{X_I} were a little weaker, than shown in the figure (or both), activity Y would occur instead. Preference for the activity motivated by the weaker instigating force should occur, in other words, whenever the ratio of the "initial gaps" is greater than the ratio of the respective instigating forces, that is, whenever $g\mathrm{X}/g\mathrm{Y} > F_X/F_Y$.

If there is little or no substitution (see above), this could come about in a series of trials in which the individual, though exposed to both F_X and F_Y, always had been expressing T_X in his choices. Each time, there is exposure to F_Y and growth in the strength of T_Y which, we have assumed (Figure 2), will persist to influence behavior on a later occasion. Each time activity X occurs, there is some consummatory force to produce some reduction in the strength attained by T_X on that trial. And if T_{A_F} is constant across trials, the level of T_X is always the same after each choice of X. But all this time, T_{Y_I}, the inertial tendency to engage in Y, is increasing in strength. Sooner or later it will have grown sufficiently so that $gX/gY > F_X/F_Y$, and then the choice of the activity instigated by the weaker force will occur. This could also come about in everyday life if a person had been tempted sufficiently more to engage in one activity than in another before the interval of observation in which the paradoxical preference is observed.

An individual's choice in the direction of the weaker instigating force may appear "stupid" to an observer of only the limited interval in the stream of a person's behavior in which the single choice occurs. It appears to be a preference for the less attractive alternative. In the domain of achievement-oriented activity, it would take the form of an occasional choice of an "easy" rather than a "moderately difficult" task by someone known to be very strong in motive to achieve. But this kind of apparently "stupid" behavior, traditionally attributed to random fluctuations in the strength of tendencies, is a lawful consequence of assumptions we have made concerning the dynamics of an action tendency: once aroused, it will persist until strengthened further either by direct instigation or by displacement, or until weakened by expression in action or substitution.

Preference will more frequently, but not always, be an expression of the tendency influenced by the stronger instigating force. Our detailed analysis of this problem (Atkinson & Birch, 1970, pp. 107–118) has shown that *it is the ratio of the magnitudes of instigating force and not the difference in their magnitudes which systematically influences the probability of choosing one alternative in preference to another.*

Perhaps most critical for an attempt to recover earlier findings concerning achievement-oriented activity within the new dynamics of action are the results obtained on a number of occasions that show greater preference for tasks of intermediate difficulty (where the probability of success is near .50) among persons who are strong in achievement motive than among those who are weak in achievement motive (Atkinson & Feather, 1966). If the old theory (Chapter 2) is now taken as a theory concerning the determinants of instigating force (i.e., $F_S = M_S \times P_s \times I_s$), the ratio of the strength of forces to achieve where $P_s = .90$ and where $P_s = .50$ should not be affected by the multiplicative factor, M_S. (Previously we had assumed that preference was a function of the magnitude of the difference which is affected by a multiplicative factor.)

There is a satisfactory explanation which does not go beyond our usual assumption that normally there are other extrinsic sources of motivation for achievement-oriented actions. We now refer to a tendency that is a composite of several different action tendencies all of which refer to the very same activity as a *compound* action tendency. For example, when $T_A = T_{A,S} + T_{A,ext}$, T_A is a compound action tendency. This comes about when the immediate stimulus situation produces instigating forces to undertake an activity in order to achieve success (F_S) and in order to attain some other extrinsic incentive (F_{ext}) such as approval for cooperation, etc. In the absence of evidence to the contrary, we have generally assumed (now to state the idea in terms of the new scheme) that some F_{ext} is constant for activities which differ in difficulty and which otherwise differ in F_S.

What is the effect of adding a constant F_{ext} to each F_S on the ratio of forces to undertake a moderately difficult task ($P_s = .50$) versus an easy task ($P_s = .90$) when M_S is strong and weak? If, for simplicity, we suppose that the ratio of forces favoring choice of intermediate difficulty is 9/3 when M_S is strong and 3/1 when it is weak, then $9/3 = 3/1$. The effect of adding a constant of 1, representing F_{ext}, to each of the forces now produces 10/4 when M_S is strong and 4/2 when M_S is weak, and $10/4 > 4/2$. The effect of adding a constant is to change the ratio of forces in each case, but the change, in the direction of equalizing the forces, is greater the smaller the absolute magnitude of the forces.

Given this analysis, the preference for intermediate levels of difficulty should be more marked among persons in whom M_S is strong, not because the absolute difference among forces to engage in activities that differ is larger (the kind of presumption we had made earlier), but because most achievement-oriented activities are overdetermined. That is, they are motivated by *compound* action tendencies. *When M_S is strong, the instigating forces to achieve have proportionality greater influence on the ratio of the total forces to undertake activities that differ in difficulty than when M_S is weak.* (See, in this regard, Smith, 1966.)

From this, we must draw the conclusion that in an *ideal* achievement-oriented situation, i.e., one that produced only instigating forces to achieve success, the generally observed preference for activities in which P_s is near .50 would hold true uniformly no matter how great the variations in strength of M_S among individuals.

The most important point in this analysis of choice or preference among alternatives, as in the earlier treatment of initiation and persistence of particular activities, is that action is not completely controlled by the magnitude of the instigating forces produced by the immediate stimulus situation. The differential states of readiness to undertake one or another activity, i.e., the strengths of various inertial tendencies, reflect the cumulative impact of prior instigation to act that have not been adequately expressed and consummated in action (or by substitution) and so are carried on into the present situation as important selective influences on behavior.

The Effect on Motivation of Deprivation

The same principle that is applied to the fate of the tendency for the unchosen alternative in a choice can account for some fundamental behavioral facts which the concept of "drive" was introduced into psychology to explain. Most notable is the fact that the tendency to eat increases as a function of the number of hours the individual has been deprived of the opportunity to eat. Deprivation of water increases the tendency to drink. Deprivation of a mate increases the tendency for sexual behavior (see, e.g., Bolles, 1967).

The traditional problem of "drive", which is grounded in these and related observations, is recovered from a different vantage point. One need not make an explicit appeal to metabolic activities that use up supplies of vital commodities and create bodily needs (though this possibility is not necessarily excluded). One can, instead, consider the traditional operational definition of hunger drive from the viewpoint of the present scheme. The experimenter provides no opportunity for an animal to eat for a given length of time. This is the extent of rigid experimental control. Thus we know that the one activity capable of producing the greatest consummatory force on the tendency to eat does not occur. Traditionally, the procedure for making animals hungry has not involved any particular control of the environmental stimulation to which the animal is exposed during the time of deprivation. So we may safely assume, without contradiction, that during the time of deprivation, the animal is exposed spasmodically to visual, olifactory, and other stimuli that are related by stimulus generalization to eating or to the pursuit of food in its history. Intermittent exposure to these various instigating forces to eat, however weak and infrequent they may be, should produce the kind of cumulative effect of increasing the tendency to eat that has been shown in Figure 2. And the amount of the increase should be a function of the time of deprivation.

The present scheme leaves room for the influence on tendency to eat (or to drink, or to copulate, etc.) of instigating forces that originate in the metabolic or hormonal processes of the organism if some behavioral phenomena should unambiguously require that we posit these forces (e.g., the effect of an internal "drive stimulus").

The effect of external inducements to eat on the strength of the tendency to eat during the deprivation period should be paralleled by similar effects when, either by design or fortuitously, an individual is prevented from engaging in other kinds of activity that would effectively consummate other kinds of tendency. Just so long as he is exposed to inducements or temptations to undertake the activity, there should be a gradual increase in the strength of the behavioral tendency. Thus an individual who is deprived of an opportunity to affiliate with others, either because of his geographic isolation or because of their consistent rejection of him for some reason, but is aperiodically exposed to the instigating force of stimuli to engage in affiliative activities, should suffer a gradual heightening of his inertial tendency to engage in activities that involve friendly commerce with other people. We mean to generalize the basic idea that prevention of activity that produces a strong consummatory force for some tendency, but not of exposure to stimuli that produce instigating force, should, as a function time (duration of exposure), produce a heightening of the tendency to engage in that kind of activity. This, we believe, is the appropriate explanation of many of the motivational effects produced traditionally by the experimental operation called *deprivation.*

Effect of Experimentally Induced Motivation on Imaginative Behavior

The results of experiments on the expression of experimentally induced motivation in thematic apperception (McClelland et al., 1953; Atkinson, 1958a) can be organized in terms of the concepts already introduced. In the first of them, individuals were systematically deprived of food for 1, 4, and 16 hours. The expression of the tendency to eat in the imaginative content of stories then written by them increased as a function of the time of deprivation. Here, paralleling the usual result for instrumental food seeking in animals, is evidence of a heightened inertial tendency to eat. The initiation of a story concerned with food-seeking activity instead of some other kind of activity, when doubtless there were many other activities suggested by the picture stimuli used to prompt stories, corresponds to the increased readiness to initiate relevant instrumental action when hunger increases. It soon became apparent that there was little reason to think otherwise than that imaginative behavior is governed by the same principles that govern instrumental striving (Atkinson & McClelland, 1948).

The procedures and results of subsequent studies that sought to demonstrate the existence of so-called "psychogenic" needs that might function in a manner parallel to the so-called "biogenic" needs of animal research deserve scrutiny in light of the present conceptualization. Let us consider, as illustrative, some results of the early experiments on the effects of the experimental arousal of *the need for achievement* (n Achievement). Among other conditions, college students wrote four imaginative stories in response to four different pictures: (*a*) in a *neutral* classroom when nothing was done either to heighten or to reduce their normal concern with achieving; (*b*) immediately following a period of explicity *achievement-oriented* performance on several intelligence-type tests which had been presented with instructions that emphasized the importance of doing well and before any knowledge of results; and (*c*) immediately following the feedback concerning such test performance which was systematically controlled so as to assure either feelings of *success* or feelings of *failure.* The underlying premise in the design of the study was that the state of motivation induced immediately before imaginative stories were written would persist long enough to influence the content of the stories as did the differences in hunger produced by food deprivation.

The average n Achievement scores for these several conditions, a measure of the frequency of achievement-related responses in the stories, were as follows: neutral, 7.33; achievement-oriented, 8.77; success, 7.92; failure, 10.10 (McClelland, Atkinson, Clark, & Lowell, 1953, p. 184). Consider them in light of the present scheme. In three of the conditions (viz., achievement-oriented, success, and failure), a strong instigating force to achieve had been introduced in the form of an instruction for an intelligence test and the confrontation with such a test. The exposure to this instigating force should have increased the strength of tendency to achieve in these three conditions relative to the neutral group, which had not been given any specific inducement to achieve over and beyond what is inherent in the classroom situation. According to the assumptions regarding displacement, the indirect or displaced effects of the instigating force to achieve on the intelligence test would amount to a simultaneous increase in the strength of many other specific tendencies to achieve. The activity of merely working at the intelligence test might have had some consummatory value for all groups. By assuming that the intensity of activity was equal in all groups, the consummatory force of working at the task is a constant among the three achievement-oriented groups. In the success condition, however, each subject was given an opportunity to engage in the additional activity of comparing his scores on the various intelligence tests with norms that were deliberately distorted so that he would experience success. Presumably, this would produce greater consummatory force than the additional activity of examining one's performance in relation to norms deliberately distorted to convey the impression of failure. In these two conditions, the experience of success and failure was systematically controlled in all the subjects. In the achievement-oriented condition, no explicit knowledge of results had been provided and, hence, no systematic control was exerted over possible covert reactions of the subjects when the tests were collected. Some individuals might have felt that they had succeeded, others that they had failed. Consequently, the achievement-oriented condition might be expected to fall between the success group, in which average consummatory force was strongest, and the failure group, in which it was weakest. The results correspond to theoretical expectations that can be derived from the present scheme concerning systematic differences in the strength of inertial tendency to achieve at the time the thematic apperception test was administered. It is of particular interest that the average n Achievement score following success was almost as low as in the neutral condition. This implies that the presumed increase in tendency to achieve, attributable to the instigating force of achievement orientation, was practically matched by the presumed decrease attributable to the consummatory force of success at the initial task. Even larger differences were obtained among groups in which the prior motivating conditions were more extreme. In a relaxed condition, when every effort was made to minimize the importance of a series of dull tasks administered very informally before the imaginative stories were written to reduce the typical instigation to achieve in a college classroom, the average n Achievement score was only 1.95 (McClelland et al., 1953, p. 184).

Other results of this experiment, which are typical of the ones obtained with different pictures in thematic apperception, illustrate the idea of a family of interrelated tendencies that share a common fate. The average n Achievement score obtained only from the stories that were written in response to a picture of two mechanics working at some kind of machine was higher than the average n Achievement score obtained when the picture contained just the heads of two men. This implies that a stronger instigating force to achieve is produced by the distinctive cues associated with work and the prior evaluations of performance in the lives of most men. The picture that contained only the heads of two men had cues that were less similar than those of the work scene to cues of specific achievement training experiences. The picture of the heads alone suggests many other kinds of activity or, in the language of the theory, defines instigating forces for many different kinds of activity.

The achievement-related activities described in stories to these particular pictures were rarely if ever instances of an individual taking an intelligence test. Yet the average n Achievement score in response to each picture was increased a comparable amount by the prior experimental induction of motivation by the stimulus of an intelligence test. The evidence of heightened tendency to achieve in many different kinds of activity following inducement to achieve at an intelligence test must be considered an instance of displacement. The instigating force to perform well at the intelligence test that was given prior to the thematic apperception task produced an increase in the strength of other tendencies that share, with the intelligence test, the anticipated consequence of successful performance in relation to a standard of excellence. This, in fact, defines the common goal of the family of tendencies that are more simply described as tendency to achieve or n Achievement. A comparison of the amount of increase in n Achievement in the two sets of stories following achievement orientation suggests that the degree of displacement between the intelligence test-taking activity and the imaginative activity suggested by a picture of men working in a shop (usually a theme about inventors) is comparable in magnitude to the degree of displacement from the test-taking activity to the kind of activity described in response to another picture of the heads of two men (usually, a theme about career planning).

The traditional experimental operation for the control of hunger drive and the technique evolved in the studies of "ego-involving" human activities to heighten motivation by failure experience have much in common. In each case, there is experimental intervention to prevent the occurrence of a so-called goal activity that would produce a substantial consummatory force to reduce the strength of tendency. In the case of food deprivation, an exposure to the instigating force of external stimuli is a fortuitous matter. The conceptual schemes of the past do not suggest that time defines the duration of a dynamic process as conceived here, in which stimuli function as instigating forces that increase the strength of tendencies that then persist in their present state until acted on by other subsequent forces. Hence, until now, there has never been any explicit theoretical reason for paying strict attention to the nature of the stimulation to which an animal is subjected during the period in which he is deprived of the opportunity to engage in the so-called consummatory activity.

In the case of the experimental induction of achievement motivation, the explicit instruction given to an individual, which emphasizes the importance of doing well because his performance will be evaluated in terms of a standard of excellence, explicitly introduces a strong instigating force to achieve at the task before him. In the case of experimental induction of affiliative motivation (Shipley & Veroff, 1952; Atkinson, Heyns, & Veroff, 1954), being surrounded by peers making ratings of one's social acceptability explicitly introduces a strong instigating force for affiliation, and so on for power, aggression, and sexual motivation (Atkinson, 1958a). A similar effect might be accomplished in a study of the tendency to eat by systematically exposing animals in the home cage to the odor of food or some other stimulus previously conditioned to eating responses, that is, one capable of producing a strong instigating force to eat during the deprivation period. Experimental procedures of this kind have already been tried in several studies (Birch, 1968; Valle, 1968) and have yielded results that are consonant with the theory.

McClelland et al. (1953) developed a method for identifying expressions of the tendency to achieve (n Achievement) in the imaginative content of thematic apperception stories by systematically varying the magnitude of the inertial tendency to achieve in groups of male college students immediately before they were given the opportunity to create imaginative stories in response to a series of pictures. The method for content analysis of imaginative stories that was developed in these experiments to yield the thematic apperceptive n Achievement score describes the various ways in which the tendency to achieve is expressed in imaginative content. This frequency measure of individual differences in strength of motive to achieve has provided the integrative link between many subsequent studies concerned with other behavioral effects of inferred individual differences in strength of motive to achieve. Similar steps have been taken to provide a basis for measurement of affiliative and power motives (Atkinson, 1958a; Winter, 1973).

When the principle of change of activity is applied directly to the initiation, magnitude, and persistence of the imaginative activity in which tendency to achieve is expressed, we must begin the interval of observation at the time the subject has just finished reading the instructions for the task and is waiting for the display of the first picture. If the ideal condition for the assessment of differences in motive has been attained (see Atkinson, 1958b) all individuals, at the time, would be equal in the strength of the inertial tendency to achieve. Then, if the tendency that sustains the initial activity of waiting for the first picture is also constant among subjects, we may take the speed of initiating an achievement-related plot, instead of some other kind of plot, as one symptom of a relatively strong instigating force to achieve. As the achievement-oriented imaginative activity continues, the strength of the tendency should move toward a level defined by F/c, which is higher if the instigating force is strong than if it is weak. Thus the magnitude or intensity of achievement-related activity should be stronger as the story is being written for those individuals for whom the instigating force is strong. Furthermore, if the tendency to achieve, now sustaining the imaginative activity in progress, is relatively strong, this activity will be more persistent and, thus, more likely to continue without interruption throughout the whole time period allotted for writing the story. All of these predicted symptoms of a strong instigating force to achieve in response to a particular picture—faster initiation of the achievement-related story, greater intensity of activity, greater persistence in the face of possible interference by other kinds of imaginative response—will enhance the likelihood of greater frequency of achievement-related imagery and more complete coverage of all the various aspects of an achievement-oriented plot in a particular story. All this will produce a higher n Achievement score for that story. (See McClelland et al., 1953, pp. 107-138; Atkinson, 1958a, Ch. 12.)

The concept of motive implies that the person who scores high in response to one kind of picture should also tend to score high in response to another kind of picture. He does (McClelland et al., 1953, p. 190; Atkinson, 1964, pp. 230-231). And the person who scores high in response to one set of pictures on one occasion should tend to score high in response to another set of pictures on another occasion. He does. And this should occur even if one test condition is relatively relaxed for all subjects and the other is given under achievement-oriented conditions for all subjects. It does (reported in McClelland et al., 1953, pp. 161, 191-194; French, 1955; Haber & Alpert, 1958). (This reading of the evidence concerning TAT n Achievement requires considerably more sophistication concerning all the other factors to be considered (see Reitman & Atkinson, 1958) than is sometimes found among reviewers of literature who have not transcended the misleading oversimplifications and myths of measurement transmitted in introductory texts on psychological measurement (e.g., Weinstein, 1969; Entwisle, 1972)).

In other words, the evidence that uses only the imaginative response measure of strength of tendency to achieve sustains the view that the differences in n Achievement observed in response to one particular picture in one particular situation refer to something more general—something that is also expressed in response to other pictures and in other situations. Of course, this does not mean that the average response of a group of subjects is the same to all pictures. It varies greatly, as it should, if other determinants of the instigating force to achieve that are more specific to the stimulus itself vary from picture to picture. And it does not mean that the average response of a group of subjects is the same in all situations. The latter should and does vary substantially as a function of the immediate success-failure history of the group and in terms of the strength of the instigating force to achieve in the test situation itself.

What, then, of the relationship of differences in the strength of motive as inferred from the thematic apperceptive n Achievement score to instrumental achievement-oriented activity? According to our principles and to the usual operating assumptions (see Atkinson & Birch, 1970, Ch. 4) that must be made to get us from the idealized conditions to the actual events that involve samples of subjects who score high and low in n Achievement, the persons who score high in n Achievement, generally, should be more willing to initiate an achievement-oriented activity and, once it is initiated, should normally perform at a higher level (unless they are too highly motivated–see Part III) and be more persistent at the activity when they are confronted with an opportunity to engage in some other kind of activity instead. This follows from the assumption that the whole family of instigating forces to achieve is stronger in them.

Illustrative of the earliest evidence that corresponds to each of these particular hypotheses are the following: (*a*) the persons who volunteer to participate in psychological tests and experiments score higher in n Achievement (Burdick, 1955), (*b*) the performance level at verbal and arithmetic tasks presented with achievement-oriented instructions is higher among persons who score high in n Achievement (for example, Lowell, 1952; Wendt, 1955; French, 1955), particularly when special measures are taken to exclude the possibility of other incentives that might produce other extrinsic instigating forces and a compound action tendency to undertake the task (Atkinson & Reitman, 1956); (*c*) the persistence in achievement-oriented performance prior to the knowledge of results, when the alternative is to leave the situation and to engage in some other kind of activity, is greater among persons who score high in n Achievement (French & Thomas, 1958; Atkinson & Litwin, 1960). To this can be added our earlier summary of how the typically greater preference for intermediate risk, or difficulty, of persons who score high in n Achievement is embraced by the new analysis of choice (Chapter 2, and Atkinson & Feather, 1966).

Resistance in a Change of Activity

Since we have already bridged the gap between this new conception of the dynamics of action and the familiar theory and facts of achievement motivation in reference to the action tendency, i.e., the tendency to achieve success, our task of reinterpretation of the source and function of the tendency to avoid failure (or a tendency to avoid success) should be easier. We retain the basic idea that the motivational significance of expecting that an activity will produce a negatively valent consequence like failure is opposition to action or resistance.

The analysis of resistance parallels that of instigation and consummation of action. It will introduce analogous terms and functions as shown in Table 1.

The basic conception may be summarized. The *inhibitory force* (I) of the immediate stimulus situation (or of a person's own covert activities and

TABLE 1

Analogous Concepts in the Treatment of Instigation of Action and Resistance to Action

Instigation of Action	Resistance to Action
Instigating Force, F	Inhibitory Force, I
Action Tendency, T	Negaction Tendency, N
Action	Resistance
Consummatory Force, C	Force of Resistance, R

experience) functions to increase the strength of a tendency *not* to engage in an activity, called a *negaction tendency* (N). A negaction tendency (N) opposes and blocks the expression of an action tendency (T) to yield a *resultant action tendency* ($\bar{T} = T\text{-}N$) that can compete with other resultant tendencies for expression in behavior. A negaction tendency (N) is diminished, or dissipated, by being expressed in resistance the way an action tendency is reduced by being expressed in action. The reduction or dissipation of a negaction tendency is attributed to the *force of resistance* (R).

Here we confront the problem of conflict that arises when a motivational impulse *to do it* (an action tendency) is directly opposed by a motivational impulse *not to do it* (a negaction tendency). We are already familiar with this general problem of mixed feelings, or ambivalence, in the achievement-oriented situation and with the concept of resultant tendency to achieve, i.e., $\bar{T}_S = T_S - N_F$.

We shall now consider the familiar theory concerning determinants of a tendency to avoid failure (Chapters 2 and 7) as instead a theory concerning the determinants of *inhibitory force* (I_F), the force to avoid failure. And we may extend to this discussion of inhibitory force what has already been said concerning *displacement* and *substitution* in reference to instigating force. The force to avoid failure in a particular activity should (as a function of its magnitude and the degree of relationship among different activities), have an indirect inhibitory effect on other activities that are functionally related to the one being blocked. It should indirectly increase the strength of a cluster or family of *negaction* tendencies which, like a family of action tendencies, can be called by the family name. Thus when we speak of a tendency to avoid failure (using the family name), we mean a set of related negaction tendencies. When we speak of a tendency to avoid rejection, we refer to a different set or family of negaction tendencies. And, as before, the term *motive* is recovered and used in reference to a family of functionally related inhibitory forces. To say that one person has a stronger motive to avoid failure than another is to say that the whole family of inhibitory forces to avoid failure is generally stronger in the one person than in the other. This means that the family of tendencies *not* to engage in activities may lead to failure, all these negaction tendencies, are more arousable and more rapidly strengthened in the one person than in the other.

In the more comprehensive discussion of *displacement* and *substitution* in reference to both instigation and resistance, we point out that the degree of relatedness of different activities may not necessarily be the same on the instigation side and on the consummation side, or in reference to instigation of activities and in reference to resistance to activities. There may, for example, be a greater spread of instigation from one activity to a wider variety of others than there is of inhibition or resistance from the one to others. So little is known, the matter is left open. It invites empirical research (Atkinson & Birch, 1970, Ch. 2, 7, and 9).

The function of a negaction tendency is to oppose an action tendency so as to block its expression in activity. This is called resistance. What is left, after taking resistance into account, $\overline{T} = T - N$, is the resultant action tendency, the amount by which the action tendency exceeds the negaction tendency. The resultant tendency $\overline{T}$ is all that is left to compete with other resultant tendencies for expression in behavior.

A negaction tendency always has a suppressive or dampening effect on an action tendency and, therefore, on activity. When the tendency not to do something (N) is just as strong as or stronger than the tendency to do it (T), i.e., when $N \geqslant T$, the resultant action tendency ($\overline{T}$) is zero. We then say that the action tendency is completely blocked or nullified. When there is no resistance at all, i.e., when $N = 0$, then the strength of resultant action tendency ($\overline{T}$) is exactly equal to the strength of the action tendency (T). And that is the case we have been discussing until now, viz., $\overline{T} = T$.

Our first task, as we seek to understand the functional role of resistance, is to consider a simple change from one activity to another and realize that it will be influenced by aversive stimuli as well as by positive inducements. The fact that activity A is initially in progress implies that $\overline{T}_{A_I} > \overline{T}_{B_I}$. The change from activity A to activity B occurs when $\overline{T}_{B_F} > \overline{T}_{A_F}$.

It can be intuitively grasped that any occurrence which would increase N_A, e.g., a punishment or a threat of punishment while activity A is in progress, would reduce $\overline{T}_A$ immediately and produce a change of activity sooner than it would otherwise have occurred. Any feature of the environment that increases N_B, on the other hand, will reduce $\overline{T}_B$ and tend to suppress or delay the change in activity. But what about a reduction in N_A or N_B? These occurrences should correspond to an increase in $\overline{T}_A$, which would delay a change of activity, or an increase in $\overline{T}_B$, which would produce a change from activity A to B sooner than otherwise.

Since we already know what causes a rise and fall in the strength of an action tendency (viz., instigating force and consummatory force), and what causes a rise in the strength of a negaction tendency (viz., inhibitory force), we need to consider the cause of reduction in the strength of a negaction tendency to complete the picture.

The Force of Resistance: The Weakening of a Negaction Tendency

The strength of a negaction tendency is diminished when it is expressed in opposition to an action tendency. It is the *force of resistance* (R), itself, that reduces the strength of a negaction tendency.

Whether a negaction tendency (N) becomes stronger or weaker depends on the relative strength of inhibitory force (I) and the force of resistance (R). When $I > R$, the strength of N increases. When $R > I$, the strength of N diminishes. When $I = R$ the strength of N becomes constant or stable.

On what does this force of resistance, which defines the rate of reduction in the strength of a negaction tendency, depend? Our present hypothesis is similar to the one offered concerning the determinants of consummatory force for an action tendency. We have proposed that the force of resistance (R) might depend on the kind of activity that is being blocked and on the strength of N that is being expressed in resistance. We use r to denote the extent to which force of resistance might vary depending upon the nature of the activity being suppressed even though we tend to treat r as a constant. The hypothesis[2] can be formulated, $R = r \cdot N$. This enables us to specify the level at which N will stabilize. It will happen when $R = I$, that is, when $r \cdot N = I$ or when $N = I/r$. In other words, *a negaction tendency will typically rise and become stable at a level that is proportionate to the strength of the inhibitory force.* The greater the threat of pain or punishment for an activity, the greater the resistance to that activity.

Effect of Resistance to the Alternative Activity

How does expectancy of failing in some activity influence the time to initiate that activity, i.e., the change from an initial activity A to the initiation of the threatened activity? Figure 5 shows initiation of an achievement-oriented activity (T_B) instigated by F_B when there is no force to avoid failure, i.e., $I_B = 0$. It also depicts the same incident when there is also a moderately strong inhibitory force, $I_B > 0$, and $\bar{T}_B = T_B - N_B$.

In the former case, the change in activity occurs when $\bar{T}_{B_F} = \bar{T}_{A_F}$, where $\bar{T}_{B_F} = T_{B_F}$. This is the familiar case of our earlier discussion.

The obvious effect of the force not to engage in activity B, I_B, is to delay the initiation of activity B. When there is resistance, the growth in strength of T_B, to undertake the task, is the same as when there is no resistance. But there is also an increase in N_B which is rapid at first because $I_B > R_B$. The rate of increase in N_B gradually diminishes because N_B, one of the determinants of R_B, the force of resistance, is growing so R_B is also growing. This continues until R_B finally equals I_B, and then N_B remains constant as shown in Figure 5.

The solid curve for the resultant tendency, $\bar{T}_B$, represents $T_B - N_B$ at every point in the time interval. The resultant tendency, $\bar{T}_B$, diminishes at the outset because N_B is growing more rapidly than T_B. But then the trend of its strength begins to turn around and increase as N_B begins to stabilize. Ultimately, when N_B has become constant, the continuing increase in the strength of the resultant tendency, $\bar{T}_B$, parallels the linear growth of T_B, for $\bar{T}_B$ now equals T_B minus a constant N_B. Before activity B can be initiated, the action tendency, T_B, must

[2]The hypothesis, as stated, is correct when $T > N$, for then the full strength of N will be expressed in resistance. If $N > T$, however, it is supposed that only the strength of negaction tendency required to nullify the action tendency, i.e., $N = T$, is expressed against it. In this case, $R = r \cdot T$, and the residual amount of negaction tendency, i.e., $N - T$, persists until needed. (See Atkinson & Birch, 1970, Chs. 7 and 9.)

grow sufficiently strong to overcome and compensate for the resistance produced by N_B. This compensatory growth, which requires the additional time of exposure to F_B to occur, is shown in Figure 5.

One can see, looking back down the slope of $\overline{T}_B$ from the point in time when the change in activity occurs, that the effect of resistance on the time of the change in activity is equivalent to the effect of a weaker inertial tendency. If we subtract the maximum strength of the negaction tendency, $N_{B_F} = I_B/r_B$, from T_{B_I}, the effect would be the same. Resistance to an activity has an effect on its initiation that is exactly opposite to that of "a hunger" for the activity.

The principle of change in activity can be revised to accommodate the influence of inhibitory force for both activity A and activity B as follows:

$$t = \frac{\overline{T}_{A_F} - (T_{B_I} - N_{B_F})}{F_B}$$

$$t = \frac{(\overline{T}_{A_F} - T_{B_I}) + \dfrac{I_B}{r_B}}{F_B} \tag{6}$$

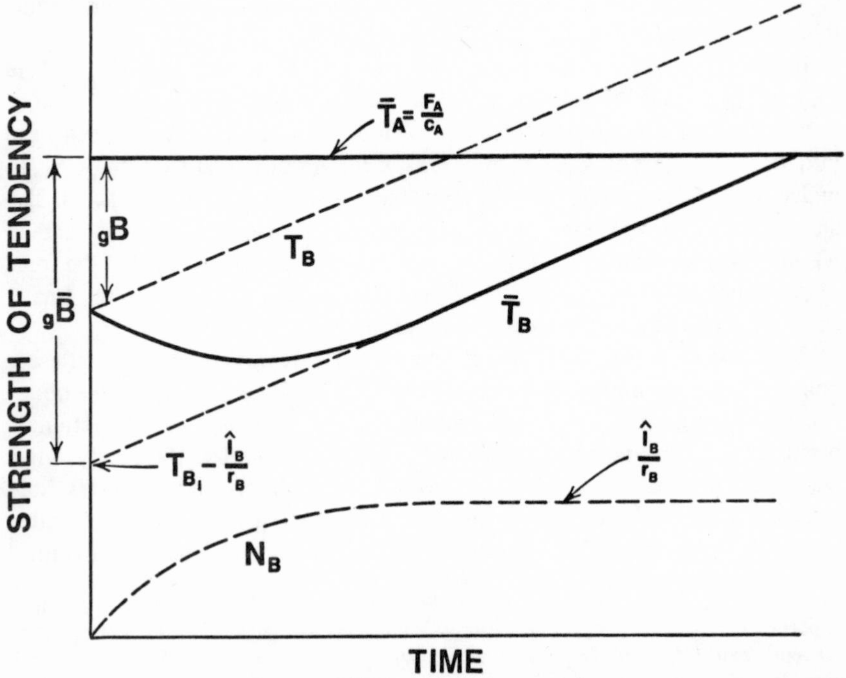

FIG. 5. The effect of resistance to an alternative activity on time to initiate that activity. See text for discussion.

Both Figure 5 and the revised principle of Equation (6) show that an inhibitory force for a new alternative has an effect equivalent to increasing the inertial gap ($\bar{T}_{A_F}$ - T_{B_I}) for that activity by an amount equivalent to the resistance that must be overcome $N_{B_F} = I_B/r_B$. This will temporarily suppress or delay the initiation of the activity. It follows that resistance to an activity will normally decrease the likelihood of its being preferred when other alternatives are available.

If the inhibitory force I_B is much stronger, as shown in Figure 6, the "temporary" suppression of a continuously instigated activity may be sufficiently long to prevent its occurrence at all if some other activity, which occurs instead, takes the person out of the stimulus situation. An example of this in the present context would be when M_{AF} is very strong relative to M_S and there are few or no extrinsic sources of motivation to engage in a competitive achievement activity. The individual resists initiating the achievement-related activity for so long that he may leave the ambivalent situation if some other instigated tendency, e.g., $\bar{T}_X$ in Figure 6, becomes dominant before the critical tendency, $\bar{T}_B$, has had time to become dominant. This, more generally, is the way that avoidance behavior can be derived without positing that a fear of punishment directly instigates the so-called avoidance response (see Atkinson, 1964, Ch. 10, pp. 285-292; Atkinson & Birch, 1970, pp. 248-250 and 350-351).

An important implication of the idea that an action tendency is "bottled up" by resistance is shown in both Figures 5 and 6. It is that there must be a compensatory growth in the strength of an action tendency, sufficient to overcome the resistance, before the activity can occur. And that is what is happening during the temporal delay (the increased duration of exposure to F_B) produced by resistance. The action tendency is becoming substantially stronger than it ever would have become without the resistance. In other words, a person who is inhibited about aggressive behavior will literally become much more angry than a less inhibited person by the time he finally initiates an aggressive reaction to a frustrating incident. And, similarly, the strength of tendency to achieve success must attain a substantially higher level before an achievement-oriented activity can be initiated by the so-called "anxious" person, i.e., the one in whom $M_{AF} > 0$. But—and *here is an important departure from the familiar theory of achievement motivation* (Chapters 2 and 7)—*the person in whom $M_{AF} > M_S$ can initiate an achievement-oriented activity without the presence of some other source of extrinsic motivation to overcome the resistance as we have felt compelled to assume in the past* (see Figure 6 in Chapter 2). The effect of inhibitory force and resistance, as here conceived, is transitory. In a constant environment, resistance only serves to delay the inevitable triumph of the action tendency even when initially $N > T$, as would be the case when $M_{AF} > M_S$, and when there are no extrinsic instigating forces to undertake the activity. This delay is usually long enough to allow some third activity, for which there is less resistance, to occur.

The actual duration of the delay attributable to resistance will depend upon the relative magnitudes of the inhibitory and instigating forces. Although in

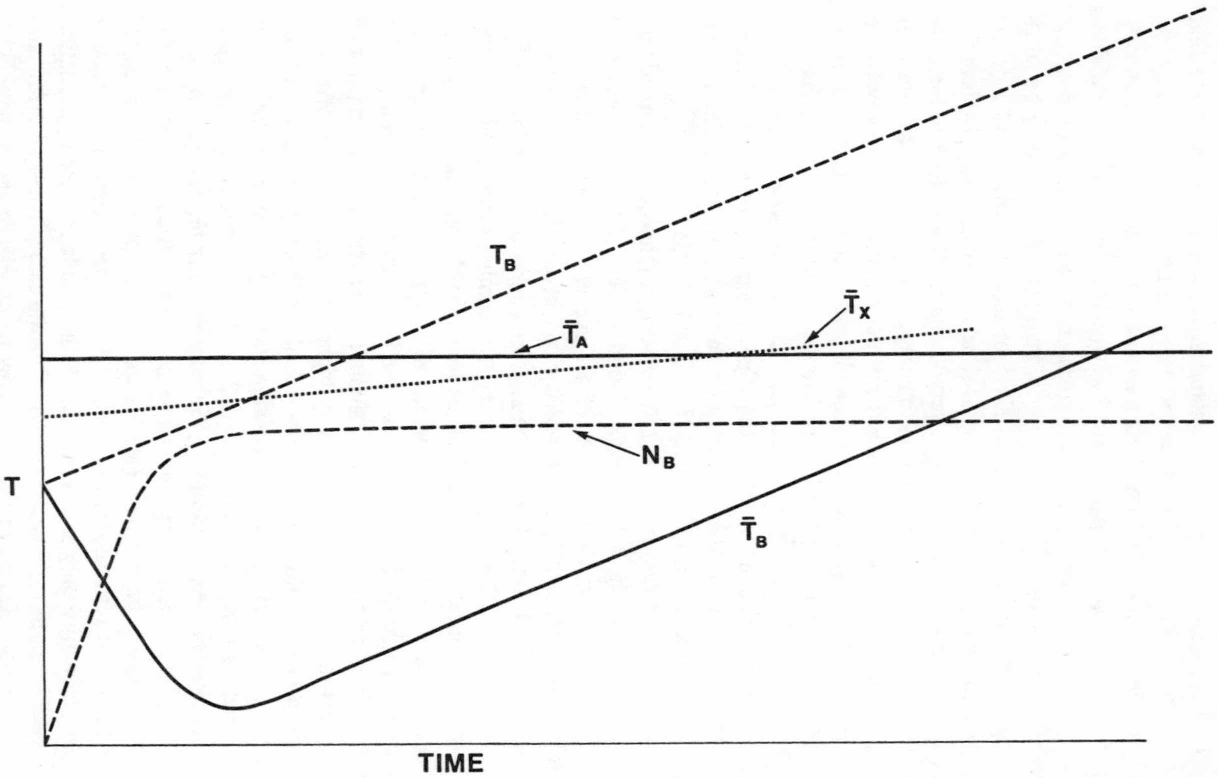

FIG. 6. The effect of very great resistance to an alternative activity on time to initiate that activity, showing the possibility that some third alternative ($\bar{T}_X$) may in fact constitute leaving the field (see text).

principle it is generally expected that a resultant tendency will always become positive, in actuality there may be instances in which inhibitory force is so strong and ubiquitous that nullification could be a long-time fate of some action tendency. Perhaps this is what constitutes repression (Atkinson & Birch, 1970, p. 217).

Effect of Resistance on Preference among Alternatives

The logic of the analysis of choice including resistance to one or both alternatives parallels the earlier analysis shown in Figure 4. It is helped by Figures 5 and 6 and the restatement of the principle of a change in activity, Equation (6) above.

Choice with resistance will depend upon which of two (or more) resultant tendencies, $\bar{T}_X$ or $\bar{T}_Y$, will take the least amount of time to dominate $\bar{T}_{A_F}$. Another special case is shown in Figure 7, but this time we have included just the amount of resistance to each of the two alternatives shown earlier in Figure 4*B* to reproduce the condition in which $t_X = t_Y$. In that case, since $gX/gY = F_X/F_Y = 2/1$, the requirement to produce the same effect as in Figure 4, but with resistance, is

$$\frac{N_{X_F}}{N_{Y_F}} = \frac{I_X/r_X}{I_Y/r_Y} = \frac{2}{1}$$

And since we treat r as a constant, the requirement is $I_X/I_Y = 2/1$. In Figure 7, these amounts of resistance to X and to Y are subtracted from the T_{X_I} and T_{Y_I} (or added to gX and gY), shown earlier in Figure 4, as stated in Equation (6) above.

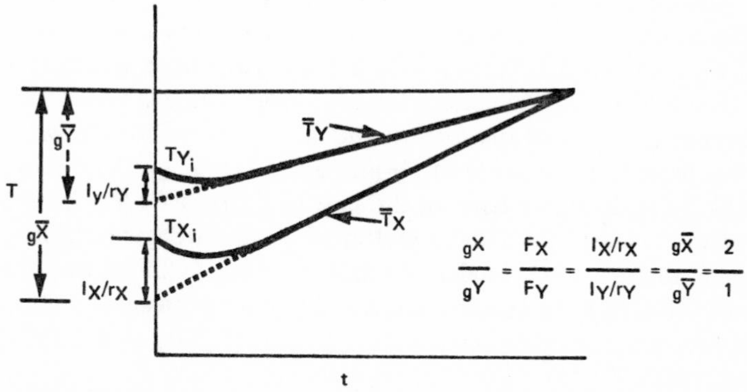

FIG. 7. *Choice with resistance.* The effect of inhibitory force is equivalent to that of a weaker initial action tendency. Resistance has no effect on preference when the ratio of inhibitory forces I_X/I_Y equals the ratio of instigating forces F_X/F_Y.

Under this special condition, when the ratio of inhibitory forces equals the ratio of instigating forces, the effect is the same as before. Activity X, the one instigated by the stronger force, will be chosen. *Choice is unaffected when the ratio of inhibitory forces equals the ratio of instigating forces.* But should the ratio of inhibitory forces exceed the ratio of instigating forces, i.e., $I_X/I_Y > F_X/F_Y$, then the choice of the less strongly instigated alternative Y would be favored. And if the ratio of inhibitory forces is less than that of the instigating forces, i.e., $I_X/I_Y < F_X/F_Y$ then the choice of the more strongly instigated alternative would be even more favored than it would be without resistance.

It follows that an inhibitory force for only one of two alternatives will always favor preference of the other and that equal inhibitory forces for two alternatives will always favor choice of the more strongly instigated one because then $I_X/I_Y = 1$, and $1 < F_X/F_Y$.

A little earlier, in applying this new conception of the dynamics of choice to preference among tasks which differ in difficulty, we made use of the conventional assumption that normally there is some source of extrinsic motivation to perform various tasks that is constant across levels of difficulty. That meant that for each of several tasks the *total magnitude of instigating force* could be represented $F_S + F_{ext}$. This would favor choice of moderately difficult tasks more when M_S was strong than when M_S was weak because the addition of a constant to each force in a ratio produces less change in the ratio with larger magnitudes. Thus $9/3 = 3/1$ became $10/4 > 4/2$ when a constant of 1 was added to each force in the ratios representing the instigating forces for moderately difficult ($P_s = .50$) and easy tasks ($P_s = .90$) when $M_S = 3$ and 1.

If the familiar theory of achievement motivation is now accepted as also a statement about the determinants of forces to avoid failure, then I_F depends upon the motive to avoid failure, the subjective probability of failure, and the incentive value of failure, or, more simply, $I_F = M_{AF} \cdot (1 - P_s) \cdot P_s$, and the ratio of inhibitory forces stemming from anticipated failure at different tasks always equals the ratio of instigating forces to achieve the anticipated success. That is, if $F_{X,S}/F_{Y,S} = 3/1$, then $I_{X,F}/I_{Y,F} = 3/1$. This means, however, that the ratio of magnitudes of the inhibitory forces to avoid failure in two activities will always exceed the ratio of the *total magnitudes of the instigating forces* when each of the latter is a composite of F_S plus a constant F_{ext}. Concretely, $3/1 > 10/4 > 4/2$. Here, then, we have an instance of $I_X/I_Y > F_X/F_Y$ implying *less* likelihood of choice of the activity motivated by the stronger instigating force (in this case, to undertake a moderately difficult task). And that, we know from a number of studies, is the effect of individual differences in anxiety (M_{AF}): the preference for moderately difficult tasks is weakened (Chapter 2, and Atkinson & Feather, 1966).

Once again the main point is that *preference among alternatives is a function of the ratio of forces and not of the magnitude of differences among tendencies, as previously supposed.*

The Effect of Resistance to an Activity in Progress

We gain an important insight concerning the effect of resistance to an activity in progress by looking again at Figure 5 as if activity B is an achievement-oriented activity. If we extrapolate ahead, beyond the point at which the change in activity occurs, for the case in which activity B is influenced only by a single action tendency, T_S, we expect the resultant tendency ($\overline{T}_B = \overline{T}_S = T_S$) to continue to increase as long as $F_S > C_S$. But in time T_S will stabilize (when $F_S = C_S$) at a level corresponding to F_S/c_S, the ratio of the instigating force to the consummatory value of the activity in progress.

Now shift attention to Figure 5, where both T_S and N_F are influencing the resultant tendency ($\overline{T}_B = \overline{T}_S = T_S - N_F$), and carry out the same extrapolation. The achievement-oriented activity is initiated later than in the other case. And by that time, T_S (the action tendency) has had to become substantially stronger than in the former case when there was no resistance. It has had to become stronger by an amount equivalent to the final strength of resistance to its expression, $N_F = I_F/r_F$. Only then will the resultant tendency $\overline{T}_S$ be sufficiently strong to exceed T_{A_F}, as in the former case, to cause the change of activity. And because the expression of the action tendency T_S continues to be bottled up by resistance equal in amount to I_F/r_F, the T_S must continue to increase until it compensates for that resistance to yield a consummatory force, $C_S = c_S \cdot \overline{T}_S$, that will equal F_S and thus stabilize the level of both T_S and $\overline{T}_S$. Only when T_S, the action tendency, attains a level equal to $F_S/c_S + I_F/r_F$ will the resultant tendency, $\overline{T}_S$, being expressed in the ongoing activity, produce a consummatory force equivalent to that in the former case when there was no resistance.

This means, generally, that *the strength of the resultant tendency sustaining an activity in progress—whether there be resistance or not—will always stabilize at a level defined by F/c.* For this to happen when there is resistance, the action tendency must continue to grow in strength until it has reached a level equal to F/c plus the resistance, I/r. Then, and only then, will $\overline{T} = F/c$.

In Figure 8, we have superimposed the resultant action tendencies from Figure 5 when there is and is not resistance, to show comparatively what should be expected concerning the initiation and level of motivation for continuous performance of an achievement-related activity, perhaps an important test in a college course, when M_S is identical in two individuals but only one of them has any M_{AF}. This means that F_S is equal for the two individuals but only one of them is exposed to I_F.

The behavioral implications are clear. The positively motivated individual will initiate the achievement-oriented activity and become more completely involved in it sooner than his more anxious peer. After a period of time, however, the strength of motivation expressed in the task, that is, $\overline{T}_S$, will be practically equivalent for the two individuals. (We can conjecture about the possibility of greater inner stress, personal cost, and fatigue in the person who is acting in the

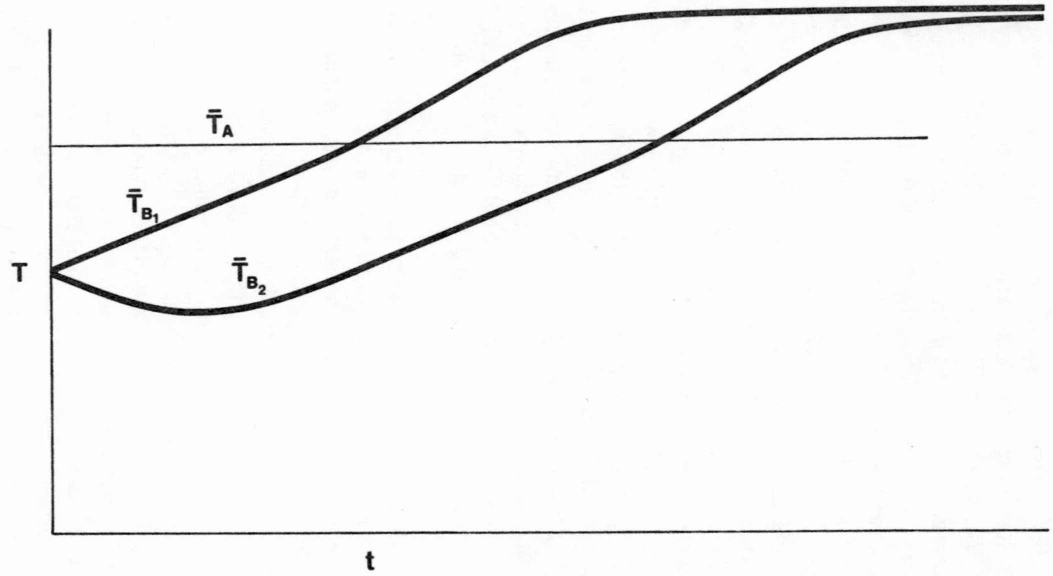

FIG. 8. The effect of resistance on initiation of an activity ($\bar{T}_{B_1} = T_B$, and $\bar{T}_{B_2} = T_B - N_B$) and the level of resultant tendency, $\bar{T}_B$, expressed in the activity.

face of strong resistance. We have previously supposed that the feeling of dread or anxiety is an aspect of this (Atkinson, 1964, Ch. 10; see also Sales, 1970, and Chapter 8, for evidence of this).

One implication of this analysis is fairly obvious in Figure 8: *most of the detrimental effects on performance attributed to the tendency to avoid failure should occur early rather than late in a test period* (presuming, of course, that the maximum level of motivation is in the low to moderate range for most individuals tested and not further complicated by the factor of "over-motivation" discussed in Chapter 11).

Now consider briefly what should happen if each of these individuals is interrupted in the course of an achievement-oriented activity by some unspecified alternative activity that, for some reason, becomes dominant. The example that comes to mind is some compelling incident outside the classroom that causes everyone to leave his seat and go to the window, i.e., to leave the immediate field of the instigating force to achieve and inhibitory force to avoid failure. (Leaving the classroom for any other reason, even at the end of the exam period and prior to knowledge of results, would serve as well for an example.)

When no longer exposed to the stimulus situation providing F_S, the tendency to achieve T_S persists unchanged and is carried ahead as an inertial tendency. But the negaction tendency N_F, which has been dampening the tendency to achieve in one of the individuals, begins to diminish as soon as that person is no longer exposed to stimuli providing inhibitory force I_F. Why does this happen? Because the negaction tendency N_F continues to be expressed in resistance to the persisting or inertial T_S. So there continues to be a force of resistance R_F. This reduces the negaction tendency when there is no longer inhibitory force to strengthen and sustain it. That is, $R_F > I_F$.

What will happen as a result? As N_F dissipates but T_S persists, the resultant tendency $\bar{T}_S$ will increase, for $\bar{T}_S = T_S - N_F$. The more anxiety-prone of the two individuals should experience a surge in $\bar{T}_S$ as N_F diminishes until $\bar{T}_S$ approaches T_S, which persists, as in the other individual, *but at a higher level.* It is then that an observer might expect to see a greater spontaneous inclination to resume the interrupted activity, paradoxically, in the one having the strong M_{AF}. If the change of activity has taken the individuals out of the achievement-related situation entirely (as when the examinations are turned in and before knowledge of results) so that resumption of this particular activity is not possible, an observer would be more likely to see initiation of some substitute activity, another member of the achievement-related family, by the individual who had been more anxious and inhibited in the test situation. Perhaps this would take the form of covert imaginative activity, the *substitutive fantasy* to which clinical psychologists from Freud onward have so often referred when tracing the vicissitudes of impulses whose direct expression has been blocked, i.e., suffered resistance. If this type of covert activity, initiated because of indirect instigation or displacement, has consummatory value (c), it may have a general cathartic value. That is, it may produce substitution and a decrease in the whole family of action tendencies called tendency to achieve.

One may legitimately ask, and we do not minimize the importance of the question nor the need for more explicit experimental study of it: What does this imply for thematic apperceptive measurement of the strength of motives? Does it imply that the level of thematic apperceptive n Achievement may sometimes overestimate the strength of M_S among individuals who are also strong in M_{AF} (as currently measured by a Test Anxiety scale) because T_{S_I} might, for the reason outlined, sometimes be temporarily stronger among such persons? Lazarus (1961) had raised this same general question earlier about the meaning of TAT n Achievement in reference to persons who have more frequently failed than succeeded in the past (see also Moulton's discussion in Chapter 4).

Our more complete treatment of resistance to an activity in progress considers thoroughly the effect of both introducing an inhibitory force after an activity is initiated and in progress, and the effect of removal of an inhibitory force that has been sustaining resistance to an ongoing activity. For the sake of completeness we include Figure 9 which shows the generally expected effects.

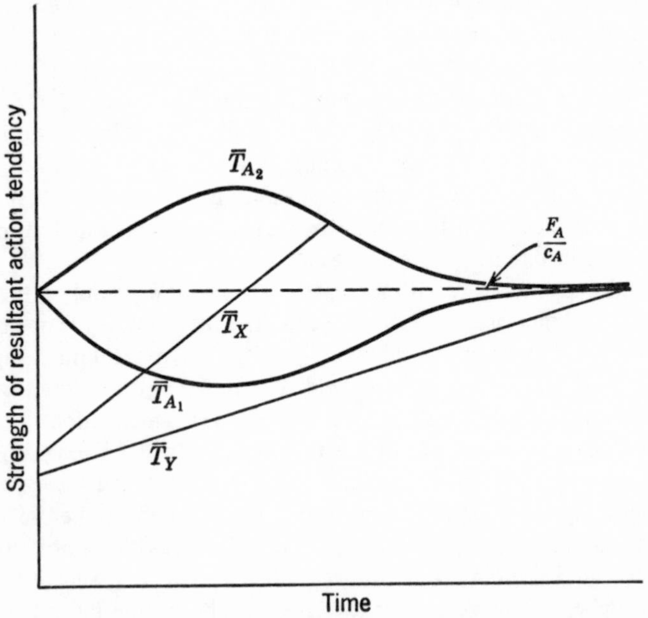

FIG. 9. Transitory periods of increased vulnerability to interruption produced by introduction of I_A in curve $\bar{T}_{A_1}$ and decreased vulnerability to interruption by the withdrawal of I_A in curve $\bar{T}_{A_2}$. The latency of a strongly instigated alternative ($\bar{T}_X$) is affected by the temporary effect of resistance to activity A, but the latency of the weaker alternative ($\bar{T}_Y$) is not. (*From Atkinson & Birch, 1970, with permission of the authors and of the publisher, John Wiley & Sons.*)

Introducing an I_A which increases N_A, for the activity in progress, produces a decrease in $\bar{T}_A$, but only a temporary one for reasons already presented. This means that a punishment, or threat of punishment, for activity in progress will produce a transitory period of increased vulnerability to interruption (i.e., a change of activity) when, but only when, the inertial tendency for some alternative is strong or when it is strongly instigated, or both. The sudden withdrawal of I_A, which sustains N_A resisting the activity in progress, produces just the opposite effect: a temporary surge in $\bar{T}_A$ (for reasons already presented) which defines a transitory period of increased intensity and involvement in the ongoing activity and decreased vulnerability to interruption by some other activity.

More relevant than this problem to analysis of achievement-oriented action is analysis of the several effects of success and failure, to which we now turn.

THE EFFECTS OF SUCCESS AND FAILURE

Success and failure in a given activity have two different effects that must be distinguished. Each of the effects has an influence, but a different kind of influence, on the subsequent motivation of an individual. One is a *cognitive learning effect,* described as a change in expectancy of success, which is related to the strength of instigating force to achieve and inhibitory force to avoid failure in an activity on a subsequent occasion. The other is an *immediate motivational effect,* assuming that success has greater consummatory value (c) than failure, on the inertial tendencies to achieve and to avoid failure immediately thereafter.

The Cognitive Learning Effect: Change in the Magnitude of Instigating and Inhibitory Force

The assumption that success strengthens and failure weakens the subsequent expectancy of success at the same and similar activities is well supported by evidence that concerns changes in the reported expectations of success following success and failure (see Jones et al., 1968) and by the interpretations of changes in the level of aspiration and persistence in the achievement-oriented activity following success and failure (Chapter 2; and Atkinson & Feather, 1966). This assumption refers to changes in the cognitive structure that correspond to the reinforcement and extinction of instigating and inhibitory forces (Atkinson & Birch, 1970, Ch. 6 and 8).

The implications of this assumption, as they apply to the problem of change in level of aspiration following success and failure, were shown in Figures 8 and 9 of Chapter 2. These figures, now reinterpreted as referring to F_S rather than to T_S, show the changes in the instigating force to achieve that correspond to an increase in the probability of success following success and a decrease following failure at a moderately difficult task. Since the incentive value of success is assumed to be the complement of the subjective probability of success, it too should change. Thus, following success there should be a weaker instigating force to undertake the same activity on a subsequent occasion, and a stronger instigating force to undertake a more difficult task according to the several assumptions of the theory of achievement motivation. Following failure, there is a decrease in the subjective probability of success at the same and similar tasks which corresponds to the changes in the instigating forces to achieve that are shown in Figure 9 of Chapter 2 for the case of failure.

Employing this simple assumption of a change in expectancy of success following success and failure, and of the complementary changes in expectancy of failure (and thus of inhibitory force to avoid failure) that is inherent in the theory of achievement motivation, Feather (1961, described in Chapter 2) predicted and found that persons who were strong in n Achievement would be more persistent in a series of repeated unsuccessful attempts to solve a puzzle when it was initially presented to them as a relatively easy task (one that 70% of college students could solve) than when it was presented as a very difficult task (one that only 5% of students could solve). His argument was that persons highly motivated to achieve would experience first a rise in instigation to achieve following failure on the initial trials, as subjective probability fell from 0.70 to 0.50, and then a gradual decline of interest following repeated failures until, at some point, the tendency to undertake the task would be weaker than the tendency to undertake another different task. When the initial subjective probability of success was 0.05, the instigation would be relatively weak to begin with and would decline immediately after the initial failures as the probability dropped toward 0. The general paradigm corresponds to the study of extinction after training.

Feather, whose study was undertaken before the influence of inertial tendencies had been proposed (Atkinson & Cartwright, 1964; Atkinson, 1964, Chap. 10), implicitly assumed that the strength of tendency to achieve success at the initiation of each of a series of trials in a failure sequence was determined *only* by what is here called the instigating force to achieve success.

The Immediate Motivational Effect: Change in Strength of Action and Negaction Tendencies

Weiner, (1963, and Chapter 17), following the general plan of the Feather experiment, was the first to attempt to isolate the two distinct effects of success and failure implied by the present scheme: (*a*) the *cognitive learning effect*, described as a change in expectancy of success, which is related to the strength of instigating force of the stimulus to undertake the activity on a subsequent trial; and (*b*) the *immediate motivational effect*, assuming that success has greater consummatory value than failure, which we refer to as the inertial tendency for a subsequent trial. Following the logic of the theory of achievement motivation, Weiner assumed that repeated success when initial subjective probability is 0.70 and repeated failure when it is 0.30 should produce comparable successive decreases in the magnitude of the instigating force to achieve. This should produce the same persistence in an achievement-oriented activity among persons strong in n Achievement if there were no differential inertial tendency. But there should be greater persistence following failure if, as is generally assumed, success has greater consummatory value than failure and the assumptions presented here concerning the influence of inertial tendency are essentially correct.

Weiner's subjects confronted the possibility of continuing with another trial on a digit symbol substitution task after repeated success or repeated failure, or of initiating, whenever they so desired, a different kind of activity (that is, non-achievement-related) instead. The question of interest was: How long would the subject continue in the achievement-oriented activity before changing to the other kind of activity? The details are given in Chapter 17.

The results showed no difference between conditions in time to finish 60 items on the first trial. This evidence of the comparable initial level of performance in the two conditions is consistent with the assumption that points equidistant from the subjective probability of success of 0.50 had been established by the initial instructions so that F_S and T_S are initially equal in the two conditions. But, on the subsequent trial, the speed of performance was greater following failure than following success, and the number of trials before the shift to the other activity was also greater following failure for persons highly motivated to achieve. Both results are implied by the assumption of greater inertial tendency following failure than following success.

The general pattern of these results is consistent with the assumptions made concerning the components of instigating force to achieve, the effect of success and failure on this instigating force, and the separate effect of success and failure on the strength of the inertial tendency to achieve. In the light of these results, one may reinterpret the earlier results of Feather as probably attributable to change both in the instigating force and in the differential inertial tendency.

Consider the two separate effects of so-called reinforced and nonreinforced trials in a typical animal learning experiment with food reward. When the food is present, the expectancy of attaining it is confirmed and strengthened, and there is an increase in the magnitude of the instigating force of the pertinent stimuli on a subsequent trial. But, since the activity of eating the food has substantial consummatory value, the consummatory force of the goal activity will function to reduce the strength of the tendency to eat and, thus, to decrease the immediate likelihood of the same response. When the food is not present in a nonreinforced trial in the extinction series, the expectancy of the goal is weakened. The corresponding decrease in the subsequent strength of the instigating force of the stimulus should decrease the probability of the response. But the absence of the food means that the animal has been deprived of the opportunity to engage in the consummatory activity, so the tendency to eat persists (instead of being reduced) and enhances the immediate likelihood of repeating the activity or of initiating some other, functionally related activity.

We believe that this latter effect probably provides a parsimonious explanation of the observed heightening of the level of performance in animals immediately after a nonreinforced trial, the phenomenon that Amsel (1958) has attributed to a frustration reaction in the animal. And we also believe that the confounding of the *learning effect* and the *immediate motivational* effect is responsible, in part, for some of the obscurities surrounding the phenomena of intermittent reinforcement.

So much for the immediate motivational effect of success and failure on the strength of an action tendency. What happens to the strength of a negaction tendency, the tendency to avoid failure that constitutes resistance to the ongoing achievement-oriented action? Weiner's research (1963, and Chapter 17) was undertaken before our conception of the dynamics of resistance had been worked out. So let us review his work briefly and then consider it from the vantage point of our present conception of resistance. In 1963, Weiner advanced the argument that success and failure should also have an immediate effect on the inertial tendency to avoid failure which functions to resist subsequent achievement-oriented action.

More recently, Weiner (1970) has collated scattered evidence from earlier studies which shows that some individuals–those who score high on tests of anxiety–typically show a decrement in level of performance after failure and enhanced level of performance after success. This is directly opposite to the typical pattern of results for less anxious or more positively motivated individuals that has been attributed to differential inertial action tendency. Weiner has explained this consistent trend among anxious individuals by assuming that success reduces both the tendency to achieve success and the tendency to avoid failure but that failure reduces neither. Hence, when individuals are classified by personality tests into subgroups according to which of the two tendencies is predominant in them, the net effects of success and failure, respectively, are (*a*) the reduction versus persistence of a resultant tendency to avoid failure (that is, resistance) among more anxious individuals, and (*b*) the reduction versus persistence of a resultant tendency to achieve success among less anxious and more positively motivated persons.

Of immediate interest is the concept of inertial resistance following failure which Weiner has suggested. Can we account for this in terms of our present analysis of the dynamics of resistance?

It is important to observe, at the outset, that success and failure are mutually exclusive outcomes of achievement-oriented activity. It is as if an animal had learned to expect either food or shock at the end of the alley on each trial. This means that during the instrumental phase of an achievement-oriented activity, the stimulus situation is the source of both instigating force (corresponding to expectancy of success) and inhibitory force (corresponding to expectancy of failure). But, *when the individual succeeds at some task, there is a change in the stimulus situation.* This change in the stimulus, which defines the outcome of the activity as successful (for example, the visual stimulus of the thrown ringer in a ring-toss game), constitutes at the same time a removal of the stimulus situation which, until that moment, had produced an inhibitory force. The individual who has just succeeded is no longer threatened with failure on that occasion. Thus, as the stimulus situation defining success produces instigating force which boosts the strength of the action tendency, the avoidant or negaction tendency, now no longer sustained and supported by the exposure to an inhibitory force, should begin to diminish immediately as a result of the continued force of resistance. As the individual engages in the consummatory activity of succeeding, the action tendency is then also reduced.

In brief, the negaction tendency (to avoid failure) is reduced by success because the inhibitory force sustaining it until that time is withdrawn, but the force of resistance, responsible for reduction of a negaction tendency, continues. The action tendency (to achieve success) is reduced by the consummatory force of succeeding.

What about the effect of failure? Again, *there is a change in the stimulus situation.* The change in the stimulus that defines the outcome as failure (for example, the visual stimulus of a miss in a ring-toss game) produces the strong inhibitory force of failure which, like a punishment, should boost the strength of the negaction tendency. But this also constitutes removal of the stimulus which until then had sustained an expectancy of success on that occasion, that is, the instigating force. Thus the magnitude of negaction tendency is immediately increased by failure, but there is no comparable increase in the action tendency. The latter persists unchanged when the instigating force to achieve success on that trial has been withdrawn.

The consequence of this difference in the two conditions should be a reduction of resistance *immediately* following success and increased resistance *immediately* following failure, as Weiner had been led to assume. Weiner's general hypothesis, developed in terms of a preliminary treatment of the concept of inertial tendency (Atkinson & Cartwright, 1964) but before the present theory of resistance had been clarified, is that success reduces the characteristic achievement-related motivation of an individual but failure does not. The diametrically opposite observed effects on the level of performance were attributed to this.

The details of the process described above may be more easily understood if we consider an analogous problem in the domain of animal behavior. Let food seeking and shock avoidance constitute the content of the action and negaction tendencies instead of success seeking and failure avoidance. And to complete the analogy, the food reward and shock punishment must be mutually exclusive outcomes of a simple instrumental activity such as running in an alley. What happens to the tendency to eat and the tendency to avoid the shock on the reward trials (that is, when the outcome is food but no shock) and on the punishment trials (that is, when the outcome is no food but shock)?

After some preliminary training with both outcomes, the stimulus of the start box and alley will be the source of both instigating and inhibitory forces. But the change in the stimulus situation following the run on the reward trials constitutes a strong instigating force to eat and the removal of the inhibitory force, since the animal has never been punished while or immediately after eating the food. The stimulus of food in the goal box immediately boosts the action tendency, and then the activity of eating reduces it. Meanwhile the negaction tendency, no longer sustained and supported by inhibitory force, should be diminished by the continued force of resistance. Both tendencies, in other words, are reduced on the reward trials.

In contrast, the change in the stimulus situation following a run on the punishment trials constitutes a sudden increase in the magnitude of inhibitory force and the withdrawal of the instigating force, since the animal has never eaten while or immediately after being shocked. The negaction tendency is given an immediate boost. The action tendency persists unchanged. Both tendencies, in other words, should be stronger immediately after the punishment trial than immediately after the reward trial.

It could be expected in both this animal case and the human case of achievement-oriented behavior that *the persistence of a negaction tendency following punishment* (*or failure*) *should be more transitory than the persistence of an action tendency.* The negaction tendency should diminish when the subject leaves the situation because it is continually expressed in resistance. A comparable reduction in an action tendency requires that it be directly expressed in activity or in substitution.

In the animal case described above, it is obvious that the kind of outcome that reduces the inertial action tendency (food reward) meets the condition for reinforcement of the instigating force. The kind of outcome that does not reduce the inertial action tendency (no reward) meets the condition for extinction of the instigating force. *The implications for behavior on an immediately subsequent trial are just the opposite for the two effects.*

But this is not also true in the case of negaction and punishment. The kind of outcome that boosts the negaction tendency and allows for continuation of resistance is punishment, and this also strengthens the inhibitory force for a subsequent occasion. And the trial without punishment is the one that produces sudden reduction of the negaction tendency and the extinction of the inhibitory force. *The effect of the change in force and the inertial effect are supplementary in the case of resistance.*

The conceptual analysis of the several motivational effects of success and failure among individuals who differ in strength of achievement-related motives provides an adequate test of anyone's understanding of this theory concerning the dynamics of action. The requirements of research design and in method of study for this problem illustrate the upgraded demand for training in personality methods, for the understanding of the relation between personality and basic behavioral process, and for skill in experimentation that is now more obviously required for systematic research on human motivation.

Let us return to Weiner's effort to disentangle the immediate motivational effects of success and failure (that is, differential inertial tendency) from their effect on learning (that is, change in magnitude of instigating and inhibitory force). Our discussion of the two kinds of effects contingent on success and failure has drawn attention to the key experimental problem if one is primarily interested in studying the differential inertial effects of success and failure. It is to control and to hold constant the magnitude of instigating force and inhibitory force on the test trial that immediately follows the critical success and failure experience. Otherwise, there is a complete confounding of effects attributable to differential inertial tendency and effects attributable to the forces.

Weiner assumed the logic of the theory of achievement motivation (see Chapter 2, and Atkinson & Feather, 1966) to achieve this kind of experimental control. We follow his justification of the design of the experiment but with comments that give our new interpretation of the conditions and results.

First, he assumed that the conditions of achievement motivation would be equivalent for a task undertaken with the initial subjective probability of success of 0.70 or 0.30. We now would consider these two conditions as equivalent in magnitude of instigating force (to achieve success) and inhibitory force (to avoid failure). Second, he assumed that repeated success when initial probability was 0.70 would produce successive increases in subjective probability having motivational implications equivalent to the ones that were produced by the successive decreases in subjective probability caused by repeated failure when the initial probability was 0.30. Third, he assumed that persons appropriately classified in terms of relative strengths of motive to achieve success and motive to avoid failure as given by the conventional diagnostic personality tests would yield results following the success and failure treatments that were either primarily indicative of the inertial tendency to achieve success or the inertial tendency to avoid failure. We consider his classification of subjects into a high n Achievement-low Anxiety group versus low n Achievement-high Anxiety group as essentially equivalent to control of the relative strength of the instigating force to achieve versus the inhibitory force to avoid failure among his subjects. The results of the former group should approximate what is expected with minimal resistance. The results of the latter group (that is, the more anxious subjects) should provide the clearest information concerning the proposed concept of inertial resistance.

The results already reported for those highly motivated to achieve—a higher level of performance and a greater persistence following failure than following success—are consistent with theoretical expectations concerning the inertial action tendency.

Among the more anxious subjects, the result was different. The level of performance measured on the trial *immediately following* the first success and first failure was significantly lower following the failure. This much is consistent with the assumption that the tendency to avoid failure, responsible for resistance, would persist following failure. But there was no evidence of less persistence in the achievement-oriented activity following failure than following success when those anxious subjects continually had the opportunity to change to another kind of task, one that did not require skill nor involve the evaluation of performance. This other expected behavioral manifestation of inertial resistance expected by Weiner was missing (see Chapter 17).

Perhaps this is to be explained as one of the paradoxical manifestations of the bottling up of an action tendency by resistance. We shall have more to say about that possibility later on when we extend this analysis beyond a simple change in activity to embrace what happens within a much longer interval of observation—in a sequence of changes from one activity to another that constitute the stream of behavior.

Personality Conceived as a Hierarchy of General Motives

The idea of describing individual differences in personality in terms of general psychogenic needs or motives probably had its origin in McDougall's (1908) conception of the individual as a bundle of instincts, that is, of goal-directed dispositions. Murray (1938), parting with the notion that psychogenic needs were necessarily instinctive, later developed this concept programmatically, arguing that a better understanding of an individual could be attained through description of him in terms of the effects he generally strives to bring about than in terms of his generalized habits or traits (Allport, 1937), which told little of his aims and goals. McClelland (1951, 1958c) included the concept of psychogenic need or motive among his proposed set of three categories for description of personality, advancing a number of sound hypotheses concerning the way in which relatively universal, non-culture-bound motives might be acquired early in life before the development of language, as a result of socialization practices connected with certain fundamental adjustment problems that arise in all societies the world over, for example, relations with people, mastery of the environment, etc.

The development of a theory of achievement motivation (Atkinson & Feather, 1966) followed the innovation in the method for the diagnosis and the measurement of the strength of human motives (McClelland et al., 1953; Atkinson, 1958a). It represented an explicit attempt to begin the specification of the nature of the interaction between personality and immediate environment implied by the Lewinian equation $B = f(P,E)$. The conceptual analysis of the dynamics of action (Atkinson & Birch, 1970) and its application to the initiation of activity, performance level, persistence, and choice, purports to be an even more precise and comprehensive specification of the behavioral implications of individual differences in the strength of a motive when the latter is taken as a shorthand reference to a family of functionally related instigating forces or inhibitory forces.

With this as historical background, let us briefly summarize what is implied when the basic structure of personality is conceived, in part at least, as a hierarchy of general motives. We have had conjectures about a heirarchy of motives for years. Now, perhaps, we can give the concept some scientific respectability. We can do this by recognizing that the hierarchy of motives defines the way in which the basic personality structure of an individual will selectively enhance the influence of some immediate environmental inducements or threats more than others. Given the guiding principle in Equation (6),

$$t = \frac{\bar{T}_{A_F} - \bar{T}_{B_I}}{F_B} = \frac{(F_{A}/c_{A} - T_{B_I}) + I_{B}/r_{B}}{F_B}$$

we can identify the three major sources of selectivity in behavior, particularly when we distinguish, in our conception of the constituents of the instigating forces (F_A and F_B) and the inhibitory forces (I_A and I_B), the relatively more general and enduring differences in personality (that is, motive) from the relatively more specific and transient situational influences that are defined by variables that refer specifically to the immediate stimulus situation (that is, as reflected in expectancy and incentive value).

First, there is the selectivity attributable to the fact that the immediate environment of the individual (the stimulus situation) tends to heighten the strength of certain tendencies to action but not of others. Second, there is selectivity attributable to persistence into the present of previously instigated but insufficiently consummated tendencies to action, the inertial tendencies that reflect the balance of past inducements to satisfactions—the effects of relative deprivation in the past. Then, finally, there is the selectivity attributable to basic personality structure, the greater arousability of the individual by environmental inducements or threats concerning one kind of activity than another and the variations in persistence in certain kinds of ongoing activity which we associate with differences in strength of motive.

What does the Principle of Change of Activity tell us in general about the consequences of differences in the strength of a motive, that is, the differences in the magnitude of a whole family of instigating forces? It tells us that when some other kind of activity is in progress and the motive of interest is in the position of F_B to prompt a change of activity, the individual with a strong motive will generally show more prompt initiation of that activity than an individual with a weak motive unless deterred by a strong inhibitory motive. And when the motive is in the position of F_A, sustaining the activity in progress, there will be greater persistence by the individual for whom that motive is strong. When the motive of interest is weak relative to others, the individual will generally be slow to initiate the activity and quick to leave it. This means, in general, that *the hierarchy of motives arranged according to their strength will greatly influence the way an individual distributes his time among different kinds of activity.* The person who is stronger in motive to achieve than in motive for affiliation will spend more time at work and less in friendly commerce with others. Given a reversal in this hierarchy of only two motives, there will be a reversal in the time distribution of activities. Given simultaneous opportunity for either of the activities, the choice will vary with the difference in motive. This is nicely illustrated in an experiment by French (1956) in which men who differed in n Achievement and n Affiliation, when asked to choose a work partner for a subsequent test of skill, chose either a friend known to be previously unsuccessful at the kind of task to be undertaken, or a stranger known to be very successful at this kind of task, in accordance with the stronger motive.

Here, we believe, lies the possibility for a useful taxonomic description of individual differences in personality that makes sound theoretical sense. A paramount objective, since the inception of the study of individual differences in n Achievement in 1947, has been to bring about an integration of the study and description of individual differences in personality and the conceptual and experimental analysis of the basic process of motivation. The dynamics of action represents another substantial step towards that objective.

THE STREAM OF ACTIVITY

Our analysis of what is involved in a simple change from one activity to another has encompassed the problems of traditional interest: the initiation of an activity, its intensity or magnitude (see Chapter 11), its persistence, and choice or preference among alternatives. These have always been matters of interest, in part because they refer to the motivational questions that arise in the incidents of everyday life. How willing is an individual to initiate this activity? Why is he more or less persistent than another person in that activity? Why does a person generally tend to prefer to do this instead of that? But the great emphasis of these particular behavioral issues also reflects the short episodic analysis of behavior that has been fostered by the long dominance of the stimulus-response mode of thought within psychology and the fact that only relatively short intervals of observation have been considered much in traditional experimental study. The psychology of the past has emphasized the separateness of these questions. The psychology of the future will clarify their interrelatedness. The short episodes that contain these problems have never before (except by Barker, 1963) been seen for what they really are–short segments in the continuing stream of an individual's activities, his life.

It is now time to extend our discussion of an interval of observation beyond a single change in activity to embrace a series of changes over a longer span of time, to identify the measurable aspects of the molar stream of activity and to see how the same concepts and principles that explain a single change of activity can be applied to a much longer time interval and to the various behavioral measures that can be derived from it.

The protocol of an observer of a sequence of changes from one activity to another by an individual over a substantial temporal interval would contain two items of information concerning the various activities that had occurred:

frequency and duration. From this information, the following measures can be derived: the frequency of occurrence of a particular activity; the total amount of time spent in that activity; the average duration of the activity when it has occurred; the operant level or rate of its occurrence during the interval; the proportion of time spent in the activity; and the relative frequency of its occurrence, given the total number of activities that occurred.

Some of these have been employed on occasion, most notably the operant level or rate by Skinnerians, but nowhere has their interrelatedness or their relationship to the measurable aspects of a simple change in activity been spelled out. We began to provide this integrative thread in *The Dynamics of Action* (Ch. 4 and 9), and more recently Birch (1972) has established the fundamental link between measurements on the molar stream of behavior and our principles concerning the dynamics of action by identifying still another and completely novel measure that can be taken from the molar stream of behavior concerning a particular activity; *the average dormant period* ($\bar{d}$) *of a particular activity.* This is the average of the durations of the time between the cessation of a particular activity and its next initiation. Any single dormant period is the time required for a tendency that has just ceased being dominant to become dominant again and to be expressed in behavior again. The dormant period thus corresponds closely to the t (time to change from one activity to another) represented in the principle of change in activity in Equation (6).

The upshot of this further theoretical development is the possibility, ultimately, of specifying with some precision how the motive hierarchy of an individual (his personality) is expressed in the operant level of various kinds of activity, the distribution of time among various activities, etc. This, we believe, will be the general direction and thrust in future empirical study of those descriptive aspects of personality that have motivational significance. The immediate need is for innovations in methods of study that encompass the problems as recast by this theoretical analysis.

In order to extend the treatment of the dynamics of action beyond the time of a change from one activity to another, two other factors must be taken into account. Each of them has to do with what happens to the strengths of tendencies immediately following a change in activity. We will discuss them briefly, inviting the reader to our more detailed treatment of the issues elsewhere (Atkinson & Birch, 1970, Ch. 4). Then we shall illustrate applications of the dynamics of action to the stream of behavior with some results from several of our earliest computer simulations of motivational problems.

At the instant when a new activity is initiated, $\bar{T}_{B_F}$ and $\bar{T}_{A_F}$ are nearly equal in strength. One might therefore expect that another change in activity would occur almost immediately. One factor that prevents this from happening is *selective attention.* The other is a time lag in the cessation of the consummatory force of an activity when it is replaced by another and in the initiation of consummatory force of the new activity. This is called *consummatory lag.*

Selective Attention

There is a more continuous exposure to instigating force that sustains an activity in progress (and to inhibitory force) than to forces for other activities because one must be in contact with and oriented toward certain discriminable and manipulable features of the environment to engage in the activity at all. Any activity involves a particular kind of commerce with the environment. Because of this, an individual is more systematically and continuously exposed to certain features of the immediate environment than to others concerning which exposure is more incidental and spasmodic. Someone engaged in an achievement-related activity has the work to be done immediately before him to goad him on. Another engaged in affiliative activity is in fairly continuous visual contact with the friend to whom he is talking, etc. Because of this selective attention, which is often the very first behavioral symptom of the initiation of an activity, the *average instigating force* for an activity in a given environment will always be stronger when the activity is occurring (F), than when it is not ($\hat{F}$). The redirection of attention at the time of a change in activity means a boost in the average instigating force for the newly initiated activity (from $\hat{F}$ to F) and a loss for the activity which has ceased (from F to $\hat{F}$). This operates to favor the tendency that has just become dominant because $F > \hat{F}$. (For simplicity, consider $\hat{F}$ equal to some percentage of F).

The Consummatory Lag

The consummatory force of a particular activity does not cease completely and immediately the instant another activity is initiated. The tendency to eat, for example, continues to be affected by consummatory force for some time after the visible signs of eating have ceased. Success in solving an arithmetic problem probably has a much shorter consummatory lag. If we think of a change in activity as a transition from involvement of the individual in one activity to involvement in another, we can appreciate that some interval of time (however short) will be required for the full consummatory value (c) of the newly initiated activity to come into play and for that of the initial activity to diminish entirely.

Both effects, the lag in the cessation and in the initiation of consummatory force at the change from one activity to another, are enhanced by the systematic shift in attention which occurs at the very same time. The combined effect is to drive the resultant tendencies involved in the change of activity apart as shown in Figure 10, thus favoring the continuation of the newly initiated activity.

In applications of the principle of a change in activity to a stream of behavior, i.e., to a series of changes, certain simplifying assumptions are made concerning both *selective attention* and the *consummatory lags.* The results are promising.

Computer Simulation of Motivational Problems

A computer program of our conception of the dynamics of action, initiated by Robert Seltzer (1973; see Appendix A) has enabled us to begin to explore the

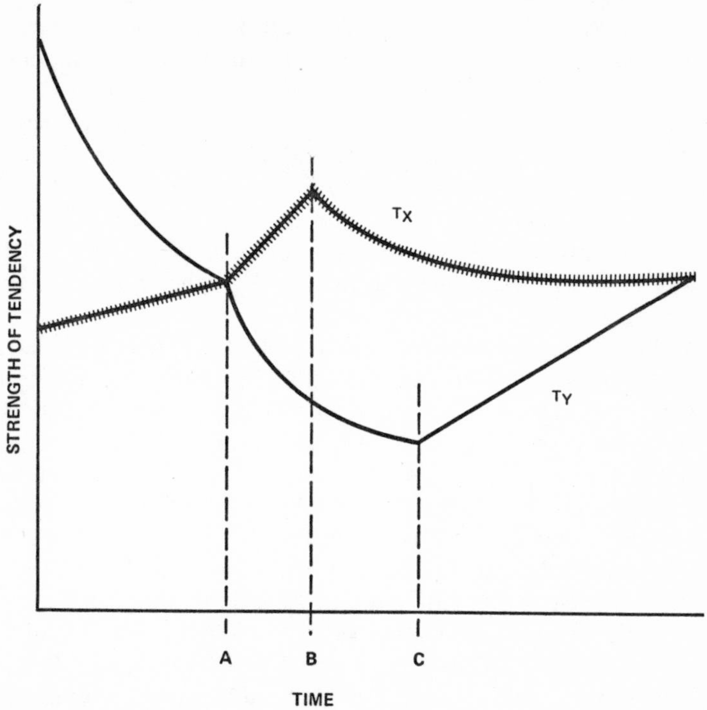

FIG. 10. The change in strength of tendencies immediately following a change in activity. A–B is the lag in the initiation of consummatory force for the new activity. A–C is the lag in cessation of consummatory force for the old activity.

implications of the theory in reference to conditions that are too complex to allow anticipating the outcome intuitively or to resolve mathematically except with an unwarranted investment of time.

The fact that we are able to do this at all attests the completeness and coherence of our specifications concerning the dynamics of action. The computer has become a collaborator in our effort to determine whether or not the application of these principles produces hypothetical results that correspond to what is already known from empirical studies of behavior in similar conditions. And, if so, it then becomes an obviously heuristic tool in identifying and generating new and nonobvious implications of the motivational process and of individual differences in personality to guide the future empirical investigations that will yield the new empirical knowledge.

Consider the case of an individual in a constant environment for a substantial length of time who is exposed to instigating forces for five different activities V, W, X, Y, and Z. They are all incompatible activities, and they belong to different families so there is neither displacement nor substitution. Let us suppose that activity X is an achievement-oriented activity, perhaps studying for an important exam next day. And all the other activities are different things that can be done instead of studying in the constant environment of a college dormitory room. These other activities V, W, Y, and Z provide the context in which we might be concerned about the time to initiate activity X, the time spent doing it, the operant level or rate of the activity, etc., as a function of the magnitude of the instigating force F_X. All the parameters for the activities that provide the context for the critical activity X (and those concerning selective attention and consummatory lags) were held constant in three conditions as we asked: How will activity X be affected by the magnitude of F_X (when $F_X = 8$; when $F_X = 16$; when $F_X = 32$)?

Figure 11*A* gives the computer-drawn plot of the trends of the several resultant tendencies, with special attention to $\bar{T}_X$ when $F_X = 8$; and Figure 11*B* gives the trends when $F_X = 32$ for comparison. Of particular interest are the very obvious differences in the initial latency of activity X, its persistence (once initiated), the frequency of its occurrence, and the total time spent in activity X. (The operant level or rate is easily derived by dividing frequency by the total duration of the interval of observation.) Table 2 summarizes the effects of variations in magnitude of instigating force with three hypothetical subjects for each magnitude of F_X (8, 16, 32). And then Table 3 summarizes the effects with identical conditions for instigation but with the addition of an inhibitory force, $I_X = 16$, for the critical activity in each case. The effect of the inhibitory force (it would be to avoid failure in our example of studying for an exam) is a delay in the first initiation of the critical activity. The amount of delay is related to the ratio of I_X to F_X in each case. But then we confront a paradoxical result in Table 3. Both the frequency and the total amount of time spent in the critical activity, once it has been initiated, are greater when there is resistance to overcome than when there is no resistance (Table 2). Closer analysis reveals that the average duration of the instances of the critical activity (i.e., time spent/frequency) is shorter when there is resistance than when there is not. And still further study shows that the average strength of $\bar{T}_X$ during these instances is less when there is resistance than when there is not. The inhibitory force has weakened the degree of involvement in the activity, has increased the variability of behavior, and, paradoxically, has increased the total time spent in that activity. How this affects the efficiency of performance (Chapter 11) while engaging in the activity is presently an open question.

All of these untested implications are a consequence of the bottling up of the action tendency, its having to become much stronger with than without resistance to be expressed at all, and the inadequate expression of it (and inadequate consummation of it) when it does control behavior in a series of shorter instances. Because the individual does not ever get as deeply involved in the critical activity, when he does initiate it in the constant environment, he is probably much more vulnerable to some interruption that would lead him completely out of the situation than his counterpart who suffers no resistance. That, at least, is our present conjecture as we consider implications of the theory

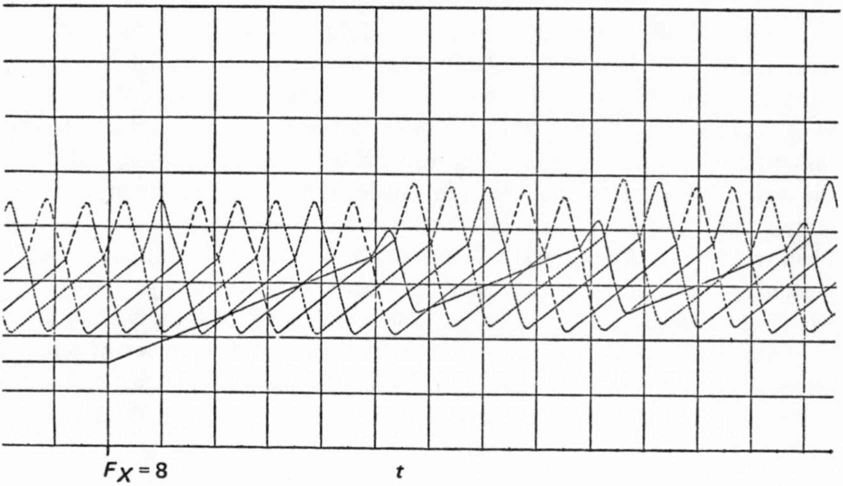

A

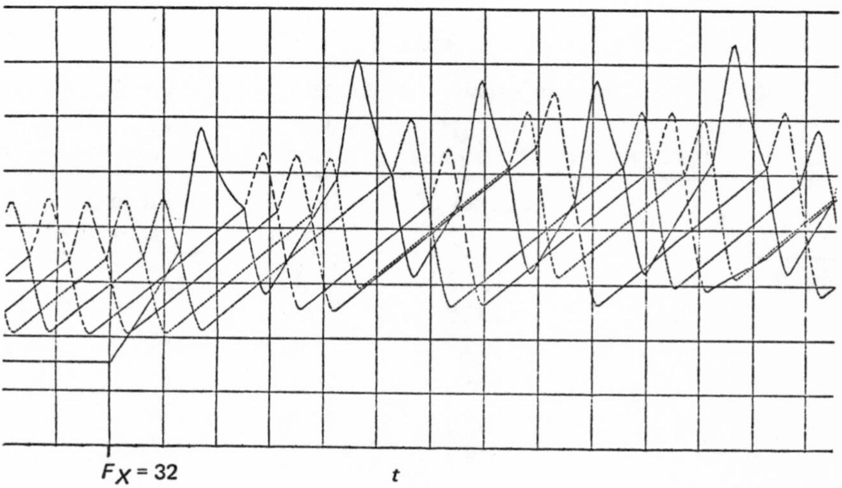

B

FIG. 11. A segment of the computer-drawn plot of the trends of resultant tendencies for five different activities in a constant environment following the onset of $F_X = 8$ in *A* and $F_X = 32$ in *B* and showing the effect of the magnitude of instigating force on the latency, time spent, and frequency of an activity (see also Table 2).

concerning the question of who will and who won't spend a great deal of time in some endeavor in the long run (Chapter 20).

Now, in closing, consider another and very familiar situation. Two hypothetical individuals, one in whom $M_S > M_{AF}$ and the other in whom $M_{AF} > M_S$, are handed the rings for the ring-toss game and invited to see how good they are (as in Atkinson & Litwin, 1960). The specification of the conditions of instigating and inhibitory force for each of five activities (corresponding to increasing distance from the peg and decreasing P_S) and the computer's report concerning the number of separate initiations and time spent in each of the several activities (shooting from each distance from the target) are summarized in Table 4. In this simulation, Mio Kawamura Reynolds recovered the now familiar greater preference for moderate risk among those in whom the motive to achieve is very strong relative to motive to avoid failure emphasized in Chapter 2 and in Atkinson and Feather (1966). Table 4 calls attention to the possibility that amount of time spent in a particular activity (e.g., taking shots from a given distance or, perhaps, pressing a lever for food) may yield a better indicator of the frequency of responses than the actual number of separate initiations of an activity in the molar stream of behavior. An individual whose inclination to shoot from the middle distance is dominant for a substantial time may, in other words, take several shots during that period.

TABLE 2

The Effect of Variations in Magnitude of Instigating Force ($F_X = 8, 16, 32$) on Latency of Activity X, Time Spent, and Frequency of Activity X under Simulated Conditions with Four Alternative Activities

F_X	Subject	Latency of activity X	Time spent in activity X[a]	Frequency of activity X[a]
8	1A[b]	109.3	19.9	2
	1B	102.8	35.6	4
	1C	106.0	26.9	3
	Mean	106.0	27.5	3
16	2A	52.9	50.4	4
	2B	58.4	50.4	4
	2C	50.0	50.4	4
	Mean	53.8	50.4	4
32	3A	25.2	91.8	6
	3B	29.7	88.4	5
	3C	32.2	107.2	6
	Mean	29.0	95.8	5.7

[a]Obtained from the last 250 time units in a 500-unit period so as not to be confounded by initial differences in latency.

[b]*Ss* A, B, and C in the treatments are matched for the time of onset of F_X for the critical activity which differed for A, B, and C to simulate the kind of variance among *Ss* in a natural situation.

TABLE 3

The Effect of an Inhibitory Force (I_X = 16) on the Latency, Time Spent, and Frequency of Activity X under Exactly the Same Conditions of Instigation as in Table 2

F_X	I_X	Subject	Latency	Time spent[a]	Frequency[a]
8	16	1A[b]	124.7	40.3	7
		1B	130.8	40.3	7
		1C	121.4	51.4	8
		Mean	125.6	44.0	7.3
16	16	2A	66.7	63.4	7
		2B	60.9	62.1	7
		2C	63.7	55.2	6
		Mean	63.8	60.2	6.7
32	16	3A	36.6	95.1	7
		3B	31.6	91.3	6
		3C	34.0	103.8	7
		Mean	34.1	96.7	6.7

[a]Obtained from last 250 time units in a 500-unit period so as not to be confounded by initial differences in latency.

[b]*Ss* A, B, and C in the treatments are matched for the time of onset of F_X and I_X for the critical activity. If differed for A, B, and C to simulate natural variance among *Ss*.

Final Comment

The Dynamics of Action (1970) provides a new and more general conceptual framework for the study of achievement-oriented action. Within this new framework, the familiar theory of achievement motivation (Chapter 2) and its elaboration by Raynor (Chapter 7) constitute a specification of the determinants of instigating force to achieve and inhibitory force to avoid failure. The processes of displacement and substitution account for the fact that the motivational impact of specific situations and specific activities has more general indirect effects on a whole family of functionally related tendencies. This provides sound theoretical justification for the use of more general terms like tendency to achieve and tendency to avoid failure in reference to families of action and negaction tendencies, and the use of general descriptive terms such as motive to achieve and motive to avoid failure in reference to how individuals differ in corresponding families of instigating and inhibitory forces.

A principle of change in activity, which is the main product of our conceptual analysis of a simple change from one activity to another, can be extended to account for the underlying dynamics of the molar stream of an individual's

TABLE 4

Computer Simulation of Effects of Individual Differences in Achievement Motivation on Risk Preference under Free Operant Conditions, e.g., Shooting from Different Distances in a Ring-toss Game

Task	P_s	50 time units		150 time units	
		Time spent	Activity initiated[a]	Time spent	Activity initiated[a]
		When $M_S = 500$ and $M_{AF} = 100$			
A	.93	0.1	0	12.6	3
B	.70	8.8	1	39.0	5
C	.50	23.6	3	49.7	6
D	.33	17.5	2	33.9	4
E	.10	0.0	0	15.6	2
		When $M_S = 100$ and $M_{AF} = 500$			
A	.93	20.9	1	37.1	4
B	.70	7.8	1	30.8	4
C	.50	0.0	0	22.2	3
D	.33	1.0	1	24.8	3
E	.10	20.2	2	35.6	4

[a]The actual frequency of shots taken, and hence the operant level, may correspond more closely to the time spent in the activity than to the number of separate initiations of the activity.

NOTE.–It is here assumed that there is neither displacement nor substitution among alternatives; that $F = F_S + F_{ext}$ and that $F_{ext} = 45$ for each alternative; that c for each activity is .1; that r for each activity is .05; that T_I and N_I for each activity are 0; that selective attention for each alternative is 1.00; that the parameters for initial and cessation lags are 10 and for each curve are .40 (see Appendix A). Simulation run and contributed by Mio Kawamura Reynolds.

activity. Computer simulation of motivational problems pertaining to measures taken from the molar stream of activity, such as operant level of an activity, time spent, etc., can now provide a valuable early check on the plausibility of various assumptions in this new conception of motivation (in light of known evidence) and a heuristic guide for the future psychology of human motivation, one that beings to do justice to the complexities of the ancient problems. Above all, it is a theory of an *active* individual, one whose behavior is a series of actions which express his constantly changing inclinations and not merely his reactions to a constantly changing pattern of stimulation.

16
SOME DETERMINANTS OF PERSISTENCE AND INITIATION OF ACHIEVEMENT-RELATED ACTIVITIES[1]

Marvin Brown[2]

This investigation is concerned with the determinants of the time taken by an individual to shift from one activity to another.[3] In particular it deals with the persistence and initiation of achievement-related activities. In the program of research on achievement motivation, this study represents a development of the analysis of persistence initiated by Feather (1961) and advanced by Weiner (1963). The theoretical importance of the present study lies in its attempt to demonstrate that the persistence of an achievement-related activity is determined *both* by factors influencing the strength of the tendency to engage in *that* activity (e.g., success/failure) and by factors influencing the strength of the

[1] This is a substantially abridged version of a more elaborate doctoral dissertation (Brown, 1967) at the University of Michigan. This study was carried out while the author held a USPHS Predoctoral Fellowship.

[2] I want to thank the members of the doctoral committee for their many helpful suggestions–Jack Atkinson, Chairman, David Birch, Dorwin Cartwright, and James Morgan.

[3] Brown was the first to demonstrate that time to change from one activity to another is influenced by variables which determine the tendencies for both the initial and subsequent activities. The whole dissertation deserves special attention for the thoroughness of its theoretical analysis (as early as 1965, when it was conceived and initiated) and the rigorous attention to details and procedural issues that are of great importance as we begin to study the stream of behavior. Since the theory of resistance had not yet been fully worked out at that time, we include here only Brown's theoretical analysis in reference to persons who are most strongly motivated to achieve. But his results and comments concerning both this group and another which scored low in n Achievement and high in Test Anxiety are included. A critical reconsideration of what should be expected for the latter group is suggested by the implications of resistance in Chapter 15 and in Atkinson and Birch (1970).–Editors.

tendency to engage in the *subsequent* activity (e.g., the nature of the next activity).

The study is based upon the conceptual analysis of change in activity (Atkinson & Cartwright, 1964) and by the early stages of Atkinson and Birch's (1970, and in Chapter 15) later elaboration. It is concerned with persistence of the activity in progress (or latency of initiation of the subsequent activity) as determined by: (*a*) the nature of the subsequent activity (achievement-related or not), (*b*) whether the activity in progress, if achievement-related, has resulted in success or in failure, and (*c*) individual differences in the relative strength of two achievement-related motives (M_S and M_{AF}).

DERIVATION OF HYPOTHESES

In order to derive testable hypotheses from the theory outlined in Chapter 15, it is necessary to make a series of assumptions which relate the theory to the specific conditions of the present study.

Extrinsic Tendencies ($T_{V,\text{ext}}$ and $T_{O,\text{ext}}$)[4]

It is assumed that in any experimental situation there exist tendencies to engage in the activities involved in that experiment, whose consequences are unrelated to the specific consequences of those activities. Such tendencies reflect *S*'s desire to be cooperative and to comply with the experimental instructions in order to gain social approval. The effect of these tendencies depends upon the specific experimental instructions which define for *S* what is expected of him. In achievement-related situations, for example, a tendency to engage in the task ($T_{X,\text{ext}}$) is assumed to exist (quite apart from $\bar{T}_{X,S}$) that is attributable to the implicit promise of approval for being cooperative and complying with the experimental instructions. It has been found in situations in which *E* and *S* interact closely or in which *E* requests *S*'s cooperation, that n Affiliation (assumed to be a major source of extrinsic motivation) substantially influences the achievement-related behavior (French, 1958b; Atkinson & Raphelson, 1956; Atkinson & Reitman, 1956; Smith, 1961; Atkinson & O'Connor, 1966; Entin, 1966; also Chapters 12, 13, and 14). In the present case, two such extrinsic tendencies, $T_{V,\text{ext}}$ and $T_{O,\text{ext}}$, are relevant.

The instructions of the present study specify that *S* engage in a series of activities, each following the onset of an appropriate signal, and imply that this

[4] This discussion uses the following notation: The first subscript refers to the *kind* of activity. Thus *V* represents a verbal task and *O* an opinions task. The second subscript refers to the assumed consequences of that activity. Thus, ach represents achievement-related, *S* represents success, and *F* represents failure. In the case of the opinions task, the goal cannot be specified and is omitted. Extrinsic consequences are represented by ext. [Editor's note: We have substituted $N_{V,F}$ for Brown's $T_{V,F}$ to make the notation of his 1965 study correspond to present usage as in Atkinson and Birch (1970) and Chapter 15. And we have done the same to indicate the resultant tendency to achieve by $\bar{T}_{VI}$.]

be done within a limited period of time. In this regard, the instructions do not distinguish between the two kinds of activity. The implication of these instructions, it is assumed, is for *S* to tend to shift from the activity in which he is currently engaged to the next activity when the stimulus for that activity is presented. If only extrinsic tendencies were instigated, it can be shown that the time to change activities should be independent of the nature of the ongoing and subsequent activities, should be equal following success and failure, and should also be equal among groups who differ in achievement-related motivation.

Tendency to Engage in Nonachievement Activity (T_O)

T_O refers to the tendency to engage in the nonachievement activity (opinions task) that is specifically attributable to the inherent characteristics of that task. *The critical characteristic of this activity is that individuals do not perceive their performance of it as instrumental to achievement.* An effort is made to avoid any evaluative connotation whatever with respect to the opinions tasks, and to keep these quite distinct from the verbal tasks. To the extent that these manipulations are effective, it can be assumed that T_O is unrelated to $\bar{T}_{V,S}$. It follows that groups which differ in achievement-related motives should not differ in the strength of any of the determinants of T_O. In addition, success and failure should not have a differential effect on the strength of T_O.

Tendency to Engage in Achievement-Related Activity ($\bar{T}_{V,S}$)

Two independent antagonistic tendencies combine additively to yield the resultant tendency to engage or not to engage in a particular achievement-related activity. These are (*a*) the tendency to achieve success ($T_{V,S}$), and (*b*) the tendency to avoid failure ($N_{V,F}$), a negative (inhibitory) tendency:

$$\bar{T}_{V,S} = T_{V,S} - N_{V,F} \tag{1}$$

To illustrate the effects of $\bar{T}_{V,S}$, let us first consider the case in which the activity in progress is achievement-related and the subsequent activity is non-achievement-related. How long will it take an individual to initiate the nonachievement activity (after the onset of the appropriate stimulus) following success as opposed to failure?

The general expression for the time to change from activity A to activity B, given the assumption that T_{A} has stabilized at an asymptotic value prior to or during the interval ${}_st_{\mathrm{B}}$ (see Chapter 15), is given in Equation (2):

$${}_st_{\mathrm{B}} = \frac{T_{\mathrm{A}_F} - T_{\mathrm{B}_I}}{F_{\mathrm{B}}} \tag{2}$$

In the present case, the components of T_{A_F}, T_{B_I}, and F_B may be represented as follows:[5]

$$_{s}t_O = \frac{[\bar{T}_{V,S_F} + T_{V,\text{ext}_F}] - [T_{O_I} + T_{O,\text{ext}_I}]}{[F_O + F_{O,\text{ext}}]} \tag{3}$$

The strength of the various extrinsic forces and tendencies has been assumed constant over activities, outcomes, and individuals. Consequently, T_{V,ext_F}, T_{O,ext_I}, and $F_{O,\text{ext}}$ are not the source of systematic differences in time to change activity ($_{s}t_O$). It has also been assumed that there are no systematic differences in either F_O or T_{O_I} following success and failure, or between individuals differing in the strength of $\bar{T}_{V,S_F}$. *Accordingly, with all these determinants considered constant, $_{s}t_O$ will be a function of $\bar{T}_{V,S_F}$ and, consequently, of the relative strength of T_{V,S_F} and N_{V,F_F}.*[6] Since $\bar{T}_{V,S}$ and $N_{V,F}$ are antagonistic tendencies, their effects are most easily seen if they are considered separately.

Tendency to Approach Success ($T_{V,S}$)

With N_{V,F_F} held constant (and for simplicity assumed to be zero), $_{s}t_O$ following success and failure should be directly related to the strength of T_{V,S_F}. It will be argued below that the strength of $T_{V,S}$ immediately prior to success and failure for a given individual is the same, but that success and failure have differential effects on $T_{V,S}$. It has already been assumed that the strength of $T_{V,S}$ has stabilized prior to both success and failure. The asymptotic strength of $T_{V,S}$ equal to $F_{V,S}/c_S$, is, in part, a function of the outcome of previous achievement-related tasks since $F_{V,S}$ is, in part, determined by P_s (see Brown, 1967, p. 21). But since the sequence of successes and failures is random for a given individual, there should be no systematic difference in the pattern of successes and failures preceding any given success or failure trial. And since there are a number of success and failure trials for each individual, it can be assumed that for each level of $T_{V,S}$ on a success trial there will be an equivalent level of $T_{V,S}$ on some failure trial.

It is generally assumed that success has greater consummatory value (c_S) for the tendency to achieve success than does failure (e.g., Zeigarnik, 1938; Lewin, 1951; McClelland et al., 1953; Weiner, 1963). Since $T_{V,S}$ is assumed equal

[5] This expression implies that instigating forces combine additively. This is approximately true *mathematically* under the special conditions of the present study. However, it should be noted that *conceptually* there is no addition of instigating forces within the theory, but only tendencies combine additively.

[6] In light of Chapter 15, Figure 8, we now presume that this statement is generally true but that differences in $\bar{T}_{V,S}$ that are attributable to differences in $N_{V,F}$ will become smaller and smaller and finally negligible when an activity has been in progress for some time. Recall that the resultant tendency $\bar{T}_A$ will finally stabilize at a level equal to F_A/c_A whether or not there is a negation tendency.–Editors.

immediately prior to success and failure, and since success is assumed to have greater consummatory value for $T_{V,S}$ than does failure, success should produce a greater reduction in the strength of $T_{V,S}$ than should failure. Therefore, *the strength of $T_{V,S}$ will be greater after failure than after success.* This is shown graphically in Figure 1.

Since ${}_st_O$ is directly related to the strength of $T_{V,S}$, the time to initiate the subsequent nonachievement activity (or the persistence of the ongoing achievement activity) should be greater following failure than following success *if only $T_{V,S}$ is considered.*

The magnitude of both $F_{V,S}$ and $N_{V,F}$ is a function of subjective probability of success (P_s). Ordinarily success leads to an increase in P_s, and failure to a decrease, and consequently there should be variation in the strength of both instigating and inhibitory forces as *S* experiences a series of successes and failures. This discussion has not considered the effects of such variation in P_s for several reasons. First, an explicit attempt is made to minimize variation in P_s and, in addition, to produce stable P_s levels of .50. Second, minor variations in P_s should be random and should not be systematically related to the strength of $\bar{T}_{V,S}$ on the success as opposed to the failure trials. Finally, since different *S*s experience different random sequences of successes and failures, minor task-to-task variation in P_s for a given person should tend to cancel out for the group of persons as a whole. To the extent that the attempted P_s manipulations were effective, P_s variation can be ignored (see Brown, 1967, Ch. 3 and 4).

Hypotheses Concerning *S*s in Whom $M_S > M_{AF}$

I. When the activity in progress is achievement-related. Let us consider first the time to initiate a nonachievement (opinions) activity following success and failure on the achievement-related activity (verbal task) in progress. This time, ${}_st_O$, is given by Equation (3). It has been argued that *S*s in whom $M_S > M_{AF}$ are those for whom the effects of $\bar{T}_{V,S_F}$ are in the same direction as those described for T_{V,S_F}. Therefore, since the strength of $\bar{T}_{V,S_F}$ is assumed to be greater after failure than after success, ${}_st_O$ should be shorter after success than after failure.

> *Hypothesis I. When the activity in progress is achievement-related and the subsequent activity is not, Ss in whom $M_S > M_{AF}$ will take longer to initiate the nonachievement activity (or persist longer on the achievement activity) following failure than following success.*

For the case in which both the ongoing and the subsequent activities are achievement-related (again for simplicity, assuming $N_{V,F} = 0$), the time to initiate the subsequent achievement activity (${}_st_{V2}$) is given by:

$$ {}_st_{V2} = \frac{[\bar{T}_{V1,S_F} + T_{V1,\text{ext}_F}] - [\bar{T}_{V2,S_I} + T_{V2,\text{ext}_I}]}{[F_{V2,S} + F_{V2,\text{ext}}]} \tag{4} $$

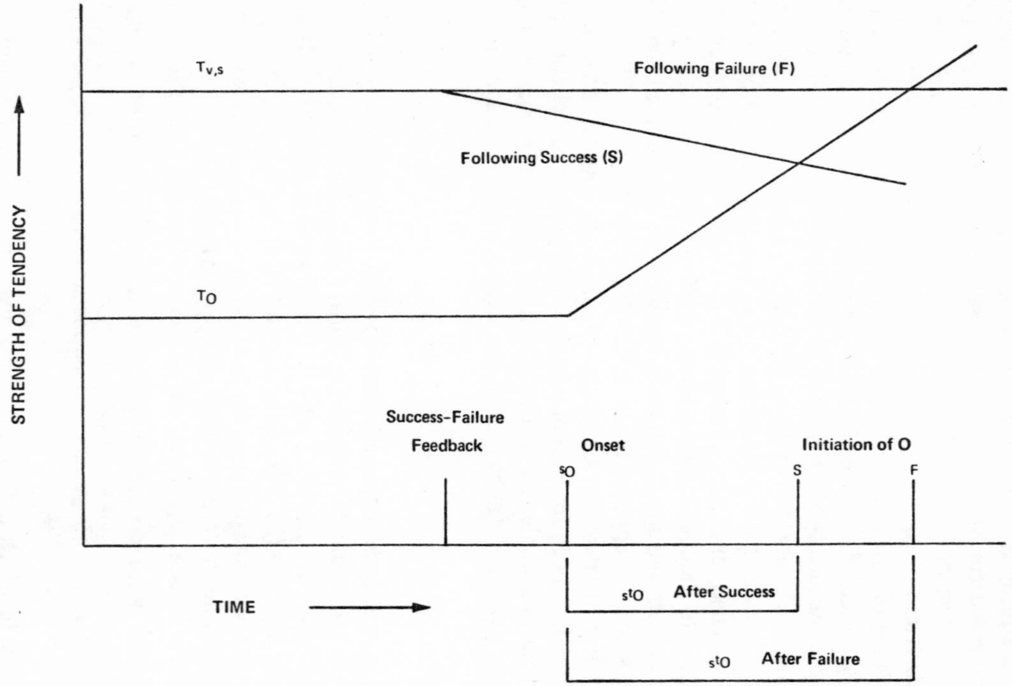

FIG. 1. Time to initiate activity O ($_st_O$) following onset of s_O according to assumed strength of $T_{V,S}$ and T_O after success and failure.

As in the previous case, the various extrinsic forces and tendencies can be ignored since they are assumed to be equal in the success and failure conditions.

Since in this case the two activities are of the same kind, the indirect instigating and consummatory forces are of considerable importance and must be taken into account. Success leads to a reduction in the strength of T_{V1,S_F} (implying less persistence of the first achievement task, *V*1), but also produces indirect consummatory forces which reduce the strength of T_{V2,S_I} (implying more persistence on *V*1). The relative magnitude of the direct and indirect effects of success and failure is, therefore, critical, since in this case the two forces have opposite effects.

It was earlier assumed (Chapter 15) that the direct consummatory force resulting from engagement in an activity is always greater in magnitude than the indirect consummatory force so produced. Consequently, the net effect of success is to reduce the strength of $\overline{T}_{V1,S_F}$ relative to $\overline{T}_{V2,S_I}$. The same argument applies to the effects of failure. Therefore, the prediction for this case parallels Hypothesis I.

> *Hypothesis II. When both ongoing and subsequent activities are achievement-related, Ss in whom $M_S > M_{AF}$ will take longer to initiate the subsequent achievement activity (or persist longer on the ongoing achievement activity) following failure than following success.*

What about the relative time to initiate achievement- and non-achievement-related activities when the activity in progress is achievement-related? The time to initiate the subsequent activity is inversely related to both the inertial tendency and the instigating force to engage in that activity [Equation (2)]. Thus, $_st_O$ is inversely related to both F_O and T_{O_I} [Equation (3)], and $_st_V$ is inversely related to $F_{V,S}$ and T_{V,S_I} [Equation (4)].

The median strength of T_{O_I} should be relatively low since the nonachievement task is completed before the next task is initiated, and should be equal to or less than the median strength of T_{V,S_I} for *S*s in whom $M_S > M_{AF}$. *S*s in whom $M_S > M_{AF}$ should have strong instigation to engage in the achievement activity relative to the nonachievement activity.[7] Accordingly, it follows that:

> *Hypothesis III. Ss in whom $M_S > M_{AF}$ will persist less on the achievement-related activity (or take less time to initiate the subsequent activity) after both success and failure when the subsequent activity is achievement-related than when it is not.*

II. When the nonachievement activity is in progress. Of interest here is the time to initiate an achievement-related activity as opposed to another non-

[7] This assumption is viewed as tentative, subject to empirical test. The major test involves obtaining preference data for the two tasks from the *S*s. If these assumptions are correct, the *S*s in whom $M_S > M_{AF}$ should indicate a preference for the achievement task, while the *S*s in whom $M_{AF} > M_S$ should indicate a preference for the nonachievement task.

achievement activity. The time to initiate the subsequent nonachievement activity ($_st_{O2}$) is:

$$_st_{O2} = \frac{[T_{O1_F} + T_{O1,\text{ext}_F}] - [T_{O2_I} + T_{O2,\text{ext}_I}]}{[F_{O2} + {_s}F_{O2,\text{ext}}]} \tag{5}$$

The time to initiate the achievement-related activity ($_st_V$) is:

$$_st_V = \frac{[T_{O1_F} + T_{O1,\text{ext}_F}] - [\bar{T}_{V,S_I} + T_{V,\text{ext}_I}]}{[F_{V,S} + F_{V,\text{ext}}]} \tag{6}$$

We wish to compare $_st_{O2}$ and $_st_V$.

Again, the various extrinsic forces and tendencies are assumed to be equal in the two cases as is the strength of T_{O1}. The strength of $F_{V,S}$ is assumed to be greater than that of F_{O2}, and the median strength of T_{V,S_I} is equal to or greater than the median strength of T_{O2_I}. Consequently, Hypothesis IV parallels Hypothesis III.

Hypothesis IV. When the nonachievement activity is in progress, Ss in whom $M_S > M_{AF}$ will initiate the subsequent activity more quickly (or persist less on the activity in progress) when the subsequent activity is achievement-related than when it is not.

[*Editor's comment:* In devising comparative hypotheses for *S*s who scored very low in n Achievement and high in Test Anxiety and who were, therefore, assumed to be ones for whom $M_{AF} > M_S$, Brown was guided by the earlier logic of the theory of achievement motivation (Chapter 2). He assumed, in other words, that the resultant tendency to achieve $\bar{T}_{V,S}$ would always be negative and have to be compensated by some other extrinsic tendency. This led him to predict that time to change from one activity would be affected just the opposite among *S*s in whom $M_{AF} > M_S$ when compared with *S*s in whom $M_S > M_{AF}$. If the implications of Chapter 15 are essentially correct, then (*a*) $\bar{T}_{V,S}$ can become positive even when $M_{AF} > M_S$ (without any extrinsic force to undertake an activity); (*b*) the level of $\bar{T}_{V,S}$ sustaining an activity will in time stabilize at the same level (i.e., F_s/c_S) whether resistance is present or not; (*c*) in a series or sequence of activities, the negation tendency (resistance) has paradoxical effects: it delays the initial occurrence of an activity, but if the environment is constant it may later on produce an increase in both the frequency and the time spent in an activity. Because of these complexities, Brown's earlier conjectural derivation for the more anxious *S*s is not included here, but his results and his interpretations of them in terms of what he had expected in 1967 are presented here.]

METHOD

Subjects

The 90 *S*s in this study were selected from a group of 364 enrolled in social and natural science introductory psychology courses at the University of Michigan during the Fall 1965 semester. Of these, 334 (92%) attended one of the three assessment sessions.

Selection of Subjects

An attempt was made to keep the *S*s from perceiving any connection between the assessment and experimental phases of the study by having another *E* conduct the assessment sessions. A Thematic Apperception Test (TAT) was administered under *neutral* conditions (McClelland et al., 1953). The slides were the same ones Feather (1961) had used and were, with one exception, also used by Weiner (1963). The self-report Test Anxiety Questionnaire (TAQ) (Mandler & Sarason, 1952) followed the TAT.

The TAT was coded blind for n Achievement by one coder and for n Affiliation by another trained coder.[8] Both had previously demonstrated interjudge reliability over .90. An estimate of coder consistency was obtained for each coder on the complete protocols of 20 *S*s, n Achievement rescoring after 4 months, n Affiliation rescoring after 6 weeks, with rank-order correlations between the two sets of scores of .93 for both motives.

The n Achievement and TAQ scores were converted to standard scores, with the difference between the two standard scores obtained for each *S*. The *S*s falling in the upper third of the resultant distribution, relatively high in n Achievement, were assumed to be those in whom $M_S > M_{AF}$. Those falling in the lower third, relatively high in Test Anxiety, were assumed to be the *S*s in whom $M_{AF} > M_S$. The *S*s for the experimental phase of the study were randomly selected from those available and run individually until the required number had been obtained.

Achievement Task

A modified anagram task was developed which permitted excellent control of performance (success and failure) without arousing *S*s suspicions and was highly ego-involving. The task consisted of a set of seven letters, two vowels and five consonants (e.g., E D C N L P A), with which *S* had to construct two four-letter words. A total of 120 seven-letter sets was pretested in several introductory psychology classes other than those from which the *S*s had been selected. The 13

[8] I am indebted to Joel Raynor for conducting the assessment sessions and for coding n Achievement and to Stuart Karabenick for coding n Affiliation. The data involving n Affiliation are peripheral to the main purpose of the study and are not discussed here. They are discussed in Brown (1967).

items whose difficulty level (percent success) was closest to 100% and the 13 closest to 0% made up the success and failure sets, respectively, with the best two items of each set making up the practice sets. In all, 94.3% of the items in the success set and only 6.6% of the items in the failure set were solved by the experimental *S*s.

Nonachievement Task

The main requirement of this task was that it have no achievement connotations. It consisted of a series of common, noncontroversial adjectives (e.g., proud, honest, smug) which *S* was instructed to rate in terms of his opinion of how desirable or undesirable it was for adult members of both sexes to behave in the ways indicated. Instructions emphasized that there was no interest in how *S* himself behaved, but only in his opinions regarding the behavior of others. The *S*s were told that these ratings were being collected as part of a study of the differences between behavior considered desirable for the same and the opposite sex, and that similar ratings were being collected from female *S*s. In order to keep the working time on the achievement and nonachievement tasks comparable, *S* was required to rate the first four (of seven) adjectives on each list.

Experimental Conditions

The experiment involved six conditions, each consisting of an ongoing and a subsequent activity. There were several replications of each condition for each *S*. The sequence of activities was random so that *S* could not predict what activity would be next before the signal for that task had been given. The various conditions and the number of replications of each are given in Table 1.

A total of 37 activities was required to complete the design. Each task in this sequence had a dual function: (*a*) it served as the ongoing activity once, and (*b*) it served as the subsequent activity when the preceding task was in progress.

The 37 activities were arranged in 15 different random sequences, each used for two *S*s in each motive group. Of the 37 activities, 22 were achievement-related (verbal test items) and 15 were nonachievement (opinions). The verbal tasks were presented in a different random sequence for each *S*, as were the opinions.

The practice series followed the same sequence for all *S*s: (*a*) verbal (success), (*b*) opinions, (*c*) verbal (failure), (*d*) verbal (failure), (*e*) opinions, (*f*) verbal (success).

Apparatus

The apparatus consisted of a large panel facing *S*. There were two compartments (one for the achievement task, the other for the nonachievement task) into which *S* deposited the tasks completed, and two others from which he took the next task to work on. Each compartment was covered by a door, which activated a timer when lifted. The contents of each compartment were indicated by appropriate labels on the doors (e.g., VERBAL TEST, DEPOSIT OPINIONS).

TABLE 1

Experimental Conditions

Condition	Ongoing activity		Subsequent activity		Replications per subject	
	Activity	Outcome	Activity	Outcome		
SA[a]	Achievement (verbal) task	Success	Achievement task	50% success	3	6
				50% failure	3	
FA	Achievement task	Failure	Achievement task	50% success	3	6
				50% failure	3	
SO	Achievement task	Success	Nonachievement task			5
FO	Achievement task	Failure	Nonachievement task			5
OA	Nonachievement (opinions) task		Achievement task	50% success	4 or 5	9
				50% failure	5 or 4	
OO	Nonachievement task		Nonachievement task			5

[a]The first letter refers to the ongoing activity (*S* = success, *F* = failure, *O* = nonachievement task) and the second to the subsequent activity (*A* = achievement task, *O* = nonachievement task).

Lights near the doors indicated the next task and where S was to deposit the task in progress.

OPERATION OF APPARATUS

Achievement Task in Progress

Success. The S took a problem from the VERBAL TEST compartment and worked on it. As he constructed a word, S wrote it down on the slip of paper and stated it aloud. When S had correctly given a second word, E initiated the success feedback. The light adjacent to the DEPOSIT VERBAL TEST compartment came on and, 1 second later, one of the lights specifying the next activity came on informing S of the task to be done next. *These two lights defined the outcome as success.* The S could then deposit the problem whenever he wished. When he deposited the slip of paper in the DEPOSIT VERBAL TEST compartment, the light adjacent to that compartment went off. When S took the next task from the compartment indicated, the light above that compartment went off.

Failure. As above, S took a problem from the VERBAL TEST compartment and attempted to solve it. After 20 seconds a *buzzer* sounded briefly indicating that Ss time was up. At the same time the light adjacent to the DEPOSIT TEST compartment came on. One second later the light specifying the next task came on. *The buzzer and the two lights defined the outcome as failure.* (The only difference between the success and failure feedback was, then, the buzzer.) The S could then wait as long as he liked before depositing the verbal task and initiating the next task. When the task was deposited in the DEPOSIT VERBAL TEST compartment the light adjacent to that compartment went off. And, as above, when S took the next task from the compartment indicated, the light above that compartment went off.

Nonachievement Task in Progress

The S took a slip of paper containing a set of adjectives to be rated from the OPINIONS compartment and began to work on the ratings. Ten seconds later the light adjacent to the DEPOSIT OPINIONS compartment came on and, 1 second after that, one of the lights signifying the next task came on. The S worked on the opinions for as long as he liked (though he had to complete the first four of each set and then deposited the slip of paper in the DEPOSIT OPINIONS compartment, turning off the adjacent light. When S took the next task the light above that compartment went off.

Time Measures

Three electric timers which could be read to the nearest .01 second were used to measure each activity cycle, i.e., from the initiation of the task (when it was taken from its compartment) to the success or failure feedback ("working time"), from that point to the depositing of the task ("deposit time") and from that point to the taking of the next task ("reaching time"). When the nonachievement task was in progress, the working and deposit times were combined since there was no success/failure feedback.

Theoretical Significance of Apparatus and Time Measures

The lights above the compartments in which the two tasks were located are assumed to have produced instigating forces to engage in the activities they signified. Thus, the light above the VERBAL TEST compartment produced an instigating force to engage in the verbal (achievement-related) task ($F_{V,S}$). Since this light remained on until *S* initiated the verbal activity, the time during which it was on represents $_st_V$ and is measured by deposit time + reaching time. Similarly, the light above the OPINIONS compartment produced an instigating force to engage in the opinions (nonachievement) task ($_sF_O$). The time during which this light was on represents $_st_O$ and is measured by working time + reaching time.[9]

Procedure

The *S*s were tested individually about 8 weeks after the assessment sessions. The experiment took about an hour to complete. *S*s from the two groups were run in random order, and at the time they were run, *E* had no knowledge of the *S*s' motive classification.

The experimental room was a small, well-illuminated cubicle. The apparatus was placed on a large table which occupied most of the room, and served as a screen between *E* and *S*.

When *S* entered the experimental room, he was told informally by *E*:

> Today you will be working on two very different kinds of tasks. But the main reason you are here is to take a new kind of verbal test—one that is likely to be related to general intelligence. You, as well as the other subjects in this study, have been selected on the basis of test scores and any other information regarding your verbal ability that is available. This information indicates that you have about a 50:50 chance of passing each of the items on the test.

The *S* was then asked to follow the printed instructions for the verbal test as *E* read them aloud. Several rules regarding acceptable answers were given, and success was defined as getting two four-letter words in 20 seconds.

Following the instructions for the verbal test, *S* was reminded that this represented the main task to be done, but that he would also be working on

[9] Analyses of the results suggested that the reaching times were not measures of the same processes as were the working and deposit times, as had been assumed. It appeared that the reaching time was a period in which *S* was getting ready to work on the next task rather than persisting in the previous one. Therefore, the reaching times are not presented here. They are shown and discussed at length in Brown (1967).

another activity—an opinions survey. In order to make the other activity credible to *S* he was told that it was desirable to keep the verbal test items spaced so that they would sometimes be alternated with the other activity. Further, *E* was also interested in the opinions in their own right since one of his other research interests, quite distinct from his interest in verbal ability, was in comparing how the males in this study differed from the (nonexistent) females in their opinions. It was stressed that, with respect to the opinions, *E* was not interested in *S* as an individual, but only as a member of the male sample. The opinions were done anonymously. All *S*s appeared to be convinced by these arguments.

The printed instructions for the opinions task were then read by *E*. These stated that *S* would be shown lists of words describing various ways of behaving, and was to rate how desirable or undesirable he thought it was for *adult* members of both sexes to behave in the ways indicated.

After *S* fully understood the nature of the two different tasks, the specific procedure and the operation of the apparatus were then explained to him.

The *S* then worked on a practice series. Any questions were answered, and *E* made certain that everything was clear. The *S* was told that from this point on there would be no further verbal communication between *E* and *S*, so that *E* would not respond to any questions once the test series began.

Success and Failure Times

On the vast majority of the predetermined successes and failures, the *S* performed as intended; but when he did not, *E* adjusted the time by a few seconds to insure the intended result. No *S* gave any indication of having noticed any variations in these times.

Manipulation of P_s

Previous studies have attempted to manipulate P_s in a variety of ways. In general, no single method has been very successful (in terms of obtaining P_s estimates from the *S*s that corresponded closely to those intended). The present study combined three different methods: (*a*) *S* was told that he had been selected on the basis of *his own* test scores, and that these scores indicated that he had a 50-50 chance of success on each of the verbal test items (adapted from Moulton, 1965); (*b*) *S* worked on a series of practice problems which, he was told, were typical of the test series, and actually succeeded on 50% of these problems (adapted from Birch, 1964); and (*c*) *S* also succeeded on 50% of the test problems (adapted from Feather, 1966).[10]

[10] The effectiveness of these manipulations was checked by having a small number of other *S*s rate their confidence of success just prior to each verbal test problem (see Brown, 1967, for a discussion of these data).

RESULTS

All *S*s were exposed to each of the six experimental conditions from five to nine times (see Table 1), so that repeated measurements of the various time intervals in each of the conditions were obtained. The median working, or deposit, and reaching times in each condition were determined for each *S*.

Achievement Activity in Progress

Table 2 shows the deposit times following success and failure on the achievement activity as a function of achievement motivation and the nature of the next activity. Failure was followed by longer deposit times (mean = 2.67 seconds) than was success (mean = 2.17 seconds). This effect is highly significant ($F_{1,58} = 14.14, p < .01$). In addition, the deposit times were significantly longer ($F_{1,58} = 5.69, p < .05$) when the next activity was the opinions task (mean = 2.49 seconds) than when it was the verbal task (mean = 2.35 seconds). These results show clearly that *the time to deposit the activity in progress was a function of both the outcome of that activity and the nature of the subsequent activity,* as expected. There were, however, no overall differences between the two motive groups. Nor did any of the interactions even approach statistical significance.

Nonachievement Activity in Progress

Table 3 shows the working time on the nonachievement activity (opinions task) as a function of the nature of the next activity. The two motive groups did not differ in the amount of time spent working on the opinions task ($F_{1,58} = 1$). There was a nonsignificant trend ($F_{1,58} = 2.07, p < .20$) for the time spent working on the opinions task to be less when a verbal task was next (mean = 32.53 seconds) than when another opinions task was next (mean = 33.39 seconds). The interaction between motive classification and nature of next task was also nonsignificant ($F_{1,58} < 1$).

TABLE 2

Deposit Times (Seconds) Following Success and Failure

n Achievement-Test Anxiety		Next activity			
		Achievement		Nonachievement	
		Success	Failure	Success	Failure
High	Mean	2.12	2.65	2.31	2.78
	S.D.	0.73	1.12	0.80	1.40
Low	Mean	2.08	2.53	2.16	2.72
	S.D.	0.93	0.53	0.87	0.87

TABLE 3

Working Time on Nonachievement Activity (Seconds)

n Achievement– Test Anxiety		Working time when next activity is: Achievement	Nonachievement
High	Mean	31.91	33.30
	S.D.	11.02	10.96
Low	Mean	33.12	33.48
	S.D.	8.32	8.42

Having summarized the general results, the specific hypotheses of the present study are tested, following the procedure suggested by Winer (1962), using the appropriate error terms of the analyses of variance (these are presented in Brown, 1967, Tables 7 and 8). The hypotheses fall into three groups: (*a*) those involving *S*s in whom it is assumed that $M_S > M_{AF}$ (*S*s relatively high in n Achievement); (*b*) those involving *S*s in whom it is assumed that $M_{AF} > M_S$ (*S*s relatively high in Test Anxiety); and (*c*) those comparing the two motive groups.

*S*s Relatively High in n Achievement

When the activity in progress is achievement-related and the subsequent activity is not, *S*s in whom $M_S > M_{AF}$ should persist longer on the achievement task following failure than following success. Table 2 shows that the mean deposit time for the *S*s relatively high in n Achievement was 2.78 seconds after failure and 2.31 seconds after success, a statistically significant difference in the direction predicted by Hypothesis I ($t = 3.73$, $df = 58$, $p < .005$, one-tail test).

When both the activity in progress and the subsequent activity are achievement-related, *S*s in whom $M_S > M_{AF}$ should persist longer on the task in progress after failure than after success (see Brown, 1967, for the derivation of the hypotheses for *S*s in whom $M_{AF} > M_S$). Table 2 shows that the mean deposit times for *S*s relatively high in n Achievement were 2.65 seconds after failure and 2.12 seconds after success. This difference, as predicted by Hypothesis II, is statistically significant ($t = 4.21$, $df = 58$, $p < .005$, one-tail test).

When the activity in progress is achievement-related, *S*s in whom $M_S > M_{AF}$ should persist longer when the subsequent task is non-achievement-related than when it is achievement-related. When the verbal task was in progress, the mean deposit time of *S*s relatively high in n Achievement was 2.39 seconds when the next activity was another verbal task and 2.55 seconds when the next activity was an opinions task. This difference, consistent with Hypothesis III, is statistically significant ($t = 1.86$, $df = 58$, $p < .05$, one-tail test).

Hypothesis IV stated that when the activity in progress is non-achievement-related, *S*s in whom $M_S > M_{AF}$ should persist longer when the subsequent activity is non-achievement-related than when it is achievement related. Table 3 shows that the mean time spent working on the opinions task was 31.91 seconds when the next task was a verbal task and 33.30 seconds when the next task was another opinions task. This difference, in the predicted direction, is statistically significant ($t = 1.88, df = 58, p < .05$, one-tail test).

In summary, all four hypotheses involving *S*s high in n Achievement are supported by the deposit time measure. With the achievement-related activity (verbal task) in progress, deposit time was longer after failure than after success both when the next activity was achievement-related and when it was not. Deposit time was longer when a nonachievement task followed the achievement task in progress than when another achievement task followed.

*S*s Relatively High in Test Anxiety

All four of the original hypotheses involving the *S*s high in Test Anxiety are contradicted by the deposit time measure. All four differences are in the direction *opposite* to that predicted—two of these being statistically significant (using two-tailed tests of significance). When the achievement-related (verbal) task was in progress, deposit time was significantly longer following failure than following success, both when the next task was achievement-related and when it was not. Regardless of the nature of the task in progress, there was a nonsignificant trend for deposit time to be shorter when the next activity was achievement-related than when it was not. Thus *S*s relatively high in Test Anxiety behave in a way similar to *S*s relatively high in n Achievement.

When the two motive groups are compared, the obtained differences in the deposit time measure are in the predicted direction, though not significant.

Previous studies (e.g., Weiner, 1963) have reported that, as would be expected, some of the differences between the two motive groups are enhanced when more extreme *S*s are compared. The analyses discussed so far were all based on *S*s selected from the extreme thirds of the distribution of n Achievement-Test Anxiety scores. In addition, the 15 most extreme *S*s of each motive group (i.e., those *S*s whose resultant n Achievement scores fell approximately in the extreme sixths of the original distribution) were selected for further analysis. Previous findings were not replicated. There was no change in the pattern of results, and little change in the significance levels of the obtained differences, as compared to those found when all the *S*s were used in the analysis.

DISCUSSION

The major result of the present study is *the clear demonstration that persistence of the achievement-related activity is determined both by the outcome of that activity (success versus failure) and by the nature of the subsequent activity (achievement-related versus non-achievement-related).* Both Feather (1961) and Weiner (1963) found differences in persistence following success and failure, but in both cases these differences were attributable only to determinants of the tendency to engage in the achievement activity in progress. Thus, Feather held the nature of the subsequent activity constant, and attributed differences in persistence to changes in P_s produced by the success and failure experiences. Weiner (1963) tried to hold both the effects of P_s and the nature of the subsequent activity constant, and assumed that the obtained differences in performance and persistence were due only to persisting (inertial) tendencies to engage in the achievement activity. *The present study is the first to obtain differences that are attributable to the nature of the next activity.* Consistent with these results is the fact that *persistence on the nonachievement activity is also a function of the nature of the subsequent activity.*

Nature of the Two Motive Groups

The results of this investigation do, however, raise an important theoretical and methodological issue concerning the nature of the two motive groups. Since the two motive groups show identical patterns of results, it might be argued that they are similarly motivated. That is, since both motive groups behave *as if* they are primarily motivated to approach success (i.e., $T_{V,S} > T_{V,F}$), it might be reasonable to assume that, in fact, $M_S > M_{AF}$ for both groups. There is considerable logical and empirical support for this argument.

First, the selection procedures employed yield *S*s whose Test Anxiety and n Achievement scores are high or low *relative to other S*s. There is no adequate measure of the magnitude of these scores *relative to each other.* The population of college students–especially those highly selected–should represent individuals who are relatively high in n Achievement and relatively low in Test Anxiety. Individuals whose motive to approach success is weak and/or whose motive to avoid failure is strong would probably not be represented in the sample. Consequently, even a *S* whose n Achievement score is low and whose Test Anxiety score is high relative to other *S*s, might well be a person whose motive to approach success was *absolutely* stronger than his motive to avoid failure.

Second, a number of studies show that *S*s defined by the selection procedures as those in whom $M_{AF} > M_S$ actually behave as if they were *S*s in whom $M_S > M_{AF}$. Thus, Atkinson and Litwin (1960) found that *S*s below the median in n Achievement and above the median in Test Anxiety (the Low-High group) seemed to *prefer* intermediate risk in a ring-toss game, though the extent of this preference was less than that of *S*s above the median in n Achievement and below the median in Test Anxiety (the High-Low group). Litwin (1966) found that both High-Low and Low-High *S*s chose risks that were within what has been accepted as the region of intermediate difficulty (P_s approximately .30 to .70) even though more extreme risks were available. Moulton (1965) found that *S*s in whom he assumed that $M_{AF} > M_S$ actually showed more typical than atypical shifts in level of aspiration. Also, O'Connor, Atkinson and Horner (1966) found that both *S*s in whom they assumed $M_S > M_{AF}$ and those in whom they assumed that $M_{AF} > M_S$ scored better on achievement tests in classes grouped on the basis of homogeneous ability than in classes heterogeneous with respect to ability.

In summary, then, there appears to be considerable empirical evidence that *S*s whose Test Anxiety score is greater than their n Achievement score are not necessarily *S*s in whom $M_{AF} > M_S$. Indeed, considered as a group, these *S*s may well have a stronger M_S than they do M_{AF}. However, the difference in the strength of the two motives is probably less for these *S*s than for those whose n Achievement score is greater than their Test Anxiety score.

Deposit and Working Times

To the extent that the foregoing arguments are valid, the present results concerning deposit and working time can be completely accounted for. If both groups of *S*s are those in whom $M_S > M_{AF}$, then the predictions would be the same for the two groups. That is, the pattern of results should be identical in the two motive groups. This is, of course, exactly what was found in the present study.

The magnitude of the effects of success and failure and of the nature of the next activity should be a function of the relative strength of M_S and M_{AF} and, consequently, of the difference between the n Achievement and Test Anxiety scores. That is, the differences manifested by *S*s less motivated to approach success should be less than those manifested by *S*s highly motivated to approach success. The present results are consistent with this expectation. Though the success-failure effects are highly significant for both motive groups, the effects attributable to the nature of the next task are only significant among *S*s relatively high in n Achievement. Furthermore, when the two groups are compared directly, the *S*s relatively high in n Achievement (assumed highly motivated to approach success) spend less time working on the nonachievement task when the next task is achievement-related and take longer to deposit the achievement task when the nonachievement task follows than do the *S*s relatively high in Test Anxiety (assumed less motivated to approach success), as expected.

This position also implies that differences between the two motive groups should be enhanced when more extreme *S*s (those showing the greatest differences between n Achievement and Test Anxiety scores) are compared. This is not found in the present study. It is interesting that Weiner's (1966b) persistence data show the same trend—the differences are not increased when more extreme *S*s are compared. Why this is so is not clear.

It should be noted that some studies (most notably that of Feather, 1961) have found differences consistent with the view that, at least in some of the *S*s, $M_{AF} > M_S$ (see also Chapters 5 and 10). Feather's selection procedure was apparently similar to that of Atkinson and Litwin (1960) and others who found no evidence of *S*s in whom $M_{AF} > M_S$.[11] The difference may represent a sampling difference, though the *S*s in all of the studies seemed to come from the same general population. In any event, Feather's results suggest that there do exist *S*s in whom $M_{AF} > M_S$ among college students. These *S*s can presumably be identified. They may be the *S*s whose Test Anxiety score exceeds their n Achievement score by a sufficiently large amount. Just what this critical difference is can only be determined empirically.

[*Editor's comment*: Brown's argument about the motivational characteristics of his sample may be correct. However, the results presented in Chapter 8, which were obtained from a sample of subjects drawn from the parent population that Brown used to obtain subjects in his experiment, suggest that in fact some *S*s (those classified simultaneously Low-High on n Achievement-Test Anxiety) did in fact have $M_{AF} > M_S$. There may be another possibility that assumes the validity of the motivational classification but has to do with the paradoxical effects of resistance to an activity in a stream of behavior in a relatively constant environment (see Table 3 in Chapter 15). It is a possibility that needs to be thoroughly considered since Brown's initial expectations were anchored in the earlier (Chapter 2) conception of how the tendency to avoid failure would influence behavior.]

[11] *Editor's note*: In fact the *S*s in these studies did not come from the same population. Feather's sample in the late 1950's was drawn from a single introductory psychology course that combined those interested in natural and social sciences, now known to differ in average n Achievement as pointed out earlier by the author. Atkinson and Litwin's late 1950's sample were all students taking a lab course in motivation, already well on their way to concentration in psychology; and Brown's sample is drawn, a decade later, from a combination of classes introducing psychology as a social or a natural science. The comparability of samples in modal personality, including those from one highly selective university to another less selective one, is a continuing problem for experimental social psychology and will be until we have better means than presently for classification of *S*s in terms of personality measures that are well calibrated.

17
THE EFFECTS OF UNSATISFIED ACHIEVEMENT MOTIVATION ON PERSISTENCE AND SUBSEQUENT PERFORMANCE[1]

Bernard Weiner[2]

Although Atkinson's (1957) model for achievement-oriented behavior (see Chapter 2) has received empirical support from many studies, it contains some apparent deficiencies. Foremost among these is that the model is completely stimulus bound. The individual is viewed as inactive, i.e., at rest, until a stimulus is presented which will instigate behavior. It is assumed that the stimulus engages a motive and initiates a cognitive, inferential process. The achievement model therefore cannot incorporate Freud's (1949) assertions concerning the persistence of an unfulfilled wish, or investigations by Zeigarnik (1938) and Ovsiankina (1928) which demonstrate the recall and spontaneous resumption of previously interrupted activities. That is, the model cannot account for the maintenance of goal-seeking, purposive behavior in the absence of the instigating external stimulus.

Atkinson and Cartwright (1964) have recently come to grips with the problem of persistence of behavior in the absence of the instigating stimulus (see also Chapter 15). They assert that a goal-directed tendency, once aroused, will persist until the goal is attained. Consequently the strength of the immediate

[1] Reprinted and abridged by permission of the Duke University Press from the *Journal of Personality*, 1965, 33, 428-442.

[2] This article is based upon a dissertation submitted in partial fulfillment of the requirements for the Ph.D. degree at the University of Michigan. The author wishes to thank John W. Atkinson, dissertation chairman, for his many criticisms and suggestions, and J. David Birch, Dorwin Cartwright, Melvin Manis, and James N. Morgan for their comments. This research was undertaken when the author was a sponsored Research Fellow at the University of Michigan. The research was also part of a project on the Determinants of Human Choice supported by the National Science Foundation (Grant No. GS-9).

tendency to act is conceived by them to be a function of the strength of previously aroused but unsatisfied motivation, called the "inertial tendency," plus the strength of the tendency aroused by the immediate stimulus situation. Atkinson and Cartwright have formalized their ideas and have incorporated persisting tendencies into Atkinson's 1957 model for achievement-related behavior. The revised model is:

$$T_A = (M_S \times P_s \times I_s + T_{Gi}) + (M_{AF} \times P_f \times - I_f)$$

T_{Gi} represents the inertial motivational component.

The implications of the assumption that a goal-directed tendency persists until the goal is attained can be most meaningfully conveyed within the context of the general procedure developed by Feather (1961) to study persistence at an achievement-related activity. Individuals are classified into motivational groups on the basis of Thematic Apperceptive Achievement scores and Test Anxiety scores. Then preselected *S*s are given an achievement-oriented task to perform, after being given instructions that they can move on, when they so desire, to an alternative activity that is nonachievement related in character. Two experimental conditions are created. In one condition norms are presented to *S*s to convey the idea that the task is relatively easy (P_s = .70), and the *S*s are allowed to succeed continually at the task. In the second condition the task is presented as relatively difficult (P_s = .30), and *S*s continually fail at the task.

Given these conditions, the strength of the tendencies to undertake the task on the first trial would be conceptualized by Atkinson's 1957 Model (Model 0) as follows:

$$(\text{When } P_s = .30)\text{: } T_A = (M_S \times .3 \times .7) - (M_{AF} \times .7 \times .3)$$

$$(\text{When } P_s = .70)\text{: } T_A = (M_S \times .7 \times .3) - (M_{AF} \times .3 \times .7)$$

When the strength of M_S relative to M_{AF} is the same for individuals in the two conditions, the strength of the resultant tendencies to undertake the task are identical in the conditions. Further, if it is assumed that the change in P_s following success is equal but opposite in direction to the change in P_s following failure, then Model 0 also would specify that the strength of motivation following success when P_s = .70 equals the strength of motivation following failure when P_s = .30.

For the conditions described in the previous paragraph, the strength of the tendencies following success and failure based on the new model proposed by Atkinson and Cartwright (Model 1) would be conceptualized as:

Success condition:

$$T_A = (M_S \times P_s + a \times I_s - a) - (M_{AF} \times P_f - a \times I_f + a)$$

Failure condition:

$$T_A = (M_S \times P_s - a \times I_s + a) - (M_{AF} \times P_f + a \times I_f - a) + T_{Gi}$$

where "a" represents the change in P_s as a result of success or failure on trial 1. Thus, according to the additional assumption of Model 1 that a goal-directed tendency will persist when the goal is not attained, the comparison between this particular Success and Failure condition should yield evidence that the strength of the tendency to undertake the achievement-related task is greater following failure than following success.

The conception of inertial motivation presented by Atkinson and Cartwright has raised a number of problems. Their discussion implies that all individuals should exhibit a greater tendency to engage in achievement-oriented behavior following failure than following success. However, the empirical evidence indicates that there is an interaction between individual differences in resultant achievement motivation and the effects of success and failure on subsequent performance. Child and Whiting (1950) found individuals high in anxiety reported that they renew goal striving following success, while individuals low in anxiety reported that they frequently "relax" following goal attainment. Weiner (1965b) found individuals high in n Achievement more frequently resume previously interrupted tasks following interpolated failure experiences than following interpolated success; individuals low in n Achievement, however, more frequently resume previously interrupted tasks following interpolated success experiences than interpolated failure. The general pattern of results reported by Lucas (1952), Mandler and Sarason (1952), Child and Waterhouse (1953), Osler (1954), Williams (1955), Burton (1957), Sarason (1957), and Katchmar, Ross, and Andrews (1958) indicates that individuals who would be classified low in resultant achievement motivation ($M_{AF} > M_S$) suffer performance decrements following failure experiences and exhibit increments in level of performance following success. On the other hand, individuals who would be classified as high in resultant achievement motivation ($M_S > M_{AF}$) exhibit increments in level of performance following failure and decrements following success experiences. Studies with schizophrenic patients also have revealed that these *S*s exhibit performance decrements following failure or censure (Rodnick & Garmezy, 1957), and it has been found that success is a better motivator for schizophrenics than is failure (Olsen, 1958).

To account for these experimental findings the author takes the view that it is the *resultant* tendency to approach or avoid a goal that persists when a goal is not attained (Model 2). This explicitly assumes the persistence of the tendency to *avoid* failure as well as the tendency to *approach* success following failure at a task. Model 2 is conceptualized as:

$$T_A = M_S \times P_s \times I_s + T^*_S + (M_{AF} \times P_f \times - I_f) + T_{-Gi}$$

T_{-Gi} represents the persisting tendency to avoid the threat of failure.

The strength of M_S relative to M_{AF}, or the direction of the aroused motivation, determines the sign or direction of the persisting tendency. If $M_S > M_{AF}$, then the resultant persisting tendency to approach an achievement-related task following nonattainment of a goal is positive, and there would be a subsequent increment in performance following a failure experience. If $M_{AF} > M_S$, then the resultant persisting tendency following failure is negative (inhibitory), and there would be a subsequent decrement in performance following failure.

Table 1 gives a numerical example which summarizes the predictions derived from the three models for the conditions described above. For illustrative purposes, it is assumed that the magnitude of the stronger motive equals 2, while the magnitude of the weaker motive equals 1. It also is assumed that on trial one the inertial component(s) equals 0, and the change in P_s following success or failure on trial one equals ± .1. Changes in these values could alter the sign and magnitude of the resultant achievement tendency, but would not change the predictions concerning the effects of success as compared with the effects of failure on subsequent performance.

Table 1 indicates that when $M_S > M_{AF}$, Model 1 and Model 2 specify that the subsequent resultant tendency to undertake the task is greater following failure when P_s is .30 than following success when P_s is .70. However, Model 0 predicts there will be no difference in the strength of the subsequent tendency in the two conditions. When $M_{AF} > M_S$, Model 0 again specifies that there will be no difference in the strength of the subsequent resultant tendency to undertake the task following success or failure. However, Model 1 specifies greater subsequent strength of motivation following failure, while Model 2 specifies the opposite: greater subsequent strength of resultant motivation following success. Thus a crucial test of the validity of Model 0 as compared with either Model 1 or Model 2 occurs when $M_S > M_{AF}$; the critical comparison between Model 1 and Model 2 occurs when $M_{AF} > M_S$.

The following experiment attempts to create the experimental conditions outlined above to test the adequacy of the three models. The main virtue of this experimental design is that the initial P_s at the task is specified; this allows the motivational effects attributable to an inertial tendency to be separated from the motivational consequences attributable to a change in P_s. Neglect of the task difficulty variable has made it difficult to evaluate fully the theoretical implications of prior studies in this area, for failure may affect both the subsequent P_s and the magnitude of the inertial tendency.

METHOD

Subjects

*S*s were 128 male college students enrolled in the introductory psychology course at the University of Michigan. The *S*s were required to participate in

TABLE 1

Relative Effects of Success and Failure on Subsequent Strengths of Resultant Achievement Motivation

Model	Trial	Motive classification	
		$M_S > M_{AF}$	$M_{AF} > M_S$
All models	One	$S^a - T_A = 2 \times .7 \times .3 - (1 \times .3 \times .7) = .21$	$T_A = 1 \times .7 \times .3 - (2 \times .3 \times .7) = -.21$
		$F^b - T_A = 2 \times .3 \times .7 - (1 \times .7 \times .3) = .21$	$T_A = 1 \times .3 \times .7 - (2 \times .7 \times .3) = -.21$
Model 0–No inertial components	Two	$S - T_A = 2 \times .8 \times .2 - (1 \times .2 \times .8) = .16$	$T_A = 1 \times .8 \times .2 - (2 \times .2 \times .8) = -.16$
$T_A = M_S \times P_s \times I_s + (M_{AF} \times P_f \times - I_f)$		$F - T_A = 2 \times .2 \times .8 - (1 \times .8 \times .2) = .16$	$T_A = 1 \times .2 \times .8 - (2 \times .8 \times .2) = -.16$
Model 1–Inertial approach component		$S - T_A = 2 \times .8 \times .2 - (1 \times .2 \times .8) = .16$	$T_A = 1 \times .8 \times .2 - (2 \times .2 \times .8) = -.16$
$T_A = M_S \times P_s \times I_s + T_{Gi} + (M_{AF} \times P_f \times - I_f)$		$F - T_A = 2 \times .2 \times .8 + .42 - (1 \times .2 \times .8) = .58$	$T_A = 1 \times .2 \times .8 + .21 - (2 \times .8 \times .2) = .05$
Model 2–Inertial approach and avoidance components		$S - T_A = 2 \times .8 \times .2 - (1 \times .2 \times .8) = .16$	$T_A = 1 \times .8 \times .2 - (2 \times .2 \times .8) = -.16$
$T_A = M_S \times P_s \times I_s + T_{Gi} + (M_{AF} \times P_f \times - I_f) + T_{-Gi}$		$F - T_A = 2 \times .2 \times .8 + .42 - (1 \times .8 \times .2 + .21) = .37$	$T_A = 1 \times .2 \times .8 + .21 - (2 \times .8 \times .2 + .42) = -.37$

[a] Success condition.
[b] Failure condition.

psychological experiments. Sixty-nine of these *S*s were selected for the final experimental hour. Of the 69 *S*s three were excluded from the final data analysis because of experimental sophistication, one refused to cooperate with the *E*, and five failed to appear. Sixty *S*s were included in the final data analysis.

Assessment of Motives

During the first experimental hour *S*s were given a Thematic Apperception Test (TAT), picture series 2, 48, 1, 7, 11, and 24 (Atkinson, 1958a). The conditions of administration corresponded to those described as neutral by McClelland, Atkinson, Clark, and Lowell (1953). After administration of the TAT, *S*s were given the Mandler-Sarason Test Anxiety Questionnaire (TAQ) (Mandler & Sarason, 1952). This is a self-report measure of situationally aroused anxiety.

The TAT protocols were scored for n Achievement according to the method of content analysis described in Atkinson (1958a). The writer's test-retest scoring reliability for these protocols over a four-month period was rho = .89 ($N = 20$).

Scores on n Achievement and Test Anxiety were transformed into *Z* scores and combined by subtracting the *Z* score on the TAQ from the *Z* score on the TAT. *S*s scoring in the upper and lower 25% of the combined distribution were selected to appear for the final experimental hour.

Procedure

*S*s were tested individually during the second experimental hour. The procedure insured that the *E* did not know the motive classification of the *S* until the entire experiment was completed.

When the *S* arrived he was informed that he would be performing two different tasks during the hour. The *S* was first given a non-achievement-related activity. The task was to answer questions about advertisements which were paired together on the basis of product, size, color, etc. The questions included: "Which ad would you be more likely to notice?" "Which ad would you be more likely to read?" etc. The directions emphasized that there were no correct answers and that there was no time limit on any question. This is explicitly a non-achievement-related orientation. This task was presented first to insure that each *S* was completely familiar with the nature of the activity.

After performing this task for approximately 10 minutes, the *E* interrupted the *S* and started him working on an achievement-related activity. This was a digit-symbol substitution task. The task was introduced as a test which could be evaluated according to a standard of excellence. Thus the instructions were explicitly achievement related. The *S* was told to work on the task, but that he could move on, whenever he so desired, to perform the advertising task again. To create this relatively free behavioral situation the *E* said: "One of the main reasons that we have these two different tasks to do this hour is that some people prefer one activity to the other, and we know we get better norms when

*S*s are interested in what they are doing. So we'll start this task, but whenever you want you can switch back to the other activity and do more of the ads. Since I am collecting norms on both activities I don't care which one you do. Just do whichever you prefer."

Each *S* received a stack of 5 X 8 cards full of digits. To succeed at the achievement task the *S* was informed that he must complete all the substitutions on the card within the allotted time period. Two conditions were created: a Success condition and a Failure condition. In the Success condition the *S* was told the task was relatively easy ("70 per cent of the college students succeed at completing these cards within the time limit"), and he was allowed to complete each card. In the Failure condition the *S* was told the task was relatively difficult ("only 30 percent of the college students succeed at completing these cards within the time period"), and he was interrupted before completing the cards.

There were two types of 5 X 8 cards. One contained 60 digits, the other contained 88 digits. The cards had identical codes consisting of the digits 1-6 and the symbols +, -, =, □, >, 0. *S*s in the Success condition received the 60-digit cards; *S*s in the Failure condition received the 88-digit cards. *S*s in the Failure condition were interrupted at that point which corresponded to the point of completion of a card for *S*s in the Success condition. Thus they were interrupted after completing about 60 substitutions, or 68% of the card. To keep *S*s from becoming suspicious the exact place of interruption was varied.

At the time of interruption the *E* pressed a stopwatch and said to *S*s in the Failure condition: "Time is up on that one." Feedback in the Success condition was: "You got that one." The *S*s then selected another 5 X 8 card or informed the *E* that they wanted to switch back to the advertising task.

Seven cards differing with respect to the sequence of digits were used. Cards were arranged so that each card was repeated every eighth trial. No *S* indicated any recognition of repeated cards.

Two dependent variables were employed to measure strength of motivation: persistence of behavior, i.e., number of trials at the achievement-related task before switching to the alternative activity; and level of performance, i.e., the time required to complete 60 digit-symbol substitutions.

When the *S* chose to resume the advertising task, but before he was allowed to do so, he was given a booklet which contained five different series of tasks, and was asked to choose one problem in each series which he would later attempt to complete. Each task consisted of ten similar problems which varied in the level of difficulty according to the length of the problem, e.g., "Name 1, 2, . . . or 10 cities which start with the letter 'C.'" The instructions specified that the *S* must complete the entire problem within one minute to gain any credit, and that the more difficult the problem the more credit was given for its completion. First the *S* made all five choices. Approximately 15 seconds were allowed for each choice. Then he was allowed to work on his five selections. The tasks were: unscrambling words to make a sentence, arithmetic problems, naming cities, making words out of letters, and counting backwards. The selections were used to determine each *S*'s risk-preference. The risk-preference task was included to provide a direct basis for integration of the present study with earlier, related studies which have demonstrated that *S*s in whom $M_S > M_{AF}$ show greater preference for tasks of intermediate difficulty than *S*s in whom $M_{AF} > M_S$.

RESULTS

Level of Performance

Table 2 shows the level of performance (mean time to complete 60 digit-symbol substitutions) on trial 1 and trial 2.

Examination of the level of performance on trial 1 by *S*s in the Success and Failure conditions provides a basis for determining whether the strength of resultant achievement motivation was initially equal in the two conditions. The mean difference between the level of performance in the Success and Failure conditions for *S*s in whom $M_S > M_{AF}$ is .83 seconds ($t = .81, df = 31, p < .60$). Among *S*s in whom $M_{AF} > M_S$, the mean difference in level of performance between *S*s in the Success and Failure conditions is .35 seconds ($t = .29, df = 24, p < .70$). Thus there is no significant difference in the level of performance on the first trial between groups with comparable motive scores.

An analysis of variance of the difference in level of performance on trial 1 minus trial 2 indicates that there is a significant interaction, $F(1,55) = 9.89$, $p < .01$, between motive classification and the experimental conditions. Further analysis reveals when $M_S > M_{AF}$ the level of performance following failure is

TABLE 2

Time (in Seconds) to Complete 60 Digit-Symbol Substitutions on Trial 1 and Trial 2

Condition		Motive classification			
		$M_S > M_{AF}$		$M_{AF} > M_S$	
		Trial 1	Trial 2	Trial 1	Trial 2
	N	19	19	12	12
Success	*M*	60.10	66.63	60.58	62.75
	SD	7.80	10.20	10.20	11.83
	N	14[a]	14[a]	14	14
Failure	*M*	60.93	64.33	60.93	70.43
	SD	9.06	8.45	8.83	13.0

[a]Level of performance for one *S* could not be accurately evaluated.

greater than the level of performance following success, although the difference is not statistically significant ($t = 1.41, df = 31, p < .20$). When $M_{AF} > M_S$, the level of performance is significantly greater following success than following failure ($t = 2.19, df = 24, p < .05$).

Persistence at the Achievement Task

Because some *S*s did not voluntarily quit the achievement task, nonparametric statistics were used for the analysis of persistence of behavior. Among *S*s in whom $M_S > M_{AF}$, the median number of trials (cards attempted) at the achievement task was 11.5. Eleven of these 34 *S*s (32%) persisted to the maximum number of trials which time allowed (20) and had to be interrupted by the *E*. The data indicates that *S*s in whom $M_S > M_{AF}$ persist longer following continual failure than following continual success, although this difference is not statistically significant ($p < .14$, two-tailed, Fisher Exact Test). Further analysis, which considers only *S*s scoring in the upper half of this selected sample on resultant achievement motivation ($N = 17$), shows that persistence is significantly greater ($p < .02$, two-tailed, Fisher Exact Test) following continual failure than following continual success.

Among *S*s in whom $M_{AF} > M_S$, the median number of trials attempted was 12.5. Twelve of the 26 *S*s (46%) persisted to the maximum number of trials. The difference in persistence between the two conditions for *S*s in whom $M_{AF} > M_S$ does not approach statistical significance ($p < .50$, Fisher Exact Test).

Additional analyses were performed on only those *S*s ($N = 37$) who voluntarily quit the achievement task. An analysis of variance reveals that among these *S*s there is a significant interaction, $F(1, 33) = 9.93$, $p < .01$, between motive classification and the experimental condition. *S*s in whom $M_S > M_{AF}$ persist significantly longer following continual failure than following continual success ($t = 3.53, df = 21, p < .01$), while *S*s in whom $M_{AF} > M_S$ persist longer following success than following failure, although this difference is not statistically significant ($t = 1.16, df = 12, p < .30$).

Risk Preference

Problems on the risk-preference task were ranked from 1-10 according to level of difficulty, and each *S* was given a "difficulty of choice" score by summing the difficulty levels of his five choices. There was no significant difference in difficulty level of choice between *S*s in the Success and Failure conditions ($\chi^2 = .26, df = 1, p < .50$). Therefore choices of all *S*s on a particular task were combined into a single distribution, and the median choice for each task was determined.

Deviation of *S*s' choices about the median were compared by computing each *S*'s absolute deviation from the median on a given task, and adding his deviations for the five tasks. In a prior study (Atkinson & Litwin, 1960) the total deviation score was computed by summing the choice-median/average deviation on each task. However, preliminary analysis showed that this conventional index correlated .97 ($N = 14$) with the more economical one employed in the present analysis. Comparing total deviation scores with a Mann-Whitney U test indicates that *S*s high in resultant achievement motivation exhibit smaller deviations from the median choice (greater preference for tasks of intermediate difficulty) than *S*s low in resultant achievement motivation ($z = 1.97, p < .05$).

DISCUSSION

The results cast doubt on the adequacy of the model for achievement-oriented behavior presented by Atkinson in 1957. That model, which does not include an inertial component, led to the prediction of no difference in persistence or level of performance following success when the initial P_s is .70 or failure when the initial P_s is .30. On the other hand, while the results for level of performance and persistence of behavior do not reach statistical significance in all comparisons, the directions of the results strongly support Model 2. Because of the inclusion of a component to represent persisting resultant tendencies, that model predicted differential reactions to failure for *S*s high or low in resultant achievement motivation.

An interesting aspect of the data was that over 38% of the *S*s persisted twenty trials (1,200 substitutions) at the digit-symbol task. Orne (1962) dramatically demonstrated that *S*s will perform boring tasks for a great length of time if they feel that this is expected of them. It may be that in this experiment the individuals who persisted 20 trials perceived that the *E* was more interested in performance at the substitution task, and a "good" *S* was one who continued at the activity in progress. If this type of compliance is unrelated to motive group or success or failure experiences, then a constant score is added to all conditions. Further analysis in this study demonstrated that differences in persistence of behavior were being masked by this group.

Further Theoretical Implications

The primary objective of this study was to investigate the motivational consequences of nonattainment of a goal (failure). However, the theoretical developments may advance the conceptualization of the effects of goal attainment (success). Atkinson and Cartwright specify that success reduces the tendency that has been aroused by the immediate stimulus situation. If it is assumed that success also reduces the strength of persisting tendencies, then the models which include an inertial component among the determinants of behavior could incorporate data from studies by Lissner (1933), Mahler (1933), and Henle (1944) which demonstrate that there is a decrease in the tendency to resume previously interrupted activities following the attainment of other, related goals. That is, goal attainment has substitute value.

Prior studies also have shown that goal attainment may instigate further behavior (Child & Whiting, 1950; Weiner, 1965b). Further, Murray (1954), in a clinical setting, found that the frequency of hostile responses directed toward significant authority figures increases following the expression of aggressive responses which are directed toward other, less significant authority figures. The apparent contradiction between studies showing goal attainment may have substitutive or instigating properties parallels the apparently contradictory data which indicates that level of performance may increase or decrease following nonattainment of a goal. This suggests that the enhancing or decremental effect of goal attainment also may be related to the relative strength of the approach and avoidance tendencies to strive for the goal.

In this paper the conception of persisting motivation has been applied specifically within the context of achievement-related behavior. Additional data suggests that this concept is relevant to other domains of behavior. In animal studies Amsel (1958) has found that nonattainment of an expected goal leads to a subsequent increase in response speed; Berkowitz (1964), working in the area of aggression, recently argued that "preventing the completion of the activated sequence heightens the arousal state and this increases the strength of any subsequent aggressive responses"; and Hartup (1963), summarizing the literature on dependency, concluded that dependency behavior increases as a result of previously nonreinforced trials. There could be heuristic value in viewing these findings within the theoretical framework presented in this paper.

18

ROLE OF SUCCESS AND FAILURE IN THE LEARNING OF EASY AND COMPLEX TASKS[1]

Bernard Weiner[2]

In a series of apparently conclusive studies, Spence and his colleagues (Spence, Farber, & McFann, 1956; Spence, Taylor, & Ketchel, 1956; Taylor & Chapman, 1955) demonstrated that *S*s high in anxiety (drive) perform better than *S*s low in anxiety on easy paired-associates tasks. Conversely, on difficult paired-associates tasks, highly anxious *S*s perform worse than *S*s low in anxiety. These data have been cited by Spence (1958) to support the Hull-Spence theoretical position, which conceives behavior to be a function of Drive X Habit.

In these verbal learning studies the preexperimental associations between the stimulus-response members in the list and the degree of intralist response competition determined the difficulty of task. In the easy list, the responses to be associated with the stimuli were high in the *S*'s response hierarchy when he started the task, and intralist competition was minimal. In the difficult list, the responses to be associated with the stimuli initially were relatively low in the *S*'s response hierarchy, while response associates high in his hierarchy were included as members of other S-R pairs. Further, intralist response competition was maximized by including synonymous stimulus words in the list. The generalization between these stimuli gave rise to associations between nonpaired S-R units.

Spence (1958) reasons that during the learning of the easy list the probability of the correct response being elicited by a stimulus is very high, while the

[1] Reprinted and abridged by permission of the author and the American Psychological Association from the *Journal of Personality and Social Psychology*, 1966, 3, 339–343.

[2] The research was supported by Grant 4945-0010-4909-61 from the Graduate School of the University of Minnesota. The author wishes to thank Sherrie Lindborg, Ann Lyon, and Robert Rosenbaum for their aid in conducting this study, and J. David Birch and James J. Jenkins for their suggestions.

probability of a stimulus eliciting an incorrect response is low. The multiplicative relation between drive and habit therefore specifies that heightened drive will facilitate performance. On the other hand, on the difficult task many incorrect responses are associated with the stimuli. Increasing the level of drive is expected to increase the amount of response competition, and cause decrements in the level of performance. Spence employs this analysis to argue that the data from the paired-associates studies confirm predictions derived from the Drive × Habit conception.

The theoretical position of Spence et al. ignores the cognitive and affective processes which occur as the subject attempts to learn these easy and difficult lists. It is likely that the rapid learning of the easy list indicates to the *S* that he is succeeding. That is, on the basis of the frequent number of correct responses he may evaluate his performance positively. On the difficult list the *S* may perceive his performance as a failure. That is, because of the many incorrect responses he may evaluate his performance negatively. Previous studies (Child & Whiting, 1950; Katchmar, Ross, & Andrews, 1958; Lucas, 1952; Mandler & Sarason, 1952; Sarason, 1957; Weiner, 1965a) have shown that highly anxious *S*s exhibit relative increments in level of performance following success. Conversely, failure depresses the subsequent performance of these *S*s. For *S*s low in anxiety, failure has been demonstrated to enhance subsequent performance, while success produces later performance decrements. Thus the findings of Spence et al. can be included among the research which has demonstrated interactions between individual differences in level of anxiety and the effects of success and failure on subsequent performance.

This experiment was undertaken to determine whether the findings from the paired-associates studies cited above are really to be attributed to the differential reactions which high- and low-anxious individuals exhibit to success and failure experiences. To ascertain this, the inherent relation between the easy task-success experience and difficult task-failure experience was experimentally severed. *S*s learning an easy list of paired associates were told that they were performing poorly relative to others. In this manner the easy task was paired with a failure experience. *S*s learning a difficult paired-associates task were told that they were doing well relative to others, thus pairing the difficult task with a success experience. If the differential reactions to success and failure experiences are the essential determinants of behavior in this situation, then on the easy task highly anxious *S*s experiencing failure should perform *worse* than *S*s low in anxiety experiencing failure. On the difficult task, highly anxious *S*s experiencing success should perform *better* than *S*s low in anxiety experiencing success. The experimental design consequently provides a definitive test of the alternative explanation of the Spence et al. data.

METHOD

One hundred and ninety-five male students enrolled in the introductory psychology course at the University of Minnesota were given a group administration of a Thematic Apperception Test (TAT) Picture Series 2, 48, 1, 7, 11, and 24 (Atkinson, 1958a) and the Mandler-Sarason Test Anxiety Questionnaire (TAQ; Mandler & Sarason, 1952). The TAT was scored for n Achievement according to the method of content analysis described in Atkinson (1958a). The correlation between the TAT and TAQ was $r = -.07$. Following the current procedure (Atkinson, 1964) scores on the two measures were converted into Z scores and score on the TAQ was subtracted from score on the TAT, yielding an index of resultant (approach-avoidance) achievement motivation. *S*s scoring in the upper and lower 25% of this combined distribution were selected for the experiment. Of the 98 *S*s selected to appear for the second experimental hour, 62 were tested.

Procedure

The experimental procedure followed as closely as possible that described in Spence, Farber, and McFann (1956). *S*s had six trials of practice on a 15-unit paired-associates list of nouns. The conditions of administration of the practice list were relaxed (McClelland, Atkinson, Clark, & Lowell, 1953) to minimize subjective success or failure at that task. *S*s were told that the purpose of the practice trials was to familiarize them with the apparatus and procedure. *S*s with 0 or more than 50 correct anticipations during the practice list were eliminated from the data analysis. Only one *S* had to be eliminated because of his performance on the practice list.

Following the practice trials the *E* said:

> Starting on this trial the practice is over, and your performance does count. From now on your performance will be assessed and compared to the performance of other college students. We have found that people differ in their ability to learn this list, and that students who do well at this are able to perform well at a variety of other tasks. So your performance will be a good indicator of your general ability.
>
> Many students wonder how well they are doing on the list. So for your own information I will stop the machine every few trials and tell you how many mistakes (correct answers) you made and how you are doing as compared to other college students.

Thus the conditions of test administration corresponded to those described as achievement oriented (McClelland et al., 1953). The *S*s then attempted to learn an easy or difficult paired-associates list of adjectives (Spence, Taylor, & Ketchel, 1956).

Success and failure were manipulated by employing false norms. In the easy list-failure condition the task was introduced as very easy. *S*s were told that,

> The average college student learned this list within four trials, so you should have very little difficulty mastering it.

Following every even-numbered trial *S*s were told how many incorrect responses (x) they actually made, and that,

> Most college students at this point are making only $1/2\,x$ mistakes.

This was done as efficiently as possible to minimize the time interval between trials. In the difficult list-success condition the task was introduced as very difficult. The *S*s were told that the average college student required 30 trials to learn the list. On every third trial starting with Trial 2 the *S*s received feedback on how many correct responses (x') they made. *S*s also were told that,

> Most college students at this point are making only $1/2\,x'$ correct responses.

In cases where odd numbers of correct or incorrect responses were made, the *E* rounded the reported norms downward. When the number of errors was increased between trials, the reported norm was the number given on the previous trial. The lists were presented at a 2:2 rate on a Hull-type memory drum. The criterion was two successive trials without an error.

RESULTS

In Figure 1 the mean percentage of correct anticipations for the four experimental groups are plotted for the first 12 trials. Inspection of Figure 1 reveals that on the easy list where failure was experienced *S*s high in resultant achievement motivation performed better than *S*s low on this measure. On the difficult list where success was experienced, *S*s low in resultant achievement motivation performed better than *S*s high on this measure. An analysis of variance of the number of trials required to reach criterion indicates that there is a significant interaction, $F = 8.06$, $df = 1/57$, $p < .01$, between motive groups and experimental conditions. Further analysis reveals that the difference in performance between the groups who experience failure at the easy task is significant, $t = 2.57$, $df = 26$, $p < .02$. Among *S*s who experience success at the

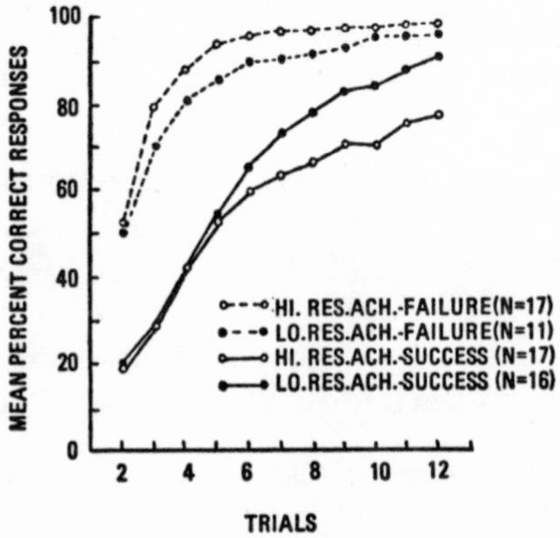

FIG. 1. Percentage of correct responses as a function of resultant achievement motivation and failure at an easy task or success at a difficult task.

TABLE 1

Mean Number of Trials to Criterion among Subjects Scoring in the Upper and Lower 25 Percentile on the TAQ

Anxiety	Easy list (failure)			Difficulty list (success)		
	N	*M*	*SD*	*N*	*M*	*SD*
High	9	9.55	3.78	12	14.83	6.57
Low	12	7.08	1.85	10	20.10	7.35

difficult task, the difference in performance between the two motive groups also approaches statistical significance, $t = 2.02$, $df = 31$, $p < .10$.

In the studies conducted by Spence et al. the Manifest Anxiety (*MA*) scale was used to classify individuals into motivational groups. Accordingly, in this study *S*s were classified as high or low in anxiety.

Of the 61 *S*s tested 43 were in the upper or lower 25% of the total distribution on the TAQ. Table 1 shows the mean number of trials to reach criterion for these four experimental groups. The pattern of results is identical to that disclosed when resultant achievement motivation was employed to classify *S*s into motive groups. An analysis of variance indicates that there is a significant interaction, $F = 5.00$, $df = 1/39$, $p < .05$, between level of anxiety and the experimental conditions. Further analysis reveals that among *S*s who experienced success while learning the difficult list, those classified as highly anxious performed better, $t = 1.79$, $df = 20$, $p < .10$, than *S*s low in anxiety. On the easy task in which failure was experienced, *S*s high in anxiety performed worse, $t = 1.90$, $df = 19$, $p < .10$, than *S*s low in anxiety.

DISCUSSION

These results strongly suggest that it is erroneous to cite prior research in this area as validating evidence for drive theory. The important determinants of behavior in this situation are the cognitive and motivational consequences resulting from success or failure at the task, rather than the individual's drive level interacting with the structure of the task per se.

In defense of drive theory it might be argued that in this study the *MA* scale was not used to assess individual differences in level of drive. However, the *MA* scale and TAQ are significantly related; the reported correlations range from .32 (Alpert & Haber, 1960) to .53 (Raphelson, 1957). Further, the drive mechanism has been hypothesized to be an internal emotional response (Spence, 1958), and the TAQ is a better predictor of changes in skin conductance in test situations than is the *MA* scale (Raphelson, 1957). Spence (1964) also has recently emphasized the necessity of environmental determinants in the arousal of anxiety; the TAQ is a measure of the tendency to respond with anxiety in test situations. It therefore must be concluded that the TAQ is an adequate measure of anxiety (drive).

The results do provide further validity for a model proposed by Weiner (1965a) which elaborates ideas originally formulated by Atkinson (1957) and recently modified by Atkinson and Cartwright (1964) (see also Atkinson & Birch, 1970; Chapter 15). They suggest that previously aroused but unsatisfied motivation persists following nonattainment of a goal. To incorporate persisting motivational tendencies into Atkinson's earlier theory of achievement motivation, Atkinson and Cartwright postulate that the tendency to undertake an achievement-related task is determined by the magnitude of the tendencies to approach or avoid that task, plus the magnitude of the previously aroused and persisting motivation.

If the ideas of Atkinson and Cartwright are expanded to include the notion that both the tendency to approach success and the tendency to avoid failure persist following nonattainment of a goal (Weiner, 1965a), then the theory specifies that following failure differential reactions will be exhibited by individuals high ($M_S > M_{AF}$) or low ($M_{AF} > M_S$) in resultant achievement motivation. When $M_S > M_{AF}$, the resultant achievement-oriented tendency is positive; the resultant persisting motivation following nonattainment of a goal therefore is positive. Consequently, these individuals should exhibit increments in level of performance following failure. When $M_{AF} > M_S$, the resultant achievement-oriented tendency is negative; the resultant persisting motivation following nonattainment of a goal is therefore inhibitory. These individuals should exhibit decrements in level of performance following failure. This conception accounts for the data in this study indicating that following failure individuals in whom $M_{AF} > M_S$ perform worse than individuals in whom $M_S > M_{AF}$.

The theory presented by Atkinson and Cartwright focuses upon the consequences of nonattainment of a goal, while the effects of goal attainment on subsequent performance are not stressed. If it were postulated that success reduces the magnitude of the persisting goal-oriented tendencies, then the model could incorporate data indicating that goal attainment has substitute value (Henle, 1944; Lissner, 1933; Mahler, 1933). Yet this conception is insufficient, for success has instigative as well as substitutive properties. As a general hypothesis, it is suggested that following goal attainment there is a decrement in the magnitude of both the persisting tendency to approach success and the persisting tendency to avoid threat of failure. The diminution in the strength of these tendencies is proportionate to the strength of motivation sustaining the original activity. When $M_S > M_{AF}$, the decrement in the magnitude of the persisting approach motivation is greater than the reduction in the magnitude of the persisting avoidance motivation. Consequently, these individuals should exhibit decrements in level of performance following success. When $M_{AF} > M_S$, the decrement in the strength of the persisting avoidance tendency is greater than the reduction in the strength of the persisting approach tendency. These individuals should exhibit increments in level of performance following success. This conception accounts for the differential reactions which subjects high or low in resultant achievement motivation exhibit following success experiences.

These ideas have been used effectively to explain paradoxical findings in the areas of substitution and psychotherapy (Weiner, 1965b), and may prove helpful in reconciling other seemingly contradictory data. For example, aggressive fantasy goal attainment sometimes has cathartic value and reduces subsequent aggressive behavior (Berkowitz, 1964), and at times leads to modeling behavior and a subsequent increase in aggressiveness (Bandura & Walters, 1963). These opposite findings may be due to differences in the motivational characteristics of the samples tested. Given overtly aggressive children, as might be found in the lower class, it is hypothesized that fantasy goal attainment will have cathartic value, inasmuch as the magnitude of the approach tendency is greater than the magnitude of the avoidance tendency. On the other hand, given a sample in whom aggressive responses are inhibited, as might be found in middle-class children, fantasy goal attainment would be expected to result in a subsequent increment in the tendency to act aggressively. In that sample the magnitude of the avoidance tendency is greater than the magnitude of the approach tendency. Similarly, if an aggressive action is thwarted because of fear of retaliation, lower-class children would be expected to exhibit subsequent increments in overt aggression, while middle-class children should exhibit subsequent decrements in aggressive expression. That is, there would be an interaction between the effects of attainment and nonattainment of a goal and the strength of the tendencies to approach and avoid the goal object.

PART V
MOTIVATION AND ACHIEVEMENT

The program of research on achievement motivation and behavior that began in the late 1940s has always encouraged an integration of our understanding of the determinants of aspiration and action in well-controlled experiments and the analogous life situations to which the conception of human motivation for achievement should apply. In the present volume, and explicitly in this concluding section, we draw on the insights from 25 years of empirical study to present a conception of how motivation influences the achievement of an individual both in some immediate critical test of his competence and cumulatively over a period of years in a lifetime.

The two final chapters provide summaries of what we think we have learned and guiding ideas for future study. We have explored enough to feel reasonably confident that there are three major sources of an individual's motivation for achievement: the pattern or hierarchy of motives he brings to a situation (the basic personality); the beliefs he holds (with varying degrees of certainty) that his action will have particular kinds of immediate and/or distant future consequences which constitute either inducements to act or resistance to be overcome; and the persistent carry-over from recent events of either unsatisfied motivation to achieve or unresolved resistance to achievement-oriented activity. The complexity of this conception of the determinants of motivation and behavioral effects, which has been presented in Chapters 7, 11, and 15 of this volume, credibly represents the multiplicity of interacting factors which account for individuality in achieving.

In Chapter 19, which deals with career striving, the various components that have been identified in experimental analysis of motivation are related to striving in pursuit of long-term goals. The concept of *contingent career path* is used to integrate the analysis of an individual's motivation with that of the functional significance of career striving in a society. Here is a conceptual bridge between our work and the continued sociological analysis of education and occupational attainment (see, e.g., Blau & Duncan, 1967; Rosen, Crockett, & Nunn, 1969; Sewell, Haller, & Ohlendorf, 1970; Spaeth, 1970; Sewell, 1971; Hauser, 1971; Wolfe, 1971; Duncan, Featherman, & Duncan, 1972; Crockett & Schulman, 1973). This chapter, drawing on all of the components of motivation treated earlier in the book, is a further expression of our earlier-stated hope of drawing psychological and sociological conceptions together at their point of contact, viz., in the conceptual analysis of the behavior of persons in particular concrete situations (Atkinson, 1958b, p. 616).

In the concluding chapter, two critically important issues are faced: the question of what is being measured by the so-called ability test; and the distinction between achievement in the short run (a critical test) and *cumulative achievement* (productivity over a span of years in some endeavor).

We are now sufficiently well along in the psychology of human motivation to call into question the simplistic interpretations of the mental test movement, and to advance a credible hypothesis concerning how ability and motivation jointly influence the level of intellective performance that has traditionally been called a test of intelligence or of ability, and also the long-term performance here called cumulative achievement. We urge, in doing this, a reappraisal of the underlying assumptions of traditional psychometrics within social psychology, in relation to which the former represents a technology needing a firmer theoretical foundation.

As an expression of our continued interest in methodological innovation, and also as a reminder that in any study of motivation not only one or two simple hypotheses but a whole theory of motivation and behavior is put to the test, we append two programs for computer simulation of motivational problems in terms of the theory that is explicitly stated in this volume and in *Dynamics of Action* (Atkinson & Birch, 1970).

19

MOTIVATION AND CAREER STRIVING[1]

Joel O. Raynor[2]

In this paper I would like to focus attention on the role that a conceptual analysis of career striving can play in attempts to integrate two of the dominant themes of this volume–the determinants of strength of tendency (or, in the newer language of the dynamics of action, of strength of instigating force) to act in an achievement-oriented situation, and the relationship between strength of tendency and performance–in trying to predict an individual's life accomplishments. To do so we must first recognize that "achievement" in a person's life can be meaningfully viewed as a process over time in which a whole series of interrelated activities and their consequences combine to produce a judgment, either by the person or by others, concerning accomplishment in life. Striving for "success in life" is the most general expression of achievement imagery (see McClelland et al., 1953, 1958). My concern here focuses on the motivational determinants of pursuit of long-term goals in "career paths." Such long-term striving guides the selection of immediate achievement-related activity and provides a bench mark for evaluation of achievement over time. It arouses tremendous sources of motivation for some individuals and involves potent forms of "success" and "failure."

The distinction between immediate performance and cumulative achievement is first made conceptually by Atkinson (see Chapter 20) and represents recognition that behavior in an interrelated series of activities now deserves

[1] This paper was written while the author was supported by NSF Grant GS-2863.

[2] I am indebted to John W. Atkinson and Elliot E. Entin for their critical comments on an earlier version of the chapter.

separate systematic treatment. My own thinking about this problem first focused on how such an interrelated series influences the strength of motivation sustaining immediate activity (see Raynor, 1969, and Chapter 7). It then shifted toward consideration of the effects of continued success in a contingent path on the level of motivation at successive steps along different kinds of paths (opened, closed, increasing, decreasing, and constant probability: see Chapter 7). The present paper expands this initial analysis to consideration of a variety of sources of motivation that are aroused in the dominant kinds of paths in society—career paths—and how these components of motivation might combine to produce the total motivation of an individual at various stages along different kinds of career paths. However speculative this analysis may be at present, it will hopefully provide a framework for the concrete application to striving over an individual's lifetime of the analysis of the relationship between motivation and achievement put forward in the concluding chapter by Atkinson (see Chapter 20).

The present discussion will be placed within the context of an individual's striving to achieve career success through socially acceptable behavior in a particular culture into which he or she has been socialized. I will first speculate about the more general nature and functioning of societal career paths, and then about the more specific details of the cognitive structures I have termed contingent and noncontingent future orientation, which in this context constitute the individual's perception of and knowledge about the career paths of a society. While arguments along these lines now represent guiding hypotheses rather than empirical generalizations, the successful investigation of contingent and noncontingent paths in laboratory situations (e.g., see Chapter 10; also Chapter 7, for a review of more recent research) and the study of future orientation in academic settings (see Chapters 8 and 9; summarized in Chapter 7) suggests that the present analysis already has a firm empirical foundation. In any case, the assumptions and hypotheses put forward here have implications that are subject to verification or disproof through predictions they yield concerning immediate and/or cumulative achievement of individuals in pursuit of careers. Perhaps, also, they are subject to verification through the effects of attempts to change an individual's cognitive structuring or knowledge of a career by various training or intervention programs. My object is to stimulate research guided by systematic theory.

Two major arguments are to be presented. The first is that the nature of career activity is such that many (but not all) career paths provide a situation offering all of the incentives that have thus far been identified as sources of motivation for achievement-oriented activity, whether excitatory or inhibitory in action implications. Thus recent conceptual and empirical developments concerning competence (Chapter 4), future orientation (Part II), interpersonal competition (Chapters 6 and 13), fear of success (Chapter 6), fear of social rejection (Chapter 6), the relationship between motivation and performance efficiency (Part III), and the distinction between immediate and cumulative achievement (Chapter 20), all have a direct application to the analysis of career striving. There are two additional conceptually relevant phenomena that I will discuss in the context of career activity as potentially serious health-related consequences of motivation for a career. One of these is termed "compulsive career striving." Its symptoms are too much time spent and and effort expended in career-related activity. The other is termed "up-tight career striving." Its symptoms are a desire to do anything but engage in career-related activity, coupled with dread of career failure, but a refusal to give up the career path. These two phenomena are caused, respectively, by too much positive and negative motivation for a career. They are consequences of the interaction between an individual's basic personality dispositions (e.g., motives) and his cognitive structure (e.g., knowledge) that relates various activities to each other in a functional way that will be termed a "contingent career path."

The second argument put forward is that the nature of career striving as an interrelated series of activities engaged in repeatedly over time means that the concept of career has an important bearing on the issue of time spent in one kind of activity rather than another (see Atkinson and Birch, Chapter 15), now considered (along with efficiency of performance) as one of the critical determinants of cumulative achievement (see Atkinson, Chapter 20). Put simply, the stronger the motivation for a career, the greater the time spent in career-related activity, other things equal. This means that cumulative achievement should generally be greater for individuals in pursuit of a career than for those not so motivated in a particular society, and should be greater for individuals with a constellation of several positive motives that are engaged by multi-incentive contingent rather than noncontingent career paths. While "other things" are never equal, and the conceptual analysis provided here and in Chapters 15 and 20 is far from simple, the significance of "career" as a selective agent in behavior can no longer be neglected in the systematic study of achievement motivation. Put another way, the narrow focus of an individual in one area of competence to the exclusion of other pursuits that is continued over a long period of time so that interruption to do something else inevitably is followed by return to that or similar activity–which is the hallmark of striving along a career path–represents perhaps the most clear-cut prescription for cumulative success to emerge from the increasingly more complicated analysis of motivation and achievement that the data and conceptual schemes presented in this volume demand.

CONTINGENT FUTURE ORIENTATION AND CAREER STRIVING

The integrating link between theory of achievement motivation (see Chapters 2 and 7) and "career" as a motivational construct is provided by the concept of future orientation (see Part II). Careers are interrelated sets of skill-demanding activities that are engaged in by individuals over time. Extrinsic rewards such as money, power, prestige, security, public acclaim, approval of family and friends, to name a few of the obvious ones, have come to be dependent upon good performance (demonstrations of competence) in such areas of knowledge or skill. Thus pursuit of a career involves the acquisition of (*a*) special competence that goes beyond the "layman's" abilities in that area, and (*b*) eventually the rewards that such competence commands. "Career success" requires (at least) the successful demonstration of performance over a sufficiently long period of time in the same area of expertise to merit a favorable judgment concerning cumulative achievement.

An important distinction between career paths has to do with whether they involve contingent or noncontingent future orientation. Many areas define career success in terms of "promotions" or "advancements" to higher levels of opportunity for the display of competence, and the corresponding increase in extrinsic rewards that such increased competence demands. While Peter and Hull (1969) have put forward the "Peter Principle" humorously noting that "promotions" may not always lead to greater demonstrations of competence, they do involve the *opportunity* for such accomplishment. While advancement is often based on factors other than prior demonstrated merit, *the anticipation that eventual success in such a contingent career path involves movement to higher levels of knowledge, skill, or proficiency with its concomitant larger extrinsic rewards provides in my opinion the greatest single source of motivational impetus for career striving.* Ratings of status and/or prestige of a career should reflect the differential amounts of skill and extrinsic rewards generally perceived to be associated with different career paths.

Consideration of contingent career paths also requires taking note of the role of "gatekeepers" whose function is to evaluate an individual's performance in a contingent career path to determine whether it merits further advancements, continuation at the same level (of responsibility, monetary and other extrinsic remuneration), demotion to a lower level, or a decision to terminate pursuit of the career through loss of the opportunity to continue in that field or specialty. Under such circumstances, immediate performance in a career path bears on the crucial issue (for the individual pursuing the career) of *earning the opportunity to continue.*

In the present discussion I will assume a "strict" contingent path, where immediate success is known to guarantee the opportunity for subsequent career striving, and immediate failure is known to guarantee future career failure through loss of the opportunity to continue in that career path. This will allow a direct extension of previous theory and research on contingent future orientation to the analysis of career striving. It should be clear that I am not assuming that all individuals see themselves faced with contingent career paths, or that "objectively" all career paths involve contingent future orientation. Some individuals may see their career pursuit in noncontingent terms, in which case the arousal of motivation (but not necessarily time spent) in career-related activity should be the same as for a single, isolated activity. There are also a wide variety of what can be termed "partial contingent paths" involving various elements of contingent and noncontingent future orientation whose motivational significance probably lies somewhere between that of these two extremes[3] but whose consideration in a systematic program of research has just begun.[4] *Contingent future orientation represents a unique feature of career striving that is related to the functional role of careers in society.*

SOCIETAL SIGNIFICANCE OF CONTINGENT CAREER PATHS

Career striving is a general part of our society and, I suspect, of any ongoing social organization that has existed for any extended period of time. Careers offer inducements for individuals to acquire skills that have come to be viewed as "necessary," "valuable," and/or "desirable" in a particular culture. Since special competence is relatively rare in the general adult population and initially lacking in the younger members of a social system, inducements have evolved that are extrinsic to the particular nature or substance of the skill in question in order to attract and then to insure persistence in various sequences of activities that are needed in society. These inducements (or incentives) are most often offered so that the greater the difficulty and/or time spent in acquiring the skill, the greater the extrinsic rewards to be eventually obtained. *Contingent* career paths serve to insure that scarce resources and/or large amounts of common ones are reserved as incentives contingent upon competence rather than incompetence, to be obtained only through a series of prior activities and evaluations (gates) and delayed at least until the prerequisite skills have been acquired and "certified" by appropriate gatekeepers. The nature of this structural arrangement demands delay of gratification in the early stages of skill acquisition, simply because rewards are available in but small amounts early in the contingent path and in larger amounts for those who are successful in moving along the path to the later steps. This arrangement is probably due to the fact that in the early stages of a career path, while the individual is acquiring the prerequisite skills, his contribution to the "social welfare" is not particularly great, and is rewarded accordingly. A strict contingent path also insures nongratification concerning many extrinsic incentives (some of which can only be obtained by successful career pursuits) for all those individuals who do not

[3] In life, as in baseball, you often get a second and third chance before striking out–and you may or may not get another chance to bat in the same "ballgame" (career).

[4] Robert Jurusik, Howard Pearlson, Ira Rubin, Richard Sorrentino, and Kenneth Wegman have all pointed out to me the fact that contingent and noncontingent future orientations do not exhaust the possibilities for cognizing the future. Wegman has conducted the first investigation (unpublished data) on partial contingent paths to be guided by the general ideas included in this paper. Vroom's (1964) concept of positive and negative instrumentality represents a continuum from noncontingent to contingent future orientation without specifying the explicit functional relationships that would be represented by such partial contingent arrangements.

successfully pass the early hurdles of skill acquisition and evaluation. Legal sanctions (punishments) are available and are used on occasion to deny those individuals who fail to obtain appropriate certification the opportunity for subsequent activity in that area. The individual who is to function effectively in such a delayed-incentive system may have to acquire a particular combination of motivational and cognitive structure that will be discussed shortly.

The fact that later steps in a contingent career path offer much larger extrinsic rewards than do the early steps has two other (related) functional consequences. Once acquired, skills tend to be utilized to make up for the individual's (oftentimes) years of relative deprivation, that is, the long period characterized by attainment of only small extrinsic rewards during skill acquisition in a career area. It also becomes increasingly more difficult to change career paths once the initial steps of "apprenticeship" have been successfully negotiated. The individual would have to give up relatively large extrinsic rewards which are now dependent upon immediate rather than (as previously in the earlier stages) future success for another period of relative deprivation in the preliminary stages of another contingent career path. In this way society has evolved so as to insure that resources devoted to training the young for specialized areas of competence tend not to be wasted on those who will not subsequently use them.

My previous conception of contingent future orientation (see Chapter 7) failed to emphasize what I now see as the critical role of extrinsic motivation and gatekeepers in sustaining motivation for such a path. The list of potential extrinsic rewards for successful career striving presented earlier in this paper suggests that these may play the largest role in the arousal and maintenance of career motivation. One of the important questions for future research concerns the relative contribution of achievement-related versus extrinsic motivation to career striving. Also important and previously neglected is the motivational significance of knowing that gatekeepers will or will not in fact do their job of gatekeeping according to publicly pronounced rules. One can speculate whether *contingent* career paths with their hierarchy of prerequisites, gates, and gatekeepers would exist at all if not so structured by society and imposed and maintained by the current generation of gatekeepers replete with their procedures for examination, qualification, and certification. Would such cognitive structures and/or actual practices evolve in society or be imposed by individuals either already certified or seeking additional motivational impetus for their own striving?

It seems clear that the control exercised by gatekeepers in society over career striving comes from their ability to *deny the opportunity* for subsequent striving along the career path through enforcement of standards developed by professional societies and governmental agencies, backed by legal, moral, and ethical sanctions. What is not clear is whether such a system is an inevitable part of the exercise of competence in a social system. *There does not seem to be any reason inherent in most skill activity for prior success or failure to determine whether or not the individual has earned the opportunity to try again at the same or a similar task, even if it be of greater difficulty than the first.* For example, failing to jump over a high-bar set at 6 feet in no way relates to the opportunity for trying to jump over that bar at 7 feet, except if the person were injured in the initial attempt so as to now be physically unable to jump again. However, *the rules of a track meet that are imposed by the judges* might stipulate that failure at any particular height means loss of the opportunity to continue in the competition. In this sense all motivation aroused by *contingent* paths might be thought of as "extrinsic" to achievement-related concerns, that is, to evaluation by the individual of his performance by use of terms such as "success" and "failure" with reference to the difficulty defined by the demands of a task. On the other hand, it would seem that society comes to place a high positive value on competence over incompetence, particularly when the exercise of skill involves the welfare of others. Medical practice would seem, for example, to require the evolution of some system for the monitoring of skill, since most cultures place a premium on physical well-being, and therefore would seek protection from individuals who are incompetent or unqualified to heal. It would seem only to be a matter of time before the establishment and maintenance of a medical hierarchy that functions to a large extent as a strict contingent career path for skill acquisition. I don't know whether this represents an accurate picture of cross-cultural knowledge concerning the practice of medicine (or law), although it is an interesting question. The extent of the existence of contingent career paths in other areas of competence and in other social or cultural groups remains an important empirical question whose answer will determine the extent of application of the major arguments of the present paper. However, that contingent career paths do exist in ways functionally equivalent to that described in Chapter 7 is a basic assumption of all that follows (see Chapters 8 and 9).

Use of extrinsic incentives as inducements for striving in contingent career paths in a particular culture is coordinated (ideally) with the dominant child-rearing practices that function to develop capacities (e.g., motives) in individuals to appreciate and therefore to strive for those extrinsic incentives that are used as "payoffs" for adult career striving. This coordination is accomplished to a greater or lesser extent through parental and more general social emphasis on "cultural values," mediated by custom, tradition, and, in modern society, mass communication. The "collusion" between those involved in preparing the young for career striving in contingent paths and those who enforce the gates of contingent careers is not necessarily apparent to those involved, nor is it necessarily very great. The extent of lack of coordination becomes apparent when large proportions of the younger generation "drop out" of the traditional network of contingent career paths that define the majority of career striving in a culture, or in fact fail to enter these paths. Such a "generation gap" probably involves a disparity in perceptions of the value of rewards that are offered by "traditional" career striving. This represents a quite different "problem" from one where the young person "wants to" pursue a career in the sense that he can appreciate the extrinsic rewards offered by career success but is unable to sustain career striving because he is overwhelmed by chronic anxiety created in resistance (inhibitory or negation tendency) to skill-demanding activity or because he has failed to develop appropriate psychological mechanisms–here proposed as identification with a "career image" and the conceptualization of a long-term step-path relationship. The latter two points will be discussed in the sections that immediately follow.

SIGNIFICANCE OF CAREER STRIVING FOR SELF-EVALUATION AND EGO-IDENTITY

The potency of motivation for career striving is not just based on the coordination of extrinsic rewards with the development of the young's capacity to appreciate them or the obvious arousal of achievement motivation in career paths that will be discussed shortly. Erickson (1963) has pointed out the link between ego-identity and career striving. Information concerning career possibilities, their expected behaviors and rewards, forms an important basis for the decision and subsequent commitment to an "image" or sense of self that provides an answer to the question "Who am I?" The pursuit of a career, whether done consciously or evolving out of successful activity in one area of competence rather than another (see Chapters 4 and 7 for discussions of competence and confidence, respectively) is a major "decision" in a person's life. The concept of "career role" as defining these behaviors and expected outcomes can be seen as related to this process, for roles provide ready-made identities for individuals who pursue a particular career path. When roles are related by the individual to long-term career pursuits, these behavior-outcome possibilities take on motivational significance. They now become part of the behavioral options available to the individual as means to strive for career success. This analysis identifies the functional significance of the concept of role within a theory of an individual's motivation (see also Atkinson, 1958b). Adult "role playing" that is sustained by a desire for career success may be indistinguishable from other career-related activity. The career role in fact becomes part of the person's sense of self so that career striving represents a major means of obtaining self-esteem. The "career image" defines a person with respect to his place in society and becomes a source of motivation for present activities which constitute career striving because success in the career means attainment of the various goals that define who the person is. This represents a source of motivation that has previously been neglected in the study of achievement motivation, although Horner's (1968, and Chapters 6 and 13) concern with the issues of sex roles and motivation (what I would now call the careers of "masculinity" and "femininity") has served as an important stimulus for the development of some of the ideas presented here.[5] Her work, linking the earlier discussion of sex roles and the character of an individual's motivation, began to focus my attention on the more general issue treated here.

The conceptual analysis of the determinants of motivation for a career that involves a person's sense of self or identity may not need to appeal directly to terms like "ego-identity." Rather, these may represent but additional sources of motivation to be viewed in terms of expectations and values (the latter always partly a function of the motives of an individual) which constitute the instigating forces that move him in one direction rather than another in particular life situations. What is effective "extrinsic motivation" for one person may not be for another. This depends upon *the basic personality structure,* i.e., the dispositions established in early socialization–affiliation, power, autonomy, etc. Atkinson and Birch (1970, and Chapter 15) make this point when they say that the time spent in activities will reflect the individual's hierarchy of motives. *I am suggesting that the time spent in activities that comprise "career striving" may reflect a primary meaning of ego identity.* Alternatively, the addition of such instigating forces might need to be coordinated with consideration of another level of personality disposition, such as "self" or "self-awareness," which would function when aroused as a higher-order disposition that directs striving to fulfill the individual's dominant motives (as he sees them) and/or self-image in one direction (career path) rather than another. This might correspond to the functional significance of conscious awareness, "thinking about," or "paying attention to" something as an instigating force to do it (see Atkinson & Birch, 1970, and Chapter 15).

THE DEVELOPMENT OF STEP-PATH SCHEMA FOR CAREER ACTIVITY

Children from a very early age try out "career roles" such as doctor, nurse, policeman, fireman, etc., although realistic striving for one of them does not begin until after a whole series of "identities" have been explored and either some initial differentiating competence has been developed and/or appropriate extrinsic motivation is aroused for one career path rather than another. In various ways and to various extents, children and adolescents learn about the adult world of "work," "occupation," and "career." Parents, grandparents, relatives, friends, children's readers, folk images, teachers, and, in modern society particularly, mass media "heroes" are sources of information about and provide role models for the acquisition of the appropriate (and not so appropriate) behavior and expected consequences of career-related activity,

[5] Steiner's (1971) conception of the alcoholic in pursuit of a long-term career goal is an illustration of how the present conception would apply to other than achievement-related concerns.

where "appropriate" is seen in terms of the societal perspective of later adult striving in acceptable avenues of pursuit. However, the *structure* rather than the content of knowledge about career striving may be the most critical factor. The extent to which the young person learns to view or acquires knowledge about the long-term rather than the short-term consequences of these activities as offering the most valuable rewards for the demonstration of competence may determine whether later career striving can be sustained. My hypothesis is: *the acquisition of a general step-path schema which relates the achievement of large rewards to skills exhibited in a sequence of interrelated activities over a long period of time, and having a specific substantive focus constitutes the necessary prerequisite cognitive structure for successful striving in the career paths of a society*. Put differently, what must be learned are the "rules of the game" of career striving, be it noncontingent or contingent in nature, or some combination of both. The ability to "delay gratification" may be the behavioral indicator of this learned schema or knowledge about the anticipated size and ordering of rewards. The fact that motivation for the entire series of steps converges or is channelled into motivation for the immediate next step means that *immediate as well as future (delayed) gratification is possible,* the latter being contingent upon prior successful performance. It is this knowledge (or belief) that may provide the prerequisite psychological structure for career striving.

Combining the several arguments that have been developed, I propose that successful socialization for career striving means that the young person has acquired (*a*) a schema or plan in the form of knowledge about the activity-outcome structures of a noncontingent or contingent path that he subsequently anticipates as part of (or imposes on) career striving, and (*b*) standards of self-evaluation that are related to the achievement of long-term career goals as a means of obtaining self-esteem. Murray and Kluckholm (1953) refer to this general process as the development of "serial programs" for the attainment of distant future goals. The study of the acquisition of such schema should, if the above hypothesis is correct, provide a new direction for the understanding of the antecedents of religious and cultural differences that have been noted with regard to career planning and future orientation (see Morgan, 1964; Veroff & Feld, 1970), which are often correlated with the strength of the achievement motive (see McClelland, 1961).

MOTIVATIONAL SIGNIFICANCE OF CONTINGENT CAREER PATHS

I assume that career activity involves competition with standards of good performance inherent in an area of competence defined by the nature of the task or skill. I have already argued that contingent career paths regulate valuable rewards in a society, that certain conditioning experiences and cognitive learning in childhood and adolescence may prepare the person to strive for those large extrinsic incentives he has learned to appreciate that are dependent upon success in later steps of career paths, and that a person's sense of self (ego identity) and therefore his self-esteem are very often defined by his image of and commitment to one of the careers available in a particular culture. These taken together would be sufficient to make it likely that a certain proportion of individuals would strive to enter (through apprenticeship training) and then to pursue traditional career paths. They are also attracted to those careers that evolve in response to technological advance for which appropriate extrinsic incentives soon become available and therefore are perceived as contingent upon successful activity in that area. In addition, since contingent paths define the serial order of tasks in the career area so that opportunities for future successes depend upon more immediate success, pursuit of a career inevitably arouses "instrumental" achievement-related tendencies (see Chapter 7). These, in addition to intrinsic achievement motivation, contribute to the strength of expressed motivation in the immediate activity in a contingent career path. Also, since many more "slots" exist for individuals in the early as opposed to the later stages or steps of most contingent career paths, the attraction of many individuals by large extrinsic incentives means that interpersonal competition is normally an inherent aspect of career striving. It is often anticipated that some individuals will be forced out of any particular career path. Motivation aroused by interpersonal competition, either trying to gain the approval of others, or to avoid their social rejection, or perhaps aggressive competitive striving in order to beat the other person out of a slot that only one of two (or more) individuals can fill, should be a relevant aspect of motivation for a career. Thus I propose that components of immediate and instrumental achievement-related and extrinsic motivation whose particular strengths depend upon the individual's particular constellation or hierarchy of basic motives, the nature of the perceived career path, and the particular stage of career striving, combine to produce motivation for career striving.

Achievement-Related Motivation

The fact that the opportunity for subsequent achievement striving in a contingent career path is determined by prior successful performance means that instrumental achievement motivation is inevitably aroused in a contingent career path, even if the predominant proportion of motivation for career striving is extrinsic to achievement-related concerns (success and failure in the immediate task per se). Individuals primarily motivated to achieve success, or "success-oriented" ($M_S > M_{AF}$; see Atkinson & Feather, 1966, Ch. 20), may have a substantial amount of achievement motivation aroused for career striving that equals or exceeds the amount aroused by extrinsic incentives, depending upon whether their other (extrinsic) motives are strong or weak. Since the possibility of career success inevitably raises the possibility of career failure, individuals considered to be "failure-threatened" ($M_{AF} > M_S$; see Atkinson & Feather, 1966, Ch. 20) should have substantial amounts of inhibitory motivation aroused that constitute resistance which subtracts from other (extrinsic and achievement) positive motivation that initially attracts such an individual to a contingent career path. While success-oriented individuals should be attracted to contingent career paths because these tend to maximize interest and excitement to be obtained in the long run from skillful competitive activity while satisfying whatever extrinsic motives may be particularly strong, the failure-threatened individual should avoid, if possible, contingent career paths because of the penalty in terms of chronic anxiety that such an individual must pay for satisfying his extrinsic motives in such long-term *competitive* pursuits. In fact, the relative scarcity of "strict" contingent paths in any society, in comparison to situations where any success means the opportunity to continue while a failure just requires another try at success (one specific example of a "partial" contingent path), is most probably related to attempts to mitigate the strong aversive feelings that are aroused in failure-threatened individuals and to a lesser extent in other positively motivated individuals with some moderate strength of the motive to avoid failure. Although not as yet systematically investigated, it is likely that some partial contingent arrangements arouse positive but not negative instrumental achievement-related motivation, so that from the viewpoint of social functioning the best aspect of a contingent path is retained (the arousal of excitatory motivation in a delayed-incentive system) while eliminating the worst (the negative reaction of stress and anxiety in pursuit of long-term career goals).[6] Such partial contingent arrangements may take on several variants, such as allowing some number of failures before loss of the opportunity at each step in the path. There are several fairly common variations of the contingent-

[6] Until recently I have assumed that the strength of achievement-related motivation that is aroused in these so-called "partial contingent paths" would fall at some point intermediate between that aroused in a contingent as compared to a noncontingent path. Therefore it seemed likely that the use of situations in which some number of unsuccessful tries were anticipated as possibilities before failure would signal loss of the opportunity to continue, might offer a humane means of arousing positive, *but not inhibitory*, motivation to attain long-term future goals. However, Elliot Entin has pointed out to me that this conceptual analysis may be in error. He argues that if these situations merely raise an individual's subjective probability of success in each step along a path that otherwise is still seen in contingent terms, then application of theory as presented in Chapter 7 leads to the paradoxical prediction that such partial contingent paths as described above would arouse *more* rather than less achievement-related motivation in comparison to a contingent path of equivalent length (see Chapter 7, Figures 3 and 4). Consequently the failure-threatened individual would be *more inhibited* when he anticipated being allowed some number of tries before a failure meant loss of the opportunity to continue than when failure in the first try would have that implication. Entin and I may be able to evaluate this hypothesis when results of our research on "contingency management" arrangements in college teaching become available. Experimental analysis of this question using modifications of the research paradigms used by Raynor and Rubin (1971, and Chapter 10) and Entin and Raynor (1973) should be given high priority in light of the possibility that this much more commonly found arrangement might have motivational effects similar to those found previously for "strict" contingent paths.

noncontingent path distinction which are now being studied by several investigators.

Interpersonal Competition

Career striving provides a potent situational inducement for the arousal of the tendency to avoid success in women (see Horner, 1968, and Chapter 6), primarily because interpersonal competition in career activity of our culture is most often against men or masculine standards of performance and successful competition often takes on aggressive achievement-related overtones. The achievement-oriented "career woman" who is also high in fear of success should face a conflict between achievement of the long-term extrinsic and achievement-related incentives contingent upon career success on the one hand and the loss of her conception of "femininity" and fear of consequent social rejection by males due to her very success on the other. The relationship between sex-role, sex-identity, and career striving appears not to offer a simple explanation for the sex differences in results of research on achievement motivation (see Horner, Chapter 6). However, I believe that a more complete analysis of career-related role images and general cultural values concerning traditional "masculine" and "feminine" career paths will allow a greater understanding and identification of those situational determinants of the arousal of fear of success, as well as its antecedents in child-rearing practices. In addition, concepts like "masculinity" and "femininity" themselves can be conceptualized in terms of careers requiring the acquisition of specific role-related behaviors over time to an adequate level of competence. Such roles take on motivational significance when the individual "identifies" with one in answer to the question "Who am I?" An analysis of the individual's anticipation of the consequences of fulfilling one role rather than another (the "feminine" woman who is inhibited from aggressive competitive striving because this endangers her chances to find an acceptable spouse) in long-term pursuit of a career may provide the basis for integration of the concept of fear of success with notions of sex-role behavior and that of long-term career striving in the more traditional sense used in this paper.

The fear of social rejection in men (see Horner, Chapters 6 and 13) may be another source of inhibitory motivation that is aroused by anticipation of career failure. Fear of "being a loser" and a "social outcast" often are associated with the inability to "hack it" in the traditional area of career striving. The extent to which such motivation is aroused in achievement-related behavior is unclear and deserves future study. So does the possibility that fear of success is aroused in a very talented man who is also strong in n Affiliation. He might anticipate generating resentment in those he wishes to be friendly with by "winning too big" in career-related pursuits. This may inhibit his striving for success so as not to lose the opportunities to satisfy his affiliative concerns.

MOTIVATION IN INITIAL, INTERMEDIATE, AND LATE STAGES OF CAREER STRIVING

One of the implications of concepts such as open and closed paths, as well as increasing, decreasing, and constant probability paths (see Chapter 7), is that motivation along a path may change as a function of continued success because the individual's cognitive structure mediates a change in the instigating forces of the remaining steps in the path, a change that is independent of previous success per se. For example, the number of remaining steps to a final or ultimate career goal in a closed contingent path should influence the strength of motivation sustaining the immediate step faced by the individual at that stage in his career striving. Also, since extrinsic rewards are anticipated according to a delayed-incentive system in many contingent career paths, strength of extrinsic motivation should change as a function of (successful) movement from the early stages of skill acquisition to intermediate and late stages of career striving. The particular patterning of achievement-related and extrinsic incentives as anticipated by the individual at any step of a contingent path should therefore interact with his particular constellation of relevant motives to determine total aroused motivation for activity at that step.

Before considering some of these patterns of interaction, it is worth making some general points about the arousability of motivation as a function of the particular stage of striving. Particularly relevant is the difference between closed and open contingent career paths as they might influence the amount of total achievement-related motivation. Many careers are so structured that their hierarchy of advancement has a clearly defined final or upper plateau, while others are seen as essentially open-ended. (Of course, the individual's view of the path, rather than some objective description of it by an outside observer, is the important psychological variable.) If previous speculation is correct (see Chapter 7), then the same task in the preliminary stages of skill acquisition of a closed contingent path should arouse substantially more achievement-related motivation (whether positive or negative depends upon the relative strengths of achievement-related motives) than the same task in the intermediate and certainly the final stages of that closed career path, where the path essentially consists of a single, isolated activity (the last). In addition, preliminary attempts by Elliot Entin and myself to create open and closed contingent paths in a laboratory-type situation confirm the assumption through the results obtained that it is the *effective length* of a contingent path, rather than the objective count of the number of steps, that determines whether anticipation of some future step contributes motivation sustaining immediate activity. Since subjective probability of success along the path (now assumed a multiplicative function of the subjective probabilities of success at each step in the path) is presumed to determine whether a component tendency is aroused (total probabilities of less than .01 are now arbitrarily assumed not to contribute motivation sustaining immediate activity), and the individual's view of his own abilities (competence) should influence these subjective probabilities, determination of the momentary motivation for achievement-related striving in a contingent path must consider: (*a*) the particular stage along the path, (*b*) the subjective probabilities at each step along the path, (*c*) the total subjective probability along the path to the step whose motivational significance is in question, (*d*) the individual's competence judgments in this area (which may influence P_s directly or represent an independent factor–probably the former), and (*e*) individual differences in achievement-related motives.

Consideration of an extrinsic delayed-incentive system in conjunction with a closed achievement-related path suggests that there are two independent gradients of arousability of motivation that operate in opposite directions as the individual moves successfully from early to middle to late stages (which can be arbitrarily represented by dividing the number of steps of a closed contingent path into thirds). Achievement-related motivation should decrease while extrinsic motivation should increase as a function of continued success, given no change in the cognitive structuring (subjective probabilities) along the path. Thus simple predictions of an increase or decrease in total motivation are not possible (they would also have to take into account any changes in cognitive structures as a function of success, and new information that might change the perceived value of the path) without consideration of the individual's entire pattern of relevant motives (those for which appropriate incentives are perceived in the career path situation) to determine the relative strengths of achievement-related and extrinsic motivation as well as the final strength of motivation for career striving at that stage in the path.

We can identify particular "personality types" in an attempt to apply these principles to concrete instances. The success-oriented individual who is relatively weak in other relevant extrinsic motives should have total motivation that is predominantly achievement-related so that predictions based only on the arousal of achievement motivation should apply, while success-oriented individuals who are strong in these other motives should have substantial amounts of both kinds of motivation. For this latter individual the relative amounts of achievement-related and extrinsic motivation will vary as a function of the stage of career striving in a closed contingent path, with achievement-related motivation proportionately greater in the early stages and extrinsic motivation proportionately greater in the later stages. The total amount of motivation at any stage for this individual may or may not be the same, depending upon the specific strengths of the two and the slope of their respective gradients, which can be determined according to the assumptions and equations presented in Chapter 7.

It is worthwhile to contrast the above predictions with those for motivation in an open contingent career path. Here achievement-related motivation should not decrease as a function of continued success, because additional possibilities for continued career-related striving become apparent as the individual moves along the career path. We would then expect that total motivation will reflect the predicted increase in extrinsic motivation that should occur as in the closed contingent path, so that there would be a net rise in motivation for career striving from early to middle to later steps (comparable stages of the closed contingent path). However, our experience in inducing open and closed paths suggests that it is necessary to take seriously the implication of theory that, other things equal, the effective length of a path will be greater for paths having high than low subjective probability of success at each step along the path (see Chapter 7). This means that what may appear to the experimenter to be a closed path of 20 steps may in fact really represent an open path of effective length 10, since subjective probabilities of eventual success at the last 10 steps are so low as seen from the first step that they do not contribute motivation sustaining immediate activity in the initial stages of striving. As the individual continues to succeed, both subjective probabilities along the path and total subjective probabilities of reaching distant steps will increase, thus contributing components of motivation aroused by those additional steps that initially failed to influence immediate striving. A dynamic process takes place over time that continually alters the instigating force properties of a particular contingent path depending upon perceived difficulty along the entire path.

When we consider the failure-threatened individual in closed and open contingent paths who is either high or low in extrinsic motivation, predictions will depend largely upon the theoretical conception of the fate of resistance over time (see Atkinson and Birch, Chapter 15). However, it seems apparent that the failure-threatened person also strong in relevant extrinsic motives has a decided advantage over the comparable person weak in extrinsic motives in terms of being able to sustain career striving, *but at a price of chronic anxiety and tension that should be great in contingent career paths,* particularly if they are perceived as open in nature.

SELECTIVE FUNCTION OF CAREER STRIVING

Both contingent and noncontingent career paths organize an interrelated series of activities over time in terms of larger units of activities which, if interrupted by some other activity, have a higher likelihood of being resumed than a comparable activity not part of a path. This means that both of these cognitive arrangements have an important bearing on time spent in activity during a person's lifetime. Here the distinction between noncontingent and one-step or single activity paths should be important. A single activity is engaged in once, for whatever period of time, but motivation for resumption of that activity will not be influenced by its functional relationship to other activity as in a noncontingent path, where a particular activity will be resumed (other things equal) simply because it is part of a step-path structure leading to those extrinsic (delayed) incentives of a career path. While motivation (both achievement-related and extrinsic) for contingent career paths should be substantially stronger than for noncontingent career paths, and hence time spent in career-related activity greater in the latter, noncontingent paths should influence time spent to make it greater in career activity than in a single-episode activity of a one-step path. Since time spent in activity in conjunction with performance efficiency in that activity are considered by Atkinson (see Chapter 20) as the two variables directly contributing to cumulative achievement, the selective role of noncontingent as well as contingent career paths needs to be taken into account in trying to predict accomplishment of different individuals over time.

How often do we hear complaints from persons pursuing a career that they would like to do this, that, or the other thing, if only the day had more time? In fact, they have as much time to apportion as anyone else to non-career-related behavior. But the perception of career striving as an interrelated series of activities that must be engaged in repetitively over time in order to (at least) fulfill the requirements of competent immediate performance, and, of course, to advance in a contingent career hierarchy, limits the behavioral options perceived to be available. Pursuit of a career provides ready-made decisions concerning the resumption of activity on a routine basis that must be considered in trying to predict the stream of behavior of an individual over time.

The selective role of career also has important implications for the sheer number of behavioral changes (and whatever cognitive work that is involved in making "decisions") that has been discussed by Toffler (1970) in reference to what he terms "overchoice." Put simply, the concept of career allows us to conceptualize why chemists don't often write books on psychology, carpenters don't often take examinations to allow them to practice law, and teachers don't often go to dental school. The concept of an interrelated sequence of activities that "hang together" because of their functional relationship either to each other (in a contingent path) or to the attainment of extrinsic rewards (in a noncontingent path) is a necessary part of a theory that would hope to deal with achievement in people's lives rather than in laboratory settings, where the behavioral options are determined by the experimenter rather than the individual who serves as subject, whereas it is the other way around in life situations. The extent to which there is a limit placed on behavioral options is not a function just of the behavioral tendencies that are aroused, but also of the functional relationship of activities over time to the pursuit of long-term goals.

COMPULSIVE STRIVING IN CAREER PATHS

The success-oriented individual who is also high in extrinsic motives and who is striving for success in a delayed (extrinsic) incentive contingent career path is particularly susceptible in the initial stages to what I will term *compulsive career striving.* This is a common ailment of college students and junior executives whose symptoms are time spent and energy expended in career-related activity that is far beyond what can be sustained over an extended period of time. The result is what is termed the "nervous breakdown," the exhaustion of the physical and emotional reserves of the body. The disturbing part of this phenomenon is that the individual who is "pulled by the future" (rather than driven by the past) in this way is most often not aware of any problem until it is too late, because for him this pattern of activity is seen as "normal." The behavioral syndrome, which is a motivational disease of increasing importance in contemporary life, is in fact often typical of those individuals who are most successful in the early stages of contingent career striving. It will become obvious below why they are often so successful so soon, but they very often "burn themselves out" long before they have the opportunity to pursue a career long enough to compile a record of sustained cumulative achievement.

The compulsive career striver most probably is susceptible to the phenomenon of performance decrements due to too much positive motivation in immediate career-related performance in an evaluative situation where he perceives "all the marbles to be at stake" in terms of earning the opportunity to continue along the contingent career path (see Part III). This individual will literally be "turned on" to the point where behavior requiring a more relaxed or calm approach will be impossible. The feedback obtained from finding out that long hours in more relaxed (nonevaluative) circumstances leads to more productive immediate performance (writing reports, preparing briefs, etc.) only furthers the likelihood that this individual will devote still greater and greater proportions of time to career-related activity, particularly in an open contingent career path. The syndrome works as follows: due to an increase in subjective probability of success for each step along the path resulting from prior success, total achievement-related and extrinsic motivation increases without any loss of future possibilities for success, which produces greater immediate performance decrements due to trying too hard, which further increases time spent in more leisurely career-related activity that has led to the prior success and which in fact again produces success, thereby further increasing subjective probability of success, which increases the length of the path and increases total positive motivation still more. The individual eventually becomes totally involved in career pursuits to the exclusion of almost all other activity.

UP-TIGHT CAREER STRIVING

There is an equally serious health-related problem stemming from the fact that large components of extrinsic motivation as well as (this time inhibitory) achievement-related motivation are aroused in contingent career paths, particularly ones that have final or ultimate extrinsic goals. This concerns the individual who is stronger in the motive to avoid failure than the motive to achieve success (the "failure-threatened" personality) but who is also strong in many relevant extrinsic motives. This individual experiences just the opposite behavioral problem from that of the compulsive career striver–inability to concentrate and devote much time to career-related activity while suffering severe attacks of anxiety (when under contingent evaluative conditions) produced by arousal of resistance in anticipation of career failure. This person would prefer to give up pursuit of success in a contingent career path, and probably does (eventually) if a less anxiety-provoking means of satisfying his extrinsic motives can be found. But while engaged in career striving this individual suffers, and his suffering is what prompts many to decry the structural arrangement here termed contingent career paths, whether found in the university, in government, or in business.

A particularly severe case of up-tight career striving results for an individual who is failure-threatened and high in extrinsic (positive) motives who is also high in fear of social rejection and/or high in fear of success.

Like the compulsive career striver, the up-tight individual has developed a motivational disease (the latter is probably often correlated with psychosomatic disorders) that can be reduced or eliminated by a change in the cognitive structuring of a career path. Both kinds of individual require a reduction in the amount of motivation aroused for career striving, the former in positive motivation, the latter in inhibitory motivation. Of course, there is another alternative—elimination of contingent career paths. That is, on the one hand, the individual can be changed, either through resocialization concerning path-goal relationships or trained not to focus attention on or "think about" the long-term implications of immediate activity while he is engaged in it. On the other hand, society's structuring of step-path relationships can be altered—by elimination of prerequisites, use of pass-fail criteria for passing hurdles, allowing an unlimited number of tries along a path regardless of prior demonstrations of (competent or incompetent) performance. Such changes might have to be coupled with an educational program aimed at firmly establishing knowledge about these "new rules of the game," for some individuals may be so accustomed to imposing long-term contingent paths on immediate activity that mere informational input would have little effect. I see a critically important direction for future research in the further development guided by systematic theory of experimental training programs (Kolb, 1965; McClelland & Winter, 1969) that would spur the discovery of those components of instigating force of achievement-related motivation that can be changed (and, if so, by what techniques and over what period of time) and those that cannot be readily altered, if at all. The development of successful programs to change the level of aroused achievement motivation would inevitably contribute important new insights into the development and function of future orientation as well as into the other factors that contribute to sustaining career striving.

20

MOTIVATIONAL DETERMINANTS OF INTELLECTIVE PERFORMANCE AND CUMULATIVE ACHIEVEMENT[1]

John W. Atkinson

Some of us look back with justifiable pride in what has been achieved by fellow humans, all of us descendants of Australopithecus. Others look around and are justifiably distraught by a keen sensitivity to suffering in the world that decries the great discrepancy between human aspiration and actuality. They are depressed by how slowly, if at all, the giant goal discrepancy (to use our technical term) seems to be diminished. Whether one feels mainly a rich sense of vicarious pride in human achievement, or mainly depression, even rage, or has the feelings alternately or mixed, depends, most likely, on how lucky one has been in the two crucial rolls of the dice over which no individual exerts any personal control. These are the accidents of birth and background. One roll of the dice determines an individual's heredity; the other, his formative environment. Race, gender, time and place of birth in human history, a rich cultural heritage or not, the more intimate details of affluence or poverty, sensitive and loving parents and peers, or not, all of them beyond one's own control, have yielded the basic personality: a perspective on the life experience, a set of talents, some capacities for enjoyment and suffering, the potential or not of ever making a productive contribution to the community that could be a realistic basis for self-esteem.

Among those who have been following the full story of life on earth as it is being recovered and told with increasing clarity in recent years, there seems to be general agreement on one thing, at least. Civilization, the cumulative human achievement, distinguishes our experience from that of other animals with whom

[1] The new work reported here was supported by a grant-in-aid of my research by the ACT (American College Testing Program) Research Institute during 1971–73.

we share (often too selfishly) the opportunity for life on this planet. Interest in one or another opportunity for expression of talent–the arts and literature, philosophy, religion, the sciences, and technology, industry, politics–either from outside, as aesthete, interested observer, or historian, or from inside, as active participant in an enterprise, exhausts the list of intellectual pursuits of man. Add to it all of the other exciting, intrinsically satisfying, and highly skillful uses of mind and body together called sports and crafts and just plain essential productive work, and one has defined the scope of behavioral phenomena to which the words *motivation for achievement* apply.

In the closing paragraphs of *One Day in the Life of Ivan Denisovich,* Alexander Solzhenitsyn (1963) reminds us that achieving is essential for man. Even in the utter degradation of Stalin's arctic prison camp, a man finds inherent satisfaction in what he is able to accomplish:

> Shukhov went to sleep, and he was very happy. He'd had a lot of luck today. They hadn't put him in the cooler. The gang hadn't been chased out to work in the Socialist Community Development. He'd finagled an extra bowl of mush at noon. The boss had gotten them good rates for their work. *He'd felt good making that wall* [italics added]. They hadn't found that piece of steel in the frisk. Ceasar had paid him off in the evening. He'd bought some tobacco. And he'd gotten over that sickness.
>
> Nothing had spoiled the day and it had been almost happy.

This closing chapter is written after 25 years of scientific interest in the measurement and the expressions of the uniquely human need for achievement. It ends a book that has attempted to summarize what some of us have learned, so far, studying the behavioral effects of individual differences in achievement-related motivation. This is a different question from–How does an achievement motive or disposition to be anxious develop in a person? Or, what are the social origins and consequences of achievement motivation? We have tried, in each of the books summarizing some new phase in the work following *The Achievement Motive* by McClelland et al. in 1953, to distinguish the several important but separate questions.

My aim, and that of most of my co-workers at Michigan, has been to study the functional significance of individual differences in personality. Once they are measured, *so what*? That is the question. We have attempted to embed the measurement and study of differences in personality in a theory of motivation, one which would complete the specification of the guiding hypothesis that is a legacy from Kurt Lewin, $B = f\,(P,E)$, referring to the interaction of personality and immediate environment in the contemporaneous determination of an individual's behavior. This is what David Birch and I now refer to as *the dynamics of action* (Chapter 15, pp. 209-210).

Through the years, we have tried to make it explicit that traditionally there have been two big questions in the study of motivation: (*a*) what are the components or determinants of a tendency to act in a certain way? (*b*) How is competition and conflict among tendencies resolved and expressed in action?

Now, in this book, we have rephrased the questions and pulled together all that we have to offer as answers concerning motivation for achievement-related action. Within the context of our conception of the dynamics of achievement-oriented action (Chapter 15), which is mostly our new answer to the second question, the "old" theory of achievement motivation (Chapter 2) with its elaboration (Chapter 7) has become part of the answer to the first question, rephrased: What are the components or determinants of the instigating and inhibitory forces that influence an individual's achievement-related activity?

Theory concerning the dynamics of action, focusing as it does on temporal changes in the relative strength of motivating tendencies, accounts for initiation, persistence, preference, operant level, relative frequency, and time spent in various activities. It answers the questions–*which* activity will occur, *when,* and for how long? To this must be added an additional assumption, one that answers the question–*how well* will the activity be executed? It is an assumption concerning how the strength of the tendency motivating an activity at a particular time influences the *efficiency* of performance (Chapter 11).

Here, in the final chapter, we can bring it all together in a way that deals specifically with the generally accepted notion that achievement in any field of endeavor depends upon both talent, or ability, and motivation. Having already made the point that motivation is a determinant of efficiency of performance while working at some task (Chapter 11), and also a determinant of how much time an individual will give to some endeavor (Chapter 15), we can now sharpen the distinction between achievement in the restricted sense of *level of performance on some given task* (e.g., an examination in a college course, a scholastic aptitude test, a given baseball game, etc.) and *cumulative achievement* over a much longer span of time (e.g., the overall academic record in college, the lifetime batting records of a baseball player, social mobility, an invention, a work of art, success in a career, success in a social movement).

One can anticipate from the way the distinction has been introduced that motivation influences *level of performance on a specific task* and *cumulative achievement* in different ways. This is shown graphically in Figure 1.

When our interest is the functional significance of individual differences in personality, we are not concerned with the important *developmental* question which is summarized under *The Past* in Figure 1. But others are (for references, see McClelland, 1951, Ch. 12; McClelland et al., 1953; Atkinson, 1958a; Veroff, 1965; Heckhausen, 1967; Smith, 1969).[2] The personality (as it applies to achievement-oriented activity) encompasses individual differences in ability

[2] And even as this volume goes to press, we (Willy Lens and Atkinson, 1973) have seen that Figure 1 can be modified so as to distinguish *two* different cumulative effects: one on the environment (achievement as here conceived) and another correlated effect on the self, viz., a growth in ability. This means that Figure 1, when so elaborated, identifies the role of motivation in the *developmental* question of growth in ability. It is implied that sooner or later one should always expect to find a positive correlation between the *true level of ability* and *strength of motivation* for the type of activity in question.

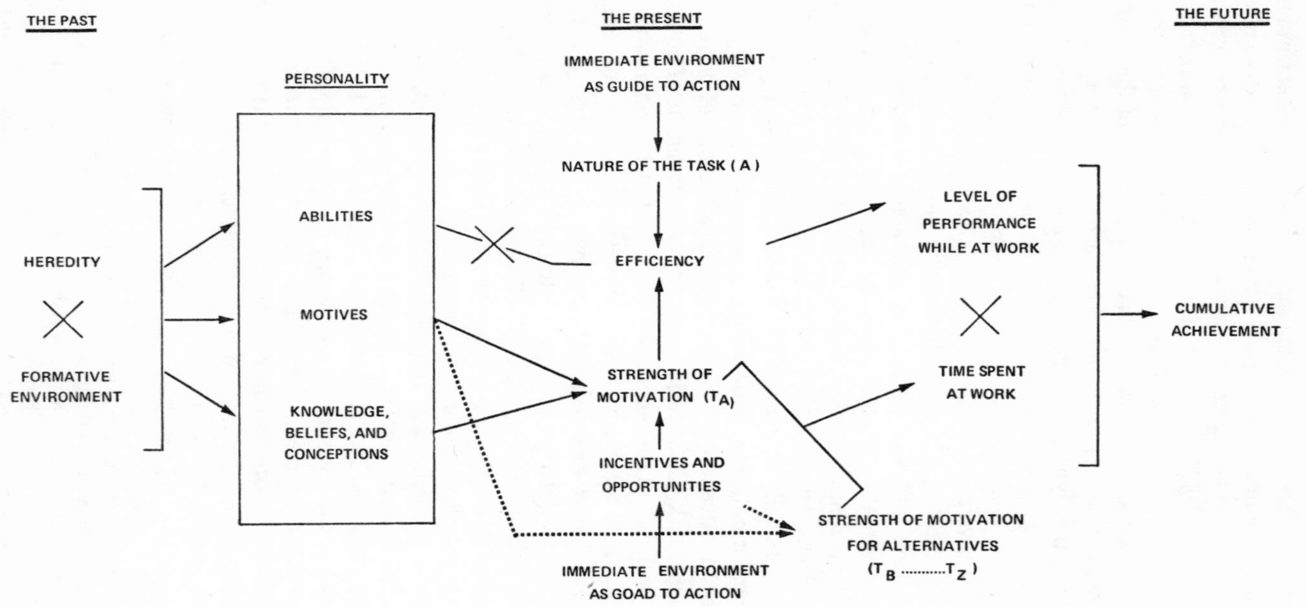

FIG. 1. The dual role of motivation as a determinant of cumulative achievement. Level of performance while at work is attributed to ability, the nature of the task, and the effect of strength of motivation (T_A) on efficiency of performance. Time spent at work depends upon the strength of motivation for the critical task (T_A) relative to the number and strength of motivation for other activities ($T_B \ldots T_Z$).

based on heredity and prior opportunity and training: individual differences in motives, a hierarchy of them as conjectured by Murray (1938) and Maslow (1954, 1970) and in McClelland's (1951, Ch. 12; also 1958c) impressive argument justifying the notion of a limited set of transcultural motives. In addition, personality embraces the cognitive structure of the individual, his knowledge, beliefs, and conceptions. This, we think, is where Rotter's (1954) belief in *internal versus external control of reinforcement* should fit, and Moulton's (Chapter 4) concept of individual differences in *competence,* which influence specific expectations of success in given activities. Of course, here is where future orientation, the long term path-goal conception emphasized by Raynor (Chapter 7), is represented as a descriptive attribute of personality.

We neither deal with the development of abilities, motives, knowledge, beliefs, and conceptions, nor do we deal explicitly with the much broader social context within which the whole paradigm fits. Included in the latter are the social organization, institutions of a particular society, and group memberships that influence the formative environment, the immediate environment of one's day to day life, and, on the other end, the social consequences of one's cumulative achievement, its impact on those social institutions. This latter problem in reference to achievement motivation is the special concern of sociology (Rosen, Crockett, & Nunn, 1969; Duncan, Featherman, & Duncan, 1972) and the special emphasis of David McClelland and his colleagues (McClelland, 1961; McClelland & Winter, 1969). We can, however, find in Figure 1 an account of the achievement-related behavior of an individual whose own cumulative achievement represents getting a higher education (Sewell, 1971), or upward social mobility (Crockett, 1962, 1964), or an entrepreneurial success (McClelland, 1961), beginning with a personality (as given and assessed) interacting with the immediate environment, and expressed in efficient and persistent activity.

Consider Figure 1. What defines the level of cumulative achievement? Our answer is twofold: the level of performance while engaged in an endeavor, whatever it is, and the sheer amount of time devoted to it instead of to other activities. Here, immediately, as we work backwards in the causal chain, we confront the *dual* role of motivation in achievement. On the one hand, the level of performance while engaging in an activity depends upon Ability $\times$ Efficiency, and the latter is influenced by the strength of motivation being expressed in the activity (Chapter 11). If we define an individual's present level of ability for a certain kind of activity (e.g., verbal, mathematical, spatial, etc.) as his level of performance when he is optimally motivated for the task, we may introduce the idea of *a coefficient of efficiency* (Coefficient of efficiency = Level of performance/Level of ability) which may vary from 0.0 to 1.00 depending upon the strength of motivation at the time of performance.

In Figure 2*A* we have redrawn a familiar curve from Chapter 11 showing the presumed relationship of strength of motivation to efficiency of performance,

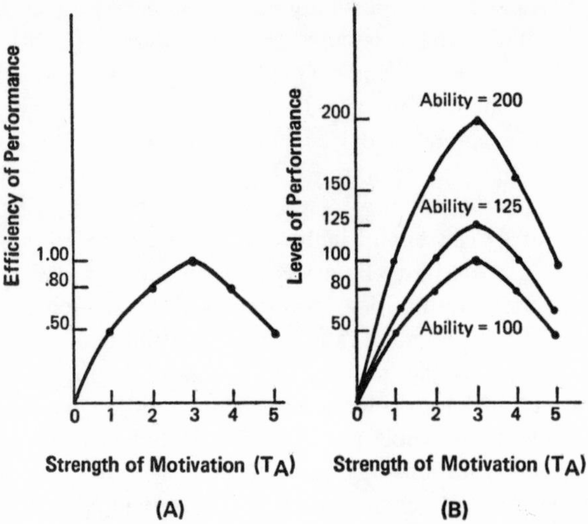

FIG. 2. (*A*) The effect of strength of motivation on efficiency of performance, and (*B*) the effect of strength of motivation on level of performance when level of performance = ability × coefficient of efficiency.

whatever the level of ability. And in Figure 2*B*, we show the effect of strength of motivation on level of performance for three levels of true ability.

Some very important implications are immediately clear. If the two individuals identified as highest and lowest in ability were, for example, taking a diagnostic test of mathematical ability, and both were optimally motivated (level 3 in Figure 2*B*), then one would score 200 and the other 100. These test scores would manifest the true difference in present ability. But suppose that the more able person had been tested under conditions that *for him* produced much weaker motivation (level 1) or much stronger motivation (level 5). Then he too would score 100 on the diagnostic test of mathematical ability. It is quite apparent that the observed levels of performance, the test scores, if taken as estimates of true levels of ability, can produce the wrong conclusions concerning the relative ability of two individuals when motivation is ignored. An able but highly anxious person, or an able but very positively motivated person, could actually perform *less well* on a diagnostic test of some ability than one of his more optimally motivated but less able peers. In Figure 1, that would be the individual having a true ability of 125 but either very weak (level 1) or very strong (level 5) in motivation compared to an optimally motivated peer whose true ability is 100.

There has been much current discussion of the real meaning of differences in various intelligence, ability, and aptitude test scores, particularly in regard to racial differences (e.g., Jensen, 1969; Eysenck, 1971). The argument has emphasized almost exclusively the developmental issue–heredity versus formative environment. It is essential to emphasize that *the mental test movement for many years has implicitly made the claim, without adequate justification and certainly in the absence of knowledge, that the level of motivation is either optimal for everyone being tested, or constant, or only negligibly different among all individuals at the time of performance.*

The evidence from our 25 years of research on effects of differences in achievement-oriented motivation challenges the habitual toleration of the simplicity of the mental tester's theoretical account of behavior. The stakes have become too high. It is apparent that we now have more and better theory of motivation than we ever have had of intelligence. *Until proven otherwise, any measured difference in what has been called general intelligence, scholastic aptitude, verbal or mathematical ability, etc., which is always obtained from performance under achievement-oriented if not multiple-incentive conditions, can be given a motivational interpretation with no less scientific justification than the traditional aptitudinal interpretation.*

The most obvious injustice, if the hypothesis concerning performance decrement attributable to *overmotivation* continues to be sustained, is the underestimation of true ability in a highly able person who is also very highly motivated for productive achievement. We can see this as we turn our attention to the other influence that motivation has on cumulative achievement, its effect on time spent in the critical activity (e.g., academic work, or work related to a career.)

In Figure 1, as in Chapter 15 on the dynamics of achievement-oriented action, the point is made that doing one thing instead of another (preference), and continuing to do it, or coming back to it often and for long stretches of time (persistence and/or time spent in an activity), depend on the *relative strengths* of the tendency to engage in the critical activity and tendencies for other alternative activities. And these differences, in turn, are determined by the *relative strengths* of instigating and inhibitory forces for various activities which express, in part, the *relative strengths* of basic motivational dispositions in people.

From computer simulations of time spent in various activities, given a number of alternatives with differences in strength of instigating force for the activities, based on *The Dynamics of Action* (Atkinson & Birch, 1970), one can state the generalization shown in Figure 3 concerning the effect of the total strength of positive motivation for a given activity in a given environment (i.e., $F_A = (F_S + F_{ext})$ on proportion of total time spent in that activity. It is a linear relationship (the argument is developed in Appendix B).

This means, very simply, that insofar as sheer persistence and time spent in an activity contributes to cumulative achievement, the effect of strength of positive motivation for an activity on cumulative achievement is linear. But, as is made explicitly clear in Figure 1, the level of performance (Ability X Efficiency) while at work is the other important factor. To predict cumulative achievement, we need to put all of the pieces together: differences in *true* ability, differences in

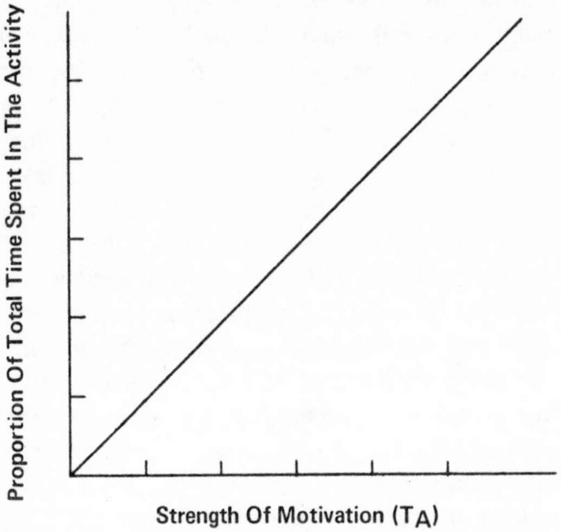

FIG. 3. The effect of strength of positive motivation for some activity (T_A) on proportion of time spent in the activity (see Appendix B for derivation).

motivational dispositions (motives, knowledge, beliefs, conceptions), nature of the task, incentives, and opportunities in the immediate environment. And last, but certainly not least, we must include in our calculations all of the factors in the life of an individual that influence the strength of his motivation to engage in other alternative activities, ones that take time away from what we are interested in here, his achievement-oriented activities.

In other words, on the motivational side, the whole hierarchy of motives within an individual personality and the richness of his environment in the incentives offered and the opportunities for expression and enjoyment of competing, non-achievement-related activities are as important for a full explanatory account of cumulative achievement as those abilities, motives, incentives, and opportunities that refer specifically to the achievement-related endeavor of critical interest.

This says no more than what is obvious. But the obvious is so often ignored. Some college students do less well academically than someone might have predicted because they spend so much time doing other interesting things, not because they are deficient in either achievement-related skills or motivation, but because they have a variety of other strong motivations that have an equally important influence on their distribution of time among various activities.

This same point can be made, but in a backhanded way, by saying that one could assure maximal cumulative academic achievement by selecting highly talented and optimally (i.e., only moderately) motivated students but *only ones who had virtually no other interests to compete for their time.* Then all they would ever do is academic work. And since they become only moderately involved in it, i.e., they are never too eager and pressing, they would be operating at peak intellectual efficiency all of the time. Perhaps this same idea can be applied more generally to great human achievements that require almost total commitment in a lifetime of concentrated effort. The essence of "genius" may sometimes lie in the unique combination of superior talent and a moderately strong single-mindedness, i.e., a real lack of interest in anything but the creative endeavor.

Now that the basic ideas are out, the discussion needs the focus of a concrete problem. So let us consider the questions of *overachievement* and *underachievement* (Thorndike, 1963) in the academic setting. In the field of mental testing and prediction of academic success, the *overachiever* is the fellow who is a real nuisance for the predictive validity of the ability test because his cumulative achievement is so much higher than expected. Perhaps he is a student who barely made it over the critical hurdle of the minimum college aptitude scores to get admitted, or one for whom a modest C record in college is predicted from his test scores. Yet he ends up with all the academic honors, outperforming most others for whom there had been great expectations based on the ability test scores. The *underachiever* is a test-taking star but a long-term bust.

A simple numerical illustration of this problem for a hypothetical sample of 20 persons who differ in their present *true* ability and motivation is presented in Table 1. The illustration is based explicitly on the analysis of the dual role of motivation stated in Figure 1 and the functional relationships assumed in Figures 2 and 3. The latter, it will be recalled, correspond to generalizations growing out of empirical work (Chapter 11) and the new theoretical conception of the dynamics of action (Chapter 15).

To make the illustration relatively simple yet realistic, these three additional assumptions are made: (*a*) when a student takes a college aptitude test, he spends all of his time working at the task before him; (*b*) the average strength of motivation (T_A) expressed in normal, everyday academic work is typically weaker for all individuals than when taking an important test; (*c*) all individuals are equivalent in the number and strength of motivation for other activities that might compete with academic work.[3]

In Table 1, 20 hypothetical persons are given names which involve a letter (A, B, C, D, E) corresponding to their true level of ability (100, 80, 60, 40, 20), and a number (5, 4, 3, 2, 1) corresponding to the strength of their own motivation (T_A) for the intellective task in the ability test situation. The 20 persons are

[3] I have not forgotten that highly anxious students may have the dampener released and therefore be more highly motivated in normal work than for test-taking. We will discuss implications for them a little later. And I do not mean to minimize variance among *S*s in motivation for nonacademic activities by an effort to keep this first illustration simple. A computer program and its use for simulations of more complex conditions are reported in Appendix B, and I will summarize some results of simulations later in this chapter.

TABLE 1

True Ability and Motivation as Determinants of the Level of Intellective Performance (e.g., on an Ability Test) and Cumulative Academic Achievement (e.g., Grade Average in College): A Hypothetical Numerical Illustration Emphasizing the Dual Role of Motivation Assumed in Figures 1, 2, and 3

	Ability test situation					Conditions of normal academic work				
Name of subject[a]	True ability	Motivation	Efficiency	Level of test performance	True ability	Motivation[b]	Efficiency	Level of performance	Time spent in work	Cumulative achievement
A3	100	3	1.00	100	100	2	.80	80	2	160–
A4	100	4	.80	80	100	3	1.00	100	3	(300)
A2	100	2	.80	80	100	1	.50	50	1	50–
B3	80	3	1.00	80	80	2	.80	64	2	128
B4	80	4	.80	64	80	3	1.00	80	3	(240)
				$-Q_1$						
B2	80	2	.80	64	80	1	.50	40	1	40–
C3	60	3	1.00	60	60	2	.80	48	2	96
A5	100	5	.50	50	100	4	.80	80	4	(320)
C4	60	4	.80	48	60	3	1.00	60	3	180
C2	60	2	.80	48	60	1	.50	30	1	30–
				–Md						

B5	80	5	.50	40	80	4	.80	64	4	(256)
D3	40	3	1.00	40	40	2	.80	32	2	64
D4	40	4	.80	32	40	3	1.00	40	3	120
D2	40	2	.80	32	40	1	.50	20	1	20
C5	60	5	.50	30	60	4	.80	48	4	(192)
				$-Q_3$						
D5	40	5	.50	20	40	4	.80	32	4	128
E3	20	3	1.00	20	20	2	.80	16	2	32
E4	20	4	.80	16	20	3	1.00	20	3	60
E2	20	2	.80	16	20	1	.50	10	1	10
E5	20	5	.50	10	20	4	.80	16	4	64

[a] *S*s are named according to their true level of ability (A = 100, B = 80, C = 60, D = 40, E = 20) and their strength of motivation (T_A) in the ability test situation. See Figure 1 to identify determinants of T_A.

[b] It is assumed here that all *S*s are less strongly motivation during normal work (–1) than in the test situation.

listed in order of their ability test scores, i.e., *the level of their intellective performance in that particular test situation.*

The first person on the list is A3. His true level of ability is 100 (the highest), and his strength of motivation (T_A) in the test situation is 3, a moderate and optimal level. His efficiency in execution of the intellective task is 1.00 (see Figure 2), so his level of performance, his test score, is 100.

One may next glance down the list of *S*s arranged in order of their test performance and note that all *S*s having level A of ability score highest except A5, who is well down the list because his motivation is so strong that his performance is very inefficient. The same pattern is apparent for the Bs, and the Cs. *It is always the most highly motivated one who performs substantially less well than the others of comparable ability.* It is obvious, even at first glance, that the ability test score is underestimating his true level of ability relative to that of others.

If one follows A3, the fellow who scored highest on the ability test, through his years of academic work to see what he accomplishes, one is somewhat disappointed. His cumulative level of achievement of 160 ranks only 7th out of 20. (Oh well! Regression toward the mean is to be expected when one has less than perfectly reliable tests. And what is more, there may be heterogeneity in the criterion variable. So say our textbooks on psychometrics.)

If we look more closely at the conditions of normal academic work for A3, we see that his level of motivation is now 2, less than optimal. This means that his efficiency is now only .80 (instead of 1.00) and so his level of performance while doing intellective work is now 80 (instead of 100). And since his motivation for the task is only 2, he spends proportionately less time than others in his work (see Figure 3). So his cumulative achievement (level of performance × time spent) is a disappointing 160.

Look down the column for cumulative achievement, which corresponds in my illustration to grade average in a year of college. The academic stars, those who represent the upper quartile, have their cumulative achievement circled so we can get some notion of who and where they are relative to the original ordering according to ability test score.

All five very high achievers (viz., A5, A4, B5, B4, C5, in order of overall academic record) have one thing in common. It is *not* a uniformly high level of true ability. It *is* a uniformly high level of motivation, so high, in fact, that all were beyond the optimal level of motivation while taking the diagnostic test of ability. This means (Figure 2), that they were relatively inefficient in their intellective performance, and their true current level of ability is underestimated by the ability test score. It also means that in normal work, *when the average level of motivation is less than on the test,* their intellective performance is more efficient than when taking the test, so their level of performance in normal work is higher than in the test situation. And since the relative strength of their motivation for academic work also influences persistence, time spent in academic versus other activities, they put more time into their work than others.

In other words, the person who is generally very highly motivated (relative to others) will be more efficient in normal work than in a test situation and will spend proportionately more time in normal work than his less motivated peers.

The very best performer is A5 because he combines the highest level of talent and motivation for the task. The biggest surprise is C5, who makes it into the top quartile on cumulative achievement (192) with only average level of true ability but who, on the diagnostic test, barely missed falling into the lowest quartile. This is the one, C5, that we had in mind at the outset when we imagined the *overachiever* who is such a nuisance for the predictive validity coefficient of our conventional intelligence -, ability -, aptitude tests. He probably was admitted to college at all only because some keen admissions officer sensed a hidden potential that didn't show in the test scores. Or perhaps it was a very sophisticated admissions officer who noted that this fellow had always done very well in the long run (his grade average in high school was always good) despite those very, very doubtful ability test scores.

Who are the *underachievers,* the biggest disappointments for the admissions officer? They are (in addition to A3) A2, B2, and C2, whose cumulative achievement is identified by (−). All these scored above the median on the diagnostic test, and all dropped into the lowest third of the class on cumulative academic performance. What do they have in common? Again the explanation is motivational. All were relatively weak in motivation taking the test but not so weak as to be *very* inefficient. But in normal everyday academic life, if that motivation for academic work is weaker still, they don't get involved in studying often enough to accomplish much. And when they do, their motivation for the task is so weak, i.e., they are so little involved in it, that their efficiency is even lower than when they were taking the crucial test.

In his analysis of the nature of the problem of *overachievement* and *underachievement,* Thorndike (1963), citing work by Diener (1960), calls attention to the fact that students who have higher percentile rank on a scholastic aptitude test than grade point average (underachievers) and the opposite group (overachievers) differ as much on the aptitude test as on the measure of cumulative achievement. Thus, he correctly concludes, "the 'underachievers' could just as truly be called 'overintelligent,' and the 'overachievers' called 'underintelligent' [p. 13]."

The corresponding point is made in a comparison of the most extreme "overachievers" and "underachievers" in our illustrative case in Table 2.

In Table 1 the actual linear correlation between *level of test performance* and *cumulative achievement* is .37. In this case we assumed that strength of motivation was less, for everyone, in normal work than in the critical test situation. We know, from everything we have done in studying achievement-related motivation, that this is not likely to be the case for particularly anxious persons. We know from practically every chapter in the book that persons in whom the strength of motive to avoid failure (or perhaps to avoid success) exceeds the strength of motive to achieve, will normally suffer

TABLE 2

Diagnostic Test Scores and Cumulative Achievement of Most Extreme "Overachievers" and "Underachievers" in Hypothetical Situation Depicted in Table 1 Following the Argument of Thorndike (1963, p. 13)

	Overachievers			Underachievers	
S	Test score	Cumulative achievement	*S*	Test score	Cumulative achievement
A5	50	320	A2	80	50
B5	40	256	B2	64	40
C5	30	192	C2	48	30
D5	20	128	A3	100	160
Mean:	35	224	Mean	73	70

more resistance to a task when it is perceived as critically important to their future than when this is less salient or obvious, as in everyday work. So we have pursued a similar analysis assuming that strength of motivation (T_A) becomes *stronger* in normal work than when taking the critical test. In this case there are some cases of substantially better cumulative achievement for persons considered disappointments in Table 1. For example, A2, B2, and C2 all become optimally motivated (level 3) in normal work if the main effect of the test situation has been to dampen and depress their level of motivation, as we generally suppose concerning very anxious persons. The levels of their cumulative achievement would then become 300 (instead of 50), 240 (instead of 40), and 180 (instead of 30) for A2, B2, and C2, respectively. And even D2 and E2, who have relatively less true ability, would show cumulative achievements of 120 (instead of 20) and 60 (instead of 10) *if* they became less anxious, less suppressed, less dampened out, in normal work than when taking the critical diagnostic test.[4]

[4] Specifically, for this example, we assume that strong arousal of a negaction tendency (to avoid failure or success) will dampen the level of motivation throughout all or most of the test period but that this negative component is absent or negligible in normal work. The latter assumption is questionable. We make it here to simplify this illustrative discussion of the dual function of motivation in achievement. At this writing, simulation work in progress is exploring the important and nonobvious implication of the dynamics of action (Atkinson & Birch, 1970, p. 305) that if an activity is once initiated in the face of strong resistance in a constant environment, then more rather than less time will be spent in that activity than if there were no resistance to it. See again Tables 2 and 3 and the accompanying text in Chapter 15. It has become increasingly clear that the composition of the resultant tendency expressed in action, as well as its strength, has important implications. For the present, we ignore the complication to make a more general point.

From our computer simulations of this second case and still others using a program developed by James Sawusch based on Figure 1 and included with a description of the conditions assumed in the appendix, we can make these general statements:

1. When motivation for the critical activity is stronger in a test situation than in normal work, the linear correlation of diagnostic test score with cumulative achievement is .36 ($N = 20$).

2. When the motivation for the critical activity is weaker in a test situation than in normal work, the linear correlation of diagnostic test score with cumulative achievement is .95 ($N = 20$).

3. When the level of motivation is the same in both test situation and in normal work, the linear correlation of diagnostic test score with cumulative achievement is .89 ($N = 20$).

4. When we create a distribution of individuals in which the more positively motivated people (item 1 above) are represented three times as often as the presumably more anxious individuals (item 2 above)—the kind of inference we are led to make from the overall pattern of results on achievement motivation in research on male college students—the linear correlation between ability test score and cumulative achievement is .48 ($N = 80$).

5. Finally, when we repeat these conditions (item 4) but also introduce random variation and sampling from a normal distribution concerning number and strength of motivations for other competing activities ($T_B \ldots T_Z$ in Figure 1), instead of assuming that factor to be constant among *S*s, along with random samples from normal distributions of true ability and strength of motivation for the critical task (T_A), the product-moment correlation between diagnostic test score and cumulative achievement becomes .33 in this most realistic simulation (see Appendix B).

We are encouraged in our analysis to note that the median of actually obtained correlations between verbal and mathematical scholastic aptitude scores and academic performance in the freshman year of college ranges between .40 and .48 for the two sexes when there is substantial heterogeneity in the test scores of the colleges studied (Angoff, 1971, p. 129), and as low as .26 to .32 when there is considerably less heterogeneity. The correlation of ACT scores with college grades ranges from .20 to .56 (American College Testing Program, 1973, Vol. I, p. 128). This gives us a satisfying sense of being on the right track.

One only gets out of a computer, whether it be in merely processing data according to the traditional assumptions of mental-testing, or a more elaborate theory concerning the motivation of behavior, *the implications of what one has put into it.* In this analysis, we have assumed a symmetric inverted-U function to describe the effect of motivation on efficiency. The relationship may, in fact, be more asymmetric. We have assumed, again in the absence of proof, that our new conception of the dynamics of action is essentially correct about how motivation influences persistence and time spent in an activity. We have assumed relatively small changes + or - in strength of motivation between the test situation and normal work. And we have probably seriously underestimated the range of differences, and therefore the relative influence, of the number and strength of tendencies for other time-demanding activities.

Our simulated results are merely the implications of these assumptions. They provide a guide for creative new empirical investigations and, perhaps, for secondary analysis of old data. The analysis as a whole is a conceptual tool for thinking about still other possibilities. For example, what about a C1, a student of average ability who is terribly frozen by anxiety in a certain kind of test setting but who might conceivably become an effective C3 under the nonstressful conditions of normal work. His diagnostic test score would be only 30, at the edge of the lowest quartile, but his cumulative achievement would be 180, at the edge of the highest quartile in the distribution in Table 1.

Are there any members of our society for whom this might be the expected pattern when and if they are given the opportunity to yield evidence of cumulative achievement (see Katz, 1967)?

SUMMARY AND CLOSING ARGUMENT

Motivation influences both efficiency in the execution of an activity (and therefore the level of performance) and persistence or, more generally, the time spent in a particular endeavor. Thomas Edison is supposed to have claimed, "Genius is 1% inspiration and 99% perspiration." Though I glance every day at a plaque hanging near my desk with this bold claim, and continue to be influenced by it, I think perhaps it overstates the case for sheer effort, dogged persistence, yesterday's will power, the dedication and commitment of almost total time and energy to some enterprise. My preliminary analysis of the determinants of cumulative achievement suggests that 50% of the variance is attributable to average level of performance while at work and 50% to the amount of time spent in the work. (There are 24 hours in a day for everyone, but some live longer than others.) The level of performance is 50% the result of differences in true ability and 50% the result of differences in strength of motivation mediated by the latter's influence on efficiency of performance. Time spent in the endeavor is attributable 50% to strength of motivation for the critical enterprise and 50% to the number and strength of inclinations for incompatible activities.

Roughly speaking, this would partition the variance in cumulative achievement (Edison's meaning of genius) as follows: 25% to true ability (inspiration?), 50% to motivation for the critical endeavor (perspiration?), and 25% to motivation for alternative activities that also make human life an interesting and intrinsically enjoyable experience (distraction?).

Until we reach that blessed day to which Herrnstein (1971) has called attention, when the formative environment as an opportunity for development of ability has become equal (and hopefully optimal) for all members of the society (and therefore no longer a source of variance in *true* ability), we must suppose that heredity as a determinant of *true* ability, per se, is responsible for something less than all of the 25% of differences in the cumulative achievement of an individual assigned to it here. Heredity may, of course, have an important direct influence on motives—recall McDougall's (1908) emphasis, that of the ethologists (Tinbergen, 1951), and that of contemporary behavioral genetics (Hirsch, 1962). In addition, heredity *undoubtedly* has very important indirect effects on the development of motivational dispositions that badly need to be studied and systematically recognized *as such.* Suppose, for example, that some genetic trait such as the shape of the nose, or the color of the skin, or the various qualities which together constitute the local definition of beauty, provoke stereotyped emotional reactions from significant others in the social context of the early formative years? There would then be gene-linked social learning experiences in those formative years and beyond (see again Katz, 1967). This kind of influence of heredity on the development of personality is suggested in the paradigm, $P = f(H \times E)$ of Figure 1.

Even the most awesome and rigorous-sounding of contemporary arguments about the degree of hereditability of IQ, which seem always to imply or to state something very definite about innate differences in *true ability,* must be condemned as simplistic and specious once one begins to comprehend that ability and motivation have been utterly confounded in that unique achievement-oriented performance that has been dignified from the very beginning by the imposing label "intelligence test." That it should have been called this at all is a historical accident. Serious interest in measurement of individual differences in ability preceded equally serious interest in measurement of individual differences in motivation by about half a century. Consideration of "intelligence" began long before scientific psychology had developed any sophistication whatever about the causal complexities of behavioral phenomena.

Does this mean that we should have used some variant of the words "motivational determinants of *intelligence*" in the title of all experiments and surveys since about 1950 showing the behavioral effects of anxiety (Mandler & Sarason, 1952; Taylor, 1956; Spence, 1958; Sarason et al., 1960; Spielberger, 1966) or achievement motivation (McClelland et al., 1953; Atkinson, 1958a; Atkinson, 1964; Atkinson & Feather, 1966; Smith, 1969) right from the outset? Perhaps so. It is certainly obvious that *now is a time for that kind of change in titles.* The semantics of psychology can produce significantly misleading social implications.

The practical application of the products of the ability test movement has managed all these years to do without any explicit psychology of motivation beyond the addition of commonsensical tests of vocational interests beginning with Strong (1931, 1943). *The conceptual scheme which underlies the processing of test data is a theory of behavior, and not a very sophisticated one.* It has yielded a picture of individuals who express abilities and interests in behavior (but hardly ever the same behavior). And we have been repeatedly told in popular textbooks that except for the fact of unreliable measurement and heterogeneity in the test and/or the criterion, the prediction of cumulative achievement from diagnostic tests of ability would indeed be much better than it is. In fact, it has not gotten any better in most of the now 70 odd years of its history.

Ability, it bears repeating, has never been measured directly or independently of the very same kind of performance one wants to explain with the concept. The scores of every *so-called* intelligence -, ability -, aptitude -, or achievement test are always measures of relative level of intellective performance on some kind of task under some particular kind of social motivating conditions. One really needs a whole social psychology to make completely coherent sense out of what happens in that setting. *Mental testing is, or should be, a subfield of social psychology.*

We now know that people are more or less strongly motivated to engage in the task depending upon the interaction of their own motivational characteristics and the incentive character of the situation. Individuals (even in as homogeneous a group as the frequently studied college sophomore) differ greatly in motivation because there are so many components of motivation in terms of which they can differ. (Did anyone ever seriously anticipate that human motivation would ultimately turn out to be a one- or two-dimensional problem once it was systematically studied?)

As we conceive the problem today, individuals may differ in strength of relatively general and enduring motives (having an early origin) to achieve, to gain social approval, to avoid failure, to avoid success, etc. They may differ in their subjective probability of success facing the challenge of a given task. They may differ in terms of whether or not they see the immediate activity as a step in a path to some distant future goal. They may differ in bringing (or not) some persistent, unsatisfied craving to achieve into a new situation that has its origin in relative past deprivation, failure.

Methods are available for measuring or manipulating these various motivational influences *independently of the kind of achievement-oriented intellective performances they are introduced to help explain.* And all of these various motivational determinants are strung together in a rather coherent theory of motivation which is explicit and complete enough to be taught to a computer for the sake of allowing simulations of behavior under fairly complex hypothetical conditions.

Ability has no measure independent of the kind of achievement-oriented task performance from which it has always been inferred. It has, in other words, always been completely confounded with motivational influences on performance.

Mental testers often decry the relative crudity of contemporary techniques for measurement of motivation, (e.g., the thematic apperceptive method). Always, it seems, they conveniently forget that the beginning of scientific physics (from which they have willingly taken a logic of measurement that may be inappropriate for behavioral science) involved having to estimate temporal duration by counting the beat of one's own pulse! The promising results and conceptions that emerged using such crude tools as this and the amount of dripping water to measure time defined the need for something better. When, later, the something better was invented, it was called a clock.

The study of individual differences in ability and the study of individual differences in motivation share an interest in the same dependent behavior, the level of intellective performance in an achievement-oriented test situation. Crude *independent* measurement of an explanatory variable seems, however modest a step, something more than no independent measurement of an explanatory variable.

The theoretical conception of achievement presented here, though unquestionably in error in respects unknown to me now, does nevertheless summarize rather well what I think we have learned about achievement-related motivation in 25 years. Despite the crudity of the technique (content analysis of imaginative behavior) that has provided an integrative thread from one study to another (when appropriately employed), and despite the small scale of the experiments, they have *together* been heuristic in yielding a fund of integratable evidence, suggestions for a more coherent theory of motivation, and the important distinction between the influence of motivation on level of performance of a given task and its influence on cumulative individual achievement.

From my perspective, the oversimplified account of test behavior and achievement yielded by the mental test movement in psychology is anachronistic. The practical success must of course be acknowledged. (Riding a horse was considered by all to be an improvement over walking.) But so, too, must the plateau in its development be candidly faced. (We await the invention of the automobile, to say nothing of jet aircraft.) Its further development requires a new idea.

The social significance now being attached to interpretation of test scores makes it imperative that we state the most tenable hypotheses concerning the functional significance of differences in motivation and that we understand their implications concerning equitable uses of tests in decision-making concerning the distribution of rare life-enhancing opportunities, and implications that are directly relevant to discussion of the primary social issue of our time.

PSYCHOLOGY TOMORROW

The scientific psychology of the future will be more than the sum of the separate parts of today's psychology, more than the sum of the two separate disciplines that Cronbach (1957) helped to identify. The sad price of their isolation from one another–studying individual differences with the product-moment correlation coefficient, studying behavioral processes by experimentation with random samples–is that we now have two very inadequate sets of half-truths to show for all the time and effort. One of them, the mental-test movement, has reached a dead end because it is anchored too exclusively in a logic of measurement taken from physics and often (perhaps more often than not) unwarranted in reference to behavioral phenomena. Its early, continued, modest practical success has made of it a substantial, profitable, inert professional establishment.

The other tradition, experimental psychology, though oriented towards basic science, has somehow managed to survive by identifying "basic" with a white lab coat and without either noticing or doing much about the fact that *people often react in diametrically opposite ways, not merely in different degrees, to the same variation in treatments.* In addition, it is still entangled in the short episodic view of behavior and a causal logic that is its heritage from the time of Descartes' (1637) conjecture about the reflex which served nineteenth century physiology so well. The complete psychology of tomorrow is not likely to be constructed by those who late in life must overcome the handicap of impoverished early specialized training and limited orientation toward the subject matter.

I have always believed, and still do, that integration of the study of individual differences and basic behavioral processes can begin to occur most readily in a science of motivation aimed at specification and empirical documentation suggested by the paradigm, $B = f(P,E)$. It requires some training in each of the two traditional disciplines (but not too much), apprenticeship with two kinds of technique (but not too much of either), and a conceptual orientation that never loses sight of either the P or the E but which focuses interest on the comma, the nature of the interaction. That is where the action is.

A complete and unified psychology will require comparable specification and empirical documentation of another interaction in the developmental paradigm $P = F(H,E_F)$ in which personality is conceived as the product of genetic (H) and formative (E_F) cultural background. I have argued elsewhere that the problem of motivation is logically prior to the problem of development (in Smith, 1969, pp. 200-206).

THE UBIQUITY OF INTERACTION EFFECTS

When all the rest of it has blown away, the single most important implication of a quarter of a century of work on achievement motivation will stand: its demonstration of the ubiquity of the interactive effects of personality and situational determinants of behavior. This implies, stated baldly, that neither the study of individual differences, ignoring the role of variations in situational conditions, nor the study of the effects of systematic variations in the environment, ignoring the role of differences in personality, will ever yield a science of motivation because the theoretically significant result so often lies in the interaction. There may be small successes, when there is substantial homogeneity in the population studied on the critically important dimensions. Then we can have an experimental psychology of the modal personality of a particular society at a particular time in history. I believe the early success of

Lewin et al. (1944) in the study of level of aspiration can be attributed largely to the fact that their subject samples, drawn from in and around German and, later, American universities in the decades prior to World War II, were homogeneously high in n Achievement and low in anxiety. The typical (most frequent) change in aspiration following success and failure attests to the fact. But what if the distribution of people had then been more equally balanced regarding $M_S > M_{AF}$ and $M_{AF} > M_S$ because many more members of the society had the opportunity to attend college and to join the sample of sophomores in the experiments?

If one imagines an experimental design having two rows, representing an important difference in personality, and two columns, representing an important manipulation of the immediate situation, our experience is that the result lies not in mean differences between the rows, or between the columns, but in the interaction of row (personality) and column (situation).

One needs to recall the diametrically opposite trends across treatments of persons who differ in achievement-related motivation: beginning in recall of interrupted tasks, the Zeigarnik effect (Atkinson, 1950, 1953); then in level of performance under varied conditions of incentive (Atkinson & Reitman, 1956; Reitman, 1957; Smith, 1961; Entin, 1968; Horner, 1968; Sales, 1970) all described in Part III; as dramatically shown in persistence following failure at easy and difficult tasks (Feather, 1962, described in Chapter 2), and following continued success at easy tasks versus continued failure at difficult ones (Weiner, 1965a, and Chapter 17); in performance and in liking or disliking heterogeneous versus ability-grouped classes (Atkinson & O'Connor, 1963, described in Chapter 2); in the motivational impact of conceiving an immediate task as a step in a path to some future goal (Part II); in performance of women in interpersonal competitional and noncompetitional settings (Horner, 1968, and Chapter 6). The list is not complete but is certainly sufficient to document the fundamental point. A careful examination of the work done by others on effects of individual differences in anxiety following Taylor (1951, 1953) and Mandler and Sarason (1952) will lead to a similar conclusion (see Spielberger, 1966).

This ubiquity of interactive effects is so far being missed in the rebirth of interest in social motivation (audience, coaction, competition) spurred by Zajonc (1965). It needs the paradigm presented in Table 3 in Chapter 11, or one like it, if today's experimental social psychology is to transcend the limitations of traditional experimental psychology. Certainly the development of differences in personality and the behavioral expression of those differences—both of which always occur in a social context—must be at the very core of a complete social psychology. Those who consider themselves *experimental* social psychologists must look to see what has already happened since 1950 in *experimental study of personality*. The science is needlessly suffering a decrement in its own performance that is attributable in part to semantics and in part to nonsensical early overspecialization in its graduate training programs. The thrust for execution of empirical research, which of course requires a sharp focusing of interest, is now occurring too soon. There is more to teach and much more to be learned by undergraduate majors and first-year graduate students *today* than there was in the early phase of rapid growth of the field following World War II.

The study of achievement-oriented activity continues to offer the greatest promise for development of a new interaction-oriented psychology because the problem of achievement has been and still is a central issue in human history; because the cumulative achievement of individuals (educational attainment, social mobility) are central interests of sociology, which studies the larger context within which the motivated stream of an individual's activities (the psychologist's interest) occurs; because the applied problems of motivation in education and industry are of increasing concern in a postindustrial society that is finally trying to provide equal opportunity for all–to say nothing of preindustrial societies; and, last but certainly not least, because it involves a kind of activity and setting that is more feasible for research, and less ethically objectionable than some others, in and around educational institutions where most *basic* scientific research on human motivation must be accomplished.

Our aim in this book has been to provide another up-to-date summary of work on the dynamics of achievement-oriented action since *A Theory of Achievement Motivation* with Norman T. Feather in 1966. The main emphasis has been the new conceptual developments–the elaboration of the old theory by Joel Raynor, the treatment of the long-neglected Yerkes-Dodson phenomenon, and the new dynamics of action with David Birch. Our hope is that this fresh and more complete conceptual framework will sharpen the definition of directions for empirical innovation and excite renewed interest in their pursuit.

For our study of achievement-oriented action, this book will mark a turning point: a transition from thinking and working in the creative context of discovery and construction, to thinking and working in the critical context of verification, of proof and disproof. It is this latter, self-corrective phase of science, *once ideas have been stated completely enough and clearly enough to be vulnerable to the harsh judgment of factual evidence,* that assures the discovery and correction of error. This is the only real protection against stale and sterile dogma, the only real guarantee of continual development towards greater clarity, coherence, simplicity, and empirical validity of our understanding of human motivation. The uncertainty about how it will come out, yet the ultimate assurance of greater enlightenment no matter how it does come out, can sustain the spark of achievement motivation in anyone.

APPENDIX A
COMPUTER PROGRAM WRITTEN TO SIMULATE THE DYNAMICS OF ACTION[1]

Robert A. Seltzer and James R. Sawusch

```
C     THIS PROGRAM IS A COMPUTER SIMULATION OF THE ATKINSON AND BIRCH
C     THEORY OF MOTIVATION:  "THE DYNAMICS OF ACTION" (J. W. ATKINSON
C     & J. D. BIRCH.  JOHN WILEY & SONS, INC.  1970).  THIS PROGRAM
C     WAS WRITTEN BY R. A. SELTZER & J. R. SAWUSCH IN FORTRAN IV "G"
C     (IBM RELEASE 20.1) FOR THE IBM 360/67 DUAL-PROCESSOR COMPUTER
C     OPERATING UNDER THE MICHIGAN TERMINAL SYSTEM (MTS) AT THE
C     UNIVERSITY OF MICHIGAN.  THIS PROGRAM HAS BEEN WRITTEN OVER A
C     3 YEAR PERIOD.  IT IS THE 4TH REVISION.  IT IS PRIMARILY FOR
C     TERMINAL USE.  IT ASKS FOR INPUT.
C                              ROBERT A. SELTZER & JAMES R. SAWUSCH
C                              THE UNIVERSITY OF MICHIGAN
C                              SUMMER  1972
C
C     DATA SET REFERENCE #1 & #2 SHOULD BE REFERENCING THE SAME
C     I/O SCRATCH FILE.  THEY ARE FOR TEMPORARY STORAGE OF THE SUMMARY
C     OUTPUT STATISTICS.
C
C     DATA SET REFERENCE #5 & #6 ARE REGULAR FORTRAN I/O DEVICES.
C
C     DATA SET REFERENCE #7 & #8 SHOULD BE REFERENCING THE SAME
C     I/O SCRATCH FILE.  THE ARE FOR TEMPORARY STORAGE OF PROTOCOL
C     OUTPUT STATISTICS.
C
C     TOTAL BYTES OF OBJECT CODE IS APPROXIMATELY 25,000 FOR THIS COMPILER.
C
C     THE FOLLOWING "INTEGER", "REAL", AND "COMMON" STMTS
C     SHOULD BE INSERTED AT THE BEGINNING OF EACH SUBPROGRAM.
C     (THEY WERE OMITTED TO SAVE SPACE.)
C
      INTEGER TIME,N,I,J,K,PRTOKL,P,M,CHEK(25,20),F,CHECK(25),Q,L,OTRCG(
     125),XJ,FULL,SUMARY,USED,NM,NO,OTRCGP(25),LP,TEND,PIFO,XZB(100),XZC
     2(100),XZD(100),U,NAMLST
      REAL MOTIVE(25,25,25),START(25,25,25),SEL(25),T,UNIQUE(8),MAXI,LAG
     1(25),CVAL(25),TKO,ELAPSE,FTIME,XZA(100),XZE(100),DON(25),DPICK(25)
     2,NAMCNT,FULCNT,SUMCNT
      COMMON TIME,N,I,J,K,PRTOKL,M,CHEK,F,CHECK,Q,L,JF,OTRCG,OTRCGP,LP,X
     1J,FULL,SUMARY,FULCNT,SUMCNT,USED,NM,NO,MAXI,LAG,CVAL,SEL,T,MOTIVE,
     2START,U,TKO,PIFO,TEND,XZA,XZB,XZC,XZD,XZE,DON,DPICK,FTIME,LAGON,EL
     3APSE,LAGS,ZAP,UNIQUE,SIGI(25),SIGC(25),XINCI(25),XINCC(25),NAMLST,
```

[1]We'd like to acknowledge with gratitude the assistance of Professor J. David Birch at the University of Michigan. His aid and moral support were invaluable.

```
     4NAMCNT
      CALL INIT
C     THE FOLLOWING DO LOOP IS THE MAIN SIMULATED TIME ADVANCE.
      DO 8 P=2,20000
      IF (T.GE.TIME) GO TO 9
      T=T+1.
      FULCNT=FULCNT+1.
      SUMCNT=SUMCNT+1.
      NAMCNT=NAMCNT+1.
      DO 2 J=1,N
      C=0.
      G=0.
      V=0.
      W=0.
      DO 1 K=1,N
      E=MOTIVE(7,K,J)*MOTIVE(3,K,K)
C     "C" IS THE TOTAL INDIRECT INSTIGATING FORCE ON J.
      C=E+C
      H=MOTIVE(9,K,J)*MOTIVE(5,K,K)*(MOTIVE(1,K,K)-MOTIVE(2,K,K))
C     "G" IS THE TOTAL INDIRECT CONSUMMATORY FORCE ON J.
      G=H+G
      R=MOTIVE(8,K,J)*MOTIVE(4,K,K)
C     "V" IS THE TOTAL INDIRECT INHIBITORY FORCE ON J.
      V=R+V
      S=MOTIVE(10,K,J)*MOTIVE(6,K,K)*MOTIVE(2,K,K)
C     "W" IS THE TOTAL INDIRECT FORCE OF RESISTANCE ON J.
      W=S+W
1     CONTINUE
C     THE FOLLOWING TWO STATEMENTS COMPUTE DELTA T AND DELTA N.
C     DELTA T, MOTIVE(17,J,J), EQUALS THE DIRECT INSTIGATING FORCE
C     PLUS THE TOTAL INDIRECT INSTIGATING FORCES (FROM DISPLACEMENT)
C     MINUS THE DIRECT CONSUMMATORY FORCE AND MINUS THE TOTAL INDIRECT
C     CONSUMMATORY FORCES (FROM SUBSTITUTION).  DELTA N, MOTIVE(18,J,J),
C     PARALLELS DELTA T FOR THE NEGACTION TENDENCIES.
      MOTIVE(17,J,J)=MOTIVE(3,J,J)+C-(MOTIVE(5,J,J)*(MOTIVE(1,J,J)-MOTIV
     1E(2,J,J)))-G
      MOTIVE(18,J,J)=MOTIVE(4,J,J)+V-(MOTIVE(6,J,J)*MOTIVE(2,J,J))-W
2     CONTINUE
      DO 3 J=1,N
      MOTIVE(1,J,J)=MOTIVE(1,J,J)+MOTIVE(17,J,J)
      MOTIVE(2,J,J)=MOTIVE(2,J,J)+MOTIVE(18,J,J)
      MOTIVE(13,J,1)=MOTIVE(13,J,2)
      MOTIVE(13,J,2)=MOTIVE(13,J,3)
C     THE NEXT STMT COMPUTES EAR T.
      MOTIVE(13,J,3)=MOTIVE(1,J,J)-MOTIVE(2,J,J)
3     CONTINUE
      DO 4 J=1,N
      DO 4 K=1,19
4     CHEK(J,K)=CHEK(J,K+1)
      CALL CHECKS
      LP=L
      DO 5 J=1,L
C     OTRCGP IS THE VARIABLE NAME OF THE PRIOR ONGOING TENDENCY GROUP
C     OTRCG IS THE CURRENT ONGOING TENDENCY GROUP.
5     OTRCGP(J)=OTRCG(J)
      CALL CNGO
      IF (CHEK(1,20).NE.CHEK(1,19)) GO TO 6
      GO TO 7
6     CALL CROSS
7     CALL INOUT
      CALL CHANGE
      ZAP=0.
8     CONTINUE
9     CONTINUE
      END
      SUBROUTINE INIT
C     SUBROUTINE INIT READS IN VARIABLES, INITIALIZES VALUES, AND PRINTS
C     OUT BEGINNING VALUES FOR ALL MAIN VARIABLES.
      DATA YES/'YES'/
      FULL=20001
      SUMARY=20001
      PRTOKL=0
      NAMLST=20001
      ZAP=0.
      T=1.
      FULCNT=1.
      SUMCNT=1.
      NAMCNT=1.
      USED=0
```

```
      WRITE (6,80)
      READ (5,93) N
      WRITE (6,91)
      READ (5,92) UNIQUE
C     NEXT 4 STMTS ZERO START MATRIX.
      DO 1 K=1,23
      DO 1 J=1,N
      DO 1 I=1,N
1     START(K,J,I)=0.
      FTIME=0.
      PIFO=0
      DO 2 I=1,N
C     NEXT 12 STMTS INITIALIZE VALUES FOR T,M,F,I,C,R FOR EACH  BEHAVIOR
      WRITE (6,81) I
      READ (5,82) START(1,I,I)
      WRITE (6,83)
      READ (5,82) START(2,I,I)
      WRITE (6,84)
      READ (5,82) START(3,I,I)
      WRITE (6,85)
      READ (5,82) START(4,I,I)
      WRITE (6,86)
      READ (5,82) START(5,I,I)
      WRITE (6,87)
      READ (5,82) START(6,I,I)
      WRITE (6,79)
      READ (5,82) SEL(I)
      WRITE (6,67)
      READ (5,82) START(11,I,I)
      WRITE (6,33)
      READ (5,82) SIGI(I)
      WRITE (6,68)
      READ (5,82) START(12,I,I)
      WRITE (6,34)
      READ (5,82) SIGC(I)
2     START(13,I,3)=START(1,I,I)-START(2,I,I)
C     THE NEXT 34 LINES SPECIFY SUBSTITUTION AND/OR DISPLACEMENT.
      WRITE (6,69)
      READ (5,92) ANSWER
      IF (ANSWER.NE.YES) GO TO 5
      WRITE (6,70)
      DO 3 I=1,N
      DO 3 J=1,N
      IF (I.EQ.J) GO TO 3
      WRITE (6,71) I,J
      READ (5,82) START(7,I,J)
3     CONTINUE
      WRITE (6,72)
      DO 4 I=1,N
      DO 4 J=1,N
      IF (I.EQ.J) GO TO 4
      WRITE (6,71) I,J
      READ (5,82) START(8,I,J)
4     CONTINUE
5     WRITE (6,73)
      READ (5,92) ANSWER
      IF (ANSWER.NE.YES) GO TO 8
      WRITE (6,74)
      DO 6 I=1,N
      DO 6 J=1,N
      IF (I.EQ.J) GO TO 6
      WRITE (6,71) I,J
      READ (5,82) START(9,I,J)
6     CONTINUE
      WRITE (6,75)
      DO 7 I=1,N
      DO 7 J=1,N
      IF (I.EQ.J) GO TO 7
      WRITE (6,71) I,J
      READ (5,82) START(10,I,J)
7     CONTINUE
8     DO 9 I=1,N
9     LAG(I)=1.+AMAX1(START(11,I,I),START(12,I,I))
      LAGON=100
C     NEXT 4 STMTS ZERO COMPATABILITY MATRICES.
      DO 10 K=14,16
      DO 10 I=1,N
      DO 10 J=1,N
      START(K,I,J)=0.0
```

```
10     CONTINUE
C      THE NEXT 3 STMTS MAKE EACH BEHAVIOR COMPATABLE WITH ITSELF!
       DO 11 K=14,16
       DO 11 I=1,N
       START(K,I,I)=1.0
11     CONTINUE
C      NEXT 9 STMTS SPECIFY RESULTANT COMPABILITY MATRIX.
       WRITE (6,76)
       READ (5,92) ANSWER
       IF (ANSWER.NE.YES) GO TO 13
       WRITE (6,77)
       DO 12 I=1,N
       DO 12 J=1,N
       IF (I.EQ.J) GO TO 12
       WRITE (6,78) I,J
C      "ITEMP" IS THE INTEGER EQUIVALENT OF A REAL NUMBER.
       READ (5,89) ITEMP
       START(16,I,J)=ITEMP
12     CONTINUE
13     WRITE (6,88)
       READ (5,92) ANSWER
       IF (ANSWER.EQ.YES) TIME=500
       IF (TIME.NE.500) WRITE (6,90)
       IF (TIME.NE.500) READ (5,94) TIME
       WRITE (6,35)
       READ (5,92) ANSWER
       IF (ANSWER.EQ.YES) USED=1
       WRITE (6,36)
       READ (5,92) ANSWER
       IF (ANSWER.NE.YES) GO TO 14
       WRITE (6,37)
       READ (5,94) FULL
14     WRITE (6,38)
       READ (5,92) ANSWER
       IF (ANSWER.NE.YES) GO TO 15
       WRITE (6,37)
       READ (5,94) SUMARY
15     WRITE (6,39)
       READ (5,92) ANSWER
       IF (ANSWER.NE.YES) GO TO 16
       PRTOKL=1
16     WRITE (6,40)
       READ (5,92) ANSWER
       IF (ANSWER.NE.YES) GO TO 17
       WRITE (6,41)
       READ (6,94) NAMLST
C      THE FOLLOWING DO LOOP PUTS ALL START MATRIX INTO MAIN
C      WORKING MATRIX, MOTIVE.
17     DO 18 K=1,23
       DO 18 J=1,N
       DO 18 I=1,N
18     MOTIVE(K,J,I)=START(K,J,I)
       WRITE (1) (START(19,I,I),I=1,N),(START(20,J,J),J=1,N)
C      NEXT STMTS OUTPUT INITIAL SUMMARY DATA
       WRITE (6,42) UNIQUE
       WRITE (6,43)
       WRITE (6,44) (MOTIVE(1,I,I),I=1,N)
       WRITE (6,45) (MOTIVE(2,I,I),I=1,N)
       WRITE (6,46) (MOTIVE(3,I,I),I=1,N)
       WRITE (6,47) (MOTIVE(4,I,I),I=1,N)
       WRITE (6,48) (MOTIVE(5,I,I),I=1,N)
       WRITE (6,49) (MOTIVE(6,I,I),I=1,N)
       WRITE (6,50) (SEL(I),I=1,N)
       WRITE (6,51) (MOTIVE(11,I,I),I=1,N)
       WRITE (6,52) (SIGI(I),I=1,N)
       WRITE (6,53) (MOTIVE(12,I,I),I=1,N)
       WRITE (6,54) (SIGC(I),I=1,N)
       WRITE (6,55)
       WRITE (6,98)
       DO 19 I=1,N
19     WRITE (6,95) (I,(MOTIVE(7,I,J),J=1,N))
       WRITE (6,56)
       WRITE (6,98)
       DO 20 I=1,N
20     WRITE (6,95) (I,(MOTIVE(8,I,J),J=1,N))
       WRITE (6,57)
       WRITE (6,98)
       DO 21 I=1,N
21     WRITE (6,95) (I,(MOTIVE(9,I,J),J=1,N))
```

```
      WRITE (6,58)
      WRITE (6,98)
      DO 22 I=1,N
22    WRITE (6,95) (I,(MOTIVE(10,I,J),J=1,N))
      WRITE (6,96)
      WRITE (6,98)
      DO 23 I=1,N
23    WRITE (6,59) (I,(MOTIVE(16,I,J),J=1,N))
      WRITE (6,97) TIME
      IF (USED.EQ.0) WRITE (6,60)
      IF (USED.EQ.1) WRITE (6,61)
      IF (FULL.NE.20001) WRITE (6,62) FULL
      IF (FULL.EQ.20001) WRITE (6,29)
      IF (SUMARY.NE.20001) WRITE (6,63) SUMARY
      IF (SUMARY.EQ.20001) WRITE (6,30)
      IF (PRTOKL.NE.0) WRITE (6,64)
      IF (PRTOKL.EQ.0) WRITE (6,31)
      IF (NAMLST.NE.20001) WRITE (6,65) NAMLST
      IF (NAMLST.EQ.20001) WRITE (6,32)
C     WRITE FULL OUTPUT COLUMN LABELS.
      IF ((T.EQ.1).AND.(FULL.NE.0)) WRITE (6,66)
      DO 24 I=1,N
24    CVAL(I)=MOTIVE(5,I,I)
      NM=N-1
      NO=N+1
      DO 25 I=1,20
      DO 25 J=1,25
25    CHEK(J,I)=0
      CALL CHECKS
      CALL ONGO
      DO 26 I=1,N
26    CHEK(I,19)=CHEK(I,20)
      WRITE (8) T,CHEK(1,20)
      DO 27 I=1,N
      IF (I.EQ.CHEK(1,20)) GO TO 27
      MOTIVE(3,I,I)=MOTIVE(3,I,I)*SEL(I)
      MOTIVE(4,I,I)=MOTIVE(4,I,I)*SEL(I)
      MOTIVE(5,I,I)=0.
27    CONTINUE
      CHECK(1)=CHEK(1,20)
      CALL INOUT
      IF (USED.EQ.0) RETURN
      DO 28 I=1,L
      MOTIVE(3,OTRCG(I),OTRCG(I))=START(3,OTRCG(I),OTRCG(I))
      MOTIVE(4,OTRCG(I),OTRCG(I))=START(4,OTRCG(I),OTRCG(I))
28    MOTIVE(5,OTRCG(I),OTRCG(I))=START(5,OTRCG(I),OTRCG(I))
      RETURN
C
29    FORMAT (1X,'NO FULL OUTPUT')
30    FORMAT (1X,'NO SUMMARY OUTPUT')
31    FORMAT (1X,'NO PROTOCOL OUTPUT')
32    FORMAT (1X,'NO NAMELIST INPUT')
33    FORMAT (1X,'INITIATION LAG CURVE PARAMETER (USE .4 FOR DEFAULT)?')
34    FORMAT (1X,'CESSATION LAG CURVE PARAMETER (USE .4 FOR DEFAULT)?')
35    FORMAT (1X,'IS SELECTIVE ATTENTION APPLIED TO ALL ONGOING TENDENCI
     1ES?')
36    FORMAT (1X,'OUTPUT CAN BE FULL, SUMMARY, AND/OR PROTOCOL:'/'TYPE "
     1YES" OR "NO" FOR EACH:  FULL OUTPUT?')
37    FORMAT (1X,'EVERY "X" TIME UNITS.  SPECIFY "X" AS A 5 DIGIT INTEGE
     1R?')
38    FORMAT (1X,'SUMMARY OUTPUT?')
39    FORMAT (1X,'PROTOCOL OUTPUT?')
40    FORMAT (1X,'DO YOU WISH TO DYNAMICALLY CHANGE VARIABLES'/1X,'(REAL
     1IZE THAT YOU WILL HAVE TO KNOW THE PROGRAM NAME FOR'/1X,'EACH VARI
     2ABLE NAME YOU CHANGE)?')
41    FORMAT (1X,'AT WHAT TIME INTERVAL DO YOU WISH TO ENTER NEW VALUES'
     1/1X,'(SPECIFY AS A 5 DIGIT INTEGER)?')
42    FORMAT (/////32X,08A4//)
43    FORMAT (15X,'1',9X,'2',9X,'3',9X,'4',9X,'5',9X,'6')
44    FORMAT (1X,'ACTION TEN',6(F9.4,1X))
45    FORMAT (1X,'NEGACTION ',6(F9.4,1X))
46    FORMAT (1X,'INSTIG FOR',6(F9.4,1X))
47    FORMAT (1X,'INHIB FORC',6(F9.4,1X))
48    FORMAT (1X,'CONSUM FOR',6(F9.4,1X))
49    FORMAT (1X,'FORCE OF R',6(F9.4,1X))
50    FORMAT (1X,'SELECT ATT',6(F9.4,1X))
51    FORMAT (1X,'INITIA LAG',6(F9.4,1X))
52    FORMAT (1X,'I LAG CURV',6(F9.4,1X))
53    FORMAT (1X,'CESSAT LAG',6(F9.4,1X))
```

```
54     FORMAT (1X,'C LAG CURV',6(F9.4,1X))
55     FORMAT (//22X,'DISPLACEMENT  ACTION'/)
56     FORMAT (//22X,'DISPLACEMENT  NEGACTION'/)
57     FORMAT (//22X,'SUBSTITUTION  ACTION'/)
58     FORMAT (//22X,'SUBSTITUTION  NEGACTION'/)
59     FORMAT (3X,I2,3X,10(F3.1,3X))
60     FORMAT (1X,'SELECTIVE ATTENTION IS APPLIED ONLY TO THE DOMINANT TE
      1NDENCY.')
61     FORMAT (1X,'SELECTIVE ATTENTION IS APPLIED TO ALL THE ONGOING TEND
      1ENCIES.')
62     FORMAT (1X,'FULL OUTPUT EVERY ',I5,' TIME UNITS.')
63     FORMAT (1X,'SUMMARY OUTPUT EVERY ',I5,' TIME UNITS.')
64     FORMAT (1X,'PROTOCOL OUTPUT.')
65     FORMAT (1X,'INPUT WILL BE REQUESTED AT ',I5)
66     FORMAT ('1',4X,'TIME',4X,'X',4X,'DELTA IX',4X,'TX',4X,'DELTA NX',4
      1X,'NX',4X,'BAR TX'/)
67     FORMAT (1X,'INITIATION CONSUMMATORY LAG PERIOD?')
68     FORMAT (1X,'CESSATION CONSUMMATORY LAG PERIOD?')
69     FORMAT (1X,'DO YOU WISH TO SPECIFY DISPLACEMENT:'/1X,'TYPE "YES" O
      1R "NO"?')
70     FORMAT (1X,'ACTION TENDENCY DEGREE OF DISPLACEMENT BETWEEN TENDENC
      1IES:')
71     FORMAT (1X,I2,' AND ',I2,' :')
72     FORMAT (1X,'NEGACTION TENDENCY DEGREE OF DISPLACEMENT BETWEEN TEND
      1ENCIES:')
73     FORMAT (1X,'DO YOU WISH TO SPECIFY SUBSTITUTION:'/1X,'TYPE "YES" O
      1R "NO"?')
74     FORMAT (1X,'ACTION TENDENCY DEGREE OF SUBSTITUTION BETWEEN TENDENC
      1IES:')
75     FORMAT (1X,'NEGACTION TENDENCY DEGREE OF SUBSTITUTION BETWEEN TEND
      1ENCIES:')
76     FORMAT (1X,'DO YOU WISH TO SPECIFY THE RESULTANT COMPATIBILITY MAT
      1RIX:'/1X,'TYPE "YES" OR "NO"?')
77     FORMAT (1X,'SPECIFY "1" FOR COMPATIBLE RELATIONSHIPS AND "0" FOR'/
      11X,'INCOMPATIBLE RELATIONSHIPS:')
78     FORMAT (1X,I2,' WITH ',I2,' :')
79     FORMAT (1X,'SELECTIVE ATTENTION?')
80     FORMAT (/1X,'THIS IS A SIMULATION OF THE ATKINSON AND BIRCH THEORY
      1:'/1X,'THE DYNAMICS OF ACTION.  ALL DATA IS TO BE REAL'/1X,'NUMBER
      2S (WITH DECIMAL POINT) EXCEPT WHERE SPECIFIED AS INTEGER.'///1X,'H
      3OW MANY BEHAVIORS ARE TO BE SIMULATED (TWO DIGIT INTEGER)?')
81     FORMAT (//1X,'FOR BEHAVIOR NUMBER ',I2,' SPECIFY THE FOLLOWING:'//
      11X,'INITIAL ACTION TENDENCY?')
82     FORMAT (F10.4)
83     FORMAT (1X,'INITIAL NEGACTION TENDENCY?')
84     FORMAT (1X,'INSTIGATING FORCE?')
85     FORMAT (1X,'INHIBITORY FORCE?')
86     FORMAT (1X,'CONSUMMATORY VALUE?')
87     FORMAT (1X,'RESISTANCE VALUE?')
88     FORMAT (1X,'SIMULATED TIME EQUAL 500?  TYPE "YES" OR "NO"?')
89     FORMAT (I1)
90     FORMAT (1X,'SPECIFY TIME AS A 5 DIGIT INTEGER?')
91     FORMAT (//1X,'SPECIFY ONE UNIQUE IDENTIFIER FOR YORSELF AND'/1X,'T
      1HIS RUN (UP TO 8 CHARACTERS)?')
92     FORMAT (15A4)
93     FORMAT (I2)
94     FORMAT (I5)
95     FORMAT (3X,I2,2X,10(F5.3,1X))
96     FORMAT (//22X,'RESULTANT COMPATIBILITY MATRIX'/)
97     FORMAT (//1X,'TOTAL TIME UNITS = ',I5)
98     FORMAT (9X,'1',5X,'2',5X,'3',5X,'4',5X,'5',5X,'6',5X,'7',5X,'8',5X
      1,'9',5X,'10')
       END
       SUBROUTINE INOUT
C      THIS SUBROUTINE DETERMINES WHEN INPUT AND OUTPUT IS DESIRED.
       NAMELIST /DATA/ MOTIVE,START,TIME,PRTOKL,USED,PRTC,SEL
       IF (FULCNT.GE.FULL) GO TO 5
       IF (FULL.EQ.1) GO TO 5
1      IF (SUMCNT.GE.SUMARY) GO TO 6
2      IF (NAMCNT.GE.NAMLST) GO TO 12
C      IS THIS THE FINAL RUN THROUGH.
3      IF ((SUMARY.NE.20001).AND.(T.GE.TIME)) GO TO 13
4      IF ((PRTOKL.EQ.1).AND.(T.GE.TIME)) GO TO 18
       RETURN
C      HERE STARTS FULL OUTPUT.
C      THE NEXT STMT IS THE MAIN FULL OUTPUT STMT.
5      WRITE (6,20) (T,((I,MOTIVE(17,I,I),MOTIVE(1,I,I),MOTIVE(18,I,I),MO
      1TIVE(2,I,I),MOTIVE(13,I,3)),I=1,N))
       IF (ZAP.EQ.1) WRITE (6,30) (T,CHEK(1,19),CHEK(1,20),CHEK(1,19),ELA
```

```
     1PSE)
      FULCNT=0.
      GO TO 1
C     HERE STARTS SUMARY OUTPUT.
C     NEXT STMT WRITES SUMMARY DATA TITLES.
6     WRITE (6,21)
      READ (2) (MOTIVE(22,I,I),I=1,N),(MOTIVE(23,I,I),I=1,N)
      DO 7 I=1,N
      DON(I)=MOTIVE(19,I,I)-MOTIVE(22,I,I)
7     DPICK(I)=MOTIVE(20,I,I)-MOTIVE(23,I,I)
      WRITE (1) (MOTIVE(19,I,I),I=1,N),(MOTIVE(20,J,J),J=1,N)
      I=1
8     J=1
      IF (J.EQ.I) J=J+1
      IJKL=DPICK(I)
      IJKM=MOTIVE(20,I,I)
      IJKN=MOTIVE(21,I,J)
      WRITE (6,22) (I,DON(I),MOTIVE(19,I,I),IJKL,IJKM,IJKN,I,J)
9     J=J+1
      IF (J.EQ.I) J=J+1
      IF (J.GT.N) GO TO 10
      IJKN=MOTIVE(21,I,J)
      WRITE (6,23) (IJKN,I,J)
      GO TO 9
10    I=I+1
      IF (I.GT.N) GO TO 11
      GO TO 8
11    SUMCNT=0.
      WRITE (6,32)
      GO TO 2
C     NAMELIST READ IN OF NEW DATA.
C     INPUT IS DONE VIA A FORTRAN NAMELIST.  THE FIRST SPACE
C     OF EACH CARD IS BLANK.  THE SECOND SPACE OF THE FIRST CARD
C     HAS AN "&" IN IT, FOLLOWED BY THE NAME OF THE NAMELIST
C     ("DATA"), FOLLOWED BY A SPACE, THE VARIABLES TO BE CHANGED FOLLOW
C     EACH TERMINATED BY A COMMA.  THE LAST CHARACTERS ARE "&END".
C     A SAMPLE NAMELIST FOLLOWS:
C      &DATA MOTIVE(4,1,1)=0.0,START(4,1,1)=0.0,NAMLST=500.,
C     FULL=200,...,SEL(8)=.25,&END
C
12    WRITE (6,24)
C     20000 IS THE MAXIMUM SIMULATED TIME, THEREFORE, UNLESS
C     "NAMLST" IS SPECIFIED AT DYNAMIC INPUT, THE REQUEST FOR
C     INPUT WILL OCCUR ONLY ONCE.
      NAMLST=20000
      READ (5,DATA)
      WRITE (6,25) T
      GO TO 3
C     FROM HERE TO #64 WRITES CUMULATIVE SUMMARY STATISTICS.
13    WRITE (6,26)
      I=1
14    J=1
      IF (J.EQ.I) J=J+1
      IJKM=MOTIVE(20,I,I)
      IJKN=MOTIVE(21,I,J)
      WRITE (6,27) (I,MOTIVE(19,I,I),IJKM,IJKN,I,J)
15    J=J+1
      IF (J.EQ.I) J=J+1
      IF (J.GT.N) GO TO 16
      IJKN=MOTIVE(21,I,J)
      WRITE (6,31) (IJKN,I,J)
      GO TO 15
16    I=I+1
      IF (I.GT.N) GO TO 17
      GO TO 14
17    CONTINUE
      GO TO 4
C     FINAL PROTOCOL OUTPUT STARTS HERE.
18    READ (7) TKO,TEND
      WRITE (6,28) TKO,TEND
      DO 19 I=1,PIFO
      READ (7) (XZA(I),XZB(I),XZC(I),XZD(I),XZE(I))
      WRITE (6,29) ((XZA(I),XZB(I),XZC(I),XZD(I),XZE(I)))
19    CONTINUE
      RETURN
C
20    FORMAT (1X,F7.1,25(T13,I2,4X,F6.1,2X,F7.1,2X,F6.1,2X,F7.1,2X,F7.1/
     1))
21    FORMAT (2X,'X',1X,'TIME IN X',2X,'TOTAL TIME',2X,'FREQ X WAS DOM',
```

```
     12X,'TOTAL FREQ',2X,'FREQ FROM X TO Y'/4X,'FROM LAST',5X,'IN X',21X
     2,'X WAS DOM'/)
22    FORMAT (1X,I2,1X,F7.1,4X,F7.1,8X,I3,12X,I3,6X,I3,6X,I2,' TO ',I2)
23    FORMAT (54X,I3,6X,I2,' TO ',I2)
24    FORMAT (1X,'ENTER NEW DATA AS NAMELIST VARIABLES:')
25    FORMAT (1X,'INPUT DATA ACCEPTED AT ',F6.1)
26    FORMAT (///17X,'FINAL CUMULATIVE SUMMARY STATISTICS'///2X,'X',3X,'
     1TOTAL TIME IN X',3X,'FREQ X WAS DOMINANT',3X,'FREQ FROM X TO Y'/)
27    FORMAT (1X,I2,6X,F7.1,16X,I3,11X,I3,6X,I2,' TO ',I2)
28    FORMAT ('1',1X,F7.1,' IS THE TIME.  THE INITIAL ACTIVITY IS ',I2)
29    FORMAT (/1X,'TIME = ',F6.1,'  CHANGE OCCURED FROM ',I2,' TO ',I2,'
     1  TIME IN ',I2,' WAS ',F5.1)
30    FORMAT (//1X,'A CHANGE IN ACTIVITY HAS OCCURED AT ',F8.1,/1X,'TIME
     1 UNITS FROM ',I2,' TO ',I2,' .  TIME IN ',I2,' WAS ',F6.1//)
31    FORMAT (46X,I3,6X,I2,' TO ',I2)
32    FORMAT (1X)
      END
      SUBROUTINE ONGO
C     THIS SUBROUTINE DETERMINES THE ONGOING TENDENCY GROUP USING THE
C     RESULTANT COMPATIBILITY MATRIX.
C     THE DOMINANT TENDENCY, DETERMINED IN CHECKS, IS FIRST.
      L=1
C     OTRCG (1) IS THE # OF THE MOST DOMINANT TENDENCY, OTRCG(L) ARE
C     THE #'S OF THE L ONGOING BEHAVIORS.
      OTRCG(1)=CHEK(1,20)
C     THE NEXT 6 STMTS DETERMINE IF THERE ARE ANY OTHER TENDENCIES
C     COMPATABLE WITH THE MOST DOMINANT.
      DO 1 J=2,N
      IF (MOTIVE(16,CHEK(1,20),CHEK(J,20)).EQ.1.) L=L+1
      IF (MOTIVE(16,CHEK(1,20),CHEK(J,20)).EQ.1.) OTRCG(L)=CHEK(J,20)
1     CONTINUE
      IF (L.EQ.1) RETURN
2     DO 4 K=2,L
      DO 4 M=1,L
      IF (K.GE.M) GO TO 4
      IF (MOTIVE(16,OTRCG(K),OTRCG(M)).EQ.1.) GO TO 4
      DO 3 I=M,L
3     OTRCG(I)=OTRCG(I+1)
      GO TO 5
C     "L" IS THE # OF ONGOING BEHAVIORS.
4     CONTINUE
      RETURN
5     CONTINUE
      L=L-1
      GO TO 2
      END
      SUBROUTINE CHECKS
C     SUBROUTINE CHECKS DETERMINES ORDER (GREATEST TO LEAST) OF
C     RESULTANT TENDENCIES.
      MAXI=0
      DO 1 J=1,N
1     MOTIVE(13,J,4)=MOTIVE(13,J,3)
      DO 5 I=1,N
C     NEXT 3 STMTS ASSIGN "MAXI" TO THE VALUE OF THE GREATEST
C     RESULTANT TENDENCY ON THE FIRST PASS, 2ND GREATEST ON THE 2ND PASS
      DO 2 K=1,N
      IF (MAXI.LT.MOTIVE(13,K,4)) MAXI=MOTIVE(13,K,4)
2     CONTINUE
      DO 3 L1=1,N
      IF (MOTIVE(13,L1,4).EQ.MAXI) GO TO 4
3     CONTINUE
C     "L1" IS A LOCAL VARIABLE WHICH IS THE VALUE OF THE BEHAVIOR # OF
C     THE GREATEST RES. TEND. ON THE FIRST PASS, THE 2ND GREATEST PASS,
4     CHEK(I,20)=L1
      MOTIVE(13,L1,4)=0.
      MAXI=0
5     CONTINUE
C     THE NEXT STMT UPDATES "TOTAL TIME" IN THE DOMINANT ACTIVITY.
      MOTIVE(19,CHEK(1,20),CHEK(1,20))=MOTIVE(19,CHEK(1,20),CHEK(1,20))+
     11.
      RETURN
      END
      SUBROUTINE CHANGE
C     THIS SUBROUTINE UPDATES INFORMATION; ESPECIALLY LAGS AND
C     CONSUMMATORY VALUE.
      LAGON=LAGON+1
C     VARIABLE "USED" DENOTES HOW TO USE THE ONGOING GROUP.
C     SELECTIVE ATTENTION IS APPLIED TO ALL BUT THE DOMINANT ACTIVITY.
      DO 1 I=1,N
```

```
      MOTIVE(3,I,I)=START(3,I,I)*SEL(I)
1     MOTIVE(4,I,I)=START(4,I,I)*SEL(I)
      MOTIVE(3,CHEK(1,20),CHEK(1,20))=START(3,CHEK(1,20),CHEK(1,20))
      MOTIVE(4,CHEK(1,20),CHEK(1,20))=START(4,CHEK(1,20),CHEK(1,20))
      IF (USED.EQ.0) GO TO 3
C     IF "USED" = 1, THEN THE NEXT STMTS FOLLOW THE PATTERN
C     OF THE PRIOR STMTS FOR THE ENTIRE COMPATIBILITY GROUP.
      DO 2 I=1,L
      MOTIVE(3,OTRCG(I),OTRCG(I))=START(3,OTRCG(I),OTRCG(I))
      MOTIVE(4,OTRCG(I),OTRCG(I))=START(4,OTRCG(I),OTRCG(I))
2     CONTINUE
C     THE SECOND HALF OF CHANGE DEALS WITH LAGS AND CONSUMATORY VALUE.
C     LAGS IS A VARIABLE WHICH IS SET TO THE LONGEST LAG PERIOD OF ALL
C     THE TENDENCIES.
C     LAG(I) IS THE NUMBER OF TIME UNITS + 1 EACH TENDENCY "I" HAS BEEN
C     ITS LAG PERIOD.
C     LAGS EQUALS 0 IN THE HIGHLY THEORETICAL CASE WHERE ALL TENDENCIES
C     ZERO LAG PERIODS.  LAGON EQUALS 1 ONLY WHEN CONTROL HAS JUST
C     TRANSFERRED FROM CROSS AFTER A CHANGE IN ACTIVITY.
3     LAGS=0.
      DO 4 J=11,12
      DO 4 I=1,N
C     LAGS IS SET TO THE MAXIMUM OF ALL THE LAG PERIODS.
4     IF (LAGS.LT.MOTIVE(J,I,I)) LAGS=MOTIVE(J,I,I)
      DO 5 I=1,N
5     LAG(I)=LAG(I)+1.
      IF ((LAGS.EQ.0).AND.(LAGON.NE.1)) RETURN
      IF (LAGS.EQ.0) GO TO 9
C     IF THERE ARE NO TENDENCIES IN THEIR LAG PERIODS THEN RETURN.
      IF (LAGON.GT.LAGS) RETURN
C     IF A CHANGE IN ACTIVITY HAS OCCURED IN THE LAST TIME UNIT, CONTROL
C     GOES TO STEP 16.
      IF (CHEK(1,19).NE.CHEK(1,20)) GO TO 9
C     THE NEXT STMTS UPDATE THE CONSUMMATORY VALUE OF THOSE
C     TENDENCIES IN THEIR LAG PERIODS.
      DO 8 I=1,N
      DO 6 J=1,L
      IF (I.EQ.OTRCG(J)) GO TO 7
6     CONTINUE
      IF (LAG(I).GT.MOTIVE(12,I,I)) GO TO 8
      XPON=-0.5*(((-2.5*(MOTIVE(12,I,I)-LAG(I))/MOTIVE(12,I,I))/SIGC(I))
     1**2)
      MOTIVE(5,I,I)=CVAL(I)-CVAL(I)*EXP(XPON)
      GO TO 8
7     IF (LAG(I).GT.MOTIVE(11,I,I)) GO TO 8
      XPON=-0.5*(((-2.5*(MOTIVE(11,I,I)-LAG(I))/MOTIVE(11,I,I))/SIGI(I))
     1**2)
      MOTIVE(5,I,I)=EXP(XPON)*(START(5,I,I)-CVAL(I))+CVAL(I)
8     CONTINUE
      GO TO 21
C     A CHANGE IN ACTIVITY OCCURED IN THE LAST TIME INTERVAL.  CONSUMMAT
C     VALUE IS FIGURED ACCORDING TO THE ONGOING COMPATIBILITY GROUP.
C     CERTAIN KEY VALUES MUST BE RESET (CVAL).
9     DO 20 I=1,N
      DO 10 J=1,LP
      IF (I.EQ.OTRCGP(J)) GO TO 15
10    CONTINUE
      DO 11 J=1,L
      IF (I.EQ.OTRCG(J)) GO TO 13
11    CONTINUE
      IF (MOTIVE(12,I,I).NE.0.0) GO TO 12
      MOTIVE(1,I,I)=(START(3,I,I)*SEL(I))/START(5,I,I)
      MOTIVE(5,I,I)=0.0
12    IF (LAG(I).GT.MOTIVE(12,I,I)) GO TO 20
      XPON=-0.5*(((-2.5*(MOTIVE(12,I,I)-LAG(I))/MOTIVE(12,I,I))/SIGC(I))
     1**2)
      MOTIVE(5,I,I)=CVAL(I)-CVAL(I)*EXP(XPON)
      GO TO 20
13    IF (MOTIVE(11,I,I).NE.0.0) GO TO 14
C     "I" IS ONGOING WITH ZERO INITIATION LAGS.
      MOTIVE(5,I,I)=START(5,I,I)
      GO TO 20
C     THE NEXT 6 STMTS APPLY IF "I" IS CURRENTLY ONGOING AND THE
C     INITIATION LAG PERIOD IS GREATER THAN ZERO.
14    CVAL(I)=MOTIVE(5,I,I)
      LAG(I)=1.
      XPON=-0.5*(((-2.5*(MOTIVE(11,I,I)-LAG(I))/MOTIVE(11,I,I))/SIGI(I))
     1**2)
      MOTIVE(5,I,I)=EXP(XPON)*(START(5,I,I)-CVAL(I))+CVAL(I)
```

```
      LAGON=1
      GO TO 20
15    DO 16 J=1,L
      IF (I.EQ.OTRCG(J)) GC TO 18
16    CONTINUE
      IF (MOTIVE(12,I,I).NE.0.0) GO TO 17
C     "I" IS NEWLY SUBDOMINANT AND HAS ZEBC CESSATION LAGS.
      MOTIVE(1,I,I)=(START(3,I,I)*SEL(I))/(START(5,I,I)*START(1,I,I))
      MOTIVE(5,I,I)=0.0
      GO TO 20
C     "I" IS NEWLY NOT ONGOING WITH CESSATICN LAG GREATER THAN ZERO.
17    CVAL(I)=MOTIVE(5,I,I)
      LAG(I)=1.
      XPON=-0.5*(((-2.5*(MOTIVE(12,I,I)-LAG(I))/MOTIVE(12,I,I))/SIGC(I))
     1**2)
      MOTIVE(5,I,I)=CVAL(I)-CVAL(I)*EXP(XPCN)
      LAGCN=1
      GO TO 20
18    CONTINUE
      IF (MOTIVE(11,I,I).NE.0.0) GO TC 19
C     "I" IS ONGOING WITH ZERO INITIATION IAG.
      MOTIVE(5,I,I)=START(5,I,I)
      GO TO 20
19    IF (LAG(I).GT.MOTIVE(11,I,I)) GC TO 20
C     "I" IS ONGOING AND INITIATION LAG IS GREATER THAN ZERO.
      XPON=-0.5*(((-2.5*(MOTIVE(11,I,I)-LAG(I))/MOTIVE(11,I,I))/SIGI(I))
     1**2)
      MOTIVE(5,I,I)=EXP(XPCN)*(START(5,I,I)-CVAL(I))+CVAL(I)
20    CONTINUE
21    RETURN
      END
      SUBROUTINE CROSS
C     CROSS MAGNIFIES ONE TIME INTERVAL ANC SPLITS IT INTO TEN PARTS.
      DIMENSION MDEC(25), TEMP1(25), TEMP2(25)
      DO 1 J=1,N
      MOTIVE(3,J,J)=MOTIVE(3,J,J)*0.1
      MOTIVE(4,J,J)=MOTIVE(4,J,J)*0.1
      MOTIVE(6,J,J)=MOTIVE(6,J,J)*0.1
      MOTIVE(1,J,J)=MOTIVE(1,J,J)-MOTIVE(17,J,J)
      MOTIVE(13,J,10)=MOTIVE(13,J,3)
1     MOTIVE(2,J,J)=MOTIVE(2,J,J)-MOTIVE(18,J,J)
C     UP TO STEP 2 DIVIDES CONSUMATORY VALUES UP INTO SMALLER UNITS
C     OVER ONE TENTH TIME UNITS AND OVER THE LAG PERIODS.
      DO 7 I=1,N
      IF (CHEK(1,19).EQ.I) GO TO 4
      IF ((LAG(I)-1).GT.MOTIVE(12,I,I)) GC TC 3
      LAG(I)=LAG(I)-1
      IF (MOTIVE(12,I,I).EQ.0.0) GO TO 2
      XPON=-0.5*(((-2.5*(MOTIVE(12,I,I)-LAG(I))/MOTIVE(12,I,I))/SIGC(I))
     1**2)
      MOTIVE(5,I,I)=CVAL(I)-CVAL(I)*EXP(XPON)
2     MOTIVE(5,I,I)=MOTIVE(5,I,I)*0.1
      MDEC(I)=1
      GO TO 7
3     MOTIVE(5,I,I)=0.
      MDEC(I)=0
      GO TO 7
4     LAG(I)=LAG(I)-1
      IF (MOTIVE(11,I,I).EQ.0.0) GO TO 5
      XPON=-0.5*(((-2.5*(MOTIVE(11,I,I)-LAG(I))/MOTIVE(11,I,I))/SIGI(I))
     1**2)
      MOTIVE(5,I,I)=EXP(XPON)*(START(5,I,I)-CVAL(I))+CVAL(I)
5     MOTIVE(5,I,I)=MOTIVE(5,I,I)*0.1
      IF (LAG(I).GT.MOTIVE(11,I,I)) GO TO 6
      MDEC(I)=1
      GO TO 7
6     MOTIVE(5,I,I)=START(5,I,I)*0.1
      MDEC(I)=0
7     CONTINUE
      T=T-1.
      FULCNT=FULCNT-1.
      SUMCNT=SUMCNT-1.
      NAMCNT=NAMCNT-1.
      DO 8 I=1,N
      IF ((MOTIVE(11,I,I).EQ.0.0).AND.(MOTIVE(12,I,I).EQ.0.0)) GO TO 8
      XINCI(I)=LAG(I)/MOTIVE(11,I,I)
      XINCC(I)=LAG(I)/MOTIVE(12,I,I)
8     CONTINUE
      DO 17 M=11,20
```

```
      Q=M
      DO 10 I=1,N
      IF ((MOTIVE(11,I,I).EQ.0.0).AND.(MOTIVE(12,I,I).EQ.0.0)) GO TO 10
      IF (MDEC(I).NE.1) GO TO 10
      XINCC(I)=XINCC(I)+(1/MOTIVE(12,I,I))*0.1
      XINCI(I)=XINCI(I)+(1/MOTIVE(11,I,I))*0.1
      IF (I.EQ.CHEK(1,19)) GO TO 9
      XPON=-0.5*((-2.5*(1-XINCC(I))/SIGC(I))**2)
      MOTIVE(5,I,I)=0.1*(CVAL(I)-CVAL(I)*EXP(XPON))
      GO TO 10
9     XPON=-0.5*((-2.5*(1-XINCI(I))/SIGI(I))**2)
      MOTIVE(5,I,I)=0.1*EXP(XPON)*(START(5,I,I)-CVAL(I))+CVAL(I)
10    CONTINUE
      T=T+.1
      FULCNT=FULCNT+.1
      SUMCNT=SUMCNT+.1
      NAMCNT=NAMCNT+.1
C     THE POSITIVE AND NEGATIVE ACTION TENDENCY INCREMENTS ARE CALCULATE
      DO 12 J=1,N
      C=0.
      G=0.
      V=0.
      W=0.
      DO 11 K=1,N
      E=MOTIVE(7,K,J)*MOTIVE(3,K,K)
      C=E+C
      H=MOTIVE(9,K,J)*MOTIVE(5,K,K)*(MOTIVE(1,K,K)-MOTIVE(2,K,K))
      G=H+G
      R=MOTIVE(8,K,J)*MOTIVE(4,K,K)
      V=R+V
      S=MOTIVE(10,K,J)*MOTIVE(6,K,K)*MOTIVE(2,K,K)
      W=S+W
      TEMP1(K)=MOTIVE(1,K,K)-MOTIVE(17,K,K)
      TEMP2(K)=MOTIVE(2,K,K)-MOTIVE(18,K,K)
11    CONTINUE
      MOTIVE(17,J,J)=MOTIVE(3,J,J)+C-(MOTIVE(5,J,J)*(MOTIVE(1,J,J)-MOTIV
     1E(2,J,J)))-G
      MOTIVE(18,J,J)=MOTIVE(4,J,J)+V-(MOTIVE(6,J,J)*MOTIVE(2,J,J))-W
12    CONTINUE
C     THE POSITIVE & NEGATIVE & RESULTANT TENDENCIES ARE CALCULATED.
      DO 13 J=1,N
      MOTIVE(1,J,J)=MOTIVE(1,J,J)+MOTIVE(17,J,J)
      MOTIVE(2,J,J)=MOTIVE(2,J,J)+MOTIVE(18,J,J)
      MOTIVE(13,J,M)=MOTIVE(1,J,J)-MOTIVE(2,J,J)
13    MOTIVE(13,J,3)=MOTIVE(13,J,M)
C     THE DOMINANT TENDENCY IS DETERMINED
      MAXI=0.
      DO 14 J=1,N
14    IF (MAXI.LT.MOTIVE(13,J,M)) MAXI=MOTIVE(13,J,M)
      DO 15 I=1,N
      IF (MOTIVE(13,I,M).EQ.MAXI) GO TO 16
15    CONTINUE
C     CHECK(M) IS THE DOMINANT TENDENCY.
16    CHECK(M)=I
      MOTIVE(19,CHECK(M),CHECK(M))=MOTIVE(19,CHECK(M),CHECK(M))+.1
C     CHECK(M) IS COMPARED TO THE PREVIOUS DOMINANT TENDENCY.
      IF ((CHEK(1,19).NE.CHECK(M)).OR.(M.EQ.20)) GO TO 18
      CALL INOUT
17    CONTINUE
C     THE TENTH OF A TIME UNIT IN WHICH THE CHANGE TOOK PLACE HAS BEEN
C     DETERMINED.
18    IF (Q.EQ.20) CHECK(Q)=CHEK(1,20)
C     NEXT STMTS FORM THE ALGORITHM WHICH ASSIGNS THE HIGHEST
C     TWO TENDENCIES TO THE CLOSEST VALUE AT THE CLOSEST
C     .1 TIME UNIT.
      D1=ABS(MOTIVE(13,CHEK(1,20),Q-1)-MOTIVE(13,CHEK(1,19),Q-1))
      D2=ABS(MOTIVE(13,CHEK(1,20),Q)-MOTIVE(13,CHEK(1,19),Q))
      D3=ABS(MOTIVE(13,CHEK(1,20),Q-1)-MOTIVE(13,CHEK(1,20),Q))
      D4=ABS(MOTIVE(13,CHEK(1,19),Q-1)-MOTIVE(13,CHEK(1,19),Q))
      IF ((D1.GE.D2).AND.(D3.GE.D4)) GO TO 19
      IF ((D1.GE.D2).AND.(D3.LT.D4)) GO TO 20
      IF ((D1.LT.D2).AND.(D3.GE.D4)) GO TO 21
      IF ((D1.LT.D2).AND.(D3.LT.D4)) GO TO 22
19    MOTIVE(1,CHEK(1,20),CHEK(1,20))=MOTIVE(1,CHEK(1,20),CHEK(1,20))-MO
     1TIVE(17,CHEK(1,20),CHEK(1,20))
C     "TEMP" IS A TEMPORARY LOCAL VARIABLE.
      TEMP=MOTIVE(13,CHEK(1,19),Q)+MOTIVE(2,CHEK(1,20),CHEK(1,20))
      MOTIVE(17,CHEK(1,20),CHEK(1,20))=TEMP-MOTIVE(1,CHEK(1,20),CHEK(1,2
     10))
```

```
      MOTIVE(1,CHEK(1,20),CHEK(1,20))=TEMP
      MOTIVE(2,CHEK(1,20),CHEK(1,20))=MOTIVE(2,CHEK(1,20),CHEK(1,20))-MO
     1TIVE(18,CHEK(1,20),CHEK(1,20))
      TEMP=MOTIVE(1,CHEK(1,20),CHEK(1,20))-MOTIVE(13,CHEK(1,19),Q)
      MOTIVE(18,CHEK(1,20),CHEK(1,20))=TEMP-MOTIVE(2,CHEK(1,20),CHEK(1,2
     10))
      MOTIVE(2,CHEK(1,20),CHEK(1,20))=TEMP
      MOTIVE(13,CHEK(1,20),3)=MOTIVE(13,CHEK(1,19),3)
      GO TO 25
20    MOTIVE(1,CHEK(1,19),CHEK(1,19))=MOTIVE(1,CHEK(1,19),CHEK(1,19))-MO
     1TIVE(17,CHEK(1,19),CHEK(1,19))
      TEMP=MOTIVE(13,CHEK(1,20),Q)+MOTIVE(2,CHEK(1,19),CHEK(1,19))
      MOTIVE(17,CHEK(1,19),CHEK(1,19))=TEMP-MOTIVE(1,CHEK(1,19),CHEK(1,1
     19))
      MOTIVE(1,CHEK(1,19),CHEK(1,19))=TEMP
      MOTIVE(2,CHEK(1,19),CHEK(1,19))=MOTIVE(2,CHEK(1,19),CHEK(1,19))-MO
     1TIVE(18,CHEK(1,19),CHEK(1,19))
      TEMP=MOTIVE(1,CHEK(1,19),CHEK(1,19))-MOTIVE(13,CHEK(1,20),Q)
      MOTIVE(18,CHEK(1,19),CHEK(1,19))=TEMP-MOTIVE(2,CHEK(1,19),CHEK(1,1
     19))
      MOTIVE(2,CHEK(1,19),CHEK(1,19))=TEMP
      MOTIVE(13,CHEK(1,19),3)=MOTIVE(13,CHEK(1,20),3)
      GO TO 25
21    MOTIVE(1,CHEK(1,20),CHEK(1,20))=MOTIVE(1,CHEK(1,20),CHEK(1,20))-MO
     1TIVE(17,CHEK(1,20),CHEK(1,20))
      MOTIVE(17,CHEK(1,20),CHEK(1,20))=MOTIVE(1,CHEK(1,20),CHEK(1,20))-T
     1EMP1(CHEK(1,20))
      MOTIVE(2,CHEK(1,20),CHEK(1,20))=MOTIVE(2,CHEK(1,20),CHEK(1,20))-MO
     1TIVE(18,CHEK(1,20),CHEK(1,20))
      MOTIVE(18,CHEK(1,20),CHEK(1,20))=MOTIVE(2,CHEK(1,20),CHEK(1,20))-T
     1EMP2(CHEK(1,20))
      MOTIVE(13,CHEK(1,20),3)=MOTIVE(13,CHEK(1,20),Q-1)
      MOTIVE(1,CHEK(1,19),CHEK(1,19))=MOTIVE(1,CHEK(1,19),CHEK(1,19))-MO
     1TIVE(17,CHEK(1,19),CHEK(1,19))
      MOTIVE(2,CHEK(1,19),CHEK(1,19))=MOTIVE(2,CHEK(1,19),CHEK(1,19))-MO
     1TIVE(18,CHEK(1,19),CHEK(1,19))
      MOTIVE(13,CHEK(1,19),3)=MOTIVE(13,CHEK(1,20),3)
      MOTIVE(17,CHEK(1,19),CHEK(1,19))=MOTIVE(1,CHEK(1,19),CHEK(1,19))-T
     1EMP1(CHEK(1,19))
      MOTIVE(18,CHEK(1,19),CHEK(1,19))=MOTIVE(2,CHEK(1,19),CHEK(1,19))-T
     1EMP2(CHEK(1,19))
      T=T-.1
      FULCNT=FULCNT-.1
      NAMCNT=NAMCNT-.1
      SUMCNT=SUMCNT-.1
      GO TO 23
22    MOTIVE(1,CHEK(1,19),CHEK(1,19))=MOTIVE(1,CHEK(1,19),CHEK(1,19))-MO
     1TIVE(17,CHEK(1,19),CHEK(1,19))
      MOTIVE(17,CHEK(1,19),CHEK(1,19))=MOTIVE(1,CHEK(1,19),CHEK(1,19))-T
     1EMP1(CHEK(1,19))
      MOTIVE(2,CHEK(1,19),CHEK(1,19))=MOTIVE(2,CHEK(1,19),CHEK(1,19))-MO
     1TIVE(18,CHEK(1,19),CHEK(1,19))
      MOTIVE(18,CHEK(1,19),CHEK(1,19))=MOTIVE(2,CHEK(1,19),CHEK(1,19))-T
     1EMP2(CHEK(1,19))
      MOTIVE(13,CHEK(1,19),3)=MOTIVE(13,CHEK(1,19),Q-1)
      MOTIVE(1,CHEK(1,20),CHEK(1,20))=MOTIVE(1,CHEK(1,20),CHEK(1,20))-MO
     1TIVE(17,CHEK(1,20),CHEK(1,20))
      MOTIVE(2,CHEK(1,20),CHEK(1,20))=MOTIVE(2,CHEK(1,20),CHEK(1,20))-MO
     1TIVE(18,CHEK(1,20),CHEK(1,20))
      MOTIVE(13,CHEK(1,20),3)=MOTIVE(13,CHEK(1,19),3)
      MOTIVE(17,CHEK(1,20),CHEK(1,20))=MOTIVE(1,CHEK(1,20),CHEK(1,20))-T
     1EMP1(CHEK(1,20))
      MOTIVE(18,CHEK(1,20),CHEK(1,20))=MOTIVE(2,CHEK(1,20),CHEK(1,20))-T
     1EMP2(CHEK(1,20))
      T=T-.1
      FULCNT=FULCNT-.1
      NAMCNT=NAMCNT-.1
      SUMCNT=SUMCNT-.1
23    DO 24 J=3,N
      MOTIVE(13,J,3)=MOTIVE(13,J,Q-1)
      MOTIVE(1,J,J)=MOTIVE(1,J,J)-MOTIVE(17,J,J)
      MOTIVE(2,J,J)=MOTIVE(2,J,J)-MOTIVE(18,J,J)
      MOTIVE(17,J,J)=MOTIVE(1,J,J)-TEMP1(J)
24    MOTIVE(18,J,J)=MOTIVE(2,J,J)-TEMP2(J)
C     PART OF THE MOTIVE BLOCK IS UPDATED.
25    MOTIVE(20,CHEK(1,20),CHEK(1,20))=MOTIVE(20,CHEK(1,20),CHEK(1,20))+
     11.
      MOTIVE(21,CHEK(1,19),CHEK(1,20))=MOTIVE(21,CHEK(1,19),CHEK(1,20))+
     11.
```

```
      MOTIVE(19,CHEK(1,20),CHEK(1,20))=MOTIVE(19,CHEK(1,20),CHEK(1,20))-
     11.1
      DO 28 I=1,N
      MOTIVE(3,I,I)=MOTIVE(3,I,I)*10.
      MOTIVE(4,I,I)=MOTIVE(4,I,I)*10.
      IF ((I.EQ.CHEK(1,19)).AND.(MDEC(I).EQ.1)) GO TO 26
      IF ((I.NE.CHEK(1,19)).AND.(MDEC(I).EQ.1)) GO TO 27
      IF (I.EQ.CHEK(1,19)) MOTIVE(5,I,I)=START(5,I,I)
      GO TO 28
26    XINCI(I)=XINCI(I)-((1/MOTIVE(11,I,I))**2)
      XPON=-0.5*((-2.5*(1-XINCI(I))/SIGI(I))**2)
      MOTIVE(5,I,I)=EXP(XPON)*(START(5,I,I)-CVAL(I))+CVAL(I)
      GO TO 28
27    XINCC(I)=XINCC(I)-((1/MOTIVE(12,I,I))**2)
      XPON=-0.5*((-2.5*(1-XINCC(I))/SIGC(I))**2)
      MOTIVE(5,I,I)=CVAL(I)-CVAL(I)*EXP(XPON)
28    MOTIVE(6,I,I)=MOTIVE(6,I,I)*10.
      ELAPSE=T-FTIME
      FTIME=T
C     ZERO AT THE CROSS POINT
      LAGON=0
      ZAP=1.
C     A DUMP OF INFORMATION TO TEMPORARY FILE FOR PROTOKL OUTPUT IS MADE
      PIFO=PIFO+1
      WRITE (8) T,CHEK(1,19),CHEK(1,20),CHEK(1,19),ELAPSE
      RETURN
      END
```

*

APPENDIX B
COMPUTER SIMULATION OF THE INFLUENCE OF ABILITY AND MOTIVATION ON TEST PERFORMANCE AND CUMULATIVE ACHIEVEMENT AND THE RELATION BETWEEN THEM

James R. Sawusch[1]

This computer simulation grew out of a paper that John W. Atkinson presented at a meeting of ACT Research Institute at Phoenix, February 25 and 26, 1972. The basic premise was that a person's level of achievement is a function of the individual's motivational dispositions, the situation, and his ability. An outline of the process is given in Figure 1 of Chapter 20.

THE THEORY

In order to construct a computer simulation, more rigorous definitions of the transformations involved are needed. First, a few labels need to be attached. The relatively stable personality dispositions will be called *motives.* The relatively transient situational factors are called *incentives.* The strength of motivation for a task (T_A) is also called the strength of tendency. The latter name is used in *The Dynamics of Action* by Atkinson and Birch (1970). Since much of what is assumed in this simulation comes from that work, the latter term will be used here also.

Heredity and prior training deal with the question of origins and development. What we are concerned with here are the contemporary determinants of behavior. On this basis, we will not be concerned with heredity and prior training as fundamental variables. We will take their present state which constitutes the ability, motives, and perception of incentives of the individual.

[1] This work was supported by a grant-in-aid from American College Testing Research Institute to J. W. Atkinson during 1971–1973.

The first step now is to combine the motives and incentives to yield a measure of the strength of a tendency. If, for activity A, there was only one motive (M, e.g., the motive to achieve success M_S) and its associated incentive (I_S), then the instigating force (F) for activity A would be: $F_A = M_S \times I_S$. From previous work by Atkinson, it seems more reasonable to work the multiple motives and incentives for any given activity (e.g., the motives to succeed, to avoid failure, for social approval, etc., each having an associated incentive). Each one of these motive-incentive pairs produces an instigating force for a certain desired consequence or outcome of the activity. If there were n different motive-incentive pairs producing n component forces, the Equation (1) would read:

$$F_A = F_1 + F_2 + F_3 + \ldots + F_n \tag{1}$$

Now, substitute for $F_1, F_2, \ldots F_n$, and the result is:

$$F_A = M_1 \times I_1 + M_2 \times I_2 + \ldots + M_n \times I_n \tag{2}$$

To go from instigating force F_A to the strength of tendency T_A involves a few other variables. T_A changes with F_A, but it also changes as a function of the consummatory force (c) and time (t). A full development of the derivation of T_A is not in the scope of this paper. The reader is referred to *The Dynamics of Action* for it (see also Chapter 15).

The efficiency of performance is treated as a function of the strength of tendency T_A. If we were to take full advantage of this, then efficiency would be a variable, changing as T_A changes over time. This seems very plausible. It would also be rather cumbersome to work with and seemed more intricate and advanced than what is required in an initial stimulation. It would be much easier to work with a constant efficiency. So we made the simplifying assumption that efficiency is a function of the asymptotic strength of a tendency. This asymptotic strength is determined by the ratio of the instigating force F to the consummatory force c. Efficiency of performance (EP) = $\mu(T_A)$. Now, substituting asymptotic $T_A = F/c$, we have

$$\text{EP} = \mu(F/c) \tag{3}$$

The situation is similar for obtaining a measure of the time spent at work. The best measure would be to use the equations for the strength of tendency for all the different possible activities over the range of time available. Time spent at work in Activity A is then the time when T_A is greater than all other Ts. However, on the basis of previous results in computer simulations based on *The Dynamics of Action,* a simpler generalization is justified. Time spent in an activity is proportional to the asymptotic level of T_A relative to the sum of the asymptotic levels of tendencies for every other available activity.

$$\text{Time Spent in A (TMSP)} = \frac{F_A/c_A}{F_A/c_A + F_B/c_B + \ldots F_n/c_n} \times \text{the Total Time Available} \tag{4}$$

As a check on the accuracy of this generalization, a product-moment correlation was computed between the time spent in an activity in simulations (based on *The Dynamics of Action*) and predicted time spent using Equation (4). There were 60 pairs over a range of F and c values, and $r = .99$.[2]

One further simplifying assumption was made: that $c_A = c_B = \ldots c_n$. This yields a simplified version of Equation (4):

$$\text{TMSP} = \frac{F_A}{F_A + F_B + \ldots + F_n} \times \text{Total Time Available (TOTME)} \tag{5}$$

It is likely not to be the case that consummatory values for all activities are the same. Small variations in c would have little effect on the usefulness of Equation (5). If $c_B \ldots c_n$ did not vary greatly from c_A, some being less than c_A and others greater, then the predicted time spent from Equations (4) and (5) would be approximately the same.

Having reduced time spent to a function of instigating forces, it is a further and consistent simplifying step to eliminate the one consummatory value remaining. This step is to change EP = $\mu(T)$ into an equation which states efficiency of performance as a function of the magnitude of instigating force instead of asymptotic tendency, i.e., $T = F/c$. This gives us:

$$\text{EP} = \mu(F) \tag{6}$$

The elimination of c as a variable is arbitrary. However, effects comparable to varying c in determining EP can be recovered (if desired) simply by manipulating the values of $M_1, M_2, \ldots M_n$ and $I_1, I_2, \ldots I_n$ and thus varying F_A. We lose the capacity to simulate variations in c given a particular F. However, for initial simulations this did not seem to be much of a price for the simplicity offered, especially since so little is known about consummatory values.

Now, it is a relatively simple matter to obtain the level of achievement. First we define *the level of performance while at work* (LP):

$$\text{LP} = \text{ABILITY} \times \text{EP} \tag{7}$$

[2] These simulations and the initial program ignore the effect of inhibitory force as a factor influencing time spent in an activity in the face of resistance. This further complication is discussed in both Chapters 15 and 20.–Editors.

Next, *level of cumulative achievement* is defined (LA):

$$\text{LA} = \text{LP} \times \text{TMSP} \tag{8}$$

Combining Equations (7) and (8) we get:

$$\text{LA} = \text{ABILITY} \times \text{EP} \times \text{TMSP} \tag{9}$$

Now, Equations (5) and (6) are used to give:

$$\text{LA} = \text{ABILITY} \times \mu\,(F_\text{A}) \times \frac{F_\text{A}}{F_\text{A} + \ldots + F_n} \times \text{TOTME} \tag{10}$$

The final step is to use Equation (2) for each F to get:

$$\text{LA} = \text{ABILITY} \times \mu\,(M_{\text{A}1}I_{\text{A}1} + \ldots + M_{\text{A}n}I_{\text{A}n}) \times \frac{M_{\text{A}1}I_{\text{A}1} + \ldots + M_{\text{A}n}I_{\text{A}n}}{(M_{\text{A}1}I_{\text{A}1} + \ldots + M_{\text{A}n}I_{\text{A}n}) + \ldots + (M_{N1}I_{N1} + \ldots M_{Nn}I_{Nn})} \times \text{TOTME} \tag{11}$$

Equation (11) is the basis of this computer simulation. With it as a starting point, the details of the simulation can now be set forth.

THE SIMULATION

The first issue to come up was what type of efficiency of performance function is to be used. A traditional (and often implicit) view of efficiency of performance expects that efficiency increases monotonically with increasing strength of tendency up to, perhaps, some upper limit beyond which efficiency becomes constant. We assumed the efficiency was increasing over the entire range of strength of tendency in our use of this type of function. It is also conceivable that efficiency would decrease monotonically with increasing strength of tendency to a lower limit.

One other type of function relating efficiency and strength of tendency was desired. It is possible that efficiency increases with strength of tendency until efficiency hits a peak of 100% (maximum efficiency in the execution of a particular activity or in the expression of a particular ability). Past this, increasing the strength of tendency leads to a decrease in efficiency. The nonmonotonic function described would look like Figure 1.

Still another nonmonotonic function in which efficiency is high for extreme levels of motivation (high and low) and low for moderate levels of motivation was also programmed. This type of curve appears in Figure 2. It should be remembered that in the actual calculating function, F_A is used in place of T_A in

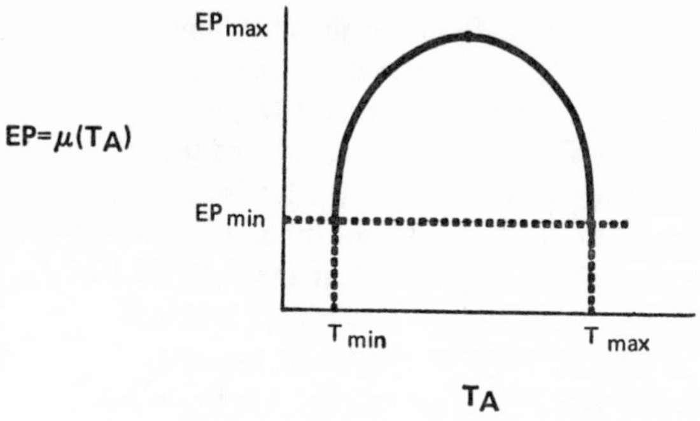

FIG. 1.

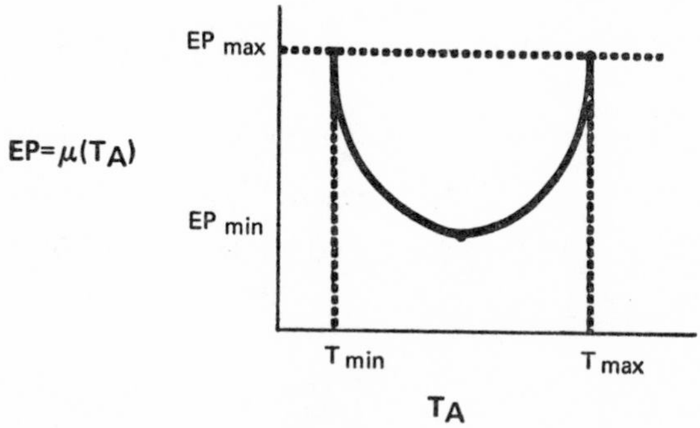

FIG. 2.

determining efficiency. The purpose of using T_A in the previous discussion was to keep the development on a more general level.

One interesting point can be noted. If efficiency is optimal (that is, 100% or 1.0), then Equation (7) can be transformed as follows:

$$\text{LP} = \text{ABILITY} \cdot \text{EP}$$
$$\text{LP} = \text{ABILITY} \cdot 1.0$$

so

$$\text{LP} = \text{ABILITY}$$

This produces the possible operational definition of ability as *the level of performance of an individual when his motivation is optimal for the task.*

The easiest way to implement these four functions is to set upper and lower bounds to the values that F_A can take on and fix the efficiency of performance at these points. From this, and a general equation for the type of function desired, the specific calculating formulas for each type of efficiency curve can be derived. These formulas were then used in the simulation.

Motives are allowed to range from 0. to 3., although any scale could be used. Incentives vary from −1. to 1. as they are thought of as a weighting factor from

-100% to 100% in decimal form. To simplify things, we decided to break F_A down into just four possible component forces. These are the force to succeed ($F_S = M_S \cdot I_S$), the force to avoid failure ($F_{AF} = M_{AF} \cdot I_{AF}$), the force for approval from others ($F_{APP} = M_{APP} \cdot I_{APP}$), and the intrinsic force for the task ($F_X = M_X \cdot I_X$). The motive and incentive labels here follow the definitions and usage in the theory of achievement motivation (Chapter 2). It should be noted that subjective probability estimates that the individual may make concerning outcomes are incorporated into the incentive parameters.

Since the incentive value of failure is negative, $F_{AF} = M_{AF} \cdot I_{AF}$ is subtracted in determining F_A. Equation (2) now becomes:

$$F_A = M_S \cdot I_S - M_{AF} \cdot I_{AF} + M_{APP} \cdot I_{APP} + M_X \cdot I_X \tag{12}$$

Maximum and minimum values of F_A can now be determined.

$$\begin{aligned} F_{A\max} &= (M_{S\max} \cdot I_{S\max}) - (M_{AF\min} \cdot I_{AF\min}) \\ &\quad + (M_{APP\max} \cdot I_{APP\max}) + (M_{X\max} \cdot I_{X\max}) \\ &= 3.0 \cdot 1.0 - 0.0 \cdot 0.0 + 3.0 \cdot 1.0 + 3.0 \cdot 1.0 \\ F_{A\max} &= 9.0 \text{ units} \end{aligned}$$

and similarly

$$F_{A\min} = 0.0$$

However, $F_A = 0$ means the subject has no motivation to enter into the activity in question. Hence efficiency = 0 when $F = 0$. This is trivial and not of any special interest. Instead, the level of $F_{A\min}$ is set at 1.0 and efficiency is explicitly defined as 0 when $F_A = 0$.

Next, the maximum and minimum efficiency values need to be set. This is entirely arbitrary since the importance of the efficiency function is in how EP varies with F_A and not in the absolute limits of EP. For simplicity, $EP_{max} = 1.0$ and $EP_{min} = .50$ (except where $F_A = 0$ and EP is defined as 0). From this the calculating formula can now be derived for any type of curve desired.

Using Equations (11) and (12) and the four efficiency formulas, the computer simulation was written. A simplified version is given below. This was written in the IBM system 360 Fortran IV language. The version here is for batch processing, although the original was written for remote terminal use.

```
      REAL MOTIVE(10,10),INCNTV(10,10),LA,T(10),LP,DATA(10,100,11)
      INTEGER A,EPGT,IND(10)
      NR=1
    3 DO 1 I=1,10
      IND(I)=0
      DO 1 J=1,10
      MOTIVE(I,J)=0.0
    1 INCNTV(I,J)=0.0
C     N IS THE NUMBER OF DATA RUNS TO BE MADE.
      WRITE (6,8)
      READ (5,9) N
```

```
C     MAIN LOOP, RUN ONCE FOR EACH SUBJECT.
      DO 645 M=1,N
C     DATA READ-IN.
      WRITE (6,10)
      READ (5,405) TOTME
      WRITE (6,13)
      READ (5,9) EPGT
      WRITE (6,14)
      READ (5,405) ABLTY
      WRITE (6,15)
      READ (5,9) A
C      IND(I) IS AN INDICATOR FOR REPLACING MOTIVE(I,J) AND INCNTV(I,J) FOR
C     ALL J FOR EACH I.
      WRITE (6,16)
      READ (5,11) (IND(I),I=1,10)
C     A NEW ROW OF MOTIVE(I,J) AND INCNTV(I,J) IS READ FOR EACH IND(I)=1.
      DO 5 I=1,10
      IF (IND(I).EQ.0) GO TO 5
      WRITE (6,17) I
      READ (5,12) (MOTIVE(I,J),J=1,10)
      READ (5,12) (INCNTV(I,J),J=1,10)
    5 CONTINUE
C     TENDENCY T(I) IS CALCULATED FROM MOTIVES*INCENTIVES .
  100 DO 106 I=1,10
      T(I)=0.
      DO 105 J=1,10
  105 T(I)=T(I)+MOTIVE(I,J)*INCNTV(I,J)
  106 IF (T(I).LT.0.) T(I)=0.0
      GO TO (200,300,400,500),EPGT
C     EFFICIENCY INCREASES LINEARLY WITH INCREASING TENDENCY.
  200 EP=0.
      IF (T(A).EQ.0.) GO TO 600
      EP=T(A)*0.0625+0.4375
      GO TO 600
C     EFFICIENCY DECREASES LINEARLY WITH INCREASING TENDENCY.
  300 EP=0.
      IF (T(A).EQ.0.) GO TO 600
      EP=1.0625-T(A)*0.0625
      GO TO 600
C     EFFICIENCY IS A PARABOLA
  400 EP=0.
      IF(T(A).EQ.0.) GO TO 600
      EP=0.5+.03125*(T(A)-5.0)**2
      GO TO 600
C     EFFICIENCY IS AN INVERTED PARABOLA.
  500 EP=0.
      IF (T(A).EQ.0.) GO TO 600
      EP=1.0-0.03125*(T(A)-5.0)**2
      GO TO 600
  600 B=0.
      DO 601 I=1,10
  601 B=B+T(I)
C     LEVEL OF PERFORMANCE (LP) AND TIME SPENT (TMSP) AND ALTERNATIVE MOTIVATION
C    (BB) ARE CALCULATED.
      LP=ABLTY*EP
      TMSP=(T(A)/B)*TOTME
      BB=B-T(A)
C     THE LEVEL OF ACHIEVEMENT (LA) IS CALCULATED.
      LA=LP*TMSP
C     DATA IS A STORAGE BLOCK FOR FUTURE USE.
      DATA(NR,M,1)=ABLTY
      DO 640 I=1,4
  640 DATA(NR,M,I+1)=MOTIVE(A,I)
      DATA(NR,M,6)=EP
      DATA(NR,M,7)=LP
      DATA(NR,M,8)=BB
      DATA(NR,M,9)=TMSP
      DATA(NR,M,10)=LA
      DATA(NR,M,11)=T(A)
      WRITE (6,18) LA
  645 CONTINUE
C      700 TO 720 ARE PRINTOUT OF DATA FOR ALL N SUBJECTS.
  700 WRITE (6,749) NR
      WRITE (6,750) TOTME
      WRITE (6,751)
      DO 705 I=1,10
      JK=10
  701 CONTINUE
      IF (INCNTV(I,JK).NE.0.) GO TO 702
```

```
      JK=JK-1
      IF (JK.EQ.0) GO TO 705
      GO TO 701
  702 WRITE (6,752) I,(INCNTV(I,J),J=1,JK)
  705 CONTINUE
      WRITE (6,753)
      DO 720 K=1,N
  715 WRITE (6,754) K,(DATA(NR,K,J),J=1,10)
  720 CONTINUE
      WRITE (6,755)
      READ (5,9) N2
      IF (N2.NE.1) GO TO 800
      NR=NR+1
      GO TO 3
  800 CONTINUE
      STOP
    8 FORMAT (//'ENTER THE NO. OF SUBJECTS.')
    9 FORMAT (I3)
   10 FORMAT (//'ENTER THE TOTAL TIME AVAILABLE (0.-10.)')
   11 FORMAT (10I2)
   12 FORMAT (10F5.2)
   13 FORMAT (1X,'WHAT TYPE OF EFFICIENCY CURVE IS TO BE USED? ')
   14 FORMAT (1X,'ENTER SUBJECTS ABILITY (0.-100.) ')
   15 FORMAT (1X,'WHICH IS THE CRITICAL TENDENCY?')
   16 FORMAT (/,'ENTER THE INDICATORS FOR EACH TENDENCY.  '/' 1 TO CHANG
     1E SOMETHING, 0 NOT TO.')
   17 FORMAT (1X,'ENTER THE MOTIVES AND THEN THE INCENTIVES FOR TENDENCY
     1 ',I3)
   18 FORMAT (/'LEVEL OF ACHIEVEMENT = ',F7.2)
  405 FORMAT (F5.1)
  749 FORMAT (///'DATA SET NO. ',I3)
  750 FORMAT (/'TOTAL TIME AVAILABLE IS ',F8.2/)
  751 FORMAT (3X,'ACTIVITY',4X,'INCENTIVE  1      2     3     4     5
     1 6      7')
  752 FORMAT (6X,I2,15X,7(1X,F5.2))
  753 FORMAT (//20X,'MOTIVE',16X,'LEVEL   ALT.    TIME   LEVEL'/'    S  A
     1BLTY     S    AF    APP    X     EFF.   PERF.   MTVN.   SPENT   ACH.'/)
  754 FORMAT (1X,I3,1X,F6.1,2X,4(F4.1,1X),1X,F5.3,2X,F6.2,2X,F6.2,2X,
     1F6.2,1X,F6.1/)
  755 FORMAT (/'IF ANOTHER DATA SET IS TO BE RUN, TYPE A 1,OTHERWISE 0')
      END
```

THE DATA

It was hypothesized by Atkinson (Chapter 20) that there might be two types of people. The first type is more highly motivated in a test situation than in normal, day-to-day situations; the second type of person is more anxious (with a corresponding decrease in the level of motivation) in the test situation than in more normal, day-to-day situations.

To translate this into data for the simulation, four possible levels of instigating force (F_A) were selected for each type of person. These four different values would cover the entire range for that type of person. For the nonanxious person, T_A's of 9., 7., 5., and 3. were used to represent the test situation (call this Case A). For the anxious person, T_A's of 7., 5., 3., and 1. were used to represent the test situation (call this Case B). The reason for the lower sequence for the anxious people is that their "Test Anxiety" reduces the level of motivation, so the sequence should cover a lower range even though in other respects they are as highly motivated as the relatively nonanxious people.

In the test situation, it was assumed that the only motivation, and hence the only instigating force, was for undertaking the activity of the test itself. Thus all other instigating forces (alternative motivation) are zero. This means that the time spent at work in the test situation is equal to the total time available.

In order to get a systematic picture of the effect of ability in determining the levels of performance and achievement, every level of instigating force (F_A) was run at each of five levels of ability (100., 80., 60., 40., 20.). This gives us a spread of combinations of levels of ability and instigating force from high and high to low and low with all possible combinations in between.

ASSUMING AN INVERTED U-FUNCTION RELATING EFFICIENCY TO MOTIVATION

The first data sets were run assuming that efficiency was an inverted U-function (parabola). Maximum efficiency (100% or 1.0) is achieved when $F_A = 5.$ and minimum efficiency (50% or .5) comes at either $F_A = 1.$ or $F_A = 9.$

The more typical day-to-day situation of normal work was treated two ways:

I. In the first (referred to with a I in the title as in Case AI or case BI), the overall magnitude of instigating force for the critical task (F_A) was assumed to be less for the nonanxious people by 2. (Case AI) as a result of no longer being in the presence of the stronger incentives of the test situation. In contrast F_A would be greater by 2. for the anxious people (Case BI) because the predominant anxiety produced by the test situation would be substantially reduced in the normal day-to-day situation. Again, this change in F_A levels is attributed to the change in incentives from the test situation to the normal work situation.

II. In a second normal work treatment (referred to with a II in the title as in Case AII or case BII), the instigating forces are assumed to remain constant from the test to the normal work situations. These data sets are identified and summarized in Table 1.

Each of these normal work situations was run at each of *three* different levels of alternative motivation (e.g., sum of instigating forces for alternative activities). These levels were 7., 9., and 13.

A second data series was run assuming an efficiency function that increased linearly with the level of instigating force (F_A). All other elements were the

TABLE 1

The Different Motivation (F_A) Levels Run for Persons Assumed to be Predominately Positive in Motivation (Nonanxious) and Relatively More Anxious

	Instigating force for critical task (F_A)		
	Test situation	Normal work I	Normal work II
Case A (nonanxious)	9., 7., 5., 3.	7., 5., 3., 1.	9., 7., 5., 3.
Case B (anxious)	7., 5., 3., 1.	9., 7., 5., 3.	7., 5., 3., 1.

same as the previous series except that only one alternative motivation level (9.) was used.

RESULTS OF SIMULATION

Table 2 summarizes the results for the several data sets as correlations between the level of achievement in the test situation (which is equivalent to level of performance since time spent = 1.0) and the level of cumulative achievement in the normal work situation. This is the series assuming the inverted-U efficiency function.

Table 3 is a summary of the results when assuming a positive linear efficiency function for otherwise the same data sets.

CONCLUSIONS AND DISCUSSION

The level of achievement in the test situation (or the level of performance since the time spent measure = 1.) is analogous to the test scores that the same

TABLE 2

Product-Moment Correlations between Test Performance and Cumulative Achievement in Normal Work for Anxious and Nonanxious People over Three Different Levels of Motivation for Alternative Activities Assuming an Inverted U-Function to Describe the Effect of Motivation on Efficiency of Performance

	Level of alternative motivation					
	7. Normal work		9. Normal work		13. Normal work	
	I	II	I	II	I	II
Case A $N = 20$ (nonanxious)	.38	.91	.36	.89	.33	.86
Case B $N = 20$ (anxious)	.94	.90	.95	.89	.97	.87

TABLE 3

Product-Moment Correlation between Level of Performance in a Test Situation and Cumulative Achievement in Normal Work Assuming a Linear Increasing Efficiency Function

	Normal work (alternative motivation = 9.)	
	I	II
Case A $N = 20$ (nonanxious)	.85	.94
Case B $N = 20$ (anxious)	.92	.83

subject would receive on a course examination, or an achievement, or an aptitude test.

The level of cumulative achievement in the long-term, normal work situation data sets correspond to such cumulative measures of achievement as grade average in a year of college work, etc. These are measures in which other activities (represented by time spent $<$ total time available) would be critically important.

The results of critical interest here are cases AI and BI where it is assumed that motivation changes from the test to normal work situations and that efficiency of performance is an inverted U-function. The results of AI and BI may be weighted by factors representing realistically the relative numbers of students of each type (anxious and nonanxious) taking achievement tests and continuing on to college. Then, when the product-moment correlation is calculated between level of test performance and cumulative achievement, the result should begin to correspond to correlations actually reported concerning aptitude or achievement test scores and average grades in a year of college work. The proportion of nonanxious to anxious students taking the achievement tests and going to college was set at 3 to 1. This estimate is inferred from the trend of results in research on achievement motivation with college students.[3] The correlation between test performance and cumulative achievement for such a sample of 80 individuals was .47 or .48, depending on whether motivation for alternative activities was set at 13 or 9 for all subjects.

In contrast, if the positive linear efficiency curve is assumed and the same proportion of anxious to nonanxious subjects is used (1 to 3), the product-moment correlation between cumulative achievement and the test performance is .80 (with alternative motivation set at 9.).

SIMULATING THE SAMPLE MORE REALISTICALLY

On the basis of the encouraging results of the first data sets for Cases AI and BI, we decided to try other data sets that would more closely approximate the student population. With a total number of subjects equal to 80, each was randomly assigned an ability level (20., 40., 60., 80., or 100.) and an alternative motivation level (3. to 27.). Both ability and alternative motivation were assumed to be normally distributed in the population so the random assignments were made by drawing from a set of values for ability and alternative motivation which had normal distributions.

Following the previously stated weighting (three of the nonanxious type of subject in the population for every anxious type), the total group of 80 was randomly split into a group of 60 nonanxious subjects and 20 anxious subjects. Within each of these subgroups the level of task motivation (T_A) was also

[3]Private communication from J. W. Atkinson.

TABLE 4

Product-Moment Correlations among Variables Presumed to Influence Cumulative Achievement in a Final Simulation Approximating Realistic Conditions for a Sample of 80 Subjects of Which 60 Are Assumed Nonanxious and 20 Relatively Anxious (See Text)

	True ability	Normal motivation	Test motivation	Normal performance	Test performance	Alternative motivation	Time spent	Cumulative achievement
True ability	1.0	-.02	-.02	.86*	.86*	.06	-.07	.50*
Normal motivation		1.0	.64*	.14	-.18	.08	.69*	.54*
Test motivation			1.0	.13	-.18	-.04	.51*	.43*
Normal performance				1.0	.74*	.11	.07	.68*
Test performance					1.0	.07	-.16	.33*
Alternative motivation						1.0	-.57*	-.38*
Time spent							1.0	.74*
Cumulative achievement								1.0

Note.–When $N = 80$, $r = .29$, $p < .01$.*

normally distributed, and again T_A levels–(1., 3., 5., 7.) or (3., 5., 7., 9.)–were assigned randomly to each subject from this normal distribution.

The product-moment correlation coefficient between cumulative achievement in normal work and the level of test performance then became .33 ($N = 80$).

Table 4 presents intercorrelations among the several variables involved in this final simulation of how motivation and ability influence both test performance and cumulative achievement when $N = 80$, three-fourths of whom are presumed to be relatively more positively motivated than anxious, and the distribution of ability, motivation for the critical task, and motivation for alternative activities are assumed to be normal and uncorrelated.

The relationships among the variables obtained in the simulation are shown schematically in Figure 3.

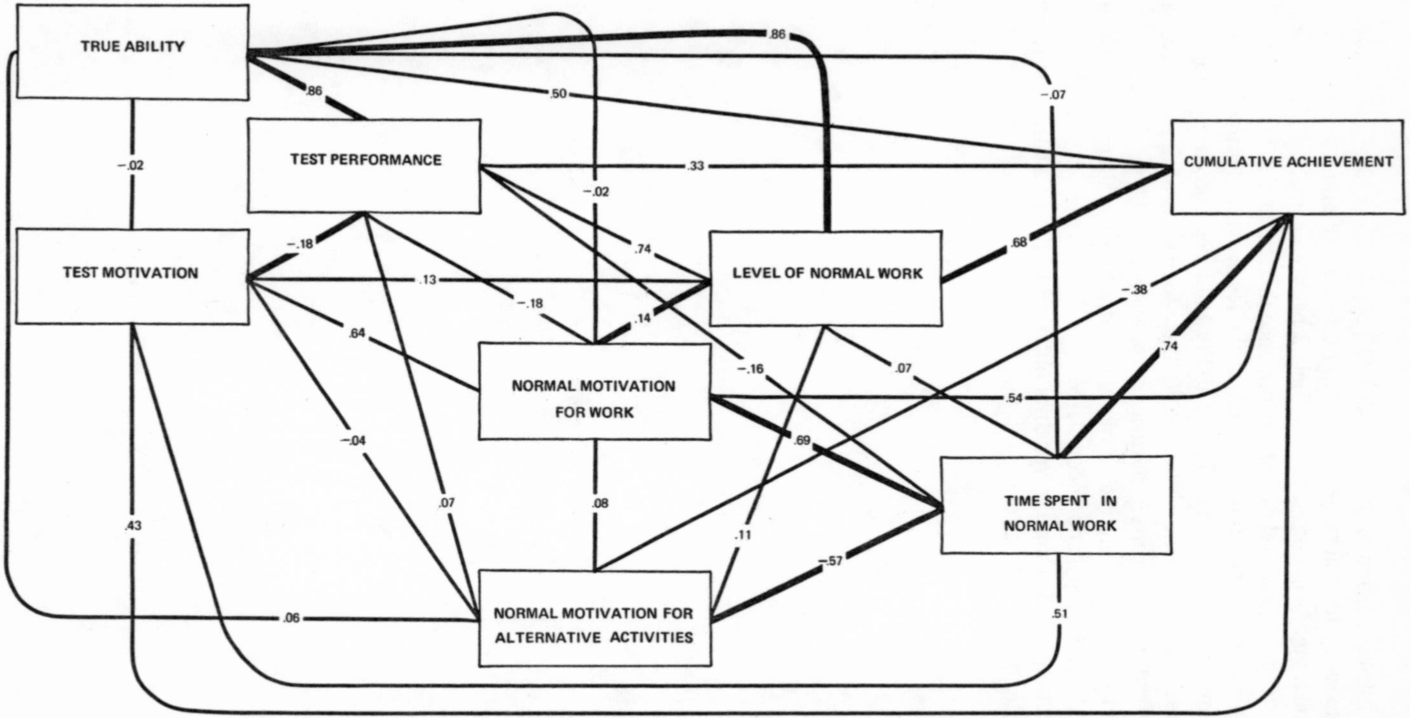

FIG. 3. Relations among variables in final realistic simulation with 80 cases based on correlations in Table 4. See test for assumptions about conditions.

REFERENCES

Allison, J. Strength of preference for food, magnitude of food reward, and performance in instrumental conditioning. *Journal of Comparative and Physiological Psychology*, 1964, 57, 217–223.

Allport, G. W. *Personality*. New York: Holt, 1937.

Allport, G. W. The ego in contemporary psychology. *Psychological Review*, 1943, **50**, 451–478.

Alper, T. G. Predicting the direction of selective recall: Its relation to ego strength and n Achievement. *Journal of Abnormal and Social Psychology*, 1957, **55**, 149–165.

Alpert, R., & Haber, R. N. Anxiety in academic achievement situations. *Journal of Abnormal and Social Psychology*, 1960, **61**, 207–215.

The American College Testing Program. *Assessing students on the way to college: Technical report for the ACT Assessment Program.* Iowa City, Iowa: ACTP, 1973.

American Management Association. Executive personality and job success. *Personnel Series*, New York, 1948, No. 120.

Amsel, A. The role of frustrative non-reward in a noncontinuous reward situation. *Psychological Bulletin*, 1958, **55**, 102–119.

Angelina, A. L. Un novo metodo par avaliar a motivacao humana. Unpublished doctoral dissertation, University of São Paulo, Brazil, 1955.

Angoff, W. H. (Ed.) *The College Board Admissions Testing Program:* A technical report on research and development activities relating to the Scholastic Aptitude Test and Achievement Tests. College Entrance Examination Board, New York, 1971.

Aronson, E. The need for achievement as measured by graphic expression. In J. W. Atkinson (Ed.), *Motives in fantasy, action, and society.* Princeton: Van Nostrand, 1958.

Astin, A. W. *Who goes where to college*? Chicago: Science Research Associates, Inc., 1965.

Atkinson, J. W. Studies in projective measurement of achievement motivation. Unpublished doctoral dissertation, University of Michigan, 1950.

Atkinson, J. W. The achievement motive and recall of interrupted and completed tasks. *Journal of Experimental Psychology*, 1953, **46**, 381–390. Also in D. C. McClelland (Ed.), *Studies in motivation.* New York: Appleton-Century-Crofts, 1955.

Atkinson, J. W. Motivational determinants of risk-taking behavior. *Psychological Review*, 1957, **64**, 359–372.

Atkinson, J. W. (Ed.) *Motives in fantasy, action, and society.* Princeton: Van Nostrand, 1958. (a)

Atkinson, J. W. Thematic apperceptive measurement of motives within the context of a theory of motivation. In J. W. Atkinson (Ed.), *Motives in fantasy, action, and society.* Princeton: Van Nostrand, 1958. (b)

Atkinson, J. W. Toward experimental analysis of human motivation in terms of motives, expectancies, and incentives. In J. W. Atkinson (Ed.), *Motives in fantasy, action, and society.* Princeton: Van Nostrand, 1958. (c)

Atkinson, J. W. Personality dynamics. *Annual Review of Psychology*, 1960, **11**, 255–290.

Atkinson, J. W. *An introduction to motivation.* Princeton: Van Nostrand, 1964.

Atkinson, J. W. An approach to the study of subjective aspects of achievement motivation. In J. Nuttin (Ed.), *Motives and consciousness in man.* Proceedings of 18th International Congress in Psychology, Symposium 13, Moscow, 1966, pp. 21–32.

Atkinson, J. W. Strength of motivation and efficiency of performance: An old unresolved problem. Paper presented at the meetings of the American Psychological Association, Washington, D.C., September 1967.

Atkinson, J. W. Measuring achievement-related motives. Unpublished final report, NSF Project GS-1399, University of Michigan, 1969. (a)

Atkinson, J. W. Change of activity: A new focus for the theory of motivation. In T. Mischel (Ed.), *Human action.* New York: Academic Press, 1969. (b)

Atkinson, J. W., Bastian, J. R., Earl, R. W., & Litwin, G. H. The achievement motive, goal setting, and probability preferences. *Journal of Abnormal and Social Psychology*, 1960, **60**, 27–36.

Atkinson, J. W., & Birch, D. *The dynamics of action.* New York: Wiley, 1970.

Atkinson, J. W., & Cartwright, D. Some neglected variables in contemporary conceptions of decision and performance. *Psychological Reports*, 1964, **14**, 575–590.

Atkinson, J. W., & Feather, N. T. (Eds.) *A theory of achievement motivation.* New York: Wiley, 1966.

Atkinson, J. W., Heyns, R. W., & Veroff, J. The effect of experimental arousal of the affiliation motive on thematic apperception. *Journal of Abnormal and Social Psychology*, 1954, **49**, 405–410. Also in J. W. Atkinson (Ed.), *Motives in fantasy, action, and society.* Princeton: Van Nostrand, 1958.

Atkinson, J. W., & Litwin, G. H. Achievement motive and test anxiety conceived as motive to approach success and motive to avoid failure. *Journal of Abnormal and Social Psychology*, 1960, **60**, 52–63.

Atkinson, J. W., & Litwin, G. H. Achievement motive and test anxiety conceived as motive to approach success and to avoid failure. In J. W. Atkinson and N. T. Feather (Eds.), *A theory of achievement motivation.* New York: Wiley, 1966.

Atkinson, J. W., & McClelland, D. C. The projective expression of needs. II. The effect of different intensities of the hunger drive on thematic apperception. *Journal of Experimental Psychology*, 1948, **38**, 643–658. Also in J. W. Atkinson (Ed.), *Motives in fantasy, action, and society.* Princeton: Van Nostrand, 1958.

Atkinson, J. W., & O'Connor, P. A. Effects of ability grouping in schools related to individual differences in achievement-related motivation: Final report. Office of Education Cooperative Research Project 1238, 1963. (Available in microfilm ($2.25) or photocopy from Photoduplication Center, Library of Congress, Washington, D.C.).

Atkinson, J. W., & O'Connor, P. A. Neglected factors in studies of achievement-oriented performance: Social approval as an incentive and performance decrement. In J. W. Atkinson and N. T. Feather (Eds.), *A theory of achievement motivation.* New York: Wiley, 1966.

Atkinson, J. W., & Raphelson, A. C. Individual differences in motivation and behavior in particular situations. *Journal of Personality,* 1956, **24**, 349–363.

Atkinson, J. W., & Reitman, W. R. Performance as a function of motive strength and expectancy of goal attainment. *Journal of Abnormal and Social Psychology,* 1956, **53**, 361–366. Also in J. W. Atkinson (Ed.), *Motives in fantasy, action, and society.* Princeton: Van Nostrand, 1958.

Bachman, J. B., Kahn, R. L., Mednick, M. T., Davidson, T. N., & Johnston, L. D. *Youth in transition.* Vol. I. *Blueprint for a longitudinal study of adolescent boys.* Ann Arbor, Mich.: Survey Research Center, Institute for Social Research, 1967.

Bales, R. F. The equilibrium problem in small groups. In T. H. Parsons, R. F. Bales, and E. A. Shils (Eds.), *Working papers in the theory of action.* Glencoe, Ill.: The Free Press, 1953.

Bandura, A., & Walters, R. H. *Social learning and personality development.* New York: Holt, Rinehart, & Winston, 1963.

Barker, R. G. *The stream of behavior.* New York: Appleton-Century-Crofts, 1963.

Bartholomew, D. J. A test of homogeneity for ordered alternatives. *Biometrika,* 1959, **46**, 36–48. (a)

Bartholomew, D. J. A test of homogeneity for ordered alternatives. II. *Biometrika,* 1959, **46**, 328–335. (b)

Bartholomew, D. J. Ordered tests in the analysis of variance. *Biometrika,* 1961, **48**, 325–332.

Bass, B. M. An analysis of the leaderless group discussion. *Journal of Applied Psychology,* 1949, **33**, 527–533.

Bass, B. M. *Leadership, psychology and organizational behavior.* New York: Harper, 1960.

Bass, B. M., & White, O. L. Situational tests: III. Observers' ratings of leaderless group discussion participants as indicators of external leadership status. *Educational and Psychological Measurement,* 1951, **II**, 335–361.

Beer, M., Buckhout, M. W., Horowitz, M. W., & Levy, S. Some perceived properties of the difference between leaders and non-leaders. *Journal of Psychology,* 1959, **47**, 49–56.

Berkowitz, L. Aggressive cues in aggressive behavior and hostility catharsis. *Psychological Review,* 1964, **71**, 104–122.

Birch, H. G. The role of motivational factors in insightful problem-solving. *Journal of Comparative Psychology,* 1945, **38**, 295–317.

Birch, D. Incentive value of success and instrumental approach behavior. *Journal of Experimental Psychology,* 1964, **68**, 131–139.

Birch, D. Verbal control of nonverbal behavior. *Journal of Experimental Child Psychology,* 1966, **4**, 266–275.

Birch, D. Shift in activity and the concept of persisting tendency. In K. W. Spence and J. T. Spence (Eds.), *The psychology of learning and motivation: Advances in research and theory.* Vol. II. New York: Academic Press, 1968.

Birch, D. Measuring the stream of activity. *Michigan mathematical psychology publication. MMPP 72-2,* Michigan Mathematical Psychology Program. Ann Arbor: University of Michigan, 1972.

Birch, D., & Veroff, J. *Motivation: A study of action.* Belmont, Calif.: Brooks-Cole, 1966.

Birney, R. C. Experimenter effect on the achievement motive. Unpublished manuscript, Amherst College, 1956.

Birney, R. C. Thematic content and the cue characteristics of pictures. In J. W. Atkinson (Ed.), *Motives in fantasy, action, and society.* Princeton: Van Nostrand, 1958.

Birney, R. C., Burdick, H., & Teevan, R. C. *Fear of failure.* New York: Van Nostrand-Reinhold, 1969.

Blau, P. M., & Duncan, O. D. *The American occupational structure.* New York: Wiley, 1967.

Bolles, R. C. *Theory of motivation.* New York: Harper & Row, 1967.

Borgatta, E. F., & Bales, R. F. Sociometric status patterns and characteristics of interaction. *Journal of Social Psychology,* 1956, **43,** 289–297.

Broadhurst, P. L. The interaction of task difficulty and motivation: The Yerkes-Dodson Law revived. *Acta Psychologica,* 1959, **16,** 321–338.

Brody, N. N achievement, test anxiety, and subjective probability of success in risk taking behavior. *Journal of Abnormal and Social Psychology,* 1963, **66,** 413–418. Also in J. W. Atkinson and N. T. Feather (Eds.), *A theory of achievement motivation.* New York: Wiley, 1966.

Broen, W. E., Jr., & Storms, L. H. A reaction potential ceiling and response decrements in complex situations. *Psychological Review,* 1961, **68,** 405–415.

Brown, D. W. The effects of anxiety, stress, and task difficulty on performance on a verbal learning task. *Journal of Psychology,* 1966, **64,** 199–212.

Brown, M. Factors determining expectancy of success and reactions to success and failure. Unpublished manuscript, University of Michigan, 1963.

Brown, M. Determinants of persistence and initiation of achievement-related activities. Unpublished doctoral dissertation, University of Michigan, 1967.

Burdick, H. The relationship of attraction, need achievement and certainty to conformity under conditions of a simulated group atmosphere. Unpublished doctoral dissertation, University of Michigan, 1955.

Burton, J. L. An empirical study of the effects of anxiety and failure-success upon the performance of a complex task. *Dissertation Abstracts,* 1957, **17,** 1386–1387.

Campbell, D. T. The indirect assessment of social attitudes. *Psychological Bulletin,* 1950, **47,** 15–38.

Cartwright, D., & Festinger, L. A quantitative theory of decision. *Psychological Review,* 1943, **50,** 595.

Child, I. L., Storm, T., & Veroff, J. Achievement themes in folk tales related to socialization practice. In J. W. Atkinson (Ed.), *Motives in fantasy, action, and society.* Princeton: Van Nostrand, 1958.

Child, I. L., & Waterhouse, I. K. Frustration and the quality of performance: III. An experimental study. *Journal of Personality,* 1953, **21,** 298–311.

Child, I. L., & Whiting, J. W. M. Effects of goal attainment: Relaxation versus renewed striving. *Journal of Abnormal and Social Psychology,* 1950, **45,** 667–681.

Christie, R. Acquiescence and education. Unpublished manuscript, Columbia University, 1958.

Clark, R. A., & McClelland, D. C. A factor analytic integration of imaginative, performance, and case study measures of the need for achievement. Unpublished paper, Wesleyan University, 1950.

Cleveland, S. E., & Fisher, S. Prediction of small group behavior from a body image schema. *Human Relations,* 1957, **10,** 223–233.

Cofer, C. N., & Appley, M. H. *Motivation: Theory and Research.* New York: Wiley, 1964.

Cottrell, N. B. Performance in the presence of other human beings: Mere presence, audience and affiliation effects. In E. C. Simmel, R. A. Hoppe, and G. H. Milton (Eds.), *Social facilitation and imitative behavior.* Boston: Allyn & Bacon, 1968.

Crockett, H. The achievement motive and differential occupational mobility in the United States. *American Sociological Review,* 1962, **27,** 191–204. Also in J. W. Atkinson and N. T. Feather (Eds.), *A theory of achievement motivation.* New York: Wiley, 1966.

Crockett, H. Social class, education, and motive to achieve in differential occupational mobility. *Sociological Quarterly,* 1964, **5,** 231–242.

Crockett, H., & Schulman, J. L. Achievement among minority Americans: A conference report. Cambridge, Mass.: Schenkman Publ. Co., 1973.

Cronbach, L. J. The two disciplines of scientific psychology. *American Psychologist,* 1957, **12,** 671–684.

Davenport, J. W. The projective expression of the achievement motive in relation to career orientation and social satisfaction in home economics freshmen. Unpublished master's thesis, University of Massachusetts, 1953.

deCharms, R., & Moeller, G. H. Values expressed in American children's readers: 1800–1950. *Journal of Abnormal and Social Psychology,* 1962, **64**, 136–142.

deCharms, R., Morrison, H. W., Reitman, W. R., & McClelland, D. C. Behavioral correlates of directly measured and indirectly measured achievement motivation. In D. C. McClelland (Ed.), *Studies in motivation.* New York: Appleton-Century-Crofts, 1955.

Descartes, R. Discourse on method [1637]. In J. Veitch (trans.), *Religion of Science Library No. 38.* Chicago: The Open Court Publ. Co., 1935.

Diener, C. L. Similarities and differences between overachieving and underachieving students. *Personnel and Guidance Journal,* 1960, **38**, 396–400.

Douvan, E. Social status and success strivings. In J. W. Atkinson (Ed.), *Motives, in fantasy, action, and society.* Princeton: Van Nostrand, 1958.

Douvan, E., & Walker, A. M. The sense of effectiveness in public affairs. *Psychological Monographs,* 1956, **70**(22, Whole No. 429).

Dubno, P. Leadership, group effectiveness and speed of decision. *Journal of Social Psychology,* 1965, **65**, 351–360.

Duncan, O. D., Featherman, D. L., & Duncan, B. *Socioeconomic background and achievement.* New York: Seminar Press, 1972.

Easterbrook, J. A. The effect of emotion on cue utilization and the organization of behavior. *Psychological Review,* 1959, **66**, 183–201.

Edwards, W. The theory of decision making. *Psychological Bulletin,* 1954, **51**, 380–417.

Edwards, W. Utility, subjective probability, their interaction, and variance preferences. *Journal of Conflict Resolution,* 1962, **6**, 42–51.

Entin, E. E. The interaction of motives and feedback method. Unpublished paper, University of Michigan, 1966.

Entin, E. E. The relationship between the theory of achievement motivation and performance on a simple and a complex task. Unpublished doctoral dissertation, University of Michigan, 1968.

Entin, E. E., & Raynor, J. O. Effects of contingent future orientation and achievement motivation on performance in two kinds of task. *Journal of Experimental Research in Personality,* 1973, **6**, 314–320.

Entwisle, D. R. To dispel fantasies about fantasy-based measures of achievement motivation. *Psychological Bulletin,* 1972, **77**, 377–391.

Erickson, E. *Childhood and society.* New York: Norton, 1963.

Eysenck, H. J. Historical and integrative: A review of *An Introduction to Motivation* by J. W. Atkinson. *Contemporary Psychology,* 1966, **11**, 122–126. (a)

Eysenck, H. J. Personality and experimental psychology. *British Psychological Society Bulletin,* 1966, 19, 62, 1–28.(b)

Eysenck, H. J. *The IQ argument.* New York: The Library Press, 1971.

Farber, I. E., & Spence, K. W. Complex learning and conditioning as a function of anxiety. *Journal of Experimental Psychology,* 1953, **45**, 120–125.

Feather, N. T. Persistence in relation to achievement motivation, anxiety about failure, and task difficulty. Unpublished doctoral dissertation, University of Michigan, 1960.

Feather, N. T. The relationship of persistence at a task to expectation of success and achievement related motives. *Journal of Abnormal and Social Psychology,* 1961, **63**, 552–561.

Feather, N. T. The study of persistence. *Psychological Bulletin,* 1962, **59**, 94–115. Also in J. W. Atkinson and N. T. Feather (Eds.), *A theory of achievement motivation.* New York: Wiley, 1966.

Feather, N. T. Persistence at a difficult task with alternative task of intermediate difficulty. *Journal of Abnormal and Social Psychology,* 1963, **66**, 604–609.

Feather, N. T. The relationship of expectation of success to need achievement and test anxiety. *Journal of Personality and Social Psychology,* 1965, **1**, 118–126.

Feather, N. T. Effects of prior success and failure on expectations of success and subsequent performance. *Journal of Personality and Social Psychology,* 1966, **3**, 287–298.

Feld, S. & Smith, C. P. An evaluation of the method of content analysis. In J. W. Atkinson (Ed.), *Motives in fantasy, action, and society.* Princeton: Van Nostrand, 1958.

Festinger, L. A theoretical interpretation of shifts in level of aspiration. *Psychological Review,* 1942, **49**, 235–250.

Festinger, L. *A theory of cognitive dissonance.* Stanford, Calif.: Stanford University Press, 1957.

Field, W. F. The effects of thematic apperception on certain experimentally aroused needs. Unpublished doctoral dissertation, University of Maryland, 1951.

Forward, J. Group achievement motivation and individual motives to achieve success, to avoid failure and to seek social approval. Unpublished doctoral dissertation, University of Maryland, 1967.

Frank, J. D. Individual differences in certain aspects of level of aspiration. *American Journal of Psychology,* 1935, **47**, 119–128.

French, E. G. Some characteristics of achievement motivation. *Journal of Experimental Psychology,* 1955, **50**, 232–236. Also in J. W. Atkinson (Ed.), *Motives in fantasy, action, and society.* Princeton: Van Nostrand, 1958.

French, E. G. Motivation as a variable in work partner selection. *Journal of Abnormal and Social Psychology,* 1956, **53**, 96–99.

French, E. G. The interaction of achievement motivation and ability in problem solving success. *Journal of Abnormal and Social Psychology,* 1958, **57**, 306–309. (a)

French, E. G. Effects of the interaction of motivation and feedback on task performance. In J. W. Atkinson (Ed.), *Motives in fantasy, action, and society.* Princeton: Van Nostrand, 1958. (b)

French, E. G., & Lesser, G. S. Some characteristics of the achievement motive in women. *Journal of Abnormal and Social Psychology,* 1964, **68**, 119–128.

French, E. G., & Thomas, F. H. The relation of achievement motivation to problem-solving effectiveness. *Journal of Abnormal and Social Psychology,* 1958, **56**, 46–48.

Freud, S. Lecture XXXIII. In *New introductory lectures on psychoanalysis.* New York: Norton, 1933. Pp. 153–186.

Freud, S. The unconscious. In *The collected papers of . . .* Vol. 4. London: Hogarth, 1949.

Gagne, R. M. *The conditions of learning.* New York: Macmillan, 1965.

Gaito, J. Unequal intervals and unequal *n* in trend analyses. *Psychological Bulletin,* 1965, **63**, 125–127.

Gardner, B. B. What makes successful and unsuccessful executives? *Advanced Management,* 1948, **13**, 116–125.

Gjesme, T. Motive to achieve success and motive to avoid failure in relation to school performance for pupils of different ability levels. *Scandinavian Journal of Educational Research,* 1971, **00**, 89–99.

Grosbeck, B. L. Toward description of personality in terms of configuration of motives. In J. W. Atkinson (Ed.), *Motives in fantasy, action, and society.* Princeton: Van Nostrand, 1958.

Gurin, G., Veroff, J., & Feld, S. *Americans view their mental health: A nationwide interview survey.* New York: Basic Books, 1960.

Haber, R. N., & Alpert, R. The role of situation and picture cues in projective measurement of the achievement motive. In J. W. Atkinson (Ed.), *Motives in fantasy, action, and society.* Princeton: Van Nostrand, 1958.

Hall, C. S., & Lindzey, G. *Theories of personality.* New York: Wiley, 1957.

Hare, A. P. *Handbook of small group research.* New York: The Free Press, 1962.

Hartup, W. W. Dependence and independence. In H. W. Stevenson (Ed.), *Child Psychology.* Chicago: University of Chicago Press, 1963.

Hauser, R. M. Socioeconomic background and educational performance. In A. J. Reiss (Ed.), The Arnold and Caroline Rose Monograph Series in Sociology. Washington, D.C.: American Sociological Assoc., 1971.

Hayashi, T., & Habu, K. A research on achievement motive: An experimental test of the "thought sampling" method by using Japanese students. *Japanese Psychological Research,* 1962, **4,** 30–42.

Hebb, D. O. Drives and the C. N. S. (conceptual nervous system). *Psychological Review,* 1955, **62,** 243–254.

Heckhausen, H. *Hoffnung und Furcht in der Leistungsmotivation.* Verlag Anton Hain: Meisenheimam Glan, 1963.

Heckhausen, H. *The anatomy of achievement motivation.* New York: Academic Press, 1967.

Heckhausen, H. Achievement motive research: Current problems and some contributions towards a general theory of motivation. In W. J. Arnold (Ed.), *Nebraska symposium on motivation.* Lincoln, Nebr.: University of Nebraska Press, 1968.

Heckhausen, H., & Weiner, B. The emergence of a cognitive psychology of motivation. In P. Dodwell (Ed.), *New horizons in psychology.* London: Penguin Books, 1972.

Henle, M. The influence of valence on substitution. *Journal of Psychology,* 1944, **17,** 11–19.

Hermans, H. J. M. The validity of different strategies of scale construction in predicting academic achievement. *Educational and Psychological Measurement,* 1969, **29,** 877–883.

Hermans, H. J. M. A questionnaire measure of achievement motivation. *Journal of Applied Psychology,* 1970, **54,** 353–363.

Hernstein, R. *I.Q. Atlantic Monthly.* 1971, 43–64.

Heyns, R. W., Veroff, J., & Atkinson, J. W. A scoring manual for the affiliation motive. In J. W. Atkinson (Ed.), *Motives in fantasy, action, and society.* Princeton: Van Nostrand, 1958.

Hirsch, J. Individual differences in behavior and their genetic basis. In E. L. Bliss (Ed.), *Roots of behavior.* New York: Harper, 1962.

Hollander, E. P. Competence and conformity in the acceptance of influence. *Journal of Abnormal and Social Psychology,* 1960, **61,** 361–365.

Hollander, E. P. Emergent leadership and social influence. In L. Petrullo and B. M. Bass (Eds.), *Leadership and interpersonal behavior.* New York: Holt, Rinehart & Winston, 1961.

Hollander, E. P., & Julian, J. W. Leadership. In E. F. Borgatta and W. W. Lambert (Eds.), *Handbook of personality theory and research.* Chicago: Rand McNally & Co., 1968.

Hollander, E. P., & Julian, J. W. Contemporary trends in the analysis of leadership processes. *Psychological Bulletin,* 1969, **71,** 387–395.

Hoppe, F. Untersuchungen zur Handlungs und Affekt-Psychologie: IX. Erfold und Misserfolg (Investigations in the psychology of action and emotion. IX. Success and Failure). *Psychologische Forschung,* 1930, **14,** 1–63.

Horner, M. Sex differences in achievement motivation and performance in competitive and noncompetitive situations. Unpublished doctoral dissertation, University of Michigan, 1968.

Hull, C. L. The goal gradient and maze learning. *Psychological Review,* 1932, **39,** 25–43.

Hull, C. L. Special Review: Thorndike's fundamentals of learning. *Psychological Bulletin,* 1935, **32,** 807–823.

Hull, C. L. Mind, mechanism, and adaptive behavior. *Psychological Review,* 1937, **44,** 1–32.

Hull, C. L. *Principles of behavior.* New York: Appleton-Century-Crofts, 1943.

Isaacson, R. L. Relation between achievement, test anxiety, and curricular choices. *Journal of Abnormal and Social Psychology,* 1964, **68,** 447–452.

Isaacson, R. L., & Raynor, J. O. Achievement-related motivation and perceived instrumentality of grades to future career success. Unpublished paper, University of Michigan, 1966.

Jacobs, B. A method for investigating the cue characteristics of pictures. In J. W. Atkinson (Ed.), *Motives in fantasy, action, and society.* Princeton: Van Nostrand, 1958.

Jensen, A. R. How much can we boost I.Q. and scholastic achievement? *Harvard Educational Review,* 1969, **39**(1), 1–123.

Jones, E. E., & Gerard, H. B. *Foundations of social psychology.* New York: Wiley, 1967.

Jones, E. E., Rock, L., Shaver, K. G., Goethals, G. R., & Ward, L. M. Pattern of performance and ability attributions: An unexpected primacy effect. *Journal of Personality and Social Psychology,* 1968, **10**, 317–340.

Julian, J. W., & Hollander, E. P. A study of some role dimensions of leader-follower relations. Technical Report No. 3, State University of New York at Buffalo, Contract Nonr. 4679, Office of Naval Research, 1966.

Julian, J. W., Hollander, E. P., & Regula, C. R. Endorsement of the group spokesman as a function of his source of authority, competence, and success. *Journal of Personality and Social Psychology,* 1969, **11**, 42–49.

Kagan, J., & Moss, H. A. *Birth to maturity.* New York: Wiley, 1962.

Kaltenbach, J. E., & McClelland, D. C. Achievement and social status in three small communities. In *Report on the Committee on Identification of Talent.* New York: Social Science Research Council, 1957.

Karabenick, S. A. The effect of consummatory behavior on the strength of an immediately subsequent instrumental response. Unpublished doctoral dissertation, University of Michigan, 1967.

Karabenick, S. A., & Youssef, Z. I. Performance as a function of achievement motive level and perceived difficulty. *Journal of Personality and Social Psychology,* 1968, **10**, 414–419.

Katchmar, L. T., Ross, S., & Andrews, T. G. Effects of stress and anxiety on performance of a complex verbal-coding task. *Journal of Experimental Psychology,* 1958, **55**, 559–563.

Katz, I. The socialization of academic motivation in minority group children. In D. Levine (Ed.), *Nebraska symposium on motivation.* Lincoln, Nebr.: University of Nebraska Press, 1967.

Kirsch, J. P., Lodahl, T. M., & Haire, M. Some factors in the selection of leaders by members of small groups. *Journal of Abnormal and Social Psychology,* 1959, **58**, 406–408.

Kish, L. Selection of the sample. In L. Festinger and D. Katz (Eds.), *Research methods in the behavioral sciences.* New York: Dryden, 1953.

Klinger, E. Fantasy n achievement as a motivational construct. *Psychological Bulletin,* 1966, **66**, 291–308.

Klinger, E. Modelling effects on achievement imagery. *Journal of Personality and Social Psychology,* 1967, **7**, 49–62.

Kolb, D. A. Achievement motivation training for under-achieving high-school boys. *Journal of Personality and Social Psychology,* 1965, **2**, 783–792.

Krumboltz, J. D. Measuring achievement motivation. A review. *Journal of Counseling Psychology,* 1957, **4**, 191–198.

Lansing, J., & Heyns, R. W. Need affiliation and frequency of four types of communication. *Journal of Abnormal and Social Psychology,* 1959, **58**, 365–372.

Lazarus, R. A substitutive-defensive conception of apperceptive fantasy. In J. Kagan and G. S. Lesser (Eds.), *Contemporary issues in thematic apperceptive methods.* Springfield, Ill.: Charles C Thomas, 1961.

Lens, W., & Atkinson, J. W. Academic achievement in highschool related to "intelligence" and motivation as measured in sixth, ninth and twelfth grade boys. Unpublished manuscript, University of Michigan, 1973.

Lesser, G. S., Krawitz, R. N., & Packard, R. Experimental arousal of achievement motivation in adolescent girls. *Journal of Abnormal and Social Psychology,* 1963, **66,** 59–66.

Lewin, K. *Conceptual representation and measurement of psychological forces.* Durham, N. C.: Duke University Press, 1938.

Lewin, K. Defining the "field at a given time." *Psychological Review,* 1943, **50,** 292–310.

Lewin, K. Behavior and development as a function of the total situation. In L. Carmichael (Ed.), *Manual of child psychology.* New York: Wiley, 1946.

Lewin, K. *Field theory in social science.* New York: Harper, 1951.

Lewin, K., Dembo, T., Festinger, L., & Sears, P. S. Level of aspiration. In J. McV. Hunt (Ed.), *Personality and the behavior disorders.* Vol. I. New York: Ronald Press, 1944.

Lindzey, G., & Heinemann, S. H. Thematic Apperception Test: Individual and group administration. *Journal of Personality,* 1955, **24,** 34–55.

Lipinski, B. G. Sex-role conflict and achievement motivation in college women. Unpublished doctoral dissertation, University of Cincinnati, 1965.

Lissner, K. Die Entspannung von Bedurfnissen durch ersatzhandlungen. *Psychologische Forschung,* 1933, **18,** 218–250.

Litwin, G. H. Motives and expectancies as determinants of preference for degrees of risk. Unpublished honors dissertation, University of Michigan, 1958.

Litwin, G. H. Achievement motivation, expectancy of success, and risk-taking behavior. In J. W. Atkinson and N. T. Feather (Eds.), *A theory of achievement motivation.* New York: Wiley, 1966.

Litwin, G. H., & Stringer, R. A. *Motivation and organizational climate.* Boston: Grad. School of Business Administration, Harvard University, 1968.

Lowell, E. L. The effect of need for achievement on learning and speed of performance. *Journal of Psychology,* 1952, **33,** 31–40.

Lucas, J. D. The interactive effects of anxiety, failure and interserial duplicaton. *American Journal of Psychology,* 1952, **55,** 59–66.

Maccoby, E. E., & Maccoby, N. The interview: A tool of social science. In G. Lindzey (Ed.), *Handbook of social psychology.* Vol. I. Cambridge: Addison-Wesley, 1954.

Mahler, W. Ersatzhandlungen verschiedener Realitatsgrades. *Psychologische Forschung,* 1933, **18,** 27–89.

Mahone, C. H. Fear of failure and unrealistic vocational aspiration. Unpublished doctoral dissertation, University of Michigan, 1958.

Mahone, C. H. Fear of failure and unrealistic vocational aspiration. *Journal of Abnormal and Social Psychology,* 1960, **60,** 253–261. Also in J. W. Atkinson and N. T. Feather (Eds.), *A theory of achievement motivation.* New York: Wiley, 1966.

Mandler, G., & Sarason, S. B. A study of anxiety and learning. *Journal of Abnormal and Social Psychology,* 1952, **47,** 166–173.

Marak, G. E. The evaluation of leadership structure. *Sociometry,* 1964, **27,** 174–182.

Marquis, D. G. Research planning at the frontiers of science. *American Psychologist,* 1948, **3,** 430–438.

Maslow, A. H. *Motivation and personality.* New York: Harper & Row, 1954; 2nd ed., 1970.

McClelland, D. C. *Personality.* New York: Wm. Sloane, 1951.

McClelland, D. C. The psychology of mental content reconsidered. *Psychological Review,* 1955, **62,** 297–302.

McClelland, D. C. Methods of measuring human motivation. In J. W. Atkinson (Ed.), *Motives in fantasy, action, and society.* Princeton: Van Nostrand, 1958. (a)

McClelland, D. C. Risk-taking in children with high and low need for achievement. In J. W. Atkinson (Ed.), *Motives in fantasy, action, and society.* Princeton: Van Nostrand, 1958. (b)

McClelland, D. C. The importance of early learning in the formation of motives. In J. W.

Atkinson (Ed.), *Motives in fantasy, action, and society.* Princeton: Van Nostrand, 1958. (c)

McClelland, D. C. *The achieving society.* Princeton: Van Nostrand, 1961.

McClelland, D. C. *Assessing human motivation.* New York: General Learning Press, 1971.

McClelland, D. C., & Atkinson, J. W. The projective expression of needs. I. The effect of different intensities of the hunger drive on perception. *Journal of Psychology,* 1948, **25,** 205–232.

McClelland, D. C., Atkinson, J. W., Clark, R. A., & Lowell, E. L. *The achievement motive.* New York: Appleton-Century-Crofts, 1953.

McClelland, D. C., Atkinson, J. W., Clark, R. A., & Lowell, E. L. A scoring manual for the achievement motive. In J. W. Atkinson (Ed.), *Motives in fantasy, action, and society.* Princeton: Van Nostrand, 1958.

McClelland, D. C., Clark, R. A., Roby, T. B., & Atkinson, J. W. The projective expression of needs. IV. The effect of need for achievement on thematic apperception. *Journal of Experimental Psychology,* 1949, **39,** 242–255.

McClelland, D. C., & Friedman, G. A. A cross-cultural study of the relationship between child-training practices and achievement motivation appearing in folk tales. In G. E. Swanson, T. M. Newcomb, and E. L. Hartley (Eds.), *Readings in social psychology.* New York: Holt, 1952.

McClelland, D. C. & Winter, D. G. *Motivating economic achievement.* New York: The Free Press, 1969.

McDougall, W. *An introduction to social psychology.* London: Methuen & Co., 1908.

McGrath, J. E., & Altman, I. *Small group research.* New York: Holt, Rinehart & Winston, 1966.

Mead, M. *Male and female.* New York: Morrow, 1949.

Mehrabian, A. Male and female scales of tendency to achieve. *Educational and Psychological Measurement,* 1968, **28,** 493–502.

Mehrabian, A. Measures of achieving tendency. *Educational and Psychological Measurement,* 1969, **29,** 445–451.

Mehrabian, A. The development and validation of measures of affiliative tendency and sensitivity to rejection. *Educational and Psychological Measurement,* 1970, **30,** 417–428.

Montague, E. K. The role of anxiety in serial rote learning. *Journal of Experimental Psychology,* 1953, **45,** 91–96.

Morgan, H. H. A psychometric comparison of achieving and non-achieving college students of high ability. *Journal of Consulting Psychology,* 1952, **16,** 292–298.

Morgan, J. N. The achievement motive and economic behavior. *Economic Development and Cultural Change,* 1964, **12,** 243–267. Also in J. W. Atkinson and N. T. Feather (Eds.), *A theory of achievement motivation.* New York: Wiley, 1966.

Morgan, J. N., Snider, M., & Sobel, M. G. *Highlights from a study on lump sum redemption settlements and rehabilitation.* Ann Arbor, Mich.: Survey Research Center, 1958.

Morris, J. Propensity for risk-taking as a determinant of vocational choice. *Journal of Personality and Social Psychology,* 1966, **3,** 328–335.

Morrison, H. W. Validity and behavioral correlates of female need for achievement. Unpublished master's thesis, Wesleyan University, 1954.

Moulton, R. W. Effects of success and failure on level of aspiration as related to achievement motives. *Journal of Personality and Social Psychology,* 1965, **1,** 399–406. Also in J. W. Atkinson and N. T. Feather (Eds.), *A theory of achievement motivation.* New York: Wiley, 1966.

Moulton, R. W. Age group and ability group norms as determinants of level of aspiration. Unpublished paper, University of California, Berkeley, 1967. (a)

Moulton, R. W. Motivational implications of individual differences in competence. Paper presented at the meetings of the American Psychological Association, Washington, D.C., September 1967. (b)

Murray, E. J. A case study in a behavioral analysis of psychotherapy. *Journal of Abnormal and Social Psychology,* 1954, **49**, 305–310.

Murray, H. A. *Explorations in personality.* New York: Oxford University Press, 1938.

Murray, H. A. *Thematic Apperception Test manual.* Cambridge: Harvard University Press, 1953.

Murray, H. A., & Kluckholm, C. Outline of a conception of personality. In C. Kluckholm, H. A. Murray, and D. Schneider (Eds.), *Personality in nature, society, and culture.* (2nd ed.) New York: Knopf, 1953.

Nisbett, R. E., & Valins, S. *Perceiving the causes of one's own behavior.* New York: General Learning Press, 1971.

Norfleet, B. Interpersonal relations and group productivity. *Journal of Social Issues,* 1948, **4**, 66–69.

Nuttin, J. The future time perspective in human motivation and learning. *Proceedings of the 17th International Congress of Psychology.* Amsterdam: North-Holland Publ. Co., 1964.

Nuttin, J., & Greenwald, A. G. *Reward and punishment in human learning.* New York: Academic Press, 1968.

O'Connor, P. A., Atkinson, J. W., & Horner, M. Motivational implications of ability grouping in schools. In J. W. Atkinson and N. T. Feather (Eds.), *A theory of achievement motivation.* New York: Wiley, 1966.

Olsen, G. W. Failure and the subsequent performance of schizophrenics. *Journal of Abnormal and Social Psychology,* 1958, **57**, 310–314.

Orne, M. T. On the social psychology of the psychological experiment: With particular reference to demand characteristics and their implications. *American Psychologist,* 1962, **17**, 776–783.

Osler, S. F. Intellectual performance as a function of two types of psychological stress. *Journal of Experimental Psychology,* 1954, **47**, 115–121.

Ovsiankina, M. Die wiederaufnahme unterbrochener handlungen. *Psychologische Forschung,* 1928, **11**, 302–379.

Peak, H. Attitude and motivation. In M. R. Jones (Ed.), *Nebraska Symposium on Motivation.* Lincoln, Nebr.: University of Nebraska Press, 1955. Pp. 149–188.

Pepinsky, N., Hemphill, J. K., & Shevitz, R. N. Attempts to lead, group productivity, and morale under conditions of acceptance and rejection. *Journal of Abnormal and Social Psychology,* 1958, **57**, 47–54.

Peter, L. J., & Hull, R. *The Peter principle.* New York: Morrow, 1969.

Poulton, C. Skilled performance and stress. In P. B. Warr (Ed.), *Psychology at work.* Harmondsworth, England: Penguin Books, 1971.

Rand, P. *Distortion and selectivity.* Oslo: Universitetsforlaget, 1963.

Rand, P. *Achievement motivation and school performance.* Oslo: Universitetsforlaget, 1965.

Raphelson, A. C. The relationships among imaginative, direct verbal and physiological measures of anxiety in an achievement situation. *Journal of Abnormal and Social Psychology,* 1957, **54**, 13–18.

Raynor, J. O. The functional significance of future goals. Paper presented at the meetings of the American Psychological Association, Washington, D.C., September 1967.

Raynor, J. O. The relationship between distant future goals and achievement motivation. Unpublished doctoral dissertation, University of Michigan, 1968. (a)

Raynor, J. O. Achievement motivation, grades, and instrumentality. Paper presented at the meetings of the American Psychological Association, San Francisco, September 1968. (b)

Raynor, J. O. Future orientation and motivation of immediate activity: An elaboration of the theory of achievement motivation. *Psychological Review,* 1969, 76, 606–610.

Raynor, J. O. Relationships between achievement-related motives, future orientation, and academic performance. *Journal of Personality and Social Psychology,* 1970, **15**, 28–33.

Raynor, J. O. Contingent future orientation as a determinant of immediate risk-taking. Unpublished paper, State University of New York at Buffalo, 1972.

Raynor, J. O., & Entin, E. E. Achievement motivation as a determinant of persistence in contingent and noncontingent paths. Unpublished paper, State University of New York at Buffalo, 1972.

Raynor, J. O., Entin, E. E. & Raynor, D. Effects of n Achievement, test anxiety, and length of contingent path on performance of grade school children. Unpublished paper, State University of New York at Buffalo, 1972.

Raynor, J. O., & Rubin, I. S. Effects of achievement motivation and future orientation on level of performance. *Journal of Personality and Social Psychology,* 1971, **17**, 36–41.

Raynor, J. O., & Smith, C. P. Achievement-related motives and risk-taking in games of skill and chance. *Journal of Personality,* 1966, **34**, 176–198.

Raynor, J. O., & Sorrentino, R. M. Effects of achievement motivation and task difficulty on immediate performance in contingent paths. Unpublished paper, State University of New York at Buffalo, 1972.

Regula, C. R., & Julian, J. W. Quality and quantity of contributions as determinants of perceived ability. Technical Report No. 6, State University of New York at Buffalo, Contract Nonr. 4679, Office of Naval Research, 1967.

Reitman, W. R. Motivational induction and behavioral correlates of the achievement and affiliation motives. Unpublished doctoral dissertation, University of Michigan, 1957.

Reitman, W. R. Motivational induction and the behavioral correlates of the achievement and affiliation motives. *Journal of Abnormal and Social Psychology,* 1960, **60**, 8–13.

Reitman, W. R., & Atkinson, J. W. Some methodological problems in the use of thematic apperceptive measures of human motives. In J. W. Atkinson (Ed.), *Motives in fantasy, action, and society.* Princeton: Van Nostrand, 1958.

Ricciuti, H. N. *The prediction of academic grades with a projective test of achievement motivation: I. Initial validation studies.* Princeton: Educational Testing Service, 1954.

Ricciuti, H. N., & Sadacca, R. *The prediction of academic grades with a projective test of achievement motivation: II. Cross validation at the high school level.* Princeton: Educational Testing Service, 1955.

Riecken, H. W. The effect of talkativeness on ability to influence group solutions to problems. *Sociometry,* 1958, **21**, 309–321.

Rodnick, E. H., & Garmezy, N. An experimental approach to the study of motivation in schizophrenia. In M. R. Jones (Ed.), *Nebraska symposium on motivation.* Lincoln: University of Nebraska Press, 1957. Pp. 109–184.

Rosen, B. C. The achievement syndrome: A psychocultural dimension of social stratification. *American Sociological Review,* 1956, **21**, 203–211. Also in J. W. Atkinson (Ed.), *Motives in fantasy, action, and society.* Princeton: Van Nostrand, 1958.

Rosen, B. C. Race, ethnicity and the achievement syndrome. *American Sociological Review,* 1959, **24**, 47–60.

Rosen, B., C., & D'Andrade, R. C. The psychosocial origins of achievement motivation. *Sociometry,* 1959, **22**, 185–218.

Rosen, B. C., Crockett, H., & Nunn, C. Z. *Achievement in American Society.* Cambridge, Mass.: Schenkman Publ. Co., 1969.

Rotter, J. B. *Social learning and clinical psychology.* Englewood Cliffs, N. J.: Prentice-Hall, 1954.

Sales, S. M. Some effects of role overload and role underload. *Organizational Behavior and Human Performance,* 1970, **5**, 592–608.

Sanford, F. H. The use of a projective device in attitude surveying. *Public Opinion Quarterly,* 1950, **14**, 697–709.

Sanford, F. H., & Rosenstock, J. Projective techniques on the doorstep. *Journal of Abnormal and Social Psychology,* 1952, **47**, 3–16.

Sarason, I. G. The effect of anxiety and two kinds of failure on serial learning. *Journal of Personality,* 1957, **25**, 383-392.

Sarason, I. G. Intellectual and personality correlates of test anxiety. *Journal of Abnormal and Social Psychology,* 1959, **59**, 272-275.

Sarason, S. B., Davidson, K. S., Lighthall, F. F., Waite, R. R., & Ruebush, B. K. *Anxiety in elementary school children.* New York: Wiley, 1960.

Scott, W. A. The avoidance of threatening material in imaginative behavior. *Journal of Abnormal and Social Psychology,* 1956, **52**, 338-346. Also in J. W. Atkinson (Ed.), *Motives in fantasy, action, and society.* Princeton: Van Nostrand, 1958.

Sears, R. R. A theoretical framework for personality and social behavior. *American Psychologist,* 1951, **9**, 476-483.

Seltzer, R. A. Simulation of the dynamics of action. *Psychological Reports,* 1973, **32**, 859-872.

Sewell, W. H. Inequality of opportunity for higher education. *American Sociological Review,* 1971, **36**, 793-809.

Sewell, W. H., Haller, A. O., & Ohlendorf, G. W. The educational and early occupational status attainment process: Replication and revision. *American Sociological Review,* 1970, **35**, 1014-1027.

Shen, E. The place of individual differences in experimentation. In Q. McNemar and M. A. Merrill (Eds.), *Studies in personality.* New York: McGraw-Hill, 1942.

Shipley, T. E., & Veroff, J. A projective measure of need for affiliation. *Journal of Experimental Psychology,* 1952, **43**, 349-356.

Shrable, V. K., & Moulton, R. W. Achievement fantasy as a function of variations in self-rated competence. *Perceptual and Motor Skills,* 1968, **27**, 515-528.

Skinner, B. F. *Beyond freedom and dignity.* New York: Knopf, 1971.

Smith, C. P. Situational determinants of the expression of achievement motivation in thematic apperception. Unpublished doctoral dissertation, University of Michigan, 1961.

Smith, C. P. Achievement-related motives and goal setting under different conditions. *Journal of Personality,* 1963, **31**, 124-140.

Smith, C. P. Relationship between achievement-related motives and intelligence, performance level, and persistence. *Journal of Abnormal and Social Psychology,* 1964, **68**, 523-532.

Smith, C. P. The influence of testing conditions and need for achievement scores and their relationship to performance scores. In J. W. Atkinson and N. T. Feather (Eds.), *A theory of achievement motivation.* New York: Wiley, 1966.

Smith, C. P. (Ed.) *Achievement-related motives in children.* New York: Russel Sage Foundation, 1969.

Smith, C. P., & Feld, S. How to learn the method of content analysis for n Achievement, n Affiliation, and n Power. In J. W. Atkinson (Ed.), *Motives in fantasy, action, and society.* Princeton: Van Nostrand, 1958.

Snedecor, G. W. *Statistical methods.* Ames, Iowa: Iowa State College Press, 1946.

Solzhenitsyn, A. *One day in the life of Ivan Denisovich.* (Translated by M. Hayward and R. Hingley with an introduction by M. Hayward and L. Labedy). New York: Praeger, 1963.

Sorrentino, R. M. An extension of theory of achievement motivation to the study of emergent leadership. Unpublished doctoral dissertation, State University of New York at Buffalo, 1971.

Sorrentino, R. M. An extension of theory of achievement motivation to the study of emergent leadership. *Journal of Personality and Social Psychology,* 1973, **26**, 356-368.

Sorrentino, R. M., & Raynor, J. O. An extension of theory of achievement motivation to the study of the emergent leadership process. Paper presented at the meetings of the Eastern Psychological Association, New York, April 1971.

Sorrentino, R. M., & Raynor, J. O. The relationship between resultant achievement motivation, task difficulty, and performance with respect to future goal orientation. Paper presented at the meetings of the Canadian Psychological Association, Montreal, 1972.

Spaeth, J. L. Occupational attainment among male college graduates. *American Journal of Sociology,* 1970, **75**, 632–644.

Spence, J. T., & Spence, K. W. The motivational components of manifest anxiety: Drive and drive stimuli. In C. D. Spielberger (Ed.), *Anxiety and behavior.* New York: Academic Press, 1966.

Spence, K. W. *Behavior theory and conditioning.* New Haven: Yale University Press, 1956.

Spence, K. W. A theory of emotionally based drive (D) and its relation to performance in simple learning situations. *American Psychologist,* 1958, **13**, 131–141.

Spence, K. W. Anxiety (drive) level and performance in eyelid conditoning. *Psychological Bulletin,* 1964, **61**, 129–139.

Spence, K. W., Farber, I. E., & McFann, H. H. The relation of anxiety (drive) level to performance in competitional and noncompetitional paired-associates learning. *Journal of Experimental Psychology,* 1956, **52**, 296–305.

Spence, K. W., Taylor, J. A., & Ketchel, R. Anxiety (drive) level and degree of competition in paired-associates learning. *Journal of Experimental Psychology,* 1956, **52**, 306–310.

Spielberger, C. D. The effects of manifest anxiety on the academic achievement of college students. *Mental Hygiene,* 1962, **46**, 420–426.

Spielberger, C. D. *Anxiety and behavior.* New York: Academic Press, 1966.

Steiner, C. *Games alcoholics play: The analysis of life scripts.* New York: Globe Press, 1971.

Stogdill, R. M. Personal factors associated with leadership: A survey of the literature. *Journal of Psychology,* 1948, **25**, 35–71.

Strong, E. K. *Change in interests with age.* Stanford, Calif.: Stanford University Press, 1931.

Strong, E. K. *Vocational interests of men and women.* Stanford, Calif.: Stanford University Press, 1943.

Taylor, J. A. The relationship of anxiety to the conditioned eyelid response. *Journal of Experimental Psychology,* 1951, **41**, 81–92.

Taylor, J. A. A personality scale of manifest anxiety. *Journal of Abnormal and Social Psychology,* 1953, **48**, 285–290.

Taylor, J. A. Drive theory and manifest anxiety. *Psychological Bulletin,* 1956, **53**, 303–320.

Taylor, J. A., & Chapman, J. P. Paired-associate learning as related to anxiety. *American Journal of Psychology,* 1955, **68**, 671.

Taylor, J. A., & Spence, K. W. The relationship of anxiety level to performance in serial learning. *Journal of Experimental Psychology,* 1952, **44**, 61–64.

Thomas, E. J., & Zander, A. The relationship of goal structure to motivation under extreme conditions. *Journal of Individual Psychology,* 1959, **15**, 121–127.

Thorndike, E. L., & Lorge, I. *The teacher's wordbook of 30,000 words.* New York: Columbia University, Teachers College, Bureau of Publications, 1944.

Thorndike, R. L. The concepts of overachievement and underachievement. New York: Columbia University, Teachers College, Bureau of Publications, 1963.

Timberlake, W. Continuous coding of general activity in the rat during repeated exposure to a constant environment and to stimulus change. Unpublished doctoral dissertation, University of Michigan, 1969.

Timberlake, W., & Birch, D. Complexity, novelty, and food deprivation as determinants of speed of a shift from one behavior to another. *Journal of Comparative and Physiological Psychology,* 1967, **63**, 545–548.

Tinbergen, N. *The study of instinct.* Oxford: Clarendon Press, 1951.

Toffler, A. *Future shock.* New York: Random House, 1970.

Tolman, E. C. *Purposive behavior in animals and men.* New York: Appleton-Century, 1932.

Tolman, E. C. Principles of performance. *Psychological Review,* 1955, **62**, 315-326.

Tompkins, S. S., & Miner, J. B. *The Tompkins-Horn Picture Arrangement Test.* New York: Springer, 1958.

Valle, F. P. Effect of feeding-related stimuli on eating. Unpublished doctoral dissertation, University of Michigan, 1967.

Valle, F. P. Effect of feeding-related stimuli on eating. *Journal of Comapratíve and Physiological Psychology,* 1968, **66**, 773-776.

Van Dusen, A. C. Measuring leadership ability. *Personnel Psychology,* 1948, **1**, 67-79. (*Psychological Abstracts,* 1948, **22**, No. 3919.)

Veroff, J. A scoring manual for the power motive. In J. W. Atkinson (Ed.), *Motives in fantasy, action, and society.* Princeton: Van Nostrand, 1958.

Veroff, J. Thematic apperception in a nationwide sample survey. In J. Kagan and G. S. Lesser (Eds.), *Contemporary issues in thematic apperceptive methods.* Springfield, Ill.: Charles C Thomas, 1961.

Veroff, J. Theoretical background for studying the origins of human motivational dispositions. *Merill-Palmer Quarterly,* 1965, **11**, 3-18.

Veroff, J., Atkinson, J. W., Feld, S., & Gurin, G. The use of thematic apperception to assess motivation in a nationwide interview study. *Psychological Monographs,* 1960, **74**(12 Whole No. 499).

Veroff, J., & Feld, S. *Marriage and work in America.* New York: Van Nostrand-Reinhold, 1970.

Veroff, J., Feld, S., & Crockett, H. Explorations into the effects of picture cues on thematic apperceptive expression of achievement motivation. *Journal of Personality and Social Psychology,* 1966, **3**, 171-181.

Veroff, J., Feld, S., & Gurin, G. Achievement motivation and religious background. *American Sociological Review,* 1962, **27**, 205-217.

Veroff, J., Hubbard, R., & Marquis, K. Components of achievement motivation as predictors of potential for economic change. Final report, Contract 91-24-70-15, U.S. Dept. of Labor, Manpower Administration. Survey Research Center, University of Michigan, Ann Arbor, Michigan, July, 1971.

Veroff, J., McClelland, L., & Marquis, K. Measuring intelligence and achievement motivation in surveys. Final report, Contract No. OEO-4180, U.S. Dept. Health, Education, and Welfare. Survey Research Center, University of Michigan, Ann Arbor, Mich., Oct., 1971.

Veroff, J., & Veroff, J. B. Reconsideration of a measure of power motivation. *Psychological Bulletin,* 1972, 78, 279-291.

Veroff, J., Wilcox, S., & Atkinson, J. W. The achievement motive in high school and college-age women. *Journal of Abnormal and Social Psychology,* 1953, 48, 103-119.

Vislie, L. Stimulus research in projective techniques. Oslo: Universitetsforlaget, 1972.

Vogel, M. An investigation of the affiliation motive in college age women using low cue strength pictures. Unpublished honors' thesis, University of Michigan, 1954.

Vroom, V. H. *Work and motivation.* New York: Wiley, 1964.

Wainer, H. A., & Rubin, I. M. Motivation of research and development entrepreneurs: Determinants of company success. *Journal of Applied Psychology,* 1969, **53**, 178-184.

Walker, E. L., & Atkinson, J. W. The expression of fear-related motivation in thematic apperception as a function of proximity to an atomic explosion. In J. W. Atkinson (Ed.), *Motives in fantasy, action, and society.* Princeton: Van Nostrand, 1958.

Weiner, B. Effects of unsatisfied achievement-related motivation on persistence and subsequent performance. Unpublished doctoral dissertation, University of Michigan, 1963.

Weiner, B. The effects of unsatisfied achievement motivation on persistence and subsequent performance. *Journal of Personality,* 1965, **33**, 428-442. (a)

Weiner, B. Need Achievement and the resumption of incompleted tasks. *Journal of Personality and Social Psychology,* 1965, **1**, 165–168. (b)

Weiner, B. Role of success and failure in the learning of easy and complex tasks. *Journal of Personality and Social Psychology,* 1966, **3**, 339–344. (a)

Weiner, B. Additional evidence for an expanded theory of achievement motivation and a re-interpretation of prior data. Unpublished paper, University of California, Los Angeles, 1966. (b)

Weiner, B. New conceptions in the study of achievement motivation. In B. Maher (Ed.), *Progress in experimental personality research.* Vol. 5. New York: Academic Press, 1970.

Weiner, B., Frieze, I., Kulka, A., Reed, L., Rest, S., & Rosenbaum, R. M. *Perceiving the causes of success and failure.* New York: General Learning Press, 1971.

Weinstein, M. S. Achievement motivation and risk preference. *Journal of Personality and Social Psychology,* 1969, **13**, 153–172.

Weiss, R. F., & Miller, F. G. The drive theory of social facilitation. *Psychological Review,* 1971, 78, 44–58.

Wendt, H. W. Motivation, effort, and performance. In D. C. McClelland (Ed.), *Studies in motivation.* New York: Appleton-Century-Crofts, 1955.

Whalen, R. E. Sexual motivation. *Psychological Review,* 1966, **73**, 151–163.

Williams, J. E. Mode of failure, interference tendencies and achievement imagery. *Journal of Abnormal and Social Psychology,* 1955, **51**, 573–580.

Winer, B. J. *Statistical principles in experimental design.* New York: McGraw-Hill, 1962.

Winter D. G. The need for power in college men: Action correlates and relationship to drinking. In D. C. McClelland, et al. (Eds.), *Alcohol and human motivation.* New York: The Free Press, 1971.

Winter, D. G. *The power motive.* New York: The Free Press, 1973.

Winterbottom, M. The relation of childhood training in independence to achievement motivation. Unpublished doctoral dissertation, University of Michigan, 1953. Also in J. W. Atkinson (Ed.), *Motives in fantasy, action, and society.* Princeton: Van Nostrand, 1958.

Wish, P. A., & Hasazi, J. E. Motivational determinants of curricular choice behavior in college males. Paper presented at the Eastern Psychological Association, Boston, April 1972.

Wolfe, D. *The uses of talent.* Princeton: Princeton University Press, 1971.

Yerkes, R. M., & Dodson, J. D. The relation of strength of stimulus to rapidity of habit formation. *Journal of Comparative and Neurological Psychology,* 1908, **18**, 459–482.

Youssef, Z. I. Association and integration in serial learning. *American Journal of Psychology,* 1967, **80**, 355–362.

Zajonc, R. B. Social facilitation. *Science,* 1965, **149**, 269–274.

Zander, A. *Motives and goals in groups.* New York: Academic Press, 1970.

Zander, A., & Forward, J. Position in group, achievement motivation, and group aspirations. *Journal of Personality and Social Psychology,* 1968, **8**, 282–288.

Zeigarnik, B. On finished and unfinished tasks. In W. D. Ellis (Ed.), *A source book of gestalt psychology.* New York: Harcourt, Brace & World, 1938.

Zeleny, L. D. Characteristics of group leaders. *Sociology and Social Research,* 1939, **24**, 140–149.

AUTHOR INDEX

Numbers in italics refer to the pages on which the complete references are listed.

Z

SUBJECT INDEX

A

G

H

N

R

S

U

V

W

Y

Z